Conservation Psychology

Conservation Psychology

Understanding and promoting human care for nature

Second Edition

Susan Clayton and Gene Myers

WILEY Blackwell

This edition first published 2015 ©2015 by John Wiley & Sons Ltd

First edition published by John Wiley & Sons Ltd 2009

Registered office: John Wiley & Sons, Ltd, The Atrium, Southern Gate, Chichester, West Sussex,
PO19 8SQ, UK

Editorial offices: 9600 Garsington Road, Oxford, OX4 2DQ, UK
The Atrium, Southern Gate, Chichester, West Sussex, PO19 8SQ, UK
111 River Street, Hoboken, NJ 07030-5774, USA

For details of our global editorial offices, for customer services and for information about how to apply for permission to reuse the copyright material in this book please see our website at www.wiley.com/wiley-blackwell.

Library of Congress Data applied for.

A catalogue record for this book is available from the British Library.

ISBN: 9781118874608

Wiley also publishes its books in a variety of electronic formats. Some content that appears in print may not be available in electronic books.

Cover image: Volunteers restoring streamside habitat. Photo courtesy of Nooksack Salmon Enhancement Association & Phil Humphries

Typeset in 10/12pt AGaramondPro by SPi Global, Chennai, India.
Printed and bound in Malaysia by Vivar Printing Sdn Bhd

1 2015

Contents

Preface to the Second Edition

The role of psychology in conservation has grown dramatically since the first edition of *Conservation Psychology*. We are delighted by this development, although it has made our attempt to cover the field even more difficult. With this edition of the book, we have accepted the impossibility of including everything in this field. Instead, guided by the interests of our likely readers, we have reordered some of the material in a way that we hope will be more accessible and highlighted new developments in applied conservation. We have also described the promising intersection between conservation psychology and positive psychology. As originally, we are grateful to all the people working on this enterprise as well as to the students and practitioners whose interest is driving new research. This edition is dedicated to those who are doing their best to apply psychological insights to conservation practice.

About the Companion Website

This book is accompanied by a companion website:

www.wiley.com/go/clayton/conservation

The website includes:

- Pdfs of all figures from the book for downloading
- Powerpoints of all tables from the book for downloading

1

Introducing the Field of Conservation Psychology

- **Conservation**
- **Psychology**
- **Human care for nature**
- **The roots of conservation psychology**
- **The utility of conservation psychology**
- **The practice of conservation psychology**
- **The organization of the book**
- **Conclusion**
- **References**

Humanity faces environmental challenges on every level from local to global. Human population growth and human activities are negatively affecting the ecological processes that support life as we know it, and the effect of these changes on human well-being will be profound. Recent quantitative assessments of the human impact on nature give a sobering picture; the Millennium Ecosystem Assessment found that that about 60% of the earth's ecosystem services are being used unsustainably. Using ecological footprint methodology, the Global Footprint Network (Global Footprint Network, 2013; http://www.footprintnetwork.org) has calculated that humanity's load on the biosphere is about 150% of earth's capacity, up from 70% in 1961. These trends result from individual behavior patterns as well as from the societal infrastructure constituted by our institutions, governance systems, and ways of interacting. At stake are two inextricably linked sets of values: concern for the present and future quality of human lives and care about the vitality of the biosphere and its other inhabitants.

We were drawn to write about conservation psychology not only by these uncompromising facts and future possibilities but also by a perception that our primary discipline, psychology, could do more to address these realities. This is clear across areas of conservation and natural resource research. We want to urgently ask: Are psychologists on those research teams? Are they prepared to intelligently deploy their skills in these new contexts (do they know their ecology and economics)? Are other social or natural science specialists ready to seek those skills (do they understand human motivations and biases)? A growing body of psychological research is relevant to conservation. Collectively, however, psychology is at best midway into effectively putting its resources at the disposal of individuals and groups working for a more healthy relation to our planet. We have yet to see a sea-change in the work of psychologists toward

Conservation Psychology: Understanding and promoting human care for nature, Second Edition.
Susan Clayton and Gene Myers.

www.wiley.com\go\clayton\conservation

addressing sustainability. This book is for the reader with some interest in psychology, whether as a psychologist or just that of a normally curious and reflective human being, and concern about contemporary threats to environmental and social well-being posed by the way humans relate to ecological systems. Our goal is to describe the many ways in which psychology is relevant to environmental sustainability and vice-versa.

Conservation

We define *conservation psychology* as the use of psychological techniques and research to understand and promote a healthy relationship between humans and the natural environment. Let us unpack the book's title. "Conservation" should not be identified with turn-of-the-twentieth century resource conservation, with its strictly utilitarian focus. Instead, we associate "Conservation" with its rebirth in the 1980s, in which it was applied to a whole new set of ideas, including landscape and continent-wide ecosystem planning, and especially to Conservation Biology. That field was born of a sense of crisis and some within it openly avowed value-laden positions (Soulé, 1985). The same goes for conservation psychology: the goal is not only to understand the interdependence between humans and nature but also to promote a healthy and sustainable relationship.

> What's in a name?
>
> There is no consensus on what to call the kind of psychological research that we discuss here. "Conservation Psychology" is well represented in books, handbooks, and organizations, but some workshops or groups have opted for "Sustainability Psychology," "Green Psychology," or other titles. Even "Environmental Psychology" is sometimes used as if it refers only to research that relates to environmental protection and conservation, although there is a wide range of environmental psychology research on topics that are almost completely irrelevant (such as workplace design or crowding). Although the name "Conservation Psychology" was carefully chosen after discussion at a few workshops in the early 2000s, the specific name is less important than the ability to find relevant research. We review research whose authors might not identify by the term conservation psychology in the hopes of making it more available to anyone interested in promoting a healthy and sustainable human–nature relationship.

The explicit value basis of conservation psychology is unfamiliar to some scientists, who would prefer to simply describe behavior rather than take a stance with a prescriptive component (cf. Crosby et al., 2004). But psychology already has a clear value basis: the goal of promoting human well-being. If choosing research questions with an eye to their relevance compromises the integrity of one's results then all of medical research would be suspected. Weak or inappropriate methodology and nonvigilant thinking are the real threats to experimental validity, not a preference for sustainable behavior. There is wide consensus about the value of the natural environment, but not always about the need for change or the direction of change in order to promote sustainability. Conservation psychology seeks to direct rigorous research toward the goal of sustainability and to rely on the results of that research to make recommendations about specific techniques.

Psychology

"Psychology" also requires explication. Many people are at first surprised when we say the two words together, "conservation psychology." But soon they get it: oh yes, environmental problems are a result of human behavioral choices, and because addressing those problems will require changes in patterns of behavior, we need to understand people. Psychology can be defined as the scientific study of mind, brain, and behavior. It is often misunderstood by the public, who – partly on the basis of exposure to "pop psychology" theories promoted by non-professionals – confuse psychology with psychiatry and with an emphasis on therapy. Although many psychologists do work to promote individual mental health, psychology as a discipline has both a broader agenda and a greater emphasis on scientific research. The two, linked, goals of psychology are to understand human behavior and to promote human well-being. Psychological research and practice are based on the assumption that the promotion of human welfare requires an understanding of human behavior that is based on rigorous empirical study.

Understanding human behavior means, in part, understanding how individuals are affected by the setting in which they find themselves. This includes the natural environment and changes in that environment due to things such as climate change, overpopulation, and the loss of wild landscapes. People spend a great deal of time and money interacting with aspects of the natural environment; indeed, a significant proportion of human behavior occurs in a setting that, if not directly in nature, invokes nature through windows, pictures, or potted plants. This means that environmental changes will affect everyday human experience. Environmental issues are social issues as well, and socially constructed perceptions of environmental change have an impact on human social behavior.

Promoting human welfare requires awareness of how intimately it is connected to the natural environment. It is well known that environmental toxins can have direct impacts on human health. Less visible are the possible effects on mental functioning. There is a large body of research documenting the detrimental effects of lead, mercury, and PCBs on cognitive functioning and sometimes social behavior (see Moore, 2003 for a review). Less directly, environmental problems will ultimately affect the well-being of everyone on the planet: global warming and overcrowding affect social behavior and intergroup conflict, and opportunities for interaction with animals and nature affect emotional well-being and stress reduction. The goal of sustainability articulated by the World Commission of Economic Development (WCED, 1987) report explicitly linked the two goals of environmental health and human development, including attention to human as well as environmental welfare.

A brief review of some key environmental problems shows the ways in which humans are implicated (see Oskamp, 2000):

- Global climate change is generally agreed to be a result of human action. There is a wide range of probable effects on humans. Direct effects include a possible effect of increased temperature on aggression (e.g., Anderson, 2012) and the probability of increased serious weather events with concomitant damage to human dwellings and built environments. Indirect effects may include eco-migrations, with concomitant increase in intergroup conflict (e.g., Hsiang et al., 2013; Reuveny, 2008), along with negative impacts on mental health due to stress, anxiety, and reduced social support (Clayton et al., 2014).
- Pollution of the air, water, and soil is a clear by-product of human manufacturing processes. Impacts include not only increased susceptibility to cancer and possible effects on

reproduction but also more psychological effects such as decreased cognitive functioning (due, e.g., to exposure to lead or mercury).

- Resource depletion, for example, the depletion of water resources and the collapse of fish populations, results from human overuse. Any of these will require a major shift in the way humans conduct their lives such as where they live and how they are employed.
- Loss of biodiversity is a result of the three problems described above as well as the increased development of wilderness to house a rising human population. An anthropocentric argument to preserve biodiversity is often couched in terms of potential benefits to humanity from, for example, as-yet-undiscovered drugs made from natural sources. But surveys show that humans value wilderness for more difficult-to-quantify reasons as well and feel that human experience would be diminished by its loss (Kellert, 1996; Manfredo, 2008).

Psychology has a broad purview, spanning topics from the biophysical to the cultural with diverse methods that range from observation of naturally occurring behavior to analysis of brain activity and hormone levels. We want to enlist this full spectrum of psychology in the urgent task of conservation. This includes the following core areas:

- *Clinical psychology* is the study of mental health and well-being, as well as abnormal behavior.
- *Developmental psychology* examines continuities and changes that are associated with growth across the lifespan, in perceptual, social, and cognitive and other areas of capabilities.
- *Cognitive psychologists* examine information processing: the mental models that people use, and the abilities and tendencies that affect the way people respond to information.
- *Social psychology* looks at interpersonal behavior, and the ways in which people are affected by others.
- *Physiological psychologists* utilize amazing new technologies to explore the neural, endocrinal, and bodily processes that underlie behavior.

There is no definitive list of specialties, and there are many other ways in which people define their subdiscipline.

Conservation psychology should not be considered as a subdiscipline, but as a field or area of focus (see Sommer, 2000, for a discussion of the difference). That field or focus is not only practical and applied, but also theoretical and fundamental. The conceptual part of conservation psychology involves persistently and deeply asking what is the human place in nature, and what is nature's place in the human being. The world today offers many ways of actually testing this: What is a human being, deprived of contact with nature, or supplied with technological simulations of nature? Is he or she missing anything? Is a nature DVD as good as a potted plant, an arboretum, a million acres of wild land for discerning in our hearts what it means to be a living creature on a living planet?

We can explore this query in terms of how it could be addressed within different core areas. Clinical psychologists can (and do) explore the positive effects on mental health of exposure to nature. Developmentalists examine the significance of early exposure to nature on the formation of an enduring environmental empathy and ethic. For cognition–brain–communication specialists: our simplified protocols for perceptual and cognitive stimuli are like nursery tunes compared to the symphonic acoustics we evolved in; what can those variations tell us that we have not even asked yet about our minds? Physiological psychologists should not neglect the impact of synergies of environmental toxins on behavior (kudos to those already doing this). Social psychologists can study ways of constructing effective and persuasive communications about the significance of nature-based experiences and design socially based behavioral interventions. Conservation psychology should attract psychologists from all the areas mentioned, as well as others not described. Organizational, health, population, and psychologists from across the spectrum can contribute to the goals of this field.

Human care for nature

The last part of our title references "care for nature." Care may sound like too casual a term, but its familiarity is a strength. We all recognize that to act with intention, to inquire, to get activated, requires that one "give a damn" – that one "care." In the midst of legitimate concern over the harm that people are inflicting upon the natural environment, it is easy to feel pessimistic about the extent to which people care about nature. As people waste energy, consume resources at an unsustainable rate, undermine life-support systems, and pollute the environment, it may seem as though they have to be threatened or enticed to engage in pro-environmental behavior, as if it were against their own self-interest. However, people do

We should clean up the environment because it's just the right thing to do	93% agree
When I see trash in places like the beach or the woods, I want to pick it up immediately	87%
I am concerned about the health of our oceans	85%
Preserving places for animals to live has its own virtues even if humans don't benefit	85%
I like to have activities in my life that bring me close to nature	85%
Nature has lots of solutions to our current problems, like more trees to make shade and more wetlands to stop flooding	84%
Personal health is the best reason to reduce pollution	83%
Wild animals need more places to live in the way they always have	83%
How essential to do something about increase in water shortages	82%
Oil companies have too much power in America today	81%
I love going to the ocean	81%
Animals have a moral right to be protected	81%
If we don't do something our oceans will be in worse shape five years from now than they are today	80%
The extinction of plants and animals threaten human life	80%
How essential to do something about garbage and grime in the environment	80%
I make a strong effort to recycle everything I can	79%
It's not fair that oil and coal companies get big tax breaks	79%
A human-caused disaster (oil spills or nuclear leaks) is a call to action to change the way we live	78%
When plant species go extinct, we could be losing drugs that could cure things like cancer or heart diseases	78%
It will not matter to children if all the lions and bears have to live in zoos	78%
Our children's lives will be worse off because of our generation's wasteful habits	78%
How essential to do something about loss of plants species that could lead to medicines	78%
I feel better knowing that people are protecting land from development forever	76%
How essential to do something about worsening health of oceans	76%
America needs to lead the world in solving environmental problems	75%

Fig. 1.1 Shared environmental values among the American public. (Ecoamerica (2011). The American Climate and Environmental Values Survey. Available at http://www.climateaccess.org/sites/default/files/ecoamerica_ACEVS%20report.pdf).

care about the environment. They demonstrate this in ratings of photographs, in descriptions of favorite places, and in survey responses (Fig. 1.1).

Does care mean anything more than personal preference? It does have a stronger sense – that of an obligation we learn to accept and own, to take into our very identity. Care is personal because it seems discretionary *what* we give a damn about; people care about all variety of things, mostly the things that are close to them and that serve to define them: other people, places, and values. Care develops within social contexts, usually in relationships. Children have a lesson in care around ages 8 to 11 years through friendships that are conditional: if care is not reciprocated, the friend soon is gone. There is similar conditionality in our relationship with the earth. In way that are recognized and in ways that are not, the natural environment takes care of our needs, suggesting that we need to think about the needs of the environment in return (Fig. 1.2).

Care is not only an emotional response, but also a type of action. We sometimes refer in the book to "care about" which denotes an emotional response, an attitude of concern. "Caring for" has a behavioral sense; we use the phrase in everyday life when we talk about caregivers and caretakers. If we care about the environment, we need to care for it. There are many ways to express care.

Care sounds like something you do privately, since we use it to talk about personal relationships. Yet, there is no question that in the stronger senses of care unveiled above – as an internalized obligatory motivation, as based in a universal valuing of cherished relationships – we care collectively too. Patriotic sentiments and action, helping to maintain one's church, involvement in community organizations all represent collective care. Caring together can mean working together to stop actions by others, but threats to nature are sometimes best addressed by caring about human-to-human relations and institutions. We mean that by our

Fig. 1.2 A reciprocal relationship with nature. Photo credit Susan Clayton.

title also. The most courageous and novel interventions for nature – by individuals in moral impasse, or by institutions in policy innovation – may be in the human–human realm.

Fully instantiated, care includes cognitive, affective, and behavioral components. In order to care about an issue, people must be informed. Regarding environmental issues, people must recognize the ways in which their behavior can affect the environment and the ways in which those environmental changes in turn will affect the things they value. Beyond thought, however, people must feel: they will experience positive emotions associated with nature, and negative ones that are stimulated by the threat of environmental degradation. Finally, people should act in ways that will express both their knowledge and their emotions, and that may tend to minimize or alleviate the environmental threats they are facing.

Probably not everything we want conservation psychology to include falls clearly under this flag of care. Even in this volume, many other angles are taken: self-interested benefits, matters of rights and justice, and strategies that simply work better with people. The richness of seeking more sustainable and harmonious relationships between people and nature and institutions cannot be reduced to any term. We use "care" here as a fundamental starting point, of giving a damn, and doing something about it. Conservation psychology cannot be about much more unless it begins with that.

The roots of conservation psychology

Within environmental studies, any list of early influential articles would probably include Garrett Hardin's (1968) piece on the "tragedy of the commons" and Lynn White's (1967) article on "The historical roots of our ecological crisis." Both of these provocative (and flawed) essays drew attention not to unexpected consequences of technological advances, but to the ways in which people thought about the environment and how that influenced their treatment of it. At about the same time, serious research on the relationship between humans and their environment led to the development of *environmental psychology* as a subdiscipline of psychology. "Environment" was defined as the physical (rather than social) context, including both natural and built components. At first, environmental psychologists primarily focused on the ways in which environments had causal impact on human behavior. With the rise of the environmental movement, there was more attention to the natural environment and more acknowledgment of the ways in which human behavior has an impact on the environment. Bonnes and Bonaiuto (2002) review the development of environmental psychology from a focus on the spatial-physical environment to concern with sustainable development. A thorough and more recent review of environmental psychology can be found in Gifford (2014).

From the beginning, environmental psychology has included researchers concerned with the health of the environment, and a great deal of research relevant to conservation psychology has been done by environmental psychologists. Detailed discussion of the relationship between environmental and conservation psychology can be found in a recent handbook (Clayton, 2012, Chapters 1 and 34). Some of the relevant psychological research has addressed the impacts of exposure to nature for individual well-being; the ways in which humans interact with nature; perceptions of nature and of environmental risks; decision making about environmental policies; conceptions of environmental ethics; and the ways in which people's self-concepts are intertwined with the natural environment. Important psychological constructs include knowledge, behavior, values, and attitudes, at the individual level; norms, incentives, barriers, and behavior settings, at the system level. Psychologists are employed by, or consult for, environmental management agencies, planning authorities, and government bodies (Reser, 2007).

The field of conservation psychology arose not in response to a lack of research, but in response to a lack of visibility and identification: both psychologists and nonpsychologists are often unaware of the body of psychological research related to sustainability. Conservation psychology also seeks to provide a community for psychologists across all subdisciplines who want to reflect their concern for the future of the planet in their professional identity.

Although the natural environment has only recently begun to attract widespread attention from psychological researchers, there have long been psychologists who have argued for its importance, as demonstrated by a quote from Alfred Adler: "We are living on the surface of this planet, with only the resources of this planet, with the fertility of its soil, with its mineral wealth, and with its climate and atmosphere. It has always been the task of mankind to find the right answer to the problem these conditions set us, and even today we cannot think that we have found a sufficient answer" (Adler, 1956, p. 131). Relatedly, psychiatrist Harold Searles stated in 1960 that "The nonhuman environment, far from being of little or no account to human personality development, constitutes one of the most basically important ingredients of human psychological existence" (p. 5). Conservation psychology proposes to carry forward the distinctive spirits of each of these insights into today's world of nature and universe of psychology.

The utility of conservation psychology

Conservation psychology encompasses both basic and applied research. Applied, because a primary goal is to address and ameliorate environmental problems. But "there is nothing so practical as a good theory," to quote Kurt Lewin (1951). Psychological research has yielded some broad conclusions that have important relevance for conservation. They include the idea that behavior is strongly affected by the consequences that follow that behavior; that people learn not only behaviors but also attitudes, values, and norms from those around them; and that people change over time, in ways that are genetically preprogrammed as well as responsive to environments. The effect of specific experiences varies according to the developmental stage at which they are encountered, and some important experiences or influences have a disproportionate impact early in development. These principles are clearly relevant to understanding the interdependence between humans and nature.

Two core aspects of human behavior are worth identifying even though they almost go without saying. One is that behavior is a function of multiple causes, many of which are irrational and/or outside conscious awareness. This means that people do not always know what's good for them, and even when they do they may not act on it; logical argument about the importance of addressing environmental threats is not enough to affect behavior. A second is that behavior is susceptible to change. Patterns of behavior that may seem like inevitable consequences of "human nature" are nevertheless malleable, responding to both unintentional and intentional influence. Even something as fundamental as reproduction shows huge variability across both time (the birthrate declined by almost 50% between 1910 and 1994 in the U.S.) and culture (ranging from 11 births per 1,000 people per year in Italy to 45 per 1,000 per year in Tanzania) (Howard, 2000). An understanding of the core influences on behavior can allow for positive interventions to promote a healthy human–nature relationship.

Between them, Saunders (2003) and Mascia (2003) articulate a set of areas for conservation psychology research that reflect psychological knowledge and our complex definition of care. Saunders argued that conservation psychology should address (1) how humans care about nature and (2) how humans behave toward nature. Mascia added the cognitive component,

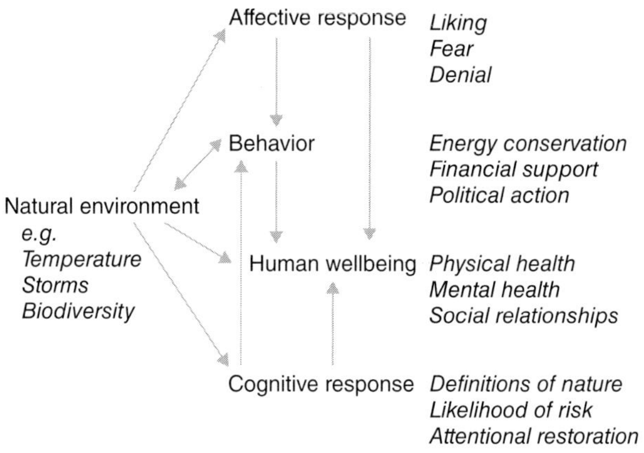

Fig. 1.3 A simplified model of the human-nature relationship.

(3) how humans develop beliefs and knowledge about nature. He also recognized that humans function within a social context by adding two more foci (4) human-to-human relationships that are relevant to conservation, and (5) the relationships between humans and social institutions. See Fig. 1.3 for a diagram of the general processes of concern to conservation psychologists, and some specific examples.

Conservation psychology aims to apply the concepts and the techniques of psychological research to conservation areas. This might include, for example:

- Using survey research to assess community attitudes toward particular conservation initiatives
- Drawing on the results of attitude change research to design persuasive messages
- Drawing on the results of behavior research to encourage sustainable behavior
- Consulting with architects and designers to provide ways for people to interact with nature
- Designing environmental education programs that will promote pro-environmental attitudes
- Conducting research on the effects of exposure to nature in order to enhance the argument for protecting nature
- Observing social interactions in order to understand the ways in which environmental values are created and transmitted

Psychology can also promote the recognition that economic motivations are not the only forces that guide behavior. Clayton and Brook (2005) discuss the ways in which self-presentation motives and other identity concerns can supersede the desire to protect the environment, and described the success of the Toyota Prius over the comparable Honda Civic hybrid as due to the way in which the Prius satisfies self-presentation concerns by making a more visible statement about its owner's environmental values than the less distinctive Civic hybrid. This analysis was later corroborated: in a survey reported in the New York Times, the top reason people gave for buying a Prius was that it "makes a statement about me" (Maynard, 2007).

A lack of psychological information can be harmful. For example, Robert Cialdini, a specialist in the psychology of social influence, has documented the "understandable, but misguided, tendency to try to mobilize action against a problem by depicting it as regrettably frequent" in public service announcements and other pro-environmental messages

(2003, p. 105). In controlled research, Cialdini and colleagues have demonstrated that such a message can identify a descriptive social norm by stating that many people engage in this negative behavior. Littering and polluting, for example, are common. Because people are highly guided by social comparison, they may choose to do as others are doing rather than to set themselves up as paragons. Thus, the well-intentioned attempts to increase pro-environmental behavior may actually backfire.

Caveats and cautions. Among the vast body of research on sustainable behavior, many studies have focused on behavior changes that are not particularly useful (Gardner & Stern, 1996). Psychologists sometimes target individual-level changes in cases where the important decisions and behaviors occur at the organizational or the governmental level. This does not mean that individual behavior is irrelevant, but that not all behavioral changes are equally significant. In some cases, target behaviors might be lobbying organizations, or voting for particular policies. Recycling paper will have a lower impact than purchasing a fuel-efficient car. In addition, claims can also be made about benefits of nature that are based on anecdote but not backed up with data, or that fail to acknowledge the complexity of the human–nature relationship. Nature presents costs as well as benefits, and there are aspects of nature that people do not like (Bixler & Floyd, 1997)! Psychologists and others need to resist the temptation to be satisfied with simple answers.

It is partly out of such origins that the field of ecopsychology emerged. Ecopsychology is rooted in concern with the ways in which people relate to nature, and the consequences for both human and environmental health. As such, it provides an important reminder that people live in nature as fish do in water, and that degradation of the environment is likely to affect people in ways that are more subtle than increased risk of cancer. Its agenda is to link personal and social change, connecting individual therapy with environmental stewardship. The relationship between ecopsychology and psychology has been contested (see Beringer, 2003; Reser, 1995). Not all ecopsychologists are trained as psychologists, and writings on ecopsychology have been criticized for a lack of scientific objectivity, referencing concepts such as spirituality and indigenous wisdom that are difficult to clearly define. More recently, ecopsychology has moved to embrace both scientific and humanistic traditions with the intent of plumbing the depths and practicality of the human place in nature (Kahn & Hasbach, 2012).

The practice of conservation psychology

Since the first edition of this book was published, conservation psychology has grown exponentially – both in its research base and in its application. Interdisciplinary workshops and symposia have brought psychologists together with other conservation professionals to discuss ways of working together. University centers, such as the Columbia University Center for Research on Environmental Decisions, or the Yale University Project on Climate Change Communication, promote research on the psychological aspects of environmental issues. Governmental and policy groups and NGOs have hired psychologists to be part of their teams. Individual psychologists, including PhD students, are reaching out to applied settings to investigate the factors that will best promote conservation (Clayton et al., 2013).

For several years, a summer Conservation Psychology Institute has been organized by Carol Saunders and sponsored by Antioch University. This institute provides conservation professionals and other interested participants with a multiday introduction to relevant psychological methods and findings in order to enable the participants to encourage environmental behavior and concern in their own work environments. Topics include cultural and individual frameworks for thinking about the human relationship with nature, message framing, behavioral interventions, and the role of natural environments in human health and well-being.

Doug McKenzie-Mohr, a key proponent of a social marketing approach to promoting pro-environmental behavior, provides many examples of applied settings in which psychology has been useful. In a 2000 article, for example, he describes an intervention to reduce peak summer water usage (McKenzie-Mohr, 2000). A first step identified barriers to efficient lawn watering. Targeted interventions then addressed these barriers by providing information and prompts and eliciting signed commitments to water less often. The social marketing condition decreased watering by 54%, compared to only 15% for a comparison group that only received the information.

The vast body of research in conservation psychology means that, even more than for the first edition, this book cannot hope to be comprehensive. Our goal, rather, is to describe the range of research topics that are included and to summarize the main points of what is currently known about the relationship between humans and the natural world.

The organization of the book

This volume is designed to present a body of research related to how and why people care for nature, in order to make it accessible and useful to both psychologists and nonpsychologists. We split the volume into three sections. The first section, "Human experiences of nature," describes a context for the human–nature relationship by examining some specific ways in which people interact with nature. We group the primary settings into "Domestic nature" (Chapter 2), "Managed nature" (Chapter 3), and "Wild nature" (Chapter 4). Each of these settings has its own unique significance and interest. Under "domestic nature," for example, we examine the abundant literature on companion animals as well as the more sparse research on gardens. We take a critical look at the evidence for benefits, as well as the mechanisms that have been suggested to explain these benefits. We also include a discussion of the very preliminary evidence concerning virtual, or simulated, nature. Managed nature includes zoos and urban parks. We describe the intended purpose of these public services and review evidence about their impact, in particular the ways in which they promote caring for nature. In the chapter on wild nature, we review the literature on the benefits of outdoor experiences and on attitudes toward wildlife. This is also where we talk about research on natural disasters. This section of the book serves as a reminder that the natural environment is a source of benefits and positive experiences as well as of stressful and even traumatic experiences and fear about environmental degradation.

In our second section, "Thinking about nature," we step back to review the ways in which people perceive and interpret their environments. Here, we address the ways in which the environment and environmental issues have psychological significance for people. Chapter 5 deals most directly with cognitive constructs: conceptions of nature, attitudes, values, and language regarding nature. Because perceptions of climate change have generated such attention, Chapter 6 focuses more sharply on the ways people think about environmental risk. Chapter 7 introduces the concept of morality. Many people consider the environment to have moral significance. How do beliefs about justice, ethics, and fairness affect the way we think about nature? In chapter 8, we examine evidence that nature has intimate, personal significance for people's sense of themselves and their personal and social identities.

In the last section, "Encouraging a sustainable relationship between humans and nature," we take a more practical look at interventions. Chapter 9 provides an overview of the extensive research on behavioral interventions – one of the most well-established areas of study within conservation psychology. Chapter 10 examines international issues, including models for community-based conservation programs and concerns about the positive and negative impacts of environmental issues on international conflict. Chapter 11 reviews the research on environmental education. The interdisciplinary connections of conservation psychology are highlighted in these chapters, and Chapters 9–11 attempt to build bridges to other communities of practice as well as other fields of study. There is much more such bridging and calibration to be done.

Finally, Chapter 12 offers a more positive view. In our own experience, as well as that of others we have spoken with, studying environmental topics may lead to a sense of pessimism or even despair. We wrote this book because of our own optimism in the face of environmental challenges, and in Chapter 12 we encourage the reader to respond in the same way. The chapter provides an overview of conservation psychology's intersections with the growing field of positive psychology, which focuses on human well-being, sense of purpose, and strengths. In addition to describing some psychological insights about sources of hope and optimism, this overview suggests directions for research addressing the human potential not only for resilience but also for flourishing in the face of environmental challenges. Human behavior is a major source of environmental problems, and human behavior can be a source of solutions as well.

Conclusion

Conservation psychology is mission driven. It suggests choosing research questions based on the promise that rigorously produced results will lead to better solutions. It is about "promoting" human well-being by way of attending to nature, because the two are inseparable. Conservation psychology aims to capitalize on the extraordinary breadth of psychology, and is an "identity" open to *every psychologist* who wants to bridge the disconnect between their professional specialty and their personal sense of responsibility toward the planet. Psychology's strength is its great scientific tradition; thus, the "understanding" embedded in our title. Conservation psychology wants to tap every variety of this talent in several possible kinds of endeavors: applied interdisciplinary conservation teamwork that can immediately use tools of psychology; using theory and findings of psychology to help recast the foundations of major institutions to be truer to human in nature, and to nature in humans.

Conservation psychology is a new and rapidly developing field. Our aim in this volume is to give a sense of the focus and purpose of conservation psychology and to summarize the research on some of the most important topics. In this way, we hope to introduce the field to those for whom it is new and to package the information in a way that makes it useful to those who might wish to join the collective of conservation psychologists as well as those who are in a position to apply what has been learned. Protecting the environment must be a collaborative effort, and communication among people with different specializations is an important first step.

At the heart of conservation psychology is a recognition of the bidirectional relationship between humans and the natural environment: how nature affects people and how they in turn affect the environment. Understanding why nature is significant to people strengthens the argument for conservation. Understanding the ways in which nature is significant to people enables the construction of initiatives that will promote conservation. In the face of the environmental challenges and changes that have already begun, evidence from psychological research has an important part to play in considerations of environmental policy.

For further information, visit these websites

Society for Environmental, Population, and Conservation Psychology, www.apadivisions.org/division-34/ (XXXX-a).
Society for Human Ecology, www.societyforhumanecology.org/ (XXXX-b).
Society for Conservation Biology's Social Science Working Group, www.conbio.org/workinggroups/SSWG/ (XXXX-c).
Environmental Design Research Association, www.edra.org (XXXX-d).
North American Association for Environmental Education, www.naaee.org (XXXX-e).
International Association for People-Environment Studies, www.iaps-association.org/ (XXXX-f).
European Psychological Association's Environmental Psychology division, www.dgps.de/fachgruppen/umwelt/ (XXXX-g).
Community Based Social Marketing, http://www.cbsm.com/ (XXXX-h).

References

Adler, A. (1956). *The individual psychology of Alfred Adler*. (H. Ansbacher & R. Ansbacher, Eds.) New York: Basic Books.
Anderson, C. A. (2012). Climate change and violence. In D. Christie (Ed.), *The encyclopedia of peace psychology*. Hoboken, NJ: Wiley-Blackwell.
Beringer, A. (2003). A conservation psychology with heart. *Human Ecology Review 10*(2), 150–153.
Bixler, R. & Floyd, M. (1997). Nature is scary, disgusting, and uncomfortable. *Environment and Behavior, 5*(2), 202–247.
Bonnes, M., & Bonaiuto, M. (2002). Environmental psychology: From spatial-physical environment to sustainable development. In R. Bechtel & A. Churchman (Eds.), *Handbook of environmental psychology*. New York: Wiley.
Cialdini, R. B. (2003). Crafting normative messages to protect the environment. *Current Directions in Psychological Science, 12*(4), 105–109.
Clayton, S. (Ed.) (2012. *The Oxford handbook of environmental and conservation psychology*. New York: Oxford.
Clayton, S. & Brook, A. (2005). Can psychology help save the world? A model for conservation psychology. *Analyses of Social Issues and Public Policy, 5* (1), 87–102.
Clayton, S., Litchfield, C., & Geller, E. S. (2013). Psychological science, conservation, and environmental sustainability. *Frontiers in Ecology and the Environment, 11*, 377–382.
Clayton, S., Manning, C. M., & Hodge C. (2014). *Beyond storms & droughts: The psychological impacts of climate change*. Washington, DC: American Psychological Association and ecoAmerica. Available at http://ecoamerica.org/wp-content/uploads/2014/06/eA_Beyond_Storms_and_Droughts_Psych_Impacts_of_Climate_Change.pdf.
Crosby, F., Clayton, S., Downing, R., & Iyer, A. (2004). Values and science. *American Psychologist, 59*, 125–126.
Gardner, G., & Stern, P. (1996). *Environmental problems and human behavior*. Boston: Allyn & Bacon.
Gifford, R. (2014). Environmental psychology matters. *Annual Review of Psychology, 65*, 541–579.
Global Footprint Network (2013). *The national footprint accounts*, 2012 edn. Oakland, CA, USA: Global Footprint Network.
Hardin, G. (1968). The tragedy of the commons. *Science, 162*, 1243–1248.
Howard, G. S. (2000). Adapting human lifestyles for the 21st century. *American Psychologist, 55*(5), 509–515.
Hsiang, S., Burke, M., & Miguel, E. (2013). Quantifying the impact of climate on human conflict. *Science, 341*, DOI: 10.1126/science.1235367

Kahn, Jr.,, P. H. & Hasbach, P. H. (Eds.) (2012). *Ecopsychology: Science, totems, and the technological species*. Cambridge, MA: MIT Press.

Kellert, S. R. (1996). *The value of life: Biological diversity and human society*. Washington, D.C.: *Island Press*.

Lewin, K. (1951). *Field theory in social science: Selected papers*. New York: Harper.

Manfredo, M. (2008). *Who cares about wildlife?* New York: Springer.

Mascia, M. (2003). Conservation psychology: challenges and opportunities. *Human Ecology Review, 10*, 163–164.

Maynard, M. (2007, July 4). Toyota hybrid makes a statement, and that sells. *New York Times*, *A1*, A11.

McKenzie-Mohr, D. (2000). Fostering sustainable behavior through community-based social marketing. *American Psychologist*, *55*, 531–537.

Moore, C. (2003). *Silent scourge: Children, pollution, and why scientists disagree*. New York: Oxford.

Oskamp, S. (2000). A sustainable future for humanity: how can psychology help? *American Psychologist*, *55*, 496–508.

Reser, J. P. (1995). Whither environmental psychology? *Journal of Environmental Psychology*, *15*, 235–257.

Reser, J. P. (2007) *Psychology and the natural environment. A position statement prepared for the Australian Psychological Society*. Melbourne: Australian Psychological Society.

Reuveny, R. (2008). Ecomigration and violent conflict: case studies and public policy implications. *Human Ecology*, *36*, 1–13.

Saunders, C. (2003). The emerging field of conservation psychology. *Human Ecology Review*, *10*, 137–149.

Searles, H. F. (1960). *The nonhuman environment in normal development and schizophrenia*. New York: International Universities Press.

Sommer, R. (2000). Discipline and field of study: A search for clarification. *Journal of Environmental Psychology*, *20*(1), 1–4.

Soulé, M. E. (1985). What is conservation biology? *BioScience*, *35*, 727–734.

White, L. (1967). The historical roots of our ecological crisis. *Science*, *155*, 1203–1207.

World Commission on Environment and Development (WCED). (1987). *Our common future*. New York: Oxford University Press.

Part I

Human Experiences of Nature

2

Domestic Nature: Cohabiting with Animals and Plants

Nature can seem to be remote from human affairs (see Chapter 5). But many people have constructed an intimate relationship with nature by making natural entities a part of their homes. A large body of research investigates people's interactions with companion and other domestic animals. Interactions with plants around the home and garden have received less study, although they clearly are meaningful to many people. We review both literatures as they reflect on the ways in which people directly care for nature, both in the sense of emotional responsiveness and in the sense of practical caretaking.

Animals in the home

Pets are a principal example of what we consider "domestic nature." The definition of a pet, however, is not simple. Eddy (2003) considered Webster's notion of a pet as a "domesticated animal kept for pleasure rather than utility." If domestication means that a species' reproduction has been controlled by people over time so as to select specific traits, then this definition applies well to the prototypical cases. But it does less well in cases where cats or dogs are bred for sale, or are allowed to go feral, or may serve both pleasure and utilitarian functions. Further, the variety of captured and tamed wild animals that some human owners would consider pets are left out.

Conservation Psychology: Understanding and promoting human care for nature, Second Edition.
Susan Clayton and Gene Myers.

www.wiley.com\go\clayton\conservation

Table 2.1 U.S. Pet ownership statistics.

	Dogs	Cats	Birds	Horses
Percent of households owning	36.5	30.4	3.1	1.5
Number of households owning	43,246,000	36, 117,000	3,671,000	1,780,000
Average number per household	1.6	2.1	2.3	2.7
Total number in the US	69,926,000	74,059,000	8,300,000	4,856,000

Adapted from AVMA, 2012.

A second entry in Webster's is intended for human–human relations: one "who is treated with unusual kindness or consideration." Extending this to nonhumans broadens our view of the relationship between people and their animal companions. Still, some animal relations may fall outside either definition: for example, the popular practice among Japanese children of keeping insects. Called "mushi," they may be referred to as pets and are anthropomorphized in media, but are rarely given names and their deaths are not grieved (Laurent, 2000). (Much more common is entomophobia, afflicting 6% (20 million) of Americans. Lockwood (2013) proposes evolutionary predispositions and also cultural priming of insect fears. Of the few who seek therapy, 90% successfully attain entomophilia, which characterizes early childhood and our species' potential to be enthralled by nature around us.)

Simple statistics available for the U.S. suggest the huge importance of domestic nature. Sixty-three percent of American households report having at least one pet. Table 2.1 shows the American Veterinary Medical Association (AVMA, 2012) estimates for 2011, based on a national survey of over 50,000 households.

In addition, the AVMA estimates about 8 million households hold a total of about 58 million fish; 1.4 million homes keep 3.2 million rabbits, and 1.3 million residences host 2.3 million turtles – among many other creatures. The economic investment is correspondingly large. Total U.S. pet expenditures for 2013 were over 55.7 billion USD (APPA, 2014). The combined trends suggest people are keeping fewer of every category of pet compared to 2008, but spending more on them. Nearly 27% of elementary school classrooms have animals other than dogs and cats (Rud & Beck, 2003). What some people consider to be excessive pet-pampering continues to expand in the recent decades, with trends such as dental braces, antidepressant drugs, designer foods, and cancer surgery for various pets (Brady & Palmeri, 2007).

History and variations in pet-keeping

Do such excesses suggest that bringing animals into the home is a frivolous side effect of affluence? The domestication of cats and dogs from their wild forebears originated in the emergence of agriculture and its stores of rodent-attracting grain in the case of cats; and possibly in the partnership of wolves raised at the hearth in the case of dogs. Dogs and cats were kept in sixteenth century England for their usefulness in shepherding, ratting, and so forth, but they were not regarded as pets. Historians, such as Ritvo (1987), attribute the increasing popularity of pets in modern times to industrialization, which made it economically feasible to support pets. By the mid industrial era, a new level was reached. Dog fanciers and breeders selected for purposeless and exaggerated features; distinctiveness and a lack of functionality among pets signaled the owner's status just as bound feet indicated membership in a privileged class among Chinese women.

An alternate account is offered by historian Grier (1999). In nineteenth century industrial cities an emerging middle-class was charting a new ideal of family life that can be called "domesticity." The home stood in contrast to the commercial domain's rough pursuit of self-interest and to masculine violence. The special mission of the home was to cultivate the countervailing virtue of gentility, which combined self-control and softened feelings. The potential of pets to encourage such kindness was extolled by parenting advisors in antebellum America as something "natural." This readily translated into the much wider humane movement.

These historical accounts are not mutually exclusive. But in light of newer ideas about our links to animals and nature, we would add that perhaps pet-keeping expresses a desire to connect with nature, even in the context of the city. Indeed, keeping pets in one's dwelling turns out to be a much wider-spread impulse than accounts focused on the West suggest. Serpell (1986, 1988) cites numerous examples from antiquity where the gentry and nobility are recorded as having kept a variety of pets, and descriptions of pet-keeping in tribal societies documented by early explorers and anthropologists. In the latter accounts, people were hesitant to give up their pets for any price; in some Amazonian Indian tribes, women suckled young animals, even bear cubs, from their own breasts. Such animals, it was reported, were never eaten. The Warao, on the Orinoco River near the Amazon, kept wild birds, monkeys, sloths, rodents, ducks, dogs, and chicken as pets, as reported in the 1970s. The M'Bbuti Pygmies of Zaire hunted with dogs, though they apparently treated them cruelly. The Comanche of North America, on the other hand, revered their dogs, which were kept for no particular use (Serpell 1988).

In looking at the contemporary and cross-cultural evidence, Serpell (1988) holds that neither utilitarian explanations nor those that describe pets as gratuitous "toys" provide a full explanation. Instead, he argues that in most cases the relationship is one of nurturance, protection, and emotional bonds. Perhaps pet-keeping expresses what Taylor (2002) calls the "tending instinct." Attachment to pets does not strongly correlate with attachment to people, positively or negatively, unless we restrict our sample to people who take pet owning to such an extreme that it may displace other people from their lives (see Paul, 2000 for an overview of this topic). For the majority of modern pet owners, pet-keeping probably augments social relationships rather than replicating or replacing them. There is another possibility: in a close look at pet-keeping in several lowland Amazonian societies, Erikson (2000) suggested that it allows a hunting society to appease the powerful animal spirits by taming and feeding, and thus balancing the relationship. Perhaps for modern people too, pets let us experience reciprocity with nature.

Relationships with pets

How do we examine the relationships between humans and their animals? Are they most similar to human–object relations, human–human relationships (such as attachment), relationships among nonhuman animals, or do human–animal relationships require their own kind of categories and methods (Kidd & Kidd, 1987)? All may be useful and tell us different things. If the animal is regarded as an object, one model may be appropriate, but if it is seen as a subjective being, alternative models are more accurate. Ethological studies of the behaviors of pets and their people have shown that for both dogs (Millot & Filiatre, 1986; Mitchell, 1987) and cats the "relationships are indeed two-way partnerships, with both parties adjusting their behaviour to that of their partners" (Turner, 2000, p. 258). Human–animal relations are indeed a special territory, and a diverse one at that.

One topic suggesting mutuality between pet and owner is play (Fig. 2.1). In careful studies of bouts of play between dogs and their owners, Mitchell (1987) found large overlap in the kinds of mutual play routines enacted by humans and both familiar and unfamiliar dogs. Both engaged in contingency games, although only people attempted manipulations and complex deceptions.

Speech with pets would appear to be only subjectively mutualistic but on closer inspection it may be more objectively so, at least with dogs. Reports from therapeutic contexts suggest children may talk to an animal (sometimes silently) in the same fashion as to a confidant (Rochberg-Halton, 1985). In a study of military families, Cain (1985) found that 77% "believed that the pet understood when they talked or confided in them" and that 73% said that their pet "communicated back to them"; half or more indicated that the pet responded to moods such as when someone was anxious or upset. During play with dogs, people use short utterances to get attention or try to control the dog (Mitchell & Edmonson, 1999). Mills (2005), outlining a cognitive approach to dog training, highlights the multichannel nature of even simple commands and the extent to which dogs may understand the concept behind commands and generalize them to novel contexts.

Looking at ordinary speech behavior with animals, it may be easy to overestimate humans' anthropomorphism. Hirsh-Pasek and Treiman (1982) suggested that people talk to dogs in similar register to how they talk to very young children. Adults do appear to be very casual in the apparent assumptions they make about animals' linguistic abilities and they attribute more higher-order intentionality the more they perceive the animal as similar to humans (Eddy et al., 1993). But there may be an important clue here. Myers (2007) argues that in social development children deploy their basic social interactive abilities in ways that reflect the differences presented on a bodily level by the animal, a pattern also observed by Millot and Filiatre (1986; see also Serpell, 2000). This ability may be refined with practice to produce nuanced

(a)

Fig. 2.1 (a, b) Myers in primary research about child–dog relationship. Photos courtesy of Olin Myers Sr.

(b)

Fig. 2.1 *(continued).*

interactions with, and understandings of, an animal (cf. Shapiro, 1989). The human "mirror neuron" system underlying human empathy (Sommerville & Decety, 2006) may be recruited when we try to understand animals. Franklin et al. (2013) found similar, though not identical, patterns of neural activation to suffering humans and suffering animals. Humans use many of the same brain areas to recognize dog and human faces (Blonder et al., 2004). But when people study dog and cat faces for emotion, they are biased to look at eyes, whereas cats and dogs use their ears as a means of communication (Sims et al., 2005). The unimportance of our own ears as expressive tools leads us to ignore this cue.

The way people speak about, as well as to, pets also reflects the nature of the relationship. Many people consider pets as family members or friends; in 2006, half of pet owners (49.7%) said they considered their pets to be family members (Cain, 1985; APPMA, 2008). Some are beginning to suggest that pets be considered "companion animals" and that the person be considered as a "guardian" rather than an "owner." A study of a random U.S. sample showed that those considering themselves "guardians" practiced significantly higher levels of spaying or neutering, registering, providing celebrations, and expressing affection toward their pet (Carlisle-Frank & Frank, 2006). This difference in language thus appears to capture different underlying value orientations and relationships to the animals. Another linguistic indicator of the personalization of pets is the use of the term "who" rather than "which" to refer to them in writing. In a study of a 100 million word corpus of writing collected from well-balanced sources in Great Britain between 1991 and 1995, Gilquin and Jacobs (2006) found that the animals most frequently referred to in this personal way were dogs, horses, cats, birds, and rabbits – pet or domestic animals. Interestingly, when style manuals did permit the use of "who," they tended to stipulate that it was allowable when the animal had been personalized with a name or other individualizing features (Gilquin & Jacobs, 2006).

Attachment to companion animals includes an emotional bond, a sense of compatibility, a sense of security, a desire to be together, and a mental representation of the other and the relationship. Attachment between humans may also vary on all these dimensions. Of course not all human–pet relationships follow one model. Blouin (2013) suggested that three orientations to pet dogs each are rooted in individual characteristics, experiences, distinct histories, and contemporary sources. They are dominionistic (low regard for pets, mainly valued for uses they provide); humanistic (elevated view of the dog to near-human status and valued for the affective bonds with it); and protectionistic (high regard for animals generally, and the pet valued as a companion who also has its own interests). Perhaps, the most tempting human–human attachment on which to model human–pet relationships is that of parent and child. Like children, pets need food and medical care, oversight in dangerous situations, and someone to explain them to authorities such as doctors, and both are subject to behaviors at the dominant partner's will such as petting and touching (Beck & Katcher, 1996). Both pets' and children's range of movement is restricted, their sexuality controlled, their excrement tolerated, and their dependence accepted.

As with children, most relationships between humans and pets are mutualistic; both parties benefit, although in different ways. Some, however, are "parasitic" relations, where one partner is benefited at a cost to the other. Neglect, abuse, hoarding, and sexual exploitation are examples. Although these patterns are often pathological, the extent to which this is the case has sometimes been exaggerated. See Herzog (2010, pp. 29–34) for a review of extensive attempts to find a "link" between childhood animal abuse and a pattern of escalating violent crime. It turns out that while some violent criminals showed this pattern, childhood animal abuse is far more common than recognized among people who turned out normal. Arluke (2006), for example, highlights the perspectives of animal hoarders in contrast to media portrayals and discusses ways in which casual animal abuse by adolescents (recollected by them as college students) served as what might be called "serious play" that let them experiment privately with adult-like power. These qualifications do not justify the abusive behaviors, but give insight into the complex social dimensions of animal cruelty.

Although it is not a pleasant topic, the study of issues such as animal abuse and euthanasia, and how this compares to the treatment of humans, provides insight into the psychological meanings of our close attachment to animals. Interestingly, concern for the abuse of both children and animals arose simultaneously in England and the US in the nineteenth Century (Unti 2002). Euthanasia of animals is routine in several contexts including animal shelters, animal research, and veterinary practice; if a bond exists between the workers and their subjects, some kind of psychic defense should emerge. In a study of 148 animal workers, Rohlf and Bennett (2005) found that 11% reported experiencing moderate levels of traumatic symptoms. Social support and time in the job seemed to buffer against this, while concern about animals' deaths predicted trauma.

Between mutualistic and parasitic relationships are "commensal" relations, such as when people care for semi-tame or feral pet animals. Many developing countries have large feral or free-roaming dog populations, which are a major contributor to human rabies infections. Studies suggest that cats hunting outdoors (including an estimated 60 million feral cats plus 35% of owned cats in the U.S.) hunt birds whether hungry or not. If only 20% to 30% of prey are birds, this still results in millions of birds killed by cats every year (Crooks & Soule, 1999). From a social and psychological point of view, the feral cat issue illustrates how people caring about different aspects of nature creates contention. People who help semiowned cats were found to have positive feelings toward them, and to believe cats are independent and thus in less need of care (Toukhsati et al., 2007), although in fact cats living outside are subject to multiple risks.

In other ways, however, relations with animals are on a more equal status, although they may provide things that humans cannot as easily (or that we cannot receive as willingly). Myers (2007) suggested that interaction with familiar animals provides children's developing sense of self with a number of important qualities including similarity-within-difference that confirms the child's own self, an implicit feeling of self-other clarification, a vivid "symbolism" of life process itself, and an early sense of connection with the nonhuman. Interaction with animals also may foster perspective-taking and empathy. As Shepard (1996) observed, animals make us human because they offer different points of comparison that clarify what it means to be human.

The ways in which animals differ from humans offer other advantages. Because animals are typically unable to enforce or apply standards of human convention or morality, we experience them as nonjudgmental. Since language is used to define, negotiate, and adjudicate an often ambiguous social reality, animals offer interaction free from such demands, tensions, and accountability. Animals thus may feel more authentic to us, since it is rare for a creature without language to conceive or send a double message. Language itself entails the potentially challenging job of putting our experiences, needs, and wishes into words; with an animal, a child or adult can simply feel a connection (or act out a feeling) without worry of articulating it. Rather than taking turns, being polite, and listening carefully, conversations can be delightfully one-sided, or alternatively, insightful. Nonetheless, despite language often having been used to signify human superiority, it is because of the very structure of human language that we can wonder and care about the subjective meanings of animals' behavior (Myers, 2007). Language is also positive and essential to our humanity, and it can be a direct avenue to deepen our empathy with animals through the exercise of the sympathetic imagination elicited by literature (Beierl, 2008). To speak and to listen are affirmations of our humanity, and denial or refusal of these actions can indicate inhumanity and injustice. Through words among humans we create shared meanings and open new domains not only of connection and compatriotism – but also of misunderstanding and separation. It is no wonder that in a complex human world, animals offer us something essential.

Health and well-being effects of domestic animals

Domestic animals contribute to human health and well-being in numerous ways. One relatively well-studied effect is on cardiovascular health (Friedmann et al., 2000). Beginning in 1980, Erica Friedmann and colleagues began to find that cardiovascular patients who were pet owners showed better survival than nonowners. Larger, more controlled studies found striking effects; for example, independent of social support or severity of illness, dog owners were 8.6 times as likely to be alive one year after heart attacks (Friedman & Thomas, 1995), but cat ownership predicted lower survival (and was associated with lower social support). Male and female pet owners were also shown to have fewer risk factors for heart disease in a study of 5,541 Australians (Anderson et al., 1992). Some benefits of pets arise fairly obviously: adopters of dogs (but neither control subjects nor those adopting cats), who showed better health ten months after adoption, reported a four-to five-fold increase frequency and amount of walking (Serpell, 1991). Increased walking among dog owners can be attributed to increased social support, motivation, companionship and empathic sense of responsibility for a family member (Higgins et al., 2013). Recent studies illuminate one of the physiological mechanisms responsible for the less obvious health effects: elderly hypertension patients showed less blood pressure elevation in a stressful situation when accompanied by a friendly dog than without the dog present (Friedmann et al., 2007). Similar effects had already been found for children ages 9 to 15 years, although college students seem less affected by the presence of a dog (Friedmann et al., 2007). Not only in stressful situations but also in everyday activities, the presence of a pet (especially a dog) lowered the ambulatory blood pressure (ABP) of elderly subjects living with hypertension (Friedmann et al., 2013). The data included ABP readings every 20 minutes, tracking of the presence of the pet and other people in the room, and a variety of controlled factors, with strong statistical results, suggesting the effect is robust. The familiarity of the dog makes a difference too; owners' blood pressure decreased significantly while subjects petted their own dogs, but not others' dogs (Baun et al., 1984). The connection between longer-term health and pet ownership, however, is weaker among the elderly (Wells, 2009).

Studies have shown more subtle effects of animals on stress reduction. Viewing an aquarium of fish has sometimes, though not always, reduced physiological measures of stress or improved patient recovery. Fairly consistently, however, fish tanks do have positive psychological effects. In the same studies of stressful conditions that found little change in blood pressure and heart rate, subjects reported feeling calmer, more comforted, and greater delight (Barker et al., 2003). Overall, the health benefits of pets may primarily come indirectly through a variety of psychological benefits associated with well-being (Crawford et al., 2006). Although findings are not consistent (probably due in part to measurement issues), companion animals have been found to reduce anxiety, increase reported happiness, and buffer stressful periods: those under stress report greater attachment to a pet, and that attachment is negatively correlated with depression.

Several studies have found that living with a pet is associated with lower levels of loneliness among elderly women (Goldmeier, 1986), women living alone (Zasloff & Kidd, 1994), and elderly respondents living at home (Roberts et al., 1996). This may not mean that obtaining a pet causes the decrease in loneliness. A quasi-experimental longitudinal study of pet adopters (Gilbey et al., 2007) found that those having obtained a pet did not report lower loneliness, controlling for gender, presence of other pets, or type of pet sought. Experiments examining the presence of animals in settings, such as nursing homes, however, have shown decreases in loneliness (Banks & Banks, 2005). A study of singly-living and married cat owners and nonowners found that spouses, but not cats, increase positive effect, whereas cats (and spouses) decreased negative effect (Turner et al., 2003). If an animal is experienced as an added burden, however, by people whose lives are too busy or who have low attachment to the animal, then it does not have positive effects for the person (nor for the animal, probably). Also, pets can pose risks to humans in the form of allergens, physical injuries, and diseases. Evidence of the positive effect of a dog on depressive symptoms comes from people with hearing impairments after receiving their service dog (Guest et al., 2006). Following on promising leads, research on the use of dogs in detecting cancers, seizures, and hypoglycemia is exploring whether the dogs use olfactory cues or mood, bodily motion, orientation, or other cues (Wells, 2009). Dogs may offer noninvasive alternatives to some technologies used presently.

Animals' positive effects on cognitive functioning have also been explored, particularly in the context of preschools, where recent trends in safety concerns have discouraged the long-standing practice of classroom pets. For example, research by Gee et al. (2010a, 2010b) has shown that preschoolers do better in the presence of a dog when doing a categorization task and performing an unprompted memory task, compared to with a stuffed dog. When required to adhere to instructions to do a motor task, preschoolers did as well with a real dog as with human help. Both evoked better performance than a stuffed dog, but not significantly so

(Gee et al., 2009). Children with special needs such as language impairment or developmental delays benefit (Gee et al., 2009, 2010a). Dogs appear to offer children with autism a preferred form of social interaction (Prothmann et al., 2009).

Social effects of companion animals

The above effects may be due in part to the animal itself, and in part to the animal's way of facilitating social interaction. Mugford and M'Comisky (1975) randomly placed either a budgerigar or a begonia in the homes of solitary elderly people and found that those with birds were significantly more socially involved at the end of the study. Being accompanied by a rabbit or turtle facilitates social interaction too, though dogs are the focus of most of the related research (Wells, 2009). The tendency of strangers to talk more frequently with a person walking a dog has been well documented (e.g., Messent, 1983). McNicholas and Collis (2000) put the facilitative effect of the mere presence of a dog to a stringent test by using a highly trained dog that did not directly initiate interaction itself. Being accompanied by the dog increased interactions with strangers in a variety of everyday settings. In another study, the researchers varied how well attired the man with the dog was. When he was "scruffily" dressed, interactions were lower, but the presence of the dog still had a positive effect. Could the presence of a dog facilitate closer relationships? A series of experiments by Guéguen and Ciccotti (2008) says yes, in these cases: soliciting money, helping a stranger pick up money, and, for young women asked if they would give their phone number to a male research confederate, complying! Although the following study used animals with whom the subjects were bonded, it could provide an explanation of this latter striking result on a neurophysiological level. Miller et al. (2009) measured oxytocin levels in men and women after interaction with their pet dogs after a stressful day at work. Oxytocin is a neuropeptide associated with social bonding, socialization, and stress relief. For women blood oxytocin levels increased at a high level of statistical significance after 25 minutes of interaction with their dogs after work compared to the same period reading nonfiction. For men, there was a decrease in oxytocin for both dog and reading conditions. All participants scored high on bonding with their dogs, suggesting different hormonal pathways are at work.

Employing a sociological analysis, Sanders (1990) explained that dogs act as sources of "mutual openness," providing a shared focus of nonthreatening attention. At other times, dog behavior in public, because it reflects on the owner, can pose significant "impression management" challenges, and owners, unable to completely deny their involvement, use a variety of "excusing tactics" (such as justifying, redefining, situating, quasi-theory explanation, demonstrative disciplining, or, as a last resort "unlinking" or denying) (Sanders, 1999). Indeed, not only do others make judgments about a person based on a pet's behavior, but also they may employ a folk psychological theory to impute personality traits based merely on the breed of dog they believe the person to own (Mae et al., 2004).

Research on the relation of personality variables to pet ownership has not found consistent differences, even when the strength of attachment is taken into consideration (Podberscek & Gosling, 2000). The researchers point out that, aside from widely different measures and methods, this may be because former pet ownership is not considered in these studies. It may be that only a small fraction of adult "nonowners" have actually never owned a pet. Further, to the extent differences are found, since all studies are cross-sectional, we do not know if we are seeing causes or effects: Do nice people become pet owners or do pet owners become nice people? Despite tempting stereotypes, studies looking for personality differences between dog and cat owners have generally shown none, perhaps because these are the most common pets and many people own or have owned both. When owners of more widely diverse animals such as birds, snakes, rabbits, ferrets, hedgehogs, horses, and turtles, or of different breeds of dog have been studied, some personality-related differences have been found (Kidd et al., 1983), but there are few studies and inconsistent findings (Podberscek & Gosling, 2000). More recently, Gosling et al. (2010) have shown that self-identification as "dog person" (as opposed to a "cat person") is moderately associated with extroversion.

Emerging studies are looking at animal personality as a measurable variable, and at the interaction between owners' personality traits and the animals' behavior (e.g., Podberscek & Serpell, 1997). A recent study found that Austrian and Hungarian dog owners rated their own and their pet's personalities similarly on the five factor personality model: openness/closedness to experience, conscientiousness versus impulsivity, extraversion versus introversion, agreeableness versus antagonism, and neuroticism versus emotional stability (Turscán et al., 2012). The results held up when the dog was assessed by an independent person. Application of these traits to dogs is contentious. Nonetheless, such studies would have special relevance if they could help reduce the rate at which dogs are returned to shelters, which ranges from about 15% to 50%. One team produced a concerted effort to determine psychological characteristics that predict a good fit between dogs and owners (Curb et al., 2013). After generating an exhaustive list of dog traits, they gave dog owners two surveys, one describing the dog's traits on eight dimensions, and the other describing the owner's personality, plus a rating of satisfaction with their dog. They found four characteristics in which a dog–person match correlated significantly with satisfaction: tendency to share possessions, love of running outside, likeliness of being destructive, and ability to get along with others. Taking these few characteristics into account could produce better adoptive matches.

It is often believed that people physically resemble their pets. College students indeed did much better than chance at matching owners and dogs for pure-bred dogs, but not for mutts (Roy & Christenfeld, 2004). Herzog (2010) considered whether the evidence for pet–owner similarity supports the theory that people and dogs (like spouses) come to resemble each other over time, or whether the pattern suggests assortative mating, as when people choose romantic partners of similar attractiveness or other characteristics to themselves. Because the observed similarities did not relate to how long the person–dog pairs had been together, and because the pattern does not hold for mutts (whose adult appearance is hard to anticipate when they were presumably obtained as puppies), the assortative mating theory is stronger. Given this finding, what cues are used to judge similarity? In a series of studies, Nakajima et al. (2009, 2013) showed that Japanese college students and adults make accurate judgments of whether a pure breed dog–person pair of facial photos includes the dog owner, or not, on about 80% of trials, much better than their odds of 50–50 by guessing. This judgment was based strongly on viewing the eye regions of the dyads; when that region was blocked, judgments fell to chance levels. Again our human subconscious biases about faces seem to be at work. Ears, however, do come into play but in a human way: long-haired women preferred dogs such as spaniels with long ears, whereas short-haired women liked short-haired breeds, in both cases rating the similar dogs as smarter, more loyal, and friendlier (Coren, 1999).

We might anticipate sex differences in involvement with animals. According to a thorough review, however, studies have shown that men and women are nearly identical in keeping pets and desiring to live with animals (Herzog, 2007, p. 15). Only modest average differences favoring women are found in attachment to pets, and women are more likely to express concern for animal rights. Across studies, the pattern is of two overlapping bell curves, with men a little lower on average and women higher on average. Coinciding with this pattern, there are disproportionately many more women at the extreme positive end of attitudes toward animals, and the same with men on the negative end (Herzog, 2010). In the broad middle, it may be that animals provide men as well as women with a way to express care and affection. Melson and Fogel (1988) found that animals were especially important for middle-childhood boys because they provide an object to nurture without feeling girlish.

Robotic animals

What if the benefits of pets were available with advanced life-like robotic animals? What is different between such "personified computational technologies" and living things? This topic, itself a subset of the field of Human–Robot Interaction, is one of three places in this chapter where we tap into the research of Peter Kahn and others to compare something "really natural" with a technologically mediated version. These examples may shed light on basic questions about the human–nature relationship. In one series of studies, Kahn (2011) and colleagues examined responses to the Sony robotic dog AIBO, which displays seemingly autonomous self-directed and self-organizing behavior. It can detect and move toward a special pink ball and varies the timing and combinations of behaviors in a way that mimics the agency of a real animal. Its appearance, however, is unmistakably technological; it has no fur, but a rather shiny and sleekly designed gray exterior.

One study looked at the spontaneous web postings of 182 participants in an online AIBO forum. The 3,119 comments showed that members thought of AIBO not only as a technology but also having life-like biological and mental states, as a companion, and as more "real" than a robot. While not alive, it seemed to provide a vivid social presence. Some recounted how they lavished affection on their AIBOs, for example. But while AIBO evoked attributions of agency, biological life, mental states, and social rapport, people seldom talked about it as if it had moral standing or accountability – concepts such as rights, meriting respect, deserving attention, or blameworthiness. Additional studies of the ways children interacted with AIBO found that preschool children attributed biological properties, mental states, social rapport, and moral standing to AIBO at fairly high rates, but these rates were very similar to their attributions to a stuffed toy dog, suggesting their answers were based on pretense for both artifacts. Behavioral coding, however, showed that the children were apprehensive and made attempts at reciprocal interactions more often with AIBO; they also used verbal directives with AIBO five times as frequently as with the stuffed dog and often startled when AIBO initiated movement (Kahn, 2011). Although the researchers were not able to rule out pretend play as accounting for the children's responses, a fundamental question is raised: when people interact with technological nature, do they think it is "real"? Research by a different team found preschoolers showed positive affect toward, and social interactions with, both a real dog and a furry robotic dog, but less toward a metallic robotic dog similar to AIBO (Howard & Vick, 2010). The furry dog seemed to blur across behavioral and verbal measures with the real dog. It seems that in many instances the criteria of what is real are not well specified, and robots may muddy the waters more.

This was the conclusion from a further study with children from three age groups between 7 and 15 years old, which compared the AIBO with a real dog (Kahn, 2011). Children were observed interacting with each and were interviewed in depth using a semistructured approach that allowed the researchers to explore the "why's" behind children's attributions and behaviors. On many measures, the children clearly differentiated AIBO and the real dog: AIBO was understood to be an artifact, was poked and prodded, and received less gentle physical gestures, whereas the real dog was clearly seen as biological, psychological, a possible companion, and having moral standing at statistically significantly higher rates. And children cited AIBO's status as an artifact as the reason they denied these properties to it. Nonetheless, surprising proportions of the children attributed aliveness (21%), mental states (56%), sociality (70%), moral standing (76%), and "could be a friend" (83%) to AIBO, although in each case the percentage was lower with each step in age. The children gave the dog much more physical attention, but half of the children did pet AIBO gently at least once. So what is going on? Perhaps personified technologies present the human mind with a new "ontological category" that does not correspond perfectly to either animate being or inanimate; social other or not (Kahn, 2011; Severson & Carlson, 2010). And yet, the children were very clear that the real dog was much more alive and subject to moral consideration. Thus, the general pattern, Kahn suggests, is that technologically simulated nature may be better than no nature at all, but not quite as good as real nature.

Connections with nature

Does keeping pets create bonds with wild nature? Myers and Saunders (2002) suggest a developmentally potent route in which children think of animals as individuals and care about them on that level and this may lead to concern for wider levels of the ecological world. The evidence, however, is mixed. Kellert (1996) described links between humanistic (pet-like) attitudes and more ecological ones only in some populations. Sometimes care for animals as individuals can conflict with caring for other levels of biological organization, as in opposition to management options for deer overpopulation (Miller, 2002). Caring for pets does not necessarily inform people about caring for wildlife (Shore, 2002, cited in Vining, 2003). But Kafer et al. (1992), using a psychometric instrument (the Pet Relationship Scales), found relationships between three affective aspects of pet attitudes and beliefs about wild animals. Adults who see their pets as members of the family, who are affectionate toward them, or who share activities with the pet are more likely to believe that humans and wild animals have similar cognitive experience and intrinsic value (correlations of about $r = 0.60$). They also prefer closer physical distances to wild animals and are less favorable to hunting and sealing (correlations of about $r = 0.25$). Vining and Merrick (2006) also report some association between attachment to pets and nonanthropocentric worldviews. Bjerke et al. (2003) found that pet owners in Trondheim, Norway expressed more liking for common urban wildlife species (birds, squirrels, hedgehogs, butterflies, ducks, geese, foxes, bumblebees, etc.) than did nonpet owners. There were no differences in liking for less attractive species such as rats, snails, and mosquitoes. Again, these findings cannot indicate a causal relationship and may reflect a general predisposition toward nature. The connection between pets and wildlife attitudes was put to a stiff test by researchers who surveyed children ages 10 to 15 in Slovakia about their knowledge of and attitudes toward three unpopular animals (Prokop & Tunnicliffe, 2010). In separate studies, the animals included a pest (potato beetle), a predator (wolf), and a disease vector (mouse); popular animals were posed as controls. Children overall knew more about but disliked the unpopular animals. But having pets at home was associated with more positive attitudes toward animals and better knowledge of them. The researchers note that the direction of causality regarding animal attitudes is unknown, but suggest that education focused on harmful animals' ecological roles and adaptations could improve understanding of how to control them. This might help constrain negative attitudes from becoming general if no specific action is available to deal with a threat.

It is clear, however, that emerging patterns in pet-keeping pose a problem for conservation when they lead to wildlife poaching and habitat destruction (e.g., tropical fish capture by blasting leads to coral reef damage). Rare animals become more valuable as they decline, fueling the illegal pet trade. With increasing affluence, developing countries such as China now have a booming pet trade, with many animals caught fresh from the wild sold in cages on street markets. Even when suitable animals are chosen, lack of knowledge about their needs and appropriate care often leads to negative consequences for the pet or for the local ecosystem. Thus, while our fascination for nature expresses something important about us, it is an appetite that itself must be tamed and educated.

Plants in the domestic sphere

The meanings and benefits of plants in domestic contexts have not received as much research attention as pets have, but there is some evidence for their impact. Certainly many people find landscaping, gardening, and houseplants important and engaging. In his history of relations to nature in early modern England, historian Keith Thomas (1983) notes the incredible emotion attached to trees on the estates of nobility. Their ancient age attested to the stability and status of the landlord, and for the same reason they were targets for vandalism, attacked as proxies for their owners. People still make personal connections to trees, as can be seen when they plant a tree to commemorate a marriage, celebrate a birth, or memorialize a death. Robert Sommer (2003) reviewed research on the way people feel about trees, concluding that "there is something deeper, spiritual, and almost ineffable about people's attachment to trees" (p. 180). In perhaps a less dramatic way, smaller plants can also have psychological and emotional significance for people, as well as having implications for the way they present themselves socially.

It is estimated that the US landscaping services industry includes about 50,000 companies with combined annual revenue of over $44 billion in 2006 (National Gardening Association). A 2006 study of 2,287 U.S. households by the National Gardening Association (NGA) found that 40%, or about 43 million households' respondents regard themselves as "gardeners," with estimated annual expenditures of about $21 billion. In 2013 expenditures were $34.9 billion after a series of years with double-digit percentage increases (Baldwin, 2014). In the United Kingdom, 67% of adults say that they are gardeners (Gross & Lane, 2007). More involved gardeners tend to be older and have no children at home. Although 18 to 34 year olds are the largest segment of the U.S. population, they participate in gardening less than others, and even 35 to 54 year olds have declined as a portion; over 55 year olds make up 46% of gardeners in 2013, compared to 31% in 2001. Gardening sales have increased over 300% since 1980 (Hyland, 2004) (Fig. 2.2).

In biophysical terms, gardening, landscaping, and indoor plants can have negative environmental impacts. They entail flows across space of material (industrially mined or "fixed" nutrients in fertilizer, topsoil, and peat mining) and organisms (conversions of ecosystems to produce flower or seed crops, transfer and sometimes depletion of native populations, and introduction of intentional and unintentional exotics), not to mention the application of toxic chemicals in the form of pesticides and herbicides. More sustainable approaches are available, and increasingly landscapers promote the use of native plants and organic pest control. Aside from their ecological impacts, these relations with plants also have impacts on their human caretakers by providing an intimate active connection to living organisms and natural processes.

Effects of indoor plants

Some houseplants provide direct health benefits. For over 25 years, NASA experimented with plants as it sought effective ways to purify air in space stations. In carefully controlled studies they found that philodendrons and spider plants were efficient at removing formaldehyde, and Gerbera daisies and chrysanthemums removed benzene (Wolverton, 1997). A Norwegian study

Fig. 2.2 Gardening is a common leisure pursuit. Photo by Susan Clayton.

of 51 office workers found that health problems decreased after plants were placed in the office (Fjeld et al., 1998). On the other hand, it should be noted that a few houseplants contain toxins and could pose hazards to pets or young children (for a database on poisonous plants, see Munro, 2014).

The mere presence of an interior plant also appears to facilitate cognitive function and positive emotion (Health Council of the Netherlands, 2004). Although Larsen et al. (1998) found that performance on a cognitive task decreased as the quantity of plants increased, participants' mood became more positive. Larsen et al. (1998) argue that their results may have been due to the repetitive and uncreative nature of their experimental task. Shibata and Suzuki (2004) looked more closely at the interaction of task demand and mood. They gave undergraduates the task of generating associations to adjectives (a cognitive demand), and gauged their mood, in the presence of a plant, a magazine stand, or an empty area. Subjects evaluated the plant as generating more calmness, less distraction, and more tranquility. Women had more positive moods under the plant condition, and their task performance was better. When plants have a positive effect on task performance, it may be because of their effect in reducing tension and arousal; the presence of plants has been shown to lower blood pressure (Health Council of the Netherlands, 2004). In Shibata and Suzuki's study, subjects' evaluation of the plant (or other object) had an effect on performance beyond the object's mere presence, showing that the effects of nature may be partly emotionally mediated. Similar benefits were found for cognitive performance after a demanding task for subjects by placing plants in a laboratory office type setting by Raanaas et al. (2011), who, like Shibata and Suzuki, interpreted their results to support Attention Restoration Theory (ART; see chapter 12).

On the other hand, other studies have supported Ulrich's (1983) psychoevolutionary stress reduction theory, including studies showing that the presence of plants increases subjects' ability to tolerate pain. Other possibilities are that plants may elevate positive mood regardless of stress or attention depletion, including possibly via the cultural or evolutionary symbolic meanings of plants and especially flowers (Bringslimark et al., 2009). These are possibilities yet to be addressed by empirical research and it could be that the indoor context of all these studies is sufficiently different from outdoor nature that other theories may be needed to explain the observations. But it is well enough established that plants in indoor settings have effects as predicted by the main theories (ART, stress reduction) to suggest they constitute "nature" enough, even though isolated from their habitats.

Window views of nature

Besides plants in or around the dwelling, a view of nature from a window has been shown to have a number of positive effects. Ulrich (1984) showed that post-gallbladder surgery patients who were placed in rooms with window views of natural elements needed fewer pain-killers, had shorter recovery times, and had fewer negative evaluations by nursing staff, as opposed to those with built views. Office workers with views of nature were more satisfied, which in turn was associated with more positive ratings of work and fewer health problems (Kaplan, 1993). And university students with a natural view from their dormitory room windows performed better on attention tests that were given in that setting than students whose view comprised built elements (Tenneson & Cimprich, 1995). Wells (2000) found that children moving into homes with windows onto a greater extent of green rather than built views, compared to their pre-move homes, showed better attentional capacity. And, in an important line of research, Taylor et al., (2002) have found that the ability to view nature from one's home can increase concentration and self-discipline. Window views of nature seem to be restorative, adding to residents' satisfaction and sense of well-being: feeling less distracted, more at peace, energized, competent, and focused (Kaplan, 2001). Views of trees were especially important in a sense of having one's attentive capacity restored. Kaplan (2001) also found that the view of a garden increases satisfaction with one's community.

In another of set of technological nature studies, Kahn (2011) compared the effects of three window conditions on subjects' heart-rate recovery after a low-level stressor. The three conditions were the subject's normal office window looking outside onto a scene with natural components; the window area blanked out; or replaced by a high-resolution monitor projecting the scene outside the office as detected by a camera mounted on the wall – in other words, a nearly identical view to the glass window. Participants recovered significantly more rapidly after the stressor for the glass window as opposed to the blank wall. Surprisingly, there was no significant difference between the technological view and the blank wall. In a follow-up field experiment where real-time virtual outside views were installed for six weeks in interior offices that lacked windows, however, subjects unanimously cited benefits and said they would recommend the devices for coworkers. (They did cite downsides: they noted the screen lacked parallax, where one's views of objects should shift with changed viewing positions, and that the cameras could invade others' privacy.) Kahn's results again fit his general finding that technological nature is better than no nature, but comes up short in comparison to "real" nature.

Plant-facilitated therapy

The psychological benefits of houseplants have been studied in the context of horticultural therapy with special populations. Plant-based therapy has been used with brain-injury patients, domestic violence victims, people with mental illness, and others. Relf (1998) outlines the major aspects of horticultural therapy including explaining why people respond to plants. Studies by Gigliotti et al. (2004, 2005) have carefully observed participants with dementia in adult day service programs using traditional and plant-based therapy techniques including cooking, crafts, and puzzles. They found that all kinds of horticultural therapy activities generated more engagement and positive affect, and less nonengagement, compared to conventional activities. Although these studies are promising, the evidence for their efficacy is not extensive (Relf, 2005) and falls short of clinical research standards. A comprehensive review of research on the health effects of nature notes that in many ways the results are suggestive, but methodological shortcomings undermine definitive conclusions (Health Council of the Netherlands, 2004). Frumkin (2004) urges an expansion of rigorous research on the therapeutic effects of plants. At the time of Annerstedt and Währborg's (2011) systematic review of nature-assisted therapies, only two randomized clinical trial studies of horticultural therapy were found, one showing no significant effect, with the other finding significant improvements in mood. For other study types 5 out of 8 reports showed positive results. Although strong recommendations for use of plants in diverse therapeutic contexts can be found, evidence of the type the medical research community demands is still sparse.

Experience and effects of gardening

Like the effects of pet ownership, the impacts of gardens range from the obvious to the more subtle. The physical activity required by gardens is a health benefit, as is eating the food a garden produces. In the context of a school-based nutrition education program, research reported by Morris et al. (2000) showed that children were willing to taste and eat more vegetables when they had helped grow them at a school garden than when they had received either no nutrition education or education without the gardening experience (we explore other aspects of greenery from children's perspective in the next chapter). The opportunity to relax in a garden and to engage all the senses can also have cognitive benefits. In interviews with gardeners aged 18 to 85, Gross and Lane (2007) found more abstract impacts, whose meanings differed according to subjects' life stages but which were salient to all the gardeners. *Escape* referred to the sense that they were removed from their usual worries and demands (compare the benefits described by Attention Restoration Theory, reviewed in Chapter 12). *Identity* acknowledged the way in which a garden is a public display of one's own effort, skill, and preferences (as suggested by the discussion of environmental identity in Chapter 8). *Ownership* fulfilled the desire to exercise control over a territory. Similarly, Clayton (2007) used surveys and factor analysis to explore benefits of gardening; she found that the primary benefits were relaxing and spending time in nature, controlling the appearance of the garden, and demonstrating effort and expertise (Fig. 2.3).

As early as 1973, Rachel Kaplan (Kaplan, 1973) found that gardeners with different kinds of gardens had somewhat different benefits. Vegetable growers put the heaviest weight on tangible productivity from their gardens, whereas gardening activities themselves were more important to others. A third kind of benefit was cognitive in nature, deriving from the intrinsic fascination of helping plants grow. In the Clayton (2007) study, gardeners who sought to appreciate nature thought their yard and gardening were more likely to express environmental concerns. Indeed, Kiesling and Manning (2010) explored whether there is a clear "environmental gardening identity" (EGID) using both Clayton's EID scale and a gardening-adapted version and other measures. The notion of EGID was partially supported, especially for gardeners whose reasons for gardening include connecting with nature – nurturing living things by working

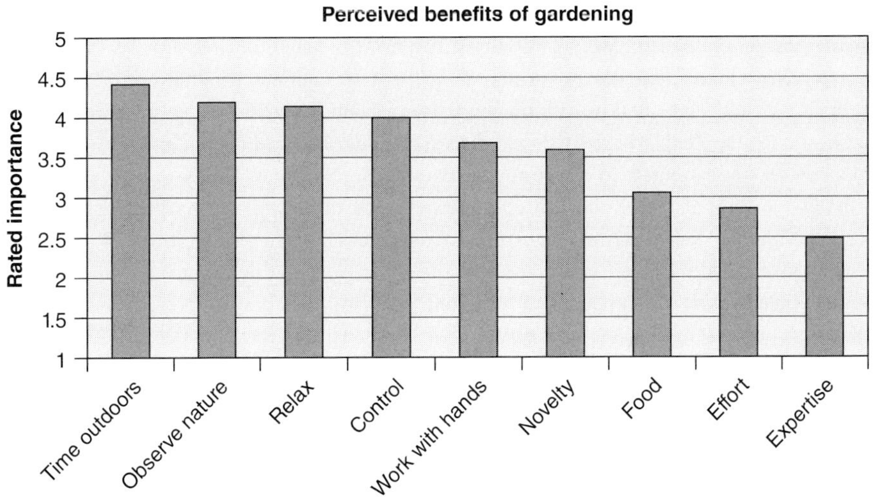

Fig. 2.3 Benefits of gardening. Based on data in Clayton, 2007.

with nature's processes. In interviews, urban domestic gardeners in Dunedin, New Zealand reiterated themes in the above paragraphs such as the garden being highly valued, health promoting, offering escape and relaxation, and (often implicitly) affording a chance to connect with and care for nature (Freeman et al., 2012). The researchers were struck by how gardeners' relationship to their gardens had morphed over their lives and became idiosyncratic expressions of the self.

Like perceptions of domestic animals, perceptions of gardens vary. Some people recognize the connection between the backyard and the broader ecosystem, whereas others think of the backyard more like an outdoor living room. Clayton (2007) asked homeowners whether they considered their gardens as an extension of their home or as part of the natural world and found a range of responses, but on the whole slightly closer to being part of the home. As a negative side effect, people do not tend to think of their gardening practices as having an impact on the ecosystem. It is possible, however that working closely with plants can connect people to wider realms of nature. A community-based gardening program for juvenile offenders not only increased horticultural knowledge, but also improved environmental attitudes, in proportion to how regularly the youth participated (Cammack et al., 2002). It is important to stress that the primary benefit of gardening identified by Clayton's (2007) sample was the opportunity to enjoy nature. Gross and Lane described the garden as a "deliberate construction of a relationship with nature" (p. 237). Taking care of the garden may not generalize to sustaining the ecosystem, but it can be an opportunity to remind people of what they value in nature.

More than most interactions with nature, gardening occurs in a social context. A garden can facilitate social interaction and a sense of community (Robbins et al., 2001). Carol Werner (2003) has looked at the social transactions that shape Americans' perceived need to maintain weed-free verdant lawns; she cites a study of citizens in the Northwestern U.S. who gave these reasons for using chemicals to maintain their lawns: a desire to be good neighbors (68%), and to have proper appearing yards (58%). Carrico et al. (2013) similarly found that household choices about fertilizer use related more to social pressure and aesthetics than environmental concerns. In the arid Southwest, Neel et al. (2014) examined the symbolic and self-presentational meanings of residential xeriscaping, such as planting cacti. Unfortunately for conservation, water-intensive landscapes generated more positive attributions of the homeowners. In the Freeman et al. (2012) study, a more hopeful direction was noted: when the researchers shared the study results with the participants, they showed an eagerness to reduce pesticide use and to adopt biodiversity-friendly practices, a special concern in endemic-rich New Zealand. Gardens are discussed and evaluated by one's neighbors and will form a part of one's identity in the community (see also Nassauer, 1988).

Finally, we look at two rather different frontiers of domestic nature: building-integrated vegetation and a web-interface controlled "telegarden." The integration of biophysical functions into buildings (and landscapes) is a trend in sustainable design. Familiar examples may be "green roofs" composed of soil and plantings that slow runoff and moderate interior temperature shifts; "rain gardens" that direct runoff into plantings and soil; more conventional plantings like ivy-covered walls; and new examples of biophilic design (Kellert et al., 2008). White and Gatersleben (2011) digitally altered images of four houses to show several conditions including different green roofs (turf, sedum, or meadow), and ivy facades – or the lack of these features, and then asked UK subjects to rate them. Some vegetated building images, particularly the meadow roof and ivy façade were significantly more preferred, and seen as more beautiful, restorative, and evoked more positive affect than the plain brick or brown controls. Glor and Clayton (2014) also found that architecture incorporating greenery was preferred and led people to feel more connected to nature. Hopefully such sentiments will give a boost to "greener" social norms as these practices are adopted.

Kahn (2011) studied users' on-line discussions around an internet-controlled robotic telegarden as one of his technological nature studies. Conversations about actual nature made up 13% of the discussion; social and technological topics dominated the conversation. For a few users, such as those lacking other kinds of mobility, the telegarden mattered greatly. Those who were interested in nature seemed to get the most out of it, so intention matters. It would be hard to argue that the telegarden provides as rich, multifaceted, and compelling an experience of nature as a real garden, but for some it was better than no garden. So it fits Kahn's repeatedly found pattern: the psychological benefits of real nature are hard to reproduce.

Conclusion

With gardening and household pets, it is easy to see how nature has become part of our social worlds, allowing us to benefit from contact with nature in our day-to-day activities. The developmental and social effects of technological forms of domestic nature in comparison to "traditional" forms have yet to be seen – if indeed either competes effectively with the predominance of "screen time" in the contemporary home (Granich and Rosenberg, 2010). As we move into the wider spheres of managed nature and wild nature, it is important to keep that social context in mind. Our relations to nature in the domestic sphere can be a metaphor for our relationship to nature on a larger scale. Gardening may not be the appropriate lens for every kind of human–nature relation, but it does highlight the need to balance science and human values. Ecological restoration projects are like gardening on a grander scale but perhaps with a humbler attitude, one that acknowledges the relevance of other values beside human utility or aesthetic preference (Higgs, 1997). With many individuals taking care of small elements of nature, humans are managing nature, in the aggregate, with all the benefits as well as responsibilities that are entailed. We turn to more public examples of managed nature in Chapter 3.

References

American Pet Products Manufacturers Association. (2008). Industry statistics and trends. Available at: http://www.americanpetproducts.org/press_industrytrends.asp (accessed 20 March n).

American Pet Products Association. (2014). Pet industry market size & ownership statistics. Available at: http://www.americanpetproducts.org/press_industrytrends.asp (accessed 20 August 2014).

American Veterinary Medical Association. (2012). U.S. pet ownership statistics. Available at: https://www.avma.org/KB/Resources/Statistics/Pages/Market-research-statistics-US-pet-ownership.aspx (accessed August 2013).

Anderson, W., Reid, P., & Jennings, G. L. (1992). Pet ownership and risk factors for cardiovascular disease. *Medical Journal of Australia 157*, 298–301.

Annerstedt, M. & Währborg, P. (2011). Nature-assisted therapy: Systematic review of controlled and observational studies. *Scandinavian Journal of Public Health, 39*(4), 371–388.

Arluke, A. (2006). *Just a dog: Understanding animal cruelty and ourselves*. Philadelphia: Temple University Press.

Baldwin, I. (2014). 2013 had the biggest increase in garden spending this century. Today's garden center, July 9. Available at: http://www.todaysgardencenter.com/ (accessed 8 August 2014).

Banks, M. R. & Banks, W. A. (2005). The effects of group and individual animal-assisted therapy on loneliness in residents of long-term care facilities. *Anthrozoös, 18*(4), 396–408.

Barker, S., Rasmussen, K, & Best, A. (2003). Effect of aquariums on electroconvulsive therapy patients. *Anthrozoös, 16*(3), 229–240.

Baun, M. M., Bergstrom, N., Langston, N, & Thomas, L. (1984). Physiological effects of human/companion animal bonding. *Nursing Research, 33*, 126–129.

Beck, A. H. & Katcher, A. H. (1996). *Between pets and people: The importance of animal companionship* (2nd ed.). West Lafayette, IN: Purdue University Press.

Beierl, H. B. (2008). The sympathetic imagination and the human-animal bond: Fostering empathy through reading imaginative literature. *Anthrozoös, 21*(3), 213–220.

Bjerke, T., Østdahl, T. & Kleiven, J. (2003). Attitudes and activities related to urban wildlife: Pet owners and non-owners. *Anthrozoös, 16*(3), 252–262.

Blonder, L. X. Smith, C. D., Davis, C. E., Kesler/West, M. L., Garrity, T. F., Avison, M. J., Andersen, A. H. (2004). Regional brain response to faces of humans and dogs. *Cognitive Brain Research, 20*(3), 384–394.

Blouin, D. D. (2013). Are dogs children, companions or just animals? Understanding variation in people's orientations toward animals. *Anthrozoös 26*(2), 279–294.

Brady, D. & Palmeri, C. (2007). The pet economy. *Business Week* Aug 6. Availabe at: http://www.businessweek.com/magazine/content/07_32/b4045001.htm (accessed 20 March 2008).

Bringslimark, T., Hartig, T., & Patil, G. G. (2009). The psychological benefits of indoor plants: A critical review of the experimental literature. *Journal of Environmental Psychology, 29*(4), 422–433.

Cain, A. (1985). Pets as family members. In Sussman, M. (Ed.), *Pets and the family* (pp. 5–10). New York: Haworth Press.

Cammack, C., Waliczek, T. & Zajicek, J. (2002). The Green Brigade: The psychological effects of a community-based horticultural program on the self-development characteristics of juvenile offenders. *HortTechnology 12*(1), 82–86.

Carlisle-Frank, P. & Frank, J. (2006). Owners, guardians and owner-guardians: Differing relationships with pets. *Anthrozoös, 19*(3), 225–242.

Carrico, A. R., Fraser, J., & Bazuin, J. T. (2013). Green with Envy: Psychological and social predictors of lawn fertilizer application. *Environment and Behavior, 45*(4), 427–454.

Clayton, S. (2007). Domesticated nature: motivations for gardening and perceptions of environmental impact. *Journal of Environmental Psychology 27*(3), 215–224.

Coren, S. (1999). Do people look like their dogs? *Anthrozoös 12*, 111–114.

Crawford, E., Worsham, N., Swinehart, E. (2006). Benefits derived from companion animals, and the use of the term "attachment." *Anthrozoös, 19*(2), 98–112.

Crooks, K. R. & Soule, M. E. (1999). Mesopredator release and avifaunal extinctions in a fragmented system. *Nature*, *400*, 563–566.

Curb, L. A., Abramson, C. I., Grice, J. W., & Kennison, S. M. (2013). The relationship between personality match and pet satisfaction among dog owners. *Anthrozoös*, *26*(3), 395–404.

Eddy, T. J. (2003). What is a pet? *Anthrozoös*, *16*(2), 98–105.

Eddy, T. J., Gallup, G., & Povinelli, D. (1993). Attribution of cognitive states to animals: Anthropomorphism in comparative perspective. *Journal of Social Issues*, *49*(1), 87–101.

Erikson, P. (2000). The social significance of pet-keeping among Amazonian Indians. In A. Podberscek, E. Paul & J. Serpell (Eds.), *Companion animals and us* (pp. 7–26). Cambridge: Cambridge University Press.

Fjeld, T., Veiersted, B. & Sandvik, L. (1998). The effect of indoor foliage plants on health and discomfort symptoms among office workers. *Indoor and Built Environment*, *7*, 204–206.

Franklin, R., Nelson, A. J., Baker, M., Beeney, J. E., Vescio, T. K., Lenz-Watson, A., & Adams, R. (2013). Neural responses to perceiving suffering in humans and animals. *Social Neuroscience*, *8*, 217–227.

Freeman, C., Dickinson, K. J. M., Porter, S., & van Heezik, Y. (2012). "My garden is an expression of me": Exploring householders' relationships with their gardens. *Journal of Environmental Psychology*, *32*(2), 135–143.

Friedmann, E. & Thomas, S. A. (1995). Pet ownership, social support, and one-year survival after acute myocardial infarction in the Cardiac Arrhythmia Suppressing Trial (CAST). *American Journal of Cardiology 76*, 1213–1217.

Friedmann, E., Thomas, S. A. & Eddy, T. J. (2000). Companion animals and human health: Physical and cardiovascular influences. In A. Podberscek, E. Paul & J. Serpell (Eds.), *Companion animals and us* (pp. 125–142). Cambridge: Cambridge University Press.

Friedmann, E., Thomas, S. A., Cook, L., Tsai, C.-C. & Picot, S. (2007). A friendly dog as potential moderator of cardiovascular response in speech in older hypertensives. *Anthrozoös*, *20*(1), 51–63.

Friedmann, E., Thomas, S. A., Son, H., Chapa, D. & McCune, S. (2013). Pets' presence and owner's blood pressures during the daily lives of pet owners with pre- to mild hypertension. *Anthrozoös*, *26*(4), 535–550.

Frumkin, H. (2004). White coats, green plants: Clinical epidemiology meets horticulture. *Acta Horticulturae*, *639*, 15–26.

Gee, N. R., Sherlock, T. R., Bennett, E. A. & Harris, S. L. (2009). Preschoolers' adherence to instructions as a function of presences of a dog and motor skills task. *Anthrozoös*, *22*(3), 267–276.

Gee, N. R., Church, M. T., Atobelli, C. L. (2010a). Preschoollers make fewer errors on an object categorization task in the presence of a dog. *Anthrozoös*, *23*(3), 223–230.

Gee, N. R., Crist, E. N., & Carr, D. N. (2010b). Preschool children require fewer instructional prompts to perform a memory task in the presence of a dog. *Anthrozoös*, *23*(2), 173–184.

Gigliotti, C. M. & Jarrott, S. E. (2005). Effects of horticultural therapy on engagement and affect. *Canadian Journal on Aging*, *24*(4), 367–377.

Gigliotti, C. M., Jarrott, S. E. & Yorgason, J. (2004). Harvesting health: Effects of three types of horticultural therapy activities for persons with dementia. *Dementia 3*(2), 161–180.

Gilbey, A., McNicholas, J., & Collis, G. (2007). A longitudinal test of the belief that companion animal ownership can help reduce loneliness. *Anthrozoös*, *20*(4), 345–353.

Gilquin, G. & Jacobs, G. (2006). Elephants who marry mice are very unusual: The use of the relative pronoun who with nonhuman animals. *Society and Animals 14*(1), 79–105.

Glor, B., & Clayton, S. (2014). Let the outside in: Impacts of biophilic design. Unpublished manuscript.

Goldmeier, J. (1986). Pets or people: Another research note. *The Gerontologist*, *26*(2), 203–206.

Gosling, S., Sandy, C. J. & Potter, J. (2010). Personalities of self-identified "dog people" and "cat people." *Anthrozoös*, *23*(3), 213–222.

Granich, J., Rosenberg, M., Knuiman, M., & Timperio, A. (2010). Understanding children's sedentary behavior: A qualitative study of the family home environment. *Health Education Research*, *25*(2), 199–210.

Grier, K. C. (1999). Childhood socialization and companion animals: United States, 1820–1870. *Society and Animals*, *7*(2), 95–120.

Gross, H. & Lane, N. (2007). Landscapes of the lifespan: Exploring accounts of own gardens and gardening. *Journal of Environmental Psychology 27*(3), 225–241.

Guéguen, N. & Ciccotti, S. (2008). Domestic dogs as facilitators in social interaction: An evaluation of helping and courtship behaviors. *Anthrozoös, 21*(4), 339–349.

Guest, C. M., Collis, G. M., & McNicholas, J. (2006). Hearing dogs: A longitudinal study of social and psychological effects on deaf and hard-of-hearing recipients. *Journal of Deaf Studies and Deaf Education, 11*, 252–261.

Health Council of the Netherlands. (2004). Nature and health: The influence of nature on social, psychological, and physical well-being. The Hague: Health Council of the Netherlands and RMNO. Publication number 2004/09E, RMNO publication number A02ae. Available at www.healthcouncil.nl.

Herzog, H. A. (2007). Gender differences in human-animal interactions: A review. *Anthrozoös, 20*(1), 7–21.

Herzog, H. A. (2010). *Some we love, some we hate, some we eat: Why it's so hard to think straight about animals*. New York: HarperCollins.

Higgins, J. W., Temple, V., Murray, H., Kumm, E. & Rhodes, R. (2013). Walking sole mates: Dogs motivating, enabling and supporting guardians' physical activity. *Anthrozoös 26*(2), 237–252.

Higgs, E. S. (1997). What is good ecological restoration? *Conservation Biology 11*, 338–348.

Hirsh-Pasek, K., & Treiman, R. (1982). Doggerel: Motherese in a new context. *Journal of Child Language, 9*, 229–237.

Howard, L. & Vick, S.-J. (2010). Does it bite? The role of stimulus characteristics on presechoolers' interactions with robots, insects and a dog. *Anthrozoös, 23*(4), 397–413.

Hyland, B. (2004). Market trends. Available at: http://www.greenscaper.net/about.php. (accessed 23 March 2008).

Kafer, R., Lago, D., Wamboldt, P. & Harrington, F. (1992). The Pet Relationship Scale: Replication of psychometric properties in random samples and association with attitudes toward wild animals. *Anthrozoös 5*(2), 93–105.

Kahn, P. H. Jr., (2011). *Technological nature: Adaptation and the future of human life*. Cambridge, MA: MIT Press.

Kaplan, R. (1973). Some psychological benefits of gardening. *Environment and Behavior, 5*(2), 142–162.

Kaplan, R. (1993). The role of nature in the context of the workplace. *Landscape and Urban Planning, 26*, 193–201.

Kaplan, R. (2001). The nature of the view from home: Psychological benefits. *Environment and Behavior 33*, 507–542.

Kellert, S. R. (1996). *The value of life: Biological diversity and human society*. Washington, DC: Island Press.

Kellert, S., Heerwagen, J. & Mador, M. (2008). *Biophilic design*. Hoboken, NJ: John Wiley.

Kidd, A. H., & Kidd, R. M. (1987). Seeking a theory of the human/companion animal bond. *Anthrozoös, 1*(3), 140–157.

Kidd, A. H., Kelly, H., & Kidd, R. (1983). Personality characteristics of horse, turtle, snake and bird owners. *Psychological Reports, 52*, 719–729.

Kiesling, F. M., & Manning, C. M. (2010). How green is your thumb? Environmental gardening identity and ecological gardening practices. *Journal of Environmental Psychology, 30*(3), 315–327.

Larsen, L., Adams, J. Deal, B., Kweon, B.-S. & Tyler, E. (1998). Plants in the workplace: The effects of plant density on productivity, attitudes and perceptions. *Environment and Behavior, 30*, 261–281.

Laurent, E. L. (2000). Children, 'insects' and play in Japan. In A. Podberscek, E. Paul & J. Serpell (Eds.), *Companion animals and us* (pp. 61–89). Cambridge: Cambridge University Press.

Lockwood, J. (2013). *The infested mind: Why humans fear, loathe and love insects*. New York: Oxford University Press.

Mae, L., McMorris, L. & Hendry, J. (2004). Spontaneous trait transference from dogs to owners. *Anthrozoös, 17*(3), 225–243.

McNicholas, J. & Collis, G. (2000). Dogs as catalysts for social interactions: Robustness of the effect. *British Journal of Psychology, 91*, 61–70.

Melson, G. F., & Fogel, A. (1988). Children's ideas about animal young and their care: A reassessment of gender differences in the development of nurturance. *Anthrozoos* *2*(4), 265–273.

Messent, P. (1983). Social facilitation of contact with other people by pet dogs. In A. Katcher & A. Beck (Eds.), *New perspectives on our lives with companion animals* (pp. 37–46). Philadelphia: University of Pennsylvania Press.

Miller, C. (2002). *Comment on Panel discussion at the first Conference on Conservation Psychology*, Chicago, IL: Brookfield Zoo.

Miller, S. C., Kennedy, C. DeVoe, D., Hickey, M., Nelson, T. & Kogan, L. (2009). An examination in oxytocin levels in men and women before and after interaction with a bonded dog. *Anthrozoös*, *22*(1), 31–42.

Millot, J.-L. and Filiatre, J.-C. (1986). The behavior sequences in the communication system between the child and his pet dog. *Applied Animal Behaviour Science*, *16*, 383–390.

Mills, D. S. (2005). What's in a word? A review of the attributes of a command affecting the performance of pet dogs. *Anthrozoös*, *18*(3), 208–221.

Mitchell, R. W. & Edmonson, E. (1999). Functions of repetitive talk to dogs during play: Control, conversation or planning? *Society and Animals* *7*(1), 55–81.

Mitchell, R. W. (1987). *Projects, routines, and enticements in interspecies play between familiar and unfamiliar dogs and people.* Unpublished doctoral dissertation, Clark University, Worcester, MA.

Morris, J., Briggs, M. & Zidenberg-Cherr, S. (2000). School-based gardens can teach kids healthier eating habits. *California Agriculture*, *54*(5), 40–46.

Mugford, R. & M'Comisky, J. G. (1975). Some recent work on the psychotherapeutic value of caged birds with old people. In R. S. Anderson (Ed.), *Pets, animals and society* (pp. 54–65). London: Balliere Tindall.

Munro, D. B. (2014). Canadian poisonous plants information system. Available at: http://www.cbif.gc.ca/eng/species-bank/canadian-poisonous-plants-information-system/?id=1370403265036 (accessed 9 August 2014).

Myers, Jr., O. E. (2007). *The significance of children and animals: Social development and our connections to other species* (Rev. ed.). West Lafayette, IN: Purdue University Press.

Myers, Jr., O. E. & Saunders, C. D. (2002). Animals as links to developing caring relationships with the natural world. In P. H. Kahn Jr., & S. R. Kellert (Eds.), *Children and nature: Psychological, sociocultural and evolutionary investigations.* (pp. 153–178). Cambridge, MA: MIT Press.

Nakajima, S. (2013). Dogs and owners resemble each other in the eye region. *Anthrozoös*, *26*(4), 551–556.

Nakajima, S., Yamamoto, M. & Yoshimoto, N. (2009). Dogs look like their owners: Replication with racially homogeneous owner portraits. *Anthrozoös*, *22*(2), 173–181.

Nassauer, J. I. (1988). The aesthetics of horticulture: Neatness as a form of care. *HortScience*, *23*, 973–977.

National Gardening Association. (2006). *National Gardening Survey*. South Burlington, VT: National Gardening Association.

Neel, R., Sadalla, E., Berlin, A., Ledlow, S., & Neufeld, S. (2014). The social symbolism of water-conserving landscaping. *Journal of Environmental Psychology*, *40*, 49–56.

Paul, E. (2000). Love of pets and love of people. In A. Podberscek, E. Paul & J. Serpell (Eds.), *Companion animals and us* (pp. 168–186). Cambridge: Cambridge University Press.

Podberscek, A. & Gosling, S. (2000). Personality research on pets and their owners: Conceptual issues and review. In A. Podberscek, E. Paul & J. Serpell (Eds.), *Companion animals and us* (pp. 143–167). Cambridge: Cambridge University Press.

Podberscek, A. & Serpell, J. (1997). Aggressive behavior in English cocker spaniels and the personality of their owners. *The Veterinary Record*, *141*, 73–76.

Prokop, P. & Tunnicliffe, S. D. (2010). Effects of having pets at home on children's attitudes toward popular and unpopular animals. *Anthrozoös*, *23*(1), 21–35.

Prothmann, A., Ettrich, C. & Prothmann, S. (2009). Preference for, and responsiveness to, people, dogs and objects in children with autism. *Anthrozoös*, *22*(2), 161–171.

Raanaas, R. K., Evensen, K. H., Rich, D., Sjøstrøm, G., & Patil, G. (2011). Benefits of indoor plants on attention capacity in an office setting. *Journal of Environmental Psychology*, *31*(1), 99–105.

Relf, P. D. (1998). People-plant relationship. In S. P. Simson & M. C. Straus (Eds.), *Horticulture as therapy: Principles and practice* (pp. 21–42). New York: Haworth Press.
Relf, P. D. (2005). The therapeutic values of plants. *Pediatric Rehabilitation 8*(3), 235–237.
Ritvo, H. (1987). *The animal estate*. Cambridge, MA: Harvard University Press.
Robbins, P., Polderman, A., & Birkenholtz, T. (2001). Lawns and toxins: An ecology of the city. *Cities, 18*, 369–380.
Roberts, C., McBride, E., Rosenvinge, H. Stevenage, S. & Bradshaw, J. (1996). The pleasure of a companion animal. In J. Nicholson & A. Podberscek (Eds.), *Further issues in research in companion animal studies* (p. 64). Callendar: SCAS.
Rochberg-Halton, E. (1985). Life in the Treehouse: Pet therapy as family metaphor and self-dialogue. In M. Sussman (Ed.), *Pets and the family* (pp. 175–189). New York: Haworth Press.
Rohlf, V. & Bennett, P. (2005). Perpetration-induced traumatic stress in persons who euthanize non-human animals in surgeries, animal shelters and laboratories. *Society and Animals, 13*(3), 201–219.
Roy, M. M. & Christenfeld, N. J. (2004). Do dogs resemble their owners? *Psychological Science, 15*(5), 361–363.
Rud, A. Jr., & Beck, A. (2003). Companion animals in Indiana elementary schools. *Anthrozoös, 16*(3), 241–251.
Sanders, C. R. (1990). The animal "Other": Self-definition, social identity and companion animals. *Advances in Consumer Research, 17*, 662–668.
Sanders, C. R. (1999). *Understanding dogs: Living and working with canine companions*. Philadelphia: Temple University Press.
Serpell, J. A. (1986). *In the company of animals*. Oxford: Blackwell.
Serpell, J. A. (1988). Pet keeping in non-Western societies: some popular misconceptions. In A. Rowan (Ed.), *Animals and people sharing the world* (pp. 33–52). Hanover, NH: University Press of New England.
Serpell, J. A. (1991). Beneficial effects of pet ownership on some aspects of human health and behavior. *Journal of the Royal Society of Medicine 84*, 717–720.
Serpell, J. A. (2000). Creatures of the unconscious: Companion animals as mediators. In A. Podbersek, E. Paul & J. Serpell (Eds.). *Companion animals and us* (pp. 108–117). Cambridge: Cambridge University Press.
Severson, R. L., & Carlson, S. M. (2010). Behaving as or behaving as if? Children's conceptions of personified robots and the emergence of a new ontological category. *Neural Networks, 23*(8–9), 1099–1103.
Shapiro, K. (1989). Understanding dogs through kinesthetic empathy, social construction, and history. *Anthrozoös, 3*(3), 184–195.
Shepard, P. (1996). *The others: How animals made us human*. Washington DC: Island Press.
Shibata, S. & Suzuki, N. (2004). Effects of an indoor plant on creative task performance and mood. *Scandinavian Journal of Psychology, 45*, 373–381.
Shore, D. (2002). Comment on Panel discussion at the first Conference on Conservation Psychology, Chicago, IL: Brookfield Zoo.
Sims, V. K., Chin, M. G., Sushil, D. J., Ellis, L. U. & Jones, R. (2005). Eye movements when judging affect in cats and dogs. Abstract of paper presented at the International Association for Anthrozoology 14th Annual Conference, July 11–12, Niagara Falls.
Sommer, R. (2003). Trees and human identity. In S. Clayton & S. Opotow (Eds.), *Identity and the Natural Environment* (pp. 179–204). Cambridge, MA: MIT Press.
Sommerville, J. A. & Decety, J. (2006). Weaving the fabric of social interaction: Articulating developmental psychology and cognitive neuroscience in the domain of motor cognition. *Psychonomic Bulletin and Review, 13*(2), 179–200.
Taylor, A. F., Kuo, F. E., & Sullivan, W. C. (2002). Views of nature and self-discipline: Evidence from inner city children. *Journal of Environmental Psychology, 22*, 49–63.
Taylor, S. E. (2002). *The tending instinct*. New York: Henry Holt.
Tennessen, C. M., & Cimprich, B. (1995). Views to nature: Effects on attention. *Journal of Environmental Psychology, 15*(1), 77–85.
Thomas, K. (1983). *Man and the natural world: A history of the modern sensibility*. New York: Pantheon.

Toukhsati, S., Bennett, P., & Coleman, G. (2007). Behaviors and attitudes toward semi-owned cats. *Anthrozoös*, *20*(2), 131–142.

Turner, D. (2000). Human-cat interactions. In A. Podberscek, E. Paul & J. Serpell (Eds.), *Companion animals and us* (pp. 257–271). Cambridge: Cambridge University Press.

Turner, D., Riger, G., Gygax, L. (2003). Spouses and cats and their effects on human mood. *Anthrozoös*, *16*(3), 213–228.

Turscán, B., Range, F., Virányi, Z., Miklósi, Á., & Kubinyi, E. (2012). Birds of a feather flock together? Perceived personality matching in owner-dog dyads. *Applied Animal Behavior Science 140*, 154–160.

Vining, J. (2003). The connection to other animals and caring for nature. *Human Ecology Review 10*(2), 87–99.

Vining, J. & Merrick, M. (2006). Pet keeping, environmental attitudes and behavior, and quality of life. Paper presented at the 14th International Conference of the Society for Human Ecology, Bar Harbor, ME, Oct. 18–21.

Ulrich, R. S. (1983). Aesthetic and affective response to natural environments. In I. Altman & J. F. Wohlwill (Eds.), *Human behavior and the natural environment* (pp. 85–125). New York: Plenum.

Ulrich, R. (1984). View through a window may influence recovery from surgery. *Science 224*, 420–421.

Unti, B. O. (2002). *The quality of mercy: Organized animal protection in the United States 1866–1930.* Unpublished doctoral dissertation, American University, Washington, DC.

Wells, D. (2009). The effects of animals on human health and well-being. *Journal of Social Issues*, *65*(3), 523–543.

Wells, N. (2000). At home with nature: Effects of "greenness" on children's cognitive functioning. *Environment and Behavior*, *32*, 775–795.

Werner, C. M. (2003). Changing homeowners' use of toxic household products: A transactional approach. *Journal of Environmental Psychology 23*, 33–45.

White, E. V., & Gatersleben, B. (2011). Greenery on residential buildings: Does it affect preferences and perceptions of beauty? *Journal of Environmental Psychology*, *31*(1), 89–98.

Wolverton, B. C. (1997). *How to grow fresh air: 50 Houseplants to purify your home or office*. New York: Penguin.

Zasloff, R. & Kidd, A. (1994). Loneliness and pet ownership among single women. *Psychological Reports*, *75*(2), 747–752.

3

Managed Nature: Zoos, Aquariums, and Public Parks

The natural environment is typically perceived as something separate from populated areas and unaffected by humans – the remote wilderness locations we discuss in Chapter 4. However, their very remoteness and isolation from human activity means that most people experience these environments infrequently. For citizens of developed countries, exposure to nature occurs predominantly in managed settings: zoos and aquariums, which display animals, and urban parks and arboretums, which present more natural green settings. (Officially, a zoo is an urban park, but because the type of experience it presents is very different, for the most part we discuss these two settings separately.)

Parks and zoos are particularly notable for the way in which they create and support a social context surrounding the interaction with nature. This social context is important in allowing people to develop a relationship with nature that is nurtured rather than inhibited by their friends and family. When nature is found in human areas, it may discourage the tendency to relegate "human" and "natural" to separate spheres and encourage a perception that a typical human lifestyle should include exposure to nature. As environmental historian Nash (2005, p. viii) put it, "A meaningful relationship with nature does not necessarily depend on a rejection of the urban context".

This chapter reviews some of the rapidly accumulating evidence suggesting that encountering these constructed displays of nature in a social context can have an important effect on people, their social interactions, and their relationships with nature.

Conservation Psychology: Understanding and promoting human care for nature, Second Edition.
Susan Clayton and Gene Myers.

www.wiley.com\go\clayton\conservation

Zoos and aquariums

Zoos and aquariums both serve to exhibit animals to human visitors. We primarily discuss them together, but it is worth noting a slight difference in their challenges. Although both bring an unfamiliar world to the visitor, the world represented by aquariums is even more profoundly unfamiliar. Carson (1961), in the 1961 edition of her 1950 best selling *The Sea Around Us,* warned that "there has long been a certain comfort in the belief that the sea, at least, was inviolate, beyond man's ability to change and to despoil" (p. x). The picture today is different. Marine science has expanded greatly, but the oceans are in trouble (International State of the Ocean Project, 2013). Abadia et al. (2004) suggest that the public has positive attitudes toward the ocean but knows little about specific ocean issues. Although people worry about its vulnerability and care about its health, the public is "not at all aware of the current degree or sources of threat" (p. 187). Likewise, a survey of 22,000 Americans by International State of the Ocean Project (2009) found a high level of support for protecting ocean health alongside widespread ignorance of the environmental issues affecting ocean health, including the impact of climate change. The mission of aquariums is to inspire conservation of a fragile world that we, as terrestrial creatures, are biased not to notice.

The goals of zoos and aquariums have evolved over the years. Although they originated purely to satisfy the curiosity of the viewers, they have developed into institutions with the combined missions of recreation, education, and conservation. They play the roles of "model citizen, wildlife conservationist, agent for conservation, and mentor/trainer" (Rabb & Saunders, 2005). Most accredited zoos put significant resources into educating people about animals and their needs, as well as into protecting animal species both in the zoo and in the wild. Zoos are very conscious of their role in affecting knowledge and attitudes. Educational programs are a core component of zoos, including school and community programs, informal education (zoo visitors' experiences), and using the public image of the zoo to deliver messages about conservation and the zoo's role (Mazur, 2001). Stoinski et al. (1998) found that more than 60% of North American zoos do visitor research, whereas more than 40% do education research. Conservation education programs run by zoos and aquariums reach almost 12 million students each year; in addition, 400,000 teachers have attended formal training workshops over the past 10 years (AZA, 2014). Although the educational mission previously emphasized teaching facts about animals, it now encompasses a focus on encouraging care and concern and inspiring conservation action – a shift reflected in the name change from the Public Education Committee to the Conservation Education Committee of the AZA in 1997 (Ogden et al., 2004).

Zoos are highly popular destinations; zoos accredited by the Association of Zoos and Aquariums attracted 175 million visitors in 2013, more than the annual attendance of all NFL, NHL, and NBA games combined (AZA, 2014). They are the most frequently visited type of museum in the world (Mason, 2000). Moreover, they draw from across society. People of all ages, ethnicities, religions, and socioeconomic classes visit zoos. Schools often incorporate zoo visits into their curricula, particularly in the early grades. Many zoos offer a "free" day every week for local residents, with the result that zoos have a broader cross-section of visitor types than other museums (Mason, 2000). Thus, zoos represent one of the principal ways in which a wide variety of people encounter nature.

There is a great deal of debate over the morality and function of the zoo. This has ranged from sometimes well-deserved criticism of the ways in which animals are treated to more fundamental challenges to the practice of confining and displaying animals. Philosopher Jamieson (1985, 1995), for example, asserts that animals' pursuit of their own interests creates a moral presumption against keeping them in captivity that can only be overridden by more substantial human interests than entertainment or even education. In his view, the conservation interests of animals may justify keeping some in captivity, but not displaying them. Others argue that this overlooks a wider class of conservation problems in which the welfare of individuals is pitted against some benefit to a composite such as a species (Norton, 1995). Although ethical arguments are not the focus of this book, data on effects on human visitors is relevant to the debate. For example, observing captive animals could make people feel sad or depressed, with the result that they try to avoid thinking about the problems of animals. More insidiously, Beardsworth and Bryman (2001) argue, zoos may have a negative effect on attitudes toward animals by rationalizing human domination over animals, suggesting that captivity is in the animals' best interest and reassuring visitors that animal species are safe from threats because zoos, as agents of human concern, are looking out for them. Very likely there has been historical change concerning such basic values, on the part of both zoos and visitors.

Contemporary empirical results are somewhat reassuring on these issues. Woods (2002) collected Australians' "best" and "worst" wildlife experiences. Among over 300 best and 300 worst captive animal experiences, respondents were consistently upset by signs of poor care of the animals. The most important "best" experiences were ones affording interaction, including being close, watching, touching, "being amongst animals," and feeding. Rather than expressing dominance, the illustrative quotes provided suggest more a sense of wonder, surprise, and connection. When "best" experiences with captive and noncaptive animals was compared, the profiles of features overall were very similar. The two main differences were "learning things" – 18.9% of captive "best" experiences as opposed to 5.5% of wild; and "natural setting" – 4.6% of captive, versus 32.8% of noncaptive. This suggests people value the learning opportunities, but do not discount the fact of captivity.

Whereas critics suggest that zoos may promote a feeling of domination over, and separation from, the animals, zoos may instead serve to enhance people's interest in animals, or their appreciation for nature. Zoos may also provide a setting for the social expression and transmission of pro-environmental values. These goals are reflected in the conservation education and activism missions of zoos (Maple, 1995) and are embodied in the mission statement of many zoos. The Wildlife Conservation Society (originally founded as the New York Zoological Society), for example, fosters activities that "change attitudes toward nature and help people imagine wildlife and humans living in sustainable interaction." The mission of the Association of Zoos and Aquariums is to " … facilitate collaborations that activate the public to connect with and take personal action to conserve wildlife and wild habitats" (statements available on the respective society websites. See also Moss & Esson, 2013, for a discussion of zoo mission statements).

Reasons for visiting

We can understand more about the perceived benefits of a zoo visit by examining the reasons people give for visiting. A number of researchers have addressed this question, finding a range of motivations that include pleasure, social interactions, and enjoyment of the animals (Holzer et al., 1998; Morgan & Hodgkinson, 1999). Learning and education are mentioned, but are not the most important factors. Concern about conservation is also occasionally referenced. In a study at the Fort Worth Zoo, Tomas et al. (2003) found evidence for six types of benefits, in order of importance: family togetherness, wildlife enjoyment (this factor included an item on "view beautiful surroundings"), wildlife appreciation and learning (this included several items related to conservation), companionship, escape, and introspection/meeting new people. Similarly, in the United Kingdom, Turley (2001) found the top reasons for visiting were to have

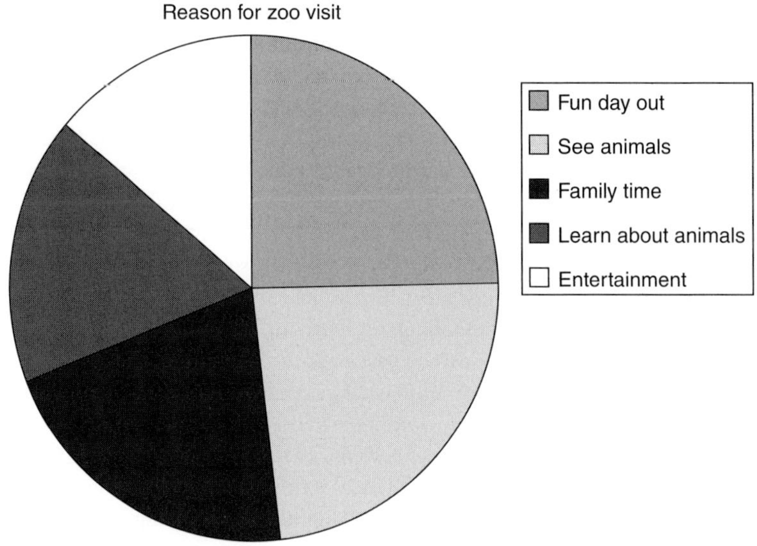

Fig. 3.1 Reasons for visiting the zoo (based on data in Moss et al., 2014).

a pleasurable day out, to experience wild animals up close, to support conservation activities of the zoo, to spend time with others, to learn about animals, and to learn about conservation. A comprehensive worldwide survey of over 6000 visitors found that a "fun day out," "seeing animals," and "family time" were the most common reasons (Moss et al., 2014). See Fig. 3.1.

Most zoo visitors (96–99%) go with other people (Turley, 2001), and very often this means family members including young children. Children not only motivate the visits; by increasing interaction among members of the visitor group, children can also enhance the experience for adults. Parents use animals to promote social interactions between themselves and their children. In Turley's study, the presence of children increased the importance of a pleasurable day out and the importance of learning about animals. Support for the conservation role of zoos was greater among older visitors. Interestingly, nonzoo visitors felt that the zoo's educational role was more important compared to ratings by the zoo visitors, which encourages the conclusion that zoos are seen as educational in theory, but as entertainment in practice.

Overall, the most important motivators of a visit to the zoo appear to be social, involving opportunities to facilitate interactions with family and friends. Opportunities for personal relaxation and enjoyment are also important. But animals, and the opportunities to learn about them, are more than incidental. People do consider zoos to be educational and conservation organizations and seek them in part for those reasons (Clayton et al., 2009; Fraser et al., 2008). Based on their visitor research, the Ocean Project report stated: "The public expects and trusts aquariums, zoos, and museums to communicate about solutions to environmental and ocean issues and to advance [ocean] conservation" (2009, p. 3). In a study that built from the attributes that visitors sought at the zoo to the consequences they perceived from these, and to the ultimate values that visitors felt were fulfilled, Klenosky and Saunders (2008) found two ultimate values related to having a good time: enjoyment and family togetherness. They also found three values that stemmed from wanting to learn about animals and nature: to grow or develop better, to encourage stewardship, and to broaden horizons. Many facets of the visit could be grouped under these main values.

Not everyone goes to the zoo for the same reason. Falk (2005) described five different types of visitors: the explorer (generally interested in discovering more about the subject and did not care whether others in their social group enjoyed the visit), the facilitator (visiting in order to satisfy the needs and desires of someone they cared about, usually their children), the professional/hobbyist (possessing a strong professional or other knowledge and interest in the topic, and motivated in learning how the information was conveyed), the experience seeker (wanted to say they had been there, or looking for experiences emblematic of the location), and spiritual pilgrim (relatively rare, visited in order to reflect, rejuvenate, or wonder). Most people (87%) could be categorized as explorer, facilitator, or both. More than half of respondents had multiple motivations for visiting.

Visitors' experience of the zoo

What do people do at the zoo? For one thing, they enjoy themselves. Zoo visits are perceived as positive and are associated with feelings of relaxation, happiness, and attentive interest in animals (Clayton et al., 2009). When Myers et al. (2004) used electronic pagers to cue visitors to complete a response booklet on emotions while viewing zoo animals, visitors reported overall quite positive feelings; on average, they reported feeling focused, excited, involved and relaxed. This combination of affect indicates active engagement with the exhibits. The spontaneous interest may stem directly from the ability of the zoo to evoke or represent nature. Like other nature-based settings, zoos may provide stress relief, relaxation, and the quality of being "away" (Mazur, 2001). As Kaplan and Kaplan (1989) have proposed for nature in general, zoo exhibits may attract attention effortlessly and thus enable the restoration of attentional capacity.

People's desire to promote social interactions is also fulfilled; a large part of the zoo experience comprises communication with other people. In an early survey, Cheek (1973) found that 40% of a national sample said that one of their primary activities in the zoo was getting to know their children better. Clayton et al. (2009) coded over 1200 verbal comments by zoo visitors in interaction with each other and found that the majority of comments seemed to be generated for the sole purpose of facilitating social interaction, for example, by simply commenting on the animal ("Look, there he is."). Other types of responses that promoted social interactions were negative comments, often made by teenagers with the apparent goal of evoking a response from another person ("Snakes! I hate snakes"), or the use of the animals to teach, often observed among parents speaking to their children ("How many giraffes do you see?"). Further evidence of the prominence of social interaction at the zoo was found by Clayton et al. (2011). In over 80% of visitor groups they studied, one person pointed out an animal to another or called attention to the animal – actions that had no informative content and merely served to make viewing the animal into a social experience. Relatedly, a study of zoo volunteers and their motivations for working at the zoo found that many of them referred to the social benefits ("You come for the animals, but you stay for the people") (Fraser et al., 2009).

The zoo also allows people to connect to the animals (Bodamer & Sankovic, 2000; Clayton et al., 2009, 2011). In studies by Clayton and colleagues (2009, 2011), a significant proportion of visitors made some comment that reflected a connection between humans and the zoo animals, whether by attempting to infer the animal's state of mind, interacting with the animal, or explicitly making a comparison between the animal's behavior or appearance and that of humans ("That gorilla looks just like Daddy!"). A study of responses to chimpanzees showed a similar proportion of comments comparing them to humans (Bodamer & Sankovic, 2000). In a number of different ways, visitors appear to make a behavioral or conceptual connection between themselves and the animals.

Impact on environmental knowledge and concern

Because of their access to a broad range of people who are predisposed to be interested in nature, zoos provide a powerful opportunity to inform people about animals and conservation issues. Studies find mixed results on the effectiveness of zoo visits in inculcating learning. When Lukas and Ross (2005) surveyed 1000 visitors to the Lincoln Park Zoo on attitudes and knowledge toward chimps and gorillas, they found that visitors exiting the building had higher knowledge scores than visitors entering. Although a study of visitors at 12 AZA zoos and aquariums over the course of three years found no evidence for a significant increase in knowledge, visitors said that the zoo supported their conservation beliefs, strengthened their connection to nature, and made them reassess their environmental behaviors. Nearly half of 1400 individuals surveyed offered comments about the elevated awareness of their role in conservation as a direct consequence of their visit (Falk et al., 2007). A recent worldwide survey of over 6000 zoo visitors found evidence of greater knowledge about biodiversity at the end of a zoo visit (Moss et al., 2014).

It may be more appropriate to consider the zoo as a place that contributes to the ongoing process of learning about the environment and conservation, affecting individuals' understanding of environmental processes and problems, more than as a place where a significant amount of information is conveyed (Falk, 2005; Tofield et al., 2003). Like other free-choice learning environments, the contribution of zoos and aquariums may be to reinforce what people already believe, and affirm their identities (Falk, 2005; Storksdieck et al., 2005). However, given what zoo-goers believe and value, zoos may be able to effectively increase awareness of specific environmental issues and ways to address them (Litchfield & Foster, 2009).

Apart from enhancing knowledge, zoos may have more indirect effects on attitudes. Some of Kellert's research has suggested this possibility. In surveys of people who engage in a range of activities with animals, zoo visitors were high on the humanistic scale, more so than birdwatchers. Zoo visitors scored relatively low on dominionistic attitudes, which were exemplified by trappers and hunters. All animal activity groups scored relatively low on the negativistic scale (Kellert, 1996). Other research has found that zoo-goers are more concerned about environmental problems, including climate change, than the general public (Clayton et al., 2013) and that zoo members are more concerned than nonmembers (Clayton et al., 2009).

Myers and Saunders (2002) proposed that zoos enable an empathic connection that can increase the desire to care for the animals at the zoo, and as a consequence, for the species and the broader ecosystem in which those animals live. As one example, research at the Bronx Zoo demonstrated that personal interactions between gorillas and visitors were positive and increased conservation concern (Hayward & Rothenberg, 2004). Ballantyne and Packer (2005) also state that although the research could be more rigorous, there is evidence that a visit does make people more aware of conservation issues. They go on to speculate that an emotional experience may be important in eliciting this effect, because emotional arousal will enhance attention to the emotional stimulus (i.e., the animal) as well as promoting recall. As described earlier, a positive emotional response does appear to be part of the zoo visit (Clayton et al., 2009; Myers et al., 2004). Luebke and Matiasek (2013) extended previous research findings in an important way when they surveyed over 500 zoo visitors and found that emotional experiences in the zoo predicted environmental concern even when controlling for visitors' preexisting attitudes. Relatedly, in a sample of over 7000 zoo visitors from multiple institutions, a sense of connection to the animal was a strong predictor of concern about climate change (Clayton et al., 2013).

One of the impacts of a zoo visit may be for people to contemplate their own relationship to the natural world. This may take place at both a conceptual and an ethical level. There is evidence that visitors to the zoo take the opportunity to reflect on the similarities as well as the differences between themselves and nonhuman animals, perhaps in order to better their understanding of what it means – and does not mean – to be human (Clayton et al., 2009). The impact of these connections has been empirically demonstrated. In two studies comparing people entering a zoo to people leaving, Schultz and Tabanico (2007) found that the people leaving showed higher ratings of an implicit connection with nature (assessed with an Implicit Associations Test; see Chapter 8). No differences were found, however, in environmental concern.

This reflection on the relationship between humans and the rest of nature may lead people to think about their responsibilities to the natural world. Fraser et al. (2008) proposed that zoo visitors use their encounters with wild animals to "explore their own environmental identities." Such identities may encourage the contemplation of how one's own actions can have a positive or negative impact on the environment, as described in the results from the American Zoo and Aquarium Association (AZA) study. Fraser (2009) found that many parents considered moral development to be part of the zoo visit, as children learned their responsibilities toward nature. In surveys of 206 zoo visitors, Clayton et al. (2009) found that perceived learning, wanting to know more, and a stated feeling of connection with the observed animal in an exhibit were all related to a desire to help the individual animal and the species. The reported feeling of a sense of connection was the strongest predictor of the desire to help. Similarly, Myers et al. (2004) found that the strongest correlations between discrete emotions and caring about saving the animal observed were feelings of caring, love, and sense of connection. This connection to the animals and increased concern for animal well-being may be facilitated by the social quality of the zoo visit. The visit to the zoo may not only remind people of their support for the well-being of animals in the wild but also provide an opportunity to affirm and communicate that support within a social group.

The impacts of a zoo visit are not the same for every visitor. Research that looked at impacts on visitors with different motivations showed that a year or two after the visit, what people remembered about it varied depending on what type of visitor they were. In the multi-institutional study described above (Falk et al., 2007), experience seekers were the only group to gain a significant amount of knowledge from a visit to the zoo. Clayton et al. (2009) found that people who came to learn about animals were more likely to say they wanted to know more about the animal and the species as opposed to those who came for entertainment or for a social outing. Compared to the visitors who came primarily to enjoy themselves, these learning-motivated visitors were more likely to say that they did learn something about the animal and the species, to agree that they felt a sense of connection to the animal, and to agree that they would like to help care for the animal and protect the species.

The impact of the zoo may be strengthened, and thus particularly visible, among people who work there. Groff et al. (2005) conducted focus groups with staff members at Disney's Animal Kingdom (which is an AZA-accredited institution), and found that they reported enhanced knowledge of conservation issues, greater support for conservation initiatives and more sustainable behavior as a consequence of coming to work at the Animal Kingdom. Many zoos have "career ladder" type programs targeting teenage workers that may capitalize on this effect. Fraser et al. (2009) conducted an in-depth study of zoo volunteers, combining interviews and surveys in order to explore the extent to which experiences as a zoo volunteer helped to create or to strengthen an environmental identity. In response to open-ended questions, some volunteers reported that they had become more committed to conservation and environmental concerns, and that they had increased their understanding of conservation issues. They also talked about their interest in continued learning about animals, and importantly, identified the community of zoo volunteers as a source of social support for this learning.

In general, the volunteers in Fraser et al.'s (2009) study described their experience as both satisfying their interest in animals and conservation and motivating them toward a fuller expression of their concern for nature, all within the social context provided by their fellow volunteers and by significant others who valued and respected their identities as zoo volunteers. In other words, it was not just their experiences at the zoo but the social context surrounding these experiences that encouraged them to feel a deeper connection and commitment to the natural world. The opportunity to socialize with people who share a love of animals and nature both validates those values and empowers people to act in ways that promote their values.

Maximizing the experience

As managed settings, zoos have the opportunity to construct their exhibits and the overall zoo experience in a way that, informed by the research, is designed to achieve the best effect on environmental learning and attitudes. Interactive experiences appear not only to be appreciated by visitors but also to have positive educational effect. Lindemann-Matthies and Kamer (2006) studied the impact of a "touch table" at a Swiss zoo. The touch table provided physical objects to explore, as well as zoo professionals who could answer questions and engage in discussion. Compared to a group who did not use the touch table, zoo visitors who visited the table were more likely to say they had learned something as well as more likely to correctly answer questions about the exhibit. This was true even at a 3-month follow-up. (There were no differences between the two groups before exposure to the touch table.) Swanagan (2000) found that visitors who had more interactive experiences with elephants (watching a demonstration or handling biofacts) expressed more support for conservation than visitors who only had passive experiences.

Given the importance of enjoyment as a motivation for zoo visits, it is important to consider visitor preferences as well as educational outcome. People spend more time viewing active than inactive animals, exhibits where animals are visible, exhibits with baby animals, and exhibits with naturalistic settings (Bitgood et al., 1988; Davey, 2006; Shettel-Neuber, 1988). Ward et al. (1998) found that people spend more time viewing larger than smaller animals and also demonstrated a preference for larger animals. Price et al. (1994) compared reactions to caged and free-ranging monkeys and found that people were more likely to ask questions and to say they had learned something at the free-ranging exhibit; they also spent more time at the free-ranging exhibit, even though it was more difficult to see the monkeys there. In a review of take-home lessons for enhancing wildlife viewing experiences, Ballantyne et al. (2007) highlighted these findings from the zoo literature:

- When people observe animals in a more "natural" setting they enjoy it more, spend more time, and learn more, perhaps due to the fact they feel more positive about the animal when confinement is less obvious.
- Observing animal behavior, including live animal presentations where animals are presented as 'ambassadors' to talk about the conservation issues of their wild counterparts, positively affected conservation learning.
- Emotionally engaging animals (symbolically meaningful, larger, anthropomorphic, young, and endangered) may serve as "indicator species" for the general public and are sometimes key ecological indicators too.
- Exhibits should include multiple levels of information and motivational themes to allow visitors with different background knowledge, experiences, and motivations to create meaning by combining their previous experiences and the issues being interpreted.

- Persuasive communication strategies, such as discussed in Chapter 9, may provide incentives to extend learning beyond the visit.
- If the conservation challenges of a species or its ecosystem are highlighted, provide information on concrete steps individuals can take in their everyday lives to further conservation goals. Studies have shown that visitors to exhibits with conservation themes have more knowledge and concern about conservation than the general public (Falk & Adelman, 2003). Carr (2005) urged zoos to develop messages that not only inform audiences of the problems but also describe what can be done to address them.

Immersion experiences are now fairly common in zoos. Some zoos have moved toward settings that embody the perspective and practice of caring in conservation, and fostering connection (see also sidebar). For aquariums, both kinds of exhibits are important. Immersion experiences at aquariums take the visitor literally under the waters to see the world from a sea creature's point of view, probably for the first time. One dramatic example is the pioneering "Jellies" exhibit at Monterey Bay Aquarium (MBA)– huge tanks in a darkened area, lit from above to reveal the jellies' bodies in motion. Evaluation by Yalowitz and Tomulonis (2004) found that the exhibit not only had a large aesthetic impact but also a conservation impact, with about half the visitors remembering something about conservation two or three months later, thus demonstrating the power of aesthetic experiences to motivate. The MBA also looked at an exhibit and program that directly tackled conservation issues and actions, the *Vanishing Wildlife* exhibit. Two to three months afterwards 79% recalled learning something about conservation, and almost 40% remembered the *Seafood Watch* guide to seafood purchase; a similar number recalled information in species at risk (Korn, R. & Associates, 2003). These exhibits show that innovative aquarium exhibits may be very effective in communicating conservation around hard-to-appreciate marine issues.

Exhibits that promote connection

When you walk into the Hamill Family Play Zoo (HFPZ) at Chicago's Brookfield Zoo, you realize this is nothing like a traditional children's zoo. There are no goats or cows or raccoons. In fact, live animals are not prominent. Instead, arranged around a central "mountain" are many activity centers, some in separate spaces off to the side. Children (ages 1 to 10 years) can pot or mist plants in the greenhouse that will be used elsewhere in the zoo, paint their faces like an animal, represent their nature experiences in the art-studio "workshop," pretend to be a veterinarian in a child-scale animal hospital, dress up as lemurs right next to real lemurs, be the zoo director either answering queries by phone from a companion across the hall or arranging a manipulable habitat model, learn about pet choices and care, or swap a good nature story for a cool bone or rock. Outside are zones for house-building play, mud play, a creek, a demonstration "sustainable" backyard, and more. There are live animals: house cats, armadillos, and others. But most conspicuous are the "Play Partners," workers trained in developmental psychology and in helping parents help their children connect with nature (Fig. 3.2).

Everything at the play zoo is designed to foster caring for and about nature. The HFPZ, designed by researcher/children's play space architect Robin Moore, won the 2001 Exhibit Award from the AZA. This mold-breaking new concept

(Continued)

(Continued)

Fig. 3.2 Hamill Family Play Zoo: Play partners share enthusiasm and facilitate development of caring attitudes (photo courtesy of Jim Schultz/Chicago Zoological Society).

was a research-based innovation that illustrates the potential of conservation psychology in applied settings. In early conceptual phases of the play zoo, Brookfield Director, zoologist Dr. George Rabb instigated extensive collaboration between in-house talent and outside experts in child development and nature. Among the key ideas eventually embodied in the design and operation of the zoo are that children relate to animals as individuals and connect individuals to habitat and ecology; that hands-on caring is a powerful experience even if only in pretend; that children are active, constructive learners; that imagination, imitation, and pretend enable identification; that children need to start with the familiar; that the family is the basic audience for conservation education; that children are losing chances to interact with nature; and that the zoo can make its own caring visible and help parents make connections to nature and pro-environmental behavior at home (Fig. 3.3).

Urban parks and green spaces

Neighborhood parks may not seem glamorous, but they are widely used and often much loved. Overall, the research suggests that they may have significant psychological benefits. It is worth remembering that the argument made for including parks in urban settings was based on

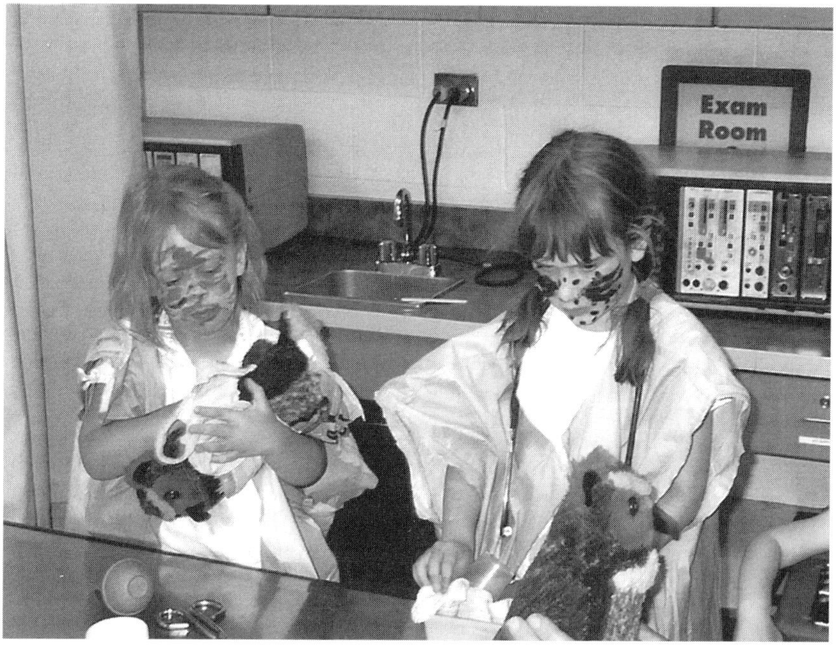

Fig. 3.3 Hamill Family Play Zoo: Pretend is a powerful form of caring (photo courtesy of Mardi Solomon).

their presumed salutary effect. America's most well-known landscape designer, Frederick Law Olmsted, had been the US Sanitary Commissioner during the Civil War and was a strong believer in the influence of physical environment on health (Maller et al., 2005). The opportunity to experience a natural environment and fresh air was expected not only to reduce disease and promote health but also to promote a healthy community by reducing the crime rate. A hundred years later, data are being collected that support those theories.

If we consider merely the quantity of use, urban parks certainly play a significant part in social life. In one study of 688 Northeast Ohio residents, 78% had visited a park in the past 12 months (Payne et al., 2002). In a national survey, respondents reported an average of 43 visits to a local park in the past year. Urban parks are intended both to provide opportunities for experiencing nature and to promote recreational opportunities, and the disparate design of urban parks – from baseball fields and skating rinks to wilderness areas – reflects this. Passive encounters with nature certainly represent a significant proportion of the visits, however. In a case study of Boston's Franklin Park, picnicking, walking, sitting, children playing, and even sitting in a car accounted for 70% of the activity recorded (Hayward, 1989).

There are differences in use of, as well as attitudes toward, parks. A study of women in Brooklyn's Prospect Park (Krenichyn, 2004) uncovered some concern with issues of safety in public areas. Bonnes et al. (2011) describe two dimensions underlying attitudes toward public parks: a positive dimension, based on the opportunities for contact with nature; and a negative dimension, based on fear of crime and urban disorder. Many people hold both attitudes, experiencing ambivalence toward the parks. In their sample of Roman residents, most people were positive about the parks, but opposition was correlated with anthropocentric attitudes and with political conservatism.

A number of studies have found ethnic differences, with African-Americans less likely to visit parks compared to Whites. (Asians show a more mixed pattern of results; they are not always included in the research, and there appear to be differences among Chinese, Japanese, and Korean respondents.) Some of these differences are due to constraints on access. Minority and low socioeconomic status (SES) citizens are less likely to live near parks and may find it more difficult to reach them. Differences emerge, however, even when access is taken into account; as seen in the next chapter, similar differences are found in attitudes toward wild nature. In a study of 1500 survey respondents, women were less likely to use the parks for exercise and considered logistics such as access to be more important. They also preferred more open and manicured settings than men do. They did not differ from men in the perceived benefits of public parks. African-Americans also prefer more managed settings than Whites do, and rate the presence of wildlife as less important. They perceive fewer social and health benefits of parks. But overall, all groups perceived far more positive than negative effects of parks on environmental, physical, social, and spiritual well-being (Ho et al., 2005; see also Payne et al., 2002).

Parks are not the only green spaces in the city. Botanic gardens are more similar to zoos in that they are highly managed and structured spaces that present elements of nature to the public. Although there is not much research on the impacts of botanic gardens, we would expect them to have some similar impacts to other urban green settings. Ballantyne et al. (2008) found that visitors sought them out for enjoyment and restoration. Unlike zoos, however, botanic gardens did not for the most part attract visitors who were hoping to learn about nature.

Parks and human well-being

The presence of urban parks may be more significant than is commonly realized for the well-being of local residents. Observations of public parks in low-income, minority communities, along with interviews of park users and local residents, led Cohen et al. (2007) to conclude that neighborhood parks are critical resources for physical activity in such areas; interviewees said that the park was the most common location for them to exercise, and exercise levels were predicted by the proximity of their residence to the park. Two large epidemiological studies in the Netherlands found that people living in areas of cities with high levels of close-by and somewhat further (1–3 km from home) green space reported fewer health problems on average. This correlation was not explained by age, sex, or socioeconomic status, but the effects were stronger among seniors, housewives, and lower-SES groups (De Vries et al., 2003; Maas et al., 2006). In Japan, a study of over 3000 Tokyo residents found that mortality rate was significantly lower for people with walkable green spaces near their residences; again, this was unrelated to age, sex, or income (Takano et al., 2002). A recent analysis looking at more than 10,000 people in the United Kingdom over almost two decades showed that the proportion of local green space was positively correlated with life satisfaction and negatively related to mental distress; these relationships held true even when controlling for income, employment, local crime rate, and a number of demographic factors (White et al., 2013a).

There are multiple reasons for the positive effects of green space. The healthy benefits of exercise are clear, although that is not the full story. Ryan et al. (2010) found that people rated increased feelings of vitality after walking along a tree-lined path, but not after walking the same distance through tunnels. Increased social contacts, better air quality, and less noise are also part of the outdoor experience (van den Berg et al., 2007). The salience of green spaces in reducing the stress-related impacts of urban noise was shown in a study of dwellings near noisy corridors by Gidloff-Gunnarsson and Ohrstrom (2007). The evidence for the positive effects of time outdoors on mood, cognitive functioning, and stress reduction is now well established. Interestingly, White et al. (2013b) found that urban parks were just as restorative as open countryside in self-reports. However, there is some evidence that the biological diversity of the park is relevant to its positive effects. In a study of urban green spaces in the United Kingdom, Fuller and colleagues (2007) found that increased number of plant species and habitat types were positively correlated with ratings of psychological well-being among visitors.

In rigorous quasi-experimental work, Frances Kuo and colleagues have demonstrated that the impact of parks extends well beyond physical health. Through comparisons of residents of low-income communities that do or do not have access to greenery but do not differ in other ways, they have found that the "greener" neighborhoods show less aggressive and violent behavior (Kuo & Sullivan, 2001), stronger social ties (Kuo et al., 1998), and stronger academic performance. Other studies have explored the impact of urban parks on community relations. When Krenichyn (2004) interviewed women in Brooklyn's Prospect Park, her interviewees reported finding social support for both relationships and activities, among both friends and strangers. This support enabled the fulfillment of athletic interests and contributed to an overall feeling of safety, which arguably could affect overall satisfaction with the community and feeling of connection to the neighborhood.

Children and green space

Children are important beneficiaries of parks and less structured nature areas, as shown by growing evidence that time in nature plays unexpected roles in child development (Kahn & Kellert, 2002). Studies have shown that children prefer natural areas for play (Maxey, 1999; Chawla, 2002; Korpela, 2002) including asphalt playgrounds reconstructed into a more natural state (Moore, 1986b). Hart (1979) and Moore (1986a), among the first to track children's use of space and interview them about it, both found that natural, neglected, and semiwild places were among the most significant to the children. Children often spontaneously construct shelters or use shrubs, bushes, trees, and other vegetation as "hide-outs" and natural refuges (Heerwagen & Orians, 2002).

Many health and developmental factors are encouraged by natural playscapes that offer complex environments for the three main types of play: functional (motor), construction, and symbolic (Frost, 1992). In contrast, traditional playgrounds foster rule-bound play that inhibits development (Frost & Klein, 1979). Motor fitness, balance, and coordination were found to be superior in a group of 5- to 7-year-old children that played in an area with trees and shrubs, as compared to a group with a conventional playground (Fjørtoft, 2004). The researcher noted that "the rough surface provides movement challenges, and topography and vegetation provide a diversity of different designs for playing and moving" (p. 22).

Natural areas provide havens when children are stressed. Korpela (1992) found that adolescents went to natural areas to calm down and gain perspective after stressful events. Studying rural 8- to 11-year olds with access to varying amounts of nearby nature (extent of natural window views, indoor plants, and outdoor plants) and controlling for family income, Wells and Evans (2003) demonstrated that "the impact of stressful life events on [children's] psychological stress is weaker under conditions of high nature than under low nature" (p. 320). Children with more nearby nature also perceived higher self-worth. The researchers suggest that nature may provide the most buffering for the children most vulnerable to distress and low self-worth. Among children with attention deficit hyperactivity disorder symptoms, Kuo and Faber Taylor (2004) found that parents of a nationally representative sample reported that their children showed reduced symptoms after activities in natural settings as compared with indoor and built outdoor settings. The positive effect of a green setting was found even after controlling for the social setting and the activity itself (e.g., reading).

Nature appears to enhance both cognitive and social outcomes for children. The attention children pay to nature, and the rich sensory information available to them in a natural setting, help to foster cognitive abilities such as concentration (Wells, 2000). The opportunity to explore a relatively unstructured physical environment is important in developing a sense of direction as well as problem-solving abilities (Wohlwill & Heft, 1987). Derr (2006) found that children in rural New Mexico "invest creativity and imagination into their place-making and other place interaction" (p. 114). Boys invented names for their areas such as "my green mountain" or "the mighty jungle," and girls made little houses or *casitas* for social activities. In traditional "hardscaped" play settings, social groupings tend to be structured according to hierarchies based solely on physical competence, but Herrington and Studtmann (1998) found that more natural landscapes encouraged fantasy play and social hierarchies based on command of language, creativity, and imagination. Plantings that create differentiated spaces or "green rooms" offer important social play opportunities. Fjørtoft (2004) reported that a prickly juniper bush was highly favored because it offered several enclosed spaces as well as a view to the outside, accommodating a group of 12 children in games of pirates, house, cowboys, etc. Kirkby (1989) made similar observations about green rooms. Finally, children's experience in nature also has implications for environmental identity and for environmental education, as discussed in other chapters.

These results all point to the importance of incorporating nature into the everyday landscapes where children spend a great deal of time (Moore & Cooper Marcus, 2008), such as by turning school playgrounds into green spaces and providing public parks for every urban neighborhood (Fig. 3.4). They also suggest that parents and others rethink the overstructuring

Fig. 3.4 Children and community members benefit from school ground greening projects (photo courtesy of Chuck Holtorf).

of children's days, and the many forces that are reducing time in nature. A lively movement to "leave no child inside" has sprung up in response to journalist Louv's (2008) book, *The last child in the woods*, which has brought this pattern to the public's attention. Although Louv's term, "nature deficit disorder," should not be taken as an indication of a real mental disorder, it is clear that children lacking substantial exposure to nature may miss out on significant benefits.

Conclusion

Managed nature is clearly an important part of human social experience, as reflected in the extensive use people make of zoos and urban parks and in the impact of these parks on human health and social functioning. These experiences not only may emerge from people's attitudes toward nature, but they also have the potential to feed back into those attitudes, strengthening people's perceived connections to the natural world and possibly their support for conservation. Many parks, and zoos in particular, also have extensive resources devoted to visitor research, involving an increasing number of psychologists. They present a valuable opportunity to understand the human relationship with nature as well as to promote a positive relationship.

References

Abadia, R., Day, B., Knowlton, N., McCosker, J., Baron, N., Katoppo, A., & Hough, H. (2004). Defying ocean's end through the power of communication. In L. Glover & S. Earle (Eds.), *Defying ocean's end: An agenda for action* (pp. 183–196). Washington, DC: Island Press.

AZA (2014). Zoo and Aquarium Statistics. Available at https://www.aza.org/zoo-aquarium-statistics/.

Ballantyne, R, & Packer, J. (2005). Promoting environmentally sustainable attitudes and behaviour through free-choice learning experiences: What is the state of the game? *Environmental Education Research*, *11*, 281–295.

Ballantyne, R., Packer, J., Hughes, K., & Dierking, L. (2007). Conservation learning in wildlife tourism settings: Lessons from research in zoos and aquariums. *Environmental Education Research 13*(3), 367–383.

Ballantyne, R., Packer, J., & Hughes, K. (2008) Environmental awareness, interests and motives of botanic gardens visitors: Implications for interpretive practice. *Tourism Management*, *29*, 439–444.

Beardsworth, A., & Bryman, A. (2001). The wild animal in late modernity: The case of the Disneyization of zoos. *Tourist Studies 1*, 83–104.

Bitgood, S., Patterson, D., & Benefield, A. (1988). Exhibit design and visitor behavior: Empirical relationships. *Environment and Behavior*, *20*, 474–491.

Bodamer, M. D., & Sankovic, J. M. (2000). "We're all cousins!" A sampling of public comments at a zoo, reflecting people's sibling relationship with chimpanzees. *Zoo Biology*, *18*, 443–448.

Bonnes, M., Passafaro, P., & Carrus, G. (2011). The ambivalence of attitudes toward urban green areas: Between pro-environmental worldviews and daily residential experience. *Environment and Behavior*, *43*, 207–232.

Carr, B. L. (2005). *Conservation education in zoos and aquariums*. Silver Spring, MD: American Zoo and Aquarium Association. Available at: http://www.izea.net/education/conservationed_aza.htm (Accessed Mar. 26, 2008).

Carson, R. (1961). *The sea around us* (revised edition). New York: Oxford University Press.

Chawla, L. (2002). Spots of time: Manifold ways of being in nature in childhood. In P. Kahn, & S. Kellert (Eds.) *Children and nature: Psychological, sociocultural and evolutionary investigations* (pp. 199–225). Cambridge, MA: MIT Press.

Cheek, N. (1973). People at the zoo. *Animal Kingdom*, *76*, 9–14.

Clayton, S., Fraser, J., & Saunders, C. (2009). Zoo experiences: Conversations, connections, and concern for animals. *Zoo Biology 28*, 377–397.

Clayton, S., Fraser, J., & Burgess, C. (2011). The role of zoos in fostering environmental identity. *Ecopsychology, 3*, 87–96.

Clayton, S., Luebke, J., Saunders, C., Matiasek, J., & Grajal, A. (2013). Connecting to nature at the zoo: Implications for responding to climate change. *Environmental Education Research, 20*, 460–475.

Cohen, D., McKenzie, T., Sehgal, A., Williamson, S., Golinelli, D., & Lurie, N. (2007). Contribution of public parks to physical activity. *American Journal of Public Health, 97*, 509–514.

Davey, G. (2006). Visitor behavior in zoos: A review. *Anthrozoos, 19*, 143–157.

De Vries, S., Verheij, R., Groenevegen, P., & Spreeuwenberg, P. (2003). Natural environments- healthy environments? An exploratory analysis of the relationship between green space and health. *Environment and Planning A, 35*, 1717–1731.

Derr, T. (2006). 'Sometimes the birds sound like fish': Perspectives on children's place experiences. In C. Spencer & M. Blades (Eds.), *Children and their environments* (pp. 108–116). Cambridge: Cambridge University Press.

Falk, J. H. (2005). Free-choice environmental learning: Framing the discussion. *Environmental Education Research, 11*, 265–280.

Falk, J. H., & Adelman, L. M. (2003). Investigating the impacts of prior knowledge and interest on aquarium visitor learning. *Journal of Research in Science Teaching 40*, 163–176.

Falk, J. H., Reinhard, E. M., Vernon, C. L., Bronnenkant, K., Deans, N. L., & Heimlich, J. E., (2007). *Why zoos & aquariums matter: Assessing the impact of a visit*. Silver Spring, MD: Association of Zoos & Aquariums.

Fjørtoft, I. (2004). Landscape as playscape: The effects of natural environments on children's play and motor development. *Children, Youth and Environments, 14*, 21–44.

Fraser, J. (2009). The anticipated utility of zoos and aquariums for developing moral concern in children. *Curator: The Museum Journal, 52*, 349–361.

Fraser, J., Gruber, S., & Condon, K. (2008). Exposing the tourist value proposition of zoos and aquaria. *Tourism Review International, 11*, 279–293.

Fraser, J., Clayton, S., Sickler, J., & Taylor, A. (2009). Belonging at the zoo: Retired volunteers, conservation activism, and collective identity. *Ageing and Society, 29*, 351–368.

Frost, J. (1992). *Play and playscapes*. New York: Delmar Publishers.

Frost, J. L., & Klein, B. (1979). *Children's play and playgrounds*. London: Allyn and Bacon.

Fuller, R., Irvine, K., Devine-Wright, P., Warren, P., & Gaston, K. (2007). Psychological benefits of greenspace increase with biodiversity. *Biology Letters, 3*, 390–394.

Gidloff-Gunnarsson, A., & Ohrstrom, E. (2007). Noise and well-being in urban residential environments: The potential role of perceived availability to nearby green areas. *Landscape and Urban Planning, 83*(2–3), 115–126.

Groff, A., Lockhart, D., Ogden, J., & Dierking, L. D. (2005). An exploratory investigation of the effect of working in an environmentally themed facility on the conservation-related knowledge, attitudes and behavior of staff. *Environmental Education Research, 11*, 371–387.

Hart, R. (1979). *Children's experience of place*. New York: Irvington Pub.

Hayward, J. (1989). Urban parks: Research, planning, and social change. In I. Altman & E. Zube (Eds.), *Public places and spaces* (193–216). New York: Plenum.

Hayward, J., & Rothenberg, M. (2004). Measuring success in the Congo Gorilla Forest Conservation Exhibition. *Curator, 47*, 261–282.

Heerwagen, J. H., & Orians, G. H. (2002). The ecological world of children. In P. H. Kahn, Jr., & S. R. Kellert (Eds.), *Children and nature* (pp. 29–63). Cambridge, MA: MIT Press.

Herrington, S., & Studtmann, K. (1998). Landscape interventions: New directions for the design of children's outdoor play environments. *Landscape and Urban Planning, 42*, 191–205.

Ho, C., Sasidharan, V., Elmendorf, W., Willits, F., Graefe, A., & Godbey, G. (2005). Gender and ethnic variations in urban park preferences, visitation, and perceived benefits. *Journal of Leisure Research, 37*, 281–306.

Holzer, D., Scott, D., & Bixler, R. (1998). Socialization influences on adult zoo visitation. *Journal of Applied Recreation Research, 23*, 43–62.

International State of the Ocean Project (2013). State of the Ocean Report. Available at http://www.stateoftheocean.org/research.cfm

Jamieson, D. (1985). Against zoos. In P. Singer (Ed.), *In defense of animals* (pp. 108–117). Oxford: Basil Blackwell.

Jamieson, D. (1995). Zoos revisited. In B. Norton, M. Hutchins, E. Stevens & T. Maple (Eds.), *Ethics on the ark* (pp. 52–66). Washington DC: Smithsonian Inst. Press.

Kahn, P., & Kellert, S. (2002, Eds.). *Children and nature*. Cambridge, MA: MIT.

Kaplan, R., & Kaplan, S. (1989). *The experience of nature: A psychological perspective*. New York: Cambridge University Press.

Kellert, S. R. (1996). *The value of life: Biological diversity and human society*. Washington, D.C.: Island Press.

Kirkby, M. (1989). Nature as a refuge in children's environments. *Children's Environments Quarterly, 6*, 7–12.

Klenosky, D. B., & Saunders, C. D. (2008) Put me in the zoo! A laddering study of zoo visitor motives. *Tourism Review International, 11*, 317–327.

Korn, R. & Associates. (2003). *Summative evaluation of Vanishing Wildlife*. Monteray, CA: Monteray Bay Aquarium.

Korpela, K. M. (1992). Adolescents' favorite places and environmental self-regulation. *Journal of Environmental Psychology, 12*, 249–258.

Korpela, K. (2002). Children's environment. In R. Bechtel & A. Churchman (Eds.), *Handbook of environmental psychology*. New York: Wiley.

Krenichyn, K. (2004). Women and physical activity in an urban park. *Journal of Environmental Psychology, 24*, 117–130.

Kuo, F., & Faber Taylor, A. (2004). A potential natural treatment for Attention-Deficit/Hyperactivity Disorder: Evidence from a national study. *American Journal of Public Health, 94*, 1580–1586.

Kuo, F., & Sullivan, W. (2001). Aggression and violence in the inner city: Effects of environment via mental fatigue. *Environment and Behavior, 33*, 543–571.

Kuo, F. E., Sullivan, W. C., Coley, R. L., & Brunson, L. (1998). Fertile ground for community: Inner-city neighborhood common spaces. *American Journal of Community Psychology, 26*(6), 823–851.

Lindemann-Matthies, P., & Kamer, T. (2006). The influence of an interactive educational approach on visitors' learning in a Swiss zoo. *Science Education, 90*, 296–315.

Litchfield, C., & Foster, W. (2009). Conservation psychology in zoos. *International Zoo Educator, 45*, 6–10.

Louv, R. (2008). *The last child in the woods*. Chapel Hill: Algonquin Books.

Luebke, J. F., & Matiasek, J. (2013). An exploratory study of zoo visitors' exhibit experiences and reactions. *Zoo Biology, 32*, 407–416.

Lukas, K., & Ross, S. (2005). Zoo visitor knowledge and attitudes toward gorillas and chimpanzees. *Journal of Environmental Education, 36*, 33–48.

Maas, J., Verheij, R., Groenewegen, P., de Vries, S., & Spreeuwenberg, P., (2006). Green space, urbanity and health: How strong is the relationship? *Journal of Epidemiology and Community Health, 60*, 587–592.

Maller, C., Townsend, M., Pryor, A., Brown, P., & St. Leger, L. (2005). Healthy nature healthy people. *Health Promotion International, 21*, 45–54.

Maple, T. (1995). Toward a responsible zoo agenda. In B. Norton, M. Hutchins, E. Stevens & T. Maple (Eds.), *Ethics on the ark* (pp. 20–30). Washington DC: Smithsonian Inst. Press.

Mason, P. (2000). Zoo tourism: The need for more research. *Journal of Sustainable Tourism, 8*, 333–339.

Maxey, I. (1999). Playgrounds: From oppressive spaces to sustainable places? *Built Environment, 25*, 18–24.

Mazur, N. A. (2001). *After the ark: Environmental policy-making and the zoo*. Victoria, Australia: Melbourne University Press.

Moore, R. (1986a). *Childhood's domain*. London: Croom-Helm.

Moore, R. (1986b).The power of nature. *Children's Environments Quarterly*, *3*, 52–69.

Moore, R. C., & Cooper Marcus, C. (2008). Healthy planet, healthy children: Designing nature into the daily spaces of childhood. In S. Kellert, J. Heerwagen & M. Mador, *Biophilic design* (pp. 153–203) Hoboken, NJ: John Wiley.

Morgan, J. M., & Hodgkinson, M. (1999). The motivation and social orientation of visitors attending a contemporary zoological park. *Environment and Behavior 31*, 227–239.

Moss, A., & Esson, M. (2013). The educational claims of zoos: Where do we go from here?. *Zoo Biology*, *32*(1), 13–18.

Moss, A., Jensen, E., & Gusset, M. (2014). *A global evaluation of biodiversity literacy in zoo and aquarium visitors*. Gland: WAZA Executive Office, 37 pp.

Myers, Jr., O. E., & Saunders, C. D. (2002). Animals as links to developing caring relationships with the natural world. In P. H. Kahn Jr., & S. R. Kellert (Eds.), *Children and nature: Psychological, sociocultural and evolutionary investigations*. (pp. 153–178). Cambridge, MA: MIT Press.

Myers, Jr., O. E., Saunders, C., & Birjulin, A. (2004). Emotional dimensions of watching zoo animals: An experience sampling study building on insights from psychology. *Curator*, *47*, 299–321.

Nash, R. (2005). Forward. In P. Barlett (Ed.), *Urban place: Reconnecting with the natural world* (pp. vii–viii). Cambridge, MA: MIT.

Norton, B. (1995). A broader look at animal stewardship. In B. Norton, M. Hutchins, E. Stevens & T. Maple (Eds.), *Ethics on the ark* (pp. 102–121). Washington, DC: Smithsonian Inst. Press.

Ogden, J., Gentile, C., & Revard, B. (2004). Trends in conservation education. *Communique*, August, 18–20.

Payne, L., Mowen, A., & Orsega-Smith, E. (2002). An examination of park preferences and behaviors among urban residents. *Leisure Sciences*, *24*, 181–198.

Price, E., Ashmore, L., & McGivern, A-M. (1994). Reactions of zoo visitors to free-ranging monkeys. *Zoo Biology*, *13*, 355–373.

Rabb, G. B., & Saunders, C. D. (2005). The future of zoos and aquariums: Conservation and caring. *International Zoo Yearbook*, *39*, 1–26.

Ryan, R., Weinstein, N., Bernstein, J., Brown, K., Mistretta, L., & Gagné, M. (2010). Vitalizing effects of being outdoors and in nature. *Journal of Environmental Psychology*, *30*, 169–168.

Schultz, P. W., & Tabanico, J. (2007). Self, identity, and the natural environment: Exploring implicit connections with nature. *Journal of Applied Social Psychology*, *37*, 1219–1247.

Shettel-Neuber, J. (1988). Second and third-generation zoo exhibits: A comparison of visitor, staff, and animal responses. *Environment and Behavior 20*, 452–473.

Stoinski, T. S., Lukas, K. E., & Maple, T. L. (1998). A survey of research in North American zoos and aquariums. *Zoo Biology*, *17*(3), 167–180.

Storksdieck, M., Ellenbogen, K., & Heimlich, J. E. (2005). Changing minds? Reassessing outcomes in free-choice environmental education. *Environmental Education Research 11*, 353–369.

Swanagan, J. (2000). Factors influencing zoo visitor's conservation attitudes and behavior. *Journal of Environmental Education*, *31*, 26–31.

Takano, T., Nakamura, K., & Watanabe, M. (2002). Urban residential environment and senior citizens' longevity in megacity areas. *Journal of Epidemiology and Community Health*, *56*, 913–918.

The Ocean Project. (2009). *America, the Ocean, and Climate Change: New Research Insights for Conservation, Awareness, and Action*. The Ocean Project: Providence, RI.

Tofield, S.; Coll, R. K.; Vyle, B., & Bolstad, R. (2003). Zoos as a source of free choice learning. *Research in Science & Technological Education*, *21*, 67–99.

Tomas, S. R., Crompton, J. L., & Scott, D (2003). Assessing service quality and benefits sought among zoological park visitors. *Journal of Park and Recreation Administration*, *21*, 105–124.

Turley, S. K. (2001). Children and the demand for recreational experiences: The case of zoos. *Leisure Studies*, *20*, 1–18.

van den Berg, A. E., Hartig, T., & Staats, H. (2007). Preference for nature in urbanized societies: Stress, restoration, and the pursuit of sustainability. *Journal of Social Issues*, *63*, 79–96.

Ward, P. I., Mosberger, N., Kistler, C., & Fischer, O. (1998). The relationship between popularity and body size in zoo animals. *Conservation Biology*, *12*, 1408–1411.

Wells, N. (2000). At home with nature: Effects of "greenness" on children's cognitive functioning. *Environment and Behavior, 32*, 775–795.

Wells, N., & Evans, G. (2003). Nearby nature: A buffer of life stress among rural children. *Environment and Behavior, 35*, 311–330.

White, M. P., Alcock, I., Wheeler, B. W., & Depledge, M. H. (2013a). Would you be happier living in a greener urban area? A fixed-effects analysis of panel data. *Psychological Science, 24*(6), 920–928.

White, M. P., Paul, S., Ashbullby, K., Herbert, S., & Depledge, M. H. (2013b). Feelings of restoration from recent nature visits. *Journal of Environmental Psychology, 35*, 40–51.

Wohlwill, J., & Heft, H. (1987). The physical environment and development of the child. In D. Stokols & I. Altman (Eds.), *Handbook of environmental psychology*, Vol. *1* (pp. 281–328). New York: Wiley.

Woods, B. (2002). Good zoo/bad zoo: Visitor experiences in captive settings. *Anthrozoös 15*(4), 343–360.

Yalowitz, S., & Tomulonis, J. (2004). *Jellies: Living art summative evaluation*. Monteray, CA: Monteray Bay Aquarium.

4

Wild Nature: Encounters with Wilderness

Whether we are experiencing it or merely talking about it, wild nature seems psychologically potent. Backcountry travelers frequently describe "peak" moments, and wild animals provoke intense positive and negative emotions. This chapter explores the meanings of wildness, describes patterns of contact with wild nature and values people hold toward it, and examines the psychological experience of key aspects of wild settings and creatures. Acknowledging the social and other influences on the experience of wild nature, we especially ask what may be the distinctive contributions of wild nature itself to experience. Along the way we consider some psychological theories that help account for these effects and examine some applications and implications.

A healthy ecosystem may require curtailing access to wilderness, or at least restraining human activities. Access to wild areas, however, arguably informs people about the values of wild nature and fuels political support for preservation. Decisions about the best way to protect wilderness require an understanding of the complex ways in which humans approach it.

Defining wild nature and wilderness

Before examining the experience of wilderness, we should consider what it means. This turns out to involve a complex intersection of psychology, history, culture, and landscape. Historian

Conservation Psychology: Understanding and promoting human care for nature, Second Edition.
Susan Clayton and Gene Myers.

www.wiley.com\go\clayton\conservation

Roderick Nash has said that "wilderness" is so heavily freighted with meaning of a personal, symbolic, and changing kind as to resist easy definition (1982, p. 1). In the US, the idea of wilderness as a deliberately preserved natural area was born of the preservationist movement of the late 19th century. It became institutionalized in the 20th century, first as the "preservation" portion of the National Park Service's mission as laid out in 1916; soon after as the "primitive area" administrative designation used by the US Forest Service; and later in the 1964 Wilderness Act. To some degree, this broad movement reflects the symbolic meanings of wilderness that derived from the Romantic period: wilderness as pure, sublime, and spiritual, and an antidote to overly civilized life. But these are by no means the only associations with wild nature. In Medieval Europe, some viewed wild areas as the antithesis of the creator's garden, and thus to be avoided as the realm of the devil, or reclaimed physically from pagan presence (Nash, 1982). Harrison (1992) argues that the forest edge literally and psychologically bounded "civilization," containing dangers both external and internal. The earliest European settlers in North America sometimes feared not only the natives of the wild, but also their own potential to let civilized behavior lapse in a land so lacking in familiar if onerous external social constraints (Nash, 1982). Alternatively, Tuan suggested a source of the idea of wilderness as beautiful and elevating:

> We owe to the city our aesthetic appreciation of nature: directly because it is in the city that artistic sensibility is cultivated; indirectly because to be keenly aware of something we need to have its antithesis, and the city is the antithesis of nature. Through the millennia of written history we repeatedly find sentiments for nature expressed in reaction to the failings of urban life.
>
> (Tuan, 1971, p. 34)

Juxtapositions such as the foregoing demonstrate that "wilderness" is a cultural construction that would probably be nonsensical to native peoples who do (or did) not see a clear distinction between their own status in nature and that of the beings and landscapes with which they coexisted (see Chapter 5). Callicott and Nelson (1998) argue that the wilderness idea many people hold today, which was articulated by the 19th century preservation movements, could only be possible in countries, such as the US and Australia, where nature could be found in a "pristine state" beyond the frontier of civilization. Unfortunately, native peoples around the globe, including in North America (Keller & Turek, 1998), have sometimes been displaced in order for lands they used to become national parks or other kinds of wilderness preserve (see Chapter 10 for a discussion of contemporary issues related to this). In the developing world, denying access may destroy political support for conservation. An important theme in environmental thought since the 20th century has been the attempt to reconcile the wilderness ethic of keeping some parts of nature free of human influence with the reality of human presence in and use of nature.

Whatever may be the cultural specificity of the concept of "wilderness," it was an unprecedented historical moment when nature was recognized by modern industrial people as worthy of protection in a wild state. Today, the US Wilderness system includes 758 designated Wilderness areas totaling over 109.5 million acres (just over half of this is in Alaska; the remainder equals an area about the size of the state of Minnesota or about 2.7% of the lower 48 states) (Wilderness.net, 2014). Even outside the designated areas, there are areas where people may still experience wildness. For example, an analysis of wilderness attributes and federal land status by Aplet et al. (2005) showed that the federal Bureau of Land Management (BLM) has only 6.5 million acres of Wilderness out of its 270 million acre holdings, but 58 million nondesignated BLM acres possess the highest Wildness Index (30) in Aplet et al.'s rating system. Official protection is important, but may not be necessary for a psychological experience of wilderness. The complexity of defining wilderness is reflected in the complexity of wilderness management. By way of practical illustration, the Wilderness Stewardship Reference System maintained by the Arthur Carhart National Wilderness Training Center and the USFS Aldo Leopold Wilderness Research Institute lists over 65 legislative, administrative, judicial, and scientific issues about which federal managers of wilderness areas must be concerned (see http://www.wilderness.net/index.cfm?fuse=WSRS&sec=intro). Nickas and Proescholdt (2005) examine problems with "nonconforming" uses of wilderness, and Woods (1998) provides a conceptual analysis of paradoxes that have unfolded from the implementation of the Wilderness Act itself. The wider set of social and economic forces impinging on wild nature globally makes it clear wild areas and creatures can continue to exist "freely" only through great human effort.

Degree of wildness can be described in terms of observable attributes. Wild nature means (1) natural composition, or an essentially complete set of native species; (2) unaltered structure, or the retention of the historic arrangement of the parts; (3) lack of pollution of water, air, soil, darkness at night, and noise; (4) capacity to provide opportunities for solitude; (5) remoteness – particularly lack of, and distance to, roads; and (6) uncontrolled processes such as fires, floods, migrations, and evolution (Aplet et al., 2005). Some minimum spatial scale is probably required, depending on which ecological or evolutionary processes are to be left to operate uncontrolled. It is the work of conservation biologists and ecologists to inform our choices regarding which areas will best preserve ecological diversity and functions. But if "wild" nature is partly humanly defined, then it cannot be described only in biophysical terms. This chapter discusses features of wild nature that describe its experience psychologically. After briefly describing wilderness use, we turn to the themes of solitude, domination by natural forces rather than by humans and their technologies, and the uncontrolled and remote qualities that lend wild nature particular qualities of challenge and risk. Especially intriguing is the possibility that wild nature, nature at its most other-than-human, offers something singular and possibly universal to our fulfillment as humans. The exploration of that possibility is a key theoretical and empirical challenge for conservation psychology.

Wilderness use and wilderness values

Approximately 12 million people visit US designated Wilderness areas annually (USFS 2013), and many others encounter wild nature on other lands or settings with minimal technological mediation. Human activities in wild nature vary along a continuum from heavily exploitative, to subsistence, to recreation, and to appreciative or aesthetic. Many people place high value on the mere existence of wild nature, even if they themselves never experience it directly. The National Survey on Recreation and the Environment (NSRE) (Cordell et al., 2008) asked a representative sample of Americans over age 16 whether they endorsed 13 values of wilderness identified by Haas et al. (1986). Table 4.1 shows the percentages who said each of the listed values was "extremely" or "very" important. The only statistically significant changes between the 1986 and 2008 studies were increases in valuing preservation of unique wild plants and animals, providing recreation opportunities, preserving areas for science, and providing tourist industry income. It is notable that in the more recent sample 50.7% indicated there is not enough Wilderness, and about 35% said the amount is "about right"; both figures showed upward trends over the previous period. Only 4% expressed the opinion there is too much Wilderness, representing a decrease. Finally, over two-thirds "strongly" or "somewhat" favored additional federal designation of wilderness in their states at both time periods, whereas those opposed

Table 4.1 Wilderness values: percent of US residents age 16 and older who said given values are extremely or very important. 1999–2000 $n = 5058$; 2006–2007 $n = 2187$.

Wilderness value	1999–2000	2006–2007
Protecting air quality	91.8	93.0
Protecting water quality	91.4	90.3
Protecting wildlife habitat	87.2	87.7
Knowing future generations will have wilderness areas	85.1	85.6
Protecting rare and endangered plants and animals	82.9	82.7
Preserving unique wild plants and animals	79.7	83.0
Providing scenic beauty	74.3	76.5
Knowing that wilderness areas exist	74.1	75.7
Having option to visit wilderness areas in future	73.2	76.2
Providing recreation opportunities	66.7	71.3
Preserving natural areas for science	57.4	64.3
Providing spiritual inspiration	58.2	57.8
Providing income for tourist industry	33.3	39.6

Source: Adapted from Cordell et al. 2008, Table 1, pp. 5–6.

constituted less than 13%. Thus, we can conclude that in the US the values of Wilderness and Wilderness protection enjoy strong public support.

Driver and colleagues developed an exhaustive scale of benefits, termed "Recreation Experience Preferences" (REP), to understand visitors' reasons for Wilderness travel. Sixteen main categories of REP include enjoying nature, physical fitness, tension reduction, escaping noise and crowds, outdoor learning, sharing values, independence, family kinship, introspection, achievement or stimulation, and other items. Studies across eight varied Wilderness areas found remarkable consistency in users' ratings on these scales. First on the preference list was to enjoy nature, followed by physical fitness, reducing tensions, escape, learning, and values sharing. These items added to satisfaction with the experience "most strongly" or "strongly" (Driver et al., 1987). Studies in the REP tradition have focused on personal benefits, including developmental, therapeutic, physical, self-sufficiency, social identity, education, and spiritual and aesthetic or creative benefits and have included structured group expeditions as well as independent wilderness excursions. These studies, summarized in Schuster et al. (2005), show positive effects from wilderness experiences for self-efficacy type constructs, personal and problem-solving skills, and some therapeutic outcomes, in programs aimed at each of these outcomes. Social identity enhancement is also found.

Understanding the constituencies for wilderness and the trends in use help focus the question of the perceived values of wilderness among its traditional constituency as well as others. Analyses of the NSRE data revealed no significant differences between rural and urban populations, with marginally significant higher values placed on spiritual inspiration and tourist income for rural respondents (Cordell et al., 2008). Earlier Johnson et al. (2005) found urban versus nonurban dwellers to differ significantly only in terms of the former showing more scientific/medicinal and existence values. Wilderness visitors are more likely to be male, to have attended college and to have higher than average incomes (Johnson et al., 2005). Immigrants were significantly less likely than native-born respondents to actively use Wilderness areas, to anticipate using them, to see a relationship to off-site environmental quality, or to perceive option values, intragenerational bequest values, or existence values. But on other items (scientific/medicinal value, intergenerational bequest, and intrinsic values), immigrants were not different than natives. Roughly similar results were found for Blacks or Latinos versus whites. Members of Asian groups showed fewer differences from whites, and while being less likely to visit or expect to visit wilderness, they were more likely to express existence and intrinsic values than whites. The strongest predictor of using and valuing wilderness in the 10 different ways measured was acculturation, measured as how long the respondent had lived in the United States.

In general, Johnson et al. (2005) conclude that while cultural differences are most pronounced in site-related values, there are relatively few differences in off-site (environmental quality) and passive values (option, bequest, and existence), especially when acculturation is taken into account. These findings suggest that nontraditional users might value wilderness if they were introduced intelligently to it, and that ethnic differences in valuing wilderness in indirect ways should not be exaggerated. Winter and Chavez (2008) found that whites and people of color agreed that natural resource areas should be used for recreation. They adapted Clayton's (2003) environmental identity scale (see Chapter 8), finding ethnic differences in one study (whites, particularly wilderness users, had higher EID scores), but not in the other. In both studies, higher EID values correlated with support for managing forest lands for environmental quality, and with perceived need for more area protected. Indeed, other methodologies show a convergence in the public's wilderness values. The largest values of wild lands derived from economic studies, again across demographic sectors, come from off-site use and passive use values (e.g., Loomis & Richardson, 2000; Bowker et al., 2005).

While studies such as those summarized above use fairly abstract questions to obtain estimates of the values of wilderness, Brown and Alessa (2005) used GIS to examine the association of values with specific areas known by respondents. They asked respondents to place dots coded to represent different wilderness values on maps of nearby lands in Alaska (including Wilderness areas but not showing their boundaries). On this local scale, strong associations emerged between Wilderness locations and indirect life-sustaining, intangible (intrinsic and spiritual), and deferred or future values. Tangible values such as economic, recreational, and subsistence tended to be located outside preserved areas. There were no differences by area (Wilderness or not) for biological diversity, learning, therapeutic, and cultural values. These results strengthen the picture derived from NSRE results of a historic shift toward the public most highly valuing nonuse, ecosystem-support benefits of wilderness.

Wilderness solitude

The experiences of people in wild nature can be characterized according to the outstanding psychological features of wilderness: solitude; encounter with natural forces and features, especially wild animals; wilderness remoteness and challenge; and the spiritual dimension of wilderness experiences. Wildness may be directly encountered alone, with a small group, or with many other people, but even when others are present, wilderness seems to contain the potential for solitude – by lagging behind on the trail, or taking a detour into an untracked area – in part because of the (relative) absence of built objects and human artifacts. Because of these contrasts with most people's daily lives, we might expect that solitude would be a psychologically compelling aspect of wild nature.

Although sometimes romanticized as blissful and transcendent, actually being alone is an uncomfortable experience for many people, particularly adolescents (Larson, 1997; Buchholz & Catton, 1999). Using surveys and interviews Bobilya and colleagues (2005) studied 126 college students' experiences during 2–3 day solos that were part of an 18-day wilderness orientation program. They found that participants' expectations were important. Generally, the students expected chances for spiritual growth and reflection (this was how the solo was framed by the leaders), as well as autonomy and rest. But students also worried about loneliness, uncertainty, lack of structure and whether they would fulfill their expectations for what was "supposed" to occur. The experience of solitude was affected not only by the wilderness setting, but also by experiences preceding the solo, such as positive or negative group interactions, which affected feelings of support, comfort, and safety while alone. The contrast between wilderness solos and everyday life "encouraged participants to reflect on their role in the universe" (Bobilya et al., 2005, p. 113) and heightened sensory experience; participants reported noticing details of nature that had escaped them before, and saw common events such as sunsets in new ways. Such attention may be enhanced by prior "micro solos" designed to focus the person on nature (Maxted, 2005).

Some of the students reported discomfort and anxiety. Similarly, Maxted (2005) enumerated adolescent solo participants' anxieties about external elements, such as wild animals, wet weather, long dark nights, unidentified sounds, and strangers; and internal fears such as not knowing how they would cope, and fear of the unknown within. Such insecurities were acknowledged much more readily after the solo than before. Maxted's participants also reported boredom. These findings highlight the challenges the wilds pose that demand practical and emotional skills. In everyday life, socialization agents, such as parents, teachers, employers, institutions, and physical settings, provide structure and control. In contrast, wild spaces offer freedom and potentially the discovery of self-reliance and responsibility. This freedom and discovery, however, are enhanced by good orchestration. Talented and attentive program designers and leaders weave together cognitive framing of the experience, group facilitation, timing, challenge level, emotional intelligence, risk assessment, and instruction with use of specific features of the setting (Knapp & Smith, 2005; Miles & Priest, 1999).

Solitude was mentioned as the one of the two most difficult aspects of a solo experience in a retrospective study of 227 people who had participated in a college wilderness expedition program (the other difficult aspect was fasting) (Daniel, 2005). Daniel also reported that a "great majority" of participants found the solo significant because of its novelty: such an experience was singular in their lives before and after. As noted by Neisser (1982, quoted in Daniel, 2005), life events are more likely to become significant if they are relatively unique and strongly emotional, as was the case for these participants. Perhaps counter-intuitively, one of the greatest benefits of wilderness solitude may be strengthened relationships with others (Buchholz & Catton, 1999). Participants in the programs described above dwelt upon their family and friends and their own roles with those significant others while alone. Whether the same would be found among those who become skilled and habituated to living in wilderness solitude is another question.

The flip side of solitude is an issue of concern to wilderness managers: crowding and its impact on visitors' experiences. In one early study, Heberlein (1977) found that crowding reduced river recreationists' satisfaction. Such evaluations were found to be relative to how long the visitor had been coming to the location (Vaske et al., 1980), suggesting something akin to the "generational environmental amnesia" (see Chapter 10). In another early project, Twight and colleagues (1981) examined preferences for privacy, measured in several dimensions (intimacy, lack of neighbors, solitude, anonymity, and seclusion). They found that backpackers preferred to be in a small group but had greater desire for privacy compared with car campers. Recent research by Cole and Hall (2010) on trail users in Washington and Oregon wilderness areas used factor analysis to differentiate the experience of privacy (in the sense of feeling isolated and away from others) from two experiences that privacy enhances (1) "release" including items relating to stress reduction as well as autonomy and (2) "personal growth" such as self-discovery, opportunities to confide in others, to work through problems, and to explore new ideas. Most hikers were in small groups, and although privacy decreased markedly the more other parties that were encountered, the beneficial functions of privacy could be experienced even where moderate levels of privacy are experienced.

Closely related to solitude is the experience of tranquility in nature, an experience that can be disrupted by noise. In a study by Mace et al. (2013), subjects watched scenes of Bryce Canyon National Park on a computer monitor while also hearing helicopter, propeller plane, or jet noise and natural sounds (the latter both alone and in combination with the others). The noises were at audible at about 50Db in a soundproof lab room, roughly equivalent to refrigerator noise. The noise conditions resulted in significantly lower ratings of scene preference, scenic beauty, naturalness, solitude, and tranquility, and higher levels of annoyance, similar to what other studies have found. Helicopter noise was most disruptive, followed by propeller planes and jet noise.

Wilderness managers have an interest in matters such as crowding and noise because the Wilderness Act mandates "outstanding opportunities for solitude." Questions about the standards for visitor experience in wilderness involve psychology and have been approached via social norm theory (Shelby et al., 1996). Examples include Visitor Impact Management (Graefe et al., 1990); Visitor Experience and Resource Protection (National Park Service, 1997); and consensual approaches to recreation management decision making such as Limits of Acceptable Change (Stankey et al., 1985; McCool and Cole, 1997). Manning et al. (2002) acknowledge that it may be difficult to identify norms for outdoor recreation because of the lack of effective social sanctioning where people are few, and because norms may not be shared across social groups. But research has documented some degree of consensus on recreation related norms. As an illustration, before running the Middle Fork of the Salmon River in Idaho each season, thousands of people receive mandatory leave-no-trace instructions. Despite almost nil official enforcement, successive groups of boaters encounter apparently unused campsites, suggesting a high degree of social group sanctioning and norm internalization (R. Hebert, personal communication).

Conservation psychology may contribute to such pragmatic problems, in part by unearthing other important variables. For example, one psychological factor influencing visitors' judgments of environmental conditions is place identity. As described in Chapter 8, Kyle et al. (2004) found that Appalachian Trail hikers with higher place identity tended to perceive social and environmental conditions as more degraded. Taken together, the evidence suggests the need to better balance and integrate biophysical indicators of ecological health with social-psychological models of values in wild lands management.

Natural forces and features

Wild nature is various, and it seems likely that humans respond to different kinds of wild nature in different ways. Even something as familiar as daily or seasonal weather variation can be considered an uncontrollable wild aspect of nature. Duffy and Verges (2010) showed that seasonal weather had significant effects on implicit associations between self and nature, which were higher in spring and fall, whereas associations between self and the built environment were higher in winter. Effects of weather in other areas, such as interpersonal affective behavior, aggression, and accident rates, are summarized by Duffy and Verges (2010). Characterizing wild nature by landscape, dramatically different psychological meanings are suggested by the metaphorical and literary associations of biomes as disparate as hot dry deserts, or cold arctic tundra; tropical forests; estuarine deltas; high mountains peaks or deep river gorges; verdant prairies; and intertidal shores. Given the 867 distinct terrestrial ecoregions identified by Olson et al. (2001), there is clearly an opportunity for research on human responses to different natural features. Further, within any given ecosystem are its wild inhabitants which evoke widely different responses. Wild forces of nature with notably different psychological dimensions are wildfire and more generally natural disasters, and wild animals.

Wildfire

Fire burning uncontrolled through dry vegetation would seem to embody wild nature's destructive power. Fire evokes a deep fear in people, and with obvious reason. Since the early 20th century conservation movement in the US, wildfires were universally suppressed when possible, consistent with a broadly utilitarian ethic that viewed them as destructive of natural resources. Forest fire-fighting budgets today have shifted dramatically toward protecting people's dwellings, particularly in the mountain west and southwest where many have settled "close to nature" in homes in the new "wild land–urban interface." Ironically, it is people's very attraction to nature that is driving this trend.

Attitudes toward fire have changed as scientists have learned of its ecological roles in many types of natural communities. US federal wild land fire policy shifted in 1995 toward allowing certain natural fires to burn. At the same time, there are institutional pressures to prevent fires or lower fire intensity, and pro-suppression attitudes remain (Aplet, 2006). Slowness to change may be reflected in the continued use of Smokey Bear and his slogan "Only you can prevent forest fire!" instead of the adoption of alternate Reddy Squirrel (proposed by the group Forest Service Employees for Environmental Ethics) and her updated saying, "Wildfire happens. Be ready!" (To his credit, Smokey has updated his web page to reflect some newer thinking.)

Researchers have applied Ajzen's (1991) Theory of Planned Behavior (see Chapter 6) to understand individuals' cognitive disposition toward fire and its management. Broad value orientations lead to attitudes, personal norms, and behavioral intentions (Knotek, 2006) that inform peoples' decision making on the individual level (i.e., whether to sacrifice loved trees in order to create a defensible space around one's cabin), as well as on the management level (whether to let a fire burn in a roadless national forest area and whether to support salvage logging after the fire). Qualitative studies of residents in Montana's fire-prone Bitterroot River valley revealed that people's place-meanings interact with their attitudes toward using fire as a tool to manage the Bitterroot National Forest (Gunderson & Watson, 2007). Many forest users accepted intense wildfire as an inevitable and desirable aspect of a forest they had intimate knowledge of, whereas others considered stand-replacing fires in special spots to be undesirable. Such social and psychological meanings have large implications for the acceptability of management decisions. In a series of case studies, Jakes and colleagues (2007) found that landscape, government, community, and citizen-level factors all contributed to how well the communities dealt with wildfire. On the psychological level, wildfire belongs with the larger set of "wild" forces of nature that deliver "natural disasters," which we address next.

Natural disasters

Natural disasters can result in personal injury, loss of home or valued possessions, injury or death of loved ones, disruptions to one's social network, and damage to physical infrastructure

(Neria & Schultz, 2012; Simpson et al., 2011). Intense negative emotions are likely to dominate people's initial response to a disaster. Distress, anxiety, and acute traumatic stress are typical. Interview participants in a study about flooding by Carroll et al. (2009) used words such as "horrifying," "panic stricken," and "petrified" to describe their experience during the flood. Some studies have found that many victims of a flood disaster express prolonged psychological distress (Green, 1995; Solomon & Green, 1992), as do people victimized by wildfire (Jones et al., 2003b).

In some cases, the psychological trauma of a disaster can lead to more severe conditions, such as major depressive disorder or posttraumatic stress disorder (PTSD; Alderman et al., 2012; Lowe et al., 2013; Mason et al., 2010). PTSD is associated with suicide, substance abuse, depression and anxiety, and aggression (Simpson et al., 2011). Less obviously, losing treasured objects when a home is damaged or destroyed can significantly impair an individual's sense of self and identity, particularly objects such as photographs or family heirlooms that relate to one's personal history (Dittmar, 2011). Flood victims in one study (Carroll et al., 2009) reported distress due to the loss of personal possessions, such as things they had made themselves or special things they had spent time and effort to procure or maintain. People who lose their home and have to be relocated after a disaster tend to experience more severe effects (Najarian et al., 2001).

Disasters affect the social environment as much as the physical environment. People whose homes, schools, or jobs are harmed in a disaster may have to be separated from one another and from their systems of social support. Parents may find themselves less able to be effective caregivers. Family relationships may suffer. Domestic abuse, for example, often increases among families who have experienced disasters (such as Hurricane Katrina or the Exxon Valdez oil spill) (Yun et al., 2010). Pre-existing hostility toward other social groups can be a precipitating factor for violence between different social groups and increase the crime rate (Agnew, 2012).

Different vulnerability refers to how not everyone is equally affected by natural disasters. Children may be more likely to report persistent distress and anxiety (Carnie et al., 2011; Simpson et al., 2011). Demographic variables also matter; people who have fewer resources are more vulnerable to the impacts (Elliott & Pais, 2006). Thus, high sensitivity is related to factors such as poverty and lower education levels. In addition to children, the elderly, disabled people, recently arrived immigrants, migrants, or refugees, and people with pre-existing mental health conditions are also at greater risk (Weissbecker & Czinez, 2011). Communities themselves can be more or less resilient to natural disasters. Social stressors, such as racism, economic inequality, and environmental injustices, weaken community ties. Lower levels of social cohesion and connectedness undermine the social capital that can help communities recover from disaster (Norris et al., 2008).

The Conservation of Resources stress theory (COR) describes the overall pattern of dealing with acute and prolonged stressors (Hobfoll, 1998, 2012). Four categories of resources provide meaning, safety and security: condition (roles, employment, etc.); personal characteristics (age, knowledge, locus of control, self-esteem, and optimism); energy (e.g., time), and objects (physical possessions). Individuals with greater or fewer resources will be correspondingly more or less vulnerable to stresses and able to recover. When a stress such as a natural disaster occurs, people "respond in a variety of ways, including mobilizing resources to minimize resource loss, avoiding the situation, attempting to improve their situation and to cope effectively, and experiencing stress and impaired psychological functioning" (Sattler et al., 2006). Because resources are linked, loss of specific resources can have wide-reaching effects. In a pair of studies conducted in El Salvador immediately following the devastating earthquakes of early 2001, Sattler and colleagues found that for a college student sample, the largest contributors to Acute Stress Disorder (ASD) were being female, experiencing prior traumatic events (which were plentiful in that country), low social support, and loss of personal characteristic, condition, and energy resources. For a community sample, loss of personal characteristic and object resources accounted best for ASD and depression. In the context of the multiple earthquakes in El Salvador, resource loss spirals and secondary stressors may also account for the ASD observed.

Negative outcomes, however, are not the only possible result. In some cases, particularly when disasters are seen as purely natural rather than resulting from human actions, communities come together in supportive ways and the result is a strengthening rather than weakening of social ties (Rao et al., 2011). People, too, may experience what has been described as "posttraumatic growth" (PTG) following a natural disaster (Tedeschi & Calhoun, 1996; see also Suedfeld, 2012). Particularly when they have benefitted from strong social support, individuals sometimes describe benefits such as strengthened social relationships, enhanced self-efficacy, or a sense of meaning (Fernando & Hebert, 2011; Roxberg et al., 2010; Yang, Lin, & Qian, 2010). Sattler and colleagues (2014) investigated both posttraumatic stress symptoms (PTS) and PTG in 3-month and 15-month in independent samples after the 2004 Indian Ocean tsunami. Similarly to Sattler's study of the El Salvador catastrophe, distress symptoms were associated with loss of personal characteristic resources, condition resources, object resources, emotion-focused coping, concerns about governmental favoritism, as well as fear of loss of one's own or another's life. Just as in the El Salvador case, however, there was evidence of PTG, which in both cases showed no correlation with stress disorders. PTG was associated with education, prior trauma experience, somatic problems, problem-focused coping and, most strongly, social support. It was negatively associated with personal characteristic loss. Sattler et al. (2014) suggest that, consistent with COR theory, response to natural disasters should include not only attending to acute losses, but also activities promoting engagement, "a positive affective-motivational state that persists in response to an enduring stressor or challenging event," that may strengthen personal resources and coping following loss (p. 234). Social support may help survivors manage negative emotions and clarify values and priorities.

These speculations regarding PTG are consistent with the broader picture emerging in positive psychology, applicable to a wide variety of trauma. Posttraumatic growth is related to "resilience, sense of coherence, hardiness, stress inoculation and toughening" (Ryff & Singer, 2003). Even enduring multiple severe events, individuals may show results such as:

> perceiving oneself as survivor rather than victim; increased self-reliance and self-efficacy; heightened awareness of one's own vulnerability and mortality; improvements in ties to others – with greater self-disclosure and emotional expressiveness, more compassion and capacity to give to others; clearer philosophy of life, renewed sense of priorities and appreciation of life, deeper sense of meaning and spirituality.
>
> (Ryff & Singer, 2003, p. 24)

Understanding more about the contexts and the conditions that enhance growth beyond trauma poses an essential research agenda to increase individuals' and communities' resources and resilience. It is worth noting that one effect of climate change will be increased frequency of disasters such as violent storms, floods, and droughts (IPCC, 2013). Efforts to adapt to climate change will need to be mindful of ways to prepare communities to cope with these events (Clayton et al., 2014).

Wild animals: attitudes and experience

Relations between humans and wild animals have deep evolutionary roots and demonstrate remarkable diversity and complexity. Wild animals are important objects for indirect experiences (mediated by institutions such as zoos) and vicarious experiences (including symbolic, literary, etc.). Conservation advocates use wild animals under various threats to motivate and inform important contributions to conservation. "Flagship" species are those which can attract a politically potent following, and whose protection may help various other components of their ecosystems. More directly, communities and groups whose choices directly impinge on wild populations have been targeted with custom designed and often highly successful wildlife-centered conservation education programs, as reported in the many studies in Jacobson (1995).

It is easy to see that different species in different ecological relations to people might spark varying attitudes. But there may also be cultural variation in interest, concern, and connection to other species. Kellert (1996) compared the way people in different countries described their value for animals (further discussed in Chapter 5). He found that most respondents in the US, Germany, and Japan placed "humanistic" value on individual animals (usually domestic or culturally important varieties), but showed low concern for wildlife species and low ecological knowledge. Most of Kellert's American respondents expressed a humanistic affinity for wildlife similar to humans –"particularly animals of large size, considerable intelligence, familiarity, and the capacity for social bonding" (1996, p. 41). Kellert noted, though, that humanistic valuing also sometimes includes animals that are unlike people, perhaps due to their availability for intimate relationships and not being subject to commercial exploitation (e.g., 65% to 70% of respondents in two whaling countries, Japan and Norway, support whaling if the species is not threatened, compared to less than half that in other countries). The "moralistic" attitude, in Kellert's (1996) description, is biased toward sentient and intelligent species, but is based less on affection than on the application of concepts of right and wrong to relations with animals. With such widely varying attitudes, symbolic meanings, and relationships to wildlife, it is unsurprising that social conflict over wildlife is common (Herda-Rapp & Goedeke, 2005).

Manfredo and colleagues (Fulton et al., 1996; Manfredo, 2008) identified four value orientations in western US populations that, in conjunction with attitudes, norms, and cultural factors, predict intentions regarding wildlife. These value orientations are "utilitarian," "mutualism," "attraction," and "concern for safety." Included in mutualism are egalitarian attitudes toward other species. Across numerous studies Manfredo has found that mutualism strongly predicts anti-fishing and anti-hunting attitudes and behavioral intentions, as well as (more weakly) partaking in nonconsumptive wildlife activities. Mutualism has been increasing in recent years as the population in the west becomes more affluent and less economically dependent on natural resources. Manfredo and Teel (2008) explain mutualism as due partly to what they regard as a human tendency to anthropomorphize. They suggest that release from economic dependence has allowed mutualistic attitudes to increase. Ironically, however, coexistence values are also expressed by some people's desire for private homes in natural-amenity-rich sites (e.g., Southern Utah; see Matarrita-Cascante et al., 2010). This has led to low-density settlement in the American west, habitat conversion and fragmentation – a possible example of disconnection between values and collective behavior.

Coinciding with this shift are increases in nonconsumptive or appreciative activities regarding wildlife in the US and internationally. At the same time consumptive uses, such as hunting and fishing, have stabilized at historically low levels in the US. The US Fish and Wildlife Service's 5-yearly report on wildlife activities for 2011 found that the number of hunters was at 6% of the US population ages 16 and older (essentially constant since 7% in 1991, the earliest strictly comparable USFWS survey). Fishing was practiced by 14% of the same sample, up 1% since 2006, although still lower than 2001 or any time before. Meanwhile, a much greater proportion of Americans 16 and older – 30% – engaged in wildlife watching as an activity. These differing activities contributed to the economy substantially in 2011, with an estimated

$41.8 billion spent on fishing, $33.7 billion on hunting, and $54.8 billion spent by wildlife watchers. Overall, 90.1 million people, or 38% of the population were active with wildlife, and their expenditures amount to 1% of the US GDP. Separate data have been collected on 6- to 15-year-olds starting in the 1980s when about 34% fished, 6% hunted, and 51% watched wildlife. Each survey since has shown gradual declines in all categories. Notwithstanding the "no child left inside" movement, the 2010 data set new lows: 28% fished, 5% hunted, and 31% watched wildlife (USFWS, 2014).

The human encounter with wild animals is clearly multifaceted. We are in the role of predator when animals are killed for income, food, status, excitement, safety, sanitation, or other motivations. People's reasons for hunting are various and, counter-intuitively, do not always rule out positive or protective emotions toward animals. In one study, 21% of hunters said they hunted to "be close to nature," fewer than do it for "sport or recreation," or "meat" (Responsive Management, 1998, n.d.). Haymond (1990) showed that although large percentages of forestland owners in South Carolina described "lifestyle enhancement values" derived from wildlife (such as observing and appreciating animals, preserving a way of life, providing a better environment for future generations, and hunting), only hunting was positively related to the number of land management practices that favor wildlife which owners implemented. These findings show that utilitarian use of animals may motivate care for their habitat.

Some species place us in the role of prey (see, e.g., McNay, 2002). Certainly, fears of animals, such as bears, large cats, and wolves, historically overblown, have slowly subsided in the US. Nonetheless, perhaps the most puzzling aspect psychologically is the disproportionate persecution and malice directed at creatures that only very rarely consume humans (Coleman, 2004). Kellert (1996), for example, noted differences in public attitudes toward three large predators: wolves, cougars, and grizzly bears. Cougars and wolves are comparably sized, have similar prey requirements, occurred historically at about the same densities across much of North America and both were subject to concerted government extermination campaigns, but today the cougar arouses much less passion than the wolf. This is especially puzzling since cougar attacks on livestock and humans (mostly children) are more frequent and better documented. Possible explanations include that wolves are more conspicuous, and that cougars did not occur in Europe, so immigrants did not harbor old world prejudices as they did toward wolves and bears. For all three species, attitudes are a complex mix, and also reflect people's reactions to government intervention on the species' behalf. Wolf reintroduction has been particularly polarizing politically.

Significant threats from or conflict with wildlife can influence attitudes toward animals and support for wildlife management strategies. Kaltenborn et al. (2006) asked residents around Serengeti National Park in Tanzania about their responses if an animal (1) was sighted near the village; (2) killed domestic livestock; or (3) threatened humans. Would they do nothing, scare the animal off, report the incident to a game officer, or kill the animal? Across the three worsening degrees of threat, higher percentages favored the more severe responses. The animal species had some effect: stronger responses were reported for lions, cheetahs, leopards, and especially the highly disliked hyenas. Interestingly, although less stringent measures were favored for a liked or preferred species, this effect was shown only for the low-threat situations. In a Norwegian study, sheep farmers with deeper attachment to their sheep had more negative attitudes toward carnivores (bears, wolves, wolverine, and lynx) (Vittersø et al., 1998). In another study, farmers from a region with high losses of sheep showed more negative attitudes toward predators than farmers from a region with lower losses. Interestingly, however, when farmers' anticipated personal losses were controlled for statistically, farmers from the high-loss region expressed more positive attitudes toward the predators (Vittersø et al., 1999). The authors speculated that farmers from high-loss regions had more sophisticated cognitive representations of the predators, perhaps reflecting the role of familiarity and knowledge in boosting perspective-taking and cognitive empathy.

It is important to acknowledge these "negative" human–animal realities for several reasons. They help counter idyllic conceptions of simple human harmony with nature, and they explain some of the diversity in attitudes toward animals. Conflicts between humans and animals over prey, space, or other resources represent common challenges to conservation (see Chapter 10). Finally, we cannot appreciate the complex emotional and cognitive achievement when people come to value, empathize with, and protect even dangerous animals unless we appreciate the negative realities that exist (see Chapter 7 on integrated biophilia).

Positive nonharmful experiences of wild animals must be common, given the large numbers of wildlife watchers reported above, but there are relatively few empirical studies of such phenomena. Fiedeldey (1994) found that the birds and mammals encountered by 91 hikers on guided nature walks in African wild lands were a significant part of the experience and deepened subjects' appreciation of ecological complexity. Several researchers have examined human encounters with dolphins. DeMares (2000) documented positive emotions in response to wild dolphins and concluded that human–wild cetacean interaction showed marked effects on people's sense of self. In-depth interviews with a small number of subjects who swam with dolphins describe attraction, as well a feeling of connection through eye contact or touch. Subjects' statements also reflect the influence of their prior conceptions (Curtin, 2006). Some studies have attempted to experimentally determine the effects of swimming with dolphins: Webb and Drummond (2001), for example, compared swimming with and without dolphins in semiwild settings. All 99 participants reported increases in well-being, but those who swam with dolphins reported greater increases and also decreased anxiety. Antonioli and Reveley (2005) measured depression and anxiety before and after a 2-week (1 h per day) program swimming with captive dolphins, compared with subjects who swam and snorkeled nearby instead; they found improvement in depression scores but not anxiety scores in the treatment group.

Unfortunately, the research supporting claims of benefits from swimming with dolphins is weak, leading to serious questions about claims of their therapeutic efficacy. Marino and Lilienfeld (1998, 2007) conducted two methodological reviews of the dolphin-assisted therapy experimental literature and found multiple threats to internal validity in even the best studies. The few studies using randomized assignment and blind rating procedures failed to control for a variety of influences that could have accounted for the results, such as novelty, placebo effects (important because dolphin swimming is marketed as highly effective), or the presence of other people. Often the actual treatment received was poorly conceptualized and monitored, and seldom were longer than immediate effects measured. On the costs side, Marino and Lilienfeld (2007) cite studies showing that both dolphins and people are injured in these encounters, and that there are risks of parasitism and infection to both parties as well.

The primacy of interaction and intimate knowledge in forging a psychological connection to wild animals was emphasized by Myers and Russell's (2003) study of the experiences of adult males who had intimate knowledge of wild black bears. Such knowledge came though everyday experience (by old-timers who grew up in an area frequented by black bears), animal tracking, bow hunting, or professional bear biology work. In comparison to suburban homeowners who had reported bears to the state wildlife agency, all those with intimate experience of bears had little fear of wild bears, yet a high degree of respect. Their knowledge was based on immediate encounters that included a bodily based reading of bear behavior, and a sense of the bear as a knowing, intentional creature. These perceptions held across not only type of activity (including the hunters) but also aspects of worldview, such as religiously informed beliefs about the "place" of humans and bears. The impact of nature comes partly through its social construction, but studies of humans and wild animals in wild settings suggest that the animals also contribute directly to the human sense of meaning.

The edge of control: wilderness remoteness and challenge

Along with the potential for positive experiences, wild nature also presents some inherent challenges, both internal and external. Indeed, key elements of wilderness are remoteness from human civilization and the diminishment of a sense of human control. What is the psychology of this aspect of wild nature?

Wilderness may present characteristics of what are called "extreme environments." Suedfeld (1991) describes these as: *extreme*, where survival is not possible unprotected and unprovisioned; *unusual* because they are different from settled areas; and *stressful* because they are difficult to access and contain objective hazards. Suedfeld's prime example is Antarctica, but mountaintops, space stations, offshore oil rigs, and many other types of situations also qualify. Despite the natural tendency to avoid such environments, there is a fundamental challenge to the wilderness experience which adventure education and wilderness therapy programs rely on to pull participants into vigorous activity in situations where they cannot hide behind their usual patterns (Luckner & Nadler, 1997). Studies of such adventure education participants, workers in Antarctica, and individuals in self-chosen wilderness excursions show that those who subject themselves to extreme environments often show similar psychosocial reactions afterwards including personal growth (Reser & Scherl, 1988; Davis-Berman & Berman, 1994), increased sense of control and competence, and fewer physical and mental health problems (Suedfeld, 1997, 2012).

To a nonparticipant, these benefits might seem insufficient to motivate a person to place themselves in such a risky situation. One traditional explanation of the motivation to go into extreme environments is that some people need to have a high level of stimulation in order to enjoy an experience, and thus they pursue high-risk recreation. Netherland psychologists van den Berg and ter Heijne (2005), for example, provided a typology of fear-relevant nature situations to their participants: Close Encounters, Forceful Situations, Overwhelming Situations, and Disorienting Situations. Those who were attracted to such situations, disproportionately male, were high in sensation-seeking. Some have interpreted such sensation-seeking to represent suppressed suicidal wishes. Koole and van den Berg (2005) found that wilderness provoked more thoughts about death than cultivated nature or city environments among their subjects in lab studies. Reminding these subjects of death lessened their perception of wilderness as beautiful, and lessened their coping responses. Whether this echoes our cultural history of alienation from wild nature as the antithesis of civilization (in which social death meant banishment to the "desert"), whether it applies to those undertaking wild nature adventure activities, or whether it is part of the more general effects of "mortality salience" in inducing self-concern and restricted world views (Solomon et al., 2004) is not clear.

But the story appears more complex than just sensation-seeking or death-denial. In interviews with 360 people who had just climbed Mt. McKinley, the highest mountain in North America, Ewert (2001) found that social aspects, image, technical aspects of climbing, and catharsis/escape were important, but risk taking was not motivationally important. The most important motives related to exhilaration, excitement, and accomplishment. Notably, patterns of motivation varied with degree of experience. In general, those with appropriate preparation may regard an extreme environment as a good place to recreate, whereas others could not imagine it being enjoyable.

Csikszentmihalyi's (1990) theory of "flow" offers a systematic and empirically based phenomenology of peak experiences and has been applied to a number of wilderness activities. Csikszentmihalyi (1975) studied accomplished individuals engaged in highly demanding and usually not extrinsically rewarding activities – people such as music composers, rock climbers, chess players, and surgeons – and found that across these very different activities, subjects described similar peak experiences at certain times. This experience, dubbed by subjects as "flow" in consciousness, has these characteristics:

1 Total concentration on the task at hand.
2 A sense that action is automatic, with action and awareness merged in the activity.
3 Clear goals and immediate feedback.
4 A sense of control such that there is no conscious awareness of control but rather no worry about lack or loss of control; a sense of freedom of choice.
5 A lessening of feelings of self-consciousness.
6 Alteration of sense of time (speeded up, slowed down, and standing still).

Flow experience produces strong positive feelings, a sense of competence, and strong intrinsic motivation to do the activity.

Flow is likely to occur when the person's skills are in balance with the challenge of a freely chosen situation (Mannell et al., 1988). More precisely, it occurs when both the skills and challenge are slightly above the person's mean on both variables, as described by Massimini and Carli's (1986) "four-channel" model (Figure 4.1). When challenge is above the person's mean and skill is below, anxiety occurs; when skills are above mean and challenge is below, boredom results; and when both are below mean, apathy occurs. It is notable that challenge and skills have physical, cognitive, and emotional dimensions. The emotional dimension is important because flow results not from the challenge or danger itself but from the person's ability to minimize it by exerting control over risks that would otherwise produce anxiety (Csikszentmihalyi, 1975). Thus, this theory provides a more subtle and systematic way of understanding the attraction and the benefits of activities in extreme environments such as wild nature may provide.

Theoretical refinements on flow theory differentiate moderate from high levels of both challenge and skill. This has led to an empirical distinction between the flow channel or state, and one of high skill but only moderate challenge, termed the "control" state. According to the "experience fluctuation model" (Massimini & Carli, 1988, Figure 4.2) what is different about these channels subjectively is that "control" is characterized by more positive effect, arousal, a sense of ease in concentration and a stronger voluntary motivation or feeling free. The flow channel is expected to be higher on activation and cognitive efficiency, but lower on levels of affect and motivation. Higher than moderate challenge and skills (i.e., flow) is associated more with extrinsic than intrinsic motivation. These predictions have mostly born out. For example, in an experiential sampling study of adolescents, Lambert et al. (2013) found that the youths' time in the flow channel was higher on concentration, activation, involvement, and lower on self-determined intrinsic motivation, whereas the control channel was higher in enjoyment, happiness, ease of concentration, and self-determined ease of concentration. Csikszentmihalyi (1990) has long regarded flow as the route to psychological growth in complexity. This process is more effortful and cognitively demanding, and once competency has been reached, more enjoyment of the activity in the control channel is possible. Advance in skill has moved the challenge from high to moderate. That advance might not take place if the move to higher challenge depends only on self-determined intrinsic motivation.

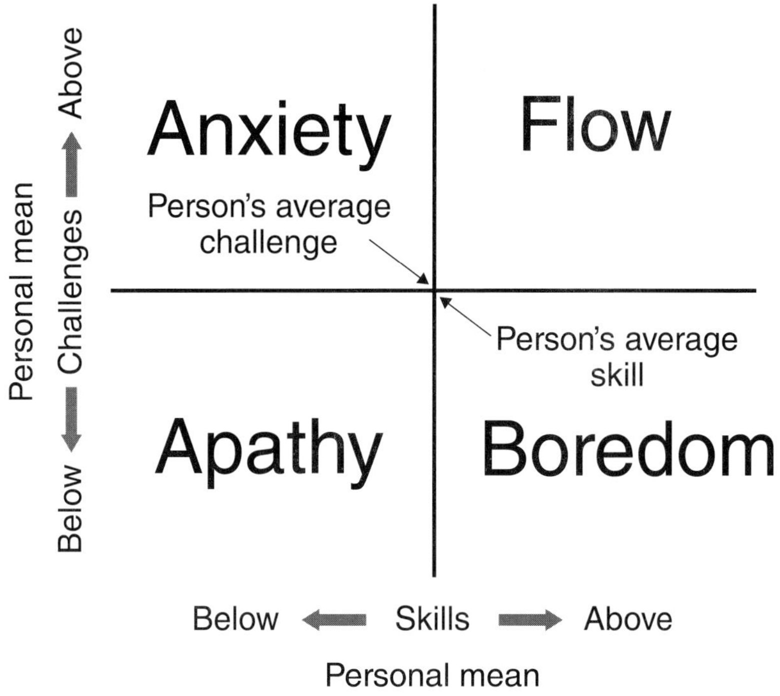

Fig. 4.1 Four-channel model of psychological flow. (Adapted from Jackson & Csikszentmihalyi, 1999.)

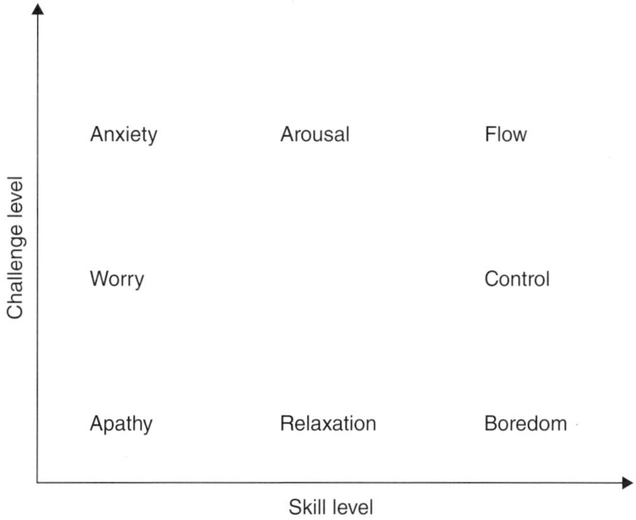

Fig. 4.2 The experiential fluctuation model. (Adapted from Massimini & Carli, 1988, Figure 16.1, p. 270. Used with permission of Cambridge University Press.)

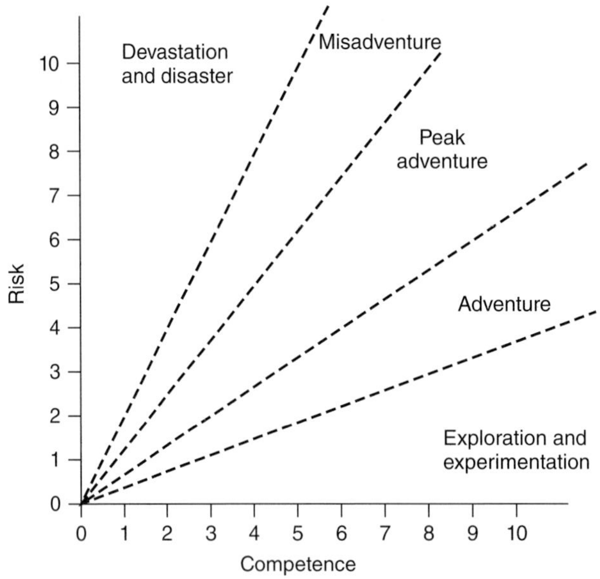

Fig. 4.3 Adventure experience paradigm. (Adapted from Martin & Priest, 1986.)

Martin and Priest's (1986) Adventure Experience Paradigm (AEP) is a similar model that predicts five types of experience ranging from "devastation and disaster" to "experimentation" depending on the balance of perceived risk and competence (see Figure 4.3). Both the AEP and the flow model have been used to study wild nature activities such as river paddling (Priest & Bunting, 1993; Jones et al., 2003a), mountain climbing (Fave et al., 2003; Stebbins, 2005), and snowboarding (Stebbins, 2005), as well as many other activities. Such research confirms the intrinsically motivating nature of these activities, and suggests that it is the activity itself, the interplay of the person's complement of skills in interaction with an environment that elicits them, that is motivating. Highly interdependent groups may experience more positive affect in a flow activity than when interdependence is lower (Walker, 2010).

Activity in wild nature, connection, and caring

Emotional associations between the highly positive flow state and the setting in which it occurs could lead not only to valuing nature but to a sense of connection to the wild setting. That is, some may act to protect wild nature because they have had peak experiences there and want to protect the opportunity for more such experiences. But is there also a direct role of nature, even in activity-centered adventure; does it lead to caring about nature for its own sake? In a meta-analysis of adventure programs, Hattie et al. (1997) note that "the highest ranking of importance for participants is the enjoyment of nature" (p. 76) and suggest that a theoretical model centered on forming relationships with nature could help explain the changes resulting from adventure programs.

The contribution of nature should be more apparent in programs that emphasize nature over activity-based adventure, such as a program run and documented by Greenway (1996) that emphasized "reconnection" with wilderness. The primary value experienced by his participants was the "perceptual shift" that occurred during time in the wilderness. Interestingly, 57% of women but only 27% of men stated that a main goal of the trip was to "come home" to nature, whereas 60% of men and 20% of women said a major goal was to conquer fear, challenge themselves, and expand limits. Women experienced the transition into the trip more easily than men, who had an easier time reentering everyday culture.

Just what is the structure of experience in wild nature? Kahn et al. (2012) proposed to map out fundamental patterns of interaction between humans and nature. Their proposal of a "nature language" (after Alexander's architectural "pattern language") consists of categories of experience that are whole but irreducible and contribute unique dimensions to human existence. The categories were generated by broad reading (from nature writing to ecology to anthropology; deducing from photos; personal experience; and a web forum). Examples from their preliminary list of 30 patterns include *sleeping under the night sky, recognition with a nonhuman other, building a shelter, experiencing the elements, being immersed in water, foraging, killing an animal, and encountering nature that can hurt us.* Kahn et al. (2012) suggest that each can have "wild," "domestic," or "perverse" instantiations. Wild ones hark back to environments of our evolution and occur in a minimally human-mediated setting. Domestic cases are more technologically mediated; some part of the full force or vividness of the wild patterns has been lost. "Perverse" includes the connotation of "psychological ill health and a normative judgment against [the experience]" (p. 63). Perverse examples may involve harm to another valued entity, or the instance is simply too impoverished compared to even domestic examples, an example being in a modern giant wave pool that is so "crowded, congested, chlorinated, and homogeneous that it undercuts the pattern of *being moved by water*" (p. 64). Wild instantiations may be at risk of loss to present and future generations in a world with less wild nature.

In the context of this chapter, an interesting question is whether such "wild" experiences contribute to connectedness to nature and pro-environmental behavior. Scott et al. (2014) studied participants in a earth-living skills gathering who reported high levels of 28 activities the researchers conceptualized as "participation in nature." This participation emphasizes consumptive or experiential relations to nature that the authors theorize entail greater intimacy and conscious dependence on wild nature, including activities such as eating wild animals or using plants as food or medicine, walking barefoot, exposing one's skin to the elements, spending extended time in wilderness, going without bathing or shaving for several days, navigating by sun or stars, and skills such as fire-starting, hide tanning, or clothes-making completed with only wild raw materials. Granting that the sample of this exploratory study is not representative of the general population, the authors found that "participation in nature" correlated with an item measuring pro-environmental decision making. Interestingly, the most frequently mentioned and most common top motivation attendees gave for coming to the gathering was "I want to feel more connected to nature" (equally frequent but second ranking was to "become more self-sufficient"). Direct experience may be the most powerful way to feel and understand one's embeddedness in and dependence upon ecological systems. Further research on more experiential relations to nature will increase our understanding of the significance of wild nature as well as its absence.

Provocative insights into the positive psychological experience of wild nature were revealed by Beringer's (2000a) qualitative study of five people, previously active in nature-based adventuring, who had lost mobility (for 10 years or more) due to traumatic, life-changing spinal cord injuries. Beringer described how these subjects felt "distanced" from nature by their disability, but became more active observers with heightened sensitivity to nature. And although therapeutic regimes removed them from nature, and access constraints were frustrating, her subjects felt strongly that nature or outdoor pursuits accelerated healing. "Individuals seem to be able to forget and be free from their physical limitations, if only temporarily, while in nature" (Beringer, 2000a, Table II). Psychically and palpably they felt "moved by nature" when they were able to access natural areas. An explanation based on risk taking or activity seems irrelevant for the benefit her para- and quadriplegic subjects described. Instead, natural places were more prominent. Based on this study, Beringer (2000a) suggests 12 ideas about how nature heals; that is, by conveying: sense of continuity and stability; support; positive feedback, perspective, exploration of self and body; slowing-down effect; freedom from social judgment; self-worth; transcendence; and calming and euphoria.

Wild nature and spiritual experience

Experiences in nature of both intense challenge-induced "flow" as well as more subtle and nature-centered effects may be considered "transcendent" states of consciousness. Experiences that transcend the mundane, human-centered sphere have long been of interest in psychology. Some early figures even saw connections between spirituality and nature. James (1902) noted that solitude in nature may be conducive to religious experience, particularly mysticism. Laski (1961), examining the contexts of ecstasy among religious and nonreligious people, found that nature was the most common trigger among nonbelievers and the third-most common among Christians. Among early depth psychology theorists, Carl Jung paid the greatest attention to nature, and considered elements of nature in myth and dreams as archetypes or ideas embedded deep in the human psyche: dreams "originate in a spirit that is not quite human, but is rather a breath of nature" (Jung, 1964, p. 36). Schroeder (2006) noted that Jung "viewed the wilderness as a symbol of the unconscious mind itself, and has regarded the relationship between modern civilization and nature as an outward reflection of the relationship between the conscious ego and the unconscious psyche" (p. 15). Thus, in the unconscious "the division between our own minds and wild nature is not entirely clear-cut" (p. 17), and despite our alienation, time in wilderness and sensitivity to its emergent symbolic meanings can "reconnect us with the deepest part of our own minds" (p. 18) (see also Schroeder, 1996). The idea has old historical roots. Despite the generally negative connotations of wilderness in early Christianity, Nash notes that "a succession of Christian hermits and monks (literally, one who lives alone) found the solitude of the wilderness conducive to meditation, spiritual insight and moral perfection" (1982, p. 18). [For a cogent discussion of secular versus specific spirituality (grounded in a metaphysically defined "sacred" realm), and the implications for the investigation and facilitation of wilderness experience, see Beringer, 2000b.]

It is difficult, but not impossible, to empirically study the spiritual dimensions of wilderness experience. An early attempt was by Rosegrant (1976), who distinguished between *mystical* experiences, "brief ineffable intuition[s] that the experiencer is one with the universe"; *meaningful* experiences that a person feels may "have a long-term importance for his life"; and *communion*, or the sense of being mutually accepting toward and accepted by the other (pp. 302–303; 309). Rosegrant was curious to test a speculation advanced by Aaronsen (1967) that mountaintops, deserts, and other settings where one can see "interrelationships between objects and each other and objects and space" are conducive to communion and mystical experience. Comparing the experiences of Outward Bound solo participants in two locations differing in their affordance of such an overview (one on a mountaintop, the other in dense brush along a creek), Rosegrant found that subjects at the mountain solo sites did report more communal states of relating to nature. Meaningful experiences were modestly more likely on the mountain. In both settings, nature was not without potency.

Table 4.2 Reported dimensions and feelings related to spirituality.

Dimensions of spiritual and spirituality feelings associated with spirituality	
Ineffable	Empowered
Intangible	Hopeful
Centering force	Grounded and secure
Heightened sensory awareness	Wonder and awe
Timelessness	Humility

Source: Reprinted from Fredrickson and Anderson (1999), Copyright 1999, with permission from Elsevier.

Fredrickson and Anderson (1999) used grounded-theory procedures to study participants in women-only backcountry experiences in powerful but contrasting natural settings: the Boundary Waters Canoe Area Wilderness (BWCA) of northern Minnesota, and Arizona's Grand Canyon. The all-female character of the group was important, but of primary interest were several facets of being in a vast remote wilderness area, including direct contact with nature, periods of solitude, and the inherent physical challenge. Contact with wild nature gave the women a "great sense of freedom and release from simply having the opportunity to go out and explore, rediscovering the sights and sounds of nature" (p. 30). Different aspects were cited by participants at the two locations: wildlife in the BWCA, and the open sky in the Grand Canyon. A common theme in solitude was contemplating larger questions in their lives. With one or two exceptions, the participants lacked previous wilderness experience, and thus were unaccustomed to the physical challenges, which again differed dramatically between the flat, forested, and wet north, and the steep, open, and dry south locations. Some found merely engaging in these challenges to be spiritually inspirational, and experienced a recovery of parts of themselves left behind in their youth. The researchers also explicitly asked about the women's thoughts and feelings about spirituality. Characteristics that emerged are summarized in Table 4.2.

The participants experienced the locations as spiritual due to the social context as well as the ecological site. Social factors, such as sharing stories of daily experience, played a very important role in the women's appreciation of their wild places. But an interesting difference emerged regarding the locations. Those describing the BWCA's meaningful aspects talked about the setting as "an organic whole" or gestalt such as the "green wall" along the edge of lakes, rather than seeing individual trees (p. 35), whereas the Grand Canyon group spoke about "individual features" more. The authors suggest that this may be because the BWCA lacks opportunities to take in a panoramic vista where isolated features stand out and are important for navigation. This suggests the varying psychological affordances of different environments.

Vining and Merrick (2012) reported on 34 in-depth interviews with self-selected individuals who described experiencing environmental epiphanies, which the researchers defined as "an experience in which one's perception of the essential meaning of their relationship to nature shifts in a meaningful manner" (see also Merrick, 2008). While this definition stresses the dimension of knowledge, insight, or significance, epiphanies are also often ineffable and strongly emotional. Of the sample, indeed, 85% included positive emotions. Many but not all of the accounts occurred in preserved areas such as parks or wildernesses, and only 26.5% were experienced during a routine activity or environment. Vining and Merrick (2012) generated a typology of environmental epiphanies which overlaps somewhat with the other schemes of spiritual experience in this section:

1. Aesthetic – vivid or awestruck descriptions of being struck by the beauty of a place. Subjects were slightly older, and the experience takes the subject by surprise. The perception of the place itself changes afterwards, and this type elicited discussion of environmental issues and behaviors; it was the least emotionally intense type.
2. Intellectual epiphanies occurred while reading, and entailed something novel or divergent such as other living things, spiritual issues, etc. They had a strong "aha" feeling and produced widespread changes in environmental behavior.
3. Realization epiphanies "occur when one realizes a concept of which one was aware but did not fully grasp" and apparently were the most frequent type (percentages were not given). They occurred in unusual settings, often recreational, and lasted longer than others.
4. Awakening epiphanies entail a new vividness as if one had been asleep before, similar to realization but with more intensity. These were reported in conjunction with physical exertion, were drawn out, and were likely to be felt by people who had other epiphanies. They also created a bond to the place and represented turning points in life.
5. Connectedness epiphanies were felt as mystical and spiritual, including a sense of becoming one with nature or a higher power. Although sudden they were associated with some effort to have such an experience. Physical exertion, very high levels of emotion, changed perceptions of place, and new environmental behaviors were described. The most intense type, these included the only examples of physical sensations such as tingling. Subsequent epiphanies were likely.

Subjects felt epiphanies were compelling and took them seriously, but they tended to keep them private, wanting to avoid having their stories discounted or rejected due to the sense of magic or the strong emotion that went with them. Since epiphanies deal with grasping at a deeper level something about the human place in nature, and since they are powerful and include reports of changed environmental behavior, they merit further study.

Williams and Harvey (2001) undertook a quantitative study of experiences in forest environments in order to identify the forms of transcendence that occur there and to understand the qualities of forest environments that shape these experiences. They described six types of forest experience, which varied on dimensions which they interpreted as: fascination, novelty, and compatibility. Of the six types of forest experience, one type, described as "diminutive experiences," though rare, had a high level of transcendence. These moments were characterized by fascination with "compelling elements of the environment: tall trees, vast views, high waterfalls, extreme of heat or cold" (p. 255) and were accompanied by feelings of insignificance and humility. Rather than producing a relaxed feeling of belonging, the environment seems potent, novel, complex, and inscrutable, and often contained a single compelling point of attention.

Williams and Harvey called a second type of very absorbing and transcendent experience "deep flow," which occurred in relatively open, familiar settings for which subjects felt affection and belonging. These environments, less novel and more compatible than those evoking diminutive feelings, induced flow in the sense of effortless attention and ease. Four other experience types were not transcendent but of interest: "non-transcendent experiences" were typified by low fascination, novelty, and compatibility, and occurred in environments that were hard to move through, familiar and not potent seeming; "aesthetic experiences" (high novelty, low compatibility, and less sense of insignificance); "restorative-familiar" (low novelty and attachment to place); and "restorative-compatibility" (high compatibility and a less emotionally intense form of deep flow). The authors note:

> Nature does not move us simply because of activities undertaken in natural settings. Each natural landscape is a unique and complex system of matter, energy, human purpose and action.... Our understanding of the spiritual meaning of nature depends on recognizing the situational characteristics that contribute to deep emotional experiences in natural environments.
>
> (Williams and Harvey, 2001, p. 256)

Wilderness-based growth and therapeutic programs

Wilderness experience programs probably number over 1000 in North America, based on projections of Ewert and McAvoy (1999) and serve predominantly adolescents and youth. Programs span those focused on purely educational goals, personal-growth programs, and therapeutic programs (Friese et al., 1998). While wilderness-based education programs will be touched on in Chapter 11, the focus here is on the latter two, which have historical precedents dating back to the late 19th and early 20th centuries. Current wilderness behavioral healthcare programs draw most of their participants by referral from psychotherapists or counselors, with one-fifth as many youth referred through the juvenile justice system (Russell, 2003). All three types of programs draw on the characteristics of wilderness discussed above.

Nature is certainly not the only factor contributing to such programs. By understanding the other major components, it is possible to see how wilderness may work in synergy with them to facilitate personal growth and/or therapeutic goals. In contrast to older models of the wilderness growth/ therapy process as stage-like, Russell (Russell & Farnum, 2004; Russell, 2012) argues that four major factors combine concurrently but dynamically across the course of a wilderness program to generate psychological benefits in participants, as summarized in Table 4.3. Wild nature, as proposed in Attention Restoration Theory (see Chapter 12), provides a combination of a sense of being away from one's usually stressful life, and a sense of "soft fascination" which draws and holds noneffortful attention yet is not so overwhelming as do preclude reflective thought. Thus, nature itself is an effective agent in therapeutic and growth outcomes.

The other three components are intertwined with activities that are most effective when carried out in wild nature. The participant's active self is fostered by the physical activity and its health benefits, and by tasks that must be mastered in backcountry living, leading to improved self-esteem, self-efficacy, and internal locus of control. The group is a vehicle for social learning, development of responsibility, collaboration, and collective efficacy. In the wilderness, group members manifestly depend on each other. Important to this are the leaders who provide models of responsibility, focus, healthy social skills and self-challenge, and positive behaviors. Leaders are critical in facilitating the group in overcoming preconceived biases and joining together to support each other and to achieve goals. Active reflection is inherent in the series of outdoor activities such as backpacking, climbing, ocean sailing, or solo experiences that present novel and graduated challenges. Especially in therapy and personal-growth programs, the participants' responses to the activities may provide metaphors in directed discussions to reflect on and gain insight into personal patterns. In the wilderness context, consequences of behavior may be "natural," removing facilitators from the position of blame and helping participants focus on their own choices. (Notably this discussion excludes programs, sometimes caricatured as "boot camps," that use harsh practices or punishments and that violate basic standards of therapeutic practice and ethics.)

Russell (2012) qualifies this four-category theory of wilderness experience by noting that each program presents a unique configuration of these and many other factors (such as

Table 4.3 Factors in the concurrent model of wilderness experience.

Category	Time of peak intensity	Proposed effects
Nature	Beginning of program	The wilderness environment, acting alone, can be seen as a restorative environment for youth who have high levels of anxiety who and are stressed from mental fatigue caused by too much direct attention.
Active self	Middle-late	By combining the effects of actively accomplishing physically demanding tasks designed to increase in difficulty and scope while allowing opportunities for immediate feedback and success, the wilderness works as a therapeutic medium to foster an enhanced sense of the self.
Social group	Late	Research has shown that wilderness experiences conducted in small group settings over extended periods of time help break down preconceived stereotypes and self-doubt, allowing youth to experience a unique and intense feeling of community and belongingness.
Activity reflection	Variable	The adventure-based activities themselves provide meaning and context for individual and group learning and are used to aid direct and indirect transfer of learning back to youths' daily lives.

Source: From Russell (2012), Table 22.1, p. 433. By permission of Oxford University Press, USA.

possible roles of trained psychotherapists, staffing configuration, duration, client type, etc.). The wilderness context is both an irreducible contributor and facilitative of all aspects of such programming.

The evidence for positive outcomes of such programs is extensive, leading to overall confidence in their potential effects. This holds generally for personal development outcomes, and for positive effects of groups as varied as cancer survivors, adolescent sex offenders, addiction, abuse victims, and adjudicated youth / antisocial behavior. However, few studies include random assignment, and the effect of nature itself can be difficult to tease out in such complex therapeutic settings. Some studies find no impact of the wilderness experience, indicating the need for more research on which factors are most important for certain populations (Frumkin, 2001; Russell, 2012).

Conclusion

This chapter has surveyed several aspects of the psychology of wild nature, especially describing the uses and values of wilderness, and the human experience of wild lands, forces, and creatures.

Wild nature is highly valued in the US, increasingly for indirect and intangible reasons, and it appears these values are shared broadly. Activities in wild nature are also popular. While the term "wild" has a certain relativity, areas or features with certain characteristics appear to produce fairly consistent psychological regularities in experience. These include solitude, natural forces and features that function independently of people, and remoteness presenting potential stresses and challenges. The literatures on these areas sometimes confound the natural, social, and activity aspects of the experience, and there is still little known about the psychological significance of the many different types of natural ecosystems, forces, and wild creatures. Nonetheless, features of wild nature have long been perceived by at least some people as promoting experiences that give a sense of transcendence of the familiar human world, and union with a wider world, suggesting the unique ways in which nature has psychological significance. This is an area of great interest to conservation psychologists and others working to increase caring and connection to nature.

References

Aaronsen, B. S. (1967). Mystic and schizophreniform states and the experience of depth. *Journal for the Scientific Study of Religion 6*, 256–252.

Agnew, R. (2012). Dire forecast: A theoretical model of the impact of climate change on crime. *Theoretical Criminology, 16*(1), 21–42.

Ajzen, I. (1991). The theory of planned behavior. *Organizational Behavior and Human Decision Processes, 50*, 179–211.

Alderman, K., Turner, L. R., & Tong, S. L. (2012). Floods and human health: A systematic review. *Environment International, 47*, 37–47.

Antonioli, C. & Reveley, M. A. (2005). Randomized controlled trial of animal facilitated therapy with dolphins in the treatment of depression. *British Medical Journal, 331*, 1231–1234.

Aplet, G. H. (2006). Evolution of wilderness fire policy. *International Journal of Wilderness, 12*(1), 9–13.

Aplet, G. H., Wilbert, M. & Morton, P. (2005). Wilderness attributes and the state of the National Wilderness Preservation System. In H. K. Cordell, J. C. Bergstrom, & J. M. Bower (Eds.), *The multiple values of wilderness* (pp. 91–111). State College: Venture Publishing.

Beringer, A. (2000a). Being moved by nature: Adventure therapy and spinal cord injury rehabilitation. *Proceedings of the 2nd International Adventure Therapy Conference, Augsburg, Germany, March 20–24.*

Beringer, A. (2000b). In search of the sacred: A conceptual analysis of spirituality. *Journal of Experiential Education, 23*(3), 157–165.

Bobilya, A. J., McAvoy, L. H. & Kalich, K. R. (2005). Lessons from the field: Participant perceptions of a multi-day wilderness solo. In C. E. Knapp & T. E. Smith (Eds.), *Exploring the power of solo, silence and solitude* (pp. 103–119). Boulder, CO: Association for Experiential Education.

Bowker, J. M., Harvard III,, J. E., Bergstrom, J. C., Cordell, H. K., English, D. B. K. & Loomis, J. B. (2005). The net economic value of wilderness. In H. K. Cordell, J. C. Bergstrom & J. M. Bowker (Eds.), *The multiple values of wilderness* (pp. 161–180). State College, PA: Venture Publishing.

Brown, G. & Alessa, L. (2005). A GIS-based inductive study of wilderness values. *International Journal of Wilderness, 11*(1), 14–18.

Buchholz, E. & Catton, R. (1999). Adolescent's perceptions of aloneness and loneliness. *Adolescence, 34*(133), 203–213.

Callicott, J. B. & Nelson, M. (Eds.). (1998). *The great new wilderness debate*. Athens, GA: University of Georgia Press.

Carnie, T., Berry, H., Blinkhorn, S., & Hart, C. (2011). In their own words: Young people's mental health in drought-affected rural and remote NSW. *Australian Journal of Rural Health, 19*(5), 244–248.

Carroll, B., Morbey, H., Balogh, R., Araoz, G. (2009). Flooded homes, broken bonds, the meaning of home, psychological processes and their impact on psychological health in a disaster. *Health and Place, 15*(2), 540–547.

Clayton, S. (2003). Environmental identity: A conceptual and an operational definition. In S. Clayton & S. Opotow (Eds.), *Identity and the natural environment* (pp. 45–65). Cambridge, MA: MIT Press.

Clayton, S., Manning, C. M., & Hodge C. (2014). *Beyond storms & droughts: The psychological impacts of climate change*. Washington, DC: American Psychological Association and ecoAmerica. Available at http://ecoamerica.org/wp-content/uploads/2014/06/eA_Beyond_Storms_and_Droughts_Psych_Impacts_of_Climate_Change.pdf.

Cole, D. N. & Hall, T. E. (2010). Privacy functions and wilderness recreation: Use density and length of stay effects on experience. *Ecopsychology, 2*(2), 67–75.

Coleman, J. (2004). *Vicious: Wolves and men in America.* New Haven: Yale Univ. Press.

Cordell, H. K., Betz, C. J., Stephens, B., Mou, S. & Green, G. T. (2008). *How do Americans view wilderness – Part 1.* Athens, GA: USDA Forest Service Southern Research Station, University of Georgia, Athens, & Univ. Tennessee, Knoxville. Available at http://warnell.forestry.uga.edu/nrrt/nsre/IRISWild/IrisWild1rpt.pdf.

Csikszentmihalyi, M. (1975). *Beyond boredom and anxiety.* San Francisco: Jossey-Bass.

Csikszentmihalyi, M. (1990). *Flow: The psychology of optimal experience.* New York: HarperCollins.

Curtin, S. (2006). Swimming with dolphins: A phenomenological exploration of tourist recollections. *International Journal of Tourism Research, 8*(4), 301–315.

Daniel, B. (2005). The life significance of a wilderness solo experience. In C. E. Knapp & T. E. Smith (Eds.) *Exploring the power of solo, silence and solitude* (pp. 85–102). Boulder, CO: Association for Experiential Education.

Davis-Berman, J. & Berman, D. S. (1994). *Wilderness therapy: Foundations, theory and research.* Dubuque, IA: Kendall/Hunt.

DeMares, R. (2000). Human peak experience triggered by encounters with Cetaceans. *Anthrozoös, 13*(2), 89–103.

Dittmar, H. (2011). Material and consumer identities. In S. J. Schwartz, K. Luyckx, and V. L. Vignoles (Eds.), *Handbook of identity theory and research, Vol. 2* (pp. 745–769). New York: Springer.

Driver, B. L., Nash, R. & Haas, G. (1987). Wilderness benefits: a state of knowledge review. In R. C. Lucas (Ed.), *Proceedings: National wilderness research conference: Issues, state-of-knowledge, future directions* (pp. 294–319). Ogden, UT: USDA Forest Service, Intermountain Research Station. General Technical Report INT-220.

Duffy, S. & Verges, M. (2010). Forces of nature affect implicit connections with nature. *Environment and Behavior, 42*(6), 723–739.

Elliott, J. R. & Pais, J. (2006). Race, class and Hurricane Katrina: Social differences in human responses to a disaster. *Social Science Research 35*, 295–321.

Ewert, A. (2001). Playing at the edge: Motivation and risk taking in a high-altitude wilderness-like environment. *Journal of Human Performance in Extreme Environments, 6*(1), 12–20.

Ewert, A. & McAvoy, L. (1999). The effects of wilderness settings on organized groups: A state-of-knowledge paper. In S. F. McCool, D. N. Cole, W. T. Borrie & J. O'Loughlin (Eds.), *Wildernesss science in a time of change – vol. 3* (pp. 13–26). Ogden, UT: USD Forest Service, Rocky Mountain Research Station.

Fave, A. D., Bassi, M. & Massimini, F. (2003). Quality of experience and risk perception in high-altitude rock climbing. *Journal of Applied Sport Psychology, 15*(1), 82–98.

Fernando, D. M., & Hebert, B. B. (2011). Resiliency and recovery: Lessons from the Asian tsunami and Hurricane Katrina. *Journal of Multicultural Counseling and Development, 39*, 2–13.

Fiedeldey, A. (1994). Wild animals in a wilderness setting: An ecosystemic experience? *Anthrozoös, 7*(2), 113–123.

Fredrickson, L. M., & Anderson, D. H. (1999). A qualitative exploration of the wilderness experience as a source of spiritual inspiration. *Journal of Environmental Psychology, 19*, 21–39.

Friese, G., Hendee, J. C. & Kinziger, M. (1998). The wilderness experience program industry in the United States: Characteristics and dynamics. *Journal of Experiential Education, 21*(1), 40–45.

Frumkin, H. (2001). Beyond toxicity: Human health and the natural environment. *American Journal of Preventative Medicine, 20* (3), 234–240.

Fulton, D. C., Manfredo, M. J. & Lipscomb, J. (1996). Wildlife value orientations: A conceptual and measurement approach. *Human Dimensions of Wildlife, 1*(2), 24–47.

Graefe, A., Kuss, F. & Vaske, J. (1990). *Visitor impact management: The planning framework*. Washington DC: National Parks and Conservation Association.

Green, B. L. (1995). Long-term consequences of disasters. In S. E. Hobfoll & M. W. de Vries (Eds.), *Extreme stress and communities: Impact and intervention* (pp. 307–324). Dordrecht, The Netherlands: Kluwer.

Greenway, R. (1996). Wilderness experience and ecopsychology. *International Journal of Wilderness, 2*(1), 26–30

Gunderson, K. I. & Watson, A. (2007). Understanding place meanings on the Bitterroot National Forest, Montana. *Society and Natural Resources, 20*(8), 705–721.

Haas, G. E., Hermann, E. &Walsh, R. (1986). Wilderness values. *Natural Areas Journal, 6*(2): 37–43.

Harrison, R. P. (1992). *Forests: The shadow of civilization*. Chicago: University of Chicago Press.

Hattie, J., Marsh, H. W., Neill, J. T. & Richards, G. E. (1997). Adventure education and Outward Bound: Out-of-class effects that have a lasting effect. *Review of Educational Research, 67*, 43–87.

Haymond, J. L. (1990). Wildlife attitudes of early adopters who own forestland. *Society and Natural Resources, 3*, 11–18.

Heberlein, T. (1977). Density, crowding, and satisfaction: Sociological studies for determining carrying capacities. In *Proceedings: River recreation management and research symposium* (pp. 67–76). USDA Forest Service General Technical Report NC-28. Ogden, UT: USDA Forest Service.

Herda-Rapp, A. & Goedeke, T. L. (2005). *Mad about wildlife: Looking at social conflict over wildlife*. Leiden: Brill.

Hobfoll, S. E. (1998). *Stress, culture, and community: The psychology and philosophy of stress*. New York: Plenum Press.

Hobfoll, S. E. (2012). Conservation of resources and disaster in cultural context: The caravans and passageways for resources. *Psychiatry, 73*, 227–233.

Intergovernmental Panel on Climate Change (IPCC). (2013). Climate change 2013: The physical science basis. Available at http://www.ipcc.ch/report/ar5/wg1/#.UtLo2WRDuaR.

Jackson, S. & Csikszentmihalyi, M. (1999). *Flow in sports*. Champaigne, IL: Human Kinetics.

Jacobson, S. (Ed.). (1995). *Conserving wildlife: International education and communication approaches*. New York: Columbia University Press.

Jakes, P., Kruger, L., Monroe, M., Nelson, K. & Sturtevant, V. (2007). Improving wildfire preparedness: Lessons from communities across the U.S. *Human Ecology Review, 14*(2), 188–197.

James, W. (1902). *The varieties of religious experience*. New York: Modern Library.

Johnson, C., Bowker, J. M., Cordell, H. K., & Bergstrom, J. C. (2005). Wilderness value differences by immigration, race/ethnicity, gender and socioeconomic status. In H. K. Cordell, J. C. Bergstrom & J. M. Bowker (Eds.), *The multiple values of wilderness* (pp. 143–159). State College, PA: Venture Publishing.

Jones, C. D., Hollenhorst, S. & Perna, F. (2003a). An empirical comparison of the four channel flow model and adventure experience paradigm. *Leisure Sciences, 25*(1), 17–31.

Jones, R. T., Ribbe, D. P., Cunningham, P. & Weddle, J. D. (2003b). Psychosocial correlates of wildfire disaster: Post disaster adult reactions. *Fire Technology, 39*, 103–117.

Jung, C. G. (1964). Approaching the unconscious. In C. G. Jung (Ed.), *Man and his symbols* (pp. 1–94). New York: Dell Publishing.

Kahn, P. H., Jr.,, Ruckert, J. H., & Hasbach, P. H. (2012). A nature language. In P. H. Kahn, Jr.,, & P. H. Hasbach (Eds.), *Ecopsychology: Science, totems, and the technological species* (pp. 55–78). Cambridge, MA: MIT Press.

Kaltenborn, B. P., Bjerke, T., Nyahongo, J. W. & Williams, D. R. (2006). Animal preferences and acceptability of wildlife management actions around Serengeti National Park, Tanzania. *Biodiversity and Conservation 15*: 4633–4649.

Keller, R. H., Jr., & Turek, M. F. (1998). *American Indians and the national parks*. Tucson: University of Arizona Press.

Kellert, S. R. (1996). *The value of life: Biological diversity and human society*. Washington, D.C.: Island Press.

Knapp, C. E & Smith, T. E. (Eds.). (2005). *Exploring the power of solo, silence and solitude*. Boulder, CO: Association for Experiential Education.

Knotek, K. (2006). Understanding social influences on wilderness fire stewardship decisions. *International Journal of Wilderness, 12*(1), 22–25.

Koole, S. L. & Van den Berg, A. E. (2005). Lost in the wilderness: Terror management, action orientation and nature evaluation. *Journal of Personality and Social Psychology, 88*(6), pp. 1014–1028.

Kyle, G., Graefe, A., Manning, R., & Bacon, J. (2004). Effects of place attachment on users' perceptions of social and environmental conditions in a natural setting. *Journal of Environmental Psychology, 24*, 213–225.

Lambert, J., Chapman, J., & Lurie, D. (2013). Challenges to the four-channel model of flow: Primary assumption of flow support the moderate challenging control channel. *The Journal of Positive Psychology, 8*(5), 395–403

Larson, R. W. (1997). The emergence of solitude as a constructive domain of experience in early adolescence. *Child Development, 68*(1), 80–93.

Laski, M. (1961). *Ecstasy*. Bloomington, IN: Indiana University Press.

Loomis, J. B. & Richardson, R. (2000). Economic values of protecting roadless areas in the United States. Accessed 22 Aug 2007 from http://www.wilderness.org/Library/Roadless.cfm.

Lowe, S. R., Manove, E. E., & Rhodes, J. E. (2013). Posttraumatic stress and posttraumatic growth among low-income mothers who survived Hurricane Katrina. *Journal of Consulting and Clinical Psychology, 81*(5), 877–889.

Luckner, J. L. & Nadler, R. S. (1997). *Processing the experience: Strategies to enhance and generalize learning*. Dubuque, IA: Kendall/Hunt.

Mace, B. L., Corser, G. C., Zitting, L. & Denison, J. (2013). Effects of overflights on the national park experience. *Journal of Environmental Psychology, 35*, 3–39.

Manfredo, M. (2008). *Who cares about wildlife*. New York: Springer Press.

Manfredo, M., & Teel, T. (2008). Integrating concepts: Demonstration of a multi-level model for exploring the rise of mutualism value orientations in post-industrial society. In M. Manfredo (Ed.), *Who cares about wildlife* (pp. 191–217). New York: Springer Press.

Mannell, R. C., Zuzanek, J. & Larson, R. (1988). Leisure states and "flow" experiences: Testing perceived freedom and intrinsic motivation hypotheses. *Journal of Leisure Research, 20*(4), pp. 289–304.

Manning, R., Lawson, S., Newman, P. Laven, D. & Valliere, W. (2002). Methodological issues in measuring crowding-related norms in outdoor recreation. *Leisure Sciences, 24*, 339–348.

Marino, L. & Lilienfeld, S. O. (1998). Dolphin-assisted therapy: Flawed data, flawed conclusions. *Anthrozoös, 11*, 22–32.

Marino, L. & Lilienfeld, S. O. (2007). Dolphin-assisted therapy: More flawed data and more flawed conclusions. *Anthrozoös, 20*, 239–249.

Martin, P. & Priest, S. (1986). Understanding the adventure experience. *Journal of Adventure Education 3*(1), 18–21.

Mason V., Andrews H., Upton D. (2010). The psychological impact of exposure to floods. *Psychology, Health & Medicine, 15*(1), 61–73.

Massimini, F. & Carli, M. (1986). La selezione psichologica umana tra biologia e cultura. In F. Massimini & P. Inghilleri (Eds.), *L'esperienza quotidiana* (pp. 65–84). Milan: Franco Angeli.

Massimini, F. & Carli, M. (1988). The systematic assessment of flow in daily experience. In M. Csikszentmihalyi & I. Csikszentmihalyi (Eds.), *Optimal experience: Psychological studies of flow in consciousness* (pp. 266–287). New York, NY: Cambridge University Press.

Matarrita-Cascante, D., Stedman, R. & Luloff, A. E. (2010). Permanent and seasonal residents' community attachment in natural amenity-rich areas: Exploring the contribution of landscape-related factors. *Environment and Behavior, 42*(2), 197–220.

Maxted, J. (2005). Coming home: Adolescents and the nature-based solo. In C. E. Knapp & T. E. Smith (Eds.), *Exploring the power of solo, silence and solitude* (pp. 121–136). Boulder, CO: Association for Experiential Education.

McCool, S., & Cole, D. (1997). Proceedings-Limits of acceptable change and related planning processes: Progress and future direction. USDA Forest Service General Technical Report INT-371. Ogden, UT: USDA Forest Service.

McNay, M. E. (2002). *A case history of wolf-human encounters in Alaska and Canada (Wildlife Technical Bulletin 13)*. Juneau, AK: Alaska Dept. of Fish and Game.

Merrick, M. (2008). *Environmental epiphanies: Exploring the shifts in human nature interactions*. Unpublished doctoral dissertation, University of Illinois at Urbana-Champaign, Urbana.

Miles, J. C. & Priest, S. (1999). *Adventure Programming* (2nd ed). State College, PA: Venture Publishing.

Myers, Jr., O. E. & Russell, A. (2003). Human identity in relation to wild Black bears: A natural-social ecology of subjective creatures. In S. Clayton & S. Opotow (Eds.), *Identity and the natural environment* (pp. 67–90). Cambridge, MA: MIT Press.

Najarian, L. M., Goenjian, A. K., Percovitz, D., Mandel, F., & Najarian, B. (2001). The effect of relocation after a natural disaster. *Journal of Traumatic Stress, 14*, 511–526.

Nash, R. (1982). *Wilderness and the American mind*. New Haven, CT: Yale University Press.

National Park Service (1997). *VERP: The Visitor Experience and Resource Protection (VERP) framework: A handbook for planners and managers*. Denver: NPS Denver Service Center.

Neisser, U. (1982). *Memory observed: Remembering in natural contexts*. San Francisco: W. H. Freeman.

Neria, P. & Schultz, J. M. (2012). Mental health effects of hurricane Sandy characteristics, potential aftermath, and response. *Journal of the American Medical Association, 308*(24), 2571–2572.

Nickas, G. & Proescholdt, K. (2005). Keeping the wild in wilderness. *International Journal of Wilderness, 11*(3), 13–18.

Norris, F. H., Stevens, S. P., Pfefferbaum, B., Wyche, K. R., & Pfefferbaum, R. L.(2008). Community resilience as a metaphor, theory, set of capacities, and strategy for disaster readiness. *American Journal of Community Psychology, 41*, 127–150.

Olson, D., Dinerstein, E., Wikramanayake, E., et al. (2001). Terrestrial ecoregions of the world: A new map of life on earth. *Bioscience, 51*(11), 933–938.

Priest, S. & Bunting, C. (1993). Changes in perceived risk and competence during whitewater canoeing. *Journal of Applied Recreation Research, 18*(4), 265–280.

Rao, L.-L., Han, R., Ren, X.-P., Bai, X.-W., Zheng, R., Liu, H., Wang, Z.-J., Li, J.-Z., Zhang, K., & Li, S. (2011). Disadvantage and prosocial behavior: The effects of the Wenchuan earthquake. *Evolution and Human Behavior, 32*, 63–69.

Reser, J. P. & Scherl, L. M. (1988). Clear and unambiguous feedback: A transactional and motivational analysis of environmental challenge and self-encounter. *Journal of Environmental Psychology, 8*(4), 269–286.

Responsive Management (1998). *Wildlife and the American mind*. Harrisburg, VA: Responsive Management.

Responsive Management (not dated). Hunters and hunting: Public opinion on hunting. Web page located at: http://www.responsivemanagement.com/hunting.html#pubop., Accessed 14 Dec 2006.

Rosegrant, J. (1976). The impact of set and setting on religious experience in nature. *Journal for the Scientific Study of Religion, 15*(4), 301–310.

Roxberg, Å., Burman, M., Guldbrand, M., Fridlund, B., & Barbosa da Silva, A. (2010). Out of the wave: The meaning of suffering and relieved suffering for survivors of the tsunami catastrophe. An hermeneutic-phenomenological study of TV-interviews one year after the tsunami catastrophe, 2004. *Scandinavian Journal of Caring Sciences, 24*, 707–715.

Russell, K. C. (2003). A nation-wide survey of outdoor behavior healthcare programs for adolescents with problem behaviors. *Journal of Experiential Education, 25*(3), 322–331.

Russell, K. C. (2012). Therapeutic uses of nature. In S. Clayton (Ed.), *Oxford handbook of environmental and conservation psychology* (pp. 428–444). New York: Oxford University Press.

Russell, K. C. & Farnum, J. (2004). A concurrent model of the wilderness therapy process. *Journal of Adventure Education and Outdoor Learning, 4*, 39–55.

Ryff, C. D. & Singer, B. (2003). Flourishing under fire: Resilience as a prototype of challenged thriving. In C. L. M. Keyes & J. Haidt (Eds.), *Flourishing* (pp. 15–35). Washington DC: American Psychological Association.

Sattler, D. N., Glower de Alvarado, A. M., Blandon de Castro, N., Van Male, R., Zetino, A. M., & Vega, R. R. (2006). El Salvador earthquakes: Relationships among acute stress disorder symptoms, depression, traumatic event exposure, and resource loss. *Journal of Traumatic Stress, 19*, 879–893.

Sattler, D. N., Assanangkornchai, S., Moller, A., Kesavatana-Dohrs, W., & Graham, J. M. (2014). Indian Ocean Tsunami: Relationships among posttraumatic stress, posttraumatic growth, resource loss, and social support at three and fifteen months. *Journal of Trauma and Dissociation: Systemic Trauma Special Issue 15*, 219–239.

Schroeder, H. W. (1996). Psyche, nature and mystery: Some psychological perspectives on the values of natural environments. In B. L. Driver, D. Dustin, T. Baltic, G. Elsner, & G. Peterson (Eds.), *Nature and the human spirit* (pp. 81–96). State College, PA: Venture Publishing.

Schroeder, H. W. (2006). Symbolism, experience and the value of wilderness. *International Journal of Wilderness, 13*(1), 13–18.

Schuster, R. M., Tarrent, M., & Watson, A. (2005). The social values of wilderness. In H. K. Cordell, J. C. Bergstrom, & J. M. Bowker (Eds.), *The multiple values of wilderness* (pp. 113–142). State College, PA: Venture Publishing.

Scott, B. A., Amel, E. L. & Manning, C. M. (2014). In and of the wilderness: Ecological connection through participation in nature. *Ecopsychology, 6*(2), 81–91.

Shelby, B., Vaske, J. & Donnelly, M. (1996). Norms, standards, and natural resources. *Leisure Sciences, 18*, 103–123.

Simpson, D. M., Weissbecker, I., & Sephton, S. E. (2011). Extreme weather-related events: Implications for mental health and well-being. In I. Weissbecker (Ed.), *Climate change and human well-being: Global challenges and opportunities* (pp. 57–78). New York: Springer.

Solomon, S. D., & Green, B. L. (1992). Mental health effects of natural and human made disasters. *PTSD Research Quarterly, 3*, 1–8.

Solomon, S., Greenberg, J., & Pyszczynski, T. (2004). The cultural animal: Twenty years of terror management theory and research. In J. Greenbert, S. Koole & T. Pyszczynski (Eds.), *Handbook of experimental and existential psychology* (pp. 13–34). New York: Guilford Press.

Stankey, G., Cole, D., Lucas, R., Peterson, M., Frissell, S., & Washburne, R. (1985). The limits of acceptable change (LAC) system for wilderness planning. USDA Forest Service General Technical Report INT-176. Ogden, UT: USDA Forest Service.

Stebbins, R. A. (2005). *Challenging mountain nature: Risk, motive and lifestyle in three hobbyist sports*. Calgary: Detselig Enterprises.

Suedfeld, P. (1991). Levels of anxiety in polar environments. *Journal of Environmental Psychology, 11*(3), 265–275.

Suedfeld, P. (1997). Homo invictus: The indomitable species. *Canadian Psychology, 38*(3), 164–173.

Suedfeld, P. (2012). Extreme and unusual environments: Challenges and responses. In S. Clayton (Ed.), *Oxford handbook of environmental and conservation psychology* (pp. 348–371). New York: Oxford University Press.

Tedeschi, R. G., & Calhoun, L. G. (1996). The Posttraumatic Growth Inventory: Measuring the positive legacy of trauma. *Journal of Traumatic Stress, 9*, 455–471.

Tuan, Yi-Fu. (1971). *Man and Nature*. Washington D.C: Association of American Geographers.

Twight, B. W., Smith, K. L. & Wissinger, G. H. (1981). Privacy and camping: Closeness to the self vs. closeness to others. *Leisure Sciences, 4*(4), 427–441.

U.S. Fish and Wildlife Service (2014). *2011 National survey of fishing, hunting and wildlife-associated recreation (revised)*. Washington, DC: USFWS.

U.S. Forest Service. (2013). Wilderness. http://www.fs.fed.us/recreation/programs/cda/wilderness.shtml. Accessed 9 Dec 2014.

van den Berg, A. E. & ter Heijne, M. (2005). Fear versus fascination: An exploration of emotional responses to natural threats. *Journal of Environmental Psychology, 25*,(3), 261–272.

Vaske, J., Donnelly, M. & Heberlein, T. (1980). Perceptions of crowding and resource quality by early and more recent visitors. *Leisure Sciences, 3*(4), 367–381.

Vining, J. & Merrick, M. (2012). Environmental epiphanies: Theoretical foundations and practical applications. In S. Clayton (Ed.), *Oxford handbook of environmental and conservation psychology* (pp. 485–508). New York: Oxford University Press.

Vittersø, J., Kaltenborn, B. P. & Bjerke, T. (1998). Attachment to livestock and attitudes toward large carnivores among sheep farmers in Norway. *Anthrozoös, 11* (4), 210–217.

Vittersø, J., Bjerke, T. & Kaltenborn, B. P. (1999). Attitudes toward large carnivores aamong sheep farmers experiencing different degrees of depredation. *Human Dimensions of Wildlife, 4*(1), 20–35.

Walker, C. J. (2010). Experiencing flow: Is doing it together better than doing it alone? *Journal of Positive Psychology, 5*(1), 3–11.

Webb, N. L. & Drummond, P. D. (2001). The effect of swimming with dolphins on human well-being and anxiety. *Anthrozoös 14*(2), 81–85.

Weissbecker, I., & Czinez, J. (2011). Humanitarian crises: The need for cultural competence and local capacity building. In I. Weissbecker (Ed.), *Climate change and human well-being: global challenges and opportunities* (pp. 79–96). New York: Springer.

Wilderness.net (2014). The National Wilderness Preservation System, Fast facts. http://www.wilderness.net/NWPS/fastfacts. Accessed 22 July 2014.

Williams, K. & Harvey, D. (2001). Transcendent experience in forest environments. *Journal of Environmental Psychology, 21*, 249–260.

Winter, P. L. & Chavez, D. J. (2008). Wildland recreationists' natural resource management priorities and preferences: a connection to environmental identity. In D. J. Chavez, P.l. Winter & Absher, J. D. (Eds.), *Recreation visitor research: studies of diversity*. Albany, CA: United States Department of Agriculture, Forest Service, Pacific Southwest Research Station, Wildland Recreation and Urban Cultures. General Technical Report PSW-GTR-XXX.

Woods, M. (1998). Federal Wilderness preservation in the United States. In J. B. Callicott & M. Nelson (Eds.), *The great new wilderness debate* (pp. 131–153). Athens, GA: University of Georgia Press.

Yang, F., Lin, M.-Y., & Qian, M.-Y. (2010). A study of the relationship between posttraumatic growth and social support in children and adolescents following Wenchuan earthquake. *Chinese Journal of Clinical Psychology, 18*, 614–617.

Yun, K., Lurie, N., & Hyde, P. S. (2010). Moving mental health into the disaster-preparedness spotlight. *New England Journal of Medicine, 363*(13), 1193–1194.

Part II

Thinking About Nature

5

Attitudes, Values, and Perceptions

- **Core understandings of nature**
- **Values**
- **Attitudes**
- **Perceptions**
- **Evolutionary perspectives**
- **Conclusion**
- **References**

At the core of the human relationship with the natural world are the ways in which people understand and value nature. Although most of us have an intuitive sense of what nature is and what it means to us, there is wide variability among both individuals and societies. Yet these understandings are crucial in motivating people to protect their environments. This chapter examines some core ways in which people think about the natural environment as well as discussing theories that attempt to explain these understandings.

Core understandings of nature

Although conceptions of nature are informed by both personal experience and scientific understanding, nature and the natural environment are social constructs. Beliefs about what nature is, as well as the way in which nature is valued, are created within a historical and cultural context. For example, Carolyn Merchant (1980) has argued that the dominant view of nature is confounded with perceptions of the feminine (as in "Mother Nature"). The result, according to Merchant as well as other ecofeminists, is a pervasive attitude that nature is a source of perpetual nourishment that can be exploited and violated.

More concretely, most people define nature as that which is not under the control of humans. Thus, although one could argue that human constructions are just as much a part of nature as bird nests or termite mounds, the environment is felt to be natural when it is free from obvious human impact (Simmons, 1993). This simple conception has profound consequences for ecosystem management. It encourages an approach to the preservation of wilderness that removes all humans and all traces of human occupation, while conversely suggesting that there is no need to provide for or protect nature in an urban setting. It also sets up a zero-sum

Conservation Psychology: Understanding and promoting human care for nature, Second Edition.
Susan Clayton and Gene Myers.

www.wiley.com\go\clayton\conservation

competition between humans and the rest of nature: if humans use a site, it is no longer natural; if it is preserved as natural, it is off-limits to humans. This approach threatens and alienates those whose occupations involve interactions with nature such as farmers, hunters, fishers, and ranchers.

In contrast to the human/nature distinction found in the developed world, pretechnological societies may have sharply different conceptions. Anthropologist Annabelle Sabloff (2001) writes, "In most if not all of the native peoples anthropologists have studied, the natural world was perceived … to be integral to their own and could not be separated out from their cultural life" (p. 34). Bang et al. (2007), for example, found that Menominee (American Indian) parents were more likely to teach their children that they were part of nature compared to European American parents, who taught their children to respect nature; other research showed that Native Americans were more likely than European Americans to take the perspective of nonhuman elements of nature (Medin et al., 2013).

> In our Indian way of thinking, everything is equal, the earth is a living thing …
> In the other way, the earth is our unending grocery store.
>
> Lori New Breast, co-founder of Blackfeet Women Against Fracking (in Black, 2014, p.49)

Defining nature as free from human impact does not imply that people accurately assess that impact. Aesthetic judgments suggest that people prefer natural scenes with some degree of human management rather than ones in which nature has been allowed to run wild and messy. Williams and Cary (2002) asked a random sample of Australian respondents to rate photographs of different types of natural landscape and found that although "perceived naturalness" of landscapes was valued, there was no relationship between the preference ratings and the ecological health of the landscapes as rated by professional ecologists. Among Rome residents in another study, satisfaction with local green spaces was related to their availability, defined as the amount of public green space per capita in the neighborhood, but not to the biodiversity of those spaces (Bonnes et al., 2007).

Regardless of the way in which nature is defined, views of nature are predominantly positive. People tend to pick natural settings when asked to describe a "favorite place" or "a place they would like to be" (Korpela et al., 2001) a result that is found across cultures. For example, when Newell (1997) asked 223 students in the United States, Ireland, and Senegal to identify a valued and favorite place, approximately 60% of respondents from each country named natural environments. Herzog and colleagues (e.g., Herzog et al., 2002; Herzog & Chernick, 2000) have found that people consider natural settings to have great restorative potential and to be more tranquil, and less dangerous, than urban settings.

Values

Values are general preferences for end states or ways of acting; they serve as goals that apply across different contexts and underlie more specific attitudes, preferences, and behaviors. (See Dietz et al., 2005, for a more extensive review of definitions and uses of the term "value" in discussions of environmental issues.) People may value, for example, beauty, peace, or wealth in varying degrees. Overall, across different countries and cultures, there is a high level of agreement that nature has value. Kahn (1999) has found such results in a number of studies, which we discuss in Chapter 7.

On what bases do people value nature? One of the earliest and most widely used schemes for categorizing values was developed by Stephen Kellert, whose studies on this topic are summarized in his 1996 volume, *The value of life: Biological diversity and human society*. Initially based on interviews, but repeated with various sets of survey questions, in many different studies and settings over many years, Kellert identified nine to ten basic values explaining the human affiliation with the natural world, which he suggests may have evolutionary roots. In American society, humanistic values were given the highest ratings. Humanistic values are embodied in the emotional attachments people form toward natural entities, most often companion animals. Moralistic values, assigning ethical standing to nature and natural entities and derived from a worldview of human kinship with nature, are also strong. Table 5.1 shows the rough order of prevalence of 8 value types in the general US population.

The third most highly rated set of values in Kellert's research was described as "negativistic," comprising feelings of fear, disgust, and dislike for elements of nature. It is important to recognize the prevalence of these negative emotions toward nature. Even negative emotions, however, reflect a type of engagement rather than disinterest, and as such may represent an opportunity to attract people's interest. Negatively viewed species, such as bats and snakes, attract a great deal of attention in zoos, for example, and this fascination may engage people's attention long enough for them to learn about the animals and their needs. See the discussion of biophobia described below.

Michael Manfredo and his colleagues (Manfredo, 2008) built on previous work by examining values specifically toward wildlife in the United States. They found that overall value orientations could be classified along two dimensions: domination and mutualism. People who endorse domination tend to be in favor of hunting and the utilization of animals, whereas those who lean toward mutualism are more supportive of animal rights. It is possible to endorse both (or neither) value orientations, although people more often clustered around one or the other. It is worth noting that value orientations differ systematically with geographical region of the country, and that modernization appears to drive a shift from domination toward mutualistic values for wildlife.

Kempton et al. (1995) also studied American values toward nature, through in-depth interviews of 46 people representing different interest groups, supplemented by follow-up

Table 5.1 Kellert value types in order of prevalence in American society.

- Humanistic (primary interest/affection for individual animals, pets)
- Moralistic (right and wrong of treatment of animal and nature, strong opposition to cruelty/exploitation)
- Negativistic (active avoidance due to indifference, dislike, fear)
- Utilitarian (concern for the practical and material value of animals and or habitat)
- Ecologistic (concern for environment as a system, for interrelations between wildlife and natural habitats)
- Naturalistic (interest/affection for wildlife and outdoors)
- Dominionistic (interest in mastery and control)
- Scientific (interest in the physical attributes and biological functioning)

From Kellert, 1996.

surveys of a representative sample of 142 others. Like Kellert, they found a strong moralistic component, concluding that "... American perspectives on global environmental change are based on fundamental moral and religious views" (p. 2–3). Surprisingly, they also found that the people in their general public sample held values similar to those espoused by people belonging to the environmental group the Sierra Club, although the public's views were not quite as internally consistent.

Whereas Kellert focuses on the type of benefit humans receive from nature, Carolyn Merchant (1992) noted that different beneficiaries can be identified. Values may be distinguished according to whose interests are privileged. Merchant described three ways in which nature can be valued: for its own sake (eco- or biocentric values), for the sake of other humans (anthropocentric or altruistic), or for an individual's own benefit (egocentric). Research has confirmed the existence as well as the distinctiveness of these value orientations. People who value nature for its own sake are likely to have different standards for the ways in which humans should treat nature, as compared to people who value nature for the benefits it provides to humans.

Much of the research into the values that underpin environmental attitudes and behavior is based on the work of Shalom Schwartz and his colleagues (e.g., Schwartz, 1992). Schwartz proposes that there are universal value types and that people can be characterized by the different ways in which they prioritize those values. Starting with 56 possible values, Schwartz's research has revealed ten distinct groupings of value types: power, achievement, hedonism, stimulation, self-direction, universalism, benevolence, tradition, conformity, and security. These derive from universal needs of the person as a biological organism, the requirements of social interaction, or the effective functioning of groups. Subsumed in these are values such as social justice (within universalism), freedom (self-direction), honesty and forgiveness (benevolence), humility (tradition), and obedience (conformity).

This fundamental value structure, which has been found in multiple countries around the world, aligns these value types according to their positions on two dimensions. The first dimension reflects self-enhancement versus self-transcendence, describing the extent to which a value prioritizes one's own interests versus the interests of others. The second dimension is traditionalism versus openness to change. The self-transcendence values include ones associated with environmentalism, including "a world of beauty," "protecting the environment," and "unity with nature," as well as others more purely altruistic, such as "a world at peace" and "equality"; these values have been associated with pro-environmental behavior (Schultz, 2001). Stern, Dietz, and Guagnano (1995) have modified the scale to more clearly distinguish the altruistic from the biocentric values.

Considering human value for nature begs the question of how that value can be measured. When products from nature are traded in a market, the prices they command reflect economic value in the given transaction. Much of environmental economics has been concerned with quantifying the "external" values not included in market prices. (See sidebar for one example.) (Fig. 5.1).

> A computer program has been developed to assess the economic value of trees, figuring in the costs associated with planting and upkeep and the benefits they provide by increasing property values, removing CO_2 from the air, and reducing energy consumption by providing cooling shade. A recent examination by the New York City Parks Department concluded that New York City's street trees provide about \$122 million in benefits annually, or a return of \$5.60 for every dollar that is spent.
>
> (Randall, 2007)

Fig. 5.1 Demonstrating the value of trees. (Photo by Susan Clayton.)

Often nature provides public goods (such as ecosystem services) for which markets do not exist; the challenge then is to estimate their monetary values by other means (Hanley & Barbier, 2009). Ecological economists' calculations of the value of ecosystem services now play key roles in conservation planning. To assess the value of natural objects that are not bought and sold, studies often ask how much people are willing to pay for nature, through what are called *contingent valuation methods*. Willingness to pay (WTP) involves asking people to identify the amount they would pay for continued access to a natural resource, or the knowledge that it would continue to exist. The WTP measure is not a perfect representation of nature's economic value. It is influenced by some variables (e.g., the framing of the question as a possible gain or loss) that should not affect it, and unaffected by some variables (e.g., the amount of nature being protected) that should (Kahneman, 1986), suggesting that it taps a more psychological assessment of value. WTP research, however, provides evidence that nature does have concrete value for people, as well as illuminating some of the variables that affect this value. In an interesting validation of such measures, a study of visitors to public green spaces in Sheffield, England found that WTP for increased biodiversity was higher for people who reported more psychological benefits from the area such as emotional attachment, sense of identity, or opportunities for reflection (Dallimer et al., 2013).

Although they are difficult to assess, values are important drivers of public policy, affecting environmental management practices and monetary expenditures. The regulations created to implement the US Oil Pollution Act of 1990 explicitly affirm that "passive use values" such as those determined by contingent valuation may be considered in determining natural resource damages. We examine the role of values in predicting pro-environmental behavior in Chapter 9.

Attitudes

Attitudes are evaluative reactions to objects or behaviors based on beliefs about those objects or behaviors. In social psychological theory, attitudes arise out of general values and primitive beliefs and are more immediate predictors of behavior. Attitudes serve to summarize and integrate our values and beliefs as they apply to a particular issue. In the United States, national surveys consistently show positive attitudes toward nature. Support for environmental protection is widespread and has persisted across decades.

What explains these positive environmental attitudes? The *biophilia hypothesis*, developed by sociobiologist E.O. Wilson (1984; Kellert & Wilson, 1993), proposes that evolutionary pressures led humans to develop a genetically based predisposition to take a strong interest in and affiliate with nature, including plants, animals, and landscape features. Behaviors and emotional experiences are not directly heritable; that is, they are not encoded in our genes but are responses to external stimuli. The tendency to respond to certain stimuli in certain ways, however, can have a genetic basis. Genotypes that promoted attention and emotional responses to natural objects could have conferred adaptive value and thus come to predominate if such attention and feelings promoted effective responding to those elements of nature that support life (edible plants and safe havens) and those that represent threats (dangerous predators and poisonous snakes).

As just implied, nature can prompt not only positive but also negative responses, termed "biophobia." In our evolutionary past, it would have added to one's reproductive success (or fitness) to fear organisms that were potentially fatal and contexts that were dangerous. This could have led to a prepared learning for biophobias; it is easier to learn a fear response to a dangerous natural object than to a dangerous manufactured object. In support of this, experimental studies show it takes longer to unlearn a reinforced fear response to an image of a spider or snake than of an object like a gun (Öhman et al. 1985; Cook et al. 1986). Even today, fears of snakes and spiders are among the most common and easily acquired phobias (Ulrich, 1993) – despite the fact that modern people are more likely to be killed by guns, car crashes, or other threats that were unfamiliar to our ancestors. The thought of being lost and alone in dark wilderness is fearsome even for rural dwellers (Bixler & Floyd 1997). Research supports the suggestion that there is a biological basis to these fears. Studies comparing people with different degrees of genetic relatedness show that genetic factors are implicated in animal phobias; if a close relative has a fear of snakes, you are more likely than an unrelated person to share that fear (Kendler et al., 1992, cited in Ulrich 1993). The persistence of these primitive fears, and our intense fear and fascination with dangerous animals, may be further evidence for biophobia.

Despite the possibility that we have inherited a love of nature, there are still individual differences in attitudes about environmental issues (see Gifford & Sussman, 2012). Overall, demographic variables are only weakly related. Younger and more highly educated respondents tend to be more pro-environmental (Bodur & Sarigöllü, 2005; Xiao & Dunlap, 2007). Women show more concern for the environment, on average (Milfont & Duckitt, 2004; Zelezny et al., 2000), but the effect is small and is not always found. A number of writers have suggested that ethnic groups differ in their attitudes toward the environment. In general, behaviors have been found to show small differences (e.g., Parker and McDonough, 1999), but attitudinal differences are less clear. Members of environmental groups are more likely to be white and of a higher socioeconomic status than the general population, but that may reflect differences in the tendency to join advocacy/issue-oriented organizations rather than in the underlying attitude toward the environment (Morrison & Dunlap, 1986).

In an analysis of national survey data, Johnson, Bowker, and Cordell (2004) found gender and ethnic differences both in environmental behaviors (such as reading, recreation, and membership in environmental groups) and attitudes (endorsement of the New Environmental Paradigm, described below). Ethnic differences in behavior remained even after attitudinal differences were controlled. Johnson et al. conclude that the context for environmental behaviors varies among ethnic groups; both the ease of performing a behavior and the meaning symbolized by that behavior are different for the different groups. In other words, the behavioral expression of an attitude will vary according to the social context and the amount of behavioral control, a point we return to below.

The search for a general predisposition toward the natural environment has generated many different ways of measuring environmental attitudes. Milfont and Duckitt (2004), using a wide range of items, obtained evidence that environmental attitudes cluster into two independent but related themes: preservation, based on a biocentric valuing of nature; and utilization, reflecting an anthropocentric value. It is perhaps most useful to consider specific environmental attitudes as resulting from a more generalized worldview. A worldview is an integrated set of beliefs about what is real, what is knowable, what is valuable, and what it means to be human.

Social scientists began using the idea of worldview to understand environmental issues with the publication of Riley Dunlap and Kenneth Van Liere's psychological scale, called the *New Environmental Paradigm* (Dunlap & Van Liere, 1978; later revised by Dunlap, Van Liere, Mertig, & Jones, 2000 as the New Ecological Paradigm). See Table 5.2. Dunlap and his colleagues described a worldview concerning the human relationship with nature and proposed that the Western world had experienced a paradigm shift from the "dominant social paradigm," which stressed continued economic growth, human domination over nature, and confidence in technology, to a "new environmental paradigm," emphasizing the fragility of nature and the need for limits on the growth of human society, and denying a human right to rule the rest of nature. The revised NEP has been widely used, gets a high level of endorsement in Western society, and is associated with pro-environmental behavior. Thus, the worldview it describes seems both to be widely accepted and to help explain people's support for the environment.

Table 5.2 Some items from the new ecological paradigm scale.

We are approaching the limit of the number of people the earth can support.
Humans were meant to rule over the rest of nature. (Reverse scored)
Humans are severely abusing the environment.
Human ingenuity will insure that we do NOT make the earth unlivable. (Reverse scored)

From Dunlap et al. (2000).

A worldview is usually considered to arise in part from one's cultural heritage. Environmental worldviews show consistent relations to other social belief systems. A recent multinational study of students in England, Denmark, and the United States found that support for the dominant social paradigm was negatively associated with environmental attitudes (Kilbourne et al., 2001). Heath and Gifford (2006), in a Canadian sample, found that support for free-market ideology was negatively associated with environmentalism. In a sample of Australian students, social conservatism and the belief that "money is good" were negatively associated with environmentalism (Hodgkinson & Innes, 2000). Finally, egalitarianism (as contrasted with individualism) has also been linked with environmentalism (Steg & Sievers, 2000).

Two other models of the way in which culture affects environmental worldview have received mixed support. Inglehart (e.g., 1995) proposed that societies need to reach a level of affluence that allows them to endorse postmaterialist values before they will give priority to environmental objectives. According to Inglehart, people who live in nonindustrial or industrializing countries will focus on satisfying immediate needs such as security and economic well-being. Only after societies have achieved a certain level of stability will they have the luxury to emphasize more abstract goals such as freedom and environmental protection.

This hypothesis has been investigated at both the societal and the individual level. Inglehart found that support for environmental protection was greatest in countries that held postmaterialist values, and other studies have shown a similar effect. Göksen et al., (2002), for example, surveyed over 1000 Istanbul residents and found the anticipated relationship between individuals' postmaterialist values and their environmental concern. Other research, however, has found no connection (e.g., Stern et al., 1999), or a more complex relationship. Dunlap and Mertig (1996), using a dataset with 22,000 respondents from 24 countries stratified by per capita income level, found that large majorities in all countries see environmental problems as at least somewhat serious. All problems were rated as more serious by residents of poor countries, who were most likely to rate local and national conditions as serious. Thus, it would be incorrect to conclude that environmental concern is restricted to wealthy countries.

A cultural dimension that has been frequently studied in psychological research is the distinction between individualist and collectivist cultures (e.g., Markus & Kitayama, 1991). Individualistic cultures emphasize the self as independent, distinguish between personal and communal goals, and focus on personal utility. Collectivist cultures think of the self as interdependent with others, believe that personal and communal goals are aligned, and emphasize interpersonal norms and obligations. It has been argued that collectivist values are more compatible than individualist ones with environmentalism, and some studies have found greater endorsement of the NEP in collectivist countries (Schultz et al., 2000a; Vikan et al., 2007). However, countries that are classified as having primarily collectivist worldviews, such as China and Japan, are not typically found to endorse environmental initiatives more strongly than individualistic countries such as the United States. (Deng et al., 2006; Eisler et al., 2003). On average, the Japanese show a lower moralistic value for nature compared to Americans (Kellert, 1996); and despite its supposed nature-friendly Taoist tradition, China has in fact heavily degraded its resources over many centuries.

Anthropologist Florence Kluckhohn and social psychologist Fred Strodtbeck (1961) suggested that all cultural belief systems embody one of three basic descriptions of the human–nature relationship. Some cultures incorporate the basic belief that humans are elevated over nature and superior to it and thus can and should dominate it. Others hold that humans and nature exist in harmony, and still others frame humanity as subordinate to the more powerful natural world of beings and forces. Such basic root metaphors are abstractions from complex systems of belief that systematically differ from one religious tradition to another (although they also vary across individuals and situations). Kluckhohn and Strodtbeck's work stands as a reminder that sensitivity to religious worldviews is necessary when studying the experience of nature in other cultural settings.

The fact that many ascribe spiritual or moral value to nature leads to the question whether religiosity is associated with support for nature. In an influential 1967 essay, historian Lynn White suggested that traditional Christian religiosity would undermine environmentalism, because the Judeo-Christian worldview emphasized human domination over nature. Studies that find a relationship do tend to show that measures of religiosity, such as regular churchgoing, are negatively associated with environmentalism in America (e.g., Gardner & Stern, 2002; Schultz et al., 2000b).

Gardner and Stern, however, conclude that the relationship is due to the social conservatism associated with churchgoing. Their analyses show that religious beliefs have only a weak negative relationship to environmental behavior when controlling for age, gender, education, income, and political liberalism (see also Sherkat & Ellison, 2007). White also argued that the more respectful attitude toward nature found among Eastern religions would encourage greater protection for the environment, a relationship that has not been found. Overall, religious beliefs may have some connection with environmentalism, but this connection is overshadowed by other social factors surrounding religious practice.

In some of the best research to date on culture and environmental cognition and behavior, Atran et al (2005) showed that beliefs in the sacredness of local nature were important in the rate of deforestation practiced by three different ethnic groups in the Guatemalan state of Petan. We discuss this example in more detail in chapter 10.

Perceptions

The most fundamental way in which people respond to their environment is by perceiving its properties. The usual "information processing" view of perception posits an external world of physical energies that must be transduced to brain association centers, where it gives rise to an internal mental representation that bears no inherent relation to the original stimulus. As Hume (1739/1938) and the early empiricists concluded, the mental world of mind is fundamentally different from the world outside. This does not mean that "nature" is just a product of our mental constructions. Such problems result from our ways of conceptualizing.

One alternative account is termed *ecological* because of its holistic rather than atomistic focus. An ecological perspective on perception is oriented around a basic principle: sensation and perception are holistic and relational, and an approach to perception that separates the person from the environment is inadequate. With roots in early 20th Century psychologist William James' work (e.g., 1890/1981), and especially in the more recent work of James J. Gibson (1979) and Eleanor Gibson (1969; 1997), ecological psychology is essentially a theory of perception, but its implications are so fundamental that the wider term may be justified. The Gibsons' fundamental departure from the problematic duality of subject and object was to consider organism and physical environment not as entities to be analyzed by separate principles, but as mutually and reciprocally defined. In developing the notion of "perceptual systems," they were moving toward an analysis that accounts for the structure and functions of perception.

The Gibsons addressed one of the confusions generated by standard accounts of perception: how the material can become mental. Aristotle also addressed this question in his work on psychology, *de Anima* (1973). Perception, which sets animals apart from plants, is the capacity to take on the form of an object without incorporating its matter. In Aristotle's analogy, the shape of a seal is left in wax onto which the seal was pressed; the form but not the substance is preserved. Building on this tradition, the Gibsons developed the notion of direct perception as a variant of philosophical realism, or the assumption that we experience things as they actually exist rather than the usual assumption that external objects can be known only by inference, and the mind can directly "know" only its own contents (Gibson 1979; Gibson 1997).

This theory was not a simple realism, but one that recognized the relational nature of perception. For example, James Gibson demonstrated "optical flow," or the "visual streaming or outflow of environmental features" when moving forward, or the converging flow when looking to the rear (Heft 2001, p. 119). Similarly relational is our perception of the self. We see parts of our own bodies (which we also perceive by proprioception, balance, and cutaneous sensation) in context; visual information changes in correspondence to motion of our head. Neisser (1988) termed the self known within its perceptual context as the "ecological self." Gibson also examined the familiar phenomena of "occluding edges": when one object is gradually juxtaposed or revealed by another in relation to their movements, the occluded object is experienced as persisting even when not in view. Studies of infants show that they learn by age three months to smoothly track continued trajectories of viewed objects with various paths (occluded, varied acceleration, etc.), demonstrating that they recognized the continuity of the object behind the discrete images (von Hofsten 1997). Together with perceptual inference based on generalized rules, perception, von Hofsten argues, "is designed to provide detailed predictions of what is imminently going to happen" (1997, p. 180).

Gibson argued that perception is not just a series of momentary snapshots of a sliver-thin "now" but encompasses a bit of the past as well as the future. The usual account of perception must rely strongly on inference and memory, as the mechanisms that make just-preceding stimuli available to create a full mental representation of the environment. By contrast, the ecological approach says the environment serves as its own representation, and perceptual awareness allows one to inspect an environment further. It distinguishes memory and imagination as forms of awareness that are nonperceptual: memory is denied the chance of further inspection, and imagination can be elaborated only through sheer cognition. Thus, perceptual awareness is functionally different from other cognitive phenomena (Heft 2001). In perception, we are able to actively and directly "pick up" information by exploring our environment. The fact that the information is there to be picked up illustrates Gibson's brand of "ecological realist" direct perception:

> The act of picking up information ... is a continuous act, an activity that is ceaseless and unbroken. The sea of energy in which we live flows and changes without sharp breaks.... Discrete percepts, like discrete ideas, are as mythical as the Jack of Spades.
>
> (Gibson 1979 p. 240, quoted in Heft 2001 p. 177)

Rather than considering perception in passive/information processing (stimulus-receptor) terms, the ecological approach emphasizes how perception derives from action in the world. To consider vision as an example, recent theory and findings look at vision in terms of active organism–environment adaptation. Our visual system evolved for a world of movement and motion. Action gives rise to perception, rather than the common sense view of perception making action possible. In a classic experiment, young kittens were placed in one of two treatment conditions when their eyes opened a few days after birth. Some kittens were harnessed to little wagons that they hauled around as they navigated their environment. Other kittens were paired with the wagon-pullers, by being secured in the wagons. Thus, both kittens had a similar visual input, but very different motor experiences. After a few days, the all the kittens were allowed to roam. Those that had been pulling the wagons navigated easily, but the ones that had had passive experiences bumped into things – they had not learned to "see" (described in Humphrey, 1984).

O'Regan and Noë (2001) have argued against a (traditional) mental-representational view of vision:

> Instead of assuming that vision consists in the creation of an internal representation of the outside world whose activation somehow generates visual experience, we propose to treat vision as an *exploratory activity* .... The central idea of our new approach is that *vision is a mode of exploration of the world that is mediated by knowledge of what we call sensorimotor contingencies.*
>
> (O'Regan and Noë, 2001, p. 940, emphasis in original)

Their theory is that the sensory-derived nerve signals, once in the brain, are not themselves "labeled" as (e.g.) "visual" or "auditory," although we might expect they are from gross neural anatomy. Rather, the brain sorts out the senses by detecting what kinds of actions or changes in other inputs the signals are contingent upon. As a simple example, visual percepts are affected by eye blinks, but auditory stimuli are not. The brain integrates the inputs that share contingencies into coherent visual experience, coherent hearing, etc. Contingencies are determined by the attributes of objects – consider the differences between touching versus seeing a three-dimensional object. Blind people whose sight has been restored report being dumbfounded at the sight of small photographs of faces, since they are not able initially to integrate their experience of the contingencies of touching a face with the experience of seeing such a small representation of one (O'Regan & Noë 2001). The implication of this line of research is that we directly perceive the world, *which thus serves as its own continuous* "representation" *as we act.* What is learned, for example by the kittens mentioned above, is how the rules of the different senses interact with the world's features. Our experience of the world is not fully mediated through our cognitive processes, but is fundamentally integrated with objective physical reality.

A key ecological concept is the idea of affordances (E. Gibson 1982). An affordance is "the perceived functional significance of an object, event, or place for an individual," or a "perceptual meaning" (Heft 2001, p. 123). It is not simply a physical stimulus, for it is defined in relation to the animal's perception; it is a perceivable property of the world whose patterns of occurrence in space and time are matched by the animal's life activities (Reed, 1996). At the same time, affordances are "properties of environmental features existing independently of a perceiver" (Heft, 2001, p. 124), and in principle describable by natural science. Affordances are linked to ecological theory by way of the concept of the niche, or set of environmental features needed by a particular organism (Reed 1996). An example would be a tree cavity of the right placement, opening, size, and so forth to serve as a nest for a particular bird species. The close adaptation of the organism to its niche (subjectively apprehended as an affordance) is a product of evolution.

Affordances can further be clarified by contrast with conceptual meanings. The perceptual meanings of an object (affordances) relate directly to all the purposes it can serve; these meanings depend on the user's intentions, but also are constrained by the possible uses to which it can be put. Heft (2001) uses the example of how a book might be used as paper weight, doorstop, and so on, but not other things (say, a cup). Conceptual meanings, on the other hand, can be separated from everyday realities, giving them powers to create as well as to distort, for example, in ideologies.

The effect of ecological psychology is to "displace" significant portions of what has been assumed to take place in the organism or "in the head" out into the environment. Any given thing, object or layout can in principle be specified by a set of invariants that are available to be picked up (Rader, 1997). Objects lie within nested sets of affordances; within such a structure, their meaning is directly perceived. Examples might be an animal choosing an individual prey out of a herd found in its typical hunting grounds, or a person selecting an appropriate tool within the context of a particular fabrication project. In both cases, nested information is directly picked up from the environment.

Some cultural artifacts embody cognitive processes directly (D'Andrade, 1984), and thus play a role in explaining the acquisition of "mental skills" previously unpossessed; the individual acquires skills required to use the embodied information (Heft, 2001, p. 357). Indeed, in psychology, we may have mistaken some of these very tools as metaphors for more basic mental processes. This may be the case with maps, and the related concept of "cognitive maps," presumed to contain representations of the configuration of an area. Certainly, we retain images and other knowledge of places we have navigated. But in the standard perception/information processing account, such a mental map is necessary even when actively navigating. Gibson, on the other hand, suggests that knowing an extended route or how a place is laid out derives from actively using its sequence of perspectives, or its "nested sequences of transitions connecting vistas, a flow of information generated by a perceiver moving through the environment. [This] perspective structure concurrently specifies movement of the self through the environment" (Heft, 2001, p. 187).

The perspective of ecological psychology can be summarized through several general propositions laid out by Eleanor Gibson (1997), including: organism–environment reciprocity, as shown by affordances; perception–action reciprocity, as shown by studies supporting the "pick-up" of information; "tasks," or larger functional units of behavior that have goals, rules, and constraints; ecologically nested units of tasks and affordances; control or agency by the organism; prospectivity or the future-looking, predictive quality of perception and behavior; and flexibility. The implication for conservation psychology is that our view of human perception as dominated by our supposedly unique mental abilities may have underestimated our intimate perceptual and cognitive linkage with our concrete surroundings. Action in the world is the primary basis of perception and cognition.

Evolutionary perspectives

The highly interdependent account of organism and environment proposed by ecological perception theory invites an evolutionary explanation of its origins, though such an account is not required. Evolutionary psychology has arisen as a way of understanding a wide variety of human behaviors. Evidence of several kinds has been assembled to support the idea that features of mind and behavior evolved because they enhanced the fitness (or number of surviving offspring) of individuals or groups possessing them (Geary, 2007). Evolutionary psychologists search for "modular" parts of the mind, or stable complexes of perception, thoughts, and behavioral and learning biases that pertain to specific domains of the environment (Barkow et al., 1992). Such modules have been supported for tasks including understanding other minds, and for ecology including physics and biology. In addition, various cognitive and social biases or tendencies may be explained as adaptations, as in the case of the biophilia hypothesis described above.

Evolutionary psychology assumes that innate psychological mechanisms or modules arose in response to the "environment of evolutionary adaptiveness" (EEA). This environment, generally the late Pleistocene in which *Homo sapiens* emerged from descendants of the *H. habilis* lines, posed adaptive problems for our ancestors concerning: reproductive challenges such as mating patterns and mate choice; social group functioning such as cooperation, competition, and sensitivity to cheating; capacity to learn spoken language; categorizing living things; and preferences or aversions for aspects of nature. Each of these poses specific information processing problems; the job of research is to develop and experimentally test models of cognitive programs capable of solving them. If followed rigorously, the methods of evolutionary psychology should avoid the problem of creating "just so" stories of adaptationism, where any feature can be rationalized to have emerged from a putative selective pressure (Gould & Lewontin, 1979). Evolutionary psychology is a fecund source of hypotheses and answers about the human mind's adaptedness to such problems (Barkow et al., 1992; see Cosmides & Tooby, 1997 for a short primer).

The argument that the mental faculties of the brain should be viewed as selected structures goes back to Darwin (1871), who pointed to continuities between humans and others species. On the level of brain anatomy, studies of the sensory areas of the brain in animals with different ecological specializations show enlargement for specializations related to feeding strategy, for example. The enlarged associative areas of the brain are related to social group complexity, according to the social brain hypothesis. Old World monkey species, which tend to live in complex social groups, have larger volumes of the brain's neocortex than do New World monkeys that do not live in such social groups (Geary, 2007). Evolutionary psychology has been applied to many problems associated with social exchange and threat, such as cooperation, trust, reciprocity, and detecting cheaters. These have relevance to the social dimensions of conservation, as discussed in Chapters 9–12.

Returning to the biophilia hypothesis, if it was adaptive to form attachments to landscapes, there should be a tendency for people to prefer landscapes that are more able to support the things we need to live: food, water, and shelter. Research has supported this hypothesis. In numerous experimental studies, people have been shown to prefer landscapes with water to those without, and they like flowering trees, which suggest fertile vegetation. Some research has suggested that people prefer savannah landscapes (Kaplan & Kaplan, 1989), but more recent research, carefully controlling for natural scene features, has not supported the savannah hypothesis. Han's (2007) study of Texan undergraduates, in combination with earlier studies, gave stronger support for a "forest hypothesis." Even more predictive than biome, however, were the levels of three physical features in the scenes: openness, complexity, and water (Figs. 5.2 and 5.3).

Integrating this with the ecological perspective, people seem to like landscapes offering two affordances. Prospect, or the opportunity to see some distance away, means that a person in that landscape is less likely to be ambushed by a predator or an enemy. Refuge, or the availability of a shelter or hiding place, would have provided protection from the elements or detection by predators (see Appleton, 1975). Heerwagen and Orians (1993) have suggested that people look for cues in a landscape to see whether it will fill their needs. These cues include availability of resources, which can be signaled by flowering plants and the presence of water; the availability of shelter; and the ability to navigate successfully across a landscape as opposed to being lost in a morass of untracked underbrush. Kaplan (1993) has also found that people do not like landscapes that are characterized by extreme openness (and thus no refuge) or by blocked views and dense vegetation (and thus no prospect). She argues that people evaluate landscapes in terms of how well the landscapes satisfy human needs for understanding and exploration.

Many of the biophilic/biophobic preferences postulated for humans should also apply to other species, particularly closely related ones, and perhaps to an even greater degree if the species rely less on learning. Verbeek and de Waal (2002) summarize evidence that nonhuman

Fig. 5.2 A landscape without preferred features. (Photo by Susan Clayton.)

Fig. 5.3 A landscape with preferred features. (Photo by Susan Clayton.)

Table 5.3 Characteristics of folk biological systems that interact with experience and culture.

- Biological categories determined by inner unchanging essence
- Categories show some hierarchical structuring
- Level of "basic" categories: Genus or species
- Behavioral and ecological similarities inferred from taxonomic relatedness
- Biological and psychological characteristics distinguished
- Reproduction, growth, illness, and death characterize living things

primates are highly attuned to their natural habitats and are very good at obtaining the resources they depend on and avoiding hazards. Primates appear to rely on emotional assessment of and arousal in response to nature, as would be predicted if biophilia is emotionally mediated. Verbeek and de Waal also provide anecdotes of captive primates relishing the chance to be in and explore outside areas. It appears we are not the only primate that may enjoy the outdoors, and even take an interest in other species as well as our own (Preston & de Waal 2002).

The argument for genetic predispositions is provocative but not definitive. A genetic explanation can be supported only by a few kinds of evidence, and as yet, evidence for biophilia falls short. Snake and spider phobia learning rules are most strongly supported by behavioral experimental evidence. While prospect–refuge theory provides a plausible explanation for certain preferences, more research is needed to determine how cross-culturally universal such preferences are. Given the extremely varied biomes to which human cultures have adapted, it is also conceivable that landscape preference is shaped by experience.

Probably the best-developed line of evidence from evolutionary psychology regarding the human relation to nature is biological thinking. Building on a substantial corpus of studies, Medin and Atran (2004) hypothesized that humans have a mental "folk-biological system" (FBS) attuned to living things and enabling categorization, interpretations, and inferences and about this domain of experience (Table 5.3). For example, there is evidence for specializations for food finding and preferences across many species (Geary 2007). The human FBS was presumably shaped by early foraging subsistence patterns. Humans, as generalist feeders, have to learn and remember successful food items. Human groups everywhere categorize their local flora and fauna, and cultures in natural environments develop complex classifications systems and ways of predicting the growth and behavior of other species. Such systems are similar to scientific classifications, although the degree of elaboration depends on how socially or economically important the taxonomic group is in the culture (Atran 1998).

Among the more strongly supported findings is that people universally believe that members of biological categories share an inner essence, reflected by common patterns of body shape, behavior, growth, and ecological niche. People believe that superficial changes could not change the plant's or animal's underlying essence. This belief enables inferences, such as patterns of relatedness to unfamiliar species, and a correlation between taxonomic category, and internal anatomy. Knowledge of a species of fish will not be used to predict characteristics of birds, but only of other fish. But accurate predictions are knowledge dependent. Similarly, there are variations by culture and expertise as to which biological level (species, genus, and family) is regarded as the essential type. Interestingly, people tend to believe that essence resides at the rank of species or genus (e.g., oak) rather than the life-form (i.e., tree) (Atran et al. 2005). Essentialism may explain why the theory of evolution is counterintuitive to many people.

Some elements of the FBS develop early in children, including essentialism; the beliefs that biological or bodily characteristics are inherited whereas psychological traits such as beliefs are not; that illness is a biological process (including contamination, contagion, and symptoms); and that growth and healing characterize living things (Backscheider et al., 1993; Coley et al., 2002; Rosengren et al., 1991). Children divide living things into "natural kinds" according to the assumption that some unchanging essence defines each kind, and think of the relatedness between different kinds (such as species of dog), and about reproduction, based on these natural kind categories. Their concepts about living things are distinct from those they apply to artifacts and nonliving things (Inagaki & Hatano, 1987; Coley, 1995), and they understand that living things cause their own actions, grow, feed, age, and die (Massey & Gelman, 1988; Hatano & Inagaki, 1997). This "naïve biology" emerges early, by age 5, and is robust. Following an evolutionary psychology perspective, a native cognitive module relating to living things and categorization may underlie it, but it is also dependent on experience.

Some have argued that young children tend to base their explanations of living processes on behavioral similarity to people, and this is replaced in later years by physiological and biological concepts (Carey, 1985; Hatano & Inagaki 1997; Inagaki & Hatano, 1987). Ross and colleagues (2003), however, compared urban majority culture children (similar to the populations used in most previous studies, including Carey's), with rural children of the same culture, and with rural Menominee (Native American) children. Their results showed that only the urban children tended to import a human model into thinking about animals' behaviors, whereas even the youngest rural majority culture children reasoned in biological terms. All ages of the Menominee used biological and ecological concepts in thinking about animal behavior, demonstrating the importance of experience and culture in giving substance to the naturalist intelligence.

To the extent these developmental patterns have been studied cross-culturally it is clear that the FBS interacts with cultural knowledge systems (Atran et al., 2005). There is some evidence for neural correlates of the FBS, such as injuries to some brain areas producing selective disabilities to recognize names or pictures of living versus nonliving things. Other evidence, for example, using brain imaging, however, has not been conclusive (Geary, 2007). Psychologist Howard Gardner (1999) does consider the mass of evidence related to specialized cognition of biological phenomena sufficient to merit a category of "naturalist" intelligence in addition to his original seven types. (See Chapter 11 for more on children's attainment of biological and ecological knowledge.) Atran et al. (2005) are cautious not to prematurely conclude that the FBS is an innate evolved-in adaptive module. For instance, they note important interactions of the module's biases with cultural beliefs, and they admit that their theory only partially predicted findings.

Evolutionary psychology has been criticized on a number of grounds. For example, it may be unnecessarily complex; general intelligence and learning may be more efficient ways to solve many problems than multiplying specialized modules. The conception of the Pleistocene EEA may be artificially constraining; some adaptations may have arisen earlier. Further, if a selective pressure is inferred from adaptive practices of hunter-gatherers, the notion is circular, as well as assuming an equivalence of (highly variable) hunter-gatherers and earlier prehistoric conditions (Foley, 1995). Irons (1998) argues that an alternate concept, the Adaptively Relevant Environment, is more appropriate because it denotes specific parts of the environment to which specific modules respond. On a methodological level, it is not clear why psychologists should privilege hypotheses about the functions of specific mental features derived from speculation about evolutionary settings. Understanding the mind is a wide-ranging task. While evolutionary psychology may advance some new hypotheses and has brought together new constellations of findings, we must still work to describe how the human mind is set up to solve the problems we encounter in life, including how we relate to nature.

Conclusion

This chapter has reviewed some important aspects of the ways in which people think about nature. People tend to think of nature as separate from humans, although that is more true of developed, Westernized countries. As suggested by the biophilia hypothesis, people like and value nature, and particularly have preference for landscapes that might contribute to human well-being. The ecological perspective indicates that we perceive environments in ways that support our functioning within those environments. An evolutionary perspective links our perceptions and preferences to our genetic heritage. The implications of such a link are unclear, but suggest that our responses to natural environments may be more fundamental than attitudes that are formed by culture and experience. Because of the profound ways in which our patterns of thinking and acting are interconnected with natural environments, changes in our experiences of nature may have impacts that are more subtle and powerful than we realize.

References

Appleton, J. (1975). *Experience of landscape*. New York: Wiley.

Aristotle (1973). De anima. In J. A. Smith, Trans. & R. Mckeon, (Eds.) *Introduction to Aristotle*. Chicago: University of Chicago Press.

Atran, S. (1998). Folkbiology and the anthropology of science: Cognitive universals and cultural particulars. *Behavioral and Brain Sciences, 21*, 547–609.

Atran, S., Medin, D. L. & Ross, N. O. (2005). The cultural mind: Environmental decision making and cultural modeling within and across populations. *Psychological Review, 112*, 744–776.

Backscheider, A., Shatz, M., & Gelman, S. (1993). Preschoolers' ability to distinguish living kinds as a function of regrowth. *Child Development 64*: 1242–1257.

Bang, M., Medin, D., & Atran, S. (2007). Cultural mosaics and mental models of nature. *PNAS 104*, 13868–13874.

Barkow, J. H., Cosmides, L. & Tooby, J. (1992). *The adapted mind: Evolutionary psychology and the generation of culture*. New York: Oxford.

Bixler, R. & Floyd, M. (1997). Nature is scary, disgusting, and uncomfortable. *Environment and Behavior, 5*, p. 202–247.

Black, G. (2014). The great divide. *OnEarth, 36*(1), 41–50.

Bodur, M., & Sarigöllü, E. (2005). Environmental sensitivity in a developing country. *Environment and Behavior, 37*, 487–510.

Bonnes, M., Uzzell, D., Carrus, G. & Kelay, T. (2007). Inhabitants' and experts' assessments of environmental quality for urban sustainability. *Journal of Social Issues, 63*, 59–78.

Carey, S. (1985). *Conceptual change in childhood*. Cambridge, MA: MIT Press.

Coley, J. D. (1995). Emerging differentiation of folkbiology and folkpsychology: Attributions of biological and psychological properties to living things. *Child Development 66*: 1856–1874.

Coley, J. D., Solomon, G. & Shafto, P. (2002). The development of folkbiology: A cognitive science perspective on children's understanding of the biological world. In P. Kahn & S. Kellert (Eds.) *Children and nature: Psychological, sociocultural and evolutionary investigations* (pp. 65–91). Cambridge, MA: MIT Press.

Cook, E., Hodes, R., & Lang, P. (1986). Preparedness and phobia: Effects of stimulus content on human visceral conditioning. *Journal of Abnormal Psychology, 95*, 195–207.

Cosmides, L. & Tooby, J. (1997). Evolutionary psychology: A primer. Available at: http://www.cep.ucsb.edu/primer.html (acccessed 28 July 2014).

D'Andrade, R. G. (1984). Cultural meaning systems. In R. Shweder & R. A. Levine, *Culture theory* (pp. 88–119). Cambridge: Cambridge University Press.

Dallimer, M., Tinch, D., Hanley, N., Irvine, K., Rouquette, J., Warren, P., Maltby, L., Gaston, K., & Armsworth, P. (2013). Quantifying preferences for the natural world using monetary and nonmonetary assessments of value. *Conservation Biology*, *28*, 404–413.

Darwin, C. (1871). *The descent of man, and selection in relation to sex*. London: John Murray.

Deng, J., Walker, G. J., & Swinnerton, G. (2006). A comparison of environmental values and attitudes between Chinese in Canada and Anglo-Canadians. *Environment and Behavior*, *38*, 22–47.

Dietz, T., Fitzgerald, A., & Shwom, R.. (2005). Environmental values. *Annual Review of Environmental Resources*, *30*, 335–372.

Dunlap, R. E. & Mertig, A. G. (1996). Global concern for the environment: Is affluence a prerequisite? *Journal of Social Issues*, *51*, 121–37.

Dunlap, R. E., & Van Liere, K. (1978). The "new environmental paradigm." *Journal of Environmental Education*, *9*, 10–19.

Dunlap, R. E., Van Liere, K., Mertig, A., & Jones, R. (2000). Measuring endorsement of the New Ecological Paradigm: A revised NEP scale. *Journal of Social Issues*, *56*, 425–442.

Eisler, A. D., Eisler, H., & Yoshida, M. (2003). Perception of human ecology: cross-cultural and gender comparisons. *Journal of Environmental Psychology*, *23*, 89–101.

Foley, R. (1995). The adaptive legacy of human evolution: A search for the environment of evolutionary adaptation. *Evolutionary Anthropology*, *4*, 194–203.

Gardner, G., & Stern, P. (2002). *Environmental problems and human behavior*. Boston: Allyn & Bacon.

Gardner, H. (1999). *Intelligence reframed: Multiple intelligences for the 21st century*. New York: Basic Books.

Geary, G. C. (2007). *The origin of mind*. Washington, DC: American Psychological Association.

Gibson J. J. (1979). *The ecological approach to visual perception*. Boston: Houghton-Mifflin.

Gibson, E. J. (1969). *Principles of perceptual learning and perception*. Cambridge, MA: MIT Press.

Gibson, E. J. (1982). The concept of affordances in development: A renascence of functionalism. In W. A. Collins (Ed.), *The concept of development: The Minnesota Symposium on Child Development, 15* (pp. 55–81). Hillsdale, NJ: Lawrence Erlbaum.

Gibson, E. J. (1997). An ecological psychologist's prolegomena for perceptual development: A functional approach. In C. Dent-Read & P. Zukow-Goldring (Eds.), *Evolving explanations of development: Ecological approaches to organism-environment systems* (pp. 23–45). Washington, DC: American Psychological Association.

Gifford, R., & Sussman, R. (2012). Environmental attitudes. In S. Clayton (Ed.), *The Oxford handbook of environmental and conservation psychology* (pp. 65–80). New York: Oxford University Press.

Göksen, F., Fadaman, F., & Zenginobuz, E. (2002). On environmental concern, willingness to pay, and postmaterialist values: Evidence from Istanbul. *Environment and Behavior*, *34*, 616–633.

Gould, S. & Lewontin, R. (1979). The spandrels of San Marco and the Panglossian paradigm: A critique of the adaptationist programme. *Proceedings of the Royal Society of London, Series B*, *205* (1161), 581–598

Han, K-T. (2007). Responses to six major terrestrial biomes in terms of scenic beauty, preference and restorativeness. *Environment and Behavior*, *39*, 529–556.

Hanley, N., & Barbier, E. (2009). *Pricing nature: cost-benefit analysis and environmental policy*. Edward Elgar, Cheltenham.

Hatano, G. & Inagaki, K. (1997). Qualitative changes in intuitive biology. *European Journal of Psychology of Education 12* (2): 111–130.

Heath, Y., & Gifford, R. (2006). Free-market ideology and environmental degradation: The case of belief in global climate change. *Environment and Behavior*, *38*, 48–71.

Heerwagen, J., & Orians, G. (1993). Humans, habitats, and aesthetics. In S. Kellert & E. O. Wilson (Eds.). *The biophilia hypothesis* (pp. 138–172). Washington, D.C.: Island Press.

Heft, H. (2001). *Ecological psychology in context: James Gibson, Roger Braker, and the legacy of William James's radical empiricism*. Mahwah, NJ: Lawrence Erlbaum.

Herzog, T., & Chernick, K. (2000). Tranquility and danger in urban and natural settings. *Journal of Environmental Psychology, 20*, 29–39.
Herzog, T., Chen, H. & Primeau, J. (2002). Perception of the restorative potential of natural and other settings. *Journal of Environmental Psychology, 22*, 295–306.
Hodgkinson, S., & Innes, M. (2000). The prediction of ecological and environmental belief systems: The differential contributions of social conservatism and beliefs about money. *Journal of Environmental Psychology, 20*, 285–294.
Hume, D. (1739/1978). *A treatise of human nature*. Oxford: Oxford University Press.
Humphrey, N. (1984). *Consciousness regained*. New York: Oxford University Press.
Inagaki, K. & Hatano, G. (1987). Young children's spontaneous personification as analogy. *Child Development 58*: 1013–1020.
Inglehart, R. (1995). Public support for environmental protection: Objective problems and subjective values in 43 societies. *PS: Political Science, 15*, 57–71.
Irons, W. (1998). Adaptively relevant environments versus environment of evolutionary adaptiveness. *Evolutionary Anthropology, 6*, 194–204.
James, W. (1890/1981). *The principles of psychology*. Cambridge, MA: Harvard.
Johnson, C. Y., Bowker, J. M., & Cordell, H. K. (2004). Ethnic variation in environmental belief and behavior. *Environment and Behavior, 36*, 157–186.
Kahn, P. H. (1999). *The human relationship with nature*. Cambridge, MA: MIT Press.
Kahneman, D., (1986). Comments on the contingent valuation method. In: Cummings, R. G., Brookshire, D. S., Schulze, W. D. (Eds.), *Valuing environmental goods: An assessment of the contingent valuation method*. Rowman and Littlefield, Savage, MD.
Kaplan, R. (1993). The role of nature in the context of the workplace. *Landscape and Urban Planning, 26*, 193–201.
Kaplan, R., & Kaplan, S. (1989). *The experience of nature: A psychological perspective*. Cambridge University Press.
Kellert, S. R. (1996). *The value of life: Biological diversity and human society*. Washington, D.C.: Island Press.
Kellert, S., & Wilson, E. O. (1993, Eds.). *The biophilia hypothesis*. Washington, D.C.: Island Press.
Kempton, W., Boster, J., & Hartley, J. (1995). *Environmental values in American culture*. Cambridge, MA: MIT Press.
Kilbourne, W. E., Beckmann, S. C., Lewis, A., & Van Dam, Y. (2001). A multinational examination of the role of the dominant social paradigm in environmental attitudes of university students. *Environment and Behavior, 33*, 209–228.
Kluckhohn, F. R. & Strodtbeck, F. L. (1961). *Variations in value orientations*. Evanston, IL: Row, Peterson.
Korpela, K. M., Hartig, T., Kaiser, F. G., & Fuhrer, U. (2001). Restorative experience and self-regulation in favorite places. *Environment and Behavior, 33*, 572–589.
Manfredo, M. (2008). *Who cares about wildlife?* New York: Springer Press.
Markus, H. R. & Kitayama, S. (1991). Culture and the self: Implications for cognition, emotion and motivation. *Psychological Review, 98*, 224–252.
Massey, C. & Gelman, R. (1988). Preschoolers' ability to decide whether a photographed unfamiliar object can move itself. *Developmental Psychology 24*(3): 307–317.
Medin, D. L. & Atran, S. (2004). The native mind: Biological categorization and reasoning in development and across cultures. *Psychological Review, 111*, 960–983.
Medin, D., Ojalehto, B., Marin, A., & Bang, M. (2013). Culture and epistemologies: putting culture back into the ecosystem. In M. Gelfand, C. Y. Chiu, & Y.-Y. Hong (Eds.), *Advances in Culture and Psychology Series*. New York: Oxford University Press.
Merchant, C. (1980). *The death of nature: Women, ecology, and the scientific revolution*. San Francisco: Harper & Row.
Merchant, C. (1992). *Radical ecology*. New York: Routledge.
Milfont, T. L., & Duckitt, J. (2004). The structure of environmental attitudes: A first- and second-order confirmatory factor analysis. *Journal of Environmental Psychology, 24*, 289–303.

Morrison, D., & Dunlap, R. (1986). Environmentalism and elitism: A conceptual and empirical analysis. *Environmental Management, 10*, 581–589.

Neisser, U. (1988). Five kinds of self-knowledge. *Philosophical Psychology, 1*, 35–59.

Newell, P. (1997). A cross-cultural examination of favorite places. *Environment and Behavior, 29*, 495–514.

Öhman, A., Dimberg, U. & Öst, L.-G. (1985). Animal and social phobias: Biological constraints on learned fear responses. In S. Reiss & R. Bootzin (Eds.), *Theoretical issues in behavior* (pp. 123–175). New York: Academic Press.

O'Regan, J. K. A., Noë, C. (2001). A sensorimotor account of vision and visual consciousness. *Behavioral and Brain Sciences, 24*, 939–1031.

Parker, J. & McDonough, M. (1999). Environmentalism of African Americans: An analysis of the subculture and barriers theories. *Environment and Behavior, 31*, 155–177.

Preston, S. D. & de Waal, F. B. M. (2002). Empathy: Its ultimate and proximate bases. *Behavioral and Brain Sciences, 25*, 1–20.

Rader, N. (1997). Change and variation in responses to perceptual information. In C. Dent-Read & P. Zukow-Goldring (Eds.), *Evolving explanations of development: Ecological approaches to organism-environment systems* (pp. 129–257). Washington, DC: American Psychological Association.

Randall, D. (2007). Perhaps only god can make a tree, but only people could put a dollar value on it. *New York Times, A24*.

Reed, E. S. (1996). *Encountering the world: Toward an ecological psychology*. New York: Oxford University Press.

Rosengren, K. S., Gelman, S. A., Kalish, C. W. & McCormick, M. (1991). As time goes by: Children's early understanding of growth in animals. *Child Development 62*: 1302–1320.

Ross, N., Medin, D., Coley, J. D. & Atran, S. (2003). Cultural and experimental differences in the development of folkbiological induction. *Cognitive Development 81*(1), 25–47.

Sabloff, A. (2001). *Reordering the natural world*. Toronto: University of Toronto Press.

Schultz, P. W. (2001). The structure of environmental concern: Concern for self, other people, and the biosphere. *Journal of Environmental Psychology, 21*, 327–339.

Schultz, P. W., Gamba, R. J., & Unipan, J. B. (2000a). Acculturation and ecological worldview among Latino Americans. *The Journal of Environmental Education, 31*, 22–27.

Schultz, P. W., Zelezny, L., & Dalrymple, N. J. (2000b). A multinational perspective on the relation between Judeo-Christian religious beliefs and attitudes of environmental concern. *Environment and Behavior, 32*, 576–591.

Schwartz, S. H. (1992). Universals in the content and structure of values: Theory and empirical tests in 20 countries. In M. Zanna (ed.), *Advances in Experimental Social Psychology (Vol. 25)*. New York: Academic Press: 1–65.

Sherkat, D., & Ellison, C. (2007). Structuring the religion-environment connection: Identifying religious influences on environmental concern and activism. *Journal for the Scientific Study of Religion, 46*, 71–85.

Simmons, I. (1993). *Interpreting nature: Cultural constructions of the environment*. New York: Routledge.

Steg, L., & Sievers, I. (2000). Cultural theory and individual perceptions of environmental risks. *Environment and Behavior, 32*, 250–269.

Stern, P., Dietz, T., & Guagnano, G. (1995). The new environmental paradigm in social-psychological context. *Environment and Behavior, 27*, 723–743.

Stern, P., Dietz, T., Abel, T., Guagnano, G. & Kalof, L. (1999). A value-belief-norm theory of support for social movements: The case of environmentalism. *Human Ecology Review 6*, 81–97.

Ulrich, R. (1993). Biophilia, biophobia, and natural landscapes. In Kellert, S., & Wilson, E. O. (Eds.). *The biophilia hypothesis* (pp. 73–137). Washington, D.C.: Island Press.

Verbeek, P. & de Waal, F. B. M. (2002). The primate relationship with nature: Biophilia as a general pattern. In P. Kahn & S. Kellert (Eds.) *Children and nature: Psychological, sociocultural and evolutionary investigations* (pp. 1–27). Cambridge, MA: MIT Press.

Vikan, A., Camino, C., Biaggio, A. & Nordvik, H. (2007). Endorsement of the New Ecological Paradigm: A comparison of two Brazilian samples and one Norwegian sample. *Environment and Behavior, 39*, 217–228.

Von Hofsten, C. (1997). On the early development of predictive abilities. In C. Dent-Read & P. Zukow-Goldring (Eds.), *Evolving explanations of development*. Washington, D.C.: American Psychological Association.

White, L. (1967). The historical roots of our ecological crisis. *Science, 155*, 1203–1207.

Williams, K., & Cary, J. (2002). Landscape preferences, ecological quality, and biodiversity protection. *Environment and Behavior, 34*, 257–274.

Wilson, E. O. (1984). *Biophilia*. Cambridge, MA: Harvard University Press

Xiao, C., & Dunlap, R. (2007). Validating a comprehensive model of environmental concern cross-nationally. *Social Science Quarterly, 88*, 471–493.

Zelezny, L, Chua, P., & Aldrich, C. (2000). Elaborating on gender differences in environmentalism. *Journal of Social Issues, 56*, 443–457.

6

Perceptions of Environmental Problems

- **Risk perception**
- **Biases in information processing**
- **Language and discourse**
- **Understanding environmental problems**
- **Attributions of responsibility**
- **Linking perceptions to behavior**
- **Conclusion**
- **References**

Modern environmental scientists may feel like Cassandra: blessed with the ability to foresee the future, but cursed in that no one will believe them. Public perceptions of environmental risks are frequently inconsistent with scientific understandings, with detrimental consequences for the societal response to these risks. The human mind is amazingly effective, but human rationality is imperfect: the way we think is affected by cognitive limits, leading to the use of heuristic shortcuts, and biased by emotions and values. Except in situations where people deliberately engage in sustained and critical inquiry, their understanding of a problem is probably based not on a thorough review of information, but on a selection of information that has been screened through preexisting ideas, shaped by the media and by their social interactions, and interpreted on the basis of personal and cultural biases.

Risk perception

A great deal of research has examined perceptions of environmental threats. In general, people have been shown to be inaccurate at assessing risks, inflating the probabilities of some events and underestimating others (cf. Slovic et al., 1980). Most environmental degradation is not available to human senses. Although an accident at a nuclear power plant or an oil spill may be highly visible, the slow increase in average global temperature or incremental loss of species is not. Thus the human perception of threats is highly subject to biases and dependent on framing. In addition to the impact of scientific information, Leiserowitz (2005) describes public risk perceptions as based on imagery, trust, values, worldview, personal experience, and emotion.

Conservation Psychology: Understanding and promoting human care for nature, Second Edition.
Susan Clayton and Gene Myers.

www.wiley.com\go\clayton\conservation

Information can be obtained from the mass media, but the media also serve to define an issue as important or not through the amount of coverage they give. The more coverage of climate change in the mass media, for example, the greater public concern about the issue (Brulle et al., 2012). Over the past decades, the media have paid increasing attention to environmental issues, so it is not surprising that most people are familiar with environmental problems. For example, in 2013, the Pew Global Attitudes Project reported that more than 50% of over 30,000 people surveyed around the world considered climate change to be a major threat to their country agreement (Pewglobal.org). Not surprisingly, there was substantial variability among countries (see Figure 6.1). Similarly, media coverage of such dramatic environmental disasters as the nuclear meltdown in Chernobyl, the Exxon Valdez oil spill, the Union Carbide toxic gas release in Bhopal, and Hurricane Katrina has sensitized people across the planet to the possibility of environmental threat.

The media can provide information, but they can also frame the issue in misleading ways. Dispensa and Brulle (2003) demonstrated that the US media suggest more uncertainty about anthropogenic climate change than did the media of other advanced nations; a more recent study found that US media still suggest more uncertainty than do the media in Spain, although it seems to be on the rise in both countries (Bailey et al., 2014). Even more directly, an analysis by the Union of Concerned Scientists found that 72% of climate change coverage on the Fox News channel, a conservative news network in the US, was misleading (compared with 30% for CNN and 8% for MSNBC; "Fox News Needs More Science," 2014).

The images people associate with environmental problems largely come from the media, and change over time as the media coverage changes. Smith and Leiserowitz (2012) tracked affective imagery of survey respondents from 2002 through 2010 and found that melting ice was the strongest image in 2002, but decreased over time, whereas the idea of "naysayers" became the modal response in 2010. References to the ozone layer also changed over time, becoming very rare in 2010. Smith and Leiserowitz attribute these effects not only to increased coverage in the media, reducing the tendency for people to confuse global warming with the hole in the ozone layer, but also to the heavy media focus on "climategate" and other attempts to question the

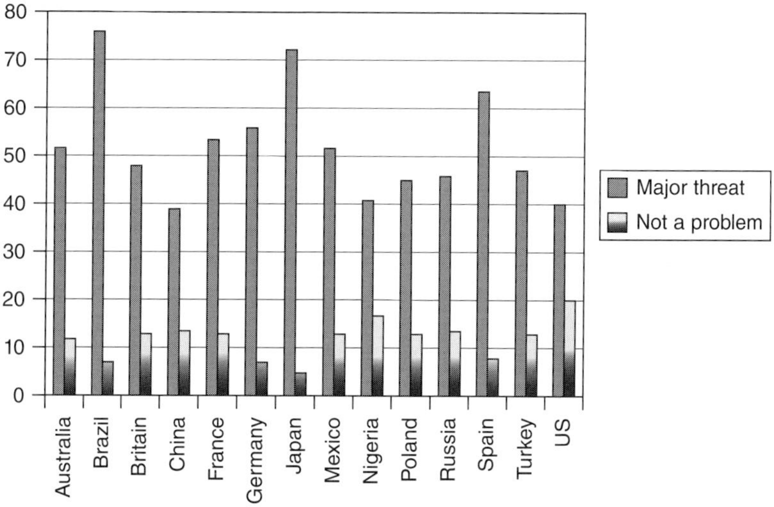

Fig. 6.1 Answers to the question, "Is global warming a problem?" (Based on data from the Pew Global Attitudes Project, 2013.)

credibility of climate scientists. Similarly, survey respondents in Pittsburgh and Seattle knew more about the causes of global warming in 2009 than in 1992, but they also demonstrated increased skepticism and more confusion about the relationship between weather and climate (Reynolds et al., 2010).

Overall, the public in general tends to feel that environmental threats will have a greater impact on the global than on their own local environment (e.g., Broder & Connelly, 2007; Chuk-Ling Lai & Tao, 2003; Leiserowitz, 2005), a phenomenon that is associated with psychological "distance." The distance of an issue can be spatial (the effects will be elsewhere), temporal (the effects will be in the future), social (the effects will be felt by other people), or conceptual (the effects are uncertain). In general, the distance of an issue is negatively related to concern about that issue as well as to preparedness to take action (Spence et al., 2012). Thus, reminding people about environmental impacts that will be sooner, or more local, can lead to greater concern. In an experimental demonstration of this, Arnocky et al. (2014) reduced temporal distance by asking participants to think about themselves 4 years in the future and found that this increased environmental concern, probably by reducing people's tendency to focus on the present. Interestingly, a representative survey of the British population in 2010 suggests that perceptions of climate change are becoming less distant, with more than 50% of the sample describing impacts as likely to be felt locally and 41% saying that impacts are already being felt (Spence et al., 2012).

Studies repeatedly show that laypeople rate environmental risks differently than do scientific or risk professionals. In part, this reflects differential access to information. For this reason, professionals may believe they simply need to impart their knowledge to the public. However, discussions of risk are about more than information; they include a subtext about power, social control, and values (Cvetkovich & Earle, 1992). Where professionals may see an environmental threat as a purely scientific/economic issue, the lay public may also be concerned about ethics, responsibility, and inclusion (Vaughan & Siefert, 1992). Members of the public may also consider outcomes that are not factored into the professionals' assessment. Thus, it is important not to dismiss the fears of the public as simply irrational, or wrong.

Slimak and Dietz (2006) surveyed risk professionals and the general public to find their ratings of 24 environmental threats. In general, the public responded more to things that were of low probability but high consequence (hazardous waste and sewage), whereas risk professionals responded to things that were probable but had incremental impact (global warming, invasive species, loss of wetlands, and decreased biodiversity). People tend to show more fear of technological hazards compared to other environmental risks (e.g., Walsh-Daneshmandi & MacLachlan, 2000), perhaps because the former are more clearly a product of human influence. In a study by Brown et al. (2005), American undergraduates rated an environmental loss as more serious if it was caused by humans than if there was a natural cause. Among human-caused events, those due to growth were considered less serious than those due to carelessness or illegal behavior. In general, people are more willing to accept risks perceived as necessary consequences of countervailing benefits.

Not surprisingly, a greater threat is perceived when people are aware of a risk and perceive the associated consequences as severe (Slovic et al., 1980). Controllability of the risk is also important (Adeola, 2007; Chuk-Ling Lai & Tao, 2003). Hazards that are unfamiliar, unobservable, uncontrollable, and with potentially fatal consequences are more feared than those that do not have these attributes. Increased fearfulness, however, does not always increase risk perception. When an outcome is seen as very threatening and people perceive that there is little they can do about it, they may respond with denial: disbelief or simply choosing not to think about it (Gifford, 2011). We explore this point further below.

People are more likely to be aware of threats that are immediate and/or personally relevant, and thus less psychologically distant. Personal experience, observation, or knowledge; spatial proximity; and length of residence are all associated with recognition of a possible local hazard (Edelstein, 2002; Whitmarsh, 2008). In Texas, driving distance from a creek predicted awareness of environmental problems: those who lived closer were more likely to express concern about the water's safety. Income, length of residence, and gender (male) also predicted awareness, as did general concern about the environment (Brody et al., 2004). Other studies, however, have found women to be more worried about environmental risks than men (Edelstein). Minority groups have also been found to perceive greater environmental risk (Flynn et al., 1994). Minority groups do, on average, experience greater exposure to environmental hazard (Bullard, 2000); in addition, they tend to have lower trust in government and authorities to protect them from these risks (Adeola, 2000).

Unsurprisingly, cultural differences have been found in risk perception. Europeans, for example, are more concerned about genetically modified food than are Americans. Some of this may reflect the fact that national media tend to highlight different issues. Studies that show differences between native-born and foreign-born residents of the US (e.g., Adeola, 2007), however, suggest that differences in risk perception reflect more than the salience of particular threats. Like nature itself, risk is a socially constructed concept. Differences between cultures reflect differences not only in access to information, but also in levels and types of potential harm or exposure, as well as in social trust and faith in technology. The existence of different issue publics, or interpretive communities, indicates the way in which underlying beliefs about science, government, and social relationships affect responses to environmental risks.

A well-documented difference in the perception of environmental problems is that found between members of right-wing and left-wing political groups. For example, in a mail survey of 673 Americans, Leiserowitz (2005) found that a White, male, conservative, religious, anti-egalitarian group represented a distinctive set of "naysayers" concerning the risk of climate change. McCright and Dunlap (2011) replicated this finding in a study of 10 Gallup surveys, with a total sample size of up to 10,000. Borick and Rabe (2010) found that political orientation was the best predictor of attitudes toward climate change in the U.S., outweighing even education; similar results have been found in the United Kingdom (Corner et al., 2012).

Cultural differences in risk perception may reflect more than ingroup bias. Other research has shown that cultural differences in tendencies toward hierarchical and individualistic, as compared to egalitarian and communitarian, worldviews, are associated with different levels of belief about the extent of climate change and the extent to which human behavior is responsible; those who are more individually oriented tend to show less concern (Kahan et al., 2011; Smith & Leiserowitz, 2012). In an Australian sample, Price et al. (2014) found that cultural differences in environmental perceptions were best characterized as a distinction between an individualistic perspective, which emphasized an environment that was elastic and relatively unaffected by humans and a more collective perspective, emphasizing the potential for humans to either harm or protect the environment. This difference was also associated with differences in environmental concern and pro-environmental behavior, which were stronger among people who perceived the environment as responsive to human influence.

Is there such a thing as overall concern about the environment, or do people respond to each issue differently? Xiao and Dunlap (2007), evaluating survey data from the US and Canada, found that there was a single underlying construct that explained responses to eight different aspects of environmental concern, which would suggest a tendency to a general environmental concern. The one exception was that concern for issues affecting the local community showed a distinct pattern, probably indicating the impact of personal experience.

Biases in information processing

Today's media and internet-savvy society provides too much information for anyone to attend to, let alone integrate and apply. Psychologists Herbert Simon and Daniel Kahneman have each, separately, won a Nobel Prize for identifying the limits on human rationality and describing some of the shortcuts, or heuristics, people use to cope with the information overload. Some of these shortcuts may have arisen in regard to adaptive pressures in our early environments, Van Vugt et al. (2014) describe humans as hampered by "stone age biases" such as a tendency toward self-interest, shortsightedness, and a lack of concern about things that cannot be directly perceived.

Unfortunately, these shortcuts and biases can lead us astray. A sample of information processing biases is listed in Table 6.1.

Some of these biases are particularly applicable to environmental issues. For example, people give more weight to a possible loss than a possible gain, a finding that is described in *prospect theory* (Kahneman & Tversky, 1979). When thinking about environmental quality it is worth recognizing that people tend to adapt to an existing state, so that a level of pollution (e.g.,) that may have been inconceivable to a previous generation may be accepted as the status quo by the current generation. The effect is that a move toward sustainability may be seen as an environmental gain, rather than as an avoidance of an environmental loss. Meanwhile, the lifestyle changes that are required may be seen as entailing a cost or perceived decrease in living standard. The loss in comfort is seen as more significant to people than the gain in environmental quality. This is quite clearly illustrated in programs for energy efficiency, where homeowners are less swayed by being informed about the potential gain in savings they could realize through more effective insulation, than by being told about the money they are losing. One program encourages energy companies to describe the loss as "like a basketball-sized hole in your wall" – a phrase that vividly illustrates the loss of heat due to inadequate insulation.

People have a tendency to discount risks whose negative effects will be felt in the distant future – an aspect of psychological distance (Frederick et al., 2002). This tendency to short-term thinking may have a basis in our evolutionary heritage: our ancestors were more likely to survive if they focused on immediate threats and often did not live long enough to benefit from any consideration of long-term outcomes (e.g., Ornstein & Erlich, 1989). People vary in the degree to which they think about the future. Milfont and Gouveia (2006) measured individuals' tendency to consider future consequences in a Brazilian sample and found that people with

Table 6.1 A sample of information processing biases.

Decision-making biases	Probability biases	Social biases
Confirmation bias	Anchoring	Actor-observer bias
Contrast effect	Attentional bias	Egocentric bias
Temporal discounting	Availability	False consensus
Illusion of control	Gambler's fallacy	Fundamental attribution error
Impact bias	Hindsight bias	Halo effect
Information bias	Illusory correlation	Ingroup bias
Loss aversion (sunk costs)	Neglect of base rates	Just-world beliefs
Neglect of probability	Optimism bias	Outgroup homogeneity
Mere exposure	Recency effect	Self-serving bias
Status quo bias	Primacy effect	Self-fulfilling prophecy

a future orientation were more likely to engage in environmentally protective behaviors (see also Arnocky et al., 2014).

A bias whose pervasive influence has been extensively documented is the *availability* heuristic. Estimates of probability are affected by how cognitively available an event is, that is, how easy it is to think of an event. It is easier to think of events that happen more often; to this extent, availability is a useful heuristic. However, it is also easier to think of events that we have personally experienced, events that have been highlighted in the media (even in fictional media, like the movies), and events that have been vividly depicted. Loss of biodiversity is difficult to envision. Global warming, however – thanks in part to Al Gore's award-winning movie, *An Inconvenient Truth* – is not. One of the successes of this movie was in linking vivid images to the consequences of global climate change. Other ways in which availability can lead us astray are demonstrated by research showing that people are more likely to believe in global warming when there has been recent warm weather and even when they are in the presence of dead plants (Borick & Rabe, 2014; Guéguen, 2012).

Because the salience of risks is influenced by the sensory vividness with which they are perceived, the use of vivid imagery of environmental damage may make risks more apparent. Keller et al. (2006) found that providing affect-laden photos of damage from a flood increased the perceived risk of flooding. Similarly, when Meijinders et al. (2001) showed Dutch adults videos with frightening images about the effects of global warming, the participants showed more fear of climate change compared to participants who did not see the videos. In addition, those who saw the frightening images were more affected by the informational content of the video than were those who did not. Meijinders et al. concluded that only the fear induced by the video motivated participants to attend to the information provided.

Caution in the use of threatening or disturbing imagery is warranted because adaptive responses are encouraged by medium levels of arousal, but inhibited by overarousal (Berlyne, 1960). Emotion may encourage attention, but emotional biases may interfere with people's ability to evaluate environmental issues adaptively. These biases can be summarized as the desire to believe that what we want to be true is true, and conversely, the desire not to think about things that we do not want to be true. Winter (2000, Winter & Koger, 2004; see also Gifford, 2011) describes how psychological defenses interfere with the rational perception of environmental realities. Defensive thinking results when our basic wants, such as the desire for comfort and pleasure, are incompatible with our rational or moral judgment. Faced with a conflict between a desire for self-gratification through unsustainable behavior and the knowledge that the environment is threatened by such behavior, we repress our awareness of the conflict, deny the threats that face us, displace them onto other communities, and rationalize our continued unsustainable behavior as having no alternative. Denial and other defensive thinking are particularly likely when people believe they can do nothing to lessen the danger (see further discussion in Chapter 7). Thus, telling people what they can do to reduce a threat is likely to be more effective than emphasizing the magnitude of the threat in getting people to respond to it.

We can understand the role of emotion in risk response through protection–motivation theory, which integrates emotion, stress, and coping (Lazarus, 1966). According to this theory, when a threat is perceived the first step is "threat appraisal": Are valued goals threatened by a high severity and high probability event? Depending on the answer, the threat is appraised as high or low. Next, the person appraises their own ability to respond ("perceived response efficacy") and the costs and benefits of doing so. This "coping appraisal" results in either a high or low sense that one can cope with the threat. Reser and Swim (2011) use this model to examine the way individuals might respond to climate change, noting that both threat appraisals and coping appraisals are affected by social factors. Research by O'Neill et al. (2013) suggests that frightening imagery in communications about climate change may reduce people's perception that there is anything they can do to confront a problem.

The combined result of these two appraisal steps is a choice of coping strategy. If the threat is low, a coping response is unlikely regardless of high or low resources for coping. If the person perceives both high threat and high coping, they will approach the situation in a problem-solving fashion, assessing and deploying resources to deal with the threat, making changes, and acting as needed. If, however, the person perceives high threat and believes they have low coping ability, they will use emotion-focused coping. In emotion-focused coping, the person tries to lessen or tolerate fear, anxiety, and helplessness by emotional means such as avoidance, denial, wishful thinking, religious faith, fatalism, and normalization/desensitization – believing the situation is normal and becoming numb.

Ironically, an experience of environmental contamination, for example, through exposure to toxins in one's neighborhood, may not only increase awareness of and sensitivity to environmental hazards but also result in a perceived loss of control (Edelstein, 2002). Although active attempts to deal with the problem can increase perceived control, the emotional experience may be so strong that denial, which helps to cope with the emotion, may be more likely than problem-focused responses. Because these strategies are self-protective and self-focused, emotional coping strategies generally work against individual or collective problem solving. Based on extensive studies of communities that have experienced environmental contamination, Edelstein (2002) suggests that the formation of local networks may simultaneously help cope with both the unpleasant emotions and the underlying problem, noting substantial evidence that the formation of local groups has psychological benefits for the participants.

Biases in information processing do not represent implacable barriers to effective environmental response. Rather, as argued by Van Vugt et al. (2014), they should be seen as guiding strategies for communicating information effectively. Language allows choices in how to frame environmental problems and decisions and it is important to recognize the ways in which wording can influence people's response to environmental risks.

Language and discourse

To a significant degree, our thinking about nature is affected by our language and the wider social conversations we have about the environment. As explained by Dryzek (1997), environmental discourses arise because of the social nature of environmental problems: that is, the different interests, positions and "shared ways of apprehending the world" (p. 8) that develop as various social actors encounter each other. Discourses persist over time but are also dynamic, interactive, and vary in their dominance. Their dominance comes partly from institutions (legal systems, etc.) that are built around their premises and then persist as social patterns, often by garnering resources. Understanding discourses helps make sense of the complex landscape of environmental issues.

Table 6.2 presents some main discourses discussed by Dryzek, compared according to four key ideas: what are considered the important entities in reality; what is natural (inevitable or intrinsic) in the relations between these entities; who or what are the principal actors and their motivations; and what linguistic devices are most typical of the discourse. As can be seen from Table 6.2, the discourses vary dramatically along these dimensions. "Survivalist" discourses stress scarcity and consequent conflict for control over dwindling resources – conflicts typically dominated by those with power. "Promethean" discourses are confident in the prerogative and promise of economic and technological progress to shape nature or make it obsolete. Other discourses stress the power of different human institutions to produce adaptive responses, although the dynamics and aims differ. The more "ecological" discourses may agree on the complexity of nature and the need for responsive institutions, but they diverge on the fundamental metaphors.

Metaphors are one example of cognitive framing devices. By highlighting some similarities between two things, they also obscure others. Metaphors also have high emotional power because the comparison may evoke fear, disempowerment, supreme confidence, and so on. The importance of cognitive framing in political discourse has been highlighted by linguist Lakoff (2004), and his work has been applied to environmental campaigns (see The Frameworks Institute, http://www.frameworksinstitute.org/). Based on a study of the reactions of people to the "language of conservation," for example, the Nature Conservancy and the Trust for Public Land found that some framings encouraged conservation while others turned people off (Weigel et al., 2004). Referring to "Conservation easements" was less favorable than "Land preservation agreements," the latter connoting a mutual act rather than a legalistic context. This study, as others, found that referring to oneself as an "environmentalist" engendered skepticism and more people identified with the term "conservationist." Typical of social discourses, such connotations and consequently the best framings will vary over time and situation.

A specific impact of language that has been the focus of research is the use of the term "global warming" versus "climate change." Scientists have predominantly been using the term "climate change" both because it is more accurate than the idea of monotonic warming, and also because of a concern that "global warming" sounds positive to people who envision being wrapped in a cuddly blanket. However, recent surveys by the Yale Project on Climate Change Communication (Leiserowitz et al., 2014) have found that, at least in the United States, respondents were more likely to say global warming was a bad thing, it would lead to greater harm, and they were more worried about it, compared to climate change. They also gave it higher political priority.

Understanding environmental problems

As shown by the confusion over the terms global warming and climate change, recognizing a threat does not always mean understanding that threat. Past research, for example, found that many Americans confuse global climate change with ozone depletion, although this seems to be less true today (Bord et al., 2000; Kempton et al., 1995; Leiserowitz & Smith, 2010). Interestingly, Bord et al. found that an accurate understanding of the causes of global warming was not related to a belief that global warming exists – misinformation about causes was just as predictive of a belief in global warming. However, accurate information was the best predictor of an intention to do something about it. A 2012 review of environmental knowledge showed that it was very uneven, with some understanding but many gaps (Robelia & Murphy).

It is not surprising that people's views of nature appear fairly simplistic. Coyle (2005) reported poor performance by American adults on the National Environmental Education and Training Foundation's 12-question environmental "report card," administered in 1997 and 2000 to random national samples (NEETF & Roper, 2001). Only 28%, for example, knew that nonpoint sources (runoff) cause most water pollution rather than factories. Only 41% could recognize the correct definition of biodiversity, and 53% chose the correct primary benefit of wetlands. If nine correct answers (75%) were considered "passing," then 33% achieved this fairly low hurdle. (See further discussion of environmental knowledge in Chapter 11.) Further complicating public understanding of ecology is the changing and complex nature of the field. Coyle notes that 80% of adults are influenced by outdated or incorrect

Table 6.2 Environmental discourses.

Discourse	Basic entities recognized or constructed	Assumptions about natural relationships	Agents and their motives	Key metaphors and rhetorical devices
Survivalism	Finite resources Carrying capacity Population Elites	Hierarchy and control	Elites Motivation "up for grabs"	Overshoot Collapse Commons Spaceship earth Doom and redemption
Promethean	Nature as only brute matter Markets, Prices Energy Innovation	Hierarchy of humans over all else Competition	Everyone Material self-interest	Mechanistic Technology
Administrative rationalism	Liberal capitalism Administrative state Experts Managers	Nature subordinate to humans People subordinate to state Experts and managers	Experts and managers Motivated by public interest, defined in unitary terms	Mixture of concern and reassurance The administrative mind
Democratic pragmatism	Liberal capitalism Liberal democracy Citizens	Equality among citizens Political relationships Cooperation Competition	Many different agents Material self-interest Multiple conceptions of public interest	Public policy as a result of forces Policy like scientific experimentation Feedback
Economic rationalism	"*Homo economicus*" Markets Prices Property Governments (not citizens)	Competition Hierarch based on expertise Subordination of nature	Self-interest Government officials motivated by public interest	Mechanistic Stigmatizing of regulation Freedom Horror stories

Sustainable development	Nested social and ecological systems Capitalist economy Limits?	Subordination of nature Economic growth, environmental protection, distributive justice	Many agents at different levels, notably transnational and local rather than the state Public good	Organic growth Progress Reassurance
Green romanticism	Global limits Inner nature Nature Unnatural practices Ideas	Natural relationships between humans and nature which have been violated Equality with nature	Human subjects, some more ecologically conscious than others Agency exists in nature too	Many biological and organic metaphors Passion Intuition
Green rationalism	Global limits Nature as complex ecosystems Rational humans Institutional structures	Equality among people Complex interconnections	Many individual and collective actors Multidimensional motivation Agency in nature downplayed	Organic metaphors Appeals to reason Potential rationality of social structures Progress

Source: Combined from tables in Dryzek (1997).

environmental beliefs. Within ecology the very idea that we can demarcate "ecosystems" is contested, although it is fundamental to the methods many ecologists use. Unless the public understands the role of these debates in scientific inquiry, the effect may be for people to feel even less inclined to rely on scientists to determine what is and is not natural.

Attributions of responsibility

Regardless of how people perceive environmental threats, the impact of this perception will be moderated by their perception of who is responsible for addressing them, as indicated by the fourth column of Table 6.2. Among a sample of German adults, Böhm (2003) found that people feel neither personally responsible nor personally threatened by environmental risks, overall. Surveys suggest that although people are willing to take some action to address environmental problems, they perceive the primary responsibility as lying with the government (e.g., Broder & Connelly, 2007). For example, among a representative sample of 1400 Americans in 1997 and 1998, a large majority (77%) believed in the existence of global warming. Fifty-nine percent said that the US government should do something to address the problem (similar proportions said US business and foreign governments should do something to address it). Only 44% said the average person should do something to deal with global warming (Krosnick et al., 2000). Bord et al. (2000), surveying Americans, found that, while people were willing to make some behavioral choices that were affected by environmental problems – about 60–70% said they might buy more a more fuel-efficient car or more energy-efficient appliances – only a small percentage would actually compromise their comfort, for example, by reducing their use of air-conditioning (42%) or driving less (31%). Similarly, a recent New York Times/CBS News poll found that 92% of Americans favor requiring car manufacturers to produce more energy-efficient cars, but only 38% support an increase in the gasoline tax (Broder & Connelly, 2007).

For some groups or cultures, causal attributions include the possibility of divine will. Among some religious groups in the US and elsewhere, the earth is considered to be outside the realm of human influence. When changes in climate (if any) are attributed to a divinity, people are unlikely to take action to mitigate those changes (Broder, 2010; Lata & Nunn, 2012).

Environmental problems are sometimes described using the metaphor of the "commons dilemma." First discussed by Hardin (1968), the commons dilemma refers to a situation in which members of a group benefit from a common resource. Because individuals do not pay for this resource, rational self-interest would lead each person to maximize his or her use of the resource. Such behavior has direct benefits for the individual while the cost of any individual's behavior, dispersed across the whole group, is insignificant. If many individuals take this behavioral approach, however, the outcome is overuse and depletion of the resource to the detriment of all. This pattern can be seen when individuals maximize their consumption of limited environmental resources such as fossil fuels, clean water, and wild-caught fish. People recognize the finite nature of the resource but do not feel personally responsible for maintaining it, and in the absence of similar curtailment by all, attempts to limit use represent a short-term sacrifice for the individual without any long-term benefit for the group. (See Chapter 10 for discussion of recent literature on the commons.)

Attempts to encourage sustainable behavior, however, are not futile. Research has shown that individuals are capable of acting in a coordinated fashion to maintain a group resource. Milinski et al. (2008) described an experiment in which people were more willing to cooperate to prevent simulated dangerous climate change when the risks of not cooperating were highest;

they suggested the importance of effectively informing people about the dangers that are faced. However, there was still a high rate of noncooperation. Regulations limiting individual use are one way of coping with the tendency toward unsustainable use. Another is to foster a sense of collective identity, which enhances the salience and value of collective well-being and may promote a sense of shared responsibility for that well-being (Kramer & Brewer, 1984). Individuals who feel highly identified with their group are more likely to voluntarily limit their own use of a collective resource in order to protect that resource for the group. This may be particularly relevant for environmental issues, which tend to promote or elicit a group-level identity (Clayton, 1998, 2000).

Linking perceptions to behavior

Both theorists and practitioners are often disappointed by the low correlation between knowledge and action. As described in Chapter 5, attitudes, such as concern about the environment, are based in part – but only in part – on perceptions and beliefs (both classified as internal representations of information), such as a perception that the environment is at risk. General tendencies toward environmental concern, in turn, may show only a limited relationship with pro-environmental actions. Several models have been developed to elucidate the links between attitudes and behavior. Ajzen (1991) formulated the Theory of Planned Behavior (TPB) in order to provide a more complete explanatory model. According to TPB, behavior is partly a function of salient attitudes, but it is also shaped by many other forces. Many causes of behavior are unintended: sometimes we have no control over our behavior, or we behave automatically in response to situational cues or habit. Behavioral intentions, however, are more internally governed. The three antecedents of behavioral intention are attitude, subjective norms, and perceived control. Attitudes, as described above, are a function of beliefs about attributes associated with the attitude object and evaluation of those attributes. Subjective norms, or normative beliefs, are concerned with the likelihood that important referent individuals or groups approve or disapprove of performing a given behavior. Perceived behavioral control refers to people's beliefs about the ease or difficulty in performing the behavior. It has been found that intentions predict behavior with a large amount of accuracy when there are not serious problems of control.

Attitudes are more likely to affect behavior when they are strong, based on personal experience, and salient. Even a strongly held attitude will be ineffective when its relevance is unclear or when other forces are stronger. Thus, many environmentalists engage in unsustainable behaviors when the environmental impacts of those behaviors is not apparent, when social norms are too strong, or when the actor does not perceive him or herself as having control over the behavior. The complex relationship between attitudes and behavior was illustrated in an analysis of an international dataset with 22,000 respondents by Brechin and Kempton (1994), who found a positive but nonsignificant correlation between willingness to pay for environmental protection and affluence, but a negative and highly significant relation between willingness to volunteer time and affluence. In other words, people in poor countries have no control over economic solutions because they do not have the money to pay for them. However, they nonetheless perceive economic problems as severe, and are willing to invest the resource they do have – time – in their solution.

The Values–Beliefs–Norms (VBN) model (Stern, 2000; Stern et al., 1999) was developed to describe how values are linked to pro-environmental behaviors. According to the VBN model, environmental values influence general beliefs or worldview about the environment, which

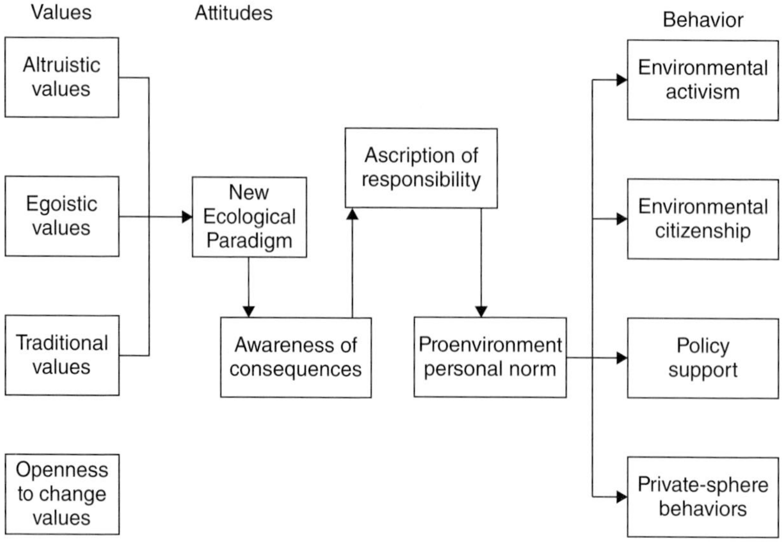

Fig. 6.2 From Stern et al. (1999).

influence beliefs about the consequences of environmental change for valued objects as well as one's perceived ability and responsibility to take action, which in turn influence personal norms about taking action. Thus, values affect perceptions, both of consequences and of responsibility, and perceptions in turn affect behavior, but only through the mediating variable of personal norm. "Personal environmental norms," or "the belief that the individual and other social actors have an obligation to alleviate environmental problems" (Stern et al., 1999, p. 91), were the one important factor across different types of behavior. (The next two chapters, on morality and identity, are relevant to the idea of personal norms.) Although values may have only a small impact on any given behavioral decision, their potential range of effect is quite large (see Figure 6.2).

Manfredo and Teel (2008) used a version of the VBN model to test values and attitudes toward wildlife. Consistent with the model, they found that values affected attitudes, which in turn predicted behavior. Chapter 9 presents a more thorough discussion of the role of values in affecting environmental behavior.

Conclusion

The large majority of people worldwide recognize the existence of threats to the environment, although many are misinformed about the specific nature of these threats or actions that can be taken to ameliorate them. Because of the ways in which specific groups filter their perceptions of threat through existing worldviews, cognitive heuristics, and emotional biases, it will take more than scientific information to redress this problem. Research suggests that there is often little or no difference in information between supporters and opponents of a technology (Freudenberg & Pastor, 1992). In order to understand the basis for the ways in which people think and care about nature, we need to take into account the social contexts and discourses within which information is received, interpreted, and constructed.

The link between attitudes or other cognitive constructs, on the one hand, and behavior, on the other, is typically weak or indirect. The way people think about the natural environment is important in understanding general tendencies, but it is not necessarily the key influence on any specific behavior affecting the environment. In Chapter 9, we discuss some of the other factors that affect environmentally relevant behavior and that may be amenable to influence.

References

"Fox News Needs More Science" (2014). *Earthwise* [the newsletter of the Union of Concerned Scientists]. Available at www.ucusa.org/scienceorspin.

Adeola, F. O. (2000). Endangered community, enduring people: Toxic contamination, health, and adaptive responses in a local context. *Environment and Behavior*, *32*, 209–249.

Adeola, F. O. (2007). Nativity and environmental risk perception: An empirical study of native-born and foreign-born residents of the USA. *Human Ecology Review*, *14*, 13–25.

Ajzen, I. (1991). The theory of planned behavior. *Organizational Behavior and Human Decision Processes*, *50*, 179–211.

Arnocky, S., Milfont, T., & Nicol, J. (2014). Time perspective and sustainable behavior: Evidence for the distinction between consideration of immediate and future consequences. *Environment and Behavior*, *46*, 556–582.

Bailey, A., Giangola, L., & Boykoff, M. (2014). How grammatical choice shapes media representations of climate (un)certainty. *Environmental Communication*, *8*, 197–215.

Berlyne, D. E. (1960). *Conflict, arousal and curiosity*. New York: McGraw-Hill.

Böhm, G. (2003). Emotional reactions to environmental risks. *Journal of Environmental Psychology*, *23*, 199–212.

Bord, R. J., O'Connor, R. E., & Fisher, A. (2000). In what sense does the public need to understand global climate change? *Public Understanding of Science*, *9*, 205–218.

Borick, C., & Rabe, B. (2010). A reason to believe: Examining the factors that determine individual belief in global warming. *Social Science Quarterly*, *91*, 777–800.

Borick, C., & Rabe, B. (2014). Weather or not? Examining the impact of meteorological conditions on public opinion regarding global warming. *Weather Climate and Society*, *6*, 413–424.

Brechin, S. R. & Kempton, W. (1994). Global environmentalism: A challenge to the postmaterialism thesis? *Social Science Quarterly 75*, 245–269.

Broder, J. (2010). Skepticism on climate change is article of faith for tea party. *New York Times*, A1, A4.

Broder, J. & Connelly, M. (2007). Public says warming is a problem, but remains split on response. *New York Times*, A23.

Brody, S. D., Highfield, W., & Alston, L. (2004). Does location matter?: Measuring environmental perceptions of creeks in two San Antonio watersheds. *Environment and Behavior*, *36*, 229–250.

Brown, T. C., Peterson, G. L., Marc Brodersen, R., Ford, V., & Bell, P. A. (2005). The judged seriousness of an environmental loss is a matter of what caused it. *Journal of Environmental Psychology*, *25*, 13–21.

Brulle, R., Carmichael, J., & Jenkins, J. C. (2012). Shifting public opinion on climate change: An empirical assessment of factors influencing concern over climate change in the U.S., 2002–2010. *Climatic Change*, *114*, 169–188.

Bullard, R. D. (2000). *Dumping in Dixie: Race, class, and environmental quality*. San Francisco: Westview Press.

Chuk-ling Lai, J., & Tao, J. (2003). Perception of environmental hazards in Hong Kong Chinese. *Risk Analysis*, *23*, 669–684.

Clayton, S. (1998). Preference for macrojustice versus microjustice in environmental decisions. *Environment and Behavior*, *30*,162–183.

Clayton, S. (2000). Models of justice in the environmental debate. *Journal of Social Issues*, *56*, 459–474.

Corner, A., Whitmarsh, L., & Xenias, D. (2012). Uncertainty, skepticism, and attitudes towards climate change: Biased assimilation and attitude polarization. *Climatic Change*, *114*, 463–478.

Coyle, K. (2005). *Environmental literacy in America*. Washington DC: NEETF.
Cvetkovich, G., & Earle, T. (1992). Environmental hazards and the public. *Journal of Social Issues, 48*, 1–20.
Dispensa, J., & Brulle, R. (2003). Media's social construction of environmental issues. *International Journal of Sociology and Social Policy, 23*, 74–105.
Dryzek, J. S. (1997). *The politics of the earth: Environmental discourses*. Oxford: Oxford University Press.
Edelstein, M. (2002). Contamination: The invisible built environment. In R. Bechtel & A. Churchman (Eds.), *Handbook of environmental psychology* (pp. 559–588). New York: Wiley.
Flynn, J., Slovic, P., & Mertz, C. (1994). Gender, race, and perception of environmental health risks. *Risk Analysis, 14*, 1101–1108.
Frederick, S., Loewenstein, G., & O'Donoghue, T. (2002). Time discounting and time preference: A critical review. *Journal of Economic Literature, 40*, 351–401.
Freudenberg, W., & Pastor, S. (1992). NIMBYs and LULUs: Stalking the syndromes. *Journal of Social Issues, 48*, 39–61.
Gifford, R. (2011). The dragons of inaction: Psychological barriers that limit climate change mitigation and adaptation. *American Psychologist, 66*, 290–302.
Guéguen, N. (2012). Dead indoor plants strengthen belief in global warming. *Journal of Environmental Psychology, 32*, 173–177.
Hardin, G. (1968). The tragedy of the commons. *Science, 162*, 1243–1248.
Kahan, D., Jenkins-Smith, H., & Braman, D. (2011). Cultural cognition of scientific consensus. *Journal of Risk Research, 14*, 147–174.
Kahneman, D., & Tversky, A. (1979). Prospect theory: An analysis of decisions under risk. *Econometrica, 47*, 313–327.
Keller, C., Siegrist, M., & Gutscher, H. (2006). The role of the affect and availability heuristics in risk communication. *Risk Analysis, 26*, 631–639.
Kempton, W., Boster, J., & Hartley, J. (1995). *Environmental values in American culture*. Cambridge, MA: MIT Press.
Kramer, R. & Brewer, M. (1984). Effects of group identity on resource use in a simulated commons dilemma. *Journal of Personality and Social Psychology, 46*, 1044–1057.
Krosnick, J. A., Holbrook, A. L., & Visser, P. S. (2000). The impact of the fall 1997 debate about global warming on American public opinion. *Public Understanding of Science, 9*, 239–260.
Lakoff, G. (2004). *Don't think of an elephant!*. White River Junction, VT: Chelsea Green.
Lata, S., & Nunn, P. (2012). Misperceptions of climate-change risk as barriers to climate-change adaptation: A case study from the Rewa Delta, Fiji. *Climatic Change, 110*, 169–186.
Lazarus, R. (1966). *Psychological stress and the coping process*. New York: McGraw-Hill.
Leiserowitz, A. (2005). American risk perceptions: Is climate change dangerous? *Risk Analysis, 25*, 1433–1442.
Leiserowitz, A., & Smith, N. (2010). *Knowledge of climate change across global warming's Six Americas*. New Haven, CT: Yale University Project on Climate Change Communication.
Leiserowitz, A., Feinberg, G., Rosenthal, S., Smith, N., Anderson A., Roser-Renouf, C. & Maibach, E. (2014). *What's in a name? Global warming vs. climate change. Yale University and George Mason University*. New Haven, CT: Yale Project on Climate Change Communication.
Manfredo, M., & Teel, T. (2008). Integrating concepts: Demonstration of a multi-level model for exploring the rise of mutualism value orientations in post-industrial society. In M. Manfredo, *Who cares about wildlife?* New York: Springer Press.
McCright, A. & Dunlap, R. (2011). Cool dudes: The denial of climate change among conservative White males in the United States. *Global Environmental Change, 21*, 1163–1172.
Meijinders, A., Midden, C., & Wilke, H. (2001). Role of negative emotion in communication about CO_2 risks. *Risk Analysis, 21*, 955–966.
Milfont, T. L. & Gouveia, V. (2006). Time perspective and values: An exploratory study of their relations to environmental attitudes. *Journal of Environmental Psychology, 26*, 72–82.

Milinski, M., Sommerfeld, R., Krambeck, H., Reed, F., & Marotzke, J. (2008). The collective-risk social dilemma and the prevention of simulated dangerous climate change. *Proceedings of the National Academy of Sciences, 105*, 2291–2294.

National Environmental Education and Training Foundation (NEETF) & Roper Starch Worldwide. (2001). *Lessons from the environment: The ninth annual national report card on environmental attitudes, knowledge, and behavior*. Washington DC: NEETF.

O'Neill, S., Boykoff, M., Niemeyer, S., & Day, S. (2013). On the use of imagery for climate change engagement. *Global Environmental Change, 23*(2), 413–421.

Ornstein, R & Ehrlich, P. (1989). *New world/new mind: Moving toward conscious evolution*. New York: Doubleday.

Price, J., Walker, I., & Boschetti, F. (2014). Measuring cultural values and beliefs about environment to identify their role in climate change responses. *Journal of Environmental Psychology, 37*, 8–20.

Reser, J., & Swim, J. (2011). Adapting to and coping with the threat and impacts of climate change. *American Psychologist, 66*, 277–289.

Reynolds, T., Bostrom, A., Read, D., & Morgan, G. M. (2010). Now what do people know about global climate change? Survey studies of educated laypeople. *Risk Analysis, 30*, 1520–1538.

Robelia, B., & Murphy, T. (2012). What do people know about key environmental issues? A review of environmental knowledge surveys. *Environmental Education Research, 18*, 299–321.

Slimak, M. W., & Dietz, T. (2006). Personal values, beliefs, and ecological risk perception. *Risk Analysis, 26*, 1689–1705.

Slovic, P., Fischoff, B., & Lichtenstein, S. (1980). Facts and fears: Understanding perceived risk. In R. Schwing & W. Albers, Jr., (Eds.), *Societal risk assessment: How safe is safe enough?* New York: Plenum.

Smith, N., & Leiserowitz, A. (2012). The rise of global warming skepticism: Exploring affective image associations in the United States over time. *Risk Analysis, 32*, 1021–1032.

Spence, A., Poortinga, W., & Pidgeon, N. (2012). The psychological distance of climate change. *Risk Analysis, 32*, 957–972.

Stern, P. (2000). Toward a coherent theory of environmentally significant behavior. *Journal of Social Issues, 56*, 407–424.

Stern, P., Dietz, T., Abel, T., Guagnano, G. & Kalof, L. (1999). A value-belief-norm theory of support for social movements: The case of environmentalism. *Human Ecology Review, 6*(2), 81–97.

Van Vugt, M., Griskevicius, V., & Schultz, P. W. (2014). Naturally green: Harnessing Stone Age psychological biases to foster environmental behavior. *Social Issues and Policy Review, 8*, 1–32.

Vaughan, E., & Siefert, M. (1992). Variability in the framing of risk issues. *Journal of Social Issues, 48*, 119–136.

Walsh-Daneshmandi, A., & MacLachlan, M. (2000). Environmental risk to the self. *Journal of Environmental Psychology, 20*, 141–149.

Weigel, L., Fairbank, J. & Metz, D. (2004). Lessons learned regarding the "Language of conservation". Memorandum to the Nature Conservancy and the Trust for Public Land. Denver CO: Public Opinion Strategies & Santa Monica, CA: Fairbank, Maslin, Maullin & Assoc.

Whitmarsh, L. (2008). Are flood victims more concerned about climate change than other people? The role of direct experience in risk perception and behavioural response. *Journal of Risk Research, 11*, 351–374.

Winter, D. (2000). Some big ideas for some big problems. *American Psychologist, 55*, 516–522.

Winter, D., & Koger, S (2004). *The psychology of environmental problems*. Mahwah, New Jersey: Erlbaum.

Xiao, C., & Dunlap, R. (2007). Validating a comprehensive model of environmental concern cross-nationally. *Social Science Quarterly, 88*, 471–493.

7

Moral Psychology and the Environment

> One of the real mistakes in the conservation movement in the last few years is the tendency to see nature simply as natural resources: use it or lose it. Yet, conservation without moral values cannot sustain itself. Unless we reach people through beauty, ethics, spiritual, or religious values or whatever, we are not going to keep our wilderness areas.
>
> George Schaller, Field biologist (Michael Bond Interview: Feral and free. *New Scientist 2598*, 05 April 2007, page 46–47)

Morality is a significant element of both attitudes and behavior toward the natural environment. Change will need to rely on ethics and not just self-interest. Although every human alive has some stake in environmental health, those with the greatest stake include future human generations and other species, as well as people who may lack the economic and political resources for effective action. Thus, conservation requires people who may not feel a direct effect of environmental change to nonetheless become morally aroused and activated. Such people feel a personal responsibility that reaches beyond self-interest to the expression of deep moral values. As we saw in Chapter 5, many people feel that environmental issues have a moral component. This chapter considers the meaning and psychological implications of such a perspective.

Background on ethical concepts

Ethics and morality are terms with complex and overlapping use. "Ethics" often refers to a more formal or philosophical approach, and morality has more "real life" flavor, whether behavioral,

Conservation Psychology: Understanding and promoting human care for nature, Second Edition.
Susan Clayton and Gene Myers.

www.wiley.com\go\clayton\conservation

psychological, or religious in emphasis. Both terms are concerned with ideas of right and wrong; with good and bad actions, outcomes, and/or intentions. What makes something a matter of morals or ethics is that it is evaluated by proscriptive or prescriptive norms. Something proscribed is forbidden or not permitted, whereas something prescribed is a matter of duty or obligation. In addition, some actions are considered supererogatory, or discretionary: these are praiseworthy actions that are considered "beyond the call of duty." Thus, out of the wide set of possible behaviors, many of which are morally "neutral," morality endows some with special significance. Another criterion of ethics is that these judgments – proscriptive, obligatory, or discretionary – are justified by appeal to human welfare, justice, or other moral values. Many ethical theories further hold that for something to be moral, it must be generalizable, applicable in principle across human groups, and not rooted in power, convention, or mere personal preference.

The different traditions of ethical thought include virtue ethics; deontological or duty-centered conceptions; consequentialist including utilitarian approaches; and ethical pragmatism. Each offers unique perspectives and potentials regarding environmental ethics and each entails somewhat different psychological considerations. In recent years, a new and particularly psychological view of morality has received attention. We will introduce it briefly here.

Social intuitionism and moral foundations theory

This perspective on moral psychology brings together strands from cultural, social, evolutionary, and comparative psychology, social–cognitive neuroscience, emotion research, classical sociology, and the philosophy of David Hume to inspire a distinct research agenda with a broadly descriptive approach. The Moral Foundations Theory (MFT) developed by psychologists Jonathan Haidt and colleagues (key papers include Haidt, 2001, 2007, 2012; Haidt & Graham, 2007; Haidt & Joseph, 2004, 2007) suggests that the close-knit groups in which humans evolved presented five morally relevant threats and related opportunities in social life, giving rise to universal mental "modules" dedicated to detecting these issues. The five, described by positive and negative poles are care/harm, fairness/cheating, loyalty/betrayal, authority/subversion, and sanctity/degradation. Each has its adaptive challenges, original and current triggers, characteristic emotions, and relevant virtues. For example, the original adaptive challenge of the care/harm root is concern for one's children, triggered by signs of distress of neediness and resulting in feelings of compassion and virtues of kindness. Today, we may also feel this response to the plight of (especially "cute") animals in harm's way. Because the temptation to cheat, inevitable in close-knit groups, could cause rifts, groups with a sense of fairness to counter this tendency would on the whole do better than groups that allowed extensive cheating. Fairness and reciprocity are regarded as important in situations of environmental wrong and redress. Loyalty keeps us in cohesive groups, defending them when threatened and engendering pride when they succeed; it is now attached to nations and sports teams as well as to "sides" in social-environmental issues. Sensitivity to authority is hypothesized to be important in forming beneficial hierarchical relations, common across social species. Respect and fear are the relevant emotional springs. Sanctity and sensitivity to degradation, associated with feelings of chastity or piety on the one hand, and disgust on the other, originally evolved to avoid contact with waste and disease and have been extended today to taboo ideas or social groups. Recently, Haidt (2012) has added a sixth foundation: liberation/oppression, an adaptive response to living in small groups where individuals may dominate or constrain others. It was originally triggered by signs of attempted domination and currently by abuse of political power or wealth. Its characteristic emotions are reactance, resentment, an urge to band together, and its relevant virtues include equality and freedom.

These modules are not necessarily specific to morality (Gigerenzer, 2010; Cushman & Young, 2011). Care/harm, for example is related closely to empathy, and concern about harm may be felt even when we know that the apparent harm (e.g., a surgeon's cuts) are for the good. Results from Haidt's Moral Foundations Questionnaire taken by Americans across the political spectrum showed that liberals elevate the care and justice dimensions but not the other moral foundations. People at the conservative end, however, gave almost equal weight to all five, giving insight into the American culture wars (although Frimer et al. (2013) found that liberals and conservatives did not differ in their evaluations of a set of morally exemplary figures). Loyalty, authority, and sanctity are, despite their potential for abuse, values that give societies valuable stability. Compared to some other bases for action, morality is more pluralistic, and thus has more room for disagreement about the good. Haidt's synthesis helps us understand the cultural diversity in moral codes.

MFT can be clarified by examining three core principles. One is simply that morality gave evolutionary advantage, particularly when indirect reciprocity, reputation, and low-cost informal punishment such as shunning are considered. The moral foundations (especially loyalty) bind and build us into teams. Cohesive teams can polarize people and "fellow-feeling" may mean out-grouping and exclusion from the scope of justice. Nonetheless, suppressing self-interest and following in the group's interest is essential to morality.

Second is "intuitive primacy." The five foundations are felt as rapid affective judgments in response to stimuli. Research demonstrates that 6- to 10-month-old infants understand helping behavior directed toward another, and prefer helper versus hinderer puppets, clearly well before they can articulate the basis for this preference. Experimental studies show people make moral judgments fast. This does not mean, however, that there is no cognition involved. Rather, it is fast "hot" cognition driven by a combination of one of the "innately specified" modules plus learned associations – culturally revisable prototypes. What people do *not* typically do is take time to reason through the different facets of right action or what will accomplish the greatest good before generating a moral response. Haidt (2001) demonstrated this in "moral dumbfounding" in experiments where subjects knew something was morally wrong even when they could not explain why. Not only did they not think first, but also they were at a loss entirely to explain their responses. Understanding such emotional wellsprings of moral behavior is one of Haidt's generative contributions.

The third main principle concerns what moral reasoning is really about. It is, in Haidt's view, used almost completely *ex post facto* for social persuasion, or rationalizing. One virtue of Haidt's work is how he leverages this model to show how readily we reach positions of moral righteousness, and how stubbornly we leave them. The theory also fits closely with dual process models such as Kahneman's (2011) synthesis (see also Chapters 6 and 10), which includes many other elements of fast intuitive processing such as confirmation bias that play into Haidt's account.

It is important to note several criticisms of this MFT/social intuitionist account (Gibbs, 2014). First, it is problematic to simply describe how people are, or how they treat "morality" and take that as a sufficient description of the domain. Haidt stresses that his is only a descriptive account, offered as a reminder of diversity, blindspots, and the importance of social cohesion rather as a normative ethical theory. In addition, it lacks a clear developmental account. On the one hand, its developmental account is nativist: evolved-in adaptive modules, whose shape in infants is taken to be an adequate description of the elicited intuition in older individuals. On the other hand, it suggests oversimplified socialization or internalization, the child acquiring the local social norms, that is, specifications of the five modules as given in his or her community.

Most importantly, missing from this is the understanding we have of how moral reasoning develops, which is not through internalization (a more nuanced account of which is given by Hoffman, 2000). It is not only through dispassionate linear calculation that reason enters the picture. The constructivist tradition shows how in childhood and later, mental schemas develop ahead of our awareness of them, synthesized by the active mind in interaction with the environment. Development can occur in jumps to new schemas of understanding that subsume and surpass the old. As it turns out, the developmental pattern, particularly the higher reaches of development, has prescriptive implications (Gibbs, 2014). Children recognize fairly early that there is such a thing as "the right" – and it depends on the cognitive achievements of understanding accuracy, noncontradiction, and reversibility (that "something I would find unacceptable if done to me is therefore not acceptable to be done to you"). These cognitive qualities of fairness allow us to distinguish distorted from "veridical" morality across all of Haidt's categories. This means that a full description of human morality must be oriented in the normative dimension.

Haidt's reduction of morality to group loyalty, primitive intuitions, and social persuasion ignores the above features of the rational mind, which need to be part of a complete description of human morality. A component of this is a better description of the corrective power of reason. Just as there are a variety of ways affect influences higher-level cognition (Blanchette & Richards, 2010) so too reasoning can independently produce a moral judgment. Functional MRI (fMRI) studies have shown that if sufficient conflict between intuitive thinking and deliberation is produced by a scenario, the choice is taken up by our deliberative intellect. Then brain areas dealing with reasoning, conflict and cognitive control dominate the process to the end (Greene et al., 2004). Consciousness may provide a working model of our memories, current social and emotional understandings, and evaluation of options in future decisions (Baumeister & Masicampo, 2010). Conscious thought is affected by unconscious System 1 processes, but in revealing ways. For people whose minds are made up about an issue, their conscious beliefs predict their later choices. For others who are undecided, however, nonconscious associations at time 1 predict both conscious thoughts and choices at time 2 (Galdi et al., 2008, cited in Keltner et al., 2014). As noted, Gibbs (2014) stresses how internally driven *moral development* brings new integrations into consciousness. Kahneman notes that investment of attention and effort in an activity improves performance on many tasks and is essential for comparison, choice, and ordered reasoning, although these are limited by available knowledge and errors in reasoning. Despite the fact System 1 thoughts (e.g., fast moral intuitions) do not generate warning signals when they are wrong, it is possible to recognize when you are in a "cognitive minefield, slow down, and ask for reinforcement from System 2" (Kahneman, 2011, p. 417). Being able to name our cognitive biases and familiarity with their conditions and dispositions can help with diagnosing them.

Finally, while Haidt's work and his explicit recommendations encourage an increase in tolerance and open-mindedness, the theory may not evade charges of ethical relativism (which Haidt claims to eschew). Ethical relativism is no longer tenable, as discussed later. And this is a point on which psychologists of both deontic and consequentialist approaches to moral psychology agree; Hoffman explained: "We no longer have the luxury of assuming every culture's values or guiding principles will pass the moral test and that each is as good as any other" (2000, p. 273).

Descriptive and/or evolutionary psychology-inspired approaches to moral psychology have invigorated and diversified the field, although it will take more research before a clearer picture is attained. Although little has been directly applied to environmental topics per se, we will point out some important intersections in the following discussions. And there are some general points we can make here. First is to realize that environmentalists have their own moral codes, which probably unconsciously contain elements that reverberate with loyalty, authority, and purity. Haidt suggests that every moral "matrix" has something sacred at its core (2012, p. 330): a sacred or "protected" value believed to possess infinite or transcendental significance that precludes trade-offs or comparisons. These cannot be defended rationally, and so are held only intuitively. Thus considering compromises, as might a utilitarian approach, can disqualify someone who treats those values as fungible (Tetlock, 2003). For example, some environmentalists may feel that it is impermissible to even consider whether any amount of monetary oil income could compensate for damage done to the Arctic National Wildlife Refuge. To even propose the idea is outrageous. A survey of conservation professional identified several "taboo" actions for managing endangered species under climate change adaptation (Hagerman & Satterfield, 2014). Nature and certain exemplars of it especially have incommensurable value. Liberals, Haidt has pointed out, apply purity/degradation to the relation of food and their bodies; similarly disgust may play a role in gut responses to pollution (see Discussion in Chapter 12 of natural beauty and awe). Environmentalists may be quite as likely to punish key members who are disloyal, as seen when prominent internal critics publish works such as "the death of environmentalism" (Shellenberger & Nordhaus, 2010). Everyone is prone to confirmation bias about core beliefs, which is a step away from a moral self-righteousness that divides and alienates.

Second, like it or not, much of the US population as well as many traditional societies around the world have strong ethics of sanctity, authority, and loyalty. Although they respond to care and justice too, those are not always the first concern. This connects to our discussion of religious values under virtue ethics, below. Following on this, third, and perhaps most important, communication must align with affect and intuition. Demonstrating what happens when it does not, Feinberg and Willer (2011) showed that framing climate change in ways that contradict deeply held intuitions that the world is just, orderly and stable results in climate change being discounted. In a set of later studies, they showed that people with strong pro-environmental beliefs see environmental issue *as* moral, and like liberals they tend to highlight ethical themes of care and harm – notes that are also stressed in environmentalist messaging (Feinberg & Willer, 2013). Consistent with Haidt's observations, however, when environmental issues were presented in the moral frame of purity/degradation, US conservatives were not significantly less concerned than liberals, but significantly more concerned than conservatives presented with the care/harm framing (Fig. 7.1) (Feinberg and Willer, 2013). In general, Haidt's advice is to get to know the other party's point of view from the inside out and create connection. From there one can appeal to their intuitions through both social and reasoned persuasion, influencing others' future intuitive responses. But to end by reiterating an earlier point about the study of morality, precisely because environmental morality would *not* show up in a straight descriptive account of many peoples' ethics, it may require a clearer normative ethical orientation to be conceptualized and studied psychologically (Kahn, 1999).

A virtue ethics of the environment

Virtue ethics is perhaps the oldest school of western ethical reflection, with clear roots in Aristotle's thinking. As the name implies, what is right is defined by character traits that are considered virtuous. It is concerned with the morality inside the individual, upon which society

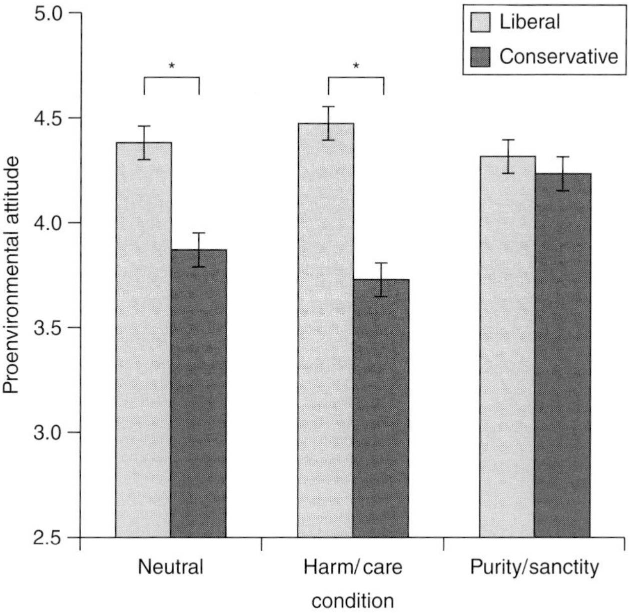

Fig. 7.1 Mean pro-environmental attitude as a function of moral-messaging condition and political ideology. Asterisks indicate between group significant differences ($p < 0.001$). From Feinberg & Willer, 2013, p. 60, copyright © 2013 by Association for Psychological Science. Reprinted by Permission of SAGE Publications.

depends but which cannot be legislated. For example, honesty is a virtue: an honest person possesses honesty as a trait and acts honestly regardless of consequences, or conflicting principles. Certain individuals might be identified as environmental heroes (Aldo Leopold) and villains (James Watt, President Reagan's first Secretary of the Interior) because of behaviors that reveal underlying moral traits. Virtue ethics answers the questions, what is the *best* life for a person and a society, and how can we achieve it (Cafaro, 2001)?

Virtue, inferred from behaviors, typically needs no justification of its intrinsic value because virtues are deeply and consensually validated by the community. Virtue ethics appears to depend strongly on inculcation of such traits during childhood, as recognized by the popular movement in the US for a "character education" approach to moral development (Likona, 1991). One weakness of virtue ethics, therefore, is that it may be undermined when a person grows up in a pluralistic community that does not agree on many virtues (MacIntyre, 1984). Lacking widespread consensus, virtues appear discretionary. Former US Vice President Dick Cheney exploited this weakness when he once said that energy conservation is virtuous and thus not required. This view of virtue ethics as tending toward locally based relativism has been criticized by philosopher Martha Nussbaum (1987), who contends that Aristotle defined the virtues by reference to spheres of human experience that matter in the flourishing of any human life. In each sphere (such as fear of damage such as death; distribution of limited resources; bodily appetites and their pleasures; association with others; intellectual life, etc.), each person has *some* attitude and behavior toward it, whether that be virtuous or deficient. Nussbaum's explication of how virtues pertain to spheres of life is very amenable to adaptation to the contemporary context of environmental relations and human flourishing (Gambrel & Cafaro, 2010).

The environmental ethicist Frasz (1993) considered a weakness of virtue ethics in prescribing behavior. Its focus on the way in which behavior evidences character rather than on the consequences of the behavior seems inflexible: it neither gives specific guidance in making decisions, nor guarantees that a person possessing a particular virtue will avoid bad choices. But there is a corresponding strength: rather than approaching environmental problems and behavioral choices in isolation, and by reference to cumbersome rule systems that miss large-scale patterns, virtue ethics is aimed at long-term broad patterns of action and the traits that produce them. Virtue theory in ethics has gained attention in the age of climate change exactly because virtuous action is *not* contingent on the behavior of others – which can divert cost-benefit decisions that favor the environment because one's impacts are but a small contribution (Jamieson, 2010). Jamieson puts it this way: "*We should focus more on* character and less on calculating outcomes. Focusing on outcomes has made us cynical calculators and has institutionalized hypocrisy" (Jamieson, 2012, p. 197, emphasis in original). One should act virtuously regardless of how others act. He recommends humility, courage, moderation, simplicity, and conservatism. Similarly, Thompson (2012) grounds environmental action in times of transformation in the virtue of responsibility.

This approach to ethics is strong because virtues are internalized and pervasively affect action not only because of socialization but also because of a person's own deliberate self-cultivation. A successfully developed virtue becomes habitual. Virtue values the small or large lifestyle changes that environmentally virtuous people routinize, and also denotes temptations in each sphere against which the virtuous must guard. In general, right action comes from character as shown when action hits the target of the virtue – and this approach contrasts with the deontological and utilitarian traditions that make conscious deliberation and choice central to the character of moral acts. Virtue ethics does not only, however, depend solely on habit but also on reason, for those matters yet lacking a habituated response. Aristotle put tremendous stress on deliberation and reflection. Among other roles, reason is needed to justify the importance of flourishing or *eudaimonia* itself. His virtue ethics is not a mere list to be blindly followed, but a set of choices based on a highly principled and contextualized analysis of life.

This combination of habituated and reflective responses in virtue ethics parallels contemporary psychology's dual-processing models of the mind (Tessman, 2013). Haidt's theory's emphasis on socialization and intuitive (habituated) responses would also fit, although evolutionary theory would be irrelevant. Compared to Haidt's approach, virtue theory puts a greater stress on conscious deliberation as a cause, rather than a rationalization, of moral choice. As Tessman (2013) stresses, conflicts between two or more intuitive responses, or between an intuitive and a reasoned response, would be central to a modern account of virtue ethics. The work of consciously sorting through such conflicts would be the kind of deliberation Aristotle had in mind. The important point is that this research shows that the virtue ethics model is psychologically realistic. It admits of conflicts but does not "require" a single best answer, acknowledging incommensurability where there is no optimum. In others ways, virtue ethics might be challenged by social psychology's observation that people are often too quick to attribute a person's behavior to internal causes (i.e., personality or character), overlooking situational factors (Harman, 1999). In fact, social psychology has found many situational determinants of behavior of which we tend not to be aware. The study of character strengths (nonmoral as well as moral) is a major focus of positive psychology (see Chapter 12).

Environmental ethicists differ on how to specify the virtues. Sandler (2005) suggests four different approaches, each with implications for environmental action. One approach extends traditional interpersonal virtues, such as compassion and gratitude, to apply to our interactions with nature. Here, we might ask what would motivate people to make such extensions, such as their views of nature or relationships with nonhuman creatures, or their perception of their own identity as a part of nature (cf. Chapter 8). A second approach relates virtues to the benefits to those possessing them. Cafaro, for example, says that virtue ethicists provide "strong self-interested reasons for treating others with respect – reasons based on a person's concern for his own virtue and flourishing" (Cafaro, 2001, p. 5). This suggests that the drive for virtue could be considered a core human motive, like the desire for control or connectedness. Third, other philosophers ground virtues in concepts of human excellence and flourishing. For example, just as a person who undermines social relationships would fail to be a virtuous human being, so too would one who habitually threatened ecological relationships. Research into how our social and ecological embeddedness binds us to nature could inform this type of virtue. Final, virtues can be specified inductively by study of the traits of outstanding individuals. Cafaro (2001) uses the exemplars of Henry David Thoreau, Aldo Leopold and Rachel Carson to illustrate the positive psychology of living respectfully and appreciatively with nature. Carfaro argues that Thoreau's vision of the good life cultivated the virtues of "health, freedom, pleasure, friendship, a rich experience, knowledge (of self, nature, God), self-culture and personal achievement" partly though contact with nature. Similarly, much of Aldo Leopold's *A Sand County Almanac* illustrates the possibilities for self-development through one's relationship to nature (Shaw, 1997). Or virtues can directly include respect for nature and "land virtues" (e.g., Sandler, 2007). In short, virtue ethics may offer a way to see our relations to nature as a route to human flourishing, a theme that runs through the field of conservation psychology and throughout this book. Some specific environmental virtues have been proposed and Table 7.1 lists several examples.

Hill (1983) chose *humility* as the one key environmental virtue, reflecting self-acceptance as a finite, mortal, dependent part of nature. Throop and Purdom (2006) apply this virtue in their argument that humility, self-restraint, and altruism should inform our thinking about wilderness and restoration. Specifically, humility may guide us toward elevating wildness (not merely naturalness) as a key criterion, and toward pursuing ecocentric rather than only anthropocentric values as the goal of land management.

Table 7.1 Possible environmental virtues.

Name of virtue	Description or examples
Prudence	Avoidance of irreversible harm; precautionary principle
Frugality/simplicity	Materialist values tempered by ecological world view and environmental impacts
Nonviolence	Avoiding and opposing harm to humans and other living things
Compassion	Compassion with equanimity toward the suffering of others, avoiding the vices of both indifference and anguish (Frakes, 2013)
Gratitude, respect, and love toward nature	Recognition of our dependence and equal status among living things
Fidelity to nature	Being "true to" nature in activities such as design, management, restoration, "saving all the parts" as the first rule of "intelligent tinkering" (Leopold, 1949)
Humility	Avoidance of arrogance and misanthropy (the devaluing of human interest; Frasz, 1993).

Virtue ethics, classically construed, appear anthropocentric. Experiences of being humbled by nature make us aware of our place in the order of things and may decenter our perspective from our own experience (Pianalto, 2013). Unlike humiliation, these experiences also involve awe, respect, and reverence toward that which humbles us, resulting in less self-absorption and self-importance and more self-acceptance. Pianalto argues that while humility does not directly make virtue ethics nonanthropocentric, it has the same effect because "a humbled attention to nature leads to an openness to and appreciation (or affirmation) of intrinsic values in nature, and because humility itself is conducive to human flourishing." In other words "the tendencies and value of humility undermine a purely anthropocentric conception of nature's value" (Pianalto, 2013, p. 143). Ecologically humble action (1) acknowledges our embeddedness in and dependence on nature, (2) is open to learning from nature, and (3) motivates us to minimize our impact on the natural world in order to preserve nature's intrinsic values. Pianalto (2013) argues that ecological humility underlies other virtuous actions toward nature such as seeking justice, or courageous action, since the interconnected world in which the ecologically humble person recognizes the source of his or her welfare provides the justification for these other virtues.

Another candidate key virtue is that of simplicity, which Gambrel and Cafaro (2010) define as "the virtue disposing us to act appropriately within the sphere of our consumer decisions" (2010, p. 90). It has several elements in addition to decreased consumption: a more conscious and deliberative consumption; a more "focused life in general"; and not only a more nuanced appreciation for other things besides material goods, but also greater appreciation of material goods. (2010, p. 90). Simplicity, Gambrel and Carfaro note, overlaps traditional virtues of temperance, frugality, prudence, and self-control that reigned in times of scarcity, but that have been replaced in an economy of apparent abundance. Simplicity sits in the middle of several extremes as shown in Table 7.2.

As an illustration, Gambrel and Cafaro critique American food consumption, which currently causes a host of health and environmental problems. Simplicity demands not (or not only) that we should eat less, but rather differently. Their suggestions for resetting our food-behaviors according to simplicity clearly engage the reflective mind in each aspect of our involvement with food. Clearly, "living simply is not necessarily simple" (2010, p. 92). It is a

Table 7.2 The virtue of simplicity as a mean between two sets of extreme vices.

Vice	Virtue Simplicity	Vice
Underconsumption (poverty)		Over consumption (gluttony)
Unthinking consumption (carelessness)		Overthinking consumption (obsession)
None; or crude consumption (asceticism)		Luxurious consumption
Inefficient or pointless consumption (wastefulness)		Hyperefficient consumption (penny-pinching)
Immoral consumption (callous, disproportional)		None; or, moral finickiness (moral foppery)

From Gambrel & Cafaro, 2010, p. 91 copyright © 2010. With kind permission from Springer Science and Business Media.

process that entails finding out how to meet our needs in a less convoluted fashion, and that will entail collective policy choices – political ones – that the term "voluntary" misses. But rules alone do not suffice in a virtue orientation. Justice and wisdom would be outcomes of this pursuit.

Whether these or any other environmental virtues are effective hinges on the empirical question of whether they enjoy community consensus. Such consensus could be found either in a broad public or in more restricted communities that share a set of basic beliefs; we will consider the evidence for each.

As we saw in Chapter 5, Americans express fairly strong environmental values. Do they actually possess the requisite virtues? American society probably discourages humility by its emphasis on control, individualism, competition, efficiency, change, and materialism (Kohls, 1984; see Schultz & Zelezny, 2003, for a consideration of how environmental messages might work *within* such values). But despite a history of viewing nature instrumentally, Americans do view it with some respect, if judged by their valuing of nature and their resolve to employ the precautionary principle (an expression of prudence) when the risks are made clear. In qualitative accounts of wilderness experience, people often make reference to the idea that they feel "small," suggesting that nature may have the ability to foster humility (see Chapter 4). Although more research is clearly needed, it seems plausible that despite great cultural diversity, Americans show some potential for humility and associated virtues regarding nature.

Humility is also held as a cardinal virtue in Christianity, Buddhism and Taoism (Wong, 2003). Thus, organized religious communities with shared spiritual worldviews might be one type of more restricted community context where humility and other environmental virtues might take stronger root. Conceptions of stewardship ethics that are grounded in the Bible may be one example where environmental virtues are taking hold in the US. Although the term stewardship is used in many different ways, it has a traditional meaning in Christian traditions where stewardship is a virtue applicable to one's relation to the church. Extending this existing virtue to creation is becoming more widespread. The Biodiversity Project et al. (2002a) found that 56% of their representative sample of 1,500 US adults agreed that "Nature is God's creation and humans should respect God's work" was an "extremely important" reason for them "personally to care about protecting the environment," second only, overall, to responsibility to future generations (58%). The subjects were also asked to choose the one most important reason, and the results are summarized in Fig. 7.2 (based on Biodiversity Project et al., 2002b, p. 17). There is a considerable literature on the relation of Christian beliefs and environmental values. Truelove and Joireman (2009) examined orthodox Christians to see what strong Christian beliefs predict. Orthodoxy was negatively related to all measures of pro-environmental behavior, but this effect was mediated completely by the subjects' awareness of the biospheric consequences of environmental problems. People high on awareness of consequences expressed stronger willingness to pay and stronger pro-environmental behavioral intentions. Thus, even extreme religious beliefs are not the sole determinant of environmental attitudes.

Other evidence of the importance of religious virtue as a force in Americans' environmental ethics is found in the declarations of the National Religious Partnership for the Environment such as the Evangelical Environmental Network's Declaration for the Care of Creation (signed by over 500 church leaders) and other initiatives. There are now multiple organizations working with religions around the world to develop stronger linkages between faith and environment. The Forum on Religion and Ecology at Yale University (http://fore.research.yale.edu/) is one hub in higher education; Harvard University Press has a book series on the theme. The Alliance of Religions and Conservation (ARC) is a secular organization that "helps the world's major faiths develop environmental programs based

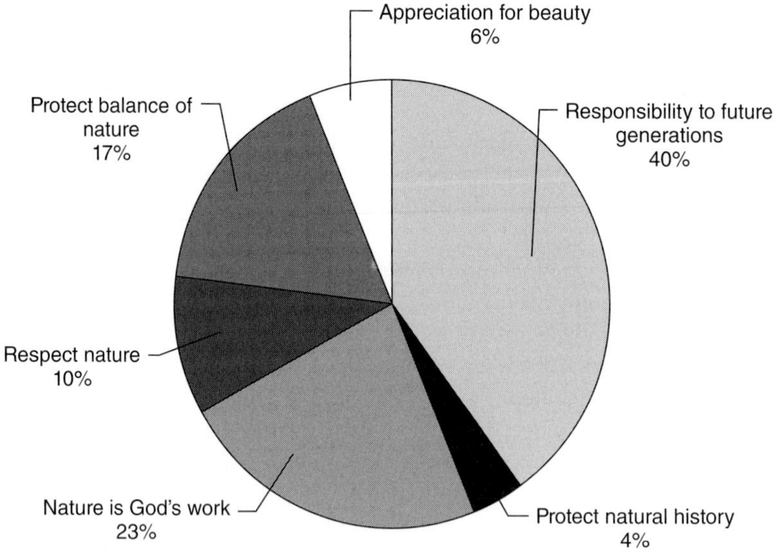

Fig. 7.2 American adults' responses to "Which is the most important reason for you personally to care about protecting the environment?" Based on data from the Biodiversity Project, 2002b, p. 17.

on their own core teachings, beliefs, and practices" (http://www.arcworld.org/). It works to foster high-level and long-term commitments as well as on-the-ground projects to bring environment into contexts like church-based formal education (over half of the schools in Africa) and food and agriculture ("Faith in Food" project). They estimate that 85% of the world follow some faith, and work with 11 major religions (Baha'ism, Buddhism, Christianity, Daoism, Hinduism, Islam, Jainism, Judaism, Shintoism, Sikhism, and Zoroastrianism). A new initiative, the Green Pilgrimage Network, sprang from two questions: "Why are the world's holiest places not its cleanest and most cared for?" and "Can the fact that they are sacred be used to make them greener?" (http://greenpilgrimage.net/). In terms either virtue ethics or Haidt's model, such efforts are promising because they recognize, honor, and engage people's most core and enduring values. The World Wildlife Foundation also has a program that reaches out to involve religious leaders in environmental initiatives (http://www.worldwildlife.org/initiatives/sacred-earth-faiths-for-conservation). Although morality is not coextensive with religion, if people's spiritual views become more ecological, environmental moral virtues and duties fall into place almost automatically (Beringer, 2003).

Virtue is always built afresh with each person's development and reflective self-cultivation. This process is open to empirical investigation. Stonehouse (2012) observed that an outdoor adventure education program for incoming students to a Christian liberal arts college in the US met Aristotle's three conditions for virtue development: moral reflection, moral practice, and sharing the moral life with others. Stonehouse's qualitative research showed that students were constantly confronted with chances for moral practice. In contrast, Martin et al. (2009) used a quantitative measure and found no improvement in courage, temperance, acceptance, compassion, and humility among a group of middle schoolers before and after a 10-week expeditionary learning experience. Perhaps, it was a poorly developed measure, but Aristotle did note that the virtues develop gradually through inculcation and arduous self-cultivation over long periods of time and are also enmeshed in context. A strength of environmental virtue ethics is that they should be tailored to fit our multitude of ways of relating to nature. Among these are the role of fulfilling experiences in nature, and appreciation of our place within it, as examined extensively by conservation psychology. As Sandler (2007, p. 112) put it, human beings "are not excellent in themselves, abstracted from the rest of the world. They are excellences in relating to the world."

Virtue ethics builds on existing internalized or deliberately cultivated moral feelings and worldviews, has the potential to generalize to many of an individual's behaviors, and contributes to both personal and community senses of responsibility and flourishing. On the other hand, it pays less attention to the outcome than the character of the actor and is weaker if community norms are absent. Nonetheless, all societies exhibit and extend existing virtues and generate new ones over time. Natural systems bind humans in increasing interdependence with each other, a situation that may be favorable to fostering virtues of the environment.

The deontic tradition and psychological research

In the modern period, ethicists have tried to ground morality on universal principles that appeal to reason. One such school of ethics, generally known as "deontological" (referring to duties), emphasizes the role of dispassionate reason following ethical principle. Philosophers in this tradition have sought to develop unitary coherent systems that can resolve confusion, often by reference to a single universalizable basic principle. At a risk of overgeneralizing, such thinkers would defend a notion of "objectively true" morality. This objectivism is not about factual accuracy, but about rational defensibility or reasonableness.

Deontological thinkers reject subjectivism, according to which one person's "right" can validly be another's "wrong" and hypocrisy or intolerance could be a "moral" position. This reduces morality to an individual preference, when in fact it is fundamentally about coordinating social existence. The ethically objective alternative to subjectivism is not absolutism. It holds, rather, that there are one or more moral principles that should generally guide action, but may be overridden by other moral principles in cases of conflict. Thus, the position provides for a moral life that is socially negotiated. But ethics is not dependent only on society or culture. If ethics was only a product of society, there would be no independent basis for criticizing the morality of any culture but one's own. Not only would any extant morality be as good as any other; ideal moralities would be less valid than any morality being practiced, even though ideals have long provided essential moral guidance. When one belonged to two or more groups with differing ethics, it would not be possible to resolve conflicting prescriptions for action. Ethical objectivism rejects this relativism as untenable.

The psychological study of morality, including development, has been strongly influenced by the deontic tradition in philosophy. Lawrence Kohlberg, for instance, carefully studied Western ethical philosophy as a preliminary to his developmental psychology research. He concluded that justice is the key ethical virtue, because: it is prescriptive (focusing on "oughts"); it favors universality by providing a minimal agreeable value (since the "good" is presumed to be different for different individuals, an objective means of interpersonal adjudication of conflicting goods is seen as a universal good, which justice provides); and its emphasis on reciprocity and equality make it "the most structural feature of moral judgment" and thus parallel to basic cognitive logical operations that develop during adolescence (Kohlberg et al., 1984a, pp. 305–306). Building on the structural developmental work of Piaget (1929/1975), Kohberg studied the conceptual structures, networks of ideas, and "mental operations" or kinds of logic children use by asking children to reason aloud about hypothetical dilemmas. In general, psychological research on morality agrees with modernist deonotological ethicists that *reasoning* is the key psychological process in morality (Turiel, 2006) because it can correct the influences of self-interest and emotion to achieve fair judgments.

Structural developmental work on environmental ethical judgment has advanced beyond Kohlberg's theories. Kohlberg had in effect defined a high standard for true morality that very few people attained. But Turiel (1983) showed that the concept of morality can be defined more simply by a person: (a) understanding and employing prescriptivity (an action can be right or wrong), (b) using justifications based on welfare, rights, and justice, and (c) generalizing, where the person maintains the action would still be right (or wrong) in another cultural setting, and despite contrary social consensus or authoritative decree. Operationalizing moral concepts accordingly with appropriate hypothetical scenarios and semistructured follow-up questions, Turiel found that most young children possess the concepts. Turiel argued that Kohlberg confounded three social knowledge *domains* that all people distinguish: matters of *morality,* which are governed by considerations listed above (plus a discretionary "beyond the call of duty" kind of morality); *conventional* matters, governed by what facilitates social life in a group and followed if supported by rules or authorities; and actions that are appropriately governed only by *personal* preference. The specific contents of what is moral versus convention may vary across social groups and cultures and time, although there appear to be some universal moral contents.

Turiel's social domain framework has shed light on the nature of moral thought in general. For example, research has shown that members of various religious groups distinguish between religious doctrine that is nonmoral and alterable by church authorities (and not expected of members of other faiths), and religious doctrines that are moral (like injunctions against killing or stealing). Tellingly, when asked if God's decree could make killing or stealing okay, children, adolescents, and young adults in these studies denied that this would make the acts morally acceptable (Turiel, 2002). This finding epitomizes the basic stance of the moral reasoning literature: that morality is not simply transmitted by doctrine and socialization, but is actively constructed by individuals in their own minds.

Do people treat environmental values consistent with this model? Hussar and Horvath (2011) applied social domain theory to determine how children categorize harm to the environment. They found that 6- to 10-year-olds judged harm to the environment more severely than social-conventional transgressions, but not as severely as human-to-human moral transgressions (all the transgressions were of ordinary everyday magnitude, such as litter, and grabbing a toy from a classmate). Notably, in justifying their judgments about environmental harm, children used more biocentric reasons than anthropocentric reasons. It is clear that environmental values must be pretty hot buttons. Carmen Tanner and colleagues (Tanner & Medin, 2004; Tanner et al., 2008; Tanner, 2009) have shown that environmental values are often strongly held or "protected." Tanner asked subjects about several realistically written scenarios: natural resources threatened by global warming, endangered species threatened by groundwater contamination, trees imperiled by habitat loss, peoples' immune systems challenged by ozone thinning, or human health versus waste minimization. In addition to questions about their threshold of participating in the action and feelings about acting or not acting, subjects had to indicate their recommendation from three alternatives. Would they: (a) undertake the suggested action only if the benefits are great enough, (b) take action no matter how small the benefits (or high the costs, in an alternate version), or (c) hold that not doing the action is okay if it saves people enough money. Choosing (b) was taken to indicate a protected value. People answering (b) were significantly more likely to act regardless of the threshold conditions (number of others also acting, and costs or benefits of acting). The character of the subjects' moral judgment responses was deontological: people holding them believe that actions should be taken (the values carry positive duties), they were reluctant to consider trade-offs and unwilling to accept incentives to change their choices, and they considered the values nonsubstitutable and inviolable. People holding deontological values were also insensitive to the framing but concerned if positive duties were not performed, whereas those higher on consequentialism were swayed by whether the outcome was portrayed as positive or negative. Those who combined both kinds of values showed framing effects and preferences for action; their attitude can be paraphrased "you have a duty to act but act in way that produces better outcomes" (Tanner et al., 2008, p. 765).

Further evidence of strong deontological environmental judgments was found in a study asking whether people would accept a hypothetical cap-and-trade climate change mitigation scheme which was presented as optimizing environmental risk and economic benefits (Sacchi et al., 2014). Those with stronger deontological (as opposed to utilitarian) stances were more likely to refuse the presented win–win solution. Follow-up studies, however, indicated that insensitivity to consequences is an underlying factor: subjects high on deontological approach were prone to accept and endorse the trade-off scheme if they were high enough on consequentialism to accept the cost–benefit analysis. Overall, the studies by both Tanner and Sacchi suggest that the two approaches are distinct rather than polar, and both might be combined in integrated moral reasoning and appeals.

More generally, however, actions causing climate change are not only perceptually and cognitively difficult to engage, but also they lack the morally and psychologically salient feature of the *intention to do harm* often associated with a deontological perspective (Markowitz and Shariff, 2012). Thus, many do not see climate change as a moral issue. The extent that college students do feel a moral obligation and consequent intention to act, however, depends on how much they believe climate change is anthropogenically caused, presumably relating to guilt (Markowitz, 2012). The consequences of climate change (for people and nonhuman nature) were not as important in seeing it as a moral issue.

As shown in Fig. 7.3, nature does elicit some deontological prescriptions. Continuing the structural developmental tradition, Peter Kahn and colleagues have conducted a series of studies on the development of environmental moral reasoning. These studies, summarized in *The human relationship to nature* (Kahn, 1999), give us the best available look at how anthropocentric and biocentric reasoning develop across different cultures. Kahn found that children from six years to young adults almost universally judged polluting a water body to be wrong, provided moral justifications, and generalized their judgments. That is, they placed polluting in the moral domain. In response to this and other questions such as relations to domestic animals, conceptions of what is natural, and ideas about harmony with nature, interviews revealed that about 95% of children's reasoning was anthropocentric (centered on human well-being) and 5% was biocentric (concerned with the intrinsic value of nature). The same general pattern was found for children in a village on the Amazon River, in Manaus, a city on the Amazon, in a predominantly poor and African American neighborhood in Houston, and among middle class American children.

The structural developmental perspective assumes that children's conceptual structures develop through interaction with their environment, so the low biocentric reasoning of children in the remote village is surprising; children in contact with unspoiled nature might be expected to understand and appreciate the inherent values of its inhabitants. Kahn and colleagues did find greater biocentric reasoning among adolescent and college age subjects in a study in Portugal, in response to questions tapping the welfare and importance of wild animals. Kahn has speculated that early in life children experience concerns about harm to both humans and nonhumans, but these are undifferentiated and unelaborated; children are

Fig. 7.3 Ethical prescriptions regarding the environment. Photo: Susan Clayton.

generally sensitive to harm. Out of this, anthropocentric and biocentric structures branch, the latter focused on the intrinsic value of living beings. Later, a more mature biocentric structure may coalesce that coordinates both the earlier branches. Kahn spells out several ways children in his study achieved this coordination, for example, by finding parallels between the bodies or needs of humans and animals, and later by balancing similarities with differences, although such reasoning was demonstrated by only a modest percentage of subjects. Overall, Kahn's research demonstrated that children across diverse cultures engage in similar moral reasoning regarding the natural environment (Kahn, 2003).

Other researchers focused on biocentric moral development have found that plants may not fare as well as animals when it comes to moral consideration, perhaps because children are less able to generalize from their own experience based on perceived similarities to natural entities. Gebhard et al. (2003) found that German children between ages 6 and about 11 see trees as morally worthy objects by virtue of their being alive. Aliveness and "anthropomorphic" qualities like feeling appear to go together, creating this concern. From ages 12 to 16, however, what Gebhard and colleagues considered "anthropomorphic" concerns for plants had lost sway and plants were more likely to be valued instrumentally. Dunlap (1989) extended moral-developmental theory to interpret the moral reasoning of 12- to 18-year-old boys about dilemmas involving animals. Nevers et al. (1997) cite evidence that 6- to 11-year-old children view animals as capable of suffering, feel solidarity with them, and will defend the "interests" of organisms. Myers (2007) found that young children ages 4- to 5-years old express moral emotional concern about harms to animals they know directly.

Confirming the early potential for biophilic morality, Severson asked children: what if an earth hypothetically uninhabited by humans were invaded by life-harming aliens? Would it be okay for the aliens to harm plants and animals? She found that 85% of second graders, and 90% of fifth graders used biocentric reasoning (Severson & Kahn, 2010). These data affirm others' findings of biocentrism at earlier ages and suggest the importance of cognitive development in children's ability to recognize and balance competing moral claims in a way that maintains concern for nonhumans.

When there is conflict between humans and nature (particularly wild animals), people may show less concern for nature's welfare. Kellert (1996) found that nonurban Americans have very low moralistic attitudes toward wolves, suggesting the negative influence of perceived threats from wildlife on morality. When levels of threat to people increase, people express less opposition to stringent solutions such as killing wild animals (e.g., Kaltenborn et al., 2006) (see further discussion in Chapter 4). In two experiments, Kortenkamp and Moore (2001) found that scenarios involving ecological damage to a "wild" setting drew more nonanthropomorphic reasoning, but when the dilemma involved a social conflict subjects drew on values from social ethics such as truthfulness. Similarly, Opotow (1994) found that people were less supportive of protective measures for a beetle species if they perceived its needs as conflicting with those of humans. This suggests that biocentric reasoning may be left out unless it is coordinated with social ethics generally. Indeed, situations where our welfare is pitted against that of another species put biocentric morality to the test, and remind us why the concept of justice is so central to moral reasoning. In general, the integration of positive and negative, and human and nonhuman in moral thought, or what Kahn (1999) called "integrated biophilia," illustrates the balancing of different principles and the check on self-interest envisioned by objectivist environmental ethical theory. We need a better understanding of its emergence, especially in diverse cultural settings.

Contextual differences in moral duties

One important divergence from early moral developmental work has been the recognition that people apply distinct moral principles in different social contexts (Shweder et al., 1997). Justice morality (Shweder's "ethics of autonomy") is especially suited to the problems of social regulation encountered in relatively impersonal and role-divided western political, economic, and social institutions. But in both political thought and moral psychology, we find a tension between the needs to control social chaos and apply laws equally, and the needs to recognize individual and contextual differences, protect interdependent relationships, and leave room for compassion.

Within a community of shared values and common interests, or in close relationships, people apply a different set of moral considerations than in less intimate settings. Among psychologists, Gilligan (1982) called this a moral orientation of care; Shweder et al (1997) identified a similar cross-cultural "ethics of community"; Snarey and Keljo (1991) use the German sociologist Tönnies' (1887/1957) term "Gemeinschaft" (as opposed to "Gesellschaft" or "society"); and Eckensberger and colleagues use "personal" as opposed to "transpersonal" (Breit et al., 2003) to designate this more particularistic ethic. These psychologists describe a form of principled morality with central values including concord or understanding; happiness integrally linked to well-being of the community; valuing of tradition; family and community obligations, roles, and relationships as basic to being; and the unity of all life. The "we" of the community might well encompass dependent humans and nonhuman others who, although they do not participate directly in the processes of interpersonal coordination that give rise to higher moral judgments, might be represented in discourse as important subjects of moral care. Beringer (1994) found that the "care" dimension is not merely "supererogatory" as suggested by

Kohlberg, but is a route by which nonhuman entities are included in adolescents' developing moral judgment. In later formulations of the ideal endpoint of moral development, Kohlberg suggested that justice and care need to be integrated (Kohlberg et al., 1984b, p. 340), and careful studies of reasoning about real-life dilemmas have confirmed that integration of care and justice leads to superior resolutions (Walker, 1991).

Environmental decision making may represent a distinctive context for moral reasoning. For example, a traditional way to describe a just or fair distribution of limited resources is to focus on the relationship between inputs and outcomes: those who contribute more, in effort, money, or other merit, receive more. Americans are comfortable distributing material resources, such as houses or cars, in this manner. But there is resistance to applying it to environmental costs and benefits. Should the use of national parks be restricted to those who can afford to pay? Should environmental hazards such as pollution be disproportionately inflicted on the poor? Natural resources seem to be viewed as things to which everyone is equally entitled. Research in controlled settings has indicated that appeals to equality make a more compelling argument in distributing environmental resources as compared to some other domains; notably, equality is a less successful basis for anti-environmental arguments, which tend to focus on individual entitlement (Clayton, 1994, 1996, 2000).

As suggested earlier, one way of defining the context and thus the relevant ethical standards is by identifying the relevant community. Another justice principle that is highly relevant to environmental issues concerns inclusion: the right to participate in a decision, and the right to be considered as a possible recipient of resources. Opotow's (1994) work has shown that inclusion is fundamental to environmental issues. The public might agree that everyone is entitled to share access, but disagree about whether "everyone" includes foreigners, future generations, or nonhuman animals. Those high in concern for the environment or in environmental identity (see Chapter 8) are more likely to consider the welfare of other species to be relevant in resolving environmental conflicts (Clayton 1996, 2003, 2008). The way in which moral inclusion and exclusion operate in environmental conflicts is further discussed below. A pattern across moral psychology paradigms is that perspective taking can increase inclusion. Schultz (2000) showed that taking the perspective of an animal harmed by pollution increased participants biocentric concerns above those of subjects told to remain objective. Recently, Pahl and Bauer (2013) prompted subjects to take the perspective of a young woman in the future affected by environmental changes. Compared to two other conditions, perspective-taking participants increased in three indicators of environmental behavior (Fig. 7.4).

Standards of justice matter, in general and in discussion of environmental issues. Kals (1996; see also Dreyer & Walker, 2013) found that individual perceptions of the justice of proposed environmental policies were the strongest predictor of support, more than the extent to which one would be personally affected by those policies. However, there is more than one way of defining justice and of delimiting the moral sphere. Social consensus about duties regarding welfare, rights, justice, and care will guide the way in which individuals frame conceptions of justice, and this consensus may gradually change in response to a recognition of our interdependence with nature.

The psychological investigation of moral reasoning suggests that moral action is not possible if people cannot recognize when their desires or self interest, or the selfish actions of others, conflict with duties to or regarding other entities, including nature. Some moral principles may be universally recognized, even if expressed differently across cultures; others must be socially negotiated. Although humans may be just beginning to articulate our duties regarding nature, this approach provides tools, such as a dialogic approach, to help others think carefully and relatively objectively through value conflicts involving nature.

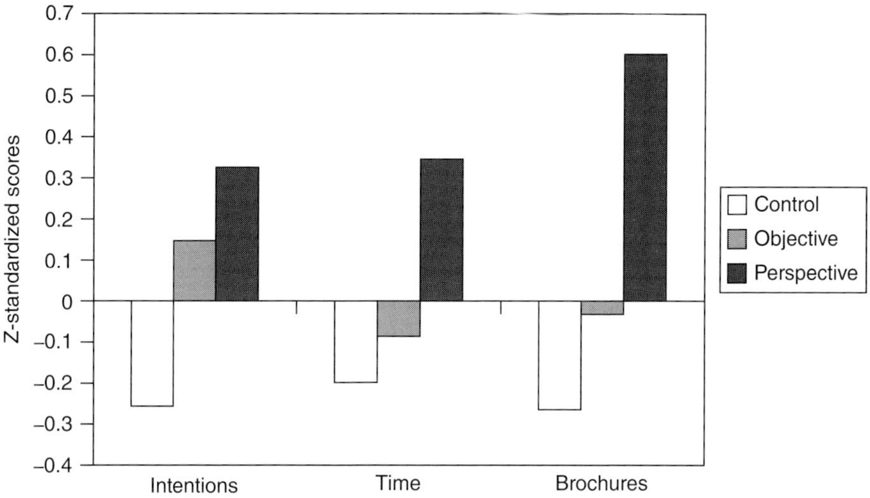

Fig. 7.4 Taking a future environmental-change victim's perspective while viewing a slide show significantly increased three behavior indicators (intentions, time spent, and brochures collected) over asking subjects to remain objective, which was higher than a no instruction condition. Effects were the same across indicators. From Pahl and Bauer (2013), p. 164, copyright © 2013 by Environmental Design Research Association. Reprinted by Permission of SAGE Publications.

Consequentialism, emotion, and socialization

A very different approach to ethics, consequentialism, is familiar under the name of utilitarianism. Consequentialists generally hold that the rightness of an act is determined not by character or by adherence to an abstract principle, but by its consequences, particularly by the "good" (happiness, utility, or benefit) it generates overall. Utilitarianism is the foundation for modern economic theory, and thus most environmental economics is concerned with how economic systems can better account for environmental costs and benefits, which have typically gone unrecognized as "externalities." Some philosophers have extended utilitarian theory to include consequences experienced by nature, most notably animals (e.g., Singer, 1975). Both the theoretical and practical adequacy of these adjustments to theory are hotly debated in economics. Also, psychological research has undercut the plausibility of the "rational actor" model of the person assumed in economic theory who chooses actions based on a reasoned comparison of consequences (Ariely, 2008; Kahneman, 2011), suggesting instead that affect and mental shortcuts play a large role in decisions.

Our main interest here is in the psychological bases of consequentialist ethics, specifically emotions and socialization. Rather than reason philosophically about what is right, the founders of utilitarianism, such as David Hume, Adam Smith and Jeremy Bentham began empirically, attempting to describe how people actually make judgments. Their observation that people respond strongly to pleasure and pain formed the basis for their calculus of the greater good: satisfaction, or "utility." Hume argued that when we experience something that feels good, we judge it to be right, and when we perceive something that feels bad, we judge it to be wrong.

Critical in this process are not just the self-interested emotions, but also the other-oriented ones, particularly what Hume called "sympathy" and we now call empathy. Our ability to share another's feelings means that when we perceive another who is benefited or harmed, we may experience that person's emotional response. This is more technically termed "state matching." If the moral spectator (as well as the recipient of the action) approves of an act, he or she attributes a positive moral virtue to the agent; a negative one if the empathic feeling was unpleasant. Sympathy thus provides the nonselfish part of our moral motivations. This is notably different from the deontological story, because reasons or principles play no role. Indeed, we typically seem to make moral judgments rapidly without conscious calculation, although subsequent thought may either validate or change our moral emotional response. Hume went further, holding that "reason is and ought only to be the slave of the passions, and can never pretend to any other office than to serve and obey them" (Hume, 1739/1978, p. 474). Emotion drives moral behavior; reason comes in afterwards in what we would call "rationalization." This view holds much in common with Haidt's theory, discussed earlier.

The emphasis on emotion makes this a very psychological approach to morality. It is also a socialization-based approach. Hume speculated that some moral traits were innate but that others were learned, and that the vices and virtues of a society may change over time as new kinds of events prompting approval or revulsion arise. In our time, several psychologists have developed theories that link empathy (or sympathy, which entails wanting to help the other) to altruistic behavior via the internalization of moral norms (e.g., Mussen & Eisenberg-Berg, 1977; Staub, 1979; Batson, 1991; Hoffman, 2000). Hoffman (2000) has researched the developmental emergence of this process, in particular by studying transgression situations, where parents use a practice called "induction" to point out the victim's distress and produce empathic guilt. Because the parents do not accuse but simply describe and explain, letting empathy do the rest of the work, the guilt produced is experienced by the child as having an internal origin, and is focused on the deed and its consequences rather than on the self. In contrast, shame focuses on the self rather than the behavior (Tangney et al., 2007) and has thus not been thought to lead to internalization. Careful research by Fung (2006) in Taiwan, however, shows that this is a cultural matter: shame is used productively in collectivistic Chinese moral socialization practices and also produces internalization.

The underlying capacity for empathy develops in stages from early automatic imitative responses at birth to mature cognitive empathy based on taking the perspective of the other, imagination, and introspection. Fascinating social-cognitive neurological studies have identified the "mirror neuron" system as a specialized process whereby we automatically represent others' actions in the same brain areas that we represent our own (for overviews, see Sommerville & Decety, 2006; Hastings et al., 2006; Preston & de Waal, 2002). Is this system active in our relations with nature? Based on observation, Myers (2007) suggested that young children experience empathic distress and moral emotional responses upon witnessing or learning about harm to animals. Franklin et al. (2013) compared MRI brain scans while subjects viewed images of humans and dogs in evident states of suffering and found broadly overlapping patterns of brain activations typical for empathy, with a greater prefrontal activation for the human images, which they speculate may reflect cognition related to theory of mind.

Concepts derived from this research were applied by Bexell (2005); Bexell et al. (2013), who tested a conservation education program in Chengdu, China, a country with very low levels of humane attitudes, and less than 1/3000 the number of humane organizations per capita as in the US (Irwin, 2003). Remarkably, when both children and adults were given the chance to observe animals carefully, discuss their cognitive abilities, and learn about caring for them, Bexell found dramatic changes toward moral inclusion of animals (Fig. 7.5) (we discuss Bexell's program further in Chapter 11). These results suggest that the basic equipment of empathy is not overridden by cultural norms, but may be available for recruitment to culturally non-valued

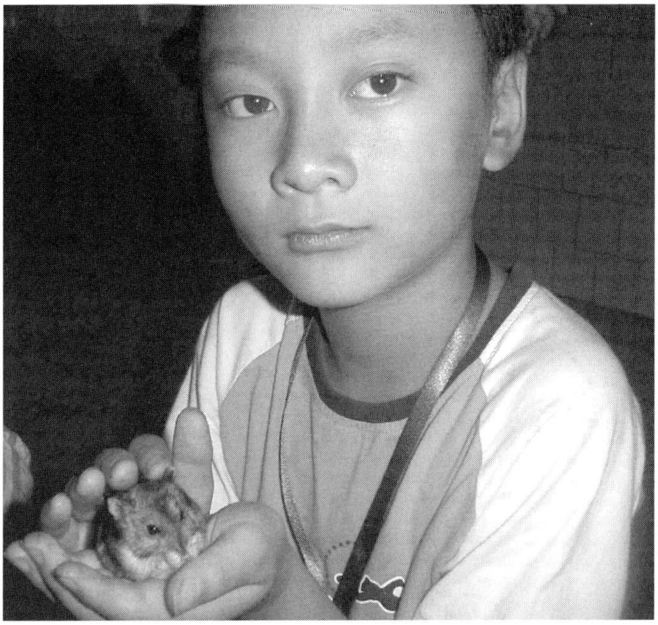

Fig. 7.5 Empathy grounds moral responsiveness: Wildlife conservation education camp, Chengdu, China. Photo courtesy of Sarah Bexell.

entities, particularly animals, given favorable conditions. The potentials of empathy with wild animals are explored in Myers et al. (2009; see also Chapter 4).

The likelihood of an empathic response to another varies with the perceived familiarity and similarity of the other to us, as well as with the salience of the cues about the other's state, the range of our own past emotional experiences, and the extent to which our knowledge helps us take the perspective of another. Notably, Bexell's (2005, 2013) intervention used all of these variables. Studies have shown higher concern for animals with anthropomorphic traits (Eddy et al., 1993; Knight et al., 2004).

Conflicts, resource dependency, or other aversive emotional reactions may decrease empathy. Considering how much these characteristics vary across the vast range of natural others and our experiences with them, it is not surprising that many people's emotional sympathies do not extend very far or very strongly away from the human and the domestic realm. A disposition toward empathy with nature has recently been shown to be a personality variable by Tam (2013) using a newly developed scale. That is, five studies spanning two societies found participants to vary in the degree to which they shared emotional experience they perceive in the natural world. This trait predicted conservation behaviors – but was distinct from other determinants of conservation behavior, and from empathy with humans. Those with more dispositional empathy with nature tended to be female, feel close to nature, and see nature as sentient. This is an exciting step toward further development of empathy and inclusion of nature in the sphere of morality. Empathy is clearly a root of morality, but it is not equivalent (Decety & Cowell, 2014).

Some of the limitations of empathy are that it is biased toward others who are familiar or similar to us, and that empathic distress can be overwhelming, causing disengagement. The phenomenon of "compassion fade" occurs when people provide decreasing levels of help or willingness to help as the number or proportion of victims in the presented plight increases.

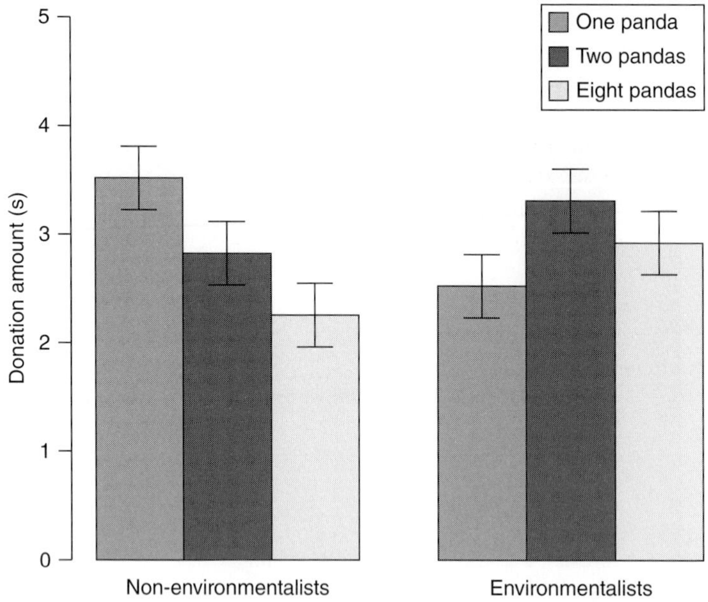

Fig. 7.6 As the number of pandas in need of aid increased, nonenvironmentalists provided significantly smaller donations, whereas environmentalists' donation did not differ significantly as a function of number of animals in need. Error bars show ±1 standard deviation. From Markowitz et al. (2013), Fig. 5, p. 403.

In general, a single identifiable victim garners greater "compassion" than two or more, and the level of help offered decreases as the proportion that will be reached by help decreases, even though the absolute number helped stays the same. These patterns are worrisome in the context of widespread problems such as climate change that include large numbers of both human and nonhuman victims. Markowitz et al. (2013) tested whether these patterns hold up for nonhuman victims, and found that they do. But compassion fade was not observed among people who self-identified as "environmentalists" – their levels of aid were remarkably consistent and tended toward proportionality with the number of animals needing aid (Fig. 7.6). Possible reasons for the difference may be that environmentalists do not count animals as an out-group, or see them in conflict with humans; or they may place a higher value on animals and care more about their lives.

The strength of the Humean approach is that emotion does seem to be what drives actual moral behavior. Without emotional drive, one might reach a clear rational conclusion about what to do, for example, upon observing someone's plight, but simply not be moved to act (this is precisely what Damasio (1994) observed in patients with an injury to a specific brain that cut off emotional input to consciousness and the reasoning brain). At the same time, caregivers and role models define what situations and objects are worthy of concern by their own actions and by whether they induce guilt or shame in the young person. Clearly, most moral socialization in modern societies concerns actions toward other humans. But the potential for the environmental ethical side is considerable. For example, in the USA and some European countries, humane attitudes have been part of middle-class socialization since the eighteenth century (Grier, 1999). Another important point is that we must pay attention to what moral responses already *are* operating – largely ones that define human–human morality – because these may dominate in situations of conflicts regarding the environment (cf. Kortenkamp & Moore, 2001). At the same time, emotional bonds with nature arise when people are offered the opportunity to develop them and they may be morally powerful also.

Emotion and reason work together, as we have argued above. On a simple level, shame- or guilt-based parental inductions typically ask the child to reflect on reasons for behavior. Meanwhile, cognition, albeit rapid and sometimes unconscious, is integral to the "primary appraisals" that generate emotions (Lazarus, 1991) and enables conscious perspective taking. If someone's level of empathy toward objects in nature can be increased, their biocentric moral reasoning as well as pro-environmental attitudes and behaviors may also increase, as demonstrated by Berenguer (2007, 2010) in experiments with Spanish college students (see also Schultz, 2000). More fundamentally, Hauser (2006) suggested that the classically dichotomized emotion and reason work with a more primary innate moral faculty that automatically analyzes actions according to an unconscious generative grammar of morality analogous to Chomskian universal linguistic grammar. After a judgment is made, both reasoning and emotion might result. This model could explain how the presence of strong emotions related to hurt (guilt, shame, and anger) or disgust can change a person's judgment of an action from the conventional to the moral sphere, whereas acts that are unintentionally harmful or disgusting but done in the course of accomplishing some greater good are perceived as permissible. That people can distinguish such cases and make rapid and precise moral judgments suggests a fine integration of emotion and cognition. When we deliberate morally, cognition about principles may correct morally misguided emotional inclinations. Compared to Haidt's, Hauser's view gives a larger role to cognition, and specifically to issues of harm, fairness, and intent.

Psychological dynamics of moral functioning

It is encouraging to think that we are moral creatures, at least some of the time. Indeed the emotional lift we get from observing virtuous action, termed "moral elevation" (distinct from happiness) is part of the moral life (Haidt, 2003; see Chapter 12). Moral elevation in response to acts of environmental heroes may be an important motivator of environmental behavior, but it has yet to be researched.

Often, however, behavior falls short of the ideal. Real moral controversies activate not only moral emotions and reasons, but also other psychological responses that may undermine optimal functioning. The complexity of environmental ethical situations may compound this: there are frequently many different values and points of view, multiple perpetrators of small actions with cumulative impact, multiple victims whose moral standing may be in question, a variety of time scales at which the outcomes differ in severity, and so on. In the heat of a moral confrontation over the environment, moral judgments entail questions such as whether anthropocentric or biocentric values are at stake, whether the agent is blameworthy, whether the consequences meet some threshold, and so on. Additional factors involve identity, emotions, communication, and social disequilibrium or disharmony. The situation is dynamic, transactional, socially and culturally structured, and the outcomes will have consequences for both the situation and the actor (Fig. 7.7). How do we behave in such situations?

As thinkers back to Plato have observed, the motivation to be moral, or to at least present the self *as* moral is extremely high (Haan et al., 1985). To be immoral, and perceived to be so, is to be placed outside the human moral community. This means a loss of dignity, standing, "face," and reciprocity with others. Because our self-perception is so deeply influenced by the messages we get about ourselves from others, it is a high risk to be perceived as having acted

Fig. 7.7 Social and cognitive disequilibrium in moral conflict. The late Joan Norman Protesting logging of Old-Growth Reserves and Inventoried Roadless Areas in the Siskiyou National Forest, Oregon, 2005. Photo: Rolf Skar.

immorally. When a moral wrong is committed, this is the social disequilibrium that occurs, and it is a more challenging aspect of morality than the cognitive demands alone (Haan et al., 1985).

The highly arousing situation of moral confrontation may swamp our ability to rationally think through the problem. Social intuitionist theory would say our responses are only fast and affective, not thought-out. But real life may include some ability to think on one's feet. So our ability to right the moral balance, regardless of our position in the controversy, will depend on what might be called "psychodynamic moral skill" as well as on our judgment. Such skills involve emotional self-regulation, or the ability to modulate our emotional reactions, or to deescalate to let our autonomic system's arousal settle down. But it also involves more habitual coping versus defensive strategies or skills. Positive coping strategies identified by Norma Haan (1977) include trying to be objective, focusing on ideas and interests rather than persons, logical analysis, tolerance of ambiguity, empathy and perspective taking, reviewing what happened, concentration, and integration of feelings and ideas. To these Alon and Omer (2006) add consolation and acceptance, alternatives to blaming and demonization. In Haan's research, subjects who used these skills found better resolutions of experimentally induced moral conflicts with friends than did those who used what Haan termed "defensive strategies": self-righteousness, withdrawal and isolation, intellectualization, projection, self-effacement, giving up, denial, and

Table 7.3 Attitudes and beliefs associated with moral exclusion.

Derogation	Normalizing violence
Dehumanization	Concealment of harm
Reducing moral standards	Desecration
Blaming the victim	Euphemisms
Self-righteousness	Condescension
Displacing responsibility	Moral engulfment
Transcendent ideologies	Deindividuation
Dominionistic values	Glorifying violence

displacement of feeling. All of these allow the person to attempt to keep intact their self-image as a moral person without admitting the possibility they did wrong. When there is a sense of mutual wrongs, but a refusal to reciprocate another's recognition that they have had a role in the problem, the imbalance is exacerbated.

Unfortunately, such negative dynamics are not only a part of acute moments of confrontation, but also can become reified in social identities and interactions. Moral disengagement (Bandura, 1990, 1999) and moral exclusion (Opotow, 1990; Opotow & Weiss, 2000) are psychological terms for what philosophers would call a denial of another's moral standing. As described by various authors (Opotow, 1990; Vollum et al., 2004; Plous, 1993), some of these behaviors and social patterns are listed in Table 7.3.

All of these may be concealed through rationalizations, or conceptual structures that legitimate or excuse the moral exclusion of others. Haidt's (2012) framework is worth attention with regard to the spirals of self-righteousness. Relatedly, Westen et al. (2006; Westen, 2007) elaborate on how when our cherished beliefs are challenged, it is our emotional brain that responds -- not our rational thought centers. Areas associated with pain respond when we feel dissonance, and pleasure if we are vindicated. Environmentalists with a strong sense that their knowledge and beliefs are superior (e.g., about fracking) have been shown to be vulnerable to self-righteous attitudes (Raimi & Leary, 2014).

Given a history in which nature has been regarded primarily as merely a means to human ends, it is not surprising that nature is often morally excluded. That some countries continue to pass and uphold laws such as the US Endangered Species Act reflects change in such cultural norms.

Chronic disputes of all kinds typically result in the moral exclusion of each group by the other. This includes environmental disputes such as the example of rangeland conflict described by Opotow and Brook (2003; Brook et al., 2003). These psychologists point out that such negative spirals can be reversed by establishing overarching identities focused on common values regarding the resource at stake, while also preserving the original identities. The original identities need to be protected, as they are fundamental to the different parties, and they form the nucleus for reaching out to others in the respective communities. Conflicts are inevitable in complex, specialized and fragmented societies with divergent interests and identities. Progress toward better conflict resolution may be enhanced by fostering communication, coping and analysis skills, and conducting conflicts in ways that reduce or work through defensiveness. These are also important in the next and final perspective on environmental ethics (see also discussion of conflict in chapter 10).

Pragmatist ethics

A growing ethical tradition focuses on approaching the human dynamics and value questions not from a particular moral theoretical point of view, but from a practice- and inquiry-oriented stance. This approach is the American-born school of thought called pragmatism, first formulated by turn-of-the-twentieth-century thinkers like Charles Sanders Peirce, William James, Oliver Wendell Holmes Jr., and John Dewey. The early pragmatists sought to understand truth as an evolving relationship between the language used in a community and the experience of its members. Language and experience were seen as active things, and truth was tested in a contest among different ideas put into action and tried and retried by a community of people attempting to solve immediate problems.

In environmental affairs, one major example of pragmatism is adaptive management, where policies and other actions are taken as experiments and data tracking the results are used to reformulate the policy (Lee, 1993). It entails community engagement with questions of fact as well as of value. The innovative and empirical spirit of this approach can be seen in the writings of philosopher Bryan Norton (1991, 2005). He has strongly criticized standard polarities in environmental ethics such as the historical preservationism of John Muir versus the conservationism of Gifford Pinchot, or, in a contemporary version of this polarity, between deontological intrinsic value (IV) biocentrists and utilitarian anthropocentric economists. Norton suggests that politically desirable solutions will be found where ecologically and economically acceptable options overlap (1991). Both the IV theorists and economists, he argues, agree on certain problematic "preexperiential ontological commitments" (Norton, 2005, p. 190) about value:

1. Both assume a dichotomy between "intrinsic" and "instrumental" values, and that intrinsic value is the basis for determining moral standing.
2. Both focus on objects rather than on processes.
3. Both are both monistic, reducing all values to a first principle or expressing them in a single metric, for example, of monetary values in the case of economics.
4. Both values are treated as placeless. As Norton puts it, "neither dollars nor 'intrinsic values' are contextualized or sensitized to the particularities and idiosyncrasies of local places" (Norton, 2005, p. 183).

When applied as rules for decisions, theories with these deep assumptions exert a leveling or homogenizing influence on behaviors, as Norton shows in examples of national policy and activism.

The alternative formulated by Norton (2005), Fuller (1992) and others (Light and Katz, 1996) is an empirical approach such as that of the pragmatists, which opens value questions, including scientific-descriptive questions, to fresh experience, and tries them "by fire" in a community problem-solving context. Such a context will reveal multiple kinds of value, some local and some larger scale, including ones grounded in a sense of place.

Norton has added the terms "transformative values" and "constitutive values" to our vocabulary. The former values are important because of their ability to spark reflection on one's overall value system (Norton, 1987). Experiences that afford such values are worth psychological study (see Chapter 4 on transformative experiences of wild nature). Constitutive values occur in relation to experiences or places whose characteristics have shaped a person fundamentally. When such values are lost, historical rootedness, community identity, home, and self are diminished.

Psychology can help in discovering values whose existence or prevalence is not addressed by philosophy. This is a kind of detection problem calling for qualitative research, and an elaboration problem calling for language and theory to support and extend what may have begun as inarticulate feelings. For example, in piloting a study of emotional experiences of zoo visitors observing animals, Myers et al. (2004) discovered many visitors felt a hard-to-articulate emotion the researchers came to denote as a sense of "special privilege." Psychological research to identify indicators for different types of values could be of use in decision making. Sayre's (1991) pragmatist approach is to determine (1) how norms come to be held in a given society; (2) the practical environmental effects of such norms; and (3) the relative desirability of alternative norms. Because it embraces diversity of values, pragmatism is a pluralistic version of morality, like Haidt's (2012). A person is assumed to be able to hold and apply justifiable but contradictory moral principles at the same time. Thus, pragmatism aims for the coexistence of differing but overlapping core values within person and/or within community. It relies on participatory processes to reduce defensiveness, increase listening, and consciously cultivate a ground of mutual respect.

Psychology can also examine this kind of learning-through-discussion with the aim of understanding and improving it. Pragmatic ethicist Anthony Weston (2007) draws from psychology in describing such techniques as reframing and lateral thinking as ways to create "room to move" in even the most vexing ethical problems. Alternatively, the emphasis in *social learning* is precisely on the level of collective process, product, and identity (Wals, 2007). Such inquiry has increased greatly in recent years, partly in response to the idea of "deliberative democracy" (e.g., Fishkin, 1991; Dryzek, 2000). Public participation in collaborative decision making has been studied in terms of the nature of processes such as successful dialog, conflict reduction, and the importance of participants having substantive knowledge (Tuler & Webler, 2006). The connection to environmental morality lies in a deepening commitment to democratic values through exercising them. Such values are essential in increasing society's ability to work through sometimes polarized value and world view differences to solve common problems. Samuelson et al. (2003) report a case study of collaborative learning in which members of different interest groups came together to discuss the restoration of a local watershed. Although they began with very different perspectives on the "right" course of action – differences rooted in their identities as farmers, residents, or resource managers – through discussion they were able to recognize shared values and develop a shared identity. They did not reach total consensus, but their sense of themselves as a collective enabled them to listen to each other and compromise rather than rigidly adhering to their initial positions. Samuelson and Barratt (2012) review theoretical models, engagement processes, evaluation criteria, and case studies of collaborative processes in environmental conflict resolution.

The ability to hear, reflect upon, choose among, and act coherently upon others' and one's own values constitutes "value-rationality" or "practical wisdom." It is central to success in solving complex real-world problems and involves a high degree of context specificity. Accordingly, pragmatic ethics is a form of situational ethics. Psychology is important here in grounding our understanding of problem solving (Brewer & Stern, 2005). Despite the emphasis on explicit models and procedures in problem-solving instruction and theory, proficient and expert problem solvers in complex fields of practice do not rely on models and rules; even advanced learners find that rules must be interpreted in order to fit a given context. Further, phenomenological analysis of the experience of experts shows that masterful performers respond to immediate context without reference to any theory or procedure, as elaborated in the work of Dreyfus and Dreyfus (1988). Experimental studies on the "deliberation without attention" hypothesis show that even ordinary consumers make complex purchase decisions (but not simple ones) better when they do not attentively deliberate on them (Dijksterhuis et al., 2006).

Problem solving requires reading the context and defining the problem in ways that offer solutions. What does this mean when applied to the values at stake in complex, contested issues? How can people's value rationality be increased? We need to understand more about how people deal with values in context. As Norton (2005, p. 397) argues:

> the identification, articulation, and measurement of... values must be undertaken... within a broad-based, participatory, iterative process, a process that must be begun, and pursued continually, within a larger adaptive management process in each particular place where community members resolve to live sustainably, according to a definition they have actively chosen.

Narrative psychology generates context-sensitive "thick" descriptions that may encourage understanding of others' viewpoints and help correct oversimplifications in the "normative" models often used by formal decision makers. Flyvbjerg (2001) argues that case study methods that address the dynamics of power, knowledge, context, identity, and collective action show the most promise to advance practical wisdom.

Like the Humean approach, pragmatism is viewed with suspicion by modernist ethicists who fear that it may legitimize relativism. Pragmatists respond that the majority in a society may be wrong, but the attempt to coerce people to comply with some ecologically determined dictate is neither proper nor effective. Instead, the best recourse is to generate and convincingly communicate data about reality and the consequences of choices, effectively widening the experiences of everyone (Norton, 2005). Pragmatism relies on psychology to measure and describe the values, change, and learning that occur.

Conclusion

It is often suggested that to meet our conservation and sustainability challenges, society must be driven by a sense of moral purpose. As this chapter shows, there is not one vision of what this might mean, but several. One places emotional or intuitive processing at the center of moral psychology and expands its foundations beyond justice and care. Another is based on the ideas of character and virtue grounded in community worldview, perhaps of a spiritual sort. Another centers on the idea that concepts related to ethical principles and knowledge underlying sound judgments are the core of morality, tempering self-interest and other personal or group biases. A fourth approach looks most closely at the psychology of emotions such as empathy, guilt, and shame; it focuses on socialization as what truly underlies moral identity and action, and thus must be understood and recruited. From these considerations, it is clear that to a great extent satisfying our environmental moral concerns depends on our ability simply to work together despite a huge variety of values, worldviews, and circumstances. In this light, our attention shifts from individual morality to our collective ability to recognize, reflect upon, and reasonably address the value questions we face. From this perspective, what is most needed is an understanding of the social processes that enable us to work together on such deeply rooted questions.

References

Alon, N. & Omer, H. (2006). *The psychology of demonization.* Hillsdale, NJ: Lawrence Erlbaum.

Ariely, D. (2008). *Predictably irrational: The hidden forces that shape our decisions.* New York: Harper Collins.

Bandura, A. (1990). Selective activation and disengagement of moral control. *Journal of Social Issues 46*(1), 27–46.

Bandura, A. (1999). Moral disengagement in the perpetration of inhumanities. *Personality and Social Psychology Review 3*(3), 193–209.

Batson, C. D. (1991). Empathic joy and the empathy-altruism hypothesis. *Journal of Personality and Social Psychology 61*, 413–426.

Baumeister, R. & Masicampo, E. J. (2010). Conscious thought is for facilitating social and cultural interactions: How mental simulations serve the animal-culture interface. *Psychological Review, 117*, 949–971.

Berenguer, J. (2007). The effect of empathy in proenvironmental attitudes and behaviors. *Environment and Behavior, 39*(2), 269–283.

Berenguer, J. (2010). The effect of empathy in environmental moral reasoning. *Environment and Behavior, 42*(1), 110–134.

Beringer, A. (1994). *The moral ideals of care and respect: A hermeneutic inquiry into adolescents' environmental ethics and moral functioning*. Frankfurt/M., Germany: Peter Lang.

Beringer, A. (2003). A conservation psychology with heart. *Human Ecology Review 10*(2), 150–153.

Bexell, S. (2005). *Effect of a wildlife conservation camp experience in China on student knowledge of animals, care, propensity for environmental stewardship, and compassionate behavior toward animals*. Unpublished doctoral dissertation, Georgia State University, Athens, GA.

Bexell, S. M., Jarrett, O. S., & Ping, X. (2013). The effects of a summer camp program in china on children's knowledge, attitudes, and behaviors toward animals: A model for conservation education. *Visitor Studies, 16*(1), 59–81.

Blanchette, I., & Richards, A. (2010). The influence of affect on higher level cognition: A review of research on interpretation, judgment, decision making and reasoning. *Cognition & Emotion, 24*(4), 561–595.

Biodiversity Project, and Belden Russonello & Stewart. (2002a). *Americans and biodiversity: New perspectives in 2002*. Madison, WI: Biodiversity Project.

Biodiversity Project, and Belden Russonello & Stewart. (2002b). *Americans and biodiversity: New perspectives: A cluster analysis of findings from a national survey*. Madison, WI: Biodiversity Project.

Breit, H., Döring, T. & Eckensberger, L. H. (2003). *Politics, law and citizens' responsibility. Justice judgments in the everyday reconstructions of environmental conflicts*. In H. Breit, A. Engels, T. Moss, & M. Troja (Eds.) *How institutions change: Perspectives on social learning in global and local environmental contexts* (pp. 179–203). Opladen: Leske and Budrich.

Brewer, G. & Stern, P. (2005). *Decision making for the environment: Social and behavioral science research priorities*. Washington DC: National Academies Press.

Brook, A. T., Zint, M. & De Young, R. (2003). Landowners' responses to an Endangered Species Act listing and implications for encouraging conservation. *Conservation Biology 17*(6), 1638–1649.

Cafaro, P. (2001). Thoreau, Leopold and Carson: Toward an environmental virtue ethics. *Environmental Ethics 22*, 3–17.

Clayton, S. (1994). Appeals to justice in the environmental debate. *Journal of Social Issues, 50*(3), 13–27.

Clayton, S. (1996). What is valued in resolving environmental dilemmas: Individual and contextual influences. *Social Justice Research, 9*, 171–184.

Clayton, S. (2000). Models of justice in the environmental debate. *Journal of Social Issues, 56* (3), 459–474.

Clayton, S. (2003). Environmental identity: A conceptual and an operational definition. In S. Clayton & S. Opotow (Eds.) *Identity and the natural environment* (pp. 45–65). Cambridge, MA: MIT Press.

Clayton, S. (2008). Attending to identities: Ideology, group memberships, and perceptions of justice. In K. Hegtvedt & J. Clay-Warner (Eds.), *Advances in group processes: Justice* (pp. 287–313). Bingley, UK: Emerald Group.

Cushman, F., & Young, L. (2011). Patterns of moral judgment derive from nonmoral psychological representations. *Cognitive Science, 35*(6), 1052–1075.

Damasio, A. (1994). *Descartes' error: Emotion, reason and the human brain*. New York: Putnam.

Decety, J., & Cowell, J. M. (2014). The complex relation between morality and empathy. *Trends in Cognitive Sciences, 18*(7), 337–339.

Dijksterhuis, A., Bos, M. W., Nordgren, L. F., & van Baaren, R. B. (2006). On making the right choice: The deliberation-without-attention effect. *Science 311*, 1005–1007.

Dreyer, S. & Walker, I. (2013). Acceptance and support of the Australian carbon policy. *Social Justice Research, 26*, 323–362.

Dreyfus, H. & Dreyfus, S. (1988). *Mind over machine: The power of human intuition and expertise in the era of the computer*. New York: Free Press.

Dryzek, J. S. (2000). *Deliberative democracy and beyond: Politics, policy and political science*. Cambridge: Cambridge University Press.

Dunlap, J. J. (1989). Moral reasoning about animal treatment. *Anthrozoös 2*(4), 245–258.

Eddy, T. J., Gallup, G., & Povinelli, D. (1993). Attribution of cognitive states to animals: Anthropomorphism in comparative perspective. *Journal of Social Issues 49*(1), 87–101.

Feinberg, M., & Willer, R. (2011). Apocalypse soon?: Dire messages reduce belief in global warming by contradicting just-world beliefs. *Psychological Science, 22*(1), 34–38.

Feinberg, M., & Willer, R. (2013). The moral roots of environmental attitudes. *Psychological Science, 24*(1), 56–62.

Fishkin, J. S. (1991). *Democracy and deliberation: New directions for democratic reform*. New Haven, CT: Yale University Press.

Flyvbjerg, B. (2001). *Making social science matter*. Cambridge: Cambridge University Press.

Frakes, C. (2013). Environmental degradation, environmental justice and the compassionate agent. In M. W. Austin (Ed.), *Virtues in action: New essays in applied virtue ethics* (pp. 119–131). New York: St. Martin's Press.

Franklin, R. G., Nelson, A. J., Baker, M., Beeney, J. E., Vescio, T. K., Lenz-Watson, A., & Adams, R. B. (2013). Neural responses to perceiving suffering in humans and animals. *Social Neuroscience, 8*(3), 217–227.

Frasz, G. B. (1993). Environmental virtue ethics: A new direction for environmental ethics. *Environmental Ethics 15*, 259–74.

Frimer, J. A., Biesanz, J. C., Walker, L. J. & MacKinlay, C. W. (2013). Liberals and conservatives rely on common moral foundations when making moral judgments about influential people. *Journal of Personality and Social Psychology, 104*(6), 1040–1059.

Fuller, R. (1992). American pragmatism reconsidered: William James' ecological ethic. *Environmental Ethics, 14*(summer), 159–176.

Fung, H. (2006). Affect and early moral socialization: Some insights and contributions from indigenous psychological studies in Taiwan. In U. Kim, K. Yang & K. Hwang (Eds.), *Indigenous and cultural psychology: Understanding people in context*. New York: Springer.

Galdi, S., Arcuri, L. & Gawronski, B. (2008). Automatic mental associations predict future choices of undecided decision-makers. *Science, 321*, 1100–1102.

Gambrel, J. C., & Cafaro, P. (2010). The virtue of simplicity. *Journal of Agricultural and Environmental Ethics, 23*(1–2), 85–108.

Gebhard, U., Nevers, P., & Billmann-Mahecha, E. (2003). Moralizing trees: Anthropomorphism and identity in children's relationships to nature. In S. Clayton & S. Opotow (Eds.), *Identity and the natural environment: The psychological significance of nature*. Cambridge, MA: MIT Press.

Gibbs, J. C. (2014). *Moral development and reality: Beyond the theories of Kohlberg, Hoffman and Haidt* (3rd ed.). Oxford: Oxford University Press.

Gigerenzer, G. (2010). Moral satisficing: Rethinking moral behavior as bounded rationality. *Topics in Cognitive Science, 2*(3), 528–554.

Gilligan, C. (1982). *In a different voice: Psychological theory and women's development*. Cambridge, MA: Harvard University.

Greene, J., Nystrom, L. E., Engell, A. D. Darley, J. M. & Cohen, J. D. (2004). The neural bases of cognitive conflict and control in moral judgment. *Neuron 44*, 389–400.

Grier, K. C. (1999). Childhood socialization and companion animals: United States, 1820-1870. *Society and Animals 7*(2), 95–120.

Haan, N., Aerts, E. & Cooper, B. (1985). *On moral grounds: The search for a practical morality*. New York: New York University Press.

Haan, N. (1977). *Coping and defending: Processes of self-environment organization*. New York: Academic Press.

Hagerman, S. M. & Satterfield, T. (2014). Agreed but not preferred: Expert views on taboo options for biodiversity conservation, given climate change. *Ecological Applications 24*:548–559.

Haidt, J. (2001). The emotional dog and its rational tail: A social intuitionist approach to moral judgment. *Psychological Review 108*, 814–834.

Haidt, J. (2003). Elevation and the positive psychology of morality. In C. L. M. Keyes & J. Haidt (Eds.), *Flourishing: Positive psychology and the life well-lived* (pp. 275–289). Washington DC: American Psychological Association.

Haidt, J. (2007). The new synthesis in moral psychology. *Science 316*, 998–1002.

Haidt, J. (2012). *The righteous mind: Why good people are divided by politics and religion*. New York: Vintage Books.

Haidt, J. & Graham, J. (2007). When morality opposes justice: Conservatives have moral intuitions that liberals may not recognize. *Social Justice Research 20*, 98–116.

Haidt, J. & Joseph, C. (2004). Intuitive ethics: How innately prepared intuitions generate culturally variable virtues. *Daedalus, 133*(4), 55–66.

Haidt, J., & Joseph, C. (2007) The moral mind: How 5 sets of innate intuitions guide the development of many culture-specific virtues, and perhaps even modules. In P. Carruthers, S. Laurence & S. Stich, (Eds.), *The innate mind: Foundations and the future* (pp. 367–391). Oxford: Oxford University Press.

Harman, G. (1999). Moral philosophy meets social psychology: Virtue ethics and the fundamental attribution error. *Proceedings of the Aristotelian society, 99*, 315–331).

Hastings, P. D., Zahn-Waxler, C. & McShane, K. (2006). We are, by nature, moral creatures: Biological bases of concern for others. In M. Killen & J. G. Smetana (Eds.), *Handbook of moral development* (pp. 483–516). Mahwah, NJ: Lawrence Erlbaum.

Hauser, M. (2006). *Moral minds: How nature designed our universal sense of right and wrong*. New York: HarperCollins.

Hill, Jr., T. E. (1983). Ideals of human excellence and preserving natural environments. *Environmental Ethics 5*, 211–24.

Hoffman, M. (2000). *Empathy and moral development*. New York: Cambridge University Press.

Hume, D. (1978). *A Treatise of human nature*. Oxford: Oxford University Press. (Original work published 1739)

Hussar, K. M., & Horvath, J. C. (2011). Do children play fair with mother nature? Understanding children's judgments of environmentally harmful actions. *Journal of Environmental Psychology, 31*(4), 309–313.

Irwin, P. G. (2003). *A strategic review of international animal protection*. In D. J. Salem, & A. N. Rowan (Eds.), *The State of the Animals II: 2003* (pp. 1–8). Washington, DC: Humane Society Press.

Jamieson, D. (2010). When utilitarians should be virtue theorists. In S. M. Gardiner, S. Caney, D. Jamieson, & H. Shue (Eds.), *Climate ethics: Essential readings* (pp. 315–331). Oxford: Oxford University Press.

Jamieson, D. (2012). Ethics, public policy and global warming. In A. Thompson & J. Bendik-Keymer (Eds.), *Ethical adaptation to climate change: Human virtues of the future* (pp. 187–202). Cambridge, MA: MIT Press.

Kahn, P. H. (1999). *The human relationship with nature*. Cambridge, MA: MIT Press.

Kahn, Jr., P. H. (2003). The development of environmental moral identity. In S. Clayton, & S. Opotow (Eds.), *Identity and the natural environment* (pp. 113–134). Cambridge, MA: MIT Press.

Kahneman, D. (2011). *Thinking, fast and slow*. New York: Farrar, Straus and Giroux.

Kaltenborn, B. P., Bjerke, T., Nyahongo, J. W. & Williams, D. R. (2006). Animal preferences and acceptability of wildlife management actions around Serengeti National Park, Tanzania. *Biodiversity and Conservation 15*: 4633–4649.

Kals, E. (1996). Are proenvironmental commitments moderated by health concerns or perceived justice?. In L. Mondata & M. Lerner (Eds.), *Current societal concerns about justice* (pp. 231–258). New York: Plenum.

Kellert, S. R. (1996). *The value of life: Biological diversity and human society*. Washington, DC: Island Press.

Keltner, D., Oatley, K. & Jenkins, J. M. (2014). *Understanding emotions* (3rd ed.). New York: Wiley.

Kohlberg, L., Levine, C, & Hewer, A. (1984a). Synopses and detailed replies to critics. In L. Kohlberg, *Essays on moral development. Vol. 2: The psychology of moral development* (pp. 320–394). San Francisco: Harper & Row.

Kohlberg, L., Levine, C., & Hewer, A. (1984b). The current formulation of the theory. In L. Kohlberg, *Essays on moral development. Vol. 2: The psychology of moral development* (pp. 212–319). San Francisco: Harper & Row.

Kohls, R. (1984). *The values Americans live*. Washington, DC: Meridian House International.

Kortenkamp, K. V. & Moore, C. F. (2001). Ecocentrism and anthropocentrism: Moral reasoning about ecological commons dilemmas. *Journal of Environmental Psychology 21*, 261–272.

Knight, S., Vrij, A., Cherryman, J., & Nunkoosing, K. (2004). Attitudes towards animal use and belief in animal mind. *Anthrozoös 17*(1), 43–62

Lazarus, R. S. (1991). *Emotion and Adaptation*. New York: Oxford University Press.

Lee, K. (1993). *Compass and gyroscope: Integrating science and politics for the environment*. Washington, DC: Island Press.

Leopold, A. (1949). *A sand county almanac*. Oxford: Oxford University Press.

Light, A. & Katz, E. (Eds.) (1996). *Environmental pragmatism*. New York: Routledge.

Likona, T. (1991). *Educating for culture*. New York: Bantam Books.

MacIntyre, A. (1984). *After virtue* (2nd ed.). Notre Dame: Notre Dame University Press.

Markowitz, E. M. (2012). Is climate change an ethical issue? Examining young adults' beliefs about climate and morality. *Climatic Change, 114*(3–4), 479–495.

Markowitz, E. M., & Shariff, A. F. (2012). Climate change and moral judgement. *Nature Climate Change, 2*(4), 243–247.

Markowitz, E. M., Slovic, P., Västfjäll, D., & Hodges, S. D. (2013). Compassion fade and the challenge of environmental conservation. *Judgment and Decision Making, 8*(4), 397–406.

Martin, B., Bright, A., Cafaro, P., Mittelstaedt, R., & Bruyere, B. (2009). Assessing the development of environmental virtue in 7th and 8th grade students in an expeditionary learning outward bound school. *Journal of Experiential Education, 31*(3), 341–358.

Mussen, P., & Eisenberg-Berg, N. (1977). *Roots of caring sharing and helping*. San Francisco: Freeman.

Myers, Jr., O. E. (2007). *The significance of children and animals: Social development and our connections to other species*, (2nd revised ed.). West Lafayette, IN: Purdue University Press.

Myers Jr., O. E., Saunders, C. D., & Bexell, S. (2009). Fostering empathy with wildlife: Factors affecting free-choice learning for conservation concern and behavior. In J. H. Falk, J. E. Heimlich, & S. Foutz (Eds.), *Free-Choice Learning and the Environment* (pp. 39–55). Lanham, MD: AltaMira Press

Myers, Jr., O. E., Saunders, C., & Birjulin, A. (2004). Emotional dimensions of watching zoo animals: An experience sampling study building on insights from psychology. *Curator 47*(3), 299–321.

Nevers, P., Gebhard, U. & Billmann-Maheca, E. (1997). Patterns of reasoning exhibited by children and adolescents in response to moral dilemmas involving plants, animals and ecosystems. *Journal of Moral Education 26*(2),169–186.

Norton, B. G. (1987). *Why preserve natural variety?* Princeton: Princeton University Press.

Norton, B. G. (1991). *Toward unity among environmentalists*. New York: Oxford University Press.

Norton, B. G. (2005). *Sustainability: A philosophy of adaptive ecosystem management*. Chicago: University of Chicago Press.

Nussbaum, M. C. (1987). Non-relative virtues: An Aristotelian approach. *WIDER Working Paper, WP, 32*. Helsinki: World Institute for Development Economic Research. Available at: http://www.wider.unu.edu/publications/working-papers/previous/en_GB/wp-32/. Accessed 2 Aug 2014.

Opotow, S. (1990). Moral exclusion and injustice: An introduction. *Journal of Social Issues 4*(1), 1–20.

Opotow, S. (1994). Predicting protection: Scope of justice and the natural world. *Journal of Social Issues, 50*, 49–64.

Opotow, S., & Brook, A. (2003). Identity and exclusion in rangeland conflict. In S. Clayton, & S. Opotow (Eds.), *Identity and the natural environment* (pp. 249–272). Cambridge, MA: MIT Press.

Opotow, S., & Weiss, L. (2000). Denial and the process of exclusion in environmental conflict. *Journal of Social Issues 56*(3), 475–490.

Pahl, S., & Bauer, J. (2013). Overcoming the distance: Perspective taking with future humans improves environmental engagement. *Environment and Behavior*, *45*(2), 155–169.

Piaget, J. (1975). *The Child's Conception of the World*. (Trans. J. & A. Tomlinson.) Towata, NJ: Littlefield, Adams & Co. (Original work published 1929)

Pianalto, M. (2013) Humility and environmental virtue ethics. In M. W. Austin (Ed.), *Virtues in action: New essays in applied virtue ethics* (pp. 132–149). New York: St. Martin's Press.

Plous, S. (1993). Psychological mechanisms in the human use of animals. *Journal of Social Issues 49*(1), 11–52.

Preston, S. D. & de Waal, F. B. M. (2002). Empathy: Its ultimate and proximate bases. *Behavioral and Brain Sciences 25*, 1–20.

Raimi, K. T., & Leary, M. R. (2014). Belief superiority in the environmental domain: Attitude extremity and reactions to fracking. *Journal of Environmental Psychology*, *40*, 76–85.

Sacchi, S., Riva, P., Brambilla, M., & Grasso, M. (2014). Moral reasoning and climate change mitigation: The deontological reaction toward the market-based approach. *Journal of Environmental Psychology*, *38*, 252–261

Samuelson, C. D. & Barratt, C. L. (2012). Collaborative processes in ecosystem management. In S. Clayton (Ed.), *Oxford handbook of environmental and conservation psychology* (pp. 598–627). New York: Oxford University Press.

Samuelson, C., Peterson, T., & Putnam, L. (2003). Group identity in water resource management. In S. Clayton & S. Opotow (Eds.), *Identity and the natural environment* (pp. 273–295). Cambridge, MA: MIT Press.

Sandler, R. (2005). Introduction: Environmental virtue ethics. In P. Cafaro, & R. Sandler (Eds.), *Environmental virtue ethics* (pp. 1–12). Lanham, MD: Rowman & Littlefield Publishers.

Sandler, R. L. (2007). *Character and environment: A virtue-oriented approach to environmental ethics*. New York: Columbia University Press.

Sayre, K. (1991). An alternative view of environmental ethics. *Environmental Ethics 13* (3), 195–213.

Schultz, P. W. (2000). Empathizing with nature: The effects of perspective taking on concern for environmental issues. *Journal of Social Issues*, *56*(3), 391–406.

Schultz, P. W., & Zelezny, L. (2003). Reframing environmental messages to be congruent with American values. *Human Ecology Review 10*(2), 126–136.

Severson, R. L., & Kahn, P. H., Jr., (2010). In the orchard: Farm worker children's moral and environmental reasoning. *Journal of Applied Developmental Psychology*, *31*, 249–256.

Shaw, B. (1997). A virtue ethics approach to Aldo Leopold's land ethic. *Environmental Ethics 19*, 53–67.

Shellenberger, M. & Nordhaus, T. (2010).The death of environmentalism. Available at: http://www.thebreakthrough.org/images/Death_of_Environmentalism.pdf

Shweder, R. A., Much, N. C., Mahapatra M., & Park, L. (1997). The "Big Three" of morality (autonomy, community, divinity), and the "Big Three" explanations of suffering. In A. Brandt, & P. Rozin (Eds.), *Morality and health* (pp. 119–169). New York: Routledge.

Singer, P. (1975). *Animal liberation: A new ethics for our treatment of animals*. New York: Random House.

Snarey, J., & Keljo, K. (1991) In a *Gemeinschaft* voice: The cross-cultural expansion of moral developmental theory. In W. M. Kurtines, & J. L. Gewirtz (Eds.), *Handbook of moral behavior and development: Vol. 1: Theory* (pp. 395–424). Hillsdale, NJ: Lawrence Erlbaum.

Sommerville, J. A., & Decety, J. (2006). Weaving the fabric of social interaction: Articulating developmental psychology and cognitive neuroscience in the domain of motor cognition. *Psychonomic Bulletin and Review*, *13*(2), 179–200.

Staub, E. (1979). *Positive social behavior and morality, Vol. 2: Socialization and development*. New York: Academic Press.

Stonehouse, P. (2012). *Rough ground of character: A philosophical investigation into character development, examining a wilderness expedition case study through a virtue ethical lens.* Unpublished doctoral dissertation, Edinburgh: University of Edinburgh.

Tam, K.-P. (2013). Dispositional empathy with nature. *Journal of Environmental Psychology, 35*, 92–104.

Tangney, J. P., Stuewig, J., & Mashek, D. J. (2007). Moral emotions and moral behavior. *Annual Review of Psychology 58*, 345–372.

Tanner, C. (2009). To act or not to act: Nonconsequentialism in environmental decision-making. *Ethics & Behavior, 19*(6), 479–495.

Tanner, C., & Medin, D. L. (2004). Protected values: No omission bias and no framing effects. *Psychonomic Bulletin & Review, 11*(1), 185–191.

Tanner, C., Medin, D. L., & Iliev, R. (2008). Influence of deontological versus consequentialist orientations on act choices and framing effects: When principles are more important than consequences. *European Journal of Social Psychology, 38*(5), 757–769.

Tessman, L. (2013). Virtue ethics and moral failure: Lessons from neuroscientific moral psychology. In M. W. Austin (Ed.), *Virtues in action: New essays in applied virtue ethics* (pp. 171–189). New York: St. Martin's Press.

Tetlock, P. (2003). Thinking the unthinkable: Sacred values and taboo cognitions. *Trends in Cognitive Science, 7*(7), 320–324.

Thompson, A. (2012). The virtue of responsibility for the global climate. In A. Thompson & J. Bendik-Keymer (Eds.), *Ethical adaptation to climate change: Human virtues of the future* (pp. 203–221). Cambridge, MA: MIT Press.

Throop, W. & Purdom, R. (2006). Wilderness restoration: The paradox of public participation. *Restoration Ecology 14*(4), 493–499.

Tönnies, F. (1957). *Community and Society.* (C. P. Loomis, Trans.). East Lansing, MI: Michigan State University. (original work published 1887)

Truelove, H. B., & Joireman, J. (2009). Understanding the relationship between Christian orthodoxy and environmentalism: The mediating role of perceived environmental consequences. *Environment and Behavior, 41*(6), 806–820.

Tuler, S. & Webler, T. (2006). Introduction: Recent research in public participation: A focus on learning. *Human Ecology Review 13*(2), 148–149.

Turiel, E. (1983). *The development of social knowledge.* Cambridge: Cambridge University Press.

Turiel, E. (2002). *The culture of morality: Social development, context and conflict.* New York: Cambridge University Press.

Turiel, E. (2006). Thought, emotions, and social interactional processes in moral development. In M. Killen & J. G. Smetana (Eds.), *Handbook of moral development* (pp. 7–35). Mahwah, NJ: Lawrence Erlbaum.

Vollum, S., Buffington-Vollum, J. & Longmire, D. R. (2004). Moral disengagement and attitudes about violence toward animals. *Society and Animals 12*(3), 209–235.

Walker, L. J. (1991). Sex differences in moral reasoning. In W. M. Kurtines & J. L. Gewirtz (Eds.), *Handbook of moral behavior and development: Vol. 2: Research* (pp. 333–364). Hillsdale, NJ: Lawrence Erlbaum.

Wals, A. E. J. (2007). *Social learning towards a more sustainable world: Principles, perspectives, and praxis.* Wageningen: Wageningen Academic Publishers.

Westen, D. (2007). *The political brain.* New York: PublicAffairs.

Westen, D., Blagov, P. S., Harenski, K., Kilts, C. & Hamann, S. (2006). Neural bases of motivated reasoning: An fMRI study of emotional constraints on partisan political judgment in the 2004 U.S. presidential election. *Journal of Cognitive Neuroscience, 18*(11), 1947–1958.

Weston, A. (2007). *Creative problem-solving in ethics.* New York: Oxford.

Wong, P. T. P. (2003). I'm glad that I'm a nobody: A positive psychology of humility. Coquitlam, BC: President's column, International Network on Personal Meaning, Nov. 2003. http://www.meaning.ca/archives/presidents_columns/pres_col_nov_2003.htm. Accessed 12 April 2007.

8

Environment and Identity

- The concept of identity
- Identity development
- Developing an affiliation with nature
- Environmental identity
- Ecopsychology and depth psychology perspectives
- Measuring environmental identity
- Place identity
- Animals and identity
- Environmental social identity
- Identity and behavior
- Putting identity to work
- Conclusion
- References

The love people have for nature is strong. As we described in Chapters 5 and 7, national surveys consistently reflect a high value for nature and its protection that is not based on instrumental concerns. Although it is true that this value does not always translate into environmentally protective behavior, it is nonetheless worth considering this love, and its implications. Why do people care about nature? What gives its emotional and moral resonance? Part of the answer lies in the deep personal significance that people find in the natural environment. Interactions with the natural environment shape the ways in which people define themselves, as individuals, as members of society, and as humans. Researchers interested in human development and identity have begun to examine the importance of nature in developing and experiencing a fully actualized sense of self, as social psychologists investigate the implications of this identity for environmentally relevant behavior.

The concept of identity

There is a substantial literature within psychology on identity: what it is, where it comes from, and what difference it makes. Identities are frameworks for organizing information about a person. They can be personal attributes; they can involve social roles and relationships; or they

Conservation Psychology: Understanding and promoting human care for nature, Second Edition.
Susan Clayton and Gene Myers.

www.wiley.com\go\clayton\conservation

can place people into social categories. We have multiple identities, whose salience may vary across time and across situations.

One of psychology's earliest and most influential writers, James (1892/1961, p. 44), described a tripartite categorization between the material, social, and personal aspects of the "objective" self, or "the sum total of all a person can call his". His definition of the material self included what was tangible: home, body, possessions. Although James did not specifically talk about nature as part of the material self, he clearly recognized that a sense of self comes from things outside the person as well as those inside, and from physical as well as social influences.

Identities are complex and multifaceted. For one thing, they are experienced both internally and externally: We have a self-concept or sense of ourselves, but we are also defined by others. The identities that come from within may not be the same as those imposed from without, but both are important and both have the potential to affect behavior. As compilations of beliefs about the self, identities are outcomes of our experiences and of the kind of aspects James described, constantly evolving over time in response to new experiences.

Identities also affect the way we respond to the world, both cognitively and emotionally. They can serve as a focusing mechanism: If something is self-relevant, it gets greater attention, as demonstrated in shorter response times and better recall (Kihlstrom et al., 1988; Markus et al., 1982). Identities have strong motivational impacts: If something is part of my self-definition, I will be invested in protecting it as well as in presenting it in the best possible light. The desire to have a coherent and positive identity leads people to value opportunities for connectedness, efficacy, and autonomy (Ryan & Deci, 2000).

One of the fundamental motivations for identity is to expand one's sense of self by forming relationships with others. These relationships are not only emotional connections, but actually change one's self-definition. When a child, for example, learns that he or she is part of a family, a community, a nation, and a species, or an adult becomes enmeshed in a romantic relationship, the experiences of these larger units become self-relevant. Such relationships can also be felt with places and with the natural world in general, leading to increased care and concern for those environments.

This chapter reviews research on the ways in which the environment, and particularly experiences with nature, affect identity development among both children and adults. We will also examine different ways of thinking about, and measuring, an environmental identity. Finally, we discuss environmental identities in practice: how they affect behavior and how they are nurtured within a social context. The impact of identity on behavior is worth considering as we ponder how to encourage care for nature. But the impact of environment on identity development also merits our attention as a reminder of *why* it is important to protect our natural environment.

Identity development

The physical environment is influential as a child develops a sense of self. Because places convey expectations for behavior and vary in their compatibility with a person's behavioral goals, familiarity with an environment will enhance the child's sense of control. Childhood memories of places evince strong emotions, in particular feelings of privacy, control, and security (Korpela, 2002). Psychoanalytically oriented theorists consider the environment as one possible object for affection and attachment. Just as a good parent can provide a secure base that gives a child the freedom to explore, so too a stable and comforting location – such as a bedroom or a treehouse – can provide a home base that allows a child to roam his or her surroundings with confidence (cf. Chawla, 1992). Conversely, instability in the environment, either through frequent moves or through some environmental disruption, may have a lasting impact on a child's identity.

Research suggests that children's identities are rooted in and enriched by relationships to natural places and to other living things. Some of the evidence for the importance of the natural environment to childhood identity development comes from research looking at children's favorite places. The geographies of childhood – the physical boundaries in which a child is allowed to venture alone or with friends – were studied earliest by Hart (1979) in the United States and Moore (1986) in the United Kingdom. These researchers mapped children's behavior and went with them to favorite and other places to learn their significance. In Fig. 8.1, Louise Chawla summarizes such findings as an expanding pattern of positive place attachments in normal development.

A variety of motivations across development encourages a balance between familiar places and the draw of the unknown. Both novel and familiar environments support identity development, providing conventional settings where social roles may be enacted, and unprogrammed spaces that offer autonomy. Contributions to identity formation vary at any moment and as the child matures.

Preschoolers depend on parents or caregivers to take them into natural settings. In middle childhood, nature can provide a particularly good site for unsupervised experimentation as children learn to manipulate objects in their environment. Damming creeks, building forts out of branches, and making mud pies are activities unconstrained by rules and instruction manuals that allow children to explore not only the physical properties of objects but also their own abilities and creativity. Friendships spur exploration, and exploration intensifies friendships

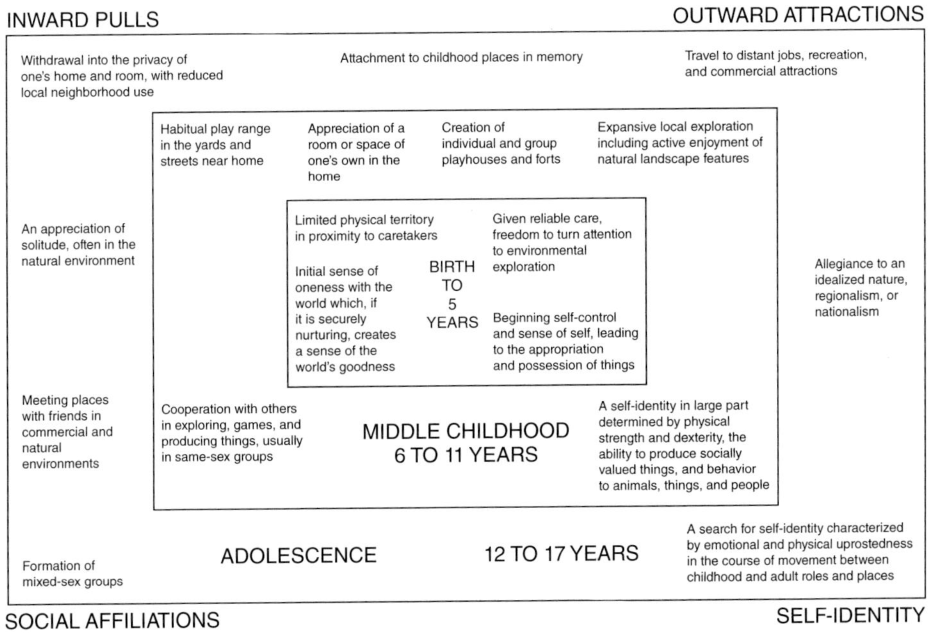

Fig. 8.1 Sources of developing place attachments in early and middle childhood and adolescence. (From Chawla, 1992, by permission of Springer Science and Business Media.)

(Moore, 1986). Bruni and Schultz (2009) found that the vast majority of their sample of 10–12 year olds associated natural areas with the self more strongly than built areas. Through middle childhood there is an outward trend, but adolescents seem to value nature less than other age groups, probably because the formation of extrafamilial social ties becomes more important and the social environment is paramount (Kaplan & Kaplan, 2002). As mixed-sex groups form, adolescent youth seek privacy in their homes and by venturing to more distant locations.

Adult autobiographies provide further evidence of the importance of nature for children. Memories of childhood show disproportionate attention to outdoor environments, given the amount of time children actually spend outdoors. Based on memories about childhood places described in contemporary autobiographies, Chawla (1986) identified four types of place attachment. (Methodological issues about using memories as data are discussed in Chawla, 1986, 1992, and 1998.) The most common was simple affection for a place. Two more types include idealization of the environment and ambivalence toward the environment – the latter based on identification with a place accompanied by recognition of its flaws or socially stigmatized status. An adolescent may find personal resonance in the social connotations of a place: nature as wild, untamed, and dangerous; sublime and awe-inspiring; or, alternatively, contaminated and repulsive. Chawla also described transcendent memories where a place was remembered as a "living presence in itself, exciting all five senses and inspiring exuberance, calm or awe" (Chawla, 1992 p. 74). These patterns suggest that nature can contribute to identity through what it represents and the emotions it evokes.

Identity may also develop from a sense of connection to other species. Myers (2007) and Myers and Russell (2003) examined the ways in which interactions with nonhuman animals affect the development of identity for both children and adults. His research began with the recognition that the identity does not develop on its own, but through interaction with and feedback from others. Myers's observations of preschool children with animals, as well as their reported experiences, talk about, and pretend play as animals revealed that children can flexibly employ their developing social abilities in interaction with a range of species. Myers argues that this process is not primarily projective, anthropomorphic, nor determined by culture, but arises as mental abilities such as mirroring, empathy, and perspective-taking encounter variations on the theme of animacy. The child's sense of self (here referring more to James' "subjective" sense of self, the on-going actor we call "I") is thus directly formed in relation to the available mixed-species community. Children expressed concern and distress when harm occurred to an animal they knew, suggesting such an extended sense of identity.

Taking this idea further, Myers and Russell (2003) showed that adults with intimate knowledge of wild animals (in this case, wild black bears) may utilize a similar suite of social skills in understanding them and shaping their identities in relationship to them. Zoo visitors, too, appear to use encounters with zoo animals to reflect upon their own identities as humans (Clayton et al., 2008). Even plants can help children to think about what it means to be human. Qualitative research by Gebhard et al. (2003) illuminated the extensive anthropomorphism evident in children's reasoning about trees and the ways in which this anthropomorphism informs their beliefs about appropriate human behavior toward nature.

Developing an affiliation with nature

Research shows that people who strongly identify with the natural environment as adults typically had special relationships with nature as children (Chawla, 2007; Degenhardt, 2002; Wells

& Lekies, 2006; Zavestoski, 2003). These relationships could encompass a special outdoors place, or a personal experience of environmental loss or degradation. Based on interviews with environmentalists about the source of their motivation to protect the environment, Chawla (1999) reported that "most people described childhood as the foundation of their relationship with the environment" (p. 17). The two most common themes were positive experiences with nature in childhood and family members who were role models for respecting the natural environment. Negative experiences of environmental loss were also mentioned by 39% of the sample. Experience of environmental destruction as an adult can also make an environmental identity stronger or more salient (e.g., Kempton & Holland, 2003), as shown by the way local leaders arise in response to environmental justice issues (e.g., Schwab, 1994).

Perhaps as important as the personal experience with nature is the association of particular environments with particular social bonds. Writers often make too strict a distinction between the social and the nonsocial environment, whereas in fact, connections to nature are usually encouraged or even initiated through connections to other people. In her analysis of environmental memories in autobiographies, Chawla (1986) found that the most common form of place attachment in children was affection due to an association with loved family members or other important social figures. Kals et al. (1999) report that emotional affinity toward nature is associated with having spent time in nature with significant others as a child. Other writers have also observed that environmentalists tend to describe parents who encouraged a love of nature. Such parents may help children to overcome common negative reactions to nature or the discomforts being outdoors may bring (Bixler & Floyd, 1997). Bixler et al. (2002) have argued persuasively that socialization, including learning basic skills, is an essential component in children having positive relations to nature.

A sense of connection to nature can also be nurtured among adults. Deep ecologists argue that it develops from personal experiences or involvement with natural entities (e.g., Diehm, 2007). In the short term, specific experiences such as time in natural settings can activate a sense of one's own connection to nature (Mayer et al., 2009; Schultz & Tabanico, 2007). Seed et al. (1988) developed a workshop called the "Council of All Beings" in which participants are encouraged to role-play the part of some nonhuman component of the natural world. Bragg (1996) examined the impact of a Council of All Beings workshop on self-concept immediately after the workshop and 6 months later. Using the Twenty Statements Test, a standard measure of self-concept, she found that a sense of ecological self was greater after the workshop. However, unless it was supported by a social network, the ecological self tended to drop back to baseline levels as time passed. It seems likely that a person needs to have a wider range of experiences – extending over time and/or throughout different aspects of one's life – in order to maintain a strong environmental identity. We need to consider the broader societal structures (such as jobs, activities, and affiliations) and discourses that support or inhibit such identity (Zavestoski, 2003).

Environmental identity

The personal relevance of nature can be closely examined among adults, who are more likely than children to reflect on, and articulate, the way nature can affect their sense of self. Comments from a Sierra Club survey that asked people why they care about the environment (available at http://www.sierraclub.org/sierra/200107/inspire.asp) show how the experience of an environmental identity can blur the boundary between self and nature:

- *My motivations for protecting the wild earth are fairly selfish.*
- *[There is a] sense of myself that I feel when I'm outdoors and nowhere else.*
- *... Something deep within all of us connects us to the natural world. ... I feel so connected to that circle [when I am out in the wilderness] ... [nature] is connected to the inner core of our being.*

These quotes suggest a sense of identity that transcends the individual and encompasses one's position as part of a living ecosystem. The philosopher Naess (1989) stressed "identification" not in the sense of indistinguishability with life processes, but in terms of our capacity to see something of the other in ourselves, to experience a sense of similarity or shared community. Writers have used terms such as "ecological self" (Bragg, 1996; Mathews, 1991; Naess, 1989) "ecological identity" (Thomashow, 1995), "environmental identity" (Clayton & Opotow, 2003; Weigert, 1997), "environmental self", or "sense of self-in-place" (Cantrill, 1998; Cantrill & Senecah, 2001). Although these terms have slightly different connotations, they all stem from the idea that the natural environment and our relationship to it can be an important part of our self-concept. Experiences with nature may be not just enjoyable, but self-relevant and potentially transformative, affecting the way we define ourselves to ourselves as well as to others.

Borden suggested that for people with a high degree of ecological concern, ecology acted as a metaphor for the sometimes sudden emergence of a new identity. In a series of studies, Borden (1985) found many correlates of high versus low environmental concern that related to self-definition or personal goals, such as a shift from "quality of life" to "quality of experience" and responsibility, suggesting pervasive changes in organizations of mind and behavior. Borden speculated that the environmental crisis is experienced as a crisis within the self. Ecological insight, often sparked by some experience in nature, can precipitate a profound and rapid dialectical reorganization of meanings about the self, making self and world part of one whole, with simultaneous deep reevaluations of responsibility and action (Borden, 2014).

Why would nature affect our sense of self? Natural, as opposed to built, environments have certain characteristics. They appear to provide an optimal level of sensory stimulation: not so low as to be boring, not so heavy as to be overwhelming. (See discussion of Attention Restoration Theory in Chapter 12.) This provides the space for self-reflection. People talk about natural environments as ones in which they are able to think about their own goals and priorities (Herzog et al., 1997; see the discussion of Norton's "transformative values" in Chapter 7). Long et al. (2003) found that people described nature as an important location for solitude experiences that promoted inner peace and self-discovery, and that it was rarely associated with such negative aspects of solitude as loneliness and anonymity. Korpela and colleagues, similarly, have found that natural settings are favored in part because they are used to reflect on personal matters and to regulate one's emotional state and self-concept (Korpela, 1989, 1992; Korpela et al., 2001).

The natural environment also may fulfill basic identity needs (Ryan & Deci, 2000). Most people feel a desire for *autonomy*, the sense that they are acting in response to their own wishes rather than merely as a tool for others. A natural environment can enhance autonomy because social regulations, oversight, and consequences are fewer. New York City residents, for example, reported that they preferred natural environments when seeking privacy (Manzo, 2005). Nisbet et al. (2011) found positive correlations between nature relatedness (a concept, discussed below, related to identity) and autonomy. In experimental research, people who were in the presence of nature scored higher on perceived autonomy than those who were not (Weinstein et al., 2009). Clayton asked students on an overnight field trip to a nature center if they felt differently about themselves out in nature and found themes related to self-direction:

- *Nature ... makes me feel like myself.*
- *I feel much more independent out here.*
- *Here in the forest I feel more like a person. I can be myself, no one here will judge me.*

Another fundamental motivation related to identity is the desire for *connection* or *belongingness*. Transcendent experiences – experiences in which a person feels a sense of transcending the limits of the self, being part of a larger collective or participating in a deeper meaning – seem to be fostered by natural environments (Williams & Harvey, 2001; Vining & Merrick, 2012; see Chapter 4). Nature provides the opportunity to think about one's role as part of a larger whole, an interdependent ecosystem. As Naess (1989) stated, "One experiences oneself to be a genuine part of all life" (p. 174). Chawla (1986) found that transcendence, defined as a profound sense of connection to nature, was a common theme in environmental memories. In research with 17–18 year old Finnish adolescents, Korpela (1989, 1992) found that children associated a sense of belongingness with their favorite places. Clayton's students also reflected a sense of connection:

- *I feel like I belong.*
- *I no longer think of myself so much as an "I" or an individual [but as] part of everything else.*
- *I feel like I get to see ... life, a community all interrelated and tied together. I am part of that.*

A third motive is the *desire to feel competent.* A perception of self-efficacy may result from the opportunity for self-sufficiency and the use of physical skills. Natural environments remind us how it feels to move around under our own steam and be responsible for satisfying our own needs (for shade, for a good view, perhaps for food and/or water). Barton and Pretty (2010), for example, found that exercise in a natural setting enhances self-esteem (see also Fredrickson & Anderson, 1999; Scherl, 1989).

As experiences with the natural environment and environmental problems transform identity, a strong environmental identity should affect the way people respond to environmental information and problems. Bragg (1996) delineates the possible consequences of an ecological self: greater sensitivity to information about the environment, feelings of connectedness or sympathy to environmental entities, and activities that promote the connection. The experience of an ecological self implies a perception of similarity, relatedness, or analogy between oneself and other elements of the ecosystem, to the extent that a person might react to threats to nature as if they were threats to themselves. Environmental identity, for example, is associated with greater environmental concern, sense of connection to zoo animals, and support for animal rights (Clayton, 2008; Clayton et al., 2011)

Ecopsychology and depth psychology perspectives

As described in Chapter 1, ecopsychologists focus on the relationship between humans and nature, and particularly how the human psyche is constituted by relationships to nonhuman nature (Kahn & Hasbach, 2012). We have emphasized the ways in which humans experience and benefit from nature; Fisher (2002) and other ecopsychologists suggest further that the problems we have caused in nature and our internal psychological ailments are part of the same pattern of psychopathology. Ecopsychologists stress therapy and what Fisher calls "recollective practices," such as vision quests, that aim at "recalling how our human psyches are embedded in and nurtured by the larger psyche of nature" (2002, p. 13). Fisher says, "if we are, in good faith, to understand the psychopathology of the human–nature relationship, we cannot avoid an examination of the social mediation *of* this relationship" (p. 21).

This perspective does not pretend to be neutral or objective. Fisher argues that ecopsychology must reject many dualisms that are built into Western thought and scientific psychology, such as the distinction between inner/outer and human/nature. Drawing on the work of phenomenological psychologist and philosopher Eugene Gendlin (1992; 1997), Fisher describes a connection between psyche and nature and provides a method by which distortions and obstacles to life process can be identified and worked through.

A different kind of theoretical tradition in psychology, perhaps best conceptualized as mythopoetic or depth psychology, suggests another way to think of the human relationship with nature in terms of the ecological self (Bragg, 1996; Mathews, 1991). Swiss philosopher Gebser (1984) examined ways of relating to nature that may be true for children and some adults, though dismissed by the mainstream social sciences (Chawla, 2002). Different human cultures and different moments in an individual's life may be characterized by different forms of consciousness in our experience of self and world.

The most basic form of consciousness is the *Archaic*, which Gebser (1984) regarded as "identical with origin" and with the consciousness of animals, probably infants, and states of reverie. One feels an identity with the world, an immersion and receptivity that is inexpressible in words. *Magic* consciousness experiences the world in terms of magical "union," a "self-aware coming together of self and other" in which one experiences the power of being connected to the world (Chawla, 2002, p. 209). Magical consciousness is vulnerable to a fear of the world's power and a resultant desire to control it – as expressed in our obsession with technologies.

Gebser also described *mythic* and *mental* forms of consciousness, both accessible through symbolic thought and communication. Myth is cyclical, associative, emotional and empathic, and multi-vocal. Mental consciousness is that governed by the "observing I/eye that assesses the environment objectively, evaluates it in the abstract, and measures it rationally and often quantitatively" (Chawla, 2002, p. 211). Mental consciousness can create dualities, which may reduce nature or other people to an object to treat without feeling. For many this is the most familiar form. Gebser denied any linear progression or hierarchy among these forms – all make necessary contributions to life – but he reserved one as representing the developmental goal. This is the *integral* form of consciousness that is able to use the others appropriately to overcome the defective forms that are creating a planetary crisis for humanity. This implies a new kind of attention not only to how we inhabit the world but also to how we mentally approach it.

Measuring environmental identity

The burgeoning recognition of the importance of environment to identity has led to the development of a number of ways to assess the connection. Clayton (2003) developed a 24-item environmental identity scale, later shortened to 11 items (see Clayton, 2012), to measure the extent to which people consider nature to form an important part of their self-concept. Items on the scale reflect the extent to which a person tends to interact with elements of the natural world, whether a person rates nature as important, whether the person thinks of him or herself as part of nature, and whether the natural environment evokes positive emotions. See Table 8.1. The scale has high internal reliability and relates in expected ways to environmental behaviors, attitudes, and group membership.

Schultz (2001) adapted an earlier measure of interdependence (Aron et al., 1992) to present people with a series of pictures of two circles, one of which represents the self and one of which represents nature. They start side by side, then overlap to an increasing extent until they are

Table 8.1 Items from the environmental identity scale.

I think of myself as a part of nature, not separate from it.
I spend a lot of time in natural settings.
Behaving responsibly toward the earth – living a sustainable lifestyle – is part of my moral code.
Learning about the natural world should be an important part of every child's upbringing.

Source: Clayton, 2003.

entirely the same. Although very different in format, Schultz's Inclusion of Nature in the Self (INS) scale is highly correlated with Clayton's EID scale, suggesting that both tap into a valid underlying construct.

Connections to nature might be implicit, operating outside conscious awareness. Schultz et al. (2004) developed a modification of the Implicit Associations Test, which measures the extent to which concepts are closely connected in a person's network of cognitive associations. This test requires people to rapidly and accurately decide if two paired terms belong together or not. For example, does an item like "flower" belong with "me or nature" or "other or built"? After rounds of this sort, the game requires choices of whether "flower" (and other terms) belong with "me or built" or "other or nature"? A person with a mental network connecting the self to nature will answer the former items more rapidly because there is a cognitive connection between "me or nature," whereas it will take more deliberation to discern that "flower" belongs with "other or nature" because "other" and "nature" are not cognitively associated. The time delay to answer questions correctly provides an estimate of the degree of how closely the person implicitly identifies with nature or with the built environment that is relatively unbiased by self-presentational concerns. Schultz et al.'s research shows acceptable reliability of the measure, and a relationship to environmental attitudes. This measure could be particularly useful when socially desirable responses are a problem.

Several other measures have been developed to assess the connections people perceive between themselves and the natural world. Kals et al., (1999) developed an emotional affinity with nature scale, which includes questions about "feelings of oneness with nature" as well as about love for nature and feelings of freedom and security associated with nature. Mayer and Frantz (2004) focused on emotional responses to nature with their Connectedness to Nature scale and found correlations with environmentalist identity and worldviews among college and community samples. Nisbet et al. (2009) developed a Nature Relatedness Scale that seems to capture the personal benefits of associations with nature (Zelenski & Nisbet, 2014). All of these measures have demonstrated some reliability and validity for research purposes. Together, they suggest that the construct of environmental identity or sense of connectedness with nature is psychologically meaningful. Tam (2013) compared these and other similar measures and found strong convergence around one common factor, a latent construct of connection to nature. The measures demonstrate modest divergence, indicating that choice of a measure should depend on the specific research question being addressed as well as characteristics of the sample.

Place identity

Environmental identity reflects the personal significance of natural environments in general. A more specific way in which the environment affects identity is captured in the concept of *place identity*. This term was first used by Proshansky (1978), where it signified "those dimensions of self that define the individual's personal identity in relation to the physical environment by means of a complex pattern of conscious and unconscious ideas, beliefs, preferences, feelings, values, goals, and behavioral tendencies and skills relevant to this environment." (p. 155). Place identity refers to the component of identity that is associated with feelings about a particular locale. It has typically been discussed with regard to a place of residence, although other places may sometimes be relevant. Identity comes from the way in which memories are intertwined with that place, so that it takes on emotional connotations and symbolic significance. Places can also be used to assert control, through a defined territory, or to express a particular self-image. Twigger-Ross and Uzzell (1996) describe the significance of a physical environment to identity in the ways it can contribute to a person's sense of distinctiveness, self-esteem, self-efficacy, and continuity.

> "... The land contains you, and you can't really differentiate between what it is and who you are."
>
> Julene Bair (2014, p. 64) on her attachment to her family land

To examine the attributes of a place that contribute to identity, Gustafson (2001) interviewed 14 Swedish residents about places that were important to them. He found three broad (and overlapping) themes that provided the basis for meaning: self, others, and environment. In other words, in addition to its utilitarian functions, a place can have personal meanings based on emotional significance and activities; based on the way in which it socially defines a person (what type of person tends to be found in this place?); and based on its natural features and climate, which may also have symbolic resonance.

Place identity is sometimes considered to be synonymous with place *attachment* (e.g., (Manzo & Devine-Wright, 2013; Stedman, 2002). Others describe place identity as a subcomponent of place attachment, which also includes place *dependence* – the extent to which one is dependent on a particular place to fulfill ones goals (Kyle et al., 2004; see Korpela, 2012). Certainly identity and attachment are related. As Belk (1992, p. 38) stated, "To be attached to certain of our surroundings is to make them a part of our extended self". On the other hand, identity and dependence may be less closely tied: Moore and Graefe (1994) defined *place dependence* as valuing a particular setting for a certain activity.

Attachment and identity have different implications. Attachment seems to emphasize the emotional ties between a person and a place, whereas identity can also include the definitional aspects whereby a person feels that alterations in an environment reflect well, or poorly, on him or her. Thus, one may care about, and take care of, an environment because one is attached to it, but one may also defend that environment because of a sense that it represents the self. Further, people may try to present an environment in the most positive way just as they would present themselves in a positive way, minimizing the flaws and even changing the environment to make it more attractive (as people do with their home landscapes). Bonaiuto et al. (1996) found that residents of British beaches with a strong local or national identity perceived their own beaches as less polluted.

Place identity differs from a more general environmental identity in more than just scope. Attachment may play a larger role in place identity, in part based on the contribution of memories of a specific place to a sense of well-being or security. Place identity also may be more affected by specific environmental threats, or the threat that one might have to leave that place. Cantrill and Senecah (2001) emphasize the relationship between a person's ideas about the self and their concepts about a place, as denoted in their term "self-in-place," which they argue may link how people appraise communications and how they behave regarding significant places. Ryan (2005) asked users of a particular urban park how they might feel about a negative change in that park, and found that they mentioned a feeling of personal loss, along with possible changes in their use of the park and environmental activism. Some of the response to a personal experience of environmental contamination, for example, from an accidental release

Box 8.1 Place identity on college campuses

One-hundred ninety randomly sampled students at the College of Wooster rated the college landscape as highly important, not only for the attractiveness and benefits it provides, but for the way in which it reflects their identity:

- *It promotes an image for the college and the atmosphere we represent* (Fig. 8.2).

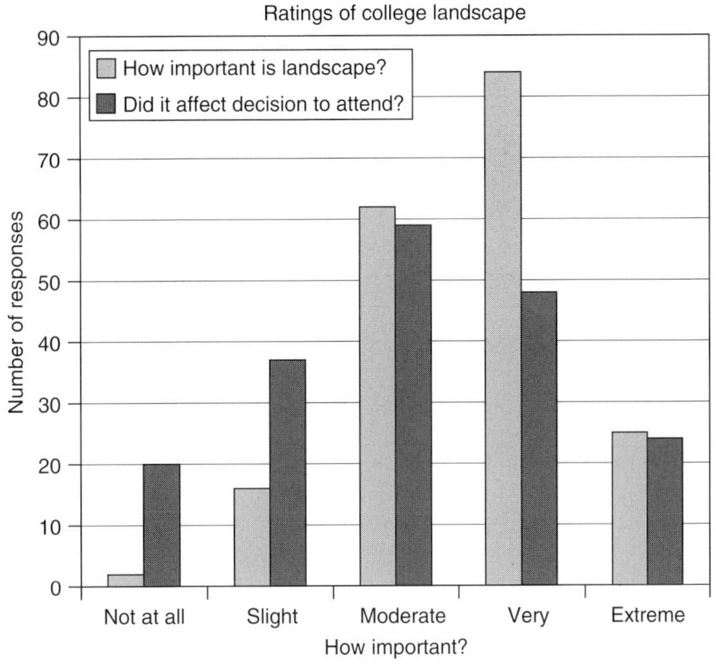

Fig. 8.2 Student ratings of the importance of the college landscape. (Unpublished data from Susan Clayton.)

At the University of Missouri, campus officials have taken advantage of the school mascot (Truman the Tiger) to promote tiger conservation with their "Tigers for Tigers" campaign (http://tigers.missouri.edu). Student identities, already linked to their alma mater, are extended to encompass the tiger and elicit support for education, research, and protection of this endangered species.

of toxic chemicals in the area or destruction of a feature of the local natural environment, may result from a sense of personal involvement, what has been referred to as a "spoiled identity" (Twigger-Ross et al., 2003).

Place identity is important to consider in implementing policies of sustainable development. Conservationists have sometimes been guilty of disregarding or even displacing the people indigenous to a place, with the aim of protecting the nonhuman residents. In addition to being ethically questionable, such policies may backfire if they lead to resistance by the local populace and/or activism by concerned outsiders. There are both positive and negative environmental consequences of a strong place identity: people may care more about threats to that place, but also be willing to simply reassign those threats to another location. (See Devine-Wright, 2011).

Are there psychopathologies of place? Hummon (1992) describes four kinds of sense of place, two of which are negative-alienation and placelessness, suggesting that some grounding in place or places is important to human identity. On a societal level, Relph (1976) argued that historical lack of attention to the experience of place in modern society has led to the loss of significant places, and the flourishing of meaningless places, embodied in kitsch, mass communication, mass culture, big business, and spaces dominated by a central authority. Since subjective meaning is integral to the concept of place, these place pathologies may be linked to cognitive deficits in the orientation of contemporary individuals to their surroundings.

Animals and identity

Like places, animals can be tied to peoples' identities. Modern evolutionary views affirm our shared biological membership in the animal kingdom (Ingold, 1988). Even for those who reject the idea that humans and animals are on a continuum because of religious beliefs or other worldview, there are many ways in which people playfully or seriously identify with animals.

Earlier we discussed how animals may be important to a developing sense of self-in-relation. If such a sense of self is grounded in interaction with the other (as social psychologists hold is the case between humans), then we might expect it to occur as well in some instances of human–animal interactions. Such systems have been studied between humans and dogs (Millot & Filiatre, 1986; Shapiro, 1989; Sanders, 1999), cats (Alger & Alger, 1997), horses (Hearne, 1986; Brandt, 2004), primates (Goodall, 1990; Strum, 1987), bears (Burghardt, 1992; Myers & Russell, 2003), and elephants (Hart, 1994), among other settings. While only suggestive, these examples support the idea that the human core self incorporates relationships to nonhuman animals. Many people's closeness to their pets reflects strong identification, as discussed in Chapter 2.

Animals may also enter identity symbolically or metaphorically, expressing something about the self. It has been a classic observation in anthropology that many cultures conceptualize humans and animals as "fellow inhabitants of the same world" (Ingold, 1994, p. 18); that is, in networks of mutual relationships, Going further, *totemism* entails the identification of social groups with animals (Lévi-Strauss, 1966), so that people in a totemic society believe that they are part of the same species as a particular plant or animal. Anthropologists Crocker (1985) and Levy-Bruhl (1966) report that the Amazonian Bororo, for example, claim to *be* red macaws – or, at least, to be metaphorically like them. This process may reflect our propensity for creating essentialist categories of unchanging entities, as described by the folk biological system discussed in Chapter 5, with social distinctions being mapped metaphorically onto animal categories (Hirschfeld & Gelman, 1994).

More broadly, many aboriginal hunter-gatherer cultures were (and some still are) *animistic*, assuming an original and persisting spiritual continuity between human and nonhuman worlds. For example, Kalahari Bushman hunters report the bodily sensation of being "in" a prey animal's body, suggesting "profound level of identification with animals" (Serpell, 2000, p. 115). In Hindu reincarnation beliefs, some part of the soul persists after death and is reborn in another form, sometimes animal. Western civilization has not outgrown such beliefs around the blurred human–animal boundary, as seen in the availability of animal telepathy experts and "channelers" that facilitate owners' communication with deceased pets, and other less esoteric forms of humanizing our pets, such as pet pedicures, cemeteries, and special "Yappy hour" gatherings (Greenebaum, 2004). The opposing tendency to animalize the self is evident too, for example, in the lively subculture of "furries" that has sprung up facilitated by the Internet. Devotees take on animal identities for real or virtual gatherings, share art and costumes depicting human–animal hybrids, and animalize their language of the body and (for some) their erotic life.

Animals affect people's social identities indirectly when a person identifies with an animal-related activity or career. Here the person may be seen by others as intimately involved with animals, for example, as a hunter, bird watcher, whaler, or animal rights crusader. The effects of such identities can be pervasive and subtle, as in the way that a person walking a dog is perceived and treated as a more socially "open" person (Robins et al., 1991). Social stereotypes develop around various animal identities too, such as that there are shared perceptions of the characteristics associated with a "cat" person, a "dog" person, or a "horsey" type. See Chapter 2 on whether such stereotypes are supported by psychological research.

Environmental social identity

Environmental identity develops not only through interactions with the natural environment but also, crucially, with the social environment. Although some nature experiences are solitary, people also experience nature in more social settings, as members of social groups and in their communities. Experiences of nature in the company of others affect our understandings of what nature signifies as well as the way we conceptualize our own relationship with nature. A relationship with the natural world may affect how a person affiliates or conflicts with others, or how other people define and perceive a person.

The social implications of place identity are particularly clear when the place with which one identifies is both a physical and a social construct. Consider, for example, a community identity – a sense of place and involvement with a residential neighborhood. Kim and Kaplan (2004) describe this kind of identity as resulting from distinctiveness, continuity, compatibility, significance, and cohesiveness of a place. They found a number of factors associated with community identity in two Maryland neighborhoods; notably, the local natural features had a strong impact. Other researchers have examined the effect of specific features of the natural environment in urban communities. Community gardens (Stuart, 2005; von Hassell, 2005) and tree-planting programs (Austin & Kaplan, 2003; Sommer, 2003) affect the way people think about their residential communities, and about their own identities as members of those communities.

A relationship toward nature may serve to define a person in the eyes of others. Sadalla and Krull (1995) asked college students to describe the probable personality of someone who engaged in a variety of behaviors that would reduce use of environmental resources: drying clothes on a clothesline, taking public transportation, and recycling. Although there were some

Fig. 8.3 Cultures may encourage defining oneself through consumption rather than environmentalism. (Photo by Susan Clayton.)

differences depending on the behavior being examined, conservation behaviors were uniformly seen to indicate lower status. Sadalla and Krull explain their finding by noting that consumption indicates higher status in most, if not all, cultures. (See Fig. 8.3.)

Other research has uncovered negative stereotypes of environmentalists, at least in the United States: Not only were typical environmentalists seen as eccentric and militant, people were less motivated to adopt pro-environmental behaviors when those were advocated by a typical environmentalist rather than by an atypical environmentalist or someone not described as an environmentalist (Bashir et al., 2013). Motivations to engage in environmentally protective behavior may include the desire to achieve a particular social identity through one's actions. For example, Griskevicius et al. (2010) found that people might act environmentally, for example, by buying "green" products, in order to increase their status. In some cases, it may be more effective to portray a behavior as motivated by concerns other than environmental ones, if environmentalism is not part of the identity that a person wants to convey.

Recognizing that the social implications of an identity as an environmentalist are not always positive, Zavestoski (2003) interviewed participants in a deep ecology workshop about strategies for maintaining their identities in the face of an unsupportive society. He found that many of them had chosen careers that were compatible with their environmental interests and that they worked hard to maintain social networks that encouraged them to express the environmentalist side of their identity. Nevertheless, many of them felt that their sense of connection with nature was not supported or respected in their day-to-day activities outside of the workshop. Zavestoski concluded that an environmental identity (he uses the term "ecological identity") must be nurtured and affirmed through social interactions in order to be fully developed and expressed.

Identity and behavior

Does identity matter? Research suggests that it does. One of the best-supported theories explaining the relationship between attitudes and behavior is the Theory of Planned Behavior (TPB; Ajzen, 1991). As described in Chapter 6, this theory proposes that behavior follows loosely from behavioral intentions, which in turn are a function of attitudes, subjective norms, and perceived control over the behavior. Recent studies have found that adding identity to the model increases its ability to explain behavior. For example, self-identity accounted for a significant proportion of variance in recycling behavior among a sample of Australian householders, above and beyond the more traditional TPB components (Terry et al., 1999): People who agreed that "recycling is an important part of who I am" and disagreed that "I'm not the sort of person who recycles" were more likely to say that they intended to recycle, and this intention, in turn, predicted whether or not they did recycle (see also Mannetti et al., 2004).

Inclusion of identity in Stern et al.'s (1999) VBN model (also described in Chapter 6) would be important for explaining committed environmentalism, perhaps by suggesting that identity can create a personal environmental norm. Clayton (2003) found that environmental identity mediated the relationship between values and behavior, and van der Werff and colleagues (2013, 2014) provide additional evidence that identity links values to behavior. Van der Werff et al. (2013) suggest that values need to be linked to the self in order to have an impact on behavioral choices.

Identity can affect responses to environmental problems by affecting attention: Typically, we monitor the condition of our own houses, yards, and children more closely than we monitor those belonging to others. Kyle et al. (2004) found that Appalachian Trail users who had a higher level of identification with that place were more likely to perceive negative environmental conditions on the trail. In surveys of adolescents working in Colorado on natural-resource-based work programs (e.g., trail maintenance), Vaske and Kobrin (2001) found that identification with the place was associated with a more general measure of environmentally responsible behavior. The personal connection to a place that represented the natural environment may have led the teens to be more aware of environmental issues.

Identity can also elicit motives related to self-presentation. As described in Chapter 1, the Toyota Prius (a hybrid car) seems to have enjoyed more sales success than other hybrids precisely because it serves as a public statement of the owner's environmental credentials. Self-presentational motives do not always have a positive impact on the environment; the "Not In My Back Yard" phenomenon refers to people's tendency to protect their own localities from environmental threats by displacing them to other sites. But a personal connection to a place can be tapped for environmental benefit. Residents of two different regions of Italy showed more support for the establishment of a local protected (natural) area when they had a strong regional identity (Carrus et al., 2005). This support was not explained by environmental attitudes. In other words, identification with the locale was enough to encourage people to support the development of a local natural area even in the absence of a general support for environmental protection. Presumably this was due to residents' desire to enhance the positive distinctiveness of a region with which they identified. Even more simply, identification with a place can lead one to feel personally implicated in threats to its well-being. Stedman (2002) surveyed property owners in Wisconsin and found that place identity predicted intention to protect the local area from overdevelopment.

Finally, a social identity as a resident of a place may be associated with taking personal responsibility for group-level outcomes and thus predict behavior as well as attitudes: Several studies assessing social identity (in an English neighborhood, a Barcelona suburb, and Olympic Village in Barcelona) found that it was positively correlated with a propensity toward sustainable behavior (such as considering ecological factors while shopping and taking responsibility for neighborhood upkeep; Pol et al., 2002; Uzzell et al., 2002; Valera & Guàrdia, 2002). Many of these studies refer to place identity or to a very specific identity as a recycler, driver, or environmentalist (a concept sometimes referred to as "environmentalist identity" or "environmental self-identity"; Kashima et al., 2014; van der Werff et al., 2013, 2014). Looking at a more general conception of environmental identity, Kals et al. (1999) found that emotional affinity toward nature predicted environmentally protective behavior and behavioral intentions in a German sample. Notably, experiences in nature had little direct effect on behavior. Instead, experiences in nature predicted emotional affinity, which in turn predicted behavior. Clayton (2003, 2008) has found that environmental identity predicted environmentally protective behavior among American college students; Kiesling and Manning (2010) found that it predicted ecological gardening practices among a community sample; and Winter and Chavez (2008) found that visitors to wilderness areas in California with higher EID scores were more supportive of managing natural resources for environmental protection (e.g., for protection of plants and improved air quality as well as the need for more areas for that purpose).

Because it involves an experience of being part of something greater than oneself, an environmental identity may encourage a sense of oneself as a member of a collective. Such a collective identity tends to encourage more group-oriented behavior (e.g., DeCremer & Van Vugt, 1999; Kramer & Brewer, 1984). This is important for environmental issues because of the need for people to take personal responsibility for what are essentially group-level outcomes (cf. Chapter 5). Due to the spatially and temporally diffuse nature of environmental threats, most people do not experience significant individual loss from those threats. However, if one is interested in the welfare of the group or even the ecosystem, the need for environmental action is clear.

The way identity entails a position with respect to different social groups has implications for how one responds to certain social and political issues, including environmental issues. Kempton and Holland (2003) found that the choice of terms people used to describe themselves was related to the actions they reported performing: Among a sample of members of environmental groups, those who described themselves as "environmentalists" were more likely to report taking civic environmental actions.

Among ranchers and farmers, environmental activists may be seen as the enemy, setting in motion a range of psychological techniques to enhance the image of their own group and delegitimize the concerns of the outgroup (cf. Chapter 7). Opotow and Brook (2003) describe the way in which group identity as a rancher, combined with a history of mistrust between ranchers and environmentalists, encouraged ranchers to oppose protection for a threatened species even while promoting their own role as environmental stewards. Attempts to resolve environmental conflict need to acknowledge the impact of competition between social groups as well as between humans and nonhuman nature. Opotow and Brook suggest that existing identities be respected but brought together under wider umbrella identities that emphasize characteristics and values shared by all the parties to the conflict. In the case of rangeland conflicts, they point to examples such as the Quivera Coalition (http://www.quiviracoalition.org), the Diablo Trust (http://www.diablotrust.org/), and the Malpai Borderlands Group (http://www.malpaiborderlandsgroup.org).

Identities do not always have the same impact on behavior. When a behavioral change is perceived as inconsistent with a person's identity – like asking a devoted car-owner to take the bus – the identity may be a source of resistance (Murtagh et al., 2012). Identities vary in sociocultural significance and implications, so that belonging to a community, for example, may or may not predict support for protecting the local environment (Devine-Wright & Howes, 2010). Individuals also vary in the extent to which they are thinking about their identities. Self-awareness has been shown to increase consistency between one's personal values and behavior (Gibbons, 1983). With regard to environmental behavior, van der Werff et al. (2014) found that the relationship between identity and behavior depended on the identity that was salient.

Putting identity to work

If identity is important to understanding the ways in which people treat their natural environments, can we usefully apply this understanding? Identities can be used to nurture conservation behavior when the natural objects being protected are tied to the self. This is one of the aims of place-based environmental education (see Chapter 11). Several programs already in existence successfully utilize identity by creating or strengthening a sense of personal connection to a particular piece of the natural environment. Programs that allow people to "adopt" a part of nature are a clear example. What does adopting mean but to make something a part of oneself or one's sphere of personal concern? Different organizations encourage individuals to adopt a particular endangered animal, or an acre of a rainforest, so that they will take a personal interest in its well-being and feel a personal responsibility to provide financial contributions. The (primarily) US program to "adopt a highway" allows groups to take responsibility for keeping a certain stretch of highway clean and in return posts the group's name on a highway sign. From its origins in Texas in 1984, the adopt-a-highway program now claims to encompass 90,000 groups in 49 different states. The program works because the clean stretch of highway is considered to project a positive image of the group's identity, and the group is motivated to maintain that stretch of highway in order to protect its public image.

One highly successful campaign asks people to take responsibility not just for a particular stretch of highway, but for the entire state. The "don't mess with Texas" campaign, sponsored by the Texas Department of Transportation, draws on the regional identity of Texas residents by using icons (e.g., cowboys) that are symbolic of Texas and language like "We Texans" and "Texans are full of state pride" to evoke a collective identity. In addition to having received multiple marketing awards, the campaign claims to be responsible for a 52% reduction in roadside litter since 1995 (www.dontmesswithtexas.org). This program also resonates with environmental virtue ethics as discussed in Chapter 7 because it extends an existing community consensus about a virtue to include treatment of nature.

Identities do not only encourage behavior; behavior can create identities. Because experiences are a source of identity, people who interpret their own behaviors as pro-environmental can strengthen their sense of themselves as environmentalists. Van der Werff et al. (2014) were able to experimentally increase the positive impact of identity on behavior by framing people's past actions in a way that led them to perceive themselves as more environmentally friendly. Thus, calling someone an environmentalist based on past behavior, under the right circumstances, can become a self-fulfilling prophecy as people adopt the label for themselves, leading to positive spillover in which the identity leads to further environmental behavior. In a field study, Poortinga et al. (2013) found evidence of this shift in identity following the introduction of a carrier bag charge in Wales. (It is important to realize that the reverse can also be true:

While it may be satisfying to call someone an enemy of the environment, it might encourage them to continue to act in ways that are unsustainable.) However, explaining others' environmental behavior as due to them being a specific type of person, such as an environmentalist, rather than in terms of their reasons for the behavior may decrease adoption of those behaviors by others who do not define themselves that way (Markowitz & Malle, 2012).

To examine the process by which environmental identities were nurtured and facilitated in a social context, John Fraser studied volunteers at the Bronx and Central Park Zoos. He found that people reported becoming volunteers because of their love for animals, but that the identity of zoo volunteer was also closely connected to a general environmental identity, based on its implications for attitudes toward animals, nature, and conservation initiatives. Just as important, volunteers reported a highly positive sense of group identity associated with being a zoo volunteer as well as strong in-group bonds with their fellow volunteers and a high degree of pride and value in the identity in their interview responses (Fraser et al., 2009). Finally, their responses suggested that the experience of volunteering both strengthened and focused their environmental identities. They reported having become active promoters of zoos and of conservation, and more committed to conservation than they were before joining the zoo. (Fig. 8.4)

Identity can also inhibit environmental care and concern. It has often been noted that political affiliation, in the United States, is one of the strongest predictors of environmental attitudes (Guber, 2013). When environmental issues are perceived as threatening to important identities, protecting those identities may be a stronger motive than protecting the environment. In the context of climate change, Norgaard (2011) provides a nuanced sociological

Fig. 8.4 A zoo volunteer with visitors at the Bronx Zoo. (Photo by Larsen Maher. Copyright WCS, reprinted by permission.)

and social-psychological analysis of the ways adults need to manage identities and associated emotions led them to deny the realities of climate change during a nearly snowless winter in Norway, and more recently in the US. Norgaard distinguishes between surface and deep emotion management, for example, suppression versus re-appraisal. The sociocultural context is critical in providing stock narratives such as national identity and innocence, and stances such as coolness, cynicism, toughness, and emotional display norms to accomplish conversational control and maintenance of a sense of "ontological security" or everyday reality in the face of evidence of climate change. This kind of analysis informed the Cambridge Carbon Conversation project's conversational settings designed to unearth and acknowledge the deeper feelings, while fostering ways for people to feel affirmed in individual and collectively chosen solution steps (http://cambridgecarbonfootprint.org/carbon-conversations/). The emotional challenges presented by societal constructions of large environmental problems and more positive ways of approaching them will be discussed in Chapter 12.

The power of collective identities, both existing and new, has often been overlooked in research on environmental identity. Conservation-minded professionals should think not just about how to tap into existing place- and environment-based identities but how to nurture an environmental identity in order to encourage more attention to and care for the natural environment. Identities develop through experience, and experiences are interpreted in part through social understandings. Giving people the opportunity to be involved together in conservation activities allows them to perceive themselves as conservationists and to be so labeled by others. As long as those labels are socially valued, they are likely to result in increased activity on behalf of nature.

Conclusion

The physical environment, particularly the natural environment, is important to identity development in both children and adults. People feel a strong attachment to the natural environment, evinced through connections to specific places, animals, and nature in general. This attachment may reflect biophilia (see Chapter 5); it may also result in part because experience with natural environments and with animals helps in self-understanding and self-regulation. Childhood experiences in nature, particularly with family members or other significant adults, may promote a value for the natural environment and commitment to protecting it that become a defining part of the mature adult's identity. However, adult experiences are also significant in strengthening, focusing, and supporting an environmental identity. A strong sense of connection to the environment has been shown to predict relevant behavior, both in regard to a specific locale and more generally.

Exposure to the natural environment occurs within a social context, both literally and figuratively. A "big picture" approach to encouraging conservation behavior suggests that we recognize, as a society, the importance of providing places and experiences that nurture environmental identity in both children and adults. It is important to protect biological diversity through preserving "wild" nature, but it may be equally important to promote environmental concern by allowing people to connect with nature in urban settings through public parks, green school grounds, arboretums, community gardens, and zoos. Far more research needs to be done to understand how such areas can be designed to encourage connection to nature.

References

Ajzen, I. (1991). The theory of planned behavior. *Organizational Behavior and Human Decision Processes, 50*, 179–211.

Alger, J. M., & Alger, S. F. (1997). Beyond Mead: Symbolic interaction between humans and felines. *Society and Animals, 5*, 65–81.

Aron, A., Aron, E. N., & Smollan, D. (1992). Inclusion of Other in the Self Scale and the structure of interpersonal closeness. *Journal of Personality and Social Psychology, 63*(4), 596–612.

Austin, M., & Kaplan, R. (2003). Identity, involvement, and expertise in the inner city: Some benefits of tree-planting projects. In S. Clayton & S. Opotow (Eds.), *Identity and the natural environment* (pp. 205–226). Cambridge, MA: MIT.

Bair, J. (2014). The great green desert. *OnEarth, 36*(1), 64.

Barton, J., & Pretty, J. (2010). What is the best dose of nature and green exercise for improving mental health? A multi-study analysis. *Environmental Science and Technology, 44*, 3947–3955.

Bashir, N., Lockwood, P., Chasteen, A., Nadolny, D., & Noyes, I. (2013). The ironic impact of activists: Negative stereotypes reduce social change influence. *European Journal of Social Psychology*, DOI: 10.1002/ejsp.1983

Belk, R. (1992). Attachment to possessions. In I. Altman & S. Low (Eds.) *Place attachment* (pp. 37–55). New York: Plenum.

Bixler, R., & Floyd, M. (1997). Nature is scary, disgusting, and uncomfortable. *Environment and Behavior, 5*, 202–247.

Bixler, R., Floyd, M., & Hammitt, W. E. (2002). Environmental socialization: Quantitative tests of the childhood play hypothesis. *Environment and Behavior, 34*, 795–818.

Bonaiuto, M., Breakwell, G. M., & Cano, I. (1996). Identity processes and environmental threat. *Journal of Community & Applied Social Psychology, 6*, 157–175.

Borden R. J. (1985) Personality and ecological concern. In D. Gray, R. Borden & R. Weigel (Eds.), *Ecological beliefs and behaviors: Assessment and change* (pp. 87–122) Westport, CT: Greenwood Press.

Borden, R. J. (2014). *Ecology and experience: Reflections from a human ecological perspective*. Berkeley, CA: North Atlantic Books.

Bragg, E. A. (1996). Towards ecological self: Deep ecology meets constructionist self-theory. *Journal of Environmental Psychology, 16*, 93–108.

Brandt, K. (2004). A language of their own: An interactionist approach to human-horse communication. *Society and Animals, 12*, 299–316

Bruni, C., & Schultz, P. W. (2009). Implicit beliefs about self and nature: Evidence from an IAT game. *Journal of Environmental Psychology, 30*, 95–102.

Burghardt, G. (1992). Human-bear bonding in research on black bear behavior. In H. Davis and D. Balfour (Eds.), *The Inevitable bond* (pp. 365–382). Cambridge: Cambridge University Press.

Cantrill, J. G., & Senecah, S. L. (2001). Using the 'sense of self-in-place' construct in the context of environmental policy-making and landscape planning. *Environmental Science and Policy, 4*, 185–203.

Cantrill, J. G. (1998). The environmental self and a sense of place: Communication foundations for regional ecosystem management. *Journal of Applied Communication Research, 26*, 301–318.

Carrus, G., Bonaiuto, M., & Bonnes, M. (2005). Environmental concern, regional identity, and support for protected areas in Italy. *Environment and Behavior, 37*, 237–257.

Chawla, L. (1986). The ecology of environmental memory. *Children's environments quarterly, 3*(4), 34–42.

Chawla, L. (1992). Childhood place attachments. In I. Altman & S. Low (Eds.), *Human behavior and environment: Advances in Theory and Research* Vol. *12*, Place attachment (pp. 63–88). New York: Plenum Press.

Chawla, L. (1998). Research methods to investigate significant life experiences: review and recommendations. *Environmental Education Research, 4*(4), 383–397.

Chawla, L. (1999). Life paths into effective environmental action. *Journal of Environmental Education, 31*(1), 5–26.

Chawla, L. (2002). Spots of time: Manifold ways of being in nature in childhood. In P. Kahn & S. Kellert (Eds.) *Children and nature: Psychological, sociocultural and evolutionary investigations* (pp. 199–225). Cambridge, MA: MIT Press.

Chawla, L. (2007). Childhood experiences associated with care for the natural world. *Children, Youth, and Environments, 17*, 144–170.

Clayton, S. (2003). Environmental identity: A conceptual and an operational definition. In S. Clayton & S. Opotow (Eds.) *Identity and the natural environment* (pp. 45–65). Cambridge, MA: MIT Press.

Clayton, S. (2008). Attending to identity: Ideology, group membership, and perceptions of justice. In K. Hegtvedt & J. Clay-Warner (Eds.) *Advances in group processes: Justice* (pp. 241–266). Bingley, UK: Emerald.

Clayton, S. (2012). Environment and identity. In S. Clayton (Ed.), *Oxford handbook of environmental and conservation psychology* (pp. 164–180). New York: Oxford.

Clayton, S., Fraser, J., & Burgess, C. (2011). The role of zoos in fostering environmental identity. *Ecopsychology, 3*, 87–96.

Clayton, S., & Opotow, S. (2003) Introduction. In S. Clayton & S. Opotow (Eds.), *Identity and the natural environment* (pp. 1–24). Cambridge, MA: MIT.

Clayton, S., Fraser, J., & Saunders, C. (2008). Zoo experiences: Conversations, connections and concern for animals. *Zoo Biology, 28*, 377–397.

Crocker, J. C. (1985). My brother the parrot. In G. Urton (Ed.), *Animal myths and metaphors in South America* (pp. 13–47). Salt Lake City, UT: University of Utah Press.

Degenhardt, L. (2002). Why do people act in sustainable ways? In P. Schmuck & W. Schultz (Eds.) *Psychology of sustainable development*. (pp. 123–148). Boston: Kluwer.

Devine-Wright, P. (2011). Place attachment and public acceptance of renewable energy: A tidal energy case study. *Journal of Environmental Psychology, 31*(4), 336–343.

Devine-Wright, P., & Howes, Y. (2010). Disruption to place attachment and the protection of restorative environments: A wind energy case study. *Journal of Environmental Psychology, 30*(3), 271–280.

DeCremer, D., & Van Vugt, M. (1999). Social identification effects in social dilemmas: A transformation of motives. *European Journal of Social Psychology, 29*, 871–893.

Diehm, C. (2007). Identification with nature: What it is and why it matters. *Ethics and the Environment, 12*, 1–22.

Fisher, A. (2002). *Radical ecopsychology: Psychology in the service of life*. Albany, NY: SUNY Press.

Fraser, J., Clayton, S., Sickler, J., & Taylor, A. (2009). Belonging at the zoo: Retired volunteers, conservation activism, and collective identity. *Ageing and Society, 29*, 351–368.

Fredrickson, L. M., & Anderson, D. H. (1999). A qualitative exploration of the wilderness experience as a source of spiritual inspiration. *Journal of Environmental Psychology, 19*, 21–39.

Gebhard, U., Nevers, P., & Billmann-Mahecha, E. (2003). Moralizing trees: Anthropomorphism and identity in children's relationships to nature. In S. Clayton & S. Opotow (Eds.), *Identity and the natural environment: The psychological significance of nature*. Cambridge, MA: MIT Press.

Gebser, J. (1984). *The ever-present origin*. (N. Bardstad, Trans.). Athens, OH: Ohio University Press.

Gendlin, E. T. (1992). The primacy of the body, not the primacy of perception. *Man and World, 25*(3–4), 341–353.

Gendlin, E. T. (1997). *A process model*. New York: The Focusing Institute.

Gibbons, F. X. (1983). Self-attention and self-report: The "veridicality" hypothesis. *Journal of Personality, 51*, 517–542.

Goodall, J. (1990). *Through a window: My thirty years with the chimpanzees of Gombe*. Boston: Houghton Mifflin.

Greenebaum, J. (2004). It's a dog's life: Elevating status from pet to "fur baby" at Yappy Hour. *Society and Animals, 12*, 117–135.

Griskevicius, V., Tybur, J. M., & Van den Bergh, B. (2010). Going Green to Be Seen: Status, Reputation, and Conspicuous Conservation. *Journal of Personality and Social Psychology, 98*(3), 392–404.

Guber, D. L. (2013)A cooling climate for change? Party polarization and the politics of global warming. *American Behavioral Scientist, 57*, 93–115.

Gustafson, P. (2001). Meanings of place: Everyday experiences and theoretical conceptualizations. *Journal of Environmental Psychology, 21*, 5–16.

Hart, L. (1994). The Asian elephant-driver partnership: The drivers' perspective. *Applied Animal Behaviour Science, 40*, 297–312.

Hart, R. (1979). *Children's experience of place*. New York: Irvington Pub.

Hearne, V. (1986). *Adam's task: Calling animals by name*. New York: Vintage.

Herzog, T. R., Black, A. M., Fountaine, K. A., & Knotts, D. J. (1997). Reflection and attentional recovery as distinctive benefits of restorative environments. *Journal of Environmental Psychology, 17*, 165–170.

Hirschfeld, L., & Gelman, S. (Eds.). (1994). *Mapping the mind: Domain specificity in cognition and culture*. Cambridge: Cambridge University Press.

Hummon, D. M. (1992). Community attachment. In I. Altman and S. M. Low (Eds.), *Human behavior and the environment: Advances in theory and research, Vol. 12, Place Attachment* (pp. 253–278). New York: Plenum Press.

Ingold, T. (1988). Introduction. In T. Ingold (Ed.), *What is an animal?* (pp. 1–16). London: Unwin Hyman.

Ingold, T. (1994). From trust to domination: An alternative theory of human-animal relations. In A. Manning & J. Serpell (Eds.), *Animals and human society* (pp. 1–22). New York: Routledge.

James, W. (1892/1961). *Psychology: The briefer course*. New York: Harper.

Kahn, Jr., P. H., & Hasbach, P. H. (Eds.). (2012). *Ecopsychology: Science, totems, and the technological species*. Cambridge, MA: MIT Press.

Kals, E., Schumacher, D., & Montada, L. (1999). Emotional affinity towards nature as a motivational basis to protect nature. *Environment and Behavior, 31*, 178–202.

Kaplan, R., & Kaplan, S. (2002). Adolescents and the natural environment: A time out? In P. K. Kahn, Jr., & S. R. Kellert (Eds.), *Children and nature* (pp. 227–257). Cambridge, MA: MIT Press.

Kashima, Y., Paladino, A., & Margetts, E. (2014). Environmentalist identity and environmental striving. *Journal of Environmental Psychology, 38*, 64–75.

Kempton, W., & Holland, D. (2003). Identity and sustained environmental practice. In S. Clayton & S. Opotow (Eds.), *Identity and the natural environment* (pp. 317–341). Cambridge, MA: MIT Press.

Kiesling, F. M., & Manning, C. M. (2010). How green is your thumb? Environmental gardening identity and ecological gardening practices. *Journal of Environmental Psychology, 30*(3), 315–327.

Kihlstrom, J., Cantor, N., Albright, J., Chew, B., Klein, S., & Neidenthal, P. (1988). Information processing and the study of the self. In L. Berkowitz (Ed.), *Advances in experimental social psychology* (vol. *21*, pp. 145–180). San Diego: Academic Press.

Kim, J., & Kaplan, R. (2004). Physical and psychological factors in sense of community. New urbanist Kentlands and nearby Orchard Village. *Environment and Behavior, 36*, 313–340.

Korpela, K. (2002). Children's environment. In R. Bechtel & A. Churchman (Eds.), *Handbook of environmental psychology*. New York: Wiley.

Korpela, K. M. (1989). Place identity as a product of environmental self-regulation. *Journal of Environmental Psychology, 9*, 241–256.

Korpela, K. M. (1992). Adolescents' favorite places and environmental self-regulation. *Journal of Environmental Psychology, 12*, 249–258.

Korpela, K. M., Hartig, T., Kaiser, F. G., & Fuhrer, U. (2001). Restorative experience and self-regulation in favorite places. *Environment and Behavior, 33*, 572–589.

Korpela, K. M. (2012). Place attachment. In S. Clayton (Ed.), *Oxford handbook of environmental and conservation psychology* (pp. 148–163). New York: Oxford.

Kramer, R., & Brewer, M. (1984). Effects of group identity on resource use in a simulated commons dilemma. *Journal of Personality and Social Psychology, 46*, 1044–1057.

Kyle, G., Graefe, A., Manning, R., & Bacon, J. (2004). Effects of place attachment on users' perceptions of social and environmental conditions in a natural setting. *Journal of Environmental Psychology, 24*, 213–225.

Lévi-Strauss, C. (1966). *The savage mind*. Chicago: University of Chicago Press.

Levy-Bruhl, L. (1966). *How natives think*. New York: Washington Square Press.

Long, C. R., Seburn, M., Averill, J. R., & More, T. A. (2003). Solitude experiences: Varieties, settings, and individual differences. *Personality and Social Psychology Bulletin*, *29*, 578–583.
Mannetti, L., Pierro, A., & Livi, S. (2004). Recycling: Planned and self-expressive behavior. *Journal of Environmental Psychology*, *24*, 227–236.
Manzo, L. C. (2005). For better or worse: Exploring multiple dimensions of place meaning. *Journal of Environmental Psychology*, *25*, 67–86.
Manzo, L., & Devine-Wright, P. (Eds.). (2013). *Place attachment: Advances in theory, methods, and applications*. London: Routledge.
Markowitz, E. M., & Malle, B. F. (2012). Did you just see that? Making sense of environmentally relevant behavior. *Ecopsychology*, *4*(1), 37–50.
Markus, H., Crane, M., Bernstein, S., & Siladi, M. (1982). Self-schemas and gender. *Journal of Personality and Social Psychology*, *42*, 38–50.
Mathews, F. (1991). *The ecological self*. London: Routledge.
Mayer, F. S., & Frantz, C. M. (2004). The connectedness to nature scale: A measure of individuals' feeling in community with nature. *Journal of Environmental Psychology*, *24*, 503–515.
Mayer, F., Frantz, C., Bruehlman-Senecal, E., & Dolliver, K. (2009). Why is nature beneficial?: The role of connectedness to nature. *Environment and Behavior*, *41*(5), 607–643.
Millot, J.-L., & Filiatre, J.-C. (1986). The behavior sequences in the communication system between the child and his pet dog. *Applied Animal Behaviour Science*, *16*, 383–90.
Moore, R. (1986). *Childhood's domain*. London: Croom-Helm.
Moore, R. L., & Graefe, A. R. (1994). Attachments to recreation settings. *Leisure Sciences*, *16*, 17–31.
Murtagh, N., Gatersleben, B., & Uzzell, D. (2012). Self-identity threat and resistance to change: Evidence from regular travel behaviour. *Journal of Environmental Psychology*, *32*, 318–326.
Myers, Jr., O. E. (2007). *The significance of children and animals: Social development and our connections to other species*, 2nd ed. West Lafayette, IN: Purdue University Press.
Myers, Jr., O. E., & Russell, A. (2003). Human identity in relation to wild Black bears: A natural-social ecology of subjective creatures. In S. Clayton & S. Opotow (Eds.), *Identity and the natural environment* (pp. 67–90). Cambridge, MA: MIT Press.
Naess, A. (1989). *Ecology, community and lifestyle*. (D. Rothenberg, Trans and Ed.). Cambridge: Cambridge University Press.
Nisbet, E. K., Zelenski, J. M., & Murphy, S. A. (2009). The Nature Relatedness scale: Linking individuals' connection with nature to environmental concern and behavior. *Environment and Behavior*, *41*(5), 715–740.
Norgaard, K. (2011). *Living in denial*. Cambridge, MA: MIT Press.
Opotow, S., & Brook, A. (2003). Identity and exclusion in rangeland conflict. In S. Clayton & S. Opotow (Eds.), *Identity and the natural environment* (pp. 249–272). Cambridge, MA: MIT Press.
Pol, E., Moreno, E., Guàrdia, J., & Iniguez, L. (2002). Identity, quality of life, and sustainability in an urban suburb of Barcelona. *Environment and Behavior*, *34*, 67–80.
Poortinga, W., Whitmarsh, L, & Suffolk, C. (2013). The introduction of a single-use carrier bag charge in Wales: Attitude change and behavioural spillover effects. *Journal of Environmental Psychology*, *36*, 240–247.
Proshansky, H. M. (1978). The city and self-identity. *Environment and Behavior*, *10*, 147–169.
Relph, E. (1976). *Place and placelessness*. London: Pion.
Robins, D., Sanders, C., & Cahill S. (1991). Dogs and their people: Pet-facilitated interaction in a public setting. *Journal of Contemporary Ethnography*, *22*, 205–227.
Ryan, R. L. (2005). Exploring the effects of environmental experience on attachment to urban natural areas. *Environment and Behavior*, *37*, 3–42.
Ryan, R. M., & Deci, E. L. (2000). Self-determination theory and the facilitation of intrinsic motivation, social development, and well-being. *American Psychologist*, *55*, 68–78.
Sadalla, E., & Krull, J. (1995). Self-presentational barriers to resource conservation. *Environment and Behavior*, *27*, 328–353.
Sanders, C. (1999). *Understanding dogs: Living and working with canine companions*. Philadelphia: Temple University Press.

Scherl, L. M. (1989). Self in wilderness: Understanding the psychological benefits of individual-wilderness interaction through self-control. *Leisure Sciences, 11*, 123–135.

Schultz, P. W. (2001). The structure of environmental concern: Concern for self, other people, and the biosphere. *Journal of Environmental Psychology, 21*, 327–339.

Schultz, W. P., Shriver, C., Tabanico, J. J., & Khazian, Azar (2004). Implicit connections with nature. *Journal of Environmental Psychology, 24*, 31–42.

Schultz, P. W., & Tabanico, J. (2007). Self, identity, and the natural environment: Exploring implicit connections with nature. *Journal of Applied Social Psychology, 37*, 1219–1247.

Schwab, J. (1994). *Deeper shades of green: The rise of blue-collar and minority environmentalism in America.* San Francisco: Sierra Club Books.

Seed, J., Macy, J., Fleming, P., & Naess, A. (1988). *Thinking like a mountain: Toward a council of all beings*. Philadelphia, PA: New Society Publishers.

Serpell, J. (2000). Creatures of the unconscious: Companion animals as mediators. In A. Podbersek, E. Paul & J. Serpell (Eds.). *Companion animals and us* (pp. 108–117). Cambridge: Cambridge University Press

Shapiro, K. (1989). Understanding dogs through kinesthetic empathy, social construction, and history. *Anthrozoös, 3*, 184–95.

Sommer, R. (2003). Trees and human identity. In S. Clayton & S. Opotow (Eds.), *Identity and the natural environment* (pp. 179–204). Cambridge, MA: MIT

Stedman, R. C. (2002). Toward a social psychology of place: Predicting behavior from place-based cognitions, attitude, and identity. *Environment and Behavior, 34*, 561–581.

Stern, P., Dietz, T., Abel, T., Guagnano, G., & Kalof, L. (1999). A value-belief-norm theory of support for social movements: The case of environmentalism. *Human Ecology Review, 6*(2), 81–97.

Strum, S. C. (1987). *Almost human: A journey into the world of baboons*. New York: Random House.

Stuart, S. M. (2005). Lifting spirits: Creating gardens in California domestic violence shelters. In P. F. Barlett (Ed.), *Urban place: Reconnecting with the natural world* (61–88). Cambridge, MA: MIT Press.

Tam, K.-P. (2013). Concepts and measures related to connection to nature: Similarities and differences. *Journal of Environmental Psychology, 34*, 64–78.

Terry, D., Hogg, M., & White, K. (1999).The theory of planned behavior: Self-identity, social identity, and group norms. *British Journal of Social Psychology, 38*, 225–244.

Thomashow, M. (1995). *Ecological identity: Becoming a reflective environmentalist*. Cambridge, MA: MIT Press.

Twigger-Ross, C. L., & Uzzell, D. L. (1996). Place and identity processes. *Journal of Environmental Psychology, 16*, 205–220.

Twigger-Ross, C., Boniauto, M., & Breakwell, G. (2003). Identity theories and environmental psychology. In Bonnes, M., Lee, T., & Boniauto, M. (Eds.) *Psychological theories for environmental issues*. (pp. 203–233). Burlington, VT: Ashgate Publishing.

Uzzell, D., Pol, E., & Badenas, D. (2002). Place identification, social cohesion, and environmental sustainability. *Environment and Behavior, 34*, 26–53.

Valera, S., & Guàrdia, J. (2002). Urban social identity and sustainability. *Environment and Behavior, 34*, 54–66.

Van der Werff, E., Steg, L., & Keizer, K. (2013). The value of environmental self-identity. *Journal of Environmental Psychology, 34*, 55–63.

Van der Werff, E., Steg, L., & Keizer, K. (2014). I am what I am by looking past the present: The influence of biospheric values and past behavior on environmental self-identity. *Environment and Behavior, 46*, 626–657.

Vaske, J., & Kobrin, K. (2001). Place attachment and environmentally responsible behavior. *Journal of Environmental Education, 32*, 16–21.

Vining, J., & Merrick, M. (2012). Environmental epiphanies: Theoretical foundations and practical applications. In S. Clayton (Ed.), *Oxford handbook of environmental and conservation psychology* (pp. 485–508). New York: Oxford.

von Hassell, M. (2005). Community gardens in New York City: Place, community, and individuality. In P. F. Barlett (Ed.), *Urban place: Reconnecting with the natural world* (91–116). Cambridge, MA: MIT Press.

Weigert, A. J. (1997). *Self, interaction, and natural environment*. Albany: State University of New York Press.

Weinstein, N., Przybylski, A. K., & Ryan, R. M. (2009). Can nature make us more caring? Effects of immersion in nature on intrinsic aspirations and generosity. *Personality and Social Psychology Bulletin, 35*(10), 1315–1329.

Wells, N., & Lekies, K. S. (2006). Nature and the life course: Pathways from childhood nature experiences to adult environmentalism. *Children, Youth, and Environments, 16*, 1–24.

Williams, K., & Harvey, D. (2001). Transcendent experience in forest environments. *Journal of Environmental Psychology, 21*, 249–260.

Winter, P. L., Chavez, D. J. (2008) Wildland recreationists' natural resource management priorities and preferences: a connection to environmental identity. In D. J. Chavez, P. L. Winter & J. D. Absher (Eds.) *Recreation Visitor Research: Studies of Diversity*. Gen. Tech. Rep. PSW-GTR-XXX. Albany, CA: United States Department of Agriculture, Forest Service, Pacific Southwest Research Station, Wildland Recreation and Urban Cultures.

Zavestoski, S. (2003). Constructing and maintaining ecological identities: The strategies of deep ecologists. In S. Clayton & S. Opotow (Eds.), *Identity and the natural environment* (pp. 297–315). Cambridge, MA: MIT Press.

Zelenski, J. M., & Nisbet, E. K. (2014). Happiness and feeling connected: The distinct role of nature relatedness. *Environment and Behavior, 46*, 3–23.

Part III

Encouraging a Sustainable Relationship Between Humans and Nature

9

Promoting Sustainable Behavior

Psychologists have long been involved in attempts to promote sustainable behavior. In some ways, these attempts have achieved less than was hoped for, yet there are many success stories to examine and imitate. Research on this topic has been so extensive that this chapter cannot hope to include everything. Our goals are to review some of the principal determinants of sustainable behavior, to discuss the interventions that target these determinants and the factors determining the success or failure of such interventions, and to provide illustrative examples of successful interventions. We close by examining some integrative attempts to evoke pro-environmental behavior.

Identifying target behaviors

Environmental degradation has multiple causes and requires multiple interventions to change human behavior. What behaviors should be the target of change? Gardner and Stern (2002); (see also Stern, 2000) rightly caution behavioral scientists to consider the potential impact of a behavioral change, noting that a lot of research attention goes to issues, such as anti-littering campaigns, that do not have a major impact on environmental health. When considering how to promote sustainable behavior, both psychologists and the general public tend to think about curtailment behaviors (ones that require us to use less) rather than efficiency behaviors (ones that perform the same function but use fewer resources), despite the fact that efficiency measures are often more effective. With limits not only on time and resources, but also on attention, it is important to choose high-impact target behaviors.

Conservation Psychology: Understanding and promoting human care for nature, Second Edition.
Susan Clayton and Gene Myers.

www.wiley.com\go\clayton\conservation

Nevertheless, even behaviors with little impact can be worth examination. Assessments of the effect of particular behavior changes should consider the long term as well as the short term, and indirect as well as direct effects. Although picking up litter may have almost no impact on the overall health of the ecosystem, an anti-littering campaign can serve to increase the salience of environmental issues (Gardner & Stern, 2002). In the right circumstances, people who take one step in a sustainable direction may proceed further along the same path. If people who engage in anti-littering behavior, for example, perceive themselves as motivated by concern for the environment, this may prompt them to take further, more effective actions (as discussed in Chapter 8). Research on the foot-in-the-door effect suggests that a small action may lead to further actions for the same cause, due to self-perception, conformity, a desire to appear consistent, and commitment (Burger, 1999). The strategy is not likely to work, however, if there are barriers to the larger behaviors, and some research suggests that positive behaviors can even backfire by allowing people to feel that they have earned the right to use more resources in a different domain (Otto et al., 2014). More research on the conditions under which small steps of commitment lead to more significant environmental actions is needed.

In addition to considering the potential impact of a behavioral change, it is important to consider the plasticity of the behavior – the extent to which it is amenable to change. A useful factor that is relevant to this question is the type of behavior that is called for. Our focus here is primarily on private-sphere actions, among which we identify three broad categories of individual behaviors: curtailment, behavior choice, and technology choice. (See Kempton et al., 1992, and Stern, 2000, for similar categorizations.)

As stated earlier, people often associate pro-environmental behavior with a reduction in consumption, or *curtailment behavior*. When people use fewer resources, they require less exploitation of the natural environment. This category encompasses reduction in purchasing (e.g., adopting a lifestyle of voluntary simplicity), reduction in water use (e.g., shorter showers), and reduction in energy use (e.g., lowering thermostat). Less frequently thought of is a very important reduction, a reduced number of children in a family; the decision whether and when to have children, and how many to have, are among the most environmentally significant choices a family can make. Curtailment behaviors are often seen as requiring a personal sacrifice. People are more likely to adopt curtailment behaviors if they can be framed in terms of the advantages that will accrue, for example in personal savings, increased comfort, or social approval, rather than the costs that are entailed. On the other hand, the idea of using fewer resources is intrinsically appealing to some people. De Young (1996), in the United States, Wilke (1991), in the Netherlands, and Fujii (2006), in Japan, all found that intrinsic satisfaction can be obtained from frugality, and that positive attitudes toward frugality are associated with the intention to engage in certain types of curtailment behaviors. (See our discussion of environmental virtues in Chapter 7 and of intrinsic motivation in Chapter 12.)

A second category of behaviors comprises *behavioral choices:* decisions not about whether or not to do something, but how to do it. Examples include using public transportation, buying organic produce, recycling, composting, managing one's land sustainably, or reusing products (e.g., buying used clothing). Although the effect of these behaviors is typically a reduced use of natural resources, the focus is not on doing or using less but on doing things in a different way, with less environmental impact. For example, people are encouraged, not to buy less food, but to buy food that has been sustainably produced. The challenge behind these behaviors is that they need to be done repeatedly in order to have an impact. Behavior change interventions must try to change someone's habits rather than merely influence a single decision.

The third category of behaviors involves *technology choices*: decisions about buying or using technological innovations, such as hybrid cars, energy-efficient appliances, low-flow showerheads, and green energy sources. These choices may be more effective than other behavior changes, because they require only one decision to have a continuing impact rather than needing to be repeatedly enacted; also the amount of energy saved through technological improvements is often greater than that saved through behavioral changes. As Stern (1992) notes, they also are often perceived as improving the quality of life rather than representing sacrifice. However, they typically involve a financial outlay that may serve as a perceptual, or a real, barrier for many consumers.

Although our focus in this chapter is the individual rather than the society, we do not mean to overlook the significance of more macro-level practices. Individuals and households consume only about one third of the energy used in the United States (Gardner & Stern, 2002; see also Department of Energy statistics, available at www.eere.energy.gov/states/us_energy_statistics.cfm#consumption). Thus, the impact of individual behavioral choices is limited. It can be more daunting to try to change behavior at the group level, but individuals can have a greater impact if they act collectively, either to implement community-level programs or to affect policy at a broader level through voting choices. We return to the issue of group-level behavior at the end of the chapter.

Influences on behavior

Most behaviors are multiply determined, influenced by things like the weather, immediate prior experience, and pure chance, as well as behavioral intentions. We review some of the causes that are most powerful as well as most amenable to interventions. Fig. 9.1 depicts these factors.

External factors

Although many people instinctively explain behavior as due to individual preferences and styles (a phenomenon known to social psychologists as the *fundamental attribution error*), the situational context is typically more influential than is realized. One of the strongest, and frequently

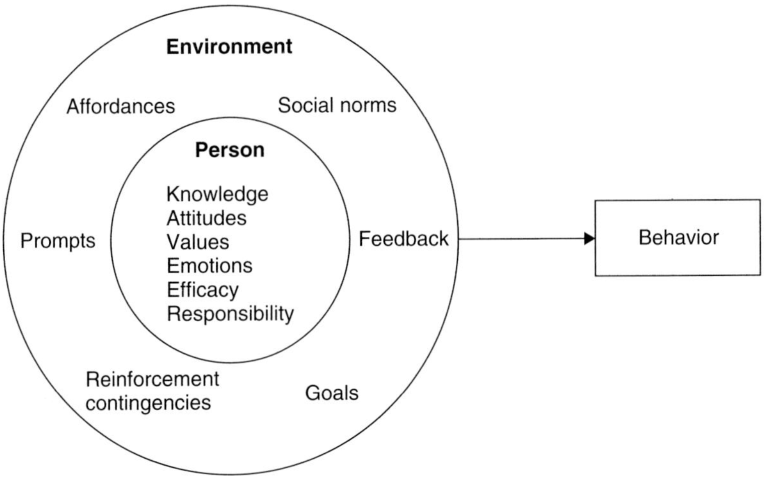

Fig. 9.1 Factors affecting behavior.

overlooked, determinants of behavior is simply what is allowed or enabled by the physical and social environment – the behavioral *affordances* (discussed in Chapter 5). Some actions that would promote sustainability are not available options in some situations. Even when actions are physically possible, a lack of information about how to perform them is an effective barrier. In either case, the motivation to perform those actions is irrelevant.

Physical circumstances may prohibit curtailment behavior. Lighting or thermostat settings, for example, are often set to fixed levels in office buildings, hotels, or rental units. People may not realize that they can reduce the temperature on their hot water heater, or know how to do so. Women often have little control over their fertility, with major consequences for the environment. Behavioral choices are also affected by the presence of behavioral options: Littering is more likely when there are no garbage cans, taking the bus may be impractical with infrequent service or missing routes, and organic produce cannot be purchased if it is unavailable. The available options are particularly important to technology choices: consumers cannot choose to buy cars that get 70 mpg if the market does not provide such cars. However, circumstances may be arranged so that unsustainable options are precluded: people will switch to unleaded gasoline if leaded gas is no longer available, and learn to bring reusable bags when stores no longer provide disposable ones.

Particular contexts not only allow or disallow sustainable behaviors; they also facilitate or hinder them. Recycling can be easy (bins provided by the city, placed in accessible locations) or difficult (consumers have to provide their own containers and transport them to a central location). Public transportation can be safe and convenient or dangerous and unreliable. Moreover, even when the consumer has multiple choices, the environmental impact can be dramatically changed by making the more sustainable option the default (e.g., Thaler & Sunstein, 2009). For example, customers are less likely to use a plastic bag if they have to request it rather than having it offered automatically. The first step in any plan to promote a more sustainable behavior should be to evaluate ways in which that behavior is currently made easy or difficult and consider whether simple changes can be made to facilitate the behavior or if more significant investments in infrastructure are necessary.

Social norms are another key determinant of behavior. People are likely to do what they see other people doing. Michel-Guillou and Moser (2006), for example, found that French farmers who used sustainable practices were influenced more by social norms than by their own environmental awareness. Such conformity is often rational. Other people may have knowledge that we ourselves lack; by imitating the behaviors of others with more experience, we take advantage of their knowledge. If my neighbor establishes a backyard wildlife habitat, I not only learn that it is a possible and perhaps acceptable thing to do, I also get procedural information about how to do it. In addition, human society rewards conformity. Because we tend to like people who behave in the same way we do and to dislike those who deviate, social support is more available to those who conform than to those who do not.

A field experiment by Nolan et al. (2008) demonstrated the power of social norms in affecting sustainable behavior. Among residents in a California town, a message describing the actual energy use of a typical homeowner was more effective in reducing energy use than a message based on environmental protection, social responsibility, self-interest, or merely behavioral information. Interestingly, a survey of (different) residents showed that they described social norms as the *least* important reason to conserve, citing environmental protection and benefits to society as the primary reasons. People are not always aware of the explanations for their own behavior.

Norms can be effective for curtailment behavior, behavioral choices, and technology choices, but it is easier to observe what someone does than to be aware of what someone is NOT doing (the products that are not purchased, the car trips that are foregone). Some effort may be needed to highlight pro-environmental norms. It may be possible to highlight information about curtailment behaviors by describing them in more active terms: for example, "I reduced my gas use by 15% by shopping once a week instead of twice." Normative information can be obtained through direct observation of behavior (modeling) or through descriptive information: for example, "87% of Americans have donated to an environmental organization." Targeting influential individuals to serve as models may be an efficient way of using norms to change behavior. Hopper and Nielsen (1991), for example, used block leaders to prompt and encourage recycling. Compared to a group that only received information or information plus prompts, the participants who had a block leader showed personal norms with increased support for recycling. These norms, in turn, predicted recycling behavior.

As noted in Chapter 1, descriptive information about norms can be conveyed unintentionally, with potentially negative effects on sustainable behavior. In a classic study, Bator and Cialdini (2000) looked at public service announcements (PSAs) designed to reduce littering in a national park. Some of these PSAs included the unintentional message that littering is common. Bator and Cialdini (2000) showed that a PSA describing littering as normative, though undesirable, was less effective than an alternative statement that avoided the normative message. Many pro-environmental messages suffer from the same problem: while deploring the current state of the environment, they suggest that it is normal to engage in anti-environmental behavior. Cialdini and his students have effectively demonstrated the power of social norms to effect positive change in the proportion of hotel guests who reuse their towels. The researchers compared the standard message, "Help save resources for future generations" with one that evoked a descriptive norm, "75% of guests who stayed in this room used their towels more than once." Whereas a modest 30% of guests reused their towels after the first message, nearly 50% reused towels in response to the second message (Nijhuis, 2007). Pairing descriptive with injunctive norms (e.g., "many of our guests value conservation") was even more effective than either message alone (Schultz et al., 2008).

Werner (2003) examined some of the processes by which social norms operate. In one study, she randomly assigned high school students to different groups that received information about switching from toxic to nontoxic household products. Groups that experienced guided group discussion, and thus the opportunity to create group norms, had more pro-environmental attitudes after the meetings compared to groups that only received information via a lecture (Werner et al., 2008). Among the high school girls, the effect of norms was completely accounted for by *perceived peer endorsement.* Endorsement, derived from content analysis of comments, included expressing preference for the nontoxics, asking questions, sharing knowledge, and giving toxics little praise. For the boys, discussion was also more effective than lecture, but others' endorsements did not mediate the relationship. Instead, the discussion seemed to stimulate them to process the information more deeply, and there was a separate normative influence as well. Clearly knowledge and social support were both effects of norms, differentially important for the two genders in this study.

The next set of influences on behavior is obvious but still undervalued: *reinforcement contingencies.* What are the positive or negative consequences of behavior for the actor? Behaviors that are rewarded are more likely to be repeated and behaviors that are punished are less likely. Through a vast body of research on behavior modification, psychologists have learned some core principles concerning the effectiveness of reinforcement schedules. One is that rewards are more effective than punishment. Punishing a behavior, for example, with a fine, may reduce people's tendency to engage in that behavior, but alternatively it may encourage people to look for ways to avoid detection, and although it tells people what they should avoid doing it does not always inform people about what they *should* do. In addition, punishment may arouse hostility and resistance if people feel that their behavior is being controlled. Pol (2002) noted that even though laws have traditionally served to punish people, recent laws have been designed to provide rewards for sustainable behavior: for example, laws surrounding the use of eco-labels can reward the distributors of sustainably produced food by granting them a marketing edge.

Many programs have been developed that use some combination of punishment and incentive to encourage sustainable behavior. Taxes and laws, for example, can provide negative consequences to discourage anti-sustainable behaviors. Garbage collection programs in which customers pay by the number and/or size of cans tend to reduce the amount of household waste that is produced. Because reduced consumption usually entails savings for the consumer, many curtailment behaviors include monetary incentives by default. Increasing the cost of a resource may decrease its use; higher gasoline taxes are often advocated for this reason. Several obstacles, however, may hinder the effectiveness of this approach. One is that increased consumption often leads to the possibility of "economies of scale:" consumers may pay more, but the cost per unit is lower. Thus even when people do not need the greater amount, they feel that it is a financially wise choice to buy it. A simple analogy can be seen with food pricing. Cookies or doughnuts are often sold at the rate of, say, 50 cents each or $2.50 for 6. As the storeowners know, the customer may feel the smart choice is to buy more than he or she originally intended. A second major barrier is that the savings may not be realized by the person controlling consumption. Hotel guests have no incentive to lower the thermostat or reduce the lighting in their rooms, because any savings will accrue to the hotel rather than to the person regulating the temperature. Finally, savings may seem too remote from the reduction in consumption for the consumer to make the connection. Although lowering the thermostat a few degrees will eventually reduce my heating bill, the savings will not show up until the bill is recalculated at the end of the year – by which time fluctuations in the price of natural gas may make it hard to see the impact.

Incentives have also been used to affect behavioral choices and technology choices; often, the incentive is provided by some institutional authority rather than representing an intrinsic part of the decision. Bottle bills – requiring a monetary deposit for beverages bought in glass bottles or cans, with the deposit to be reimbursed when the container is returned – encourage consumers to recycle containers rather than discarding them. A little creative thinking can generate nonmonetary incentives for conservation behaviors, such as reserved highway lanes for high-occupancy vehicles to reward people for carpooling. Incentives should be close in time, and clearly tied, to the behavior being rewarded. When it comes to technology choices, incentives are designed to translate the long-term savings into something that can be appreciated in the short term. Although the more efficient technology will always pay off in the long term, rebates for hybrid cars, solar panels, or even compact fluorescent lightbulbs may be necessary to encourage people to make the sometimes-substantial investments that are required.

A recent success story in Niger shows both how incentives can work and why they may not. In the 1970s and 1980s, desertification was a major problem. Trees were a valuable ecological resource, holding soil with their roots and helping to reduce water runoff. In the short term, however, individuals could gain more economic benefit by chopping the trees down for firewood or construction, or to clear the ground for planting. Because trees were considered the property of the state, farmers received no immediate value for them; with little government oversight, there were no visible costs incurred by cutting them down. More recently, the government has allowed individuals to own trees. Farmers can make money by selling pods, fruit, and bark from the trees, which is more economically rewarding than the one-time sale of the wood. The roots and leaves also enhance the productivity of the soil. Researchers report the result: over 7 million new tree-covered acres in Niger since the mid-1980s, mostly without large-scale tree-planting projects (Polgreen, 2007).

One issue to consider is whether the incentive is designed to be permanent or whether it will be removed after a period of time, during which it is hoped that the behavioral change will become habitual. A review of many studies on attempts to elicit sustainable behavior, by Dwyer et al. (1993), suggests that behaviors tend to revert to baseline levels when such temporary incentives are removed. This is not a problem for technology choices, which are typically one-time events, but is more of an issue for repeated curtailment behavior or behavioral choices.

Perhaps counterintuitively, incentives should be large enough to motivate the behavior but not too large. Research on self-perception and intrinsic motivation shows that overly large rewards for behavior can reduce the tendency to engage in the behavior when the reward is not present. People assume that the behavior must be unpleasant if such a large reward is needed. In addition, people's inferences about their own motivations are affected by the reward structure. If I have done something for which there is a large financial reward, I assume that I have engaged in the behavior in order to get the reward and that there is no other reason to engage in the behavior – leading to a reduced likelihood that I'll engage in the behavior without the reward (Bolderdijk & Steg, 2015). When there is little or no financial incentive for a behavior, the intrinsic reasons for the behavior, such as satisfaction in helping to protect the environment or moral obligation, may become more salient (De Young, 1996). Nonmonetary incentives, such as social approval, may sometimes be more effective than monetary ones because they do not as clearly undermine the intrinsic reasons for the behavior; people do not tend to believe that they are recycling to get the approval of their neighbors, even if they are.

For incentives to work, they need to have an informational as well as a motivational component. That is, people need to be aware of the opportunity to perform a particular behavior and to recognize their own success at performing the behavior, as well as to know that such behavior will be rewarded. There are many things people fail to do simply because they don't think about it. *Prompts* are reminders to people that a particular behavior is called for, ideally located both physically and temporally close to the behavior that is prompted. A classic example is the label on a light switch reminding people to turn it off, or a sign on a recycling bin saying "please recycle." (See Fig. 9.2.) Framing the prompt in a way congruent with the audience's worldview may reduce reactance. One of us observed that electrical light use was reduced in a student coop house where the light switch panels bore a prompt. In this city served by a private electrical utility, the message was effective among the students because the sticker had a caricature of a person's face, positioned so that switch was the person's nose, and the verbal message was "Flip Off Capitalist Power."

If people are positively disposed toward performing the behavior and the effort required is minimal, a reminder may be all they need. The reminder may not be effective, however, if it is perceived as rude or demanding. The psychological theory of reactance (Brehm, 1966) suggests that too-obvious attempts to control behavior often lead to a backlash. People may deliberately ignore a prompt, or engage in a prohibited behavior, in order to demonstrate their independence. De Young (1993) reports, anecdotally, that when recycling was made mandatory in one area, "homeowners [were] found to have neatly stacked recyclable bottles and cans around the inside circumference of the clear plastic bags used for recycling and then filled the center with nonrecyclable trash" (p. 498). Indeed, a general caution in all behavior change campaigns is to avoid creating a controlling environment and to promote an autonomy-supportive environment (discussed in Chapter 10).

To best guide their behavior, people need external *feedback* to know whether they have been performing it successfully. If I intend to take shorter showers or water the garden less frequently,

Fig. 9.2 Prompts on light switches are common. (Photo courtesy of Susan Clayton).

do I know if I have been effective in reducing my water usage? Individual water meters allow people to monitor their own effect and tend to result in lower water use than when people pay a flat rate (Van Vugt, 2001). In some cases, the feedback itself may provide enough reward to motivate the behavior: recycling programs often provide continuously updated information about "how many trees have been saved" by the amount of paper recycled. A target or *goal*, along with feedback about the progress toward it, can be both informative and motivational: It suggests what kind of change is possible as well as desirable, and lets people know how successful their attempts to work toward the goal have been.

Internal factors

All of the earlier factors are external to the individual – his or her personal dispositions or tendencies are not the focus. But internal tendencies and preferences do matter in determining sustainable behavior, particularly if the goal is to influence a wide range of behavior rather than a single specific action. Although they may be harder to manipulate than are external contingencies, these factors need to be considered in attempts to promote pro-environmental behavior.

The main principle of environmental education, as well as of many persuasive attempts, is that *knowledge* matters: People are more likely to act in environmentally sustaining ways if they understand the threats faced by the environment and the implications of their behavioral choices. In a thorough review of research, Hines et al. (1987) found that knowledge was a reliable predictor of environmental behavior. A more recent meta-analysis by Bamberg and Moser (2007) confirmed that problem awareness was an important antecedent of behavior. Kals and Maes (2002) note that a general ecological awareness is a powerful predictor of a wide range of sustainable behavior, including energy consumption, traffic-related behavior, and political actions. There may be a limit beyond which increasing knowledge has no impact, but at low levels of knowledge, people may lack information about the behavioral options available and/or the environmental impact of those options. Think of the confusion surrounding basic decisions such as "paper or plastic?" grocery bags. In the absence of clear information about the consequences of different behaviors, an intention to protect the environment will not be translated into effective action. Notably, the review by Hines et al. found that knowledge was even more strongly predictive of behavior among people who were environmentalists ($r = 0.69$) than those who were not ($r = 0.27$), showing the importance of adding information to intention.

Attitudes are typically expected to predict behavior. As described in Chapter 6, Ajzen's (1991) Theory of Planned Behavior describes attitudes as a key determinant of behavioral intentions; Hines et al. (1987) as well as Bamberg and Moser (2007) did find that attitudes were associated with pro-environmental behavior. Attitudes are more strongly associated with behavior when they are based on personal experience, specific to the behavior, and salient. So, if people have positive attitudes toward specific sustainable behaviors, they only need to be reminded of those attitudes (increasing salience). If their attitudes are negative, they need to be persuaded otherwise. Decades of research on attitude change have shown that it is important to consider both the source and the format of a persuasive message, as well as its content. A credible spokesperson and an attention-getting message may be as, or more, important in effecting attitude change than the informational content of the message.

Mass media campaigns are attempts at attitude change that are typically well informed by social psychological principles of persuasion. Messages in the mass media are available to a wide audience and have the opportunity to be vivid and memorable through the use of catchy music, bold visuals, dramatic scenarios, and famous actors. The spokespeople can be credible because they are attractive, expert, and/or high in social status, or alternatively they can be seen as similar to the audience member and trustworthy for that reason. Bandura (2002) describes a successful use of the mass media to reduce fertility rates in Mexico. A serial drama (soap opera) was developed to contrast the positive experiences of a small family with the marital conflicts and financial stress experienced by a large family. A number of episodes explicitly depicted how a woman could use family planning and overcome resistance from her husband, all in the context of an engrossing family drama. Evidence for effectiveness is provided by Sabido (1981, cited in Bandura), who states that new contraceptive users increased 32% in the year during which the drama was first broadcast, and the birthrate fell by 34% over a 5-year period in the viewing area for the dramas.

Another twist in the use of persuasive messages has to do with the way in which the environment is characterized. An interesting series of studies (Ahn et al., 2013; Tam, 2014; Tam et al., 2013) has shown that people show more pro-environmental behavior when nature has been anthropomorphized. That is, when nature is presented using personal pronouns, or when trash cans have faces on them, they seem to elicit a stronger response. This ties into our instinctive responsiveness to social entities, and relates to some of the efforts by zoos to promote conservation that were described in Chapter 3.

Values are also important determinants of environmental behavior (Bamberg & Moser, 2007). As described in Chapter 6, Stern et al. (1999) Value-Belief-Norm model describes the impact of personal values in determining a personal norm, or felt obligation, to act in environmentally protective ways. Values such as openness to change and concern for others are related to a variety of sustainable behaviors, including recycling, environmentally conscious purchasing, and political activism (Karp, 1996). It is not easy, or necessarily desirable, to change someone's values. However, understanding the connection between values and behavior can be useful in encouraging behavior change by targeting the values that people already hold.

Steg et al., (2014) have proposed an integrative model that links values to behavior via goals: Although everyone has hedonic (pleasure-seeking) goals, goals of personal gain, and normative goals (the desire to comply with social norms), those goals are weighted differently by people holding different sets of values. Importantly, situational cues can strengthen the importance of different values; Steg et al. suggest that normative goals can be strengthened by evidence that others are behaving in ways to uphold environmental norms, and weakened by an emphasis on financial factors.

People have strong emotional responses to the environment, which may include love and admiration as well as fear and disgust. Research suggests that *emotions* are particularly important predictors of sustainable behavior. Berenguer (2007), for example, was able to increase emotions associated with empathy (e.g., sympathy, compassion, warmth) by encouraging students to "try to imagine how [a bird or tree] feels." This empathic response, in turn, was related to a greater willingness to allocate funds to an environmental protection organization and to a stronger perceived obligation to help nature. Elisabeth Kals and her colleagues have found that both positive feelings of love for nature, and negative emotions such as indignation about the pollution behavior of others, relate to the willingness to commit to behaviors such as installing water-saving devices in the household (Kals & Ittner, 2003). Kals' research on the importance of emotions becomes even more significant in light of her finding that environmental education was able to increase an emotional response to nature, suggesting that emotions can be a useful route for encouraging sustainable behavior.

Guilt is another emotion that can motivate environmental behavior (Bamberg & Moser, 2007). What happens when guilt is evoked by information about one's environmental actions or role in environmental problems? Guilt, as discussed in Chapter 7, is important in moral development and motivation, making one want to redress the situation, but it can also be seen as a negative and unpleasant emotion to be avoided. Eco-guilt arises "when people think about times they have not met personal or societal standards for environmental behavior" and when they accept responsibility for such actions (or inactions), and is distinguishable from a more general tendency toward guilt (Mallett, 2012, p. 223). Mallett found that in fact eco-guilt does predict eco-friendly individual and collective behavior intentions, when there are no significant barriers. And, as would be anticipated by norm activation theory, eco-guilt mediates the relationship between a person's feeling a personal obligation regarding environmental behaviors, and their personal and collective behavioral intentions and behaviors. That is, awareness that we are failing to meet our standards creates eco-guilt that then motivates pro-environmental behavior (Mallett, 2012). Brook (2011), however, found that being made aware of one's impacts significantly decreased pro-environmental behavior among students learning about their ecological footprints. Only those students who based their self-esteem on environmentalism, and thus felt a personal obligation to act environmentally, were motivated by the feedback about their own impact to marginally increase their pro-environmental behavior. Guilt is related to perceptions of responsibility, which we discuss later.

One emotion to treat with some caution is fear. Although doomsday scenarios of environmental devastation might seem to encourage pro-environmental behavior, research on fear appeals shows that they can backfire. Fear-inducing strategies have been used widely for behaviors such as drinking and driving, delinquency, and health behaviors, and studies have typically found such strategies to be ineffective. The reason is that the messages often focus only on the severity of the negative consequence of the behavior. People also need to believe that there is a high probability of the fearsome consequences actually occurring before they act preventatively

(Gardner & Stern, 2002). Thus, credible information on the probability of the negative consequence needs to be verified and communicated. In addition, when people are too fearful, particularly when they think there is little they can do about the threat, they are likely to respond with denial. Fear-inducing messages attract attention but may inhibit rather than motivate action (Witte, 1998; Gardner & Stern, 2002; O'Neill & Nicholson-Cole, 2009), and warnings are ineffective except in specific conditions, with repeat warnings doing especially poorly (Joireman et al., 2009). Bain et al. (2012) found that hopeful messages, emphasizing the positive effects of climate change action on society, were more effective than fearful messages in encouraging pro-environmental behavior among those inclined to deny climate change.

A moderate amount of fear can be a useful motivating factor if people are simultaneously shown something they can do to reduce the threat. Hine and Gifford (1991) found that a moderate amount of fear about pollution, induced via the presentation of vivid slides, increased the donation of money to an environmental organization compared to a group that did not see the slides. Meijinders et al. (2001) found a similar effect in a Dutch sample: participants who saw a moderately fear-inducing video about the effects of CO_2 were more influenced by an argument about the importance of buying energy-efficient lightbulbs than were participants who merely saw an informational video. A perception of environmental risk, accompanied by information about actions that can be taken to avert the risk, can be an effective motivation for action. Based on surveys of a representative sample of 1225 US adults, O'Connor et al. (1999) found that risk perceptions had an independent effect on environmental behaviors, separate from their relationship to general environmental beliefs and knowledge.

There is no point acting when one believes one's actions will have no effect. *Self-efficacy* pertains to a person's perception that she or he is able to successfully complete an action. Bandura (1977) suggested that this belief can affect actual ability and that it also increases motivation for the task. Ajzen's (1991) Theory of Planned Behavior includes perceived behavioral control, or perceived efficacy, as a direct predictor of both behavioral intention and behavior. In the meta-analyses conducted by Hines et al. (1987) and Bamberg and Moser (2007), perceived efficacy was at least as important as knowledge or attitudes in predicting behavior. Research has shown that the belief that recycling is effective is associated with recycling (De Young, 1986) and that the belief that one can have an effect on environmental problems is a predictor of political action on behalf of the environment (Ferguson & Branscombe, 2010; Sia et al., 1985-1986). Some people have greater confidence in their own effectiveness than others. But perceived efficacy can also be manipulated. The popular book, *50 Simple Things You Can Do To Save the Earth* (Earthworks Group, 1989), was designed to reassure the mass public that they could take effective action. (See also Fig. 9.3.) Providing people with knowledge about behavioral choices can also serve to increase their perception that they have some control in bringing about a sustainable environment (Eigner & Schmuck, 2002; Geller, 1995). We discuss optimism about one's own potential to make a difference in Chapter 12.

Related to the perception that one *can* do something to address environmental problems is the perception that one *should* do something. One of the barriers in encouraging individuals to address societal problems is the diffusion of responsibility – the sense that someone else will do something; it is not my issue. In order to act, people need to feel a personal responsibility. A classic series of studies by Latané and Darley (1970) showed that even a perceived need for help might not result in helping if a large number of people are available to help and there is no clear reason why one person rather than another should take action. In several studies of Germans citizens, Kals found that an internal *attribution of responsibility* to protect nature is a significant

Fig. 9.3 Encouraging a perception of self-efficacy. (Photo courtesy of Susan Clayton).

predictor of willingness to act in pro-environmental ways. In a sample of 445 Swiss adults, feeling personally responsible for addressing pollution was associated with pro-environmental behavior (Kaiser & Shimoda, 1999). Overall, Hines et al. found a correlation between perceived personal responsibility toward the environment and behavior, and, as noted earlier, Stern et al. (1999) found a personal norm to be a direct determinant of behavior. Conversely, a sense of anonymity or depersonalization may reduce sustainable behavior.

A perception of responsibility is affected by beliefs about causality. For example, Ferguson and Branscombe (2010) found that perceived human responsibility for global warming led to collective guilt, which in turn is related to willingness to take action to address it. Bamberg and Moser (2007) also found that guilt was a precursor of attitudes and moral norms. Another strategy for increasing responsibility involves asking people to make a commitment to act in pro-environmental ways. Having promised to behave sustainably, people should now feel a responsibility to fulfill that commitment. Several reviews, have confirmed that a commitment to act increases the likelihood of acting pro-environmentally (Dwyer et al., 1993; Hines et al., 1987; Lokhorst et al., 2013). Commitments are more effective when they are written rather than verbal and public rather than private, and they must be voluntary rather than forced.

Relevant to both internal and external factors is Festinger's (1957) theory of *cognitive dissonance.* According to this influential theory, holding two psychologically inconsistent states generates an unpleasant feeling of dissonance, and people will work to eliminate it or reduce it. Inconsistencies can exist between two beliefs, or between beliefs, attitudes, or behaviors. Examples would be advocating for reductions in energy use while driving a gas-guzzler or believing that climate change is a threat while opposing measures to address it. There are many ways to avoid or reduce dissonance without changing behavior, for example, by discrediting information that is discrepant with beliefs or behaviors (denying climate change); by reevaluating the importance of an attitude or behavior (one's individual climate impact is too small to worry about); or by justifying one's behavior in other ways (arguing that inefficient cars are safer). Dissonance can also make changing behavior difficult because a new behavior may be inconsistent with existing beliefs about why one follows their usual routine. But dissonance may motivate behavior change in a direction that is more consistent with one's attitudes. This is the route that many environmental advocates want to foster by alerting people to the disjuncture between their pro-environmental attitudes and their anti-environmental behavior.

Cognitive dissonance may also be used to bring about attitude change. If behavior is changed first, the attitude may change to become consistent with the behavior. In a study by Werner et al. (1995), people who participated in a curbside recycling program developed more positive attitudes after 4 months than did those who did not participate, despite the fact that there were no apparent attitudinal differences between the groups before the program was implemented. Presumably, dissonance encouraged the attitudes to shift in order to be more consistent with the behavior. A small incentive may be more effective at inducing dissonance. As noted earlier, for a behavior change to last, a person must attribute his or her behavior change to the self; a large incentive is so clearly responsible for counter-attitudinal behavior that the person experiences little or no dissonance. Greater dissonance is also generated when a public action or statement is contrary to one's private thoughts, for example, when a commitment is written and displayed. If the new action or belief goes contrary to one's reference group (perhaps one's family), who give reasons for not joining, then there is an even stronger force to internalize the choice as one's own.

It should be noted, however, that people vary in their sensitivity to inconsistency both within and especially between cultures. Of significance for international conservation, people in cultures that foster interdependent selves, such as many Asian cultures, rather than independent selves, such as Western cultures, place less importance on cross-situational consistency and on consistency between attitude and behavior (Kim, 2002). Because an interdependent self is much more situated in one's roles, relationships, and positions, whereas an independent self's identity rests on internal attributes (Markus & Kitayama, 1991, 1998), inconsistencies are less likely to matter to the former. From the interdependent self's view, maintaining good relationships is more important than always behaving in a way that expresses one's attitudes and values. Kimura and Nakajima (2011) tested how sustainable behaviors might be motivated in collectivist cultures, centered around harmony through shared goals and duties and conformity. They suggested five techniques for persuasion in such cultures:

1 Organizing groups: Allowing people to feel like they can pursue desired behaviors without straying or disobeying the group to which they currently belong. This may require redefining a potentially ambiguous behavior as a good behavior.
2 Anonymity. This allows an individual to pursue his/her desired behavior without feeling as if they are antagonizing the group to which they belong.
3 Mutual surveillance. This takes three forms: monitored by others (acting upon social facilitation principle), watching others (to ensure a person does not feel isolated by other people in his/her society, and that others are acting in the same way), and comparing others (for the purpose of mutual aid).
4 Development of mutual aid. It is very important in a collectivist culture for people to help other group members in times of need. This may include contributing not only for oneself

but also for a person who may not be able to contribute in order to maintain consistent degrees of cooperation within the group.

5 Combine use of positive and negative feedback. Negative feelings further isolate a person, and must be avoided. Relying on punishment will tend to reduce individuals' interest in the behavior.

It is worth noting that even in individualistic cultures, individual behavior is often scarcely changed unless one feels others are acting in the same way.

Cultural differences represent one way to conceptualize variability among individuals. Countries can be said to have different personalities, as individuals certainly do. Milfont and Sibley (2012) found consistent relationships between environmental behaviors or attitudes and personality differences at both the individual and the national level: openness to experience, agreeableness, and conscientiousness were associated with environmentalism. It is a longstanding finding in psychology that personality variables are not very good predictors of any specific behavior, but when looking at broad patterns of behavior, these factors can be important.

Behavior is complicated and a large number of factors affect the tendency to engage in sustainable behavior. Prompts, goals, modeling, and cognitive dissonance seem to be particularly effective at inducing behavior change, according to a 2012 meta-analysis (Osbaldiston & Schott, 2012). It should be clear, though, that many of these factors are interdependent. Knowledge and values affect attitudes, and the reverse is also true: Once attitudes are changed, a person may then seek more knowledge to support his or her position. Perceived efficacy affects perceived responsibility. Emotions can be causes and effects: Perceived responsibility may lead to guilt; a value for nature is associated with love. Even external and internal factors are not independent. As described earlier, using incentives to motivate a behavior may undermine intrinsic motivations to act. Conversely, successful attempts at behavior change may change attitudes in a positive way, through self-perception. An effective attempt to foster sustainable behavior will integrate multiple factors. We review several of the most commonly discussed models.

Models for changing behavior

Applied behavioral analysis (ABA), an approach to promoting sustainable behavior that has been championed by Geller (1989, 2002), includes three basic principles: It is focused on an observable behavior; it looks at external rather than internal factors to improve performance; and it utilizes principles of behavioral reinforcement. The process has been described with the acronym *DO IT*: *Define* the target behavior (attending to the effectiveness as well as the feasibility of the proposed behavioral change), *Observe* the occurrence of the behavior under ordinary circumstances (and note existing barriers and reinforcements that affect the occurrence of the behavior), *Intervene* to modify the behavior (using tools such as prompts, rewards, and feedback to respond to factors identified), and *Test* the effectiveness of the intervention.

The ABA model focuses attention on external factors not because the internal factors are irrelevant, but because they are not amenable to direct intervention. Geller is clear about the need to consider internal motivations. In a 1995 article titled "Actively caring for the environment: An integration of behaviorism and humanism," he attends to some of the dispositional predictors of pro-environmental behavior, such as self-efficacy and a sense of belonging, and describes how these variables can be maximized through environmental contingencies. Self-efficacy, for example, can be increased if tasks are broken down into discrete smaller steps and people are given frequent positive feedback about their success in meeting short-term goals (Geller, 1995). Only if people "actively care," according to Geller, will they do enough to protect the environment. Both action without care, and care without action, will be insufficient.

Doug McKenzie-Mohr advocates an approach that he calls community-based social marketing (CBSM). This involves four steps: identifying barriers and benefits to an activity, developing a strategy for change, piloting the strategy, and evaluating the strategy (McKenzie-Mohr & Smith, 1999). Identifying barriers and benefits involves a close look at behavioral affordances. The strategy for change includes an emphasis on commitment, prompts, norms, incentives, and communication. CBSM is similar to ABA in its focus on manipulating external factors as well as in its emphasis on collecting information before the intervention and on assessing its effectiveness afterward. CBSM, however, does more to focus on the social context within which the intervention occurs. Social support for behavior, including supportive norms, will increase the likelihood that a behavioral intervention will work. McKenzie-Mohr's website, www.cbsm.com, includes a wide range of information as well as descriptions of successful case studies based on CBSM principles.

A third approach is based on the Elaboration Likelihood Model of persuasion (Petty & Cacioppo, 1981; Petty et al., 1995), which suggests that persuasive messages may work one of two ways: by activating superficial associations or by provoking deeper cognitive reflection. Werner (2003) developed a model of the deep elaboration type that stresses specific social factors omitted by ABA or CBSM. Her psychological-social-environmental transactional model includes these key elements (Werner, 2003):

- Embed desired change in individuals' social groups
- Use persuasive messages about behaviors embedded in the actual physical environments individuals occupy and the behavior streams or scripts they already use
- Use messages that strongly convey attitudes so that they will be "scrutinized … accessible and likely to guide behavior" (p. 37)
- Recognize that change is a dynamic process in which information is effective at different stages, and the same information may be relevant in new ways at different times
- Encourage long-term change, including institutional supports.

Any attempt to evoke behavioral change in a real social setting must be tailored to the specifics of that setting. Incentives (e.g., lower utility bills, enhanced sense of community) that matter to some groups will not matter to others (those who do not pay the utility bills, those who are not long-term residents). Some persuasive messages will work for people who have not thought about the issue, while others are better for a more informed audience. An analysis of the target behavior and target group is necessary before planning an applied intervention.

When considering a general shift in behavioral style rather than more specific behavioral changes, some useful information may be gleaned from clinical and health psychologists. Therapists often work with individuals who know that certain behavioral patterns would be preferable, but resist adopting these habits: people trying to quit smoking, exercise more, or reduce their use of alcohol. Prochaska and DiClemente (2005) devised the Stages of Change model to help understand how individuals might come to terms with the need to change their behavior and what techniques might be most effective for individuals at different stages. They identify the following:

Stage of Change	Characteristics	Techniques
Pre-contemplation	Not considering change	Encourage self-exploration Explain and personalize risks
Contemplation	Ambivalent about change	Encourage consideration of pros and cons of behavior change Identify and promote positive outcome expectations
Preparation	Planning to act within a month	Encourage small steps Ensure individual has needed behavioral skills
Action	Practicing new behavior	Focus on social support Bolster self-efficacy
Maintenance	Continued commitment to sustaining new behavior	Reinforce internal rewards
Remission	Resumption of old behaviors	Evaluate trigger for relapse

Source: adapted from http://www.cellinteractive.com/ucla/physician_ed/stages_change.html.

As individuals face the reality that current patterns of behavior are environmentally unsustainable, they may move through these stages in deciding how to modify their own habits. One can imagine how the different internal and external factors discussed earlier – knowledge, reinforcements, social norms – might be more or less effective depending on an individual's stage of change.

Collective behavior

Individuals are the ones who decide to change their behavior, but change must occur at a broader level to have a significant impact on the environment. Only by joining together can individuals elect political officials with pro-environmental positions, enact policies to protect habitats from development, or devote societal resources toward the development of greener technologies. Conceptualizing environmentalism at the group level, rather than the individual level, leads to a consideration of three categories of behaviors that Stern et al. (1999) identified as pro-environmental policy support, active citizenship, and committed activism. Policy support means an acceptance of environmental policies, whose goals may require some sacrifice; active citizenship includes low-risk actions like writing letters, joining environmental organizations, signing petitions, and staying informed; activism means political activity such as extensive involvement in movement organizations, participation in demonstrations, and collective boycotts. Research that has examined citizenship actions tends to find the more active forms are affected by the same variables as individual behaviors, but depend on knowledge and skill in action strategies, and may be more strongly linked to identity. Policy support, in addition, is related to a belief that the policy is fair (Dreyer & Walker, 2013).

A specific type of such citizenship behaviors that has received research attention is organizational environmental citizenship: People's willingness to engage in discretionary pro-environmental behavior in the workplace. Such behavior can have a double impact by establishing clear workplace norms in support of environmentally sustainable behavior. Studies have shown that organizational environmental citizenship is more likely among employees who feel committed to their organization (Paillé & Boiral, 2013) and in the presence of transformational leaders who "present a vision of a sustainable future and talk passionately and confidently about what needs to be accomplished" (Graves et al., 2013, p. 83).

Group membership may provide a bridge between individual action and societal impact. Olli et al. (2001) surveyed over 3,000 members of Norwegian environmental organizations and the general public about their environmental attitudes and behaviors, finding that belonging to a group had an impact on behavior beyond what was accounted for by attitudinal differences. Certainly one's reference groups will carry their own social norms, which may differ from the broader societal norms. Staats et al. (2004) describe an effective way to incorporate social networks into programs to promote pro-environmental behavior. One hundred and fifty Dutch citizens met in small groups over a period of 8 months to discuss possible pro-environmental behaviors and share tips. They were given periodic feedback about their effectiveness in saving energy both as individuals and as groups. Of 38 target behaviors, 20 showed improvements between the start of the program and the final data collection, 2 years later. This was not true for a control group who did not participate in the groups. Staats et al. speculate that the effect of the groups was to make people more mindful about otherwise habitual behaviors. The groups also provided social support for behavior change attempts as well as practical information.

Wiesenfeld and Sanchez (2002) describe three types of community participation: a public hearing, at which community members can voice their opinions; stakeholder negotiation, in which the interests of community members are considered in establishing some environmental position or policy; and participatory planning, in which community members are fundamentally involved in designing and implementing an environmental program. Reviewing several examples of community participation in Latin America, Wiesenfeld and Sanchez identify important fringe benefits: The community tends to experience a heightened sense of group identity as well as an increased sense of empowerment. This strengthened identity, in turn, can motivate further actions to protect the local environment. Pol (2002) went so far as to suggest that sustainability is not possible in a community that does not have a social identity.

Eigner and Schmuck (2002) describe the beginnings of an ambitious project to change the energy use of an entire German village by convincing inhabitants to convert to biomass for their heating and energy uses. Many of the suggestions for promoting the success of the project relate to the spread of social information: involving prominent sponsors, making personal contact, using existing social networks to spread information, involving the media, emphasizing the "personal conviction and authenticity" of spokespersons, and making an active effort to avoid associating the project with existing group divisions (such as political groups). Attending to the social network also involves recognizing that not all positions in that network are equally influential. Some individuals are more effective than others in prompting others to copy their actions. Those trying to mobilize community-level change should recognize the importance of involving individuals in prominent positions, who are looked up to as sources of information, and/or who come into contact with a greater number their fellow citizens than the average person (see also McKenzie-Mohr, 2000).

Many of the approaches to behavior change we have discussed emphasize highly targeted behaviors and incremental individual steps. To effectively reduce environmental impact, however, we need broad changes in lifestyle, particularly regarding consumption (Swim et al., 2011). Such shifts might draw from altruistic motivations, such as a feeling of obligation to future generations. But they might also derive from reassessing how existing values and life priorities are met. Does consumption make us happy? We discuss the possibility of a shift away from materialism in chapter 12.

Conclusion

Changing behavioral affordances is effective and durable. Incentives are effective but tend not to generalize, and behavior often returns to baseline when the incentives are removed; in addition, incentives may backfire if they encourage people to focus on financial rather than ethical aspects of behavior. Punishments may be effective but may also cause resentment and creative attempts to subvert the attempted behavioral control. Prompts and feedback are effective but people tend to habituate to prompts and the feedback needs to be maintained, perhaps incorporated as an intrinsic part of the behavioral context. Eliciting commitments tends to be an effective and lasting way to change behavior, perhaps because it serves to transfer the motivation from an external source (pleasing others) to an internal one (living up to one's promises). This, in turn, can lead people to discover or generate additional internal benefits, such as the feeling of satisfaction from fulfilling personal norms.

To achieve the kind of large-scale behavioral changes that are demanded by environmental challenges, both internal and external factors are important: people must move beyond specific behaviors to a more general way of thinking about consumption and about their impact on the environment. As more people act on their support for pro-environmental behavior, they will help to create social norms and societal infrastructure that will facilitate further progress.

References

Ahn, H.-K., Kim, H. J., & Aggarwal, P. (2013). Helping fellow beings: Anthropomorphized social causes and the role of anticipatory guilt. *Psychological Science*, DOI: 10.1177/0956797613496823

Ajzen, I. (1991). The theory of planned behavior. *Organizational Behavior and Human Decision Processes*, *50*, 179–211.

Bain, P., Hornsey, M., Bongiomo, R., & Jeffries, C. (2012). Promoting pro-environmental action in climate change deniers. *Nature Climate Change*, *2*, 600–603.

Bamberg, S., & Moser, G. (2007). Twenty years after Hines, Hungerford, and Tomera: A new meta-analysis of psycho-social determinants of pro-environmental behavior. *Journal of Environmental Psychology*, *27*, 14–25.

Bandura, A. (1977). Self-efficacy: Toward a unifying theory of behavioral change. *Psychological Review*, *84*, 191–215.

Bandura, A. (2002). Environmental sustainability by sociocognitive deceleration of population growth. In P. Schmuck & P. W. Schultz (Eds.), *Psychology of sustainable development* (pp. 209–238). Boston: Kluwer.

Bator, R., & Cialdini, R. (2000). The application of persuasion theory to the development of effective proenvironmental public service announcements. *Journal of Social Issues*, *56*, 527–542.

Berenguer, J. (2007). The effect of empathy in proenvironmental attitudes and behaviors. *Environment and Behavior*, *39*, 269–283.

Bolderdijk, J. W., & Steg, L. (2015). Promoting sustainable consumption: The risks of using financial incentives. In L. Reisch & J. Thogersen (Eds.), *Handbook of research on sustainable consumption*. Oxford, UK: Edward Elgar.

Brehm, J. (1966). *A theory of psychological reactance*. New York: Academic Press.

Brook, A. (2011). Ecological footprint feedback: Motivating or discouraging? *Social Influence*, *6*(2), 113–128.

Burger, J. M. (1999). The foot-in-the-door compliance procedure: A multiple-process analysis and review. *Personality and Social Psychology Review, 3*, 303–325.

De Young, R. (1986). Some psychological aspects of recycling: The structure of conservation satisfactions. *Environment and Behavior, 18*(4), 435–449.

De Young, R. (1993). Changing behavior and making it stick: The conceptualization and management of conservation behavior. *Environment and Behavior, 25*, 485–505.

De Young, R. (1996). Some psychological aspects of reduced consumption behavior: The role of intrinsic satisfaction and competence motivation. *Environment and Behavior, 28*, 358–409.

Dreyer, S., & Walker, I. (2013). Acceptance and support of the Australian carbon policy. *Social Justice Research, 26*, 343–362.

Dwyer, W. O., Leeming, F. C., Cobern, M. K., Porter, B. E., et al. (1993). Critical review of behavioral interventions to preserve the environment: Research since 1980. *Environment and Behavior, 25*, 275–321.

Earthworks Group. (1989). *Fifty simple things you can do to save the earth*. Berkeley, CA: Earthworks Press.

Eigner, S., & Schmuck, P. (2002). Motivating collective action: Converting to sustainable energy in a German community. In P. Schmuck & P. Schultz. (Eds.). *Psychology of sustainable development* (pp. 241–256). Boston: Kluwer.

Ferguson, M., & Branscombe, N. (2010). Collective guilt mediates the effect of beliefs about global warming on willingness to engage in mitigation behavior. *Journal of Environmental Psychology, 30*, 135–142.

Festinger, L. (1957). *A theory of cognitive dissonance*. Stanford, CA: Stanford University Press.

Fujii, S. (2006). Environmental concern, attitude toward frugality, and ease of behavior as determinants of pro-environmental behavior intentions. *Journal of Environmental Psychology, 26*, 262–268.

Gardner, G., & Stern, P. (2002). *Environmental problems and human behavior*. Boston: Allyn & Bacon.

Geller, E. S. (1989). Applied behavior analysis and social marketing: An integration to preserve the environment. *Journal of Social Issues, 45*, 17–36.

Geller, E. S. (1995). Actively caring for the environment: An integration of behaviorism and humanism. *Environment and Behavior, 27*, 184–195.

Geller, E. S. (2002). The challenge of increasing proenvironment behavior. In R. Bechtel & A. Churchman (Eds.), *Handbook of environmental psychology* (pp. 525–540). New York: Wiley.

Graves, L., Sarkis, J., & Zhu, Q. (2013). How transformational leadership and employee motivation combine to predict employee proenvironmental behaviors in China. *Journal of Environmental Psychology, 35*, 81–91.

Hine, D., & Gifford, R. (1991). Fear appeals, individual differences, and environmental concern. *Journal of Environmental Education, 23*, 36–41.

Hines, J. M., Hungerford, H. R., & Tomera, A. N. (1987). Analysis and synthesis of research on responsible environmental behavior: A meta-analysis. *Journal of Environmental Education, 18*, 1–8.

Hopper, J. R., & Nielsen, J. M. (1991). Recycling as altruistic behavior: Normative and behavioral strategies to expand participation in a community recycling program. *Environment and Behavior, 23*, 195–220.

Joireman, J., Posey, D. C., Truelove, H. B., & Parks, C. D. (2009). The environmentalist who cried drought: Reactions to repeated warnings about depleting resources under conditions of uncertainty. *Journal of Environmental Psychology, 29*(2), 181–192.

Kaiser, F. G., & Shimoda, T. A. (1999). Responsibility as a predictor of ecological behavior. *Journal of Environmental Psychology, 19*, 243–253.

Kals, E., & Ittner, H. (2003). Children's environmental identity. In S. Clayton & S. Opotow (Eds.) *Identity and the natural environment* (pp. 135–157). Cambridge, MA: MIT Press.

Kals, E., & Maes, J. (2002). Sustainable development and emotions. In P. Schmuck & P. W. Schultz (Eds.), *Psychology of sustainable development* (pp. 97–122). Boston: Kluwer.

Karp, D. G. (1996). Values and their effect on pro-environmental behavior. *Environment and Behavior, 28*, 111–133.

Kempton, W., Darley, J. M., & Stern, P. (1992). Psychological research for the new energy problems: Strategies and opportunities. *American Psychologist, 47*, 1213–1223.

Kim, M. (2002). *Non-Western perspectives on human communication.* Thousand Oaks, CA: Sage Publications.

Kimura, H., & Nakajima, T. (2011). Designing persuasive applications to motivate sustainable behavior in collectivist cultures. *PsychNology Journal 9*(1), 7–28.

Latané, B., & Darley, J. (1970). *The unresponsive bystander: Why doesn't he help?* New York: Appleton-Century-Crofts.

Lokhorst, A., Werner, C., Staats, H., van Dijk, E., & Gale J. (2013). Commitment and behavior change: a metaanalysis and critical review of commitment-making strategies in environmental research. *Environmental Behavior, 45,* 3–34.

Mallett, R. K. (2012). Eco-guilt motivates eco-friendly behavior. *Ecopsychology, 4*(3), 223–231.

Markus, H. R., & Kitayama, S. (1991). Culture and the self: Implications for cognition, emotion and motivation. *Psychological Review, 98,* 224–252.

Markus, H. R., & Kitayama, S. (1998). The cultural psychology of personality. *Journal of Cross-Cultural Psychology, 29,* 63–87.

McKenzie-Mohr, D. (2000). Fostering sustainable behavior through community-based social marketing. *American Psychologist, 55,* 531–537.

McKenzie-Mohr, D., & Smith, W. (1999). *Fostering sustainable behavior: An introduction to community-based social marketing.* Gabriola Island, British Columbia: New Society.

Meijinders, A., Midden, C., & Wilke, H. (2001). Role of negative emotion in communication about CO_2 risks. *Risk Analysis, 21,* 955–966.

Michel-Guillou, E., & Moser, G. (2006). Commitment of farmers to environmental protection. *Journal of Environmental Psychology, 26,* 227–235.

Milfont, T., & Sibley, C. (2012). The big five personality traits and environmental engagement: Associations at the individual and societal level. *Journal of Environmental Psychology, 32,* 187–195.

Nijhuis M. (2007, July/August). Everybody's doing it. *Orion Magazine,* available at www.orionmagazine.org

Nolan, J., Schultz, P. W., Cialdini, R., Goldstein, N., & Griskevicius, V. (2008). Normative social influence is undetected. *Personality and Social Psychology Bulletin, 34,* 913–923.

O'Connor, R., Bord, R., & Fisher, A. (1999). Risk perceptions, general environmental beliefs, and willingness to address climate change. *Risk Analysis, 19,* 461–471.

O'Neill, S., & Nicholson-Cole, S. (2009). "Fear Won't Do It": Promoting positive engagement with climate change through visual and iconic representations. *Science Communication, 30*(3), 355–379.

Osbaldiston, R., & Schott, J. (2012). Environmental sustainability and behavioral science: Meta-analysis of proenvironmental behavior experiments. *Environment and Behavior, 44,* 257–299.

Olli, E., Grendstad, G., & Wollebaek, D. (2001). Correlates of environmental behaviors: Bringing back social context. *Environment and Behavior, 33,* 181–208.

Otto, S., Kaiser, F., & Arnold, O. (2014). The critical challenge of climate change for psychology. *European Psychologist, 19,* 96–106.

Paillé, P., & Boiral, O. (2013). Pro-environmental behavior at work: Construct validity and determinants. *Journal of Environmental Psychology, 36,* 118–128.

Petty, R. E., Haugvedt, C. P., & Smith, S. M. (1995). Elaboration as a determinant of attitude strength: Creating attitudes that are persistent, resistant, and predictive of behavior. In R. E. Petty & J. A. Krosnick (Eds.), *Attitude strength: Antecedents and consequences* (pp. 93–130). Mahwah, NJ: Lawrence Erlbaum.

Petty, R. E., & Cacioppo, J. T. (1981). *Attitudes and persuasion: Classic and contemporary approaches.* Dubuque, IA: W.C. Brown Publishers.

Pol, E. (2002). Environmental management: A perspective from environmental psychology. In R. Bechtel & A. Churchman (Eds.), *Handbook of environmental psychology* (pp. 55–84). New York: Wiley.

Polgreen, L. (2007). In Niger, trees and crops turn back the desert. *New York Times,* Feb. 11., Section 1 p. 1.

Prochaska, J., & DiClemente, C. (2005). The transtheoretical approach. In J. Nordcross & M. Goldfried (Eds.), *Handbook of psychotherapy integration* (2nd ed.), pp. 147–171. New York: Oxford.

Schultz, P. W., Khazian, A., & Zaleski, A. (2008). Using normative social influence to promote conservation among hotel guests. *Social Influence*, *3*, 4–23.

Sia, A. P., Hungerford, H. R., & Tomera, A. N. (1985-1986). Selected predictors of responsible environmental behavior: An analysis. *Journal of Environmental Education*, *17*, 31–40.

Staats, H., Harland, P., & Wilke, H. (2004). Effecting durable change: A team approach to improve environmental behavior in the household. *Environment and Behavior*, *36*, 341–367.

Stern, P. (1992). What psychology knows about energy conservation. *American Psychologist*, *47*, 1224–1232.

Stern, P. (2000). Toward a coherent theory of environmentally significant behavior. *Journal of Social Issues*, *56*, 407–424.

Stern, P., Dietz, T., Abel, T., Guagnano, G., & Kalof, L. (1999). A value-belief-norm theory of support for social movements: The case of environmentalism. *Human Ecology Review*, *6*(2), 81–97.

Steg, L., Bolderdijk, J. W., Keizer, K., & Perlaviciute, G. (2014). An integrated framework for encouraging pro-environmental behavior: The role of values, situational factors, and goals. *Journal of Environmental Psychology*, *38*, 104–115.

Swim, J., Clayton, S., & Howard, G. (2011). Human behavioral contributions to climate change. *American Psychologist*, *66*, 251–264.

Tam, K. (2014). Are anthropomorphic persuasive appeals effective? The role of the recipient's motivations. *British Journal Of Social Psychology*, DOI: 10.1111/bjso.12076

Tam, K., Lee, S., & Chao, M. (2013). Saving Mr. Nature: Anthropomorphism enhances connectedness to and protectiveness toward nature. *Journal of Experimental Social Psychology*, *49*, 514–521.

Thaler, R., & Sunstein, C. (2009). *Nudge: Improving decisions about health, wealth, and happiness*. New York: Penguin Books.

Van Vugt, M. (2001). Community identification moderating impact of financial incentives in a natural social dilemma: Water conservation. *Personality and Social Psychology Bulletin*, *27*, 1440–1449.

Werner, C. M. (2003). Changing homeowners' use of toxic household products: A transactional approach. *Journal of Environmental Psychology 23*, 33–45.

Werner, C. M., Sansone, C., & Brown, B. B. (2008). Guided group discussion and attitude change: The roles of normative and informational influence. *Journal of Environmental Psychology*, *28*, 27–41.

Werner, C. M., Turner, J., Shipman, K., Twitchell, F. S., Dickson, B. R., Bruschke, G. V., & von Bismarck, W. B. (1995). Commitment, behavior, and attitude change: An analysis of voluntary recycling. *Journal of Environmental Psychology*, *15*, 197–208.

Wiesenfeld, E., & Sanchez, E. (2002). Sustained participation: A community-based approach to addressing environmental problems. In R. Bechtel & A. Churchman (Eds.), *Handbook of environmental psychology* (pp. 629–643). New York: Wiley.

Wilke, H. (1991). Greed, efficiency and fairness in resource management situations. In W. Stroebe & M. Hewstone, (Eds.), *European review of social psychology* (pp. 165–187). New York: Wiley.

Witte, K. (1998). Fear as motivator, fear as inhibitor: Using the extended parallel process model to explain fear appeal successes and failures. In I. P. Anderson & L. Guerrero (Eds.), *Handbook of communication and emotion* (pp. 424–451). San Diego, CA: Academic Press.

10

Community Psychology and International Biodiversity Conservation

Community constitutes an important context for conservation. "Community" has positive, even romantic, connotations for many of us, who tend to think of community as a small spatial unit, homogeneous, and with common visions. The reality is more complex. Communities need not be based on shared location; they can be interest-based, values-based, or professional; global or face to face, distant or virtual. Communities always have multiple interests and actors, and links with other entities at different scales. German sociologist Tönnies (1957) distinguished two concepts of community. *Gemeinschaft,* which emphasizes traditional norms, deep history, personality, tradition, close-knit relationships, and religious bonds, encourages putting higher value on the group's interest than one's own. *Gesellschaft* is pervaded by modernity, rationality, and science and made up of specialized roles that are coordinated via markets and bureaucracies; the actual occupants of those roles are unimportant. In either case, communities are composed of people who differ by status, power, social prestige, intentions, and world view. They may or may not be harmonious, and their relations to large-scale institutions may be positive or negative (Agrawal & Gibson, 2001).

This chapter blends two aims. One is to describe key dynamics involved in community psychology and community-based conservation. The other is to feature conservation of inhabited

Conservation Psychology: Understanding and promoting human care for nature, Second Edition.
Susan Clayton and Gene Myers.

www.wiley.com\go\clayton\conservation

landscapes, parks and protected areas, and biodiversity. Petty (2003) estimated that in all countries, between the early 1990s and 2002, 455,000 to 520,000 new community-based groups dedicated to local natural resource management were formed, involving 8 to 15 million households. In many ways, the human dimensions of these efforts are the same whether they occur in the developing world or in industrialized countries, but in other ways there are distinctive differences. In recent years, conservation innovations emerging from community-rich developing world contexts have begun to be transferred back to the industrialized world. This is an urgent frontier for the use of psychological tools, and this chapter will consider the relevance of psychological research to these applied settings. As is true throughout this book, we see human–nature issues as being human–human issues, or human–nature–human: The negative environmental effects we suffer are the result of human actions, often mediated by groups, institutions, conflict, and the welfare of others. Poverty, human rights status, and power are ultimately inseparable from the human relationship to nature. This chapter confronts the challenging intersection of human communities and perhaps the most fragile, precious, and irreplaceable environmental value: biodiversity.

International biodiversity conservation

Conservation of biodiversity has become an international enterprise, undertaken by researchers, nongovernmental organizations (NGOs), governments from the local to international level, businesses, and philanthropists. Our concern here is with programs that, in the process of directly protecting species and ecosystems, necessarily work with residents in or near areas of high conservation priority. Local people may depend directly on natural systems for their food, water, and materials, as well as for goods they trade in raw or manufactured form. They may also be employees of small or large industries with local facilities, and when tourism is present, they are involved. Such populations directly impact, and are impacted by, local ecosystems.

While this chapter focuses on people in rural areas still interacting closely with the landscape, we do not mean to minimize the responsibility of those whose interactions with nature are more indirect. Habitat loss is driven by the extensive conversion of natural areas to meet consumption demands of industrialized countries for minerals, petroleum, hydropower, trees, meat, and plantation or agricultural crops. Dietz et al. (2007) conclusively showed that the environmental intensity of countries, gauged by the ecological footprint measure, is attributable largely to population and consumption. Population growth rates are slowing but consumption growth is rising much faster. The concrete impacts of consumption often hit both biodiversity and local people and provide new incentives for resource extraction by local actors. Solving the biodiversity crisis thus requires examination of developed countries' lifestyle choices. Nonetheless, direct exploitation of nature by communities living in close dependence and market-mediated economic dependence on nature are proximate threats to biodiversity.

Official land conservation efforts originated with the establishment of national parks, preserves, and forests in the late 1800s and early 1900s in the United States and Europe. Generally, such parks were formed by legislating boundaries around areas of unusual aesthetic value, excluding people from pursuing traditional uses, and declaring recreation and preservation of the land and biota as the main purposes. This became the model for parks in other countries. Thus, when former colonies became independent, they often imposed governmental control on large areas of public land. Conservation became international with the establishment of institutions such as:

- The International Union for the Conservation of Nature (IUCN, also known as the World Conservation Union, established in 1948), which reports on species' status and coordinates teams of experts working on species survival.
- The Convention on International Trade in Endangered Species (CITES, brought into force in 1975), whose purpose is to convene nations and make rules to stem trade in endangered species.
- UNESCO's Man and Biosphere program of reserves, under which parks are recognized as having international conservation significance.
- Several large NGOs focused on preserving habitats and species, such as the Wildlife Conservation Society, the World Wildlife Fund, Conservation International, and The Nature Conservancy and Flora and Fauna International.

The Convention on Biodiversity was advanced at the 1992 United Nations Conference on Environment and Development (UNCED) in Rio de Janeiro. To date, most countries (194) are parties to the Convention (President Clinton signed in it 1993 but the United States Senate has not ratified it). UNCED emphasized the need to integrate human welfare and conservation, and sparked a surge of small but well-networked community-based NGOs worldwide. Contemporaneously with such institutions came the emergence of conservation biology as a research community focused on preserving land and species in a context of multiple threats. Conservation biologists deployed conceptual models such as island biogeography and population biology into tools such as gap analysis for designing preserves in fragmented landscapes. Augmented by increasingly accurate geographical information system (GIS) databases of species distribution, and remote-sensing (satellite) data on vegetation and land use, organizations have focused on priority areas such as "ecoregions" or "biodiversity hotspots."

Biodiversity exists on multiple levels. It is not evenly distributed across the globe, and there are different patterns of species rarity. Conservation biologists often cannot say precisely what the effects of a given species' loss would be because of unknown interdependencies. Despite these gaps in knowledge, the threats of species extinction and loss of habitat are so acute that the main goal of conservation biology seldom is merely an inventory of species. Conservation biology is a "crisis discipline" (Soule, 1985), tracking a changing target with a far less than optimal amount of resources.

From the outset, conservation biologists have recognized that biological science does not hold all the answers to conservation and have sought to work with the social sciences on the human dimensions of conservation (see the resources offered by the Social Science Working Group of the Society for Conservation Biology, http://www.conbio.org/WorkingGroups/SSWG/; see also Mascia forthcoming, Wiley). The need for the social sciences has become even more obvious as some of the early apparent successes of conservation have revealed shortcomings.

Common pool resources and models of governance

One contribution of social science, and psychology in particular, is in evaluating the different ways that common pool resources or commons are managed. Common pool resources, distinct from open access resources, are collectively owned or managed in some fashion. We will examine four major models of conservation governance applicable to the commons, each with quite different community and psychological dimensions. These four models can all be seen as alternative responses to Garrett Hardin's (1968) model of the "tragedy of the commons." As we described in Chapter 6, Hardin depicted the commons dilemma as resulting from a situation where resources are shared without rules governing use by a community, taking an English village pastureland as his historical model. Hardin suggested that because each herder would expect to receive a full unit of benefit from grazing an additional animal, but the costs would be spread across the community in the form of slightly heavier grazing, a rational cost-benefit analysis would lead the herder to graze more animals. If other herders apply the same logic, the result is an over-grazed pasture that is unable to support any cattle, and many impoverished herders who no longer have use of those common resources.

In presuming open-access conditions, Hardin reflected some typical assumptions about human nature. He was skeptical about people's ability to restrain their self-interested desires and avoid "discounting" (valuing at a lower rate) the negative consequences to others and long-term consequences to themselves. Hardin considered various possible solutions. Relying on appeals to conscience, he argued, would lead in the long run to the extinction of whatever traits give rise to conscience, since those restraining themselves would be out-competed. In considering conscience, or internalization, however, Hardin did not inquire into the underlying social factors. Another solution was privatization: sole owners will theoretically internalize total costs as well as benefits. Hardin opted for a third, "mutual coercion, mutually agreed upon," or central governance as the least undesirable option. He did not see other viable alternatives.

Hardin's influential essay appears to apply to a wide range of environmental problems, in which a resource is degraded by the extractive or polluting contributions of many isolated actors. When the incentives felt by these actors lead them to act in an individually rational but collectively irrational way, the incentives are "perverse" and we have a "social trap" situation. Because central control is consonant with the way many bureaucracies work, and since parks and species are regarded as parts of our common heritage, it is not surprising that governmental authorities stepped in to manage them.

The historical precedent in which preservation of park-like landscapes meant the exclusion of people appears to be consistent with the *central governance* method of protection. But when control of these areas was taken from local populations, people did not simply stay out. For example, in Nepal, centuries of governance by an elite led to a model of state ownership and management of forest lands. But people collected firewood and other materials needed for subsistence from government forest conservation areas illegally. Little had been done to gain people's investment in conservation. Regulation and enforcement depended on compliance, which in turn depends on the expectation of reward, or fear of punishment, rather than internalization of a norm or value. Excessive control can induce psychological reactance (Brehm, 1966) or acting to the contrary of the superimposed rule. The Nepalese system failed not only because of an impossible enforcement task, but because of psychological responses to the attempts at governmental control and a lack of individual support for the conservation goal.

In other examples, protection of wildlife has caused the displacement and impoverishment of people by excluding them from traditional resources. Fencing seems to embody the *privatization* model of management. In South Africa's 7,000+ square-mile Kruger National Park, a fence was erected in 1960 on the western border to keep wildlife in and cattle, along with human foragers and hunters, out. (Its removal began in the 1990s.) Here, the owner of the park was a governmental entity. But there are also many private wildlife or game preserves, and outright land acquisition is a major strategy favored by some conservationists. Like central governance, however, it requires costly and effective boundary enforcement and/or sufficient isolation from human incursion.

Not surprisingly from a psychological point of view, the conservation effectiveness of private land preservation depends on the intentions and social organization of the owners. Laikipia County is notable in Kenya for the fact its wildlife has not followed the national decline, and yet wildlife conservation is being conducted on private lands. Researchers used camera traps to determine the diversity of wild mammals using private lands under four different management schemes (Kinnaird & O'Brien, 2012). The highest species richness occurred in unfenced conservancies, and the next highest in rhino sanctuaries that were fenced so as to allow non-rhino species to pass in and out. Notably these types of lands employed the highest number of security guards. Moderate numbers of livestock did not affect wildlife use in these areas. High stocking levels (more than 25 per km^2), typical of both single-owner fenced ranches and unfenced communal group ranches, had the lowest biodiversity, especially of larger mammals. For owners to form intentions to tolerate large mammals, the researchers suggest, they need to directly benefit from wildlife in a range of ways including ecotourism, conservation easements, and compensation schemes (Kinnaird & O'Brien, 2012).

New conceptions of the commons

The above examples from developing countries illustrate some of the challenges that led conservationists to recognize and embrace the significance of human dimensions. We offer a more effective analytical framework to help, based on inputs from both practical and theoretical sides. On the practical side, impetus came from local groups. For example, in 1993, following the democracy movement in Nepal, forest management was decentralized and delegated partially to local Forest User Groups (Lachapelle et al., 2004); we will consider this more carefully below. Integrated Conservation and Development Projects (ICDPs) that attempt to advance both economic welfare and wildlife values represent another innovation.

On the theoretical side, our understanding of how communities of people manage commonly owned resources has changed considerably since Hardin. It turns out that Hardin's key example, the English common pasture system, was historically inaccurate and understated the actual sustainability of this ancient system. More importantly, anthropologists and political scientists have identified and studied many examples of sustainable resource management systems around the world. Psychologists have contributed research on the emergence of cooperative or selfish behavior under various conditions (e.g., Suleiman et al., 2004). This body of research does not invalidate Hardin's analysis, but as it helps delimit the settings in which it is likely to be accurate. It lets us define variables that affect the likelihood that defined groups of people will be able to manage a common resource without depleting it. Ostrom et al. (1999) explored the four property rights systems referred to above, outlining the conditions which favor common or group property arrangements and the possibility of internalization of common interests. No single management approach can be a "panacea" that fits all cases, as emphasized in a special issue of the *Proceedings of the National Academy of Sciences* (2007, vol. 104, no. 39).

Marine protected areas (MPAs) illustrate the application of this evolving body of knowledge. Over 4.2 million km^2 or about 1.17% of the world's ocean has been given protection since 1970 (Spalding et al., 2010), a large portion of this area being in about two dozen MPAs larger than 30,000 km^2. This represents progress toward the Convention on Biological Diversity (CBD) goal of 10% "conserved through effectively and equitably managed protected areas and other … conservation measures" (Secretariat of Convention on Biological Diversity, 2010). As just one example of an MPA, in coastal east Africa, free-for-all fishing had expanded with population growth and fishing equipment investments to encompass the entire coastal zone, threatening an exceptionally productive and biologically diverse system of global significance. But research by the World Wildlife Fund in the cases of Quirimbas National Park in Mozambique, Mafia Island Marine Reserve in Tanzania, and more recently the Primerias & Segundas Reserves identified variables that could provide leverage for change. Critically, a good proportion of these fish species have a moderate level of mobility. While they are not so mobile that they may migrate out of the area entirely, they do spread out as their population density increases. Thus, if a medium-sized area is designated off-limits to fishing, it can act like a natural nursery to regenerate populations that then move to surrounding fishing-permitted areas.

On the social side, the fishery resource itself was amenable to establishment of community-based protection. The resource was perceptibly threatened; fishers had seen the declining catch levels themselves. And, positively, when the MPAs began boosting populations, fishers noticed larger fish and more plentiful catches. Although the east African coastline is vast, it was possible to delineate a smaller area for protection, with boundaries that were identifiable by fishers. The intensity of use could thus be managed, and fishers' behavior could be informally observed by other community members. If the resource features were different – if the fishery were vast, hard to define, highly mobile, or difficult to predict, if degradation was not perceptible, or if behavior in the preserve were hard to observe – community management might be very difficult. Notably, some global-scale resources and behaviors affecting them resemble the latter situation.

Other factors relate to the social dynamics of the community. Too large a community of fishers would be unlikely to have the strong, enduring, and dense networks of relationships that are important for a group to evolve its own shared norms and institutions. When more formal rules are needed, people are more likely to follow them if they have participated in their creation and can collectively modify them, than if they are imposed by an unresponsive authority. In coastal east Africa groups, norms include injunctions against fishing in the MPA. With strong social networks and participation, communities form systems that protect everyone who cooperates in the management of the resource. These systems are likely to include mild penalties for violators, the effect of which is not to exclude the violator, but to mildly and temporarily ostracize them. Chronic violators are likely to be the recipients of "informal justice." Such vigilantism could undermine the system if it is applied arbitrarily. But community management systems may exist in parallel with formal institutions of justice such as regional or national laws, enforcement, and courts. Such formal institutions provide more neutral systems of arbitration, as well as essential back-ups when the community cannot effectively exclude outsiders, such as foreign large-volume fishing vessels, from using the resource. In such cases, centralized authority and local control may work positively together. Similarly, outside scientists found they had to find productive compromises with the research agenda and interests of local scientists and other community members (H. Fox, personal communication).

When fishers perceive that free riders will not be able to take advantage of them if they cooperate with management strategies and that the norms have been developed from within the group, the psychology of the situation may change from one of compliance to one of *internalization* of the group's interest. Participatory governance helps internalization because it increases commitment to the rules and a sense of ownership. This was supported by a survey of fishers from 42 communities across five countries that showed rules were followed more when they were simple and few in number. More importantly, when locals managed the MPA resource with an eye to customary arrangements, users perceived more beneficial livelihood outcomes (Cinner & Huchery, 2014). Other institutional arrangements – national park administration, or delegating to a midlevel governance unit – did not offer this social benefit, and the latter can be vulnerable to "elite capture," when decision makers escape accountability to the fishermen. Social psychology studies have shown that, given the choice, people prefer social reciprocity (communal or equitable sharing), and social trust. For reciprocity and trust to prevail in the face of market-oriented competitive individualistic societies requires institutions (rules, communication patterns, norms) that protect those showing cooperative, trustworthy behaviors. In practice, conservationists interact with overlapping and multilayered communities. Fox and colleagues (2012) summarized some of the recent lessons from MPA research. They noted ecological and social factors fostering MPA success, including: "substantial coverage of representative habitats and oceanographic conditions; diverse size and spacing; protection of habitat bottlenecks; participatory decision-making arrangements; bounded and contextually appropriate resource use rights; active and accountable monitoring and enforcement systems; and accessible conflict resolution mechanisms." Community-based solutions are not a panacea either; what works best will depend on the configuration of social, governance, and resource factors. But one larger lesson here is that "conscience" can work; control from above is not the only option.

Looking beyond MPAs to other resource types, recent empirical studies show the overlapping forces at work; for example, rules regarding resource extraction versus market forces. A set of case studies of four indigenous Kichwa communities in the Sumaco Biosphere Reserve in the Ecuadorian Amazonian (within the Tropical Andes Biodiversity hotspot) looked at conversion of forest for agriculture (Oldekop et al., 2013). The study was not able to tease out the separate effects of remoteness and size of the communities; the larger and also more remote communities were similar in forest cover to a protected park within the region. But, in general, market demand (and population) and access to markets (distance and roads) apparently overshadowed the adaptation and implementation of protective institutions in most communities. Markets elicit individual self-interested calculation. The exception was one community where reserves were strictly managed and rules regulating timber extraction existed and were enforced. All the communities had secured collective land titles and embraced general public consensus as their decision process in the 1980s, so variation in forest management needs to be understood in terms of both external (market) and internal factors, such as community decision making, norm-setting, and enforcement.

The stress imposed on traditional common resource management by market conditions has been observed elsewhere (Moran, 2006). This foreshadows future challenges for the emergence of new common property management systems, which must arise in the context of global interconnection; more pervasive markets, privatization, and individualistic values; weaker communitarian ties; and the need for multilevel/multiparty governance. The main challenges to emerging commons thus include developing shared understandings through community-building processes; the development of institutions and rules that fit the specific human–environment relations; and functional and systemic connections and integration across levels affecting the socio-ecological system(Ruiz-Ballesteros & Gual, 2012, p. 848).

Ruiz-Ballesteros and Gual (2012) provided a 3-year case study of this process based in the community of Aqua Blanco, an 8,000 hectare (ha) community of 260 people living on a river corridor within Machalilla National Park, Ecuador. The Aqua Blanco area contains three ecosystems: river valley, cloud mountain forest, and tropical dry forest. The historical context is important, as the area was dominated by a 4,000 ha *la Hacienda* from the late 19th century to the mid 1960s. This was a propertied-class system based on unsustainable extractive industry, monopoly of the best land and water, no regulation, and subjugation of laborers. A financial crisis in the 1960s bankrupted the *Hacienda* and allowed residents, who had begun a community building process on 4,000 ha outside its boundaries, to take over the water-rich and fertile valley. In the 1970s, however, the national government, responding to international trends, set up the Park, with the intent to evict the residents. Conflict followed in the 1980s between formal conservation and individualistic market choices by residents.

Remarkably, a key transition occurred in the community's conception of their relation to the environment when archeologists working in the river zone shared discoveries about the prehistoric sustainable uses of the area. The community became more pro-active and with the help of NGOs became the main actors in an emerging community-based tourism. The Park granted the community rights to the land in usufruct, thus adding the 4,000 ha of *la Hacienda* to the community's control. In 1986, the community imposed limits on household charcoal production, setting in motion a decline in the destructive practice. Charcoal production had spiked in previous decades, lacking any resource management system (including the Park's command and control attempts). Particularly significant in this resource-institution analysis are the rules that link different governance levels into a comanagement system, with a major role played by the communitarian institutions of the local community (Fig. 10.1). Also significant was a national policy promoting domestic tourism, which makes up 51% of those visiting Aqua Blanca. While in the past many resident adults had migrated to the cities, now that movement has virtually stopped, as people know the slum conditions others have encountered in the city and now have a strong stake in the tourism-based jobs and ecological sustainability their community has created. No external tourism companies operate in the community. In agreement with other literature, Ruiz-Ballesteros and Gual concluded that natural-area tourism succeeded here based on three factors: the flow of economic benefits; land tenure; and community institutions providing social and political justice. The Agua Blanca case appears to contrast with predictions that tourism conflicts with traditional extractive activities, since the latter have been reduced but continue as a part of diversified meager household incomes. Incomes are

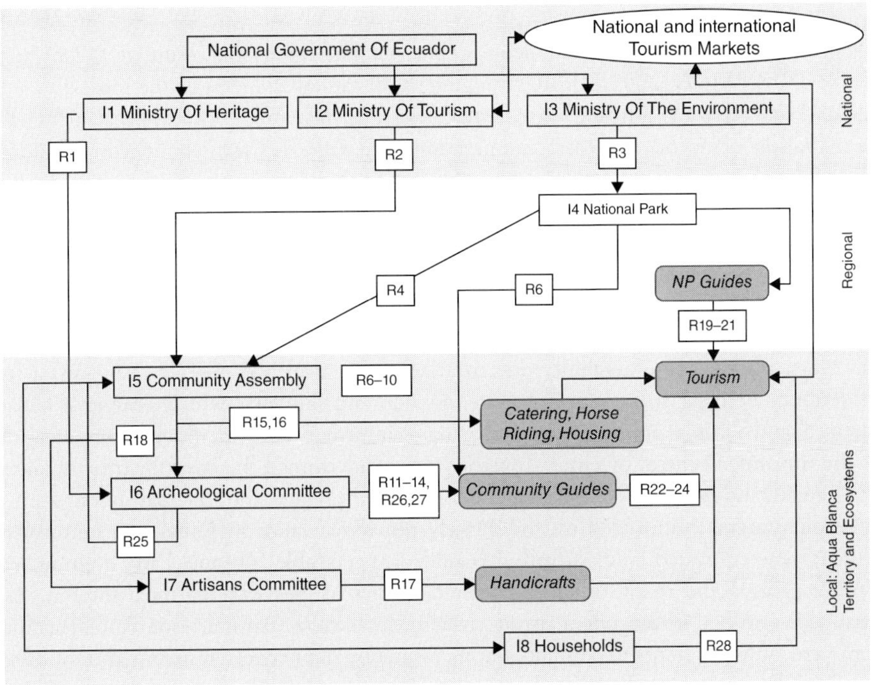

Fig. 10.1 Multilevel governance configuration composed of institutions ("I"), rules ("R"), and productive roles (gray) in tourism in Aqua Blanca, Ecuador. Arrows indicate influence; see source for content of rules (from Ruiz-Ballesteros and Gual (2012). Figure 6, p. 858, copyright © 2012. With kind permission from Springer Science and Business Media).

near-poverty level, but farming, tourism, social cohesion, and a sense of community fairness contribute to overall well-being, and participants have experienced an "ecological awakening" in their new roles (Ruiz-Ballesteros & Gual, 2012).

Social capital and its limitations

Some of the key social variables in successful commons management are captured in the concept of "social capital." A synonym might be "social cohesion," or the extent and types of objective associations and subjective bonds and shared norms among people in a community. A multidimensional concept, it has been linked to a variety of community indicators including life expectancy, resilience, the strength of civil society and democratic institutions, and environmental policy support (Coleman, 1988; Putnam, 2000; Petty, 2003; Jones et al., 2009). Several types of social capital have been identified, including the following:

- Bonding social capital, or the emotional connections and supportiveness that develop most often between people who share traits, values, or relationships.
- Bridging social capital, or the linkages among people and groups that did not choose to be together but nonetheless are. Examples include civil society institutions that bring together people with different backgrounds and interests around common concerns.
- Linking social capital, or the ability of groups to influence or gain resources from external agencies or authorities.

Social capital is fostered when people perceive that others have similar salient values (Cvetkovich & Winter, 2003); clearly, bridging social capital will thus be the most difficult to build and also often the limiting ingredient. Social trust may be important because it enables internalization of norms, increased cooperation, and reduced "transaction costs," allowing for reciprocity and in turn for long-term obligations among community members (Petty, 2003). Trust has been shown to increase cooperation in experimental studies of the commons dilemma (e.g., Messick et al., 1983).

It is not easy to build social capital. Lachapelle et al. (2004) found that the inability of the Nepalese Forest User Groups to effectively manage their resources, despite being officially empowered and networked, resulted from lack of power. This lack was expressed in three primary ways: a sense of vulnerability due to a lack of control over private resources; a sense of inferiority deriving from issues of caste, gender, and illiteracy, which programs had not addressed; and a lack of transparency or sharing of information. Underlying these perceptions was the continued control by elites. Together, they undermined the basis for trust, weakened social capital, and made individuals dependent on their private (and unequal) resources.

A similar scenario unfolded on the densely populated lands in Kabale, in southwestern Uganda; these cultivated lands surround Bwindi Impenetrable National Park, a home of the mountain gorilla and many other endangered species of great international interest. As in Nepal, this area had undergone a strong shift to decentralize natural resource management. There were, however, frequent conflicts among residents, and between residents and the administration of the national park. An analysis by Sanginga et al. (2007) suggested that social capital was not effective in managing conflicts with powerful external stakeholders, including the park and the NGOs operating in the area. Such conflicts were dealt with, on both sides, by coercion or violence – aimed either at residents, or at the park itself, as when residents set fires intending to destroy it. In-group bonding social capital may have exacerbated the conflicts, bridging social capital was formalistic and weak, and linking capital was lacking.

Context matters. The principles and issues of community-based conservation do not differ between developed versus developing countries so long as there are on-the-ground resource-dependent communities, but specific issue may vary: bushmeat, medicinals, and primary forest conversion are more common direct threats in developing countries. More fundamentally, the developing world context may be characterized by poverty, chronic disempowerment, lack of a conservation ethic, and histories of intense conflict or colonialism. Power differences between local communities and the groups that promote conservation too easily lead to imperialism, or apparent imperialism, in conservation. Today, there is debate and pressure for new approaches that can be more consistently successful.

An example from the Solomon Islands identifies the most important form of social capital for conservation (Cohen et al., 2012). The researchers conducted careful social network analysis to find out what forms of network facilitate collaboration, knowledge sharing, and knowledge use (learning) across multiactor conservation comanagement of the globally significant coastal ecosystems (Fig. 10.2). Several entities (the national fisheries agency, the national environmental agency, and an international NGO) shared the position of most highly connected node, reflecting redundancy and resilience in the network. Interestingly, networks including many nonmember entities lying outside the formal governance network were the only functional route for knowledge sharing and national-level representation of local issues, an example of "bridging" relations. Midscale managers (provincial government officials) were not well connected and ineffective. Other constraints and barriers to information exchange and learning included prioritization of personal or agency agendas, lack of common purposes for sharing, lack of trust, and commitments, mandates or momentum that prevented agencies from applying new knowledge (Cohen et al., 2012).

In a study of six countries in the developed world (Czech Republic, South Korea, South Africa, Norway, Great Britain, and the United States), Jin (2013) hypothesized that four dimensions of social capital would predict environmentally responsible behavior (ERB): (1) social trust that others will cooperate for the common good; (2) institutional trust, or the degree to

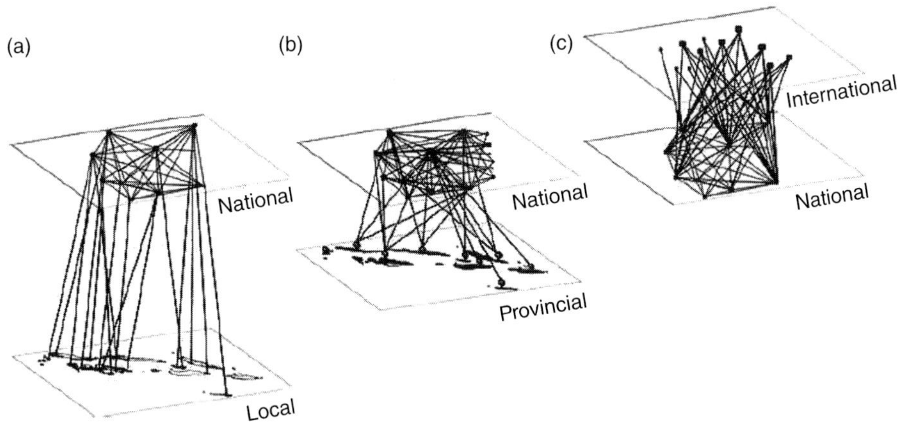

Fig. 10.2 Network analyses of the Solomon Islands Locally Managed Marine Area Network (SILMMA), showing links among national agencies and sites they comanage (a); cross-scale networking between governmental levels (b); and SILMMA members and nonmember agencies linkages to international agencies (c) (from Cohen et al. (2012), Figure 3, p. 382).

which individuals trust their legal institutions to operate in ways that benefit; (3) social norms; and (4) social networks at both individual and group levels, leading to greater flow of information and increased environmental awareness. Hypothesized links between social capital and ERB were tested with responses to the 2010 International Social Survey Program by 6,744 residents of the six countries. Not all the links were supported. Observable behaviors were more influenced by social capital than nonobservable behaviors. A more general pattern was that social capital components that involve individual activity, such as adherence to social norms and individual civic participation, promote pro-environmental behavior while components that rely on other bodies to make responsible decisions for people, such as social and institutional trust and group civic participation may hinder it, perhaps through diffusion of responsibility. On these bases, Jin stresses the importance of environmental citizenship by individuals in enabling effective governmental policies. To this end, government leaders can:

1 promote transparent communication among all governance actors that includes citizens in knowledge sharing and increased issue awareness;
2 monitor not just government performance but also include an assessment of each community's cooperative behavior;
3 promote environmental citizenship at the individual level (Jin, 2013, p. 405).

In summary, many factors influence the sustainability of community conservation management and temper the pessimism that Hardin introduced almost 50 years ago. Some conditions inhibit people's ability to self-organize successful common pool resource institutions:

1 Where individuals have no expectation of mutual trust and no means of building trust through communication and continued interaction (e.g., when outsiders cannot be effectively engaged)
2 Where mistrust is already rampant and communication and interaction do not reduce the level of distrust
3 Where many if not all individuals are willing to extend reciprocity to others but lack authority to create their own self-governing institutions, for example when they lack formal power (Ostrom et al., 1994, p. 328).

External authority may help in the creation and enforcement of contracts, but it should not be assumed that difficulties will disappear when a larger government imposes solutions, because of the known psychological pitfalls of compliance-based solutions and the importance of individual social networking, norm following, and participation. When wide geographic territories comprise the common resource, neither community-based self-governance nor central control mechanisms offer simple or comprehensive solutions. Both levels need to be coordinated, with wider economic forces taken into account also.

Psychology, culture, and local knowledge

Communities often differ in terms of their cultures, which include their social institutions, and technologies as well as psychological constructs such as beliefs, worldviews, identities, and more, but little of this has been applied to conservation. Several models of culture have been used in studies investigating culture as a variable or a moderator of environmental psychology. Across cultures, factors correlated with environmental engagement include being female, post-materialistic values, higher income and education level, environmental knowledge, and negative assessment of environmental quality (Milfont, 2012). Such studies, however, generally use an "etic" or outsider's operationalization of culture – generally a western academic one. In order to be confident in generalizing across cultures, an "emic" or internal view that acknowledges culturally specific perspectives is needed. This would address concerns with the equivalence of the measures used in terms of whether items have the same meanings across cultures, whether measures are tapping the same latent (implicit) variables, whether steps in the measurement unit are equivalent, and whether the base or "zero" point and other measurement characteristics are comparable (Milfont, 2012). Next we will explore an example of how psychology may enhance the ability of interdisciplinary conservation teams to adapt to local cultures.

The operation of psychological variables in community-based resource management has been carefully examined in an extended field research program by psychologist Doug Medin, in collaboration with cognitive anthropologists Scott Atran and Norbert Ross (Atran & Medin, 2008; Medin & Atran, 2004; Atran et al., 2005). They studied the forest management practices and beliefs of three different cultural groups in the lowlands of Petén, Guatemala, all of which practice agroforestry, the use of forests for both products of the forest via hunting and gathering, and slash-and-burn agriculture. This is not a common pool resource situation because members of each group work individual forest plots which they may rent from the local municipality. But this commonality of practice and ecologies highlights the influence of the three groups' psychological, social, and cultural differences. One group, referred to as Ixta' Maya, is native to this area; another group, the Ladinos, are immigrants to the area and are of mixed native and Spanish background. Finally, the Q'eqchi' Maya have immigrated from their nearby highland ancestral grounds to the lowland.

Atran et al. (2005) mapped the linkages between individuals and found striking differences between groups in density of social ties (Fig. 10.3). The Ixta' are the most socially atomized. They also have the fewest common institutions, and they do not coordinate their agroforestry activities with each other. The Q'eqchi', on the other hand, are very tightly knit socially, and the Ladinos represent an intermediate level of social linkages. The Q'eqchi', moreover, have the highest percentage of people that speak only their native tongue, have communal and ceremonial institutions (including sacred ties to the highlands), work their plots with their neighbors, and have some sanctions limiting things like access to copal trees.

Based on this picture of the groups' social capital, trust, and institutions, one might expect the Q'eqchi' to have the most sustainable practices, and the Ixta' the least, with Ladinos intermediate. This expectation can be tested because the researchers carefully collected data on informants' land (e.g., land use and soil quality, species diversity, tree count, and coverage) and calculated each group's average forest clearance rate. Surprisingly, the Q'eqchi' were clearing their forest plots at a rate five times that of the Ixta', whose rate is potentially sustainable. The Ladinos were clearing their forests at about twice the rate of the Ixta'.

To understand this apparent anomaly, Atran et al. (2005) looked carefully at the interaction of psychology and culture and examined the mental models or "folk ecologies" of each individual. Their Ixta' informants identified on average four times as many plant–animal interactions as did the Q'eqchi'. There were also consistent differences in the inferences informants made based on their models. All groups generalized according to folk taxonomic similarity (e.g., they reasoned that another monkey in the same folk category as the spider monkey would share its dependence on ramon fruits), and according to folk ecological similarity (e.g., that kinkajous would depend on chicle fruit in the same way spider monkeys depended on ramon fruit). But culture affected the patterns of inference. The Ixta', for example, observed symmetrical helping

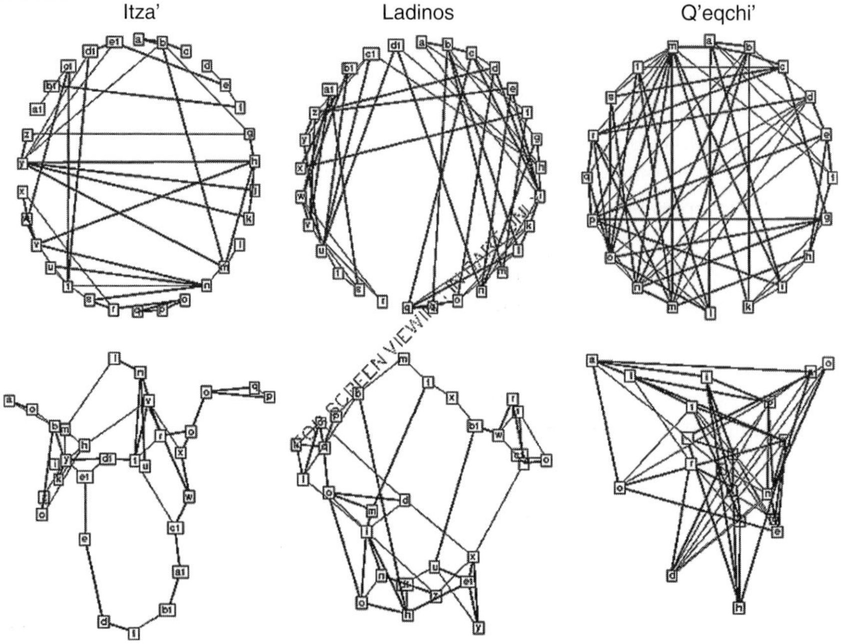

Fig. 10.3 Social networks in different cultural groups, represented schematically (top) and literally (from Atran et al., 2005. Reprinted with permission from APA Publications).

relationships between many pairs of plants and animals and tended to generalize this to cases they did not know about directly, whereas the other groups figured that plants helped animals, and were asymmetrically hurt by them. Thus, ecological thinking is shaped at a basic level by the mind's tendency to create categories of like things and then by a model of simple ecological interactions. Individuals readily assimilate new experiences to these models so that fairly elaborate ecological beliefs may be built on minimal experience.

Interestingly, the linkages between culture, forest practices, and psychological beliefs were not deterministic but passed like disease germs among populations. Consider who was consulted by members of each group if they had questions about hunting or agroforestry. Ixta' individuals asked other Ixta' who were regarded as the most expert. These people were also the most central in the social importance network shown in Fig. 10.3. Ladinos who were regarded by other Ladinos as forestry experts were well connected socially, but sought *their* information from the expert Ixta'. Tellingly, networks mapping Q'eqchi' social importance had lowest overlap with maps of forestry experts. Q'eqchi' directed questions to a Washington-based NGO or a Guatemalan governmental agency, or other Q'eqchi' men. This transmission model may help explain why Ladino forest-clearing rate was only twice as destructive Ixta': There was information flow from the more expert Ixta' to this group of newcomers.

The Q'eqchi' perceived sacred ties only to their native highlands, and felt that no supernatural sanctions applied to their actions in the lowlands. Whereas all groups believed in forest spirits, only Ixta' men believed the spirits could protect the forests. And their model of these spirits showed the closest correspondence to their model of ecological importance of plants and animals (interestingly, NGO staffs' ratings corresponded better with market value of the species than with ecological roles). Atran et al. (2005) note the implications of these spiritual beliefs for models of resource management. Although social scientists would regard forest spirits as socially constructed entities analogous to institutions, there is no social institution that metes out consequences when the spirits' wishes are violated. Instead, restraint of behavior is practiced privately by Ixta' individuals based on the belief that the resource is responsive and can act. In essence, individual Ixta' agroforesters mentally negotiate the costs and benefits of resource use with spiritual social constructs whose actions are discerned and construed by folk ecological models.

Creating ecological knowledge old and new: Traditional and modern citizen science

Anthropology has been a predominant voice for cultural considerations and cultural preservation in conservation projects partly because cultural anthropologists typically know local languages, key players, and how specific cultures work, and these days many work to empower cultural members' voices. Daryl Posey (1999), for example, studied the cultural and spiritual values of biodiversity and was an outspoken advocate of indigenous intellectual rights. Berkes (2012) and others have focused on traditional ecological knowledge (TEK): culturally (usually, orally) transmitted bodies of knowledge that have accumulated over generations, incorporating knowledge, management-relevant institutions, and a worldview based on the culture. Modern as well as "indigenous" peoples may have TEK. Scottish research participants' conceptions of "biodiversity" in Cairngorms National Park included not only their scientific knowledge, but also management, aesthetic, and normative dimensions (Fischer & Young, 2007). Moreover, citizens' mental representations of three potentially problematic local species (one large herbivorous mammal, a spider, and an invasive plant) in eight European countries were patterned and embedded in respondents' worldviews and thus societal discourses (Fischer et al., 2011).

Traditional knowledge systems do not separate empirical from moral, worldview, or spiritual components as western scientific epistemology does. This has led to intense debate over the status and purposes of using TEK in wildlife-management studies (e.g., Gilchrist et al., 2005; Gilchrist & Mallory, 2007; Brook & McLachlan, 2005), although its acceptance has increased in recent years (Berkes, 2012). In some cases, TEK has been shown to correlate strongly with scientific knowledge, for example, in detecting ecosystem changes (Aswani & Lauer, 2014), but clearly it does not always. Each kind of knowledge is fallible. Perhaps the biggest gain comes from using both forms to cross-check validity. TEK is also important for its role in maintaining human–environment relations, as well as composing part of the diversity of the collective heritage of human understanding of nature. Berkes views TEK not only as an instrumental form of knowledge but also as a form of empowerment and problem solving by groups coping with social and environmental changes. It is compatible with the uncertainty and unpredictability of the complex socio-ecological systems in which it developed, and may play an important role in collaborative community-based problem solving (Berkes, 2009).

Citizen volunteers have been employed to provide data on natural systems (Silverton et al., 2013). The Audubon Society's annual winter and breeding bird counts and the Cornell Ornithological Lab have involved citizens in research for decades. Today's conservation context – both globally and in local communities – is benefiting by great increases in such contributions as well as the use of new technologies. The design and success of conservation schemes needs to be more thoroughly assessed to inform further design and implementation. Mascia et al. (2014b) discuss how information needs in conservation may be met by several distinct types of study: ambient monitoring of local social and/or ecological conditions; assessment of how management processes are operating; performance assessment of progress toward objectives; impact evaluation to determine whether intended and unintended impacts are being caused by the intervention; and systematic review of evidence about the impacts of a given type of intervention and its impacts. Each of these necessarily involves the community, whose buy-in to what is measured may be critical in success. Thus evaluation and monitoring must be thought of in a community context.

Some ways community can be involved – or should maybe not be – were identified by Danielsen et al. (2014) who examined the CBD and 11 other international environmental agreements. From these, they identified 186 indicators for which data are needed to monitor the achievement of the agreements' goals. Of these indicators, 37% required monitoring by professional scientists, but 63% could involve community-based citizen scientists. They identified five schemes defined by the degree of scientist and local participation in the study, design, collection, and analysis of data and implementation of management schemes. Schemes A, B, and C (as labeled at the bottom of Fig. 10.4) mainly serve participants and partly or wholly serve to improve their livelihoods. Schemes D and E, on the other hand, are scientist-driven, biodiversity-oriented, and are more frequently done in protected areas. From their comparison of international agreements and the indicators they require Danielsen et al. (2014) suggest that high amounts of technical or legislative knowledge constrain the usefulness of local stakeholders. But many cases may involve community members gathering data and agreeing to goals that include both livelihoods and biodiversity.

Citizen science programs may do more than provide data, as illustrated by a program in Kerala, India, where citizen scientists documented the killing of nonvenomous helpful snakes and then communicated with villagers. They were able to prevent the killing of 276 snakes, including one that closely mimics a deadly snake (Balakrishnan, 2010). Direct ecosystem benefits derived from community-led trapping of nonnative mammals that threaten the endangered flightless kiwi birds of New Zealand (Glen et al., 2012). Psychology is important in understanding volunteer motivation; Asah and Blahna (2012), for example, found that environmental motivations were only salient predictors of participation to the extent that personal and social benefits to the volunteers were realized. These salient motivations should be identified and matched in appeals for volunteers.

Araya et al. (2009) give several examples from Namibia and South Africa involving paraecologists, eco-club volunteers, and plant custodians in three biodiversity hotspot regions, showing that such approaches are viable in developing countries where financial resources are especially scarce (Fig. 10.5). Continuous training of volunteers is essential, but the professional full-time involvement of paraecologists in time-intensive data gathering, and the insights they provide into community and livelihood contexts has made this worth the effort (Schmiedel, *et al.*, 2010).

Technologies are enabling a vastly increased capacity for data gathering for conservation, including smart-phone applications that allow the documentation and location of species. More recent developments incorporate hefty remote sensing datasets. One program (skytruth.org) recruits crowds to apply algorithms to detect tens of thousands hydraulic-fracturing wastewater ponds on google-earth maps, a process that requires human visual inspection. Another project (rfcx.org) "bugs" forests with used cell phones, left wired to small solar panels in treetops and set to periodically transmit ambient audio files. A computer scans these for frequencies indicating logging (chainsaws, trucks). Phones around the Kalaweit gibbon sanctuary in Sumatra alerted managers who drove off illegal loggers, who left the area within 2 weeks. Another collaboration (Globalforestwatch.org) uses recent high-resolution images and crowd-sources individuals who pick areas of protected forest to monitor for change, receiving alerts. The system has already been used to curtail illegal burning on concession land in Sumatra (Gibbs, 2014).

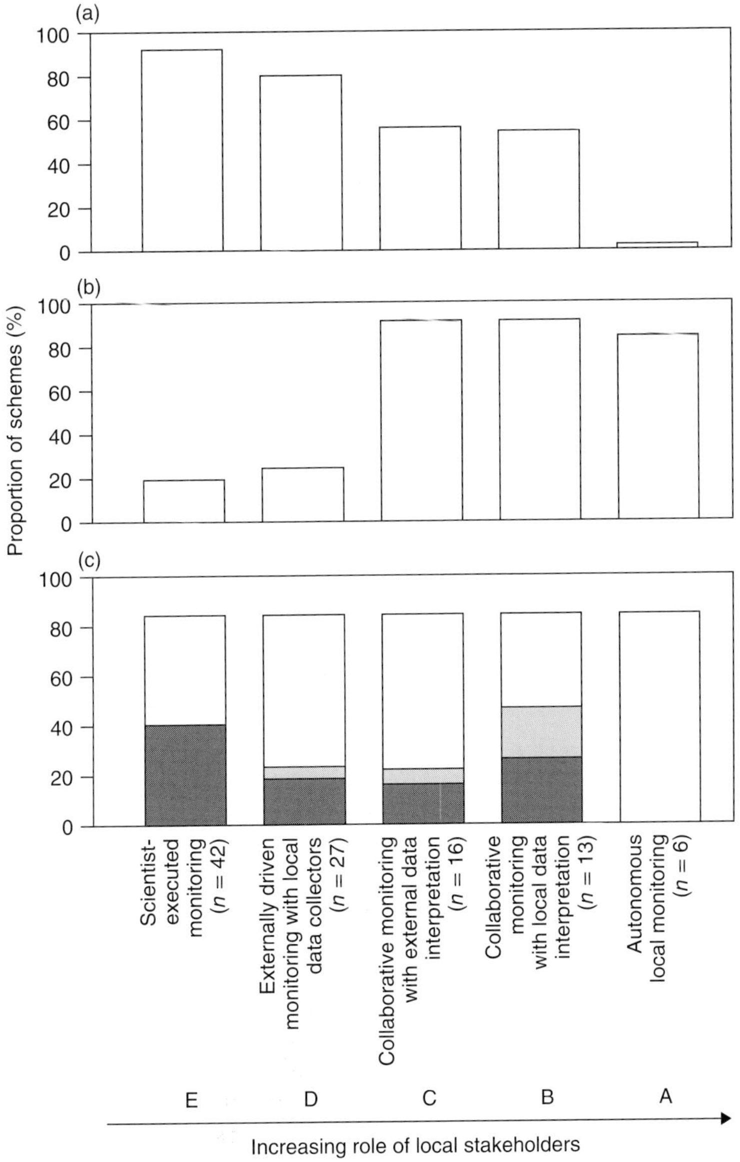

Fig. 10.4 The proportion of published environmental monitoring schemes within each type of monitoring scheme that have a biodiversity (a) or livelihoods (b) objective; and the types of governance regime (c) they operate within, including areas without protection status (white), government-managed protected areas (black), and community-managed protected areas (shaded). The relative role of local stakeholders in the monitoring schemes increases from left to right (from Danielsen et al. (2014), Figure 2, p. 19).

Fig. 10.5 Paraecologists setting up a field experiment in South Africa (photograph courtesy of Ute Schmiedel).

Accounting for the costs and benefits of conservation

Sometimes, community-based solutions fail because the exploitative pressures on a resource are too great. In other cases, the biological resources, while impacted by local activities, are not directly part of the local economy, and so local people may have little motivation to protect them. In such situations, it may work better to pay local people to conserve. But what monetary price should be placed on conservation and what form of compensation to the community in exchange for reduced pressure on the resource is appropriate? After reviewing current practice, we will ask, what is the psychology of this kind of exchange?

Putting dollar values on nature has become an important specialty in ecology and economics. Conceptually, there is a strong case that ecosystems (natural or modified) provide "ecosystem services" which people benefit from. Ecosystem services have been grouped into four categories: production of goods (foods, fiber, medicines); provision of life-support processes (such providing clean air and water, global gas balances, pollination, etc.); life-fulfilling processes (appealing to aesthetic, cultural and scientific values; see also Chapter 12); and preservation of future options (related to presently unrecognized values) (Daily et al., 2000). The value of these services is not completely lost on communities that directly depend on the ecosystem for sustenance or that understand the system's importance for a part they do depend on (Posey, 1999), and when these dependencies are observable or have been encoded in the form of cultural beliefs, ceremonies, or rituals, such as we saw in the case of the Ixta'. In many cases, however, there is no such dependence, it is not observable, or an outside group is the main beneficiary of the ecosystem. For example, many ecosystems services arise from processes that are widely distributed in the landscape, such as continuity of forest cover affecting water quality in the watershed used by a distant municipality.

Local people who do value their local biodiversity frequently try to protect it, particularly if it is linked to their livelihoods. There may, however, be obstacles to people acting on such values individually. For example, poverty in combination with poor soil may drive people to continually clear more forest. One response to this obstacle is to breed new varieties of food plant adapted to local soils; another may be to provide food or money in exchange for not clearing more land.

Payment for ecosystem (or broadly, environmental) services (PES) is a strategy that emerged in the mid-1990s to address situations where direct benefits from ecological services are not sufficient to motivate protective behavior by local actors, and where another party who does benefit wants to gain or maintain that benefit. One such strategy tries to establish linkages between biodiversity and noneconomic self-interested needs of the community, such as health, which can form the basis for a trade-off between the community, conservationists, and donors (Margoulis et al., 2001). Sometimes linkages are high, as when protecting a watershed also provides clean water. When the intrinsic linkages are low, projects may create an operational linkage. The Biodiversity Support Project identified four types of operational linkage. In the "barter" strategy, health enhancements are made in compensation for conservation work by community members. In the "entry point" approach, health needs are addressed first as a way to build trust and increase community decision-making capacity and later conservation projects use these as a foundation. The "bridge" strategy makes a strong conceptual linkage between health and conservation: conservation staff pursue health and conservation goals simultaneously and focus on education to help members understand the truly linked nature of the activities. Finally, the "symbiotic" strategy works when both staff and community members recognize the link between health and biodiversity and organizing around the health issue attains both goals (Margoulis et al., 2001, pp. 24–25). These strategies might work for other things besides health that are valued by the community, such as education (see the next section).

Another strategy estimates the dollar values of "public goods" for which no market-based values exist, such as ecological services. For example, if a forest is set aside, income from forestry may be foregone, but the value of its services can be calculated to show the benefits of conservation. These might include estimating how much it would cost to replace the value of freshwater provided by rivers, plus the monetary value first-world populations would be willing to pay to avoid the loss of rare species. Valuation methods, such as contingent valuation surveys or replacement values, are young and still debated among economists. The local community might then be compensated this amount in exchange for their agreement to protect the forest. The compensation could be translated into community needs such as a health center, small capital loans, or an ecotourism partnership. In essence, this approach recognizes that conservation imposes costs, and these costs should be covered.

PES schemes have generated intense debate. Muradian et al. (2013) warn that PES presumes markets and commodifies nature, which may crowd out or undermine local intrinsic motivations for conservation. They are also concerned about inequities and the role of political power. Wunder (2013), however, points out that PES cannot be characterized as market transactions since very seldom are competitive forces at work (the exception is carbon service trading). Rather than creating "win-wins," PES works by "take it or leave it," creating "win-settle" solutions where conservation values are attained, and the ecosystem service providers are not made worse off. Indeed, PES protects people from having conservation forced on them, because they can turn down an offered price, addressing the equity concern. Wunder contends that PES has exacting conditions, including good organization by service users, a culture that accepts payment exchanges for ecosystem features (see below), a trustful negotiating climate, and (crucially) a well-defined resource tenure regime that allows providers the control needed to "deliver." Admittedly, consistent with the psychology of intrinsic motivation, when existing motives to preserve nature are already high, PES could diminish or crowd them out. But these circumstances, Wunder contends, are not those where PES is needed. When nature-protective social norms are lacking, PES may not only incentivize and stabilize conservation but also stimulate pro-social reciprocity in the community. This debate demonstrates the need to examine conservationists' beliefs about their own tools and test these beliefs against real-world complexity.

From the psychological perspective, more than the monetary values of nature needs to be accounted for if all the values of conservation are to be fulfilled. As conservationists have increasingly realized, we need to acknowledge a wide range of costs and benefits of conservation, and how they are distributed across people. Conservation psychologists may contribute by helping to identify less material values of nature such as pride of place, ancestral home, sustainer, legacy, escape, giver of solace and restoration, and spiritual source. Psychology brings a particular awareness of the span of human values, based on social and psychological as well as material well-being (Schwartz, 1994; see Chapters 5 and 12). With a sense of the full range of important human values, we can then ask how conservation projects may positively and negatively impact these values, as they are locally conceptualized (Hunter & Brehm, 2004). Psychology can help elicit, articulate, elaborate, and find indicators for diverse values that may be nonmonetary, unvoiced, and unanticipated by any general scheme or even native language concepts. Putting such values on the table may be critical to ensuring key interests are represented.

A psychological approach means not only mapping a wide set of values, but determining the objects to which they are applied, and the frameworks people use in reasoning about them. Values are not all evaluated by the same model across cultures, as shown by Fiske and Tetlock (1997). They identified four incommensurable models of sociality: communal sharing, equality matching, authority ranking, or market pricing. Although trade-offs are proposed across these categories, the trade-off may be unacceptable. For example, if a given species has particular totemic (communal or authority-related) value, it may not be permissible to trade it on market terms. Both experimental (Clayton, 2000) and field (Syme & Fenton, 1993) research suggests that there are many cases in which people reject the allocation of environmental resources on a market basis. Or, if certain resources are communally shared, monetary compensation for impacts on them may not be regarded as appropriate. Self-direction values may be especially important in post-colonial situations, ruling out negotiation of other values according to authority-based frameworks.

Fiske and Tetlock's work assumes pluralism, where people identify with different value systems. Trade-offs may be easier if people's identities, instead, are more *cosmopolitan*; cosmopolitanism denotes multiple selves and narratives, enabling people to identify with a wider range of others, be more open to change, and embrace experimental and inclusive solutions (Earle & Cvetkovich, 1997). Application of either model means advance fieldwork to understand local value systems. But by investigating the value structure that characterizes the local group, conservation programs would reduce the chance of serious missteps.

Psychological costs of displacing populations for conservation

When land is set aside for conservation purposes, the loss of access to resources or even displacement of the local community is a cost that may not be considered by the foreign organizations or other groups whose values are most immediately served. Those bearing the costs are often poor or indigenous groups. Such cases resemble colonial or large-scale development schemes, as when the construction of dams or mines displaces thousands of villagers, or plantations remove forests for a single commercial crop. Just as in these cases, preserves are often endorsed by national or regional governments and sponsored by multilateral lending institutions such as the International Monetary Fund or the World Bank (WB). Despite policies designed to prevent or mitigate these impacts, they still occur. Failed resettlement of communities (due to opposition, despite WB protocols being followed) was a factor in the extinction of the Vietnamese population of the Javan rhinoceros (Brook et al., 2014).

The risks of projects (whether in the name of development or conservation) that involve resettling a population include: landlessness; joblessness; homelessness; marginalization; food insecurity; increased morbidity and mortality; loss of access to common property and services, and social disarticulation (Cernea, 2000). There are also psychological dimensions, as Cernea describes:

> Economic marginalization is often accompanied by social and psychological marginalization, expressed in a drop in social status, in resettlers' loss of confidence in society and in themselves, a feeling of injustice, and deepened vulnerability. The coerciveness of displacement and the victimization of resettlers tend to depreciate resettlers' self-image, and they are often perceived by host communities as a socially degrading stigma ... Psychological marginalization and its consequences ... are typically overlooked in resettlement planning. Yet, cultural and behavioral impairments, anxiety and decline in self-esteem, have been widely reported from many areas.
>
> (Cernea, 2000, pp. 18-19; emphasis in original)

The net effect of resettlement, social disarticulation, has clear psychological implications:

> Forced displacement tears apart the existing social fabric. It disperses and fragments communities, dismantles patterns of social organization and interpersonal ties; kinship groups become scattered as well. Life-sustaining informal networks of reciprocal help, local voluntary associations, and self-organized mutual service are disrupted. This is a net loss of valuable "social capital," that compounds the loss of natural, physical, and human capital .... The social capital lost through social disarticulation is typically unperceived and uncompensated by the programs causing it, and this real loss has long-term consequence.
>
> (Cernea, 2000, p. 22)

Such events threaten many values from Schwartz's typology including self-direction, achievement, tradition, security, and power. If the initial stages of project planning considered these values, weighted in ways that reflect their true importance in psychological health and functioning, the outcomes might be much better. Joshi (2012) provides a hopeful case study of the resettlement of ecologically unsustainable (and often unwilling) Gujjar communities out of the Rajaji National Park in northwest India to improve watershed management and protect biodiversity. The process addressed livelihoods, education, medical care, and women's empowerment, and was monitored and evaluated to ensure a responsive process that demonstrated some success.

The negative consequences of social disarticulation clearly work against community-based conservation. What would work in favor of it? Based on the psychological theory of self-determination (see Chapter 12), DeCaro and Stokes (2008) suggest the characteristics of "Autonomy Supportive Environments" (ASE). An ASE fosters intrinsic and internalized motivations that are aligned with a person's core interests and identity. These forms of motivation are especially important when economic incentives are not effective in promoting conservation. The characteristics of an ASE that DeCaro and Stokes identify are the following:

1 Empathic understanding, where interpersonal interactions attempt to appreciate the meaning underlying another's attitudes and behaviors. Empathy (aided by cognitive perspective

taking) ensures accurate information, communicates respect for other stakeholders, and ensures that their best interests are represented.

2 Provision of choice, where individuals' freedom to solve problems for themselves is supported by ensuring options are generated responsively (not handed down from above).
3 Transparent administration, including of any regulations. This means providing direct access to decision makers, and making the rationales, necessity, and value of rules clear.
4 Noncontrolling communication and feedback. Managers should avoid a dictatorial style and instead emphasize the voluntary nature of participation. The communicative style must convey approachability and ideals that are worth buying into.

A successful ASE provides individual and group self-determination, but is not necessarily at odds with conservation organizations or agencies having a central role. Rather, it provides foundations for collaboration and for the integration of different groups' agendas.

More broadly, the social impacts of protected areas represent an important frontier for research. For example, Mascia and Claus (2008) examined marine-protected areas and identified five types of property rights that were lost, secured, or gained. Depending on the types and bundles of rights, impacts of MPAs on governance, economy, well-being, education, and culture vary widely.

Conservation and all-too-human psychology

Three final topics drive home the message that conservationists must deal with people in all our species' complexity and contrariness. There is a wide body of psychological research on apparently irrational biases in our thinking, and psychology contributes to the multidisciplinary subjects of conservation criminology and conflict, all areas of great relevance to community-based and global biodiversity conservation.

Psychological biases and emotion

In applied conservation settings, a practitioner will benefit from some understanding of information-processing and emotional biases (Ariely, 2008). As discussed in Chapter 6, people seldom act like the rational decision makers we would like to believe, or that our economic theory says we are. On-the-ground conservationists would do well to develop awareness of their own psychological biases, as an antidote, as well as for insight into others. Psychologist Kahneman (2011; see also Chapters 6 and 7) has synthesized the research that underlies "dual process" theory, and the Elaboration Likelihood Model of attitude formation and change, as well as many other observations, into two semifictitious mental "systems." System I, as Kahneman calls the first is the "intuitive," quick, and often emotion-driven set of associations we act from much of the time. The brain is primed to want, find, and enjoy finding "associative coherence," or patterns in experience that fit together. This explains confirmation bias, which is when we seek and agree with evidence that fits our associations, and are quick to question and find faults in evidence to the contrary. In System I, the whole process seems effortless, information feels true and familiar, and we feel good about our understanding of the situation. Unfortunately, System I is frequently wrong. It bases its conclusions on what is available, ignoring absent data; it infers and invents causes and intentions behind others' behavior; it neglects probability; and it judges risk as well as arguments based on likes and dislikes. Since System I is largely automatic and out of awareness, we tend to be blind to the biases and short-circuited logic it uses. But many people are overconfident about their fast intuitive thinking. A striking example of a blind spot in conservation is the lack of awareness of protected area downgrading, downsizing, and degazettement (removal from protected status) or PADDD. Most research on protected areas has assumed that once established they are permanent features of the landscape. Revelations of the extent of PADDD shows instead they are dynamic institutions. PADDD is often driven by industrial-scale resource extraction and development and has affected 375 protected areas in 57 countries in high-priority conservation regions (Mascia et al., 2014a). Ignorance of this problem may have resulted from a desire on the part of the conservation community to disbelieve evidence that a key strategy, protected areas, was not working – an example of confirmation bias.

"System II," on the other hand involves effortful, deliberate thought, and is much more likely to catch errors. Discrepant information or a challenging mental task can spark concentration and controlled mental processing, leading to accommodation of one's associations to better deal with new information and decisions. It is improved by education, although an educated mind may only apply it in the area of deep knowledge. Nonetheless, we use it whenever we examine the information critically. Thus it is part of the deep processing that may lead to behavior change, "owned" by the person.

An understanding of the contemporary functional account of the emotions is a durable contribution to conservation. Although our folk theories say that emotion is a crude and untrustworthy guide to choices, psychology's functional theory of emotion holds that in fact emotional responses are often very adaptive. Emotions must be flexible, responsive, performance-enhancing, and not stereotypic, to serve a organism's "core relational goals" in dynamic social settings (Lazarus, 1991). Emotions provide (1) an initial assessment of the proper manner in which to respond, (2) a quick recruitment of resources needed to respond, and (3) a means of influencing others–expression (Thompson, 1993). Typically emotions operate from the quick associative System I, but they are open to elaboration, examination, communication, and creative use. Emotional and empathic know-how are not intuitive but are teachable. Understanding the role of emotion in conflict is an important tool for effective conservation work.

Illegal trade in threatened and endangered species

Recent sudden population declines in critically endangered flagship species such as rhinoceroses, tigers, and pangolins within protected areas brings home the need to enforce laws protecting biodiversity (Bennett, 2011). For example, 470 African rhinos were poached between January 2006 and September 2009. These animals are hunted for their highly valuable body parts by "organized crime syndicates using sophisticated smuggling methods… frequently operating through countries with high levels of corruption" (Bennett, 2011, p. 476). Demand from the wealthy in East Asia is driving this trade. But, based on long-standing cultural traditions, such demand is likely to be slow to change. While setting aside protected areas is essential, it is not enough. Thus Bennett calls for greatly increased and coordinated enforcement using all the tools for fighting major organized crime, as well as generating support in society and education about the full implications of illegal wildlife trade. Dutton et al. (2013) provide a thorough overview of wildlife trade and instruments for combating it.

Recognizing the values that are involved is a first step. Sometimes illegal hunting is done simply for subsistence, and hunters would stop if they had enough money and food (Pailler et al., 2009). Moro et al. (2013) used a hypothetical choice experiment format with western Serengeti informants to quantify the trade-offs between alternate forms of sustenance (cows, wages, access to microcredit, access to markets) and the hunting effort and the likelihood of being arrested. Against each of these benefits, the risks of hunting were evaluated negatively.

But there was significant variation across households, and once risks of hunting rises above a rather low threshold, higher risk did not decrease the weight put on the gain of hunting. Wealthier households, which did not attribute as much utility to hunting, are less concerned with the risk or consequences of getting caught. Thus, policies that increase wealth (microcredit, jobs) will help reduce hunting, but commercial hunting by well-off hunters requires a separate preventative measure (Moro et al., 2013).

Poaching can be a result of human–wildlife conflict, with hunters trying to protect their own property or livelihoods. Kahler et al. (2013) used spatial records of where poaching had occurred in a community-managed natural resource area in Namibia. They found that the documented sites did not correlate with where poaching informants (deliberately not considered as suspects) perceived poaching to occur. But the informants' perceptions did match places in which the stakeholders felt their livelihoods were threatened by wildlife damage, indicating that areas where livestock or agriculture and wildlife meet need increased monitoring.

Poaching has also been found to be motivated by other than subsistence or income-generation needs, including protesting conservancy rules or establishment, lack of conservancy benefits, wildlife removal, firearm training, entertainment, and retaliation for stock losses (Kahler & Gore, 2012). Cultural traditions can also add to illegal wildlife killing in retaliation to loss of livestock. In Tanzania, where perhaps 40% of the remaining African lions live, lions are commonly killed to avenge livestock attack – that is, to prevent further loss (Fitzherbert et al., 2014). Among the Sukuma people in the Mpimbwe region, however, the killing is carried out by men playing a cultural role of lion killer. The men dress with parts of other lions they have killed, come to the house of the aggrieved, perform vigorous dances, and demand (and receive) gifts as rewards for their perceived service in killing the predators. The maintenance of this role is thus an example of a collective action institution, as described by Ostrom in analyses of communal management systems. Recently, however, the density of lions near the villages has decreased, as has their prey density, suggesting that the lions are more concentrated, though still declining, in the center of the nearby Katavi National Park. The researchers found that there has been a shift from avenging to hunting among the Sakuma dancers, who may venture far to find any lion to kill. Dancers target households that are wealthy and sympathetic to the lion dancing tradition. The latter houses often have kin ties to other dancers, and may engage in reciprocally supporting this tradition. But among houses that acknowledged a shift from avenging to hunting, the data show reluctance to offer rewards, and an expression of disapproval, calling them cheaters for killing lions deep in the park. The authors note that cooperation is dependent on upholding rules and the punishment of defectors, tying this example to commons management (Fitzherbert et al., 2014).

The new field of "conservation criminology" (Gibbs et al., 2010) has bases in natural resource disciplines, criminology, and the psychology of risk and decision making, and answers the need Bennett (2011) identified, above. It is conceptualized to include a broader range of crimes than simply those violating laws in order to accommodate the wider fields of environmental risk and public perception often involved:

> Our proposed framework allows for the consideration of multiple 'victims' and 'offenders,' including anthropogenic (human) causes of environmental risk as well as threats posed to humans by the environment (e.g., human-wildlife conflict, natural disasters). As such our framework recognizes multiple causes of environmental risks (e.g., environmental risks to humans *and* the environment are rooted in social and ecological processes, structures and reactions) and is not tied to any particular solution.
>
> (Gibbs et al., 2010, p. 132)

An application of this kind of thinking is provided by Gore and colleagues' (2013) examination of corruption around wildlife crimes in Madagascar: poaching for trade or consumption; illegal timber harvest and export for furniture and musical instruments; and slash-and-burn agriculture in rare and/or extremely biodiverse ecosystems. The researchers interviewed people about conservation activities in the study area. To help ensure informants would reveal sensitive knowledge, they guaranteed confidentiality and anonymity, ensured they knew the researchers were not affiliated with any agency, and asked about the practices of *other* community members – strategies that are helpful at identifying the causes of noncompliant behavior, but not always. What Gore et al. (2013) found did not look like the typical stereotype of corruption – officials directly engaged in crime. Rather informants explained away behaviors in a variety of ways, such as there being supernatural punishments, actors being mere pawns, not wanting to disrupt a community norm of friendship, the community being the best entity to solve problems or enforce rules, the extracted materials being useless for local purposes, or a law breaker being destitute. A lack of norms is often blamed for corruption. But local participants revealed that approaches stemming from this analysis, such as laws, new levels of authority, enforcement (or its impossibility) may not speak effectively to people in corruptible positions. Instead, Gore et al. (2013) suggest experimentation with watchdogging and education to balance human and conservation needs, and with aligning reform with preexisting local informal institutions such as the community-based authority groups called "folonolona" in the Malagasy context.

Conservation, environmental threats, and conflict

Conflict is nearly a constant in human affairs. Natural objects enter the picture as both the means of conflict as well as the ends (e.g., a fight over resources). Degraded ecologies and crowding are stressors that may predispose conflict. When conflict occurs, wildlife and ecosystems as well as other humans are frequently victims. When conflict becomes armed and violent, environmental managers need ways to decrease the likelihood of further conflict and minimize the harm it causes (Shambaugh et al., 2001).

We typically are concerned about the loss of wildlife species because of the intrinsic value of the species, its role in maintaining a healthy ecosystem, or the impact on human societies that depend on that species for some sort of sustenance or cultural value. Recently, researchers have suggested that the loss of wildlife can have the indirect effect of increasing human conflict, for several reasons (Brashares et al., 2014). For one, decreasing availability of wildlife may require increased human labor to obtain the wildlife, and thus an increase in exploitative labor practices. Data have linked declining fishery harvests to human trafficking and child labor. For another, reduced availability of wildlife often makes it more valuable, and may lead to conflicts over who has the right to that wildlife, often expressed as a conflict between local residents trying to protect a resource and foreigners who try to exploit it. The increase in piracy is seen as a direct response to the declining availability of fish in areas like Somalia.

The potential impact of climate change on conflict has been noted by a number of institutions, including the military and the United Nations (e.g., CNA Military Advisory Board, 2014; United Nations, 2009). In a meta-analysis, Hsiang et al. (2013) found clear evidence for an effect of climate change on intergroup conflict as well as interpersonal violence. Both extreme temperatures and unusual amounts of rainfall (e.g., Hendrix & Salehyan, 2012) have been found to have implications for conflict. The impact on violence and aggression may be due to several mechanisms. Violence and aggression may increase when insecurity about access to basic needs such as food, water, and energy leads to competition for scarce natural resources. Ecomigration due to the changing climate may bring formerly separate communities into contact and competition for resources like jobs and land (Reuveny, 2008). Climate change may also increase conflict due to the direct impact of rising temperatures. Both lab-based experiments and quasi-experiments have demonstrated a causal relationship between heat and aggression. In other words, as the temperature goes up, so does aggression. This has led leading aggression researcher Anderson (2012) to predict a demonstrable increase in violence associated with increased average temperatures. Finally, climate change may increase violence by undermining societal and political stability. Agnew (2012) points out that the effects of climate change are likely to promote crime by "increasing strain, reducing social control, weakening social support, … increasing opportunities for crime, and creating social conflict" (p. 22).

Conflict may have multiple layers. Although the immediate dispute may concern conflicts between two communities over access to water resources, or between tigers and forest workers near a preserve in south Asia, an individual incident is surrounded by the social manifestations of attempts to manage the conflict. These may include the history of park or species preservation policies, the inclusion or exclusion of the local community, and the relations of program staff to locals. Finally, there may be still wider and longer standing disputes that hinge on identity or past cultural trauma, such as ethnic divisions, colonial or dictatorial histories underlying such conflicts. It is obviously advantageous to avoid letting conflict become so entrenched, or letting conservation needs get associated with such long-standing problems. Madden and McQuinn (2014) propose an approach to conflict transformation that attempts to address these deeper layers.

Psychology is one of the core disciplines that contribute to the broad set of knowledge and skills in conflict and peace studies, and it has been deployed creatively in conflict resolution programs. As addressed in other chapters, group identities are important in maintaining and exacerbating conflict, and moral disengagement or exclusion characterize chronic conflict. It is important not to ignore real or perceived power differences in wealth, political support, privilege, social category, access to institutions and authorities, and other resources. But it is also crucial to help parties develop empathy. Empathy is a threatening prospect when one has defined oneself as good and the enemy as bad, but the defenses against this can be addressed (Neu & Volkan, 1999).

Peace-making and peace-keeping are also important concepts. Psychologist Gordon Allport (1954) outlined principles for helping people of different ethnic backgrounds avoid conflict. These include fostering cooperation, promoting equal status among participants, and focusing group effort at solving common problems. Studies of emotion regulation, trust, distrust, neutrality, and cultural approaches to peacemaking (Lederach, 1997; www.beyondintractability.org) are matters where psychology can contribute further to creative use of conflict in conservation. Establishing conservation "peace parks" may help resolve some territorial disputes (Ali, 2007).

Conclusion

Biological and ecological knowledge alone cannot ensure successful conservation programs. Psychology and other social sciences are contributing to a growing body of knowledge about how communities can most effectively self-organize and be assisted to save biodiversity, and what kinds of programs are helpful in tying key community values and beliefs to institutions that favor biodiversity. Whenever possible it is useful to work with spiritual or other biophilic tendencies in a community, or to build universal value structures, but this cannot be relied upon in most cases (Chan et al., 2007). Thus, much of the time conservation success will depend on the adequacy of practitioners' understanding of multifaceted human dimensions and on their know-how for working with them. Psychology can offer insight into human cognition, value systems, costs and benefits, psychological biases, and conflict, all of which can inform conservation practice at every level from board room, to program planning, to field office, to on-the-ground encounters. To work in community-based conservation, one must approach the task as a learner first of all.

References

Agnew, R. (2012). Dire forecast: A theoretical model of the impact of climate change on crime. *Theoretical Criminology*, *16*(1), 21–42.

Agrawal, A., & Gibson, C. C., (2001). *Communities and the environment: Ethnicity, gender, and the state in community-based conservation*. New Brunswick, NJ: Rutgers University Press.

Ali, S. H. (Ed.). (2007). *Peace parks: Conservation and conflict resolution*. Cambridge MA, MIT Press.

Allport, G. (1954). *The nature of prejudice*. Cambridge, MA: Addison-Wesley.

Anderson, C. A. (2012). Climate change and violence. In D. Christie (Ed.), *The encyclopedia of peace psychology* (pp. 128–132). Hoboken, NJ: Wiley-Blackwell.

Araya, Y. N., Schmiedel, U., & von Witt, C. (2009). Linking' citizen scientists' to professionals in ecological research, examples from Namibia and South Africa. *Conservation Evidence*, *6*, 11–17.

Ariely, D. (2008). *Predictably irrational: The hidden forces that shape our decisions*. New York: Harper Collins.

Asah, S. T., & Blahna, D. J. (2012). Motivational functionalism and urban conservation stewardship: implications for volunteer involvement: Urban conservation stewardship. *Conservation Letters*, *5*(6), 470–477.

Aswani, S., & Lauer, M. (2014). Indigenous people's detection of rapid ecological change. *Conservation Biology*, *28*(3), 820–828.

Atran, S., & Medin, D. (2008). *The native mind and the cultural construction of nature*. Cambridge, MA: MIT Press.

Atran, S., Medin, D. L., & Ross, N. O. (2005). The cultural mind: Environmental decision-making and cultural modeling within and across populations. *Psychological Review*, *112*, 744–776.

Balakrishnan, P. (2010). An education programme and establishment of a citizen scientist network to reduce killing of non-venomous snakes in Malappuram district, Kerala, India. *Conservation Evidence*, *7*, 9–15.

Bennett, E. L (2011). Another inconvenient truth: The failure of enforcement systems to save charismatic species. *Oryx*, *45*(4), 476–479.

Berkes, F. (2009). Evolution of co-management: Role of knowledge generation, bridging organizations and social learning. *Environmental Management*, *90*, 1692–1702.

Berkes, F. (2012). *Sacred ecology: Traditional ecological knowledge and resource management* (3rd ed.). Hoboken, NJ: Taylor Francis.

Brashares, J., Abrahms, B., Fiorella, K., Golden, C., Hojnowski, C., March, R., et al. (2014). Wildlife decline and social conflict. *Science*, *345*, 376–378.

Brehm, J. (1966). *A theory of psychological reactance*. New York: Academic Press.

Brook, S. M., Dudley, N., Mahood, S. P., Polet, G., Williams, A. C., Duckworth, J. W., et al. (2014). Lessons learned from the loss of a flagship: The extinction of the Javan rhinoceros Rhinoceros *sondaicus annamiticus* from Vietnam. *Biological Conservation*, *174*, 21–29.

Brook, R. K., & McLachlan, S. M. (2005). On using expert-based science to "test" local ecological knowledge. *Ecology and Society*, *10*(2), r3. Available at: http://www.ecologyandsociety.org/vol10/iss2/resp3/ Accessed 1 Oct. 2013

Cernea, M. M. (2000). Impoverishment risks and reconstruction: A model for population displacement and resettlement. In M. M. Cernea & C. McDowell (Eds.), *Risks and reconstruction: Experiences of resettlers and refugees* (pp. 11–53). World Bank: Washington, DC.

Chan, K. M. A., Pringle, R. M., Ranganathan, J., Boggs, C. L., Chan, Y. L., Ehrlich, P. R., Haff, P. K., Heller, N. E., Al-Khafaji, K., & Macmynowski, D. P. (2007). When agendas collide: Human welfare and biological conservation. *Conservation Biology*, *21* (1), 59–68.

Cinner, J., & Huchery, C. (2014). A comparison of social outcomes associated with different fisheries co-management institutions: Fisheries co-management. *Conservation Letters*, *7*(3), 224–232.

Clayton, S. (2000). Models of justice in the environmental debate. *Journal of Social Issues, 56*(3), 459–474.
CNA Military Advisory Board. (2014). *National security and the accelerating risks of climate change*. Alexandria, VA: CNA Corporation.
Cohen, P. J., Evans, L. S., & Mills, M. (2012). Social networks supporting governance of coastal ecosystems in Solomon Islands: Social networks for ecosystem governance. *Conservation Letters, 5*(5), 376–386.
Coleman, J. S. (1988). Social capital in the creation of human capital. *American Journal of Sociology, 94*, S95–S120.
Cvetkovich, G., & Winter, P. (2003). Trust and social representations of the management of threatened and endangered species. *Environment and Behavior, 35*, 286–307.
Daily, G., Soderqvist, T., Aniyar, S., Arrow, K., et al. (2000). The value of nature and the nature of value. *Science, 289*, 395–396.
Danielsen, F., Pirhofer-Walzl, K., Adrian, T. P., Kapijimpanga, D. R., Burgess, N. D., Jensen, P. M., et al. (2014). Linking public participation in scientific research to the indicators and needs of international environmental agreements: Monitoring environmental agreements. *Conservation Letters, 7*(1), 12–24.
DeCaro, D., & Stokes, M. (2008). Social psychological principles of community-based conservation and conservancy motivation: Attaining goals within an autonomy-supportive environment. *Conservation Biology, 22*, 1443–1451.
Dietz, T., Rosa, E. A., & York, R. (2007). Driving the human ecological footprint. *Frontiers in Ecology and the Environment, 5*(1), 13–18.
Dutton, A. J., Gratwicke, B., Hepburn, C., Herrara, E. A., & Macdonald, D. W. (2013). Tackling unsustainable wildlife trade. In D. W. Macdonald & K. J. Willis (Eds.), *Key topics in conservation biology 2* (pp. 74–91). New York: Wiley-Blackwell.
Earle, T., & Cvetkovich, G. (1997). Culture, cosmopolitanism, and risk management. *Risk Analysis, 17*(1), 55–65.
Fischer, A., Langers, F., Bednar-Friedl, B., Geamana, N., & Skogen, K. (2011). Mental representations of animal and plant species in their social contexts: Results from a survey across Europe. *Journal of Environmental Psychology, 31*(2), 118–128.
Fischer, A., & Young, J. C. (2007). Understanding mental constructs of biodiversity: Implications for biodiversity management and conservation. *Biological Conservation, 136*(2), 271–282.
Fiske, A. P., & Tetlock, P. E. (1997). Taboo trade-offs: Reactions to transactions that transgress the spheres of justice. *Political Psychology, 18*(2), 255–297.
Fitzherbert, E., Caro, T., Johnson, P. J., Macdonald, D. W., & Borgerhoff Mulder, M. (2014). From avengers to hunters: Leveraging collective action for the conservation of endangered lions. *Biological Conservation, 174*, 84–92.
Fox, H. E., Mascia, M. B., Basurto, X, Costa, A., Glew, L., Heinemann, D. et al. (2012). Reexamining the science of marine protected areas: Linking knowledge to action. *Conservation Letters, 5*, 1–10.
Gibbs, C., Gore, M. L., McGarrell, E. F., & Rivers, L. (2010). Introducing Conservation Criminology: Towards interdisciplinary scholarship on environmental crimes and risks. *British Journal of Criminology, 50*(1), 124–144.
Gibbs, W.W. (2014). Spies like us. *Conservation, 15*(2), 17–23.
Gilchrist, G., Mallory, M., & Merkel, F. (2005). Can local ecological knowledge contribute to wildlife management? Case studies of migratory birds *Ecology and Society*. *10*(1), 20. Available at: http://www.ecologyandsociety.org/vol10/iss1/art20/ Accessed 1 Oct. 2013.
Gilchrist, G., & Mallory, M. L. (2007). Comparing expert-based science with local ecological knowledge: What are we afraid of? *Ecology and Society, 12*(1), r1. Available at: http://www.ecologyandsociety.org/vol12/iss1/resp1/ Accessed 1 Oct 2013.
Glen, A. S., Hamilton, T., McKenzie, D., Ruscoe, W. A., & Byrom, A. E. (2012). Kiwi *Apteryx mantelli* population recovery through community-led trapping of invasive non-native mammals in Northland, New Zealand. *Conservation Evidence, 9*, 22–27.
Gore, M. L., Ratsimbazafy, J., & Lute, M. L. (2013). Rethinking corruption in conservation crime: Insights from Madagascar. *Conservation Letters, 6*(6), 430–438.
Hardin, G. (1968). The tragedy of the commons. *Science, 162*, 1243–1248.
Hendrix, C., & Salehyan, I. (2012). Climate change, rainfall, and social conflict in Africa. *Journal of Peace Research, 49*(25), 35–50.

Hsiang, S., Burke, M., & Miguel, E. (2013). Quantifying the influence of climate on human conflict. *Science, 341*(6151). DOI: 10.1126/science.1235367.

Hunter, L. M., & Brehm, J. (2004). A qualitative examination of value orientations toward wildlife and biodiversity by rural residents of the intermountain region. *Human Ecology Review, 11*(1), 13–26.

Jin, M. (2013). Does social capital promote pro-environmental behaviors? Implications for collaborative governance. *International Journal of Public Administration, 36*(6), 397–407.

Jones, N., Sophoulis, C. M., Iosifides, T., Botetzagias, I., & Evangelinos, K. (2009). Social capital and environmental policy instruments. *Environmental Politics, 18*(4), 595–611.

Joshi, R. (2012). Gujjar community resettlement from Rajaji National Park, Uttarakhand, India. *Conservation Evidence, 9*, 3–8.

Kahler, J. S., & Gore, M. L. (2012). Beyond the cooking pot and pocket book: Factors influencing noncompliance with wildlife poaching rules. *International Journal of Comparative and Applied Criminal Justice, 36*(2), 103–120.

Kahler, J. S., Roloff, G. J., & Gore, M. L. (2013). Poaching risks in community-based natural resource management: Poaching and community-based management. *Conservation Biology, 27*(1), 177–186.

Kahneman, D. (2011). *Thinking, fast and slow*. New York: Farrar, Straus and Giroux.

Kinnaird, M. F., & O'brien, T. G. (2012). Effects of private-land use, livestock management, and human tolerance on diversity, distribution, and abundance of large African mammals: Livestock and large mammals in Kenya. *Conservation Biology, 26*(6), 1026–1039.

Lachapelle, P. R., Smith, P. D., & McCool, S. F. (2004). Access to power or genuine empowerment? An analysis of three community forest groups in Nepal. *Human Ecology Review, 11*(1), 1–12.

Lazarus, R. S. (1991). *Emotion and adaptation*. New York: Oxford University Press.

Lederach, J. P. (1997). *Building peace: Sustainable reconciliation in divided societies*. Washington, DC: United States Institute of Peace Press.

Madden, F., & McQuinn, B. (2014). Conservation's blind spot: The case for conflict transformation in wildlife conservation. *Biological Conservation, 178*, 97–106.

Margoulis, R., Myers, S., Allen, J., Roca, J., Melnyk, M., & Swanson, J. (2001). *An ounce of prevention: Making the link between health and conservation*. Washington, DC: Biodiversity Support Program.

Mascia, M. B. (forthcoming). *Conservation social science*. New York: Wiley-Blackwell.

Mascia, M. B., & Claus, C. A. (2008). A property rights approach to understanding human displacement from protected areas: The case of marine protected areas. *Conservation Biology, 23*, 16–23.

Mascia, M. B., Pailler, S., Krithivasan, R., Roshchanka, V., Burns, D., Mlotha, M. J., Murray, D. R.Peng, N. (2014a). Protected area downgrading, downsizing, and degazettement (PADDD) in Africa, Asia, and Latin America and the Caribbean, 1900–2010. *Biological Conservation, 169*, 355–361.

Mascia, M. B., Pailler, S., Thieme, M. L., Rowe, A., Bottrill, M. C., Danielsen, F., Geldmann, J., Naidoo, R., Pullin, A. S., Burgess, N. D. (2014b). Commonalities and complementarities among approaches to conservation monitoring and evaluation. *Biological Conservation, 169*, 258–267.

Medin, D. L., & Atran, S. (2004). The native mind: Biological categorization and reasoning in development and across cultures. *Psychological Review, 111*(4), 960–983.

Messick, D., Wilke, H., Brewer, M, Kramer, R., Zenke, P., & Lui, L. (1983). Individual adaptations and structural change as solutions to social dilemmas. *Journal of Personality and Social Psychology, 44*(2), 294–309.

Milfont, T. (2012). Cultural differences in environmental engagement. In S. Clayton (Ed.), *Oxford handbook of environmental and conservation psychology* (pp. 181–200). New York: Oxford University Press.

Moran, E. F. (2006). *People and nature*. Blackwell, Oxford.

Moro, M., Fischer, A., Czajkowski, M., Brennan, D., Lowassa, A., Naiman, L. C., & Hanley, N. (2013). An investigation using the choice experiment method into options for reducing illegal bushmeat hunting in western Serengeti. *Conservation Letters, 6*(1), 37–45.

Muradian, R., Arsel, M., Pellegrini, L., Adaman, F., Aguilar, B., Agarwal, B. et al. (2013). Payments for ecosystem services and the fatal attraction of win-win solutions. *Conservation Letters, 6*(4), 274–279.

Neu, J., & Volkan, V. (1999). *Developing a methodology for conflict prevention: The case of Estonia*. Atlanta, GA: Carter Center. Available at: http://www.cartercenter.org/documents/1201.pdf. Accessed 18 Apr. 2007.

Oldekop, J. A., Bebbington, A. J., Hennermann, K., McMorrow, J., Springate, D. A., Torres, B., et al. (2013). Evaluating the effects of common-pool resource institutions and market forces on species richness and forest cover in Ecuadorian indigenous Kichwa communities: Institutions and market forces. *Conservation Letters*, *6*(2), 107–115.

Ostrom, E., Gardner, R., & Walker, J. (1994). *Rules, games and common-pool resources*. Ann Arbor: University of Michigan Press.

Ostrom, E., Burger, J., Field, C. B., Norgaard, R. B., & Policansky, D. (1999). Revisiting the commons: Local lessons, global challenges. *Science*, *284*, 278–282.

Pailler, S., Wagner, J. E., McPeak, J. G., & Floyd, D. W. (2009). Identifying conservation opportunities among Malinké bushmeat hunters of Guinea, west Africa. *Human Ecology*, *37*(6), 761–774

Petty, J. (2003). Social capital and the collective management of resources. *Science*, *302*, 1912–1914.

Posey, D. A. (1999). *Cultural and spiritual values of biodiversity*. London: Intermediate Technology.

Putnam, R. D. (2000). *Bowling alone*. New York: Simon & Schuster.

Reuveny, R. (2008). Ecomigration and violent conflict: Case studies and public policy implications. *Human Ecology*, *36*(1), 1–13.

Ruiz-Ballesteros, E., & Gual, M. A. (2012). The emergence of new commons: Community and multilevel governance in the Ecuadorian coast. *Human Ecology*, *40*(6), 847–862.

Sanginga, P. C., Kamugisha, R. N. and Martin, A. M. (2007). The dynamics of social capital and conflict management in multiple resource regimes: A case of the southwestern highlands of Uganda. *Ecology and Society*, *12*(1): 6. Available at: http://www.ecologyandsociety.org/vol12/iss1/art6/. Accessed 10 Oct. 2007.

Schmiedel, U., Mtuleni, V. S., Christiaan, R. A., Isaacks, R. S., Kotze, D., Lot, M. J., *et al.* (2010). The BIOTA para-ecologist programme: Towards capacity development and knowledge exchange. In U. Schmiedel & N. Jürgens (Eds.), *Biodiversity in southern Africa. Volume 2: Patterns and processes at regional scale* (pp. 319–325). Göttingen & Windhoek: Klaus Hess Publishers.

Schwartz, S. (1994). Are there universal aspects in the structure and contents of human values? *Journal of Social Issues*, *50*(4), 19–45.

Secretariat of Convention on Biological Diversity (2010). *TARGET 11*. http://www.cbd.int/sp/targets/rationale/target-11/

Shambaugh, J., Oglethorpe, J., Ham, R., & Tognetti, S. (2001). *The trampled grass: Mitigating the impacts of armed conflict on the environment*. Washington, DC: Biodiversity Support Program.

Silverton, J., Buesching, C. D., Jacobson, S. K., & Rebelo, T. (2013). Citizen science and nature conservation. In D. W. Macdonald & K. J. Willis (Eds.), *Key topics in conservation biology 2* (pp. 127–142). New York: Wiley-Blackwell.

Soule, M. E. (1985). What is conservation biology? *BioScience*, *35*, 727–734.

Spalding, M., Wood, L., Fitzgerald, C., & Gjerde, K. (2010). The 10% target: Where do we stand? In C. Toropova, I. Meliane, D. Laffoley, E. Matthews & M. Spalding, (Eds). *Global ocean protection: Present status and future possibilities*. Brest, France: Agence des aires marines protégées, Gland, Switzerland, Washington, DC and New York, USA: IUCN WCPA, Cambridge, UK: UNEP-WCMC, Arlington, USA: TNC, Tokyo, Japan: UNU, New York, USA: WCS.

Suleiman, R., Budescu, D., Fischer, I., & Messick, D. (Eds.). (2004). Eds. *Contemporary psychological research on social dilemmas*. New York: Cambridge University Press.

Syme, G., & Fenton, D. (1993). Perceptions of equity and procedural preferences for water allocation decisions. *Society and Natural Resources*, *6*, 347–360.

Thompson, R. A. (1993). Socioemotional development: Enduring issues and new challenges. *Developmental Review*, *13*, 372–402.

Tönnies, F. (1957). *Community and society*. (C. P. Loomis, Trans.). East Lansing, MI: Michigan State University. (Original work published 1887)

United Nations. (2009). *Climate Change and its Possible Security Implications*. Report of the Secretary General. 64th Session, Item 114 of the Provisional Agenda, United Nations General Assembly, 11 September.

Wunder, S. (2013). When payments for environmental services will work for conservation: When PES will work. *Conservation Letters*, *6*(4), 230–237.

11

Environmental Education

Because modern societies devote massive resources to both formal and informal educational systems, environmental education (EE) has the potential to affect a wide range of individuals and provides an important opportunity to promote human–environment harmony. Education is part of the socialization process: Schools transmit knowledge as well as the ideals and skills necessary for citizenship. Education also aims for the development of individuals' capacities as an end in itself. Today, both of the traditional agendas of education – socialization and the fulfillment of individual potential – include the natural environment. Relevant to socialization, society is midway into a major transformation that will, if successful, change the ways all our major institutions account for our interdependence with nature. Institutions are socially constructed by the beliefs, values, and actions of the individuals making them up. Thus, all people need to be ready to participate through the way they make many everyday as well as life course decisions. Relevant to individual potential, people everywhere derive material, psychological, and spiritual benefits from nature. Experience in and learning about nature helps us realize our own humanity to the fullest. Socialization and fulfillment are intertwined. Arguably, the natural world is part of the "common patrimony" that we are obliged to pass down to succeeding

Conservation Psychology: Understanding and promoting human care for nature, Second Edition.
Susan Clayton and Gene Myers.

www.wiley.com\go\clayton\conservation

generations in good condition (Weiss, 1989). To deny others the opportunity to experience and learn about nature can be regarded as denying them part of their heritage as human beings. Thus, furthering EE is a part of the agenda for conservation psychology.

This chapter will examine what EE is, considering mainstream definitions and goals. Our emphasis will be mostly on children and youth, rather than adult audiences and community contexts, which were covered in Chapters 9 and 10. We will review evidence on support of and the need for EE, and develop four examples of recent trends to illustrate the diversity of present practice of the profession. Following this, we will discuss the psychological theories and specialized findings that help form the foundations of EE. Finally, we will briefly consider the efficacy of EE and factors that affect this, drawing on some of the excellent reviews available.

Environmental education

Education is a field whose definition and goals lie outside psychology proper. As a case in point, while some of our discussion acknowledges behavior (broadly construed) as a result of EE, whether or not behavior *should* be so considered is contentious in EE philosophy. For example, Dreyfus and Wals (1999) criticize the citizenship model for regarding education merely as a tool for environmental well-being. They argue instead for an emancipatory view of education, wherein learners construct understandings, critique underlying assumptions and worldviews, expose and alter distortions of power, and transform the world around them. In a similar vein, Courtney-Hall and Rogers (2002) identify several dissonances when environmental educators and researchers focus on modeling behavioral outcomes. As noted earlier by Robottom and Hart (1995), when EE research and practice borrow thinking and language from behavior modification, its "deterministic character contradicts one of the foremost aims of EE – or any education – the development of critical independent thinking" (p. 7). Recently, a different critique has suggested that EE is part of a liberal political agenda. But a US study found no consistent correlations between state-level EE implementation or policy with party leaning in presidential voting, composition of state legislatures, or governors' party affiliation across the years 1995, 1998, and 2005 (Crouch & Abbot, 2009). EE has also been criticized from those with strong environmental views, such as biologists Saylan and Blumstein (2011) who declared EE a failure, particularly when it comes to addressing levels of consumption in the United States. Ardoin et al. (2011), however, respond that the problem is more that EE is "broke" than "broken."

There is great diversity within the research communities of EE, as partially mapped by Sauvé (2005). New perspectives such as feminist, queer, indigenous, postcolonial, and decolonizing, and challenges to perceived neo-liberalism in mainstream EE have led to contestation, reflexivity, and divergent paradigms, as evident in a recent international handbook on research in EE (Stevenson et al., 2012; see also the 2014 special issue on Land Education, in *Environmental Education Research 20*(1)). We acknowledge these tensions and do not dispute that the task of guiding educational thought is a fundamentally ethical and critical enterprise. But as social scientists, we endorse the importance of research to test whether and how intended effects are actualized, to examine what factors maximize them, and to provide systematic ways of understanding the psychology of the learner.

EE evolved in its modern form in the 1970s, but was preceded by several historical currents drawing, for example, on American transcendentalists and conservationists, the nature study movement, experiential education, and outdoor education and the environmental movement emerging in the 1960s (Armitage, 2009; Disinger, 1983; Carter & Simmons,

2010; http://eelink.net/perspectives-timeline.html). Today, it is practiced in highly diverse settings, and is a well-developed profession around the world. Formal school systems – from pre-kindergarten to graduate level – employ a wide range of methods, from traditional courses, instructional units, supplemental materials, field trips, and community investigations (Volk & McBeth, 1998). There is also a large informal sector, which includes nature centers, environmental learning centers, residential camps, zoos and aquaria, park interpretive programs, outdoor or wilderness learning, extension programs, community projects, citizen-science projects, service-learning, professional development, industry-based training, responsible ecotourism, peer groups around a kitchen table, and more. These informal settings might include teachers using more or less structured curricula, or the learning might best be characterized as learner-directed or "free choice learning." This latter term also applies to the voluntary use of informative media such as the fine and performing arts, radio, television, digital technologies, movies, fliers, posters, newspapers, magazines, and (last but not least) books. A shift in emphasis from "education" to "social learning" would also include the many types of social interaction by which people form and exchange ideas (Wals, 2007). In essence, both learners and "teachers" engage a practical and sociocultural setting in which "knowing-in-action" is collectively distributed (Hart, 2007). Most fundamentally, individuals educate themselves and each other by reflecting on their own observations and actively seeking new kinds of experience and effects on their social environments across the lifespan.

This chapter will focus on forms of education intended to produce long-term "inner" changes in learners while recognizing that this is always embedded in cultural forms of practice. Whereas other sections of this book pertain to people's existing responses to nature, or to effecting more immediate behaviors, education focuses on people's abilities to increase their understanding greatly over the long run, thus also affecting their worldviews, attitudes, and behaviors, as well as the horizons they perceive for their own lives. As discussed in Chapter 9, Petty and Cacioppo (1981) and Kahneman (2011) suggest that people process messages differently depending on whether they think carefully about them or not. If they do not, they base their response on superficial aspects such as the phrasing of the message and the characteristics of the messenger. If they do think carefully, however, they pay attention to the quality of the arguments. Education intends to provide the challenges and supports that enable this kind of deeper reflection.

The intended outcomes of EE (as education generally) are multifaceted, as is its history. Beginning in the 1970s, a series of meetings were convened to define the international agenda. First was a UNESCO workshop that produced the founding document referred to as the Belgrade Charter. Its succinct statement of the aims of EE, which still defines the mainstream of the field, is:

> The goal of environmental education is to develop a world population that is aware of, and concerned about, the environment and its associated problems, and which has the knowledge, skills, attitudes, motivations, and commitment to work individually and collectively toward solutions of current problems and the prevention of new ones.

Environmental educators use concepts such as "environmental citizenship" or "ecological literacy" (Orr, 1991) to capture the cognitive, affective, and behavioral aspects of this goal. The cognitive components include awareness that environmental problems exist; knowledge of ecological systems that connect human actions and consequences across space and time; knowledge of one's locality or "place" and its human and cultural components; and knowledge of action strategies. Affect includes motivation to change such as feeling negative emotions upon learning of ecological destruction, a sense of empathy with nature, or understanding how environmental deterioration will affect one's health or that of one's family. It includes emotional attachment to place as well as certain attitudes about oneself, such as "self-efficacy," or feeling one can make a difference, and commitment to continue one's efforts. Behavioral aspects include private-sphere behaviors such as green consumerism, and pro-environmental policy support, citizenship behaviors, activism, and land management choices; they also include the use of political or interpersonal influence skills for collective action. The generation of a large number of environmentally educated people leads to a positive feedback loop: the recognition that together people can make a difference even though it seems that individually one can do very little. Thus wide-scale EE may address the many cumulative small causes of environmental degradation by countering a perception of helplessness.

One model of environmental citizenship that combines the elements above is that of Hungerford and Volk (1990). Like others in the field, Hungerford and colleagues conceive of EE as going beyond mere awareness and personal conduct or habits to focus on literacy, including in-depth knowledge and the ability to act collectively.

This model is based on the component objectives of EE as laid out in the Belgrade Charter and the subsequent 1977 Tbilisi Declaration: Awareness, Sensitivity, Attitudes, Skills, and Participation. However, it departs from traditional simplistic assumptions that merely giving people information (i.e., about environmental problems) will lead them to be more aware and more motivated and act more responsibly. Research does not support this view (Kollmuss & Agyeman, 2002). Instead it recognizes a distinction between information and knowledge, the latter having been integrated into the person's wider framework of concepts and orientations.

Hungerford and Volk found three types of variables in the literature, which they termed "entry level," "ownership," and "empowerment," and hypothesized that they are linked in a roughly linear fashion, eventuating in citizenship behaviors.

1 Entry-level variables are those that appear to predict responsible citizenship behavior. "Environmental Sensitivity" or "an empathic perspective on the environment" has been found to make the strongest contribution to behavior. "Knowledge of Ecology" is a prerequisite to wise environmental decision making.
2 Ownership variables contribute to the sense that environmental issues matter personally. Here, knowledge of specific *issues* – the differing values and interests of social actors in a controversy, not just ecological problems *per se* – is crucial.
3 Empowerment variables include those practical skills and traits of the person that enhance self-efficacy (cf. Chapter 9), fostering the learner's feeling that he or she can make a difference. Primary are knowledge of and skill in using political action strategies, a strong predictor of environmental behavior.

This model identifies ownership and empowerment as critical to the development of appropriate attitudes and behavior; knowledge alone is not enough. Reinforcement over time is also needed. Each of the main variables in the model is supported by research (Hines et al., 1987; Bamberg & Moser, 2007). We will consider applications of this model below.

The need for environmental education

Large numbers of Americans consider EE to be important. Coyle (2005) reports that when surveyed in 1997, 95% of adults and 96% of parents supported EE in the schools. A subsequent 2001 survey bolstered the findings, with 75% of adults saying EE is as important as math or English. Parents expected EE to prepare children to: understand environmental problems when they grow up (87% expected this effect moderately or "a great deal"); encourage volunteer community service work (86%); and contribute to a "young person's thoughtfulness, consideration, and character in the form of respect for people and places around them" (85%) (National Environmental Education and Training Foundation (NEETF) & Roper Starch Worldwide, 2001, reported in Coyle, 2005, p. 66). These three effects could be named the "citizenship," "community," and "character" arguments for EE, reflecting aspects of the traditional agendas of education. EE should not stop with schooling: 86% of respondents agreed government should support EE programs, and 80% felt private companies should train employees to solve environmental problems (Coyle, 2005). Taken together, these levels of support suggest a society that puts a high priority on EE.

A more sobering view comes from examining the types and levels of EE provided by teachers. A 2000 study found that 61% of teachers include it in their teaching, but that most of this is in the weak form called "infusion" in which environmental content is used within existing subject matters, usually science (McCrea & de Bettencourt, 2000). The amount of time devoted to EE is modest. US state-level EE requirements are modest but increasing. As of 2007, 18 states have formal EE learner objectives or outcomes; 12 states have by law or requirement that EE be taught in K-12 schools; 3 states require teacher preparation prior to certification; and 8 states test student on environmental content (usually as part of science assessments) (Campaign for Environmental Literacy, 2007).

Coyle's (2005) data also show that Americans are poorly informed about environmental issues, although they believe they are fairly well-informed. Education does help: People with a college degree were more likely to correctly answer complex items such as biodiversity, nuclear waste, and the benefits of wetlands. The NEETF/Roper studies also illustrate an interesting gender gap. Only 15% of men versus 6% of women got 11 or 12 correct (out of a total of 12), and 43% of men versus 21% of women "passed" with at least 9 of 12 correct. On the energy study and in research by other sources, similar gaps are found (Coyle, 2005). The gender difference is not explained by level of education, but might be related to involvement in science and technology: In focus groups of environmental science graduate students men and women performed the same.

A more telling difference is found between generations: Americans aged 35 to 54 (in 1997 and 2001 surveys) scored higher than those aged 18 to 34 years. This is surprising because the latter group would presumably have benefited from increased EE offered in schools during their youth, a factor largely absent in the education of older respondents. Historical cohort may make a difference here: The older group included "baby boomers" who may have been shaped by the high level of public concern accorded to environmental issues when they were in their youth (see discussion later in the chapter). The results also suggest that environmental learning may be a lifelong activity, influenced by the media. Indeed, Coyle (2005) suggests that vivid media images of pollution, persuasive consumer campaigns that outlast their purpose (such as the warning not to use aerosol cans because they contain CFCs, outdated with the CFC ban in 1978), highly visible unresolved public disputes, and "time-honored heroic efforts" such as famine relief have left an enduring stamp on people's minds that affects how they evaluate new information, often preventing the updating of knowledge. The "disconnects" noted above between perceived and actual environmental knowledge and between support for EE and its implementation, as well as the unintentional effects of powerful media, suggest that in-depth EE may be crucial for better environmental literacy.

A more direct assessment of the EE results of students themselves is possible on the basis of large studies undertaken recently in four countries (Korea, Israel, Turkey and the United States) as summarized in Marcinkowski et al. (2012). While direct comparisons are not possible across these studies, some salient findings include increases in environmental knowledge across age, low scores on cognitive skills for US and Turkish students, and high scores on environmental affect at all grade levels assessed in the United States and Turkey. The results for behavior were mixed, with younger students in the United States scoring higher. These studies represent a new level of sophistication in national assessments and present complex pictures that further research may clarify (Marcinkowski et al., 2012).

Examples of contemporary environmental education

Several trends illustrate the variety in approaches to EE.

Education for Sustainable Development (ESD)

Education for Sustainable Development (ESD) gained currency, especially outside of North America, in the years after the UN Rio Conference on Environment and Development. On March 1, 2005, the United Nations launched the "UN Decade of Education for Sustainable Development." According to McKeown, "ESD carries with it a vision for a more socially tolerant, just and equitable society in which business, industry, government, and citizens practice environmental stewardship, leave smaller ecological footprints, and are involved in community-based decision making" (2005, p. 1). The ESD agenda calls for lifelong learning, community approaches, social and ecological justice, social-niche targeting, and democratic mindedness. Implementing sustainability often entails difficult trade-offs; nonetheless, the language of sustainability is presently attractive to many, and it avoids the pitfall of posing environment and economy as mutually exclusive. According to an analysis by Jaimie Cloud (President, Sustainability Education Center), ESD and EE are not equivalent, but overlap. Overlaps between the core content of ESD and the core content of EE include ecological literacy, systems thinking, sense of place, multiple perspectives, and responsibilities of citizenship. Habits of mind shared by both areas include intergenerational responsibility, protecting the commons, looking to the future to predict implications and consequences of current practices, policies, and technologies (cited in McKeown, 2005).

Education for sustainability takes many forms, often using existing communities as sites for social learning. In general, these approaches have a focus on the socially transformative power of what Putnam (2000) calls "bridging" social capital, whereby substantial ties are built between people who would not associate out of choice. Some examples might include:

Cross-sector collaborative efforts (education, health, and business) to mobilize support for environmental education across a state or region (Washington State's E3 Initiative, http://www.e3washington.org/).

- Working with adults who are reevaluating the dominance of consumption in their lives compared to values they have discovered mean more to them (see Center for a New American Dream, http://www.newdream.org/).
- Working with business and traditionally conservative communities by working within trusted social networks. For example, former California Governor Arnold Schwarzenegger's business constituencies felt he was "on their side." Thus, he could recruit them into his ambitious state-level climate change activities (Breslau, 2007).

- Multistakeholder planning or decision-making efforts that bring together diverse social groups under wider umbrella values to resolve resource use conflicts and realize the potential of social learning (Brunner et al., 2002; Wals, 2007).
- Working within religious communities, reexamining of the role of nature in particular faith traditions, and establishing new "covenants" between the community and nature (see Chapter 7). More broadly this approach has been called "values-based" communication. A special issue of the *Canadian Journal of Environmental Education*, volume 11, 2006) addressed the intersection of religion and EE.
- Embracing trends toward urbanization and sociocultural diversity in cities, realizing these are future majority constituencies that lack ties to nature and resources (see UNESCO's Growing up in Cities project), by stressing things like nearby nature, social justice, partnerships with urban institutions, and developing leadership through wilderness expeditions for under-served youth populations. Efforts in this direction definitely transcend ESD per se. Rather, frameworks that consider student language and culture as strengths, challenge dominant ideologies, and commit to seeking social and environmental justice are responding to changing demographics (Arreguín-Anderson & Kennedy, 2013).

Despite its plusses and social momentum, ESD may be criticized for being too malleable and contested a conception to mean anything. In most depictions, ESD does not share EE's emphasis on "environmental sensitivity" or its stress on thorough ecological knowledge. Few ESD materials appear to be deeply informed by the knowledge base of educational research. As a social movement, it is attracting many newcomers, who sometimes proceed with great inspiration but shallow foundations. Dobson (2003) provides a critical analysis of the challenges of bringing the social justice aspects of "sustainability" into a discussion more focused on economic-ecological discourses. Within EE, positions on ESD vary greatly (see Stevenson et al., 2012), with some recurrent themes being the need to attend more to the people–people relations, discourses, and ethics. ESD has the potential, however, to produce innovations of genuine worth that enhance environmental health along with social justice and economic welfare. For example, Wals (2012; Wals & Jickling, 2002) has argued against the instrumentalist tendency in conservation and EE, and in favor of ESD, which must presume a democratic set of ideals focused on equity and participation, or "emancipation." Conservation psychologists and other researchers can contribute by helping tell the real successes from the rhetoric.

Classroom-based environmental education

The classroom-based approach has seen significant innovations and improvements in recent years. The North American Association for Environmental Education (NAAEE) has led efforts to raise standards and increase communication across the field. This was in part a response to a movement in the 1990s to discredit and reduce EE by accusing it of using one-sided information and scare tactics, a case that has proven to be largely anecdotal and selective (see the *Canadian Journal of Environmental Education*, volume 3, number 1, 1998). Nonetheless NAAEE and others produced a *Guidelines for Excellence* series that has defined professional standards for the field guidelines and more materials at http://eelinked.naaee.net/n/guidelines. The K-12 guidelines include: Questioning and analysis skills; Knowledge of environmental processes and systems; Skills for understanding and addressing environmental issues; and Personal and civic responsibility. As noted earlier, teacher preparation is critical. In a 2010 study, elementary teachers self-reported that their competencies and practices for teaching these skills are low and that they devoted only 1.3% of contact hours to the environment (Forbes & Zint, 2010). They believed teaching inquiry skills for science "about" the environment and the decision-making skills "for" the environment are important, but they do not distinguish between these two sets of inquiry practices. In lieu of adequate training, teachers are less likely to offer special courses on the environment, provide EE that is sufficient in scope and well sequenced across grades, teach inquiry skills, or use the environment as a more extensive integrating context for learning – approaches that are likely to yield the best results. Online EE teacher preparation courses are now plentiful.

Another school-based model that has been widely adopted in recent years is using "Environment as an Integrating Context" (EIC), also known as Environment Based Education (EBE), for learning. This effort, led by the State Education and Environment Roundtable (SEER), has closely tied the use of local communities and natural environments to the education reform agenda. Its major themes are educational best practices like constructivism; experiential, cooperative and independent learning; action and problem-based; interdisciplinary and collaborative teaching; and learner-centered pedagogies (SEER, http://www.seer.org/). These imply substantial departures from teaching as usual. To produce success SEER supports demonstration networks with ties to departments of education, environmental educators, and resource partners in 16 states. Other similar efforts exist. These programs are justified on the basis of both educational and environmental benefits, as demonstrated by increased academic achievement measures, strong environmental learning, and increased student motivation (Lieberman & Hoody, 1998). A comparison between 77 matched pairs of schools, where one member of each pair had implemented EBE systematically for at least 3 years (Bartosh, 2003; Bartosh et al., 2006), found superior performance in at least one academic area at 73 of the environmental schools as well as more experiential pedagogies in use. The most discriminating factors between teachers adopting EBE and those not include higher levels of teachers' environmental sensitivity, attitudes and knowledge; training; and seeing evidence of positive outcomes (Ernst, 2009).

Place-based education

This is an umbrella term used by several different efforts, many of them somewhat similar to the EBE model above. What distinguishes them is a focus on students learning to know and feel attached to their specific locale through experiential learning methods. The goal is not to push academic skills but to cement the child's relation to a fundamental natural inheritance and to foster personal growth in a community context. Places are characterized by their social and cultural features as much as by nature: It is a concept that reunites people fundamentally with nature, rather than promoting a dualistic notion of pure nature as a place not for humans or humans as a species that do not belong in nature (Gruenewald, 2003). Place-based EE takes time to acquaint children with natural history – other species, the elements, the landscape, and the human dwellers – and to encourage familiarity with them, by putting the learners in first-hand contact as well as by teaching (Fig. 11.1). The renaissance of natural history education is evident in the 2007 formation of the Natural History Network and its refereed *Journal of Natural History Education and Experience.*

Some approaches simply aim to give children more opportunities to choose their own activities in nature. This includes the design of more natural play spaces where students undertake unstructured activities (Moore & Cooper Marcus, 2008). German "Waldkindergarten," literally forest kindergartens (Schäffer & Kistermann, 2012; Millitz, 2004), have no buildings, but take young children into the fields and woods daily. The children's spontaneous activities are supplemented by regularized group activities and storytelling. Other varieties of place-based

Fig. 11.1 Sorting organisms from a beach seine net, students learn about intertidal natural history (photo courtesy of Courtney Blodgett).

EE occur at EE centers or nature centers that go beyond traditional ecological role-playing games, didactic instruction, or teaching of the names of organisms, to integrate the child's understanding through multiple kinds of experiences: local community elders, different users of the place, the science and the arts depicting the place, the growing of food, and their own action potentials. These combine to give the children a sense of ownership in that place.

At another end of the age and nature spectrum are wilderness-based EE programs, which incorporate significant elements such as living in pristine nature, experiencing a different lifestyle, being part of a strong community and dealing with intense challenge (D'Amato & Krasny, 2011). Outcomes of these programs blend personal development with instrumental EE goals relating to sustainability behaviors at home, and exemplify a transformational learning process (Mezirow, 2000). These and therapeutic programs depend on the characteristics of wilderness as a place as discussed in chapter 4. The few studies that have measured changes in environmental behavior as a response to these programs show similar patterns: There is some increase in pro-environmental behavior, but it wears off over time. Exceptions are among individuals who get "hooked" and continue with more experiences, although this can lead to a view of wilderness as an arena for recreation or personal development only. Studies that have explored the typically weak transfer from wilderness experience to home have found that while participants find the experience impactful and attribute valuing and feeling closer to nature to it, they also report low frequencies of sustainable behaviors and do not see a link between the backcountry and the frontcountry. Making environmental stewardship and activism skills explicit, along with guiding educational goals of the sponsoring organization, increase the degree of transfer (see Chawla & Derr, 2012 for a review).

Robert Louv's (2005) book, *The last child in the woods*, emphasized what children lose when they have insufficient exposure to their local natural environments. From the standpoint of EE, Louv's work misses the connection to citizenship and action. On the other hand, place-based approaches may do most to increase the affective and motivational variable of "environmental sensitivity," a job at which issue-based and classroom-based pedagogies are weak. Place may also have implications for assessments of educational programs: Gruenewald (2003) argues that "place-conscious education" should make education *accountable to place* as well as to academic goals.

Programs focused on biodiversity

A focus on the biodiversity crisis emerged in the 1990s, and partly following from the 1992 UN Convention on Biodiversity, many efforts have been undertaken to address the challenges. Statutory protection of species or habitats has been ineffective when local enforcement and social support are inadequate, as in many developing countries. Education may provide a promising alternative, although immediate effects on conservation targets (i.e., reduction in habitat or species population losses) have been difficult to prove (Fien et al., 1999, 2001) and may not always be the appropriate metric. Norris and Jacobson (1998) analyzed 56 reports of tropical conservation education programs published between 1975 and 1990 in order to determine the rate of program success and to evaluate the impact of factors such as location, sponsors, duration, publication, and evaluation methods. They found that only 45% of programs were "successful," defined as meeting 50% or more of their objectives. Key to success was formative and summative evaluation used for program improvement, suggesting the importance of incorporating ongoing institutional learning and consequent program adjustments into program design and funding.

Two additional routes to better results for biodiversity are stressed by Wals (1999), who advocates an approach to education that centralizes human development over ideology or narrow training, and is built on expert teachers' reflections on best practices. Based on interviews with such teachers, Wals lists these process "anchors": total immersion; diversity of learning styles; active participation; a focus on expressing values and becoming aware of others' values; balancing the local and distant aspects of the issue; a case study approach, stressing the social context as both a means and end; and learning for action. The active and socially engaged elements of this list reflect the fact that biodiversity conservation is a social issue. Thus, the stress is on creating contexts where learning can take place, and fostering group and individual choice and self-determination. That said, Wals (1999) also emphasizes multileveled content knowledge of biodiversity, from ecology, to values, to the politics of nature, and suggests how these can be built through quality learning processes.

An innovative approach to biodiversity education is found in the conservation education curricula created by Sarah Bexell for both Atlanta Zoo and the Giant Panda Breeding Research Base in Chengdu, China, as part of her dissertation work. Bexell (2005, 2013) created a model of "multiple points of contact" with animals, including careful observation of individual animals, discussion of the functions of behaviors as well as the possible subjective meanings of them, learning about animals' needs and caring for animals, appropriate pets, discussions with scientists, and exposure to selected conservation issues upon which they could take action. These activities fostered much greater empathy and perspective-taking than is usually experienced toward animals in Chinese society, and remarkably greater expressions of care generalizing to other animals. The successes of this project may depend on profound cultural changes in Chinese society as a new middle class that is not involved in farming emerges, perhaps moving beyond the historical dismissal of animals as sentient beings and allowing a suppressed ability to care for living animals to blossom in response to the curricular intervention (see also Chapter 7).

Some biodiversity education efforts targeting acute threats of biodiversity loss, rather than working on longer routes related to consumption, policy, and citizenship, were examined in the context of community-based efforts in Chapter 10. These efforts are most successful when preceded by biological, social, and psychological analyses that reveal particular opportunities or leverage points where the kinds of experiences offered by educators are likely to be effective. Rather than depersonalized and isolated information transfer, these experiences might include: targeted first-hand contact with experts, intervention via social networks, and a full scope of ecological information delivered in a well-sequenced fashion; experiences that stimulate reflection on values; analysis of the cultural and economic contexts; and a synchronized use of other behavior change strategies.

A question in EE evaluation involves the use of improvements in environmental quality or concrete conservation outcomes as measures of success (Ardoin and Heimlich, 2013). Self-reported behaviors or behavior intentions have served as poor proxies for actual impacts such as maintaining biodiversity and ecosystem resilience. Three challenges presented for such evaluation are that the issue may not be local enough to provide readily observable results; that not enough time has elapsed for effects to be observed; and that results may not be as complete as expected. Further, effects may be indirect, such as when a project serves to spark later actions; or positive effects in one sphere may be offset by negative consequences in another, leading to mixed effect on environmental quality (Short, 2009). Others question the use of such metrics as reflecting an instrumental rather than an intrinsic approach to education (Wals, 2012).

Nonetheless, a focus on concrete goals is appropriate if EE is to serve its role (Short, 2009). In a multimethod study of conservation and education practitioners, Ardoin and Heimlich (2013) found that conservation and education practitioners and organizations put a high value on education, but felt that their effectiveness was limited by barriers including a lack of demonstrable concrete results. Thus, more effective evaluation strategies and thorough transferrable case studies were desired. However, respondents recognized that education was more than just information provision. Education, if taken as a learner-guided, lifelong, and contextualized process, "bridges across social strategies" and can lead to mission-based conservation outcomes (2013, p. 112). Short (2009) draws similar implications for practice: to foster students' authentic ownership of voluntary citizen actions rather than prescribed or advocacy activities, and to use case studies documenting student-driven actions and how they arrived at these actions to combat biases that teacher coercion underlies student action.

Psychological foundations of environmental education

Although we think of education as a process of imparting knowledge, its success also depends on the psychological processes and readiness of those being educated. In this section, we will present concepts and evidence from psychology organized according to key facets of theories of EE. These include cognitive development theories, with special attention to knowledge of biology and ecology; affective and motivational factors, particularly connection to nature and feelings about the self's ability to achieve effects in the world; and actual environmental behavior, action-taking, participation and problem solving.

Cognitive development, ecology, and environmental knowledge

One of the primary psychological foundations of education is the study of cognition, referring both to the ideas or concepts people hold about their world and themselves and to the processes that describe how people think with those concepts. Where these ideas or conceptual structures come from is debated in psychology, but both innate predispositions and learning and experience make contributions.

There are regularities in how children (and many adults, even to some extent across cultures) think about living things. In Chapter 5, we discussed the "folk biological system" (FBS); the implications of this growing body of research are that children will reliably categorize living things together (and differently from other kinds of things), will notice differences related to genus- or species-level features (though this may be dependent on the transmission of cultural knowledge and limited to "important" organisms), and will probably resist the notion that biological kinds change over time, as posited by evolution. Understanding the latter, more sophisticated notions of ecology, requires that some of the naïve notions of the early FBS be directly confronted with contrary evidence.

Some research has centered on growth in children's understanding of scientific ecological concepts. Leach et al. (1995, 1996a, 1996b) studied children's explanations of systems and community ecology concepts across ages 5 to 16 years. They found that younger children especially spoke in terms of individual organisms, did not conceptualize ecosystems as interdependent groups of organisms, and thought of animals as dependent on humans to meet their needs. After age 9, such use of anthropomorphic reasoning to explain the relative abundance of organisms at different trophic levels (producers, consumers, etc.) was rare, and between ages 7 and 16 "interdependent" reasoning increased and explanations in terms of organisms' mental intentions decreased. Some children showed sophisticated knowledge of natural phenomena, but even among the oldest students and after instruction descriptive and teleological reasoning exceeded population-based interdependence reasoning.

Incomplete or incorrect ideas about food web relations, energy in ecosystems, carrying capacity, niche specificity, population dynamics, and connections of ecological concepts to everyday experience are found among children (Brody & Koch, 1989; Furuness, 1992; Munson, 1994). Similarly limited and one-way models of ecological relations were found even among 11-year-olds who completed a month-long unit that involved constructing and manipulating mini-ecosystems (Hogan, 2000). Nearly two-thirds of the students noted effects of a pollutant only when it directly contacted an organism, indicating limited knowledge and reasoning about ecological transport. The research reviewed here on ecological understanding highlights the difficulty many children have in acquiring complex scientific concepts. Children may import ideas from the domain of human action, or from simpler mechanical causal models.

It should not surprise us that ecology is hard to grasp. It is a complex science in its own right that builds on all the basic natural sciences, from physics and geology to organismal and molecular biology. Ecological processes occur on space and time scales too large or slow (e.g., geochemical cycles), too distant (far away ecosystem destruction); too subtle (changes in gas balances), too microscopic or dilute (the presence and effects of toxic materials), and too varied (not all interconnections are equally important) for people to perceive (Anderson, 2001; Trope & Lieberman, 2003). Ecology as a science is in a state of flux and growth, with earlier dogmas of balance and equilibrium being effectively overthrown in favor of disturbance, complexity and indeterminism (Drury, 1998); technological access to "big data" and integration are accelerating understanding in many areas. It is hard to maintain, however, that people can make informed value decisions without ecological and environmental knowledge. People need an extensive ecological education to be fully literate. Nonetheless, educational efforts can make the indirect direct by working within peoples' experience of local ecological interdependence (Thomashow, 2002); by employing story and metaphor (Bardwell, 1991; Kearney, 1994); and by using vivid affective imagery and language (Myers, 2006; Leiserowitz, 2003), along with more substantial curricular approaches. The importance of ecological and more general environmental knowledge in environmental behavior is both a basic tenet of EE as well as a consistently supported research finding (Rickinson, 2001; Meinhold & Malkus, 2005). Wider discourses – both academic and political – about the nature and trustworthiness of science also influence public acceptance of ecological knowledge.

Besides formal learning, informal experience in nature may be important in constructing ecological knowledge, as suggested by the research on Menominee children's biological concepts by Ross et al. (2003; see Chapter 5). It is notable that some of the greatest ecologists of the 20th century spent large amounts of time outdoors in their youth. Kahn (2002) has suggested that as our environment becomes degraded across historical time, successive generations have a poorer "baseline" of nature experience. Without realizing it, we then underestimate the full extent of degradation as we witness its continuation. He terms this "environmental generational amnesia." For instance, he found that children from Houston understood the concept of water pollution, but didn't feel that their local waterway was polluted (which it certainly was). Complete data to demonstrate generational amnesia requires both difference across generations and independently documented biological systems change which is consistent with the older generation's memories. Papworth et al. (2009) provide data partially demonstrating generational amnesia and distinguish it from similar phenomena. Kahn (2002, 2011) suggests that environmental generational amnesia has played a role in the collapse of cultures, allowing successive generations to unknowingly continue undercutting what they took to be adequate ecosystem services. When there is environmental change, one role of EE may be to reduce amnesia by providing experiences of relatively intact nature, and scientific concepts to understand it, thus helping individuals reset their baseline experience of fully functioning nature. Historical research can be undertaken and the results shared through education, helping people set better population recovery targets of marine and other species, for example (McClenachan et al., 2012).

Affective factors and EE

Research in EE has tended to support the idea that direct experience in nature is important, particularly for the affective and motivational components of environmental citizenship. Early work by Sia et al. (1985/1986) found that "environmental sensitivity," measured simply in terms of participation in outdoor activities such as camping, influenced environmental citizenship, but was not strengthened by classroom issue investigation curricula (Ramsey, 1993). We need to understand more broadly the affective dimensions of EE, and their sources. Research on "significant life experiences" (SLE) with nature as a foundation of EE started with an early study by Tanner (1980) Developmental environmental psychologist Louise Chawla (1998a, 1998b, 2001; Chawla & Derr, 2012) has played a major role in organizing, critiquing, and advancing this literature. Most studies are interviews collecting retrospective memories by environmental educators and activists in the United States and other countries (Chawla, 1999). Other studies have looked at children's experience and also extended the research across cohorts and internationally. The general picture is that experiences in nature in early to mid-childhood are a frequently mentioned factor in the career choices and values of those interviewed. This appears to also be the case in about half of the environmental educators responding to Palmer and colleagues' (1993, 1998, 1999) mail surveys in nine countries. In addition to the role of relatively "unstructured" nature experiences, other factors cited include having an adult mentor, education, books, and sometimes experience with loss of a special place (Kals et al., 1999). Taking a different research approach, Wells and Lekies (2006) examined correlations within an existing dataset of questionnaire responses from 2,004 randomly drawn people, ages 18 to 90, living in US cities. The strongest predictor of pro-environmental behaviors in adulthood was time hiking, hunting, or camping in wild nature before age 11 years, which also predicted adult environmental attitudes. Childhood participation with domestic nature (plants) predicted attitudes and (less strongly) pro-environmental behavior. Neither EE nor time in nature with other people was predictive (various kinds of others were lumped, obscuring specific influences). One limitation of the existing data was that they did not include later nature experiences, nor the ability to test whether a hidden covariate such as parents' environmental attitudes might explain the relation between time outside and later attitudes. Kals and Ittner (2003) summarized evidence from several studies by American and German researchers suggesting that experiences with or in nature can have a strong effect on attitude and behavior (Finger, 1994). Different influences are likely to be important at different points in the lifespan, such as youth organizations in adolescence and books, travel and student organizations in college (Chawla, 2012).

Just how SLE in nature have their apparent effects is important, and affective processes and positive associations probably play a role. According to a study by Cheng and Monroe (2012), a measure of children's connection to nature showed four main dimensions: enjoyment of nature; empathy for creatures; sense of oneness; and a sense of responsibility toward nature. Aesthetic feelings, including a sense of nature as unique and sensuously rich were found to be important by Billmann-Mahecha and Gebhard (2009). These researchers also point out how nature may also spawn many symbolic meanings, and it is the associated aesthetic qualities of completeness, harmony, and wholeness, which are apparent in some children's drawings of nature (Myers et al., 2003). Bixler and colleagues (2002, 2011) have argued that socialization is more important than the retrospective memories in the SLE research suggest. Social facilitation of activities, nonexplicit instruction and modeling of fascination, helping young people stay physically and mentally comfortable in nature and later learn the tips and tricks for doing so, and providing organizations for peer sharing of nature and discussion of its meaning are just some of the factors a socialization model highlights. Indeed it would be artificial to isolate the influence of others from our experiences of nature, though understanding nature's contribution per se is important for EE design.

How do the factors in the SLE research translate to EE, especially given that there are suggestions that it is informal experiences in nature that are most formative? First, because children's play in natural settings is believed to be declining (Myers, 2012; Pergams & Zaradic, 2008), EE can be designed to allow unstructured time, although to the extent it is answerable to formal schooling learning outcomes such opportunities may be limited The exceptions would be whole schools set in nature, such as the Waldkindergarten discussed earlier. Nonetheless, studies do show that nature experiences within EE are important. In the context of a qualitative program evaluation, Cachelin et al. (2009) demonstrated that only students (fourth grade) who had actual field experience with a wetland developed positive sentiments toward wetlands and wanted to return. Sensory experience was also an unexpected and major category of response, with implications for both cognition (spatial memory) and affect. The overwhelming majority of negative responses came from students who did not visit a wetland. As mentioned in Chapter 9, Kals found that EE could increase emotional response to nature. While memories reported in the SLE literature may have occurred outside of EE programs, Liddicoat and Krasny (2014) drew on the literature on episodic memory to look at memories that had persisted over 5 years after a residential outdoor EE experience. Strong positive memories were shared by the participants. The memories served directive functions in line with the goals of the EE programs, such as reflecting increased desire to return to the park where the program happened, or to support continued practice of a behavior learned 5 years ago. Memories also were used to maintain relationships with friends. Myers and Saunders (2002) proposed that affective ties to animals may provide a central developmental route to caring about larger levels of biological organization such as habitats, species, and ecological communities. Because animals are frequently used in educational settings, particularly in the early grades, the prevalence and dynamics of this pathway deserve further exploration. Finally, attention to socialization and other non-"nature" factors identified in the SLE literature is important, for example in how naturalists interpret natural history moments (Bixler et al., 2011). Not only other people (see below on socialization) but also books are cited as influences. Considering influences later in the lifespan, Mobley et al. (2010) found that greater familiarity with environmental classics such as Leopold's *A Sand County Almanac* was a significant contributor to explaining variance in responsible environmental behavior, a reminder to not ignore the higher reaches of affect, culture, and cognition.

While educational theory generally has focused on cognitive abilities, recent advances in the neuroscience of emotions are demonstrating that learning, attention, memory, decision making, social functioning, and moral reasoning are partly subsumed within emotional processes and have been called aspects of "emotional thought," or the extensive overlap of these two basic psychological functions (Immordino-Yang & Damasio, 2007). Drawing on studies of specific deficits caused by brain injuries, Immordino-Yang and Damasio make the case that education involves emotional competencies tied to calling up relevant memories, learning new associations between events and outcomes, creativity, and transfer from the schooling situation to life beyond. Without the "emotional rudder" that helps the person integrate physiological-emotional and cognitive responses within the social environment, the person cannot recognize social complexity and build an increasingly flexible and sophisticated array of responses, which they argue is at the core of learning and creativity. One qualitative discursive analysis reflecting some lessons of the research mentioned above looked at the use of emotion talk by two environmental educators. Affirming students' empathic engagement with parts of nature, articulating goals such as taking personal "emotional responsibility" for the care of nature, and demonstrating a highly positive emotional relationship to the environment are examples of the teachers' "emotional practice" (Reis & Roth, 2010).

Another affective and cognitive component of EE relates to the child's developing belief he or she is someone who can effect change either alone or with others (self-efficacy and internal locus of control are related terms, see Chapter 9; research on learned hopefulness is also relevant, see Chapter 12). This factor is important in motivation to engage in pro-environmental behavior. Designing curricula based on self-determination theory (see Chapter 12) can increase students' motivation (Darner, 2012). Educational programs should be alert to their potential impact on children's perceived control. Sobel (1996) criticized EE for promoting "ecophobia," a term that can refer to the anxieties caused when children are confronted too young with distant environmental catastrophes, or to simple fear of nature due to unfamiliarity (Matteson, 2008). Referring to the first definition, Sobel proposed a standard of "no tragedies before fourth grade" (1996, p. 27) on the assumption that information focused on problems beyond young children's own experience and competence disempowers, leading them to believe they are helpless to avert environmental catastrophe. Matteson (2008) used a quasi-experimental design with eight classes of fourth graders to see if a curriculum unit focused on rainforests and their destruction had the hypothesized effects. The results showed no effects of the curriculum per se on fear or empowerment, or on appreciation of nature, but did show more appreciation and less fear as a result of time in nature. On the other hand, Strife (2012) used open-ended questions to ask about children's knowledge and feelings about "any environmental problems" in their neighborhoods, and the same "outside your neighborhood," and their thoughts and feelings about the future. Qualitative analysis of the verbal and drawn responses of 50 10- to 12-year-old children brought to the surface vivid and frustrated statements of "sadness, fear, anger and pessimistic view of the future" (Strife, 2012, p. 49).

How empowered or helpless children become depends on how a problem is presented and how children are helped to deal with it. In fact, researchers have documented children acting on what they learn (Wals, 1994). King (1995) reports on impressive environmental activists as young as second grade, who, with coaching and support, understand the collective nature of the needed solutions and work on that level. Parallels can be drawn from actions of children in the civil rights struggles (Myers, 2013), who succeeded in sometimes heroic action because they were helped to cope emotionally with the hatred directed at them by parents and the community of activists around them.

Socialization

Social context presents strong influences on beliefs, attitudes, behavior, and education; indeed education (schooling) is an example of secondary socialization, whereas families provide offsprings' primary socialization. Other chapters deal in-depth with social influences on behavior. Here we will look at some special cases of socialization germane to EE. Above we noted Bixler et al.'s (2002) focus on socialization and nature experience; and also how some children have become environmentally active, and how the social context is important in supporting that. In generally, socialization runs from adult to child. Parents' modeling and explanations affect children's recycling behavior, although praise and sanctioning have less effect (Matthies et al., 2012). In another example, parents were the main influence on Viennese high schoolers' choices about buying organic products (Gotschi et al., 2009); peer reference groups and media were also predictive. Teachers, however, were not so influential in this case. In a sample of Danish 16- to 18-year-olds, their environmental values correlated with their parents', and their behaviors correlated even more strongly (Grønhøj & Thøgersen, 2009). In researching familial influences, the gender of the child needs to be considered. Leppänen et al. (2012) found interesting gender differences in the relationship between environmental attitudes of Finnish 15-year-olds (in 2002) and those of their mothers and fathers. Girls' attitudes related more closely to their fathers' than their mothers', but were just as positive. The attitudes of the 15-year-old boys, however, were significantly more negative than either parents' or girls'. A later study in Belgium with 15-year-olds and their parents showed strong influence from the parents on all offsprings' environmental concerns (Meeusen, 2014). This study also found that direct and indirect talk by parents about environmental concern was an important factor in transmission.

While these studies agree about the importance of parents, it should be noted that they explained less than a third of the variance. There is thus ample room for other influences including media, teachers, and other socialization agents to explain young people's environmental values. Indeed, all three of these studies noted that the younger generation had weaker environmental values or concerns than their parents. A cohort effect (rather than a developmental one) is strongly suggested by 30 years of data from the Monitoring the Future study (Wray-Lake et al., 2010), which showed increases in US adolescents' environmental behaviors (reducing driving, heating, and electricity use; and alternative transportation) in the late 1970s and early 1990s but declines otherwise from 1976 to 2005. The findings agree with Coyle's (2005) conclusions about environmental literacy in the United States, reported earlier.

Children may also influence adults, peers, and cross-age mates (Kuczynski et al., 1999), and studies have investigated the circumstances in which children's EE may "trickle down" to parents. Zampos (2011) found that nearly 60% of parents of children in two UK primary schools with sustainability education programs felt they had been somewhat or very influenced by their children. Meanwhile, 75% of the children felt they had influenced their parents "quite a bit" or more. Interestingly, 44% of the children believed (perhaps inaccurately) they knew much more than their parents about the environment, although only 12.5% believed they themselves knew a lot. Education programs that want to reach parents through their children may want to target ages at which children make key school transitions and parents are invested in supporting the new environment. The more embedded environment is in the school ethos, the stronger the transfer. Finally, parents are more likely to be affected by homework projects that require parental collaboration, allow children to be seen as experts, and concern issues that emotionally engage children, relate to their everyday lives, and are enjoyable (Ballantyne et al., 1998, 2001).

Action, participation, and problem solving

Available evidence, based on self-report studies, suggests that children do in fact engage in pro-environmental behavior. The behaviors studied are almost entirely private sphere, such as recycling, energy use, and consumer activity. Rickinson (2001) summarized available studies that described about 50% of large samples of teenagers from Australia and the Netherlands as environmentally friendly. But substantial proportions in these and other surveys also described environmentally detrimental behaviors. Australian students reported that they found the most support from others who also did the behaviors (59% reported this), followed by families (46%). Cited as sources of antagonism or indifference were close friends (40%) and teachers (32%) (Connell et al., 1998). Encouragingly, school could also be a positive factor. Specifically, students at schools with an environmental educator (but not merely an EE policy or principal support) reported higher environmental behaviors (Morris & Schagen, 1996), as did students at schools where student environmental knowledge was high (Kuhlemeier et al., 1999). Students from neighborhoods where 30% or more of the population lives below the poverty line who reported learning a lot about the environment in school also reported buying more recycled products and reducing waste (Roper Starch Worldwide, 1994).

It is important to distinguish behavior from action, which is intentionally undertaken to reflect chosen motives and reasons, and to address root causes, according to Jensen and Schnack (1997), who propose a competency-based approach. Bringing together the strands of research that show how children become capable participants, Hart (1997) distinguishes between illegitimate forms of "participation" for children, including manipulation, tokenism, and decoration, and increasingly more genuine forms that include informing children, consulting with them, and sharing initiative, decisions, and leadership (Fig. 11.2).

The foundations for genuine participation include the development of the social self, which makes possible cooperation with peers and adults. One of the key tasks of development is for children to learn to distinguish between their own and others' perspectives, moving from empathy with close friends to an understanding of the group or societal perspective. This provides the

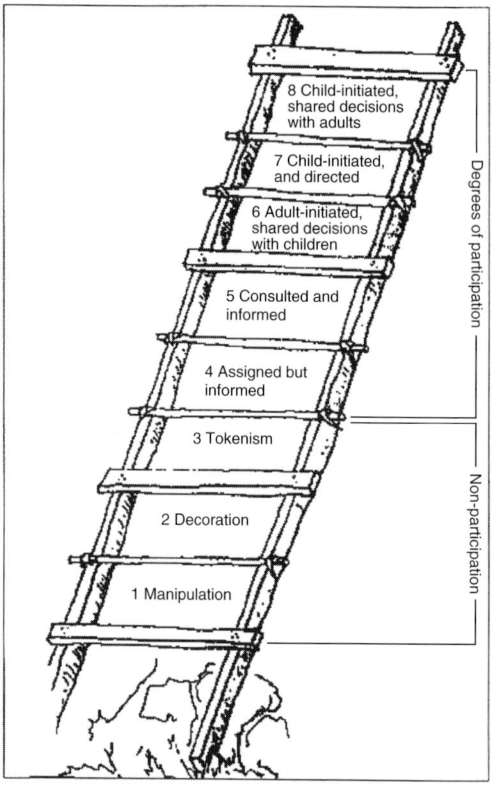

Fig. 11.2 Ladder of children's participation (from Roger Hart (1992), *Children's Participation: from Tokenism to Citizenship*. Florence: UNICEF Innocenti Research Centre).

basis for self-reflection, awareness of their own values, consciousness of a possible discrepancy between their inner and outer selves as they become oriented around peer culture, and effort to forge an identity that is more consistent with their personal beliefs and values. This social awareness needs rich and diverse contexts in which to develop. Many important gains come only when children are allowed and helped to work together toward shared ends, both with each other and with adults.

Citizenship usually requires tenacity balanced with the ability to understand and consider other points of view and interests. The conditions that foster these abilities include role models and mentors, collaborative decisions in everyday life, participation in organizations, discussion, achieving success, supportive and trusting social networks, education, action skill development, and a sense of personal significance such as comes from taking initiative or ownership of a project (Chawla & Cushing, 2007). The key recommendation from a range of studies is that children be "engage[ed] in public issues at the local level, where they can see democratic processes in action and the effects of their contributions" (Chawla & Cushing, 2007, p. 444). Many examples of youth participation projects spanning the settled continents are available. An important connection to Chapter 12 is that educators describing their practices in facilitating youth environmental action highlight multiple dimensions of positive youth development including belongingness, appropriate structure, positive social norms, efficacy, and integration with community (Schusler & Krasny, 2010).

Extending such conceptions to Wals's (2007, 2012) idea of pervasive social learning for sustainability, key features for learning across ages include:

1 The value of difference and diversity in energizing people, introducing dissonance and unleashing creativity
2 The importance of both reflection and reflexivity
3 The power of social cohesion and social capital in creating change in complex situations loaded with uncertainty
4 The power of collaborative action that strengthens the (unique) qualities of each individual (Wals, 2012, p. 637).

In addition to the social skills needed to work cooperatively, environmental citizenship requires the ability to think critically and to engage in creative problem solving. Environmental problems are what have been called ill-structured problems (Simon, 1973): They have fuzzy boundaries, complexly interconnected components, unspecified parameters, missing information, conflicting societal values, and no single solution. Research on environmental problem solving suggests that, as in other areas of skill, there are substantial differences between the solution attempts of novices and experts. Novice environmental problem solvers are likely to spend less time exploring the dimensions of the problem, are less knowledgeable about concepts and systems relevant to the problem, and less likely to address multiple dimensions of the problem (Tudor, 1989). Although few will become experts, EE could help novices develop their abilities to think about all the dimensions of problems, as well as to collaboratively explore alternatives and solutions. Myers and Beringer (2010) present evidence that college courses using in-depth place-based issue-analysis case study methods, or providing apprenticeship in action research, may be effective in developing intellectual competencies and identity traits suited to such problems. On the secondary classroom level, the Issue Investigation and Action Training (IIAT) approach of Hungerford and colleagues has been shown to develop environmental citizenship skills (Ramsey, 1993). Environmental citizenship requires a complex synthesis of scientific ecological literacy, social knowledge and skills, personal evaluation, and action skills on several levels.

Beyond the years of formal education lies adulthood. While it is true that adults appear more set in their ways, and their possible changes are constrained by their economic and other roles, there are nonetheless continuing patterns of growth throughout life. In general, adults' thinking is more contextualized; adults know their familiar settings and domains of expertise in-depth. Adults may also think more dialectically, considering many different points of view, including within the self. Labouvie-Vief and Diehl (2000) suggest an integrative tendency in adult development, where rational thought and the emotions grow into a functioning whole. Partly for the above reasons, adults as learners are quite different than children. They typically enter educational programs with self-direction and a high level of motivation to learn. They usually have their own purposes, and want to know how what they will learn will benefit them, or how they can use it. Adults bring their life experiences to the classroom and need to relate what is learned to their own set of meanings. Their experiences are a major resource for each other, and many prefer to work in groups, and use the instructor as a facilitator rather than an authority. They expect a share of the decision making, and their life circumstances may mean they are less flexible; the learning experience must fit within routines. While adult learners are independent, they also often want clear structure and expectations, efficient use of time, and a clearly knowledgeable instructor (Smith & Pourchot, 2000).

Lessons for effective practice

EE's goals include fostering individual and collective self-determination, as well as enhancing environmental knowledge, attitudes, and behavior. EE researchers have not only examined the effectiveness of EE through hundreds of scientific and program evaluation studies; they have synthesized the myriad studies and applied the results. The results refute critics who have claimed that EE is not effective (Cone & Hayes, 1980; Saylan & Blumstein, 2011). Here we will briefly summarize some of the overall findings for typical youth-focused EE.

Leeming et al. (1993) reviewed 34 studies, of which 20 reported positive or mixed results, but many had weak methodologies. Nonetheless, the studies offered some evidence about more effective techniques. Of several studies that found strong effects on behavior, all either trained subjects in the behaviors (e.g., citizenship behaviors) or involved them in the behaviors. Effects were found across a range of ages and duration of programs. Of 14 studies that targeted only attitudes, only 3 found strong positive effects on behavior. In a meta-analysis of 18 studies, Zelezny (1999) found that classroom-based programs improved reported environmental behavior more effectively than those targeting adults with methods such as labels, brochures, videos, feedback, and information. Programs including active involvement of participants, programs of at least 10 hours duration, and programs targeting participants of age 18 years or younger were all more likely to show a substantial effect on behavior.

Rickinson (2001) found that both classroom and outdoor-based EE programs can change young people's attitudes and knowledge. This review showed a bias among studies toward examining innovative programs rather than typical ones, and less than optimal study designs. Nonetheless, although one study did show a decrease in the perceived seriousness of environmental problems (Uzzell et al., 1995), overall both short-term and longer term (at retest times of 1 month to 6 years) gains in knowledge and attitude were well documented. One of the studies with the strongest designs (Bogner, 1998) showed significant gains 1 month after a German outdoor-based EE program on environmental knowledge, attitudes, and willingness to plan and take action, but this effect was only achieved by participation in a 5 day and not a 1 day version of the program. Five-day programs showed more effect on environmental attitudes among German 9- to 10-year-olds than among 11- to 13-year-olds (Liefländer & Bogner, 2014). Knowledge, attitudes, and behavior may not all be affected to the same degree. For example, some IIAT instruction did not affect environmental sensitivity (Ramsey, 1993), but did significantly affect all the other variables of the Hungerford & Volk (1990) environmental citizenship model. Like Zelezny (1999), Rickinson found that duration was a significant predictor of program effectiveness. Other important factors were location, with residential (outdoor) settings showing greater effects on attitudes, and the incorporation of preparatory and follow-up work. Rickinson speculated, however, that community involvement and sharing knowledge with the family may strengthen effects, and that residential program settings may work against long-term effects if the separation from the everyday world is accentuated.

More recent work suggests subtleties in the impacts of various program factors. In a study of seventh-grade learning associated with 2- to 3-day-long stays at a residential EE center, Smith-Sebasto and Cavern (2006) showed that adding pre- and post-trip classroom activities produced higher levels on a scale measuring positive environmental attitudes compared to just residential-only experiences, or those with only pre- or post-experiences. On a finer level, however, some possible program gains, such as comfort levels outside, were not realized, perhaps reflecting skills that are difficult to help children gain in single short stays. Children under the age of 11 years showed greater increases in their sense of connection to nature than did older children after a typical 4-day EE program with field activities such as sensory activities, catching and studying aquatic insects, and periods of "solo" quietude (Liefländer et al., 2013), adding to other evidence that EE is especially important in sixth grade and before.

In another synthesis of research on outdoor learning, Rickinson et al. (2004) affirmed the same points for success listed above, and added another: careful design of learning activities and assessment. Among the components of design were familiar routines and structure. There was disagreement about the amount of structure (such as worksheets) that best contributes to environmental learning, but structure should be aligned with learning objectives. Program planners should take participant variables into account (Rickinson et al., 2004, pp. 49–50):

- Age: Primary school students were more enthusiastic both before and after their experiences than were secondary students.
- Prior experience: For example, if students are used to highly structured lessons, they will find more open-ended investigation tasks difficult.
- Fears and phobias: These may pose a barrier to enjoying the outdoors, and require advance preparation to mitigate.
- Learning styles and preferences.
- Physical disabilities and special education needs.
- Gender: Some studies have found gender differences in some variables that influence the success of the programs, such as perceived fitness level and the importance of social relatedness and acceptance.
- Ethnic and cultural identity.

Conclusion

A familiar bumper sticker says "if you think education is expensive, try ignorance!" In fact, world expenditures on education are the largest category of public spending, outpacing even militaries. Unfortunately, our educational institutions continue to court ignorance regarding our place in nature, the many irreplaceable benefits it provides, and the promising solutions that are available already or can be developed through human ingenuity and collective resolve. While EE has a strong proven track record and is highly practical, it has not been implemented on a comprehensive and high-quality scale, and it can improve its own evaluation practices by incorporating more diverse and utilization-focused approaches, triangulation of results, and collaboration between evaluators and researchers to clarify theory, objectives, and measures (Zint, 2012).

Education is a high-investment strategy for healing humanity's troubled relations with the earth. But it is also a high-yield strategy, not only addressing sustainability but also personally enriching the lives and capabilities of all it touches.

References

Anderson, J. L. (2001). Stone-age minds at work in the 21st century science: How cognitive psychology can inform conservation biology. *Conservation Biology in Practice*, *2*, 18–25.

Ardoin, N. M., & Heimlich, J. E. (2013). Views from the field: Conservation educators' and practitioners' perceptions of education as a strategy for achieving conservation outcomes. *Journal of Environmental Education*, *44*(2), 97–115.

Ardoin, N., Simmons, B., & Hollweg, K. S. (2011). Environmental education: A critical strategy for improving environmental quality. NAAEE response to "Environmental education has failed".

Available at: http://resources.spaces3.com/b931a4fa-fb46-47a8-a427-c56f2542dce5.pdf. Accessed 16 Sept 2011.

Armitage, K. C. (2009). *The nature study movement*. Lawrence, KS: University of Kansas Press.

Arreguín-Anderson, M. G., & Kennedy, K. D. (2013). Deliberate language planning in environmental education: A CRT/LatCrit perspective. *Journal of Environmental Education, 44*(1), 1–15.

Ballantyne, R., Conneli, S., & Fien, J. (1998). Factors contributing to intergenerational communication regarding environmental programs: Preliminary research findings. *Australian Journal of Environmental Education, 14*, 1–10.

Ballantyne, R., Fien, J., & Packer, J. (2001). School environmental education programme impacts upon student and family learning: a case study analysis. *Environmental Education Research, 7*(1), 23–37.

Bamberg, S., & Moser, G (2007). Twenty years after Hines, Hungerford and Tomera: A new meta-analysis of psycho-social determinants of pro-environmental behavior. *Journal of Environmental Psychology, 27*(1), 14–25.

Bardwell, L. (1991). Success stories: Imagery by example. *Journal of Environmental Education, 23*(1), 5–10.

Bartosh, O. (2003). *Environmental education: Improving student achievement*. Unpublished Masters thesis, Evergreen State College, Olympia, Washington.

Bartosh, O., Tudor, M., Ferguson, L., & Taylor, C. (2006). Improving test scores through environmental education: Is it possible? *Applied Environmental Education & Communication, 5*(3), 161–169.

Bexell, S. (2005). *Effect of a wildlife conservation camp experience in China on student knowledge of animals, care, propensity for environmental stewardship, and compassionate behavior toward animals*. Unpublished doctoral dissertation, Georgia State University, Athens, GA.

Bexell S. M., Jarrett, O. S., & Ping, X. (2013). The effects of a summer camp program in china on children's knowledge, attitudes, and behaviors toward animals: A model for conservation education, *Visitor Studies, 16*(1), 59–81.

Billmann-Mahecha, E., & Gebhard, U. (2009). "If we had no flowers . . . ": Children, nature and aesthetics. *Journal of Developmental Processes, 4*(1), 24–42.

Bixler, R. D., Floyd, M., & Hammitt, W. E. (2002) Environmental socialization: Quantitative tests of the childhood play hypothesis. *Environment and Behavior, 34*(6), 795–818.

Bixler, R. D., James, J., & Vadala, C. (2011). Environmental socialization incidents with implications for the expanded role of interpretive naturalists in providing natural history experiences. *Journal of Interpretation Research, 16*(1), 35–65.

Bogner, F. X. (1998). The influence of short-term outdoor ecology education on long-term variables of environmental perspective. *Journal of Environmental Education, 29*(4), 17–29.

Breslau, K. (2007). The green giant. *Newsweek* (Apr. 16). Available at: http://www.newsweek.com/id/35594

Brody, M. J., & Koch, H. (1989). An assessment of 4th, 8th, and 11th grade students' knowledge related to marine science and natural resource issues. *Journal of Environmental Education, 21*(2), 16–26.

Brunner, R. D., Colburn, C. H., Cromley, C. M., Klein, R. A, & Olson, E. A. (2002). *Finding common ground*. New Haven: Yale University Press.

Cachelin, A., Paisley, K., & Blanchard, A. (2009). Using the significant life experience framework to inform program evaluation: The Nature Conservancy's Wings & Water Wetlands Education Program. *Journal of Environmental Education, 40*(2), 2–14.

Campaign for Environmental Literacy (2007). National Overview: State Level EE Legislation/Policy. Available at: http://www.fundee.org/campaigns/nclb/brief5b.htm. Accessed 9 Sept. 2014

Carter, R. L, & Simmons, B. (2010). The history and philosophy of environmental education. In A. M. Bodzin et al. (Eds.), *The inclusion of environmental education in science teacher education* (pp. 3–16). New York: Springer.

Chawla, L. (1998a). Significant life experiences revisited: A review of research on sources of environmental sensitivity. *Journal of Environmental Education, 29*(3), 11–21.

Chawla, L. (1998b). Research methods to investigate significant life experiences: Review and recommendations. *Environmental Education Research, 4*(4), 383–397.

Chawla, L. (1999). Life paths into effective environmental action. *Journal of Environmental Education, 31*(1), 5–26.

Chawla, L. (2001). Significant life experiences revisited once again. *Environmental Education Research, 7*(3), 451–461.

Chawla, L., & Cushing, D. (2007). Education for strategic environmental behavior. *Environmental Education Research, 13*(4), 437–452.

Chawla, L., & Derr, V. (2012). The development of conservation behaviors in childhood and youth. In S. Clayton (Ed.), *Oxford handbook of environmental and conservation psychology* (pp. 527–555). New York: Oxford University Press.

Cheng, J. C.-H., & Monroe, M. C. (2012). Connection to nature: Children's affective attitude toward nature. *Environment and Behavior, 44*(1), 31–49.

Cone, J. D., & Hayes, S. C. (1980). *Environmental problems and behavioral solutions*. Monteray, CA: Brooks/Cole.

Connell, S., Fein, J., Sykes, H, & Yencken, D. (1998). Young people and the environment in Australia: Beliefs, knowledge, commitment and educational implications. *Australian Journal of Environmental Education, 14*, 39–48.

Courtney-Hall, P., & Rogers, L. (2002). Gaps in mind: Problems in environmental knowledge-behaviour modelling research. *Environmental Education Research, 8*(3), 283–207.

Coyle, K. (2005). *Environmental literacy in America*. Washington, DC: NEETF.

Crouch, R. C., & Abbot, D. S. (2009). is green education blue or red? State-level environmental education program development through the lens of red- and blue-state politics. *The Journal of Environmental Education, 40*(3), 52–62.

D'Amato, L. G., & Krasny, M. E. (2011). Outdoor adventure education: Applying transformative learning theory to understanding instrumental learning and personal growth in environmental education. *The Journal of Environmental Education, 42*(4), 237–254.

Darner, R. (2012). An empirical test of self-determination theory as a guide to fostering environmental motivation. *Environmental Education Research, 18*(4), 463–472.

Disinger, J. F. (1983). *Environmental education's definitional problem. (ERIC Information Bulletin #2)*. Columbus, OH: ERIC Science, Mathematics and Environmental Education Clearinghouse.

Dobson, A. (2003). Social justice and environmental sustainability: Ne'er the Twain shall meet? In J. Agyeman, R. D. Bullard & B. Evans (Eds.), *Just sustainabilities: Development in an unequal world* (pp. 83–97). Cambridge, MA: MIT Press

Dreyfus, A., & Wals, A. (1999). Biodiversity as a postmodern theme for environmental education. *Canadian Journal of Environmental Education 4*, 155–175.

Drury, W. H. (1998). *Chance and change: Ecology for conservationists*. (Ed., J. G. T. Anderson). Berkeley, CA: University of California Press.

Ernst, J. (2009). Influences on US middle school teachers' use of environment-based education. *Journal of Environmental Education, 15*(1), 71–92.

Fien, J., Scott, W., & Tilbury, D. (1999). *Education and conservation: An evaluation of the contributions of educational programmes to conservation within the WWF Network: Reference volume*. Washington, DC: World Wildlife Fund.

Fien, J., Scott, W., & Tilbury, D. (2001). Education and conservation: Lessons from an evaluation. *Environmental Education Research, 7*(4),379–395.

Finger, M. (1994). From knowledge to action? Exploring the relationships between environmental experiences, learning and behavior. *Journal of Social Issues, 50*(3), 141–160.

Forbes, C. T., & Zint, M. (2010). Elementary teachers' beliefs about, perceived competencies for, and reported use of scientific inquiry to promote student learning about and for the environment. *Journal of Environmental Education, 42*(1), 30–42.

Furuness, L. B. (1992). How fifth graders develop an understanding of food webs. *Dissertation Abstraction International-A, 53*(11), p. 3860.

Gotschi, E., Vogel, S., Lindenthal, T., & Larcher, M. (2009). The role of knowledge, social norms, and attitudes toward organic products and shopping behavior: Survey results from high school students in Vienna. *Journal of Environmental Education, 41*(2), 88–100.

Grønhøj, A., & Thøgersen, J. (2009). Like father, like son? Intergenerational transmission of values, attitudes, and behaviours in the environmental domain. *Journal of Environmental Psychology, 29*(4), 414–421.
Gruenewald, D. (2003). Foundations of place: A multidisciplinary framework for place-conscious education. *American Educational Research Journal, 40*(3), 619–654.
Hart, R. (1997). *Children's participation: The theory and practice of involving young citizens in community development and environmental care*. London: Earthscan/UNICEF.
Hart, P. (2007). Social learning as action inquiry: Exploring education for sustainable societies. In A. E. J. Wals (Ed.), *Social learning towards a more sustainable world* (pp 313–329). Wageningen: Wageningen Academic Publishers.
Hines, J. M., Hungerford, H. R., & Tomera, A. N. (1987). Analysis and synthesis of research on responsible environmental behavior: A meta-analysis. *Journal of Environmental Education, 18*, 1–8.
Hogan, K. (2000). Assessing students systems reasoning in ecology. *Journal of Biological Education, 35*(1), 22–28.
Hungerford, H., & Volk, T. (1990). Changing learner behavior through environmental education. *Journal of Environmental Education, 21*(3), 8–21.
Immordino-Yang, M. H., & Damasio, A. (2007). We feel, therefore we learn: The relevance of affective and social neuroscience to education. *Brain, Mind and Education, 1*(1), 3–10.
Jensen, B. B., & Schnack, K. (1997). The action competence approach in environmental education. *Environmental Education Research, 3*(2), 163–178.
Kahn, P. H. Jr. (2002). Children's affiliations with nature: Structure, development ad the problem of environmental generational amnesia. In P. H. Kahn Jr. & S. Kellert (Eds.), *Children and nature: Psychological, sociocultural and evolutionary investigations* (pp. 93–116). Cambridge, MA: MIT Press.
Kahn, P. H. Jr. (2011). *Technological nature: Adaptation and the future of human life*. Cambridge, MA: MIT Press.
Kals, E., & Ittner, H. (2003). Children's environmental identity. In S. Clayton & S. Opotow (Eds.) *Identity and the natural environment* (pp. 135–157). Cambridge, MA: MIT Press.
Kals, E., Schumacher, D., & Montada, L. (1999). Emotional affinity towards nature as a motivational basis to protect nature. *Environment and Behavior, 31*(2), 178–202.
Kearney, A. R. (1994). Understanding global change: A cognitive perspective on communicating through stories. *Climate Change, 27*, 419–441.
King, D. L. (1995). *Doing their share to save the planet: Children and environmental crisis*. New Brunswick, NJ: Rutgers University Press.
Kollmuss, A., & Agyeman, J. (2002). Mind the gap: Why do people act environmentally and what are the barriers to pro-environmental behavior? *Environmental Education Research, 8*(3), 239–260.
Kuczynski, L., Harach, L., & Bernardini, S. C. (1999). Psychology's child meets sociology's child: Agency, power and influence in parent-child relations. In C. Shehan (Ed.), *Through the eyes of the child: Revisioning children as active agents of family life* (pp. 21–52). Stamford, CT: JAI Press.
Kuhlemeier, H, van den Bergh, H, & Lagerweij, N. (1999). Environmental knowledge, attitudes and behavior in Dutch secondary education. *Journal of Environmental Education, 30*(2), 4–14.
Labouvie-Vief, G., & Diehl, M. 2000. Cognitive complexity and cognitive-affective integration: Related or separate domains of adult development? *Psychology and Aging, 15*, 490–504
Leach, J., Driver, R., Scott, C., & Wood-Robinson, C. (1995). Children's ideas about ecology (1): Theoretical background, design and methodology. *International Journal of Science Education, 17*(6), 721–732.
Leach, J., Driver, R., Scott, C., & Wood-Robinson, C. (1996a). Children's ideas about ecology (2): Ideas found in children aged 5-16 about the cycling of matter. *International Journal of Science Education, 18*(1), 19–34.
Leach, J., Driver, R., Scott, C., & Wood-Robinson, C. (1996b). Children's ideas about ecology (3), Ideas found in children aged 5-16 about the interdependency of organisms. *International Journal of Science Education, 18*(2), 129–141.
Leeming, F. C., Dwyer, W. O. Porter, B. E., & Cobern, M. K. (1993). Outcome research in environmental education: A critical review. *Journal of Environmental Education, 24*(4), 8–21.

Leiserowitz, A. (2003). *Global warming in the American mind: The roles of affect, imagery and worldviews in risk perception, policy preferences and behavior*. Unpublished doctoral dissertation, University of Oregon, Eugene, Oregon.

Leppänen, J. M., Haahla, A. E., Lensu, A. M., & Kuitunen, M. T. (2012). Parent-child similarity in environmental attitudes: a pairwise comparison. *The Journal of Environmental Education, 43*(3), 162–176.

Liddicoat, K. R., & Krasny, M. E. (2014). Memories as useful outcomes of residential outdoor environmental education. *Journal of Environmental Education, 45*(3), 178–193.

Lieberman, G., & Hoody, L. (1998). *Closing the achievement gap: Using the environment as an integrating context for learning*. San Diego, CA: State Education and Environment Roundtable.

Liefländer, A. K., & Bogner, F. X. (2014). The effects of children's age and sex on acquiring pro-environmental attitudes through environmental education. *The Journal of Environmental Education, 45*(2), 105–117.

Liefländer, A. K., Fröhlich, G., Bogner, F. X., & Schultz, P. W. (2013). Promoting connectedness with nature through environmental education. *Environmental Education Research, 19*(3), 370–384.

Louv, R. (2005). *The last child in the woods*. Chapel Hill: Algonquin Books.

Marcinkowski, T., Shin, D., Nou, K.-I., Negev, M., Sagy, G., Garb, Y., McBeth, B., Hungerford, H., Volk, T., Meyers, R., & Erdogan, M. (2012). National assessments of environmental literacy. In R. B. Stevenson, M. Brody, J. Dillon, & A. E. J. Wals (Eds.), *International handbook of research on environmental education* (pp. 310–330). New York: Routledge.

Matteson, K. A. (2008). Too young for rainforests? The impact of a rainforest curriculum on elementary students' affective responses to nature. *Dissertation Abstracts International-A, 69*(04), 1267.

Matthies, E. Selge, S., & Klöckner, C. A. (2012). The role of parental behaviour for the development of behavior specific environmental norms – The example of recycling and re-use behaviour. *Journal of Environmental Psychology, 32*(3), 277–284.

McClenachan, L., Ferretti, F., & Baum, J. K. (2012). From archives to conservation: Why historical data are needed to set baselines for marine animals and ecosystems: From archives to conservation. *Conservation Letters, 5*(5), 349–359.

McCrea, E. J., & de Bettencourt, K. (2000). Environmental studies in the K-12 classroom: A teacher's view. ERIC Report ED465515.

McKeown, R. (2005). UN launches decade of education for sustainable development. *NAAEE Communicator, 35*(2), 1–6.

Meeusen, C. (2014). The intergenerational transmission of environmental concern: The influence of parents and communication patterns within the family. *Journal of Environmental Education, 45*(2), 77–90.

Meinhold, J., & Malkus, A. (2005). Adolescent environmental behaviors: Can knowledge, attitudes and self-efficacy make a difference? *Environment and Behavior, 37*, 511–532.

Mezirow, J. (2000). Learning to think like an adult. In J. Mezirow, (Ed.), *Learning as transformation* (pp. 3–33). San Francisco, CA: Jossey-Bass.

Millitz, I. (2004). *Der Waldkindergarten: Dimensionen eines paegagogischen Ansatzes* (3rd ed.). Weinheim: Beltz Verlag.

Mobley, C., Vagias, W. M., & DeWard, S. L. (2010). Exploring additional determinants of environmentally responsible behavior: The influence of environmental literature and environmental attitudes. *Environment and Behavior, 42*(4), 420–447.

Moore, R. C., & Cooper Marcus, C. (2008). Healthy planet, healthy children: Designing nature into the daily spaces of childhood. In S. Kellert, J. Heerwagen & M. Mador, *Biophilic design* (pp. 153–203). Hoboken, NJ: John Wiley.

Morris, M., & Schagen, I. (1996). *Green attitudes or learned responses?* Slough: NFER.

Munson, B. H. (1994). Ecological misconceptions. *Journal of Environmental Education, 25*(4), 30–34.

Myers, O. E. Jr. (2006). The psychology of photographic imagery in communicating conservation. Available at: http://www.linc.us/articles/Myers-PsychologyofConservationPhotography.pdf

Myers, O. E. Jr. (2012). Children and nature. In S. Clayton (Ed.), *Oxford handbook of environmental and conservation psychology* (pp. 113–127). New York: Oxford University Press.

Myers, O. E. Jr. (2013). Children, animals, and social neuroscience: Empathy, conservation education, and activism. In M. Bekoff (Ed.), *Ignoring nature no more: The case for compassionate conservation* (pp. 271–285). Chicago: University of Chicago Press.

Myers, O. E. Jr., & Beringer, A. (2010). Sustainability in higher education: Psychological research for effective pedagogy. *Canadian Journal of Higher Education, 40*(2), 51–77.

Myers, O. E. Jr., & Saunders, C. D. (2002). Animals as links to developing caring relationships with the natural world. In P. H. Kahn Jr. & S. R. Kellert (Eds.), *Children and nature: Psychological, sociocultural and evolutionary investigations.* (pp. 153–178). Cambridge, MA: MIT Press.

Myers, O. E. Jr., Saunders, C. D., & Garrett, E. (2003). What do children think animals need? Aesthetic and psycho-social conceptions. *Environmental Education Research, 9*(3), 305–325.

National Environmental Education and Training Foundation (NEETF) & Roper Starch Worldwide. (2001). *Lessons from the environment: The ninth annual national report card on environmental attitudes, knowledge, and behavior*. Washington DC: NEETF.

Norris, K. S., & Jacobson, S. K. (1998). Content analysis of tropical conservation education programs: Elements of success. *Journal of Environmental Education, 30*(1), 38–44.

Orr, D. (1991). *Ecological literacy*. Albany, NY: SUNY Press.

Palmer, J. A. (1993). Development of concern for the environment and formative experiences of educators. *Journal of Environmental Education, 24*(3), 26–30.

Palmer, J. A., Suggate, J., Bajd, B., Hart, P., Ho, R. K. P., Ofwono-Orecho, J. K. W., Peries, M., Robottom, I., Tsaliki, E., & Van Staden, C. (1998). An overview of significant influences and formative experiences on the development of adults' environmental awareness in nine countries. *Environmental Education Research, 4*(4), 445–464.

Palmer, J. A., Suggate, J., Robottom, I., & Hart, P. (1999). Significant life experiences and formative influences on the development of adults' environmental awareness in the U.K., Australia, and Canada. *Environmental Education Research, 5*(2), 181–200.

Papworth, S. K., Rist, J., Coad, L., & Milner-Gulland, E. J. (2009). Evidence for the shifting baseline syndrome in conservation. *Conservation Letters, 2*(2), 93–100.

Pergams, O., & Zaradic, P. (2008). Evidence for a fundamental and pervasive shift away from nature-based recreation. *Proceedings of the National Academy of Sciences, 105*, 2295–2300.

Petty, R. E., & Cacioppo, J. T. (1981). *Attitudes and persuasion: Classic and contemporary approaches*. Dubuque, IA: W.C. Brown Publishers.

Putnam, R. D. (2000). *Bowling alone*. New York: Simon & Schuster.

Ramsey, J. (1993). The effects of issue investigation and action training on eighth-grade students' environmental behavior. *Journal of Environmental Education, 24*(3), 31–36.

Reis G., & Roth, W-M. (2010). A feeling for the environment: Emotion talk in/for the pedagogy of public environmental education, *Journal of Environmental Education, 41*(2), 71–87.

Rickinson, M. (2001). Learners and learning in environmental education: A critical review of the evidence. *Environmental Education Research, 7*(3), 207–320.

Rickinson, M., Dillon, J., Teamey, K., Morris, M., Choi, M. Y., Saunders, D., & Benefield, P. (2004). *A review of research on outdoor learning*. London: National Foundation for Educational Research.

Robottom, I., & Hart, P. (1995). Behaviorist EE research: Environmentalism as individualism. *Journal of Environmental Education, 26*(2), 5–9.

Roper Starch Worldwide (1994). *Environmental attitudes and behaviors of American youth with an emphasis on youth from disadvantaged areas (ED 381599)* Washington, DC: NEETF.

Ross, N., Medin, D., Coley, J. D., & Atran, S. (2003). Cultural and experimental differences in the development of folkbiological induction. *Cognitive Development, 81*(1), 25–47.

Sauvé, L. (2005). Currents in environmental education: Mapping a complex and evolving pedagogical field. *Canadian Journal of Environmental Education, 10*(Spring), 11–37.

Saylan, C., & Blumstein, D. T. (2011). *The failure of environmental education*. Berkeley, CA: University of California Press.

Schäffer, S. D, & Kistermann, T. (2012). German forest kindergartens: Healthy childcare under the leafy canopy. *Children, Youth and Environments, 22*(1), 270–279.

Schusler, T. M., & Krasny, M. E. (2010). Environmental action as context for youth development. *Journal of Environmental Education, 41*(4), 208–223.
Short, P. C. (2009). Responsible environmental action: Its role and status in environmental education and environmental quality. *Journal of Environmental Education, 41*(1), 7–21.
Sia, A. P., Hungerford, H. R., & Tomera, A. N. (1985/1986). Selected predictors of responsible environmental behavior: An analysis. *Journal of Environmental Education, 17*(2), 31–40.
Simon, H. A. (1973). The structure of ill-structured problems. *Artificial Intelligence, 3–4*(Winter), 181–201.
Smith, M. C., & Pourchot, T. (Eds.). (2000). *Adult learning and development: Perspectives from educational psychology*. Boulder, CO: NetLibrary.
Smith-Sebasto, N. J., & Cavern, L. (2006). Effects of pre-and post-trip activities associated with a residential environmental education experience on students' attitudes toward the environment. *Journal of Environmental Education, 37*(4), 3–17.
Sobel, D. (1996). *Beyond ecophobia*. Great Barrington, MA: Orion Society.
Stevenson, R. B., Brody, M., Dillon, J., & Wals, A. E. J. (2012). *International handbook of research on environmental education*. New York: Routledge.
Strife, S. J. (2012). Children's environmental concerns: Expressing ecophobia. *Journal of Environmental Education, 43*(1), 37–54.
Tanner, T. (1980). Significant life experiences. *Journal of Environmental Education, 11*(4), 20–24.
Thomashow, M. (2002). *Bringing the biosphere home: Learning to perceive global environmental change*. Cambridge, MA: MIT Press.
Trope, Y., & Lieberman, N. (2003). Temporal construal. *Psychological Review, 110*, 401–421.
Tudor, M. T. (1989). *A study of the expert and novice difference in strategies to problem solve an environmental issue using a verbal response*. Unpublished doctoral dissertation, University of Wisconsin, Madison.
Uzzell, D., Rutland, A., & Whistance, D. (1995). Questioning values in environmental education. In Y. Guerrier, N. Alexander, J. Chase & M. O'Brien (Eds.), *Values and the environment: A social science perspective* (pp. 171–182). New York: Wiley.
Volk, T. L., & McBeth, B. (1998). *Environmental literacy in the U.S.: What should be … what is … getting from here to there*. Rock Springs, GA: North American Association for Environmental Education.
Wals, A. E. J. (1994). *Pollution stinks*. De Lier, the Netherlands: Academic Book Center.
Wals, A. E. J. (1999). *Environmental education and biodiversity*. Wageningen: National Reference Centre for Nature Management.
Wals, A. E. J. (2007). *Social learning towards a more sustainable world: Principles, perspectives, and praxis*. Wageningen: Wageningen Academic Publishers.
Wals, A. E. J. (2012). Learning our way out of unsustainability: The role of environmental education. In S. Clayton (Ed.), *Oxford handbook of environmental and conservation psychology* (pp. 628–644). New York: Oxford University Press.
Wals, A. E. J., & Jickling, B. (2002). "Sustainability" in higher education: From doublethink and newspeak to critical thinking and meaningful learning. *Higher Education Policy, 15*, 121–131.
Weiss, E. B. (1989). *In fairness to future generations: International law, common patrimony and intergenerational equity*. Dobbs Ferry, NY: Transnational Publishers.
Wells, N., & Lekies, K. S. (2006). Nature and the life course: Pathways from childhood nature experiences to adult environmentalism. *Children, Youth, and Environments, 16*(1), 1–24.
Wray-Lake, L., Flanagan, C. A., & Osgood, D. W. (2010). Examining trends in adolescent environmental attitudes, beliefs, and behaviors across three decades. *Environment and Behavior, 42*(1), 61–85.
Zampos, G. (2011). The role of education for sustainable development in families' sustainable consumption. In C. Shiel (Ed.), *Proceedings of the 4th International Conference. Global vision, local action: Education for sustainable development and global citizenship* (pp. 129–145). Bournemouth, England: Bournemouth University.
Zelezny, L. C. (1999). Educational interventions that improve environmental behaviors: A meta-analysis. *Journal of Environmental Education, 31*(1), 5–14.
Zint, M. (2012). Advancing environmental education program evaluation. In R. B. Stevenson, M. Brody, J. Dillon & A. E. J. Wals (Eds.), *International handbook of research on environmental education* (pp. 298–309). New York: Routledge.

12

The Positive Psychology of Conservation

> "We are continually faced with a series of great opportunities brilliantly disguised as insoluble problems"
>
> (John W. Gardner, 1912–2002)

According to the Millenium Ecosystem Assessment (2005), only 4 of 24 ecosystem services globally have shown improvement in the last 50 years. Kitzes and colleagues estimate that if US consumers were to restrict their ecological footprint to a fair and sustainable share, it would require an 80% reduction (2008, p. 468). In the face of challenges like these, is talking about positive psychology Panglossian? We think not; to the contrary, it is highly needed and one of the most promising avenues for conservation psychology. In this chapter, we offer the first comprehensive survey of the most important intersections of these two young fields.

Seligman and Csikszentmihalyi (2000) introduced positive psychology to contrast with the emphasis on problem-solving that typically characterized psychology – an important focus,

Conservation Psychology: Understanding and promoting human care for nature, Second Edition.
Susan Clayton and Gene Myers.

www.wiley.com\go\clayton\conservation

but one that directed attention away from sources of psychological strength. Corral-Verdugo (2012) suggests that conservation psychology shares this negative heritage, drawn not only from psychology but also from environmental thought. This negative tendency has not been universal; in particular, Stephen and Rachel Kaplan (1982, 1989, 1995, 2008, 2009) anticipated both the special contributions of nature to human well-being, and a model centered on human information needs that emphasizes strengths and motivations for making sense, being effective and meaningful action. But it is time to go further.

Our hope is that this chapter will help catalyze more collaborations and hybrids. As Csikszentmihalyi (2011) suggests, positive psychology offers a new framing of the human self-image; it is imperative that our ecological rootedness be integrated into that vision. Building a stronger human–nature relationship is essential if societies are to put appropriate values on healthy ecosystems, and it can begin with the positive effects nature has on people.

Nature as a positive environment

Conservation psychology contributes a distinct dimension to positive psychology by describing ways that direct or even virtual experiences of natural environments have positive mental and physical effects on people. Some examples were noted in Chapters 2–4. These can be seen as part the broader study of how all environments, including completely human-designed interior and exterior spaces, may influence many quality of life outcomes studied by positive psychology (Bonaiuto & Alves, 2012; Bonaiuto, 2013). As described in Chapter 5, "biophilia" offers an evolutionary way to think of the positive contribution of nature to human well-being. Clearly not all of nature is positive for human beings, and biophobia is a common reaction to dangerous or noxious elements of nature. As true in other areas of positive psychology, the positive side is not the whole story, and likely recruits different neurological and physiological circuitry than the negative side (Diener & Emmons, 1984). Biophobia may be quickly learned and more robust than biophilia, and narrows our responses, thus offering less potential for growth. But evidence for the positive impacts of nature is growing stronger. In this section, we will examine several kinds of benefits of natural environments (see Wells & Rollings, 2012; Russell et al., 2013; Crain & Crain, 2014; and Hartig et al., 2014 for reviews).

One kind of benefit from proximity to nature or direct interaction is physical health (Maas et al., 2006; Pretty, 2004). Studies have quantified the health benefits of activity or exercise in green settings for adults (Pretty et al., 2003) and have shown that diverse green spaces engage children in more varied forms of play and increase their motor skills (Dyment et al., 2009; Fjørtoft, 2004). Such physical effects, including reductions in obesity, can be encouraged even in indoor settings by using research-based design principles (Cosco et al., 2014). There is evidence of more complex physical benefits as well, such as the correlation of greater immunological tolerance and human microbiotic diversity with the biodiversity of where people live (Hanski et al., 2012).

Benefits of nature are also psychological. Time spent in natural environments (or even with views of nature) improves cognitive performance at attention-demanding activities. Such performances include laboratory stand-ins for difficult cognitive tasks like proofreading or remembering sequences of digits backwards (Berman et al., 2008); and in naturalistic settings, concentration, impulse control, and delayed gratification. For example, improvement in these three latter variables was observed in children after relocation from one to another public housing project that differed in the amount of vegetation near the children's new homes (Wells, 2000). Rachel Kaplan and Stephen Kaplan (Kaplan & Kaplan, 1989; Kaplan, 1995) and Terry

Hartig and colleagues (1991) developed Attention Restoration Theory (ART) to explain such effects. ART draws on the distinction between voluntary or directed attention, and involuntary attention. Many of our daily tasks require mental effort in order to direct our attention while avoiding distractions and delaying extraneous thoughts and activities. This effort draws on cognitive resources that can be exhausted. But attention can be restored in an environment with these characteristics: It gives the sense of being "away," removed from everyday activities and demands; it is "fascinating," attracting effortless attention; it has extent in time and space, so it is more than a momentary experience to be in the environment; and it is compatible with a person's current goals (even an idyllic beach is not restorative if it conflicts with one's goal to complete an urgent task). "Fascination" is of the "soft" variety, connoting low arousal and activation, versus more attention-gripping and high-arousal kinds of experiences such as watching sports competitions. An environment may feel incompatible (distinct from stressful) due to distraction, deficit of information, duty, deception, difficulty, and danger (Herzog et al., 2011). Natural environments seem to be particularly good at restoring the ability to direct attention (although dangers might decrease this effect). Indeed, research has shown that people rate natural environments as particularly good at reducing stress and at restoration (e.g., Herzog et al., 2002; Staats et al., 2003; van den Berg et al., 2007). Fascination is a particularly important quality for restoration, as revealed in an intensive diary study of young adults (Sato & Conner, 2013).

Ulrich and colleagues (1991) proposed an evolutionary or functional account of stress reduction and restoration: Humans respond unconsciously with positive emotion to settings or features that would have aided survival of our ancestors. Ulrich's early studies took place in institutionalized settings like hospitals where assignment to rooms with or without views of nature occurred rather randomly, without the influence of self-selection bias. For example, gall bladder surgery patients in rooms with a nature view asked for less pain killers, prompted fewer negative notes in nurses' files, and recovered more quickly, versus patients with a brick-wall view (Ulrich, 1984). Numerous studies have since shown similar findings, including greater positive feelings, less stressful thoughts, more time spent in "wakeful relaxation," and lower physiological measures of stress. Naturalistic research designs reinforce this pattern: Maas et al. (2009, cited in Wells & Rollings, 2012) found that Netherlanders living closer to green spaces had better perceived health, fewer complaints and less self-reported propensity for mental illness.

The Health Council of the Netherlands (2004) found that nature improved mood, enhanced concentration and self-discipline, and generally reduced stress. This stress reduction may be responsible for a wide variety of health benefits associated with nature. Even driving through a natural rather than a built environment has effects. Parsons et al. (1998) exposed people to a source of stress and then simulated a drive through a variety of environments while measuring physiological responses such as skin conductance and blood pressure. Overall, the physiological response to stress was higher in the simulated urban environments than in those that were dominated by nature. Similar physiological effects – for example, lower heart rate, lower blood pressure, and lower skin conductance activity – have been found with very brief exposure to nature, including videos of nature and office plants (Health Council of the Netherlands, 2004). As described in Chapter 2, Kahn (2011) found real nature, for example, a view out a window, to be better at reducing stress than "technological nature"(a high-resolution plasma screen live video image of the same view), which in turn was better than no window.

Time and activity in nature have positive emotional effects beyond those explained by stress reduction and attention restoration theories. Exercise in nature (such as walking, cycling, fishing, riding a boat, and conservation activities) significantly lessens mood disturbances such as anger-hostility, confusion-bewilderment, depression-dejection, and tension-anxiety (Pretty et al., 2007; Berman et al., 2012). This is consistent with findings on physical exercise in general. The study by Pretty et al. (2007) measured energy consumption per hour and over the duration of the subjects' activities, and concluded the vigorous exercise alone could not account for the benefits. Further evidence that the natural environment's effects in producing positive affect are independent of physical activity was found by Kinnafick and Thøgerson-Ntoumani (2014), with the strongest effects experienced by subjects during walking immersed in nature (as opposed to sitting in nature, lab simulations, or after the activity).

Gross and Thompson (2007) proposed five types of emotion regulation strategies: situation selection, situation modification, change of attentional focus, cognitive change, and response modulation. The first two translate readily to describe how individuals might seek out nature to increase or maintain positive emotions or decrease negative emotions. A natural environment could affect emotion regulation by boosting executive functions such as voluntary attention and self-regulation. Noting that negative emotions and attentional fatigue both adversely affect self-regulation, Johnsen (2011) suggests that nature may be doubly effective by elevating positive mood and restoring executive functioning, as well as providing an environment where people can express emotions with less concern for the social consequences. By contrast, urban environments could make some people vulnerable to downward emotional spirals. Disconcertingly, however, Nisbet and Zelenski (2011) found that people were unaware of the potential benefit of nature: Although outdoor nature walks produced better moods than walks indoors, subjects failed to anticipate how much better their moods would be outdoors.

In a survey study, Korpela et al. (2014) found that participation in nature-based recreation improved emotional well-being and they were able to rule out gender, age, household income, duration of nature visits, and the number of people in the group (social company) as mediators. Psychological states such as calmness, forgetting worries, clarifying one's thoughts, and gaining vitality and faith are experiences contributing elevated affective states.

As described in Chapter 8, natural environments encourage reflection and enhanced self-knowledge. When Fredrickson and Anderson (1999) interviewed women who had been on a trip to the Grand Canyon, they found that many talked about being free from the distractions of everyday life. Herzog et al. (1997) suggest that attention restoration may be possible in a variety of settings, including sports or entertainment contexts, but that nature is more likely to spur personal reflection. They asked college students to rate slides of a variety of settings according to how well those settings would support attentional recovery or personal reflection, and found that sports and entertainment settings were considered more conducive to recovery than reflection. Natural settings were rated highest for both goals, and urban settings were rated lowest.

Nature may also spark human creativity – expressed either through cognitive/manipulative intelligence or artistically. Childhood nature experience was thought to fund later adult creativity by Edith Cobb (1959/1977), based on her reading of autobiographies of notable creative people. Chawla (1990) tested this thesis more rigorously, and found it was supported, although only for figures in the arts or humanities (15 of the 38 in her sample). Atchley et al. (2012) gave the Remote Association Test – a problem-solving task demanding creativity – to subjects after a 4-day backpacking trip; in comparison to a group given the task before the hike, those who had completed the hike first did significantly better.

A number of questions remain (Wells & Rollings, 2012). Just how "much" nature produces stress reduction (or other benefits reviewed below)? How does nature compare to other influences on positive outcomes (Herzog & Strevey, 2008)? Characteristics of the person, the context, and the circumstances may interact to produce benefits; what moderates the effects of nature? What intervening causal variables mediate observed relationships? Some research does speak to these questions. As noted, Kahn (2011) found differences between real nature and technologically mediated nature. Swedish researchers found differences among participants already suffering from stress and/or burnout syndrome by comparing 30 minutes in Karlstad Nature Park versus viewing a 30-minute slides show of scenes from the same park (Kjellgren & Buhrkall, 2010). Although none of the physiological measures showed any differences, one psychological stress measure favored the natural environment, which also evoked more altered states of consciousness. In self-reports, those in the actual park condition reported intensified sensory perception, a feeling of harmony and union with nature, well-being and quality of life, renewed energy and wakening, "here-and-now" thinking, and a sense of tranquility. Those in the picture viewing condition described restlessness and anxiety, lack of concentration, a sense of being cut off from nature's sensory input, a longing to be in "real" nature, and positive emotions like freedom and relaxation (Kjellgren & Buhrkall, 2010).

Do variations in the ecological richness between natural settings relate to positive effects? An intriguing pair of studies leaves the answer inconclusive. Fuller and colleagues (2007) investigated the relation of biodiversity to psychological well-being. They quantified plant, bird, and butterfly species richness in urban green spaces in Sheffield, United Kingdom, and asked users of these green spaces questions about how restorative they felt their time in the areas was. The researchers found not only that people perceived species diversity fairly accurately, but that the plant and bird richness and number of habitat types were associated with aspects of restoration, including clusters of benefits they denoted as reflection, a sense of distinct identity, and a feeling of continuity with the past. A follow-up study using urban riparian green spaces in Sheffield showed that measures of well-being (reflection or gaining perspective, emotional ties to the stretch of river, and continuity with the past) correlated with subjects' perception of species richness of birds, plants, and butterflies (Dallimer et al., 2012). But these perceptions showed no relationship to actual species richness, which subjects were poor at registering and identifying. The researchers speculated that although participants perceived riparian zones as natural, they misjudged biodiversity which actually peaks at slightly higher levels of urbanization. In support of perceived "naturalness" being what actually relates to well-being, Dallimer et al. (2012) did find a positive relation between tree cover and well-being measures.

Research exploring what mediates nature's effects finds that some measure of connection to nature rather than simply exposure to nature is related to positive psychology outcomes. Scores on the Connectedness to Nature Scale correlated with a measure of psychological resilience among a self-selected but diverse sample from the northwestern United States, with some suggestion of SES affecting the relationship (Ingulli & Lindbloom, 2013). In a study demonstrating effects of nature on enhanced positive emotions and ability to reflect on a life problem, as well as on connectedness to nature, statistical analyses showed that the positive impacts were due to the sense of connection to nature, rather than to stress reduction or attention restoration (Mayer et al., 2009). Nisbet et al. (2011) used the Nature-Relatedness Scale to predict psychological well-being among undergraduates and business people, finding strong positive relationships between Nature Relatedness and positive affect, autonomy, and personal growth. The student sample also showed greater purpose in life, self-acceptance, positive relationships, and life satisfaction associated with Nature Relatedness. A third study suggested that Nature Relatedness protected students in college environmental studies courses from content-related and seasonal decrease in affect (Nisbet et al., 2011). Howell et al. (2011) found relationships between various measures of connection to nature, measures of psychological, emotional and social well-being, and mindfulness. Connectedness to nature is related to meaning in life and vitality (Cervinka et al., 2012; Ryan et al., 2010). A random-assignment experiment where the experimental group participated in nature activities, however, did not find that connectedness to nature moderated the positive effects of nature activities on positive emotion (Passmore & Howell, 2014).

The psychological relationship to nature is related to pro-sociality. Mayer and Frantz (2004) report a correlation between Connectedness to Nature and perspective-taking. The Nature-Relatedness Scale shows strong relations to consideration of future consequences, openness, agreeableness, and humanitarianism (Nisbet et al., 2009). Environmental identity reduces compassion fade (Markowitz et al., 2013). Ninety percent of environmentalists had prosocial personalities, compared with 65% of those with low environmental scores in a study by Kaiser and Bryka (2011). Connection to nature (together with environmental attitudes) mediated subjects' openness to experience (Markowitz et al., 2012).

Is nature directly responsible for these positive psychology effects, or are underlying factors? Sparked by findings that mindfulness (Howell et al., 2011; Howell & Passmore, 2013) and mysticism/spirituality (Kamitsis & Francis, 2013) may mediate the relation of nature connectedness and well-being, Zhang and colleagues (2014a, 2014b) measured the degree to which individuals perceive and engage emotionally with natural beauty. The idea here is that emotionally evocative features of a situation elicit different responses depending on one's disposition and one seeks to match situations with disposition. In one set of studies, Zhang et al. (2014a) showed that only for those high in sensitivity to natural beauty did connection to nature relate to well-being. In a second set of studies, Zhang et al. (2014b) found that those with greater proneness to perceive natural beauty were higher on agreeableness, perspective-taking, and empathy. Three other studies pitted more beautiful examples of nature (images, plants) against less beautiful examples and found that the former evoked more generous sharing, more trust, and more helping behavior. Relating this back to disposition-matching, the authors speculate that "people who are highly emotionally attuned to nature's beauty might show a greater tendency to instill a sense of purpose and meaning" in nature (2014b, p. 61), and that this may be because they are more likely to experience awe and wonder from nature.

Keltner and Haidt (2003) suggested awe is central to the experience of nature, and nature is often mentioned as an elicitor of awe (Shiota et al., 2007). Indeed, people with greater dispositional awe are higher on engagement with natural beauty (Güsewell & Ruch, 2012). Thus, connection to nature, well-being, and pro-sociality as well as pro-environmental behaviors may form a cluster around a basic disposition to experience awe and meaning in nature. The idea that aesthetics plays a role in environmental ethics and behavior is not new, and harkens back to nineteenth century Transcendentalists' and landscape artists' notion of the sublime. Iris Murdoch (1967) suggested the idea (echoed by Zhang) of "unselfing" as a response to beauty whereby beauty prompts one to transcend self-centeredness. Further research may clarify whether this is the case, and whether there are other important relations yet to be detected in the relation of nature and well-being.

Negative emotions in response to environmental challenges

Environmentalists have been criticized as prophets of doom and gloom. Is a negative message necessarily a bad thing? Chapter 6 reviewed Lazarus's theory of response to stress, which notes that people may cope in a problem-focused fashion by changing aspects of the situation, or in an emotion-focused way by using avoidance, denial, wishful thinking, fatalism, or desensitization to decrease the discomfort of the stress. For many people today, environmental degradation is an acute and chronic source of stress, which – usually combined with other stressors such as poverty, marginal health and nutrition, and lack of education – may create vicious cycles of disempowerment and fatalism, though some respond with remarkable fortitude and initiative. For other people, probably including the readers of this book, the stress comes through our *knowledge and beliefs* about environmental losses as well as direct experiences of important values that are threatened. That is, educated groups experience a cognitively mediated stress, but one that is sufficiently uncomfortable to provoke defenses (Fraser et al., 2013). How we construe these stresses and our capacities for responding adaptively to them matters very much. Our construal is affected by social influences such as what significant others do and say, cultural discourses, advocacy messages, and how the message is framed. If those of us who are less directly affected by environmental threats, but who typically have greater resources, rely solely on emotional coping, then there is little hope of solving the problems we face.

Chapter 9 reviewed the direct effects of emotions such as guilt and fear on environmental behavior. Here we focus more on the experience of these emotions, particularly as they interact with existing values, especially as among environmentalists.

Ramping up fear may make people to feel hopeless. Terror Management Theory (TMT) describes the tendency of people to react to information that threatens them existentially, such as death, by becoming defensive about the status quo or a valued worldview (Greenberg et al., 1997). Since environmental messages sometimes suggest a "doomsday" picture, researchers have investigated whether this tendency comes into play by increasing subjects' sense of "mortality salience" (by asking them to think about their own deaths) under different conditions. As long as environmental values are also made salient, the result can actually be a defensive increase in environmental behavior (Fritsche et al., 2010). But German young adults distanced themselves from nature, reducing their concern for the biospheric consequences of environmental change and declining to protect nature for its own sake – essentially centering in on their self-interest values (Fritsche & Hafner, 2012). There were, however, important caveats: Pro-environmental behaviors motivated by anthropocentric values were still effective. And mortality salience had little effect on individuals who were high on environmental identity.

In the same kind of research, young Americans were asked to write about their everyday expression of environmental values and then made more aware of their mortality. For those subjects with strong environmental values, mortality salience increased eco-guilt, and presumably also pro-environmental behaviors (Harrison & Mallett, 2013). This makes sense because for individuals holding environmental values, TMT predicts that those are what they will defend when existentially threatened. The downside is that for people with weak environmental values mortality salience did not increase guilt or motivation to protect the environment. System Justification theory has produced complementary findings: Individuals who are motivated to protect the existing socioeconomic system are also more likely to deny environmental problems and show less commitment to solving them (Feygina et al., 2010). The researchers found this factor explains the effects of political conservatism, nationalism, and gender on denial. Feinberg and Willer (2011) found that warning messages about climate change sparked denial because they contradicted beliefs that the world is just, orderly, and stable. These studies reveal some ways negative messages and "emotion-focused" coping can play out in the environmental realm. While they point to the importance of fostering strong environmental values, they also suggest that linking environmental threats to anthropocentric, self-enhancement, and patriotic values and system-sanctioned change may reach "beyond the choir."

But if guilt- and fear-inducing messages can be effective for people with high environmental values, those with passionate environmental commitments may be harmed. Fraser et al. (2013) studied the emotional experiences of environmentalists, conservationists, and environmental educators – groups both very knowledgeable about the challenges (witnessed first hand in one study), and also very emotionally attached to natural systems under threat. They found stress disorders including depression, hopelessness, anxiety, and loss of energy. The activists were aware of the risks posed by their negative emotions, but also that they were expected to suppress them. Similarly, social pressures to deny the "ontological threat" of climate change and maintain a "double reality" were identified by Norgaard (2011). It is not socially acceptable to share the grieving process activists experience, compounding their emotional toll. One danger is that activists, similar to people coping with more gut-level traumas, may pass their stress on to others (e.g., communicating gloom and doom) as a way of coping, unaware of how destructive this may be. Nature experience, recommended as resilience-building by Buzzell and Chalquist (2009), may only restimulate awareness of irreversible degradation for eco-activists and conservationists. Fraser et al.'s (2013) findings highlight the need for research on individual coping and resilience, and new practices at therapeutic and collective levels (Eaton, 2012).

Negative emotions are powerful (Baumeister et al., 2001). They focus attention, arouse the autonomic nervous system (an activation cascade involving adrenalin), and spark "fight or flight" action tendencies that are evolutionarily advantageous. Brain studies show that the valence (positive or negative) of memories is stored in the amygdalae. Emotional memories are potent because the amygdalae are sensitive to the stress hormones released into the blood when the body is aroused. Even though environmental problems may be mediated by the associative cortex where we can think the complex pieces of the puzzle together, negative emotions appear to be important in the way we respond to them. In their overview of the study of emotions and environment, Kals and Müller (2012) discuss the importance of positive attachments to nature and biophilia, but they also highlight negative emotions that may be felt directly or empathically as a result of environmental destruction – indignation, fear, loss, guilt. The experience of mourning a significant environment has even been given a name: "solastalgia" (Albrecht, 2005). These emotions have been found to motivate nature-protective behavior (Kals et al., 1999).

Positive emotions in relation to environmental behaviors

The prominence of negative feelings relates to the main contexts in which environmental concerns arise and have been studied (i.e., environmental damage or risk). But what about positive emotions? Kals and Müller note one positive feeling, "pride about personal renunciation for nature" (2012, p. 141). More readily associated with positive emotions are the "environmentally risky" behaviors – car driving, for example, provides joy, pleasure, independence, and are socially acceptable and even honored (2012, p. 140). Many such environmentally harmful behaviors are viewed as normal and pleasurable in contemporary societies, suggesting a mental association of environmentalism with negative feeling as opposed to normal life and positive emotions.

Fredrickson (2001) proposed the "broaden-and-build" theory to explain the different ways that positive emotions are evolutionarily and immediately adaptive: They broaden perspectives and action tendencies, and motivate us to do things that will build psychological and social resources for the future. Positive emotions include joy, gratitude, compassion, serenity, awe, interest, hope, pride (specific and not excessive), amusement (positive surprises and incongruities), inspiration, and love (Fredrickson, 2009). Each has distinctive broadening potentials, encompassing attitudes and thoughts as well as motivations. Joy, for example, makes one want to take everything in, get involved, play. Positive emotional states improve memory, creativity, and make people more open to new information and more accurate at complex cognitive performances. Positive feeling can reverse the narrowing caused by negative emotions and broaden a person's perspective on the triggering events. Negative emotions may be stronger but positive ones are more frequent in everyday life. It is best for a social group when positive emotions outnumber negative ones (Fredrickson & Losada, 2005). But insincere or forced positivity does not help (simply being open and accepting of one's current circumstances is better), and too small a proportion of negative emotions predicts dysfunction. So the negative is not dispensable. Negative and positive responses are not simply different ends of a spectrum; some of both are needed (Tennen & Affleck, 2003).

Positive emotions can self-amplify in a number of ways, expanding their benefits. Savoring prolongs and intensifies the experience of any of these emotions. Positive emotions can be experienced vicariously. Or two or more people can resonate, sharing expressions of the feeling. On this basis, Fredrickson (2013) redefined nonexclusive "love" as characterizing any moment where people share positive feeling, mirror it back bio-behaviorally, and feel mutual care. In contrast to "emotion-focused coping," adaptive *emotional approach coping* is the "intentional use of emotional processing and emotional expression in efforts to manage adverse circumstances" (Stanton et al., 2009, p. 225). For example, it might employ positive emotional intelligence where one empathically modulates one's own and others' arousal to accept and maintain attention to difficult situations (Salovey et al., 2009). Creating positive organizations and institutions gives contextual support to positive spirals.

The potential intersections with conservation psychology are intriguing. Carter (2011) proposed that positive emotions can broaden our vision, resourcefulness, and creativity to better address environmental problems, and help us clarify what is precious in life. Researchers have had subjects watch short film clips evoking joy/contentment, anger/fear, or neutral controls, and found significant differences in thought–action repertoires separating each condition. Although this was basic research on the "broaden" effect, it seems to have direct relevance to emotional content in environmental messages and movements. In randomized control studies, experimental participants who received training and practiced positive emotion-inducing meditation over 7 weeks showed increases in outcomes such as mindfulness, social support, self-acceptance, more sense of purpose in life, and reduced illness symptoms. Positive emotions' "build" effect was the operative factor in these outcomes (Fredrickson & Kurtz, 2011). Such findings may have relevance for building stronger organizations. Further, positive responses to nature such as awe, gratitude, and hope may attract people's care as well as help undo negative experiences and develop enduring emotional connections. Among Mexican undergraduates, positive emotions, or more broadly subjective well-being (SWB), were a consequence of sustainable behavior (Fig. 12.1) (Corral-Verdugo et al., 2011). Environmental educators may already draw on tacit knowledge that a positive emotional learning environment is much more effective than a negative one, but could benefit from the fields of positive youth development (Lerner, 2005, 2011), and positive education (Furlong et al., 2014).

Positive emotion, or more specifically happiness, has begun to take its place alongside per capita Gross Domestic Product (GDP) as a measure of economic performance of countries. In 2011, the UN General Assembly passed Resolution 65/309 inviting members to use happiness to guide policy. Subsequently, *World Happiness Report* has been produced annually by a team of academics, and Bhutan has distinguished itself by being the first and so far only country to pursue "Gross National Happiness" instead of GDP as its main development indicator. Taking this thinking a step further, O'Brien defines sustainable happiness as "happiness that contributes to individual, community, and/or global well-being without exploiting other people, the environment, or future generations" and argues that efforts to attain it will not lower our quality of life (2012, p. 1198). Integrating ecological sustainability and well-being, a rough country-level efficiency measure of this relationship is provided by the Happy Planet Index (http://www.happyplanetindex.org/), which is calculated by multiplying

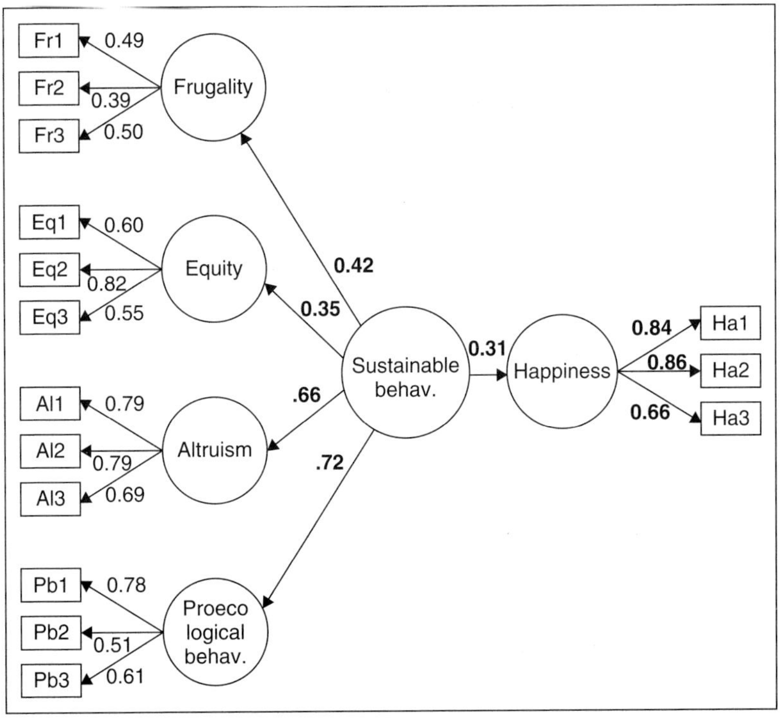

Fig. 12.1 Sustainable behaviors predict subjective well-being. (From Corral-Verdugo et al., 2011, Figure 1, p. 101.)

experienced well-being (a 1–10 rating from the Gallup World Poll) by life expectancy (UN Human Development report data), with Ecological Footprint in the denominator. Currently, high-income countries rank low because of their large footprints, while sub-Saharan African countries rank even lower because of low life expectancy and low well-being. Carter (2011) surveyed well-being indicators and found all were compatible with environmental health, so this avenue is promising.

Eudaimonism and meaning

There are reasons to qualify an endorsement of happiness. Happiness is a strongly American value: failing to appear happy can be seen as a personal shortcoming. But many cultures demonstrate varying forms of "aversion to happiness" – whether to be cautious of too much, whether it leads to bad consequences, or says something bad about the person. Also questioned are the desirability of kinds of happiness – lack of pain, pleasure, life satisfaction, worldly success, or all kinds – and how it is felt, pursued, or expressed (Joshanloo & Weijers, 2014). Expressing happiness in Eastern traditions, for example, may arouse envy, or worse. Within the West, hesitations about happiness are expressed by people who see it as individualistic and corrosive of moral ideals and community. Excesses of pleasure have evil connotations in many religions. When happiness is culturally constructed as material consumption, not only environmental but psychological harm is likely, as discussed in a later section.

Most positive emotion researchers would agree "happiness" is at best an incomplete description of well-being or flourishing. Seligman (2002) proposed four versions of the good life:

(1) the pleasant life, focused only on positive emotions; (2) the good life, where one acts authentically to use one's special character traits to obtain "gratifications"; (3) the meaningful life, which adds to the good life service to something much larger than the self; and (4) the full life, which includes all the preceding and characterizes how humans function at their best and most complex. As elucidated by Jørgensen and Nafstad (2004), this conception, and positive psychology more generally, is deeply Aristotelian in spirit. Beyond positive emotion, it embraces a holistic conception of the human being as defined by a developmental potential and realized by one's manner of living in context – particularly the pursuit of virtue but also optimal experience and functioning in all areas. Using Aristotle's term, it is a eudaimonistic approach (derived from Greek roots of true or good + spirit) to the good life, whereas an approach focused only on happiness or pleasure is called a hedonistic one.

Clearly, meaning is at the core of eudaimonistic being-well-by-doing-good. Steger (2009) defined meaning in life as "the extent to which people comprehend, make sense of, and see significance in their lives, accompanied by the degree to which they perceive themselves to have a purpose, mission or overarching aim in life" (p. 682). This combines motivational concepts like personal projects and life tasks, and cognitive ones like identity and worldview. Those who feel their lives have meaning are happier, have more well-being and life satisfaction, feel control over their lives and more engagement with work, and have stronger mental health profiles (Steger, 2012).While happiness and meaning are positively correlated and overlap, they are distinct (Baumeister et al., 2013). Happiness (and displeasure) is more rooted in biological needs, whereas meaningfulness depends more on language and culture and is integrated across time and provides more long-term benefits (Huta & Ryan, 2010; but see the behavioral genetic study by Steger et al., 2011 on biological-cultural underpinnings of meaning, religiosity, and spirituality). The difference between them helps explain the fundamental paradox of happiness: that the direct pursuit of it is likely to lead to unhappiness, noted by Epicurus. Locke recommended activities, such as acting morally, that may produce happiness incidentally (Joshanloo & Weijers, 2014). In studies where subjects completed daily and 4-week measures, Steger et al. (2008a) found that eudaimonistic behavior reports were associated with positive affect, whereas hedonic behaviors were unrelated or negatively related to positive affect. They suggest that there is no affective benefit from satisfying basic needs without a context of meaningful relationships or involvements. In the context of this book, we might ask, can some type of recognition of our ecological embeddedness provide this added benefit?

Research distinguishes between having meaning versus searching for meaning in life, with the latter more associated with anxiety and depression but also open-mindedness (Steger et al., 2008b) and with life satisfaction during adolescence and early adulthood (Bronk et al., 2009). Pro-active engagement, reaction to significant life events, and social learning were identified as three distinct pathways to a sense of purpose by Hill and colleagues (2014), and each may have pro-environmental instantiations. Generally, meaning is "most fully achieved when people actively engage in pursuits that transcend their own immediate interests" (Steger, 2009, p. 683), for example, through religion, spirituality, or work. If many people's sources of meaning lie in these predominant social institutions, environmental concern may need to work within them too, as discussed in Chapter 7. The most important source of meaning, however, is relationships (Steger, 2009), suggesting that positive interpersonal relationships and groups should be seen as both an ends and a means to environmental goals.

Ecologically speaking, we exist in relationship to nature. Thus, nature may be a transcendent realm in relation to which some people find meaning, identity, and positive affect, although this topic appears to be little addressed in the literature (see Hinds & Sparks, 2009 for an initial attempt). Supposing that some nature-identified individuals derive high meaning from their associated commitments, existing research suggests interesting questions. Baumeister et al. (2013) contrasted meaning and happiness empirically by statistically correcting for the other respective construct. They found that high happiness/low meaningfulness is associated with a carefree attitude, present and self-orientation, easily satisfied desires, being a "taker" rather than a "giver," and avoidance of argument or difficult challenges. High meaningfulness/low happiness showed the opposite: a focus on the past and future, involvement in difficult undertakings, the expectation of deep thinking and reflection, but also worry, stress, argument and anxiety (Baumeister et al., 2013). We can hypothesize that the stresses of environmental activism may be partly compensated by some of the benefits of lives high in meaning. To connect this to the work of Zhang and colleagues (2013, 2014) discussed earlier, perhaps awe at natural beauty is an emotional component specific to this form of meaning.

Indeed meaning proved protective and empowering in a study of Swedish 12-year-olds' coping with climate change. Ojala (2012) distinguished between three coping styles: de-emphasizing the seriousness of the threat; problem-focused coping, and meaning-focused coping. Children using both the latter two felt more efficacy and were more environmentally engaged. But the problem-focused approach was associated with negative affect, particularly worry. Meaning-focused coping children, on the other hand, had more life satisfaction, positive affect, purpose, and optimism. Meaning-related items on Ojala's coping scale suggest the perception that many others are taking climate change seriously, trust and faith in human society and environmental organizations, and positive reappraisal. High meaning buffered problem-focused children from negative affect. The domains in which one experiences meaning change with age and role across life stages (Delle Fave et al., 2013), so these findings clearly may not apply to other populations and in other cultures.

Materialistic values versus self-determination theory

The idea of sacrifice can connect meaning to an examination of materialistic values in contemporary life. Environmental protection is often perceived to involve sacrifice– of comfort, convenience, a job, or in the case of a developing country, the prospect of a first-world lifestyle. The green consumerism movement appears to be a response to the perceived impossibility of serious political discussion of sacrifice (Maniates, 2010). But examination of everyday life reveals many ordinary sacrifices in which people have reflected upon and voluntarily chosen the trade-offs. Peterson (2010) argues that sacrifice "demands that we give up something valued to receive something even more precious" (p. 92). The difficulty with environmental sacrifices is that only called-for sacrifices are perceived *as* sacrifices, whereas business-as-usual sacrifices, such as the ones imposed on future generations by damage to the environment, are not. It is not a matter of whether we are involved in sacrifice but of which sacrifices, which trade-offs, we choose. Meaning systems that recognize our interdependence with life and the future will place the higher value accordingly, Litfin (2010) proposes, and might lead toward collective and individual action to express a commitment to this greater good.

It seems unlikely that societies will reevaluate the pattern of all-out material consumption. Indeed, there are positive associations between income and well-being, across the decades of life (Fischer et al., 2014) and across societies and at both the individual and national level, indicating that financial status is not irrelevant to well-being although some experience of well-being is available to even the poorest (Biswas-Diener & Patterson, 2011). A synthesis of 111 independent samples from 54 countries showed the relationship is strongest in low-income countries ($r = 0.36$) and weakest in high-income countries ($r = 0.10$) (Howell & Howell, 2008).

Although research suggests there is a weak link between affluence and happiness (Aknin et al., 2009), studies of what actually does lead to life satisfaction, across societies, do not rank material consumption very high (Kasser, 2002). Significantly more important to happiness are: quality of marital and family life, friendships, and other important social relationships; meaningful work; concern for the well-being of others; and leisure to develop one's talents (Argyle, 1987; Dunn et al., 2011). Does consumerism distract us from the more important goals, and thus have deleterious psychological effects? Starting in the 1990s, Tim Kasser and colleagues began looking at the relationship between psychological well-being and materialistic values, particularly among those who put strong values on the pursuit of wealth and possessions, social recognition or fame, and appealing appearance. They developed a measure, the Aspiration Index (AI), in which research participants rate the importance of these goals along with others such as psychological growth, family and friends, and making their community or the world a better place. As Kasser summarized in his 2002 book *The high price of materialism*, the research showed that materialistic values predict lower well-being: fewer positive emotions, less satisfaction with life, lower vitality, lower self-actualization, lower self-esteem, higher depression, higher anxiety, more physical symptoms, substance use, poorer relationships, and lower psychological well-being. Relating theories of motivation to these findings and to environmental values will show their broader significance.

Materialistic values are an example of extrinsic motivation, in which an activity is undertaken in order to achieve consequences that are separate from the action, such as money, success, or social approval. In contrast, intrinsic goals, inseparable from the action, are reinforced internally by the person's own enjoyable activity and achievement; they are interesting and spontaneously satisfying. Kaplan and Kaplan (1982) and De Young (1985–1986, 1996; De Young & Kaplan, 1985–1986) were among the first to inquire into the intrinsic satisfactions of conservation behaviors, using a lens of compatibility of tasks with optimal human cognitive functioning. De Young (1996) found that a feeling of competence is a key motivation for conservation behavior. Because people find feeling incompetent unpleasant and avoid it, conservation behavior change plans may fail if they do not help people gain the procedural knowledge to do the specific tasks involved. Across studies of diverse populations, De Young (1996) found many forms of competence motivation, and highlighted two as important in reducing consumption behavior: participation and frugality. Helping others or the feeling of "being needed" also stood out (see also Kaplan, 1990).

This line of inquiry builds on the Self-Determination Theory (SDT) of motivation (Deci & Ryan, 1985, 2008). Whereas intrinsic and extrinsic motives for a given activity had been thought to be additive, research showed that they are separate types of motivation (extrinsic rewards, for example, can decrease intrinsic motivation). SDT instead distinguishes between how behavior is regulated: specifically whether it is autonomously motivated or externally controlled (rewarded, threatened, surveilled, or evaluated). The social environment is important in whether autonomy is supported or not (see discussion of Autonomy Supportive Environments in Chapter 10). Compared to controlled motivation, autonomous motivation is associated with greater persistence, performance, conceptual understanding, positive affect, healthier lifestyles, and psychological well-being. Self-determined behavior accounts for how we may internalize goals from our social environment. An extrinsic motivator may become self-determined if the person internalizes, identifies with, and integrates it as their own. Much pro-environmental behavior may be of this type, for example someone who recycles because it is part of their value system. At the core of SDT is the idea that humans strive for coherence in their cognitive model of experience and that resolving discrepancies in that model is satisfying because it allows more adequate cognitive organization. This accounts for our challenge-seeking and curiosity. SDT

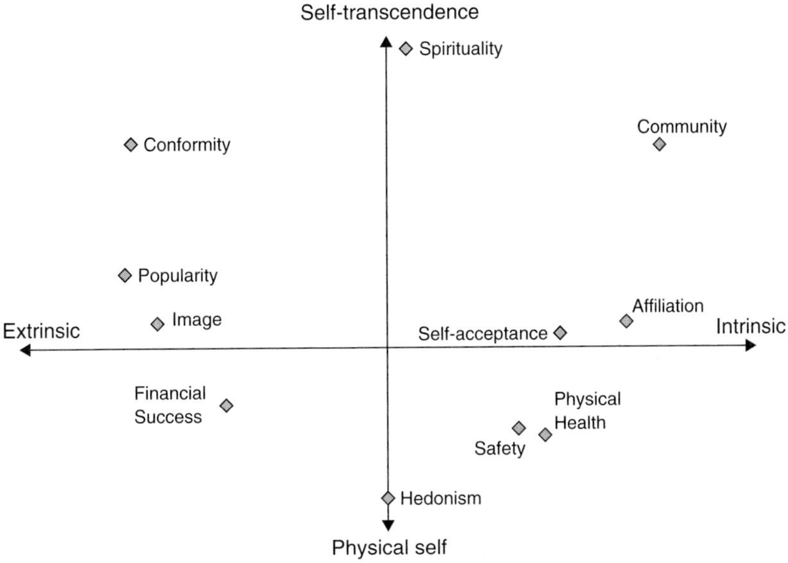

Fig. 12.2 Grouzet's circumplex of values. (From Grouzet et al., 2005, Figure 1, p. 808.)

specifies several core needs that support self-determined behavior. Safety and security are basic core needs. As described in chapter 8, Deci and Ryan (2000) posit autonomy (the need to feel that one's behavior originates in oneself), competence (feeling able to bring about desired outcomes), and social belongingness as core needs. As Maslow (1954) pointed out, when a need is not satisfied meeting it takes precedence. But some attempts to meet them may not be effective, depending on person-environment mental representations and actual interactions.

Examining materialistic values through the lens of SDT, Kasser (2002, 2009) shows that they act to thwart meeting needs. When sustenance and security are undermined, or competence and self-worth are threatened, materialistic values flower. For example, one study found that those who watched a lot of TV and compared themselves unfavorably with what they saw on TV had lower life satisfaction and strong materialistic motivations (Sirgy et al., 1998, cited in Kasser, 2002). Materialism is also related to poorer interpersonal relationships and perhaps ironically to decreased sense of autonomy and authenticity because of vulnerability to rewards, feeling pressured, compulsive buying, and placing little value on self-direction, creating a vicious circle. Looking across 15 cultures, Grouzet et al. (2005) found that a "circumplex" model of goals applied to all with slight variations regardless of culture or wealth. The model is based on two dimensions: physical self versus self-transcendence; and extrinsic versus intrinsic, similar to Schwartz's (1992) model discussed in Chapter 5. Grouzet et al.'s findings place popularity, image, and financial success opposite community feeling, self-acceptance, and affiliation (Fig. 12.2), suggesting that activating one set of values or goals makes it unlikely the opposite set can be achieved too (see also Kasser, 2011).

In summary, a society that encourages meeting basic needs through money, social-comparison, and materialism – extrinsic goals that undercut need fulfillment – invites a psychological critique calling for a societal values shift. Unsurprisingly, materialistic values are also bad for the environmental values. Hurst et al. (2013) produced a meta-analysis of studies looking at materialistic values and environmental attitudes and behavior. When adjusting for measurement reliability they found significant medium-sized negative associations between materialism and environmental measures.

Addressing materialistic values is urgent in the context of the major drivers of environmental impact, population and consumption (Dietz et al., 2007). Many countries have dramatically curbed their population growth rates leading to lowered projected world population growth. Population doubled over the 40 years prior to 2000, but is expected to increase only 50%, to 9 billion, by 2044 (U.S. Census Bureau, 2013). A doubling of consumption rates, however, could have similar environmental effects to doubling population. Emerging economies have witnessed increasing consumption rates. For example, during China's move to a more market-oriented economy, per capita consumption more than doubled, averaging 8.7% per year during 1999–2009 (Kroeber 2011). "Probably the fastest sustained growth in consumer spending ever recorded," (Kroeber, p. 331), this occurred despite private consumption being regarded as "too low" in comparison to other sectors, partly due to large amounts of materials consumed to directly build up industries.

An alternative to consumerism is to use ecologically sustainable behaviors and environments to satisfy psychological needs, and thereby achieve psychological well-being (Kasser, 2009). This could mean using policies and other means to obviate threats to basic security posed by climate destabilization, access to food, and water. Many environmental behaviors offer opportunities for competence, so long as people adopting them are helped in learning to do them. Belongingness might be addressed through localization efforts (see http://www-personal.umich.edu/~rdeyoung/). Given the greater persistence and performance of behaviors that are autonomously motivated, it seems especially important that ecologically friendly behaviors be approached this way. Brown and Kasser (2005) report on two studies (one of middle school and high school students, the other with matched samples of "voluntary simplifiers" and a mainstream population) that show strong correlations between SWB and environmentally responsible behaviors (ERB). "Happier individuals were more likely to report behavior supportive of ecological health" (p. 359). Intrinsic values and mindfulness both promoted higher SWB and ERB. And the relationship may work both ways: Weinstein and colleagues (2009) found that natural settings (vs built) increased participants' intrinsic aspirations toward generosity and decreased their extrinsic values, arguably by meeting autonomy and belonging needs. The needs of the planet appear identical to or consistent with the needs of people.

Kasser's (2011) general recommendations are to first decrease factors that encourage self-interested, materialistic values: social modeling of consumption and insecurity. Second, to promote an alternative set of values, even the ones diametrically opposed to self-enhancement values. A small but substantial movement in this direction in Western countries takes various approaches. One is to try to challenge the advertising system that manufactures needs (see The Media Foundation's popular Adbusters campaign, http://www.adbusters.org/home/). Another is to try to reduce material desires while also helping people more directly fulfill their truer values and seek time affluence. Organizations pioneering this route include the Center for a New American Dream (http://www.newdream.org/) and those promoting voluntary simplicity, such as the Northwest Earth Institute (http://www.nwei.org/). These early, apparently countercurrent efforts may lead to wider change because they provide a "social proof" of alternatives and they widen the range of options upon which cultural selection may operate. There may be more than expected public support for decreasing consumption (Bowerman, 2014). A more ambitious goal would be changing the economic system, for example, by adopting measures of economic performance that incorporate social, psychological, and ecological welfare (Kasser, 2011; Diener & Ryan, 2011).

To return to the question of sacrifice with which we began this section, Hall (2013) considered both the disempowering "gloom and doom" message framing, and "hope and possibility" frame. The latter has both human power and agency (technological optimism), and liberatory alternative lifestyle forms. Without denying the need for positive framings and narratives, Hall cautions against implying that no sacrifice is involved. On a planet already in ecological "overshoot," some cutbacks are necessary to lessen the consequences. Hall's point is that our high footprint lifestyle offers some "genuinely valuable goods" such as the ability to travel long distances to maintain social ties or broaden our cultural experiences. Thus,

> Ignoring this reality is either inaccurate in missing what it is that people value in existing ways of life, or patronizing in implying that people are essentially suffering from false consciousness about what is truly valuable in life. Yet a frame that is inaccurate or patronizing will not be persuasive.
>
> (Hall, 2013, p. 136)

Hall concludes that we must acknowledge and respect other people's existing values and not presume that there is no "true happiness, freedom, or power as things stand" (p. 138). A deeper reflection on sacrifice and rewards is called for.

Optimism and pessimism

Given the entrenchment of materialistic values plus the challenge Hall puts forth to not shy away from acknowledging having to forego things of real value to people now, should we be optimistic or pessimistic about people's response to environmental challenges? What does psychology tell us about optimism and pessimism?

There are at least three ways that optimism and pessimism have been conceptualized in recent psychology: as a result of one's dispositional self-regulation; as a consequence of the explanatory model a person uses; and as aspects of the cognitive strategies one may employ in different circumstances. Because environmentalists often engage in speculation, based on their own experiences, about whether their tactics evoke hope and action or despair and inaction it is worth reviewing these approaches and how they apply.

Self-regulation and expectancies of outcomes

The dispositional self-regulation approach is based in a model of motivation that says people organize their behavior around the pursuit of goals (Carver & Scheier, 2001). A person who experiences difficulties in his or her goal activity may stop and deliberate about the likelihood of success, thinking about conditions, prior experience, etc. This deliberation results in an *expectancy* of success in terms of self-confidence, or self-doubt at being able to achieve the goal. Confident expectancies predict further efforts, whereas doubtful ones predict disengagement or giving up. These results may apply to very specific goals, or broad ones–in the latter case leading to generalized optimism and pessimism about a whole activity or even about one's life.

Carver and Scheier (2001) suggest that a key variable is the importance of the goal in the person's hierarchy of goals. The more important the goal, the more dramatic may be the results on behavior; this may explain why one person will continue trying despite lessening results, while another at the same point would give up.

If people have consistent doubts about the possibility of success in some area, it will be very difficult to get them to keep trying, whereas others with more confidence will not give up even when difficulties are encountered. Effort should increase if expectancies of success are increased and also if individuals with low confidence can be given extra assistance throughout the process of initiating new behaviors. The importance of the goal also matters. If pro-environmental action is not a priority, little action may happen. Ironically, however, the model also cautions against making the goal *too* important, because that is where abrupt discontinuities in the confidence required are perceived. In the self-regulation perspective then, a lot depends on individual traits, and on finding a match between expectancies of success (confidence) and effort.

Explanatory style

One important strand in psychological research related to optimism originated around pessimism, or more accurately, "learned helplessness." In early research, dogs who were experimental subjects were given unpleasant shocks to their feet while contained in enclosures from which they could not escape or even leap up. After a period of learning, the lids were removed so that the dogs could leap out to avoid the shock. But those who had been helpless to escape at first were far less likely to leap out compared to dogs who had not undergone the conditioning. They had learned that attempts to avoid the shock were futile. The phenomenon has been found in many other settings and organisms as well. Human helplessness is different because even uncontrollable bad events can be construed differently, and because in circumstances such as oppression, overt passivity or submissiveness may be an adaptive response. However, humans can learn helplessness vicariously, and small groups can learn and demonstrate helplessness although their members individually show no deficit.

Seligman and colleagues (Abramson et al., 1978) later revised the theory to incorporate a cognitive dimension: how we try to explain the events that happen to us, especially the negative ones. Explanatory styles vary in terms of whether they emphasize factors that are (1) internal versus external; (2) stable versus unstable; and (3) global versus specific. If a negative experience is explained as due to factors that are internal, stable, and global (e.g., "I'm always such an idiot"), that would connote pessimism, and tend to reduce efforts to change one's own behavior to avoid the experience in future. An optimistic explanation would instead focus on external factors that are perceived as specific and changeable ("I was misinformed"). Interestingly, the opposite configuration occurs when explaining a positive outcome: Pessimists explain good events as a result of situational factors that are temporary and specific. It was just lucky things came out right that time! Optimists look at good events as resulting from their own enduring global traits (Gillham et al., 2001).

Optimistic explanatory style is associated with academic achievement, job productivity, fewer doctor visits, higher self-reported health, athletic performance, marital satisfaction, and even political victory: In 9 of 10 US elections between 1948 and 1984, the party candidacy-acceptance speeches of candidates who later lost the presidential contest were scored as more pessimistic and focused on negative events (Zullow & Seligman, 1990). Empirical studies show a strong association between pessimistic style and depressive symptoms; there is also some evidence that pessimistic explanations, especially for negative events, may be a risk factor (causative) for depression (Gillham et al., 2001). Hopelessness theory (Abramson et al., 1978) predicts depression and lack of motivation when causes of negative events are seen as stable and global; when negative or catastrophic consequences are expected; and when negative self-descriptions are used.

The implications of this theory of optimism and pessimism for environmental affairs are provocative. Consider the variables in hopelessness theory. Environmentalists often predict catastrophic consequences for the environment, attribute this degradation to global and stable factors, and imply that humans are greedy and short-sighted. Such environmentalist ideologies may be inadvertently disempowering and paralyzing.

In contrast, Zimmerman (1990) developed a theory of learned hopefulness, which is "a process of learning and utilizing problem-solving skills and the achievement of perceived or actual control" (p. 72). Zimmerman argued that *perceived control* is made up of several components, including self-efficacy (cognitive component), motivation to control (affective), and locus of control (personality). He described the conjunction of these as "psychological empowerment" and found that it was directly affected by amount of participation in neighborhood or campus volunteer organizations, in both a community sample and a student sample. Participation and empowerment were negatively correlated with alienation, in both samples. The key is to modify expectations for personal effectiveness.

Hope theory notes that false hopes are based on poorly chosen goals – either too big or maladaptive (Snyder, 2002; Rand & Cheavens, 2011). A focus on opportunities is a specific form of optimism that predicts engagement over time, even controlling for general optimism (Schmitt et al., 2013). The experience of being directly involved in making incremental positive steps (Weick, 1984), the positive motivational power of finding one's contributions are needed, and the recognition that progress can be found in a psychologically realistic fashion of "muddling" provide an antidote to impatient expectations. The adaptive management process in general (Lee, 1993) also depends on decomposing complex problems into components and tracking successes. An experience of effective participation, even if only partially successful, can train people to be optimists rather than pessimists.

Cognitive strategies

Psychologist Julie Norem (2001a, 2001b), noting that the emphasis on the power of positive thinking did not fit all people, developed a quite different approach to optimism and pessimism based on the notion that people may use different cognitive strategies in different situations. She argued that what she calls "defensive pessimism" can sometimes be highly adaptive. Defensive pessimism is shown by someone who anticipates an upcoming event in a "worst case scenario" fashion, and then actively works to foresee and prevent the various factors that could cause problems. On the other end of her scale is "strategic optimism," where one avoids thinking about what might go wrong, instead relying on a general confidence to carry them through.

These strategies are cognitive styles rather than dispositional traits; individuals vary in how much they use them according to the situation and can be encouraged to use one or the other. In one experiment, defensive pessimists who were told they should expect to do well on a test, thus short-circuiting their adaptive strategy, in fact did more poorly than an equivalent group that was not reassured. In general, strategic optimists and defensive pessimists do comparably well on a range of challenges. But the liabilities of these strategies are different. Defensive pessimists do poorly if overtaken by a positive mood, whereas strategic optimists do poorly when they are required to think about their performances beforehand.

Given its similarity to precautionary principle-based thinking, many readers with strong environmental concerns may recognize themselves in the portrait of defensive pessimists. Even so, it is likely that they use this strategy only in some domains. In areas of greater confidence, they may rely more on present-focused improvisation as do strategic optimists. The message of the cognitive strategy approach for conservation may simply be to drive home how different people adapt differently (and successfully) to similar challenges. Thus, there is a danger in assuming that a single style will work for everyone. Anxiety is an uncomfortable state for most people. Defensive pessimists have learned to harness it, but others may want to steer clear.

The benefits of optimism are well known, but there are downsides to optimism. Optimists, like everyone, are prone to use confirmation bias in selecting which information to attend to. Among those who are highly optimistic, there is a stronger tendency to under-correct when presented with information that is worse than an original estimate, a pattern confirmed in an MRI study, showing less brain activation among optimists in the areas for processing new information, leading to unrealistic estimation errors (Sharot et al., 2011). While this tendency may be good for mental health, it could mean underestimating environmental prognoses that disagree with what optimistic people would like to think. Pessimists, on the other hand, may be more realistic but at some cost to motivation and psychological health.

Optimistic and pessimistic biases in environmental issues

Comparative optimism studies look at how people believe they will fare compared to others. In general, we believe we will do better, or environmental risks will hit us less, than others. In light of these factors, Gifford and colleagues (2009) conducted a large international study investigating how cultures differ in their optimism about environmental quality on local, national, and global scales. In order to test the accuracy of respondents' assessment, national environmental quality data were assessed by an expert panel. Averaged across all 18 countries, respondents rated their present local conditions better (at statistically significant levels) than national or global conditions. Finland, Sweden, and Germany were more positive than most others, and two countries (Spain and Mexico) were more negative than others. Country by country, most demonstrated optimistic spatial bias (that conditions globally were worse than locally), a pattern observed with the impacts of climate change also (Leiserowitz, 2005; Spence et al., 2012). Responses showed robust temporal pessimism: For all spatial levels, people expected conditions to be worse 25 years in the future, and again there were significant differences between countries in their degree of pessimism, with respondents from Finland, Germany, and Canada more pessimistic than five other countries, and Australia more so than 12 other countries. Only in Romania did people feel conditions (at all 3 spatial scales) would be better in the future (Fig. 12.3). Strong positive correlations were found between experts' and respondents' ratings of national environmental conditions, suggesting the countries with more spatial optimism also have better environmental conditions. The complexity of these findings suggest interactions between on-the-ground ecological conditions, experience, and cultural and political characteristics. Interestingly, Milfont et al. (2012) found that being more oriented to the future (but not present or past) was associated with pro-environmental behaviors in a meta-analysis encompassing over 6,000 respondents from seven countries (Australia, Brazil, Germany, Mexico, New Zealand, Norway, and the United States). We might speculate that for optimism to have an effect one must also be oriented toward the future.

Toward strengths-based approaches

As we just saw, many people around the world have a pessimistic outlook on environmental trends, and a fairly accurate sense of their own country's ecological health. This is problematic if people are also pessimistic about our ability to solve these challenges, particularly if they use a pessimistic explanatory style. Many environmental discourses do portray the causes of our

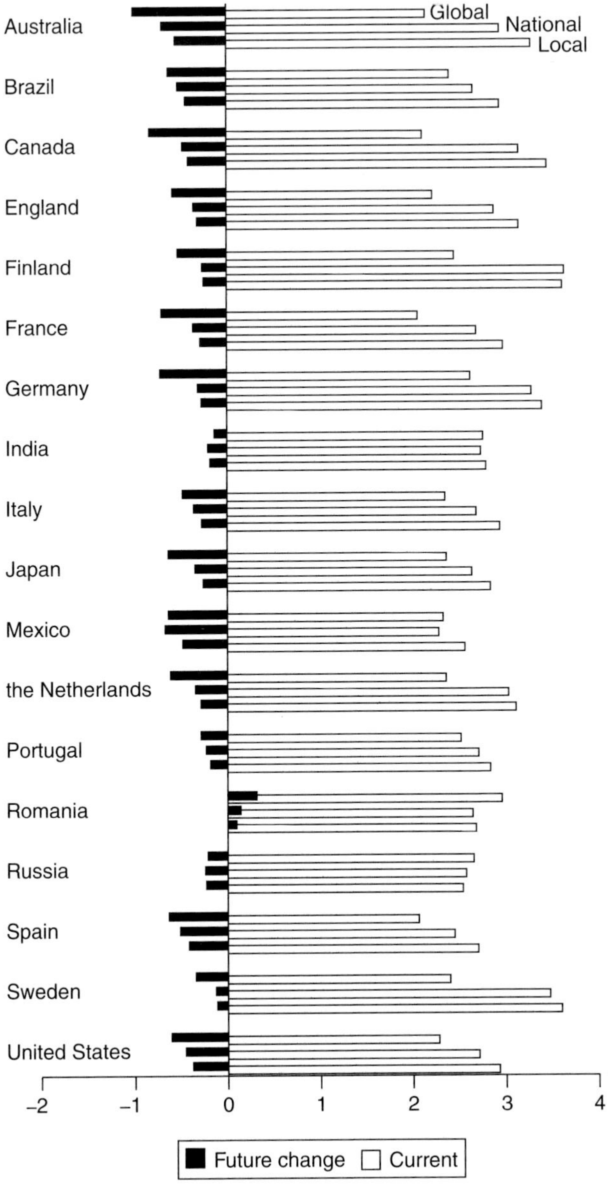

Fig. 12.3 Spatial optimism and temporal pessimism: Mean ratings of current environmental conditions (all above 0) and expected future change (mostly negative) at the local, national, and global spatial levels for 18 countries. (Reprinted from Gifford et al. 2009, p. 7, Figure 2. Copyright 2009, with permission from Elsevier.)

difficulties as stable, general, and internal: capitalism, dysfunctional bureaucracies, patriarchal societies, or human nature, are frequent targets. Just as positive psychology has been a response to an overly negative focus in psychology generally, it can also suggest new approaches in the realm of sustainability. Csikszentmihalyi (2011) asks that we question historical human self-images of supremacy, self-destructiveness, and the shallow consumerist view of happiness, choosing instead to develop a new image of humanity "by focusing attention on ideas and kinds of behavior that people [have] found desirable and valuable in most cultures" (p. 211).

We have reviewed some ways in which the good life – what feels good, what connects us to something larger than ourselves, and what meets our real needs – is consistent with sustainability. In this section, we will expand on a strengths-based approach. Strengths are preexisting capacities that lead to optimal functioning when they are employed. While it is necessary to understand, learn from, and account for human weaknesses, we cannot succeed without the power of humans at their best. We will look into human virtues and character strengths, positive morality, deep engagement and creativity, mindfulness and personal change, and collective flourishing.

Human virtue and character strengths

Character is one of the pillars of positive psychology (Seligman & Csikszentmihalyi, 2000). Positive traits connect to experience, social relationships, institutions, and leadership. Strengths of character are causes of healthy lifelong development and may buffer against negative effects of stress, trauma, and they help people thrive (Peterson & Park, 2009). Peterson and colleagues initially investigated character strengths by exhaustively reviewing contemporary and ancient sources from science and philosophy to literature, the texts of world religions, songs, even graffiti, and more. Virtue ethics (see Chapter 7) also provided guidance, and results were checked in the field in two oral cultures by Biswas-Diener (2006). The six core virtues identified, along with their subcategories, are in Table 12.1 (See Peterson and Seligman, 2004, for full description of these.)

Love, gratitude, hope, curiosity, and zest show strong relationships with psychological well-being in adult outcomes. Other profiles characterize excellence in specific domains. The character traits can be arrayed on axes of focus on self versus other and emphasis on heart versus mind (Fig. 12.4).

Many of these virtues map onto behaviors or virtues identified in the literature as associated with sustainable behaviors. Corral-Verdugo (2012; Corral-Verdugo et al., 2014) highlighted the comparisons in Table 12.2. In addition, both fields refer to responsibility, positive emotion, competency, intrinsic motivation, satisfaction, and psychological well-being.

Using Peterson's Values in Action Survey, a self-report measure of the strengths, Corral-Verdugo et al. (2014) found that in a sample of Mexican participants, all the 24 character strengths correlated as one factor with sustainable behaviors. Character virtues are not independent from each other; there may be a general trait that should be considered "virtuousness" – and it may provide a strong way to promote sustainable behavior. Harzer and Ruch (2012) found that both having positive work experiences, and a sense of "calling" about work depended on the *number* of strengths a job draws on (with a minimum of four signature strengths), so it may be promising that so many strengths align with sustainable choices.

Remarkable demonstrations of strengths include post-traumatic growth and resilience or positive adaptation in the context of significant challenge, adversity, or risk (see Chapter 4). Developmentally, resilience arises from common but powerful factors in the developmental environment such as good parenting, self-regulation skills, and community resources (Masten et al., 2009). Assessing and ensuring that these are not undermined are key to promoting resilience at individual and community levels. A striking strength of character is "grit," or a "combination of very high persistence and high passion for an objective" (Seligman, 2011, p. 118) which accounts for performance beyond the contribution of intelligence (IQ), with which it is not correlated. Grit appears to be built by persisting after failure, by the "intensity, direction

Table 12.1 Values in action classification of strengths.

Wisdom and knowledge
Creativity: thinking of novel and productive ways to do things
Curiosity: taking an interest in all of on-going experience
Open-mindedness: thinking things through and examining them from all sides
Love of learning: mastering new skills, topics, and bodies of knowledge
Perspective: being able to provide wise counsel to others

Courage
Authenticity: speaking the truth and presenting oneself in a genuine way
Bravery: not shrinking from threat, challenge, difficulty, or pain
Perseverance: finishing what one starts
Zest: approaching life with excitement and energy

Humanity and love
Kindness: doing favors and good deeds for others
Love: valuing close relations with others
Social intelligence: being aware of the motives and feelings of self and others

Justice
Fairness: treating all people the same according to notions of fairness and justice
Leadership: organizing group activities and seeing that they happen
Teamwork: working well as a member of a group or team

Temperance
Forgiveness: forgiving those who have done wrong
Modesty: letting one's accomplishments speak for themselves
Prudence: being careful about one's choice
Self-regulation: regulating what one feels and does

Transcendence
Appreciation of beauty and excellence
Gratitude: being aware of and thankful for the good things that happen
Hope: expecting the best and working to achieve it
Humor: liking to laugh and joke, bringing smiles to other people
Religiousness: having coherent beliefs about the higher purpose and meaning of life

From Peterson and Park, 2009, Table 4.1, p. 28. By permission of Oxford University Press, USA.

and duration of one's efforts toward a goal" (Duckworth et al., 2007, p. 1098). Conservation psychology may usefully help people, including environmental activists as well as others who are less active, to identify their strengths and build on them rather than focusing on weaknesses. This may lead to the discovery of routes to sustainability that are not part of the typical environmentalist profile. If environmental pessimists prove correct, understanding and promoting these strengths-in-adversity will be critical.

Other-praising emotions and positive moral psychology

Some virtuous acts have benefits beyond their direct effects by evoking positive "other-praising" emotions. We feel elevated by witnessing acts of virtue or moral beauty (kindness, charity,

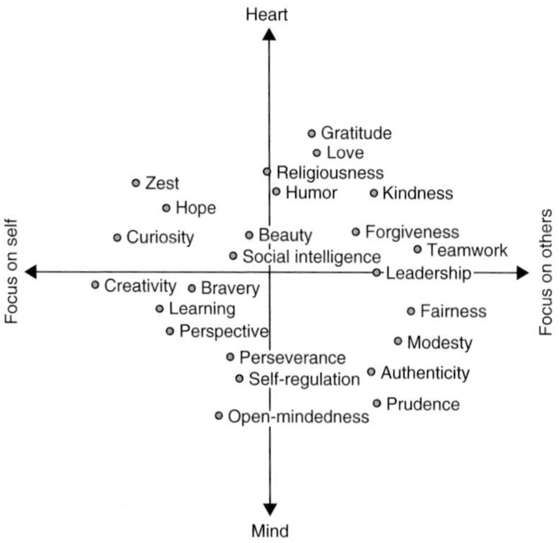

Fig. 12.4 The structure of character. (From Peterson & Park, 2009, Figure 4.1, p. 32. By permission of Oxford University Press, USA.)

Table 12.2 Character strengths and their likely links to sustainable behavior.

Positive psychology	Psychology of sustainability example or correlate (See Corral-Verdugo et al., 2014, for relevant citations)
Creativity	Pro-environmental competency
Curiosity	Environmental knowledge and skills
Open-mindedness	Considering and adopting sustainable lifestyles
Love of learning	Pro-environmental attitudes
Perspective	Pro-environmental persuasion
Bravery	Sustainable actions take effort
Perseverance	Pro-environmental deliberation
Zest	Generated by participation
Humanity, Kindness	Altruism
Social Intelligence	Pro-social competency
Justice, fairness	Equity
Teamwork	Cooperation in environmental conservation
Leadership	Environmental activism
Civic virtues	Pro-environmental norms
Forgiveness	Pro-sociality and altruism
Humility	Predicts pro-environmental behavior
Prudence	Frugality
Self-regulation	Pro-ecological behaviors
Appreciation of beauty	Influences pro-ecological behavior
Hope	Future orientation
Humor	Positive relations
Spirituality	Pro-ecological and altruistic behavior

Adapted from Corral-Verdugo (2012), copyright © 2012. With kind permission from Springer Science and Business Media. And from Corral-Verdugo et al. (2014), copyright © 2014 by Environmental Design Research Association. Reprinted by permission of SAGE Publications.

fidelity). Gratitude is felt when a benefactor is responsive to the felt needs or wishes of the recipient – in other words, is generous. And admiration is a response to display of nonmoral excellence in skill, talent, perseverance, or achievement (Haidt, 2003). Each feeling motivates characteristic positive responses. Elevation gives a warm feeling in the chest, moves one to emulate, to do good deeds, be more open to others, and to become a better person (Cox, 2010; Thomson et al., 2014; Vianello et al., 2010). Gratitude motivates one to repay, praise, and become closer to the benefactor. Admiration produces reports of chills, is energizing and inspiring, making one work harder toward success, emulate and praise the other, and want proximity to him or her (Algoe & Haidt, 2009). Thus, all can bring about higher ethical values or aspirations toward excellence on the part of the one experiencing them.

Each of these emotions might be important in furthering environmentally virtuous acts if we understand more about how they operate. Elevation is not vindication but rather involves upholding the highest standards of moral virtue and depends on the recipient of the good act being of good character. This may be the case when a part of "innocent" nature is helped. Whether this is the case and whether helping "vicious" parts of nature fails to evoke elevation are interesting questions. The presentation of large carnivores in aesthetic and nondisturbing messages suggests many environmental communicators' intuition of the answer. Approbation in response to elevation is increased when the moral deed requires high effort versus low effort (Thomson & Siegel, 2013), suggesting that we might want to avoid suggesting that environmental actions are too easy.

Markowitz (2012) conducted a series of studies to determine how gratitude may function in intergenerational terms. Because gratitude fosters indirect prosocial behaviors toward unrelated others (as opposed to indebtedness which promotes direct tit-for-tat with the giver in response to reciprocity norms) and builds social capital, gratitude could help groups overcome collective action problems like intergenerational issues. As Markowitz hypothesized, across three varied studies gratitude for the actions of others in the past led to increases in responsibility toward future others, concern for the environment, and intergenerational stewardship. Further research could elucidate the circumstances in which prosocial action encourages similar action through elevation, gratitude, or other mechanisms.

More broadly, a positive approach to studying morality is exemplar research, focused on individuals whose cases demonstrate real-world complexity in the enactment of ethical ideals. Matsuba and Pratt (2013; Matsuba et al., 2012) applied this to emerging environmentalists. Interestingly, Walker (2013) argues that such studies reveal that morality is more self-regarding than typical approaches to moral psychology suggest: The self has a meaningful stake in moral action. This is entirely consistent with the emphasis on self-cultivation in the eudaimonistic approach to virtue and well-being.

Engagement and creativity

Earlier we noted the evidence that nature may contribute to creativity, but the capacities for deep engagement and creativity are obvious human strengths in their own right, and psychology has done much to elucidate them. The study of psychological "flow" (see Chapter 4) has revealed the centrality of deep immersion in activities that challenge us to use our abilities to the utmost. Flow makes activities intrinsically rewarding, so deep engagement is a central concept in positive psychology and adds to well-being. Similarly, creativity is widely if not universally celebrated, and comes through deep engagement. The role of flow and creativity in solving the challenges of sustainability needs to be studied, applied (not only in technologies), and highlighted in the framing of these challenges.

The conditions for flow include challenges that just over-reach skills, clear proximate goals, and immediate feedback. On the face of it, however, socio-environmental challenges do not offer these features. Moreover, these challenges may inherently involve ethics. But creativity and flow do not necessarily entail ethical standards. Finally, flow and creativity are commonly understood as properties of individuals, and thus it is not clear how they are linked to social-level problems. How can we understand the nature of engagement and creativity as they are related to conservation?

Although we tend to think of creativity as achieved by a brilliant individual, sometimes in a sudden moment, in reality the process is more complex. Based on the intensive study of highly acclaimed creative individuals, Csikszentmihalyi (1996) argues that creativity is "located" at the three-way intersection of a symbolically structured domain of the culture (such as a discipline or professional practice), the creative individual who creates novelty within that domain, and the field of other experts in the domain. Culture- and society-changing creative acts are ones that change the domain as a result of their recognition and adoption by members of the field. In this way of thinking, attention is centered on the person–context relationship.

The individual, nonetheless, is not discounted. But the majority of the creative individuals studied by Csikszentmihalyi (1996) were not particularly talented, did feel themselves as creative, and rejected the label of "genius," but all had changed the culture. Many individual-level factors influence creativity, such as ideational fluency or an ease with thinking divergently, self-confidence, future orientation, and risk acceptance. Traits contributing to adult creativity are at least moderately heritable, meaning environment may not make much difference for most individuals (Simonton, 2009). But more fundamentally, development involves the active person at the center of a spiral alternation of differentiation (becoming more autonomous in competence and character) and integration (belonging in a network of meanings and relationships): it is a person-context process. The flow model incorporates this dynamic as the person naturally seeks higher level challenges. Over time one product is what Nakamura and Csikszentmihalyi (2009) call "psychological capital," or the metaskills that help a person generalize from experiences of enjoyment to diversify engagement into new areas and to find the preconditions for flow and creativity.

On the context side, large investments from education and social networks provide the scaffolding for individuals to gain deep knowledge and high skill in their domains. Thus, the social organization of knowledge is a precondition for successful novel solutions. Depending on how they are organized, fields incorporate the ethical into their domains. For example, Gardner et al. (2002) show how professional ideals and excellence weave together in the work of journalists and geneticists. Those two fabrics, however, are quite different, again showing the power of domain and field in defining creativity. Another influence of social context is that over cultural evolution, knowledge has become differentiated and more specialized. This would seem to pose a challenge for creativity in interdisciplinary areas such as environmental challenges. Creative individuals, however, thrive on crossing domains and making connections. Contact zones make more ideas available.

Indeed, today crossing domains and making connections often happens in the context of interdisciplinary teams. How do individual- and group-level factors best work together in everyday creativity? A large body of research addresses how to best harness creativity. Here are some examples. A study of interdisciplinary teams funded by the NSF showed that teams originating from the same campus were more effective, leveraging common experience and ease of meeting. Groups work well to widen the range of options – they excel at divergent thinking. But brainstorming groups get fixated and fatigued and pick a solution too early. Starting alone, and iteration, help solve these problems: begin brainstorming with a solitary phase, uninfluenced

Table 12.3 Mindfulness in contrast and comparison to related forms of consciousness.

Form	Contrast or comparison
Forms of consciousness that contrast with mindfulness	
Rumination, absorption in past, fantasy	Pull one away from present
Multitasking, preoccupation	Detract from engagement with focal present
Public self-consciousness; self-monitoring	Preoccupation with perception of self by others
Mindlessness	Automatic, compulsive, defensive behavior
Similar forms of consciousness compared to mindfulness	
Emotional intelligence	Perceptual clarity about emotional states
Big Five openness to experience	Receptive attention similar; but imagination, fantasy, aesthetic interest elements not related
Private self-consciousness	Defined by content (self-knowledge) rather than quality of consciousness
Wakefulness to cognitive tasks (Langer)	Similar but puts more emphasis on active cognitive operations
Reflexive consciousness; self-reflectiveness	Cognitive operation on aspect of self

Source: Based on Brown and Ryan, 2003

by group biases. Then in the group different perspectives spark divergent associations. But this process slows and interaction interferes with reflection. So a stop in the process to let individuals work on their own again is needed. With external pushing, the group can perform better than if left to quit when they feel done (Paulus, 2013).

This literature should be tapped for conservation and education for sustainability (Sandri, 2013). Aslan and colleagues (2014) reviewed barriers to creativity and introduced four basic creativity techniques in the journal *Conservation Biology*: routinely engaging the unfamiliar; meeting people where they are and striving to understand their perspectives; embracing and managing risk; and following the cycle of learning, struggling, and reflecting to generate and assimilate new ideas. They illustrate the boundary-crossing nature of creativity by relating Anker's (2002) historical research into the ideas of early twentieth-century ecologist A.G. Tansley. Interestingly, Tansley, who was himself analyzed by Freud, was very interested in psychoanalysis and his understanding of the psyche as arising from a material organic *system* provided the analogy for his introduction of the term "ecosystem" into ecology.

Mindfulness

Mindfulness is defined by Hanh as "keeping one's consciousness alive to the present reality" (cited in Brown & Ryan, 2003, p. 822). Consciousness, distinct from cognition, motives and emotions, includes awareness (analogous to a background "radar") and attention, which focuses awareness (brings "figure" out from "ground" of awareness). Mindfulness is a quality of open or receptive awareness and attention to internal and/or external events. It is mainly perceptual and prereflexive, and can be contrasted with various other qualities or forms of consciousness as summarized from Brown and Ryan (2003) in Table 12.3.

Different aspects of mindfulness have distinct benefits: *openness* adds cognitive and behavioral flexibility; *nonjudging* and *acting with awareness* aspects predict lower neuroticism and less absent-mindedness, respectively, and both predict lower levels of depression; *nonreactivity* is strongly correlated with self-compassion. Enhancing mindfulness has direct positive effects on self-esteem (Pepping et al., 2013).

Mindfulness is relevant to many aspects of sustainability. It adds vividness to experience, including experiences of nature. It contributes to well-being through aiding self-regulation (disregulation happens when signals are ignored or suppressed). As part of any alternative to materialistic consumer society, it can help people disengage from unwanted mindless and automatic responses, habits, and unhealthy behaviors. It strengthens autonomous functioning, ensuring choices are self-endorsed and congruent with one's needs and values, consistent with SDT (Brown & Ryan, 2003). In seeking to understand the positive relationship they found between SWB and environmentally responsible behavior, Brown and Kasser (2005) found that dispositional mindfulness (together with intrinsically oriented values) was a consistent and strong predictor. Further exploring such correlations, Amel and colleagues (2009) asked whether two facets of mindfulness, "acting with awareness" (the opposite of automatic behavior) and "observing sensations" (related to feeling connected to the world), were related to sustainable behavior choices. They found the former but not the latter was predictive, and indeed there were no outliers where low-awareness action was associated with high self-reported "green" behaviors. In other words, being on "autopilot" predicts choosing the cultural default – higher consumption in the United States. The authors speculate that the lower association of sensory observation and green behaviors suggests that ecopsychology's emphasis on connection to nature may be less relevant to actual behavior change.

Henry (2006) described effective and ineffective approaches to personal change. Those that were ineffective included: exhortation, talking about the problem, analyzing, planning, advice, negative feedback, and obsessing over an issue. We can note that these are common in environmental rhetoric and self-talk. In contrast, more effective approaches included several closely associated with mindfulness: quieting the mind, contemplation, meditation, self-acceptance, self-compassion, letting go, and reflecting and reframing (Henry, 2006). While environmentalists, like everyone, would like to be successful in their endeavors, being tied to successful outcomes invites frustration, resentment, and burnout. A mindful approach can deactivate the evaluative mindset that often implicitly underlies our actions and experiences. Thus Langer (2009) suggests mindfulness is more fundamental than other parts of positive psychology. Mindfulness keeps us open to learning and appreciative of the journey.

Collective flourishing

Positive relationships have been called the key ingredient for all of positive psychology (Seligman, 2011), which is not surprising given humans' highly social nature. Positive relationships are the most cited in what people ascribe importance to, and in to what they attribute their well-being. Every one of the topics in this chapter can be applied to organizations (Donaldson & Ko, 2010) and social collectives as well as to individuals. The roles of positive psychology as a facet of social change has received attention also (Biswas-Diener, 2011). Since the 1990s, empowerment and asset-based approaches to community and social movements have grown (Kretzmann & McKnight, 1993). Because conservation challenges always involve larger levels of social organization beyond the individual, the positive dynamics at collective levels are of crucial importance. We highlight a few emerging facets.

One key positive individual–social level link concerns how younger or less-experienced participants are prepared by older or more experienced ones. Erik Erikson's (1950) psychosocial theory of life stages denoted "generativity" as the second adulthood stage: It involves knowing and pursuing one's purposes in life, one's legacy, and being involved in the nurturance and guidance of the others. Failure to navigate the crisis of this stage results in "stagnation." Generativity is linked to parenthood, but other forms of social generativity are also important. Environmental generativity refers to the fostering of other's care and concern for the environment; recall our earlier discussion of the link to intergenerational gratitude. Environmental generativity has been found to be a motivating force behind environmental activists and an influence on parents' pro-environmental political support, independent of party alignment (Horowitz, 1996; Chan, 2009; Milfont et al., 2012; Matsuba and Pratt, 2013). In a study of environmental activists and matched controls, Matsuba and colleagues concluded that "people who devote much time to environmental causes seem to do so because they are concerned about the future state of our world, their role in contributing to that state, and the implication ... on future generations" (2012, 1109–1110). A related theme in positive development research is positive mentorship (Nakamura et al., 2009). The good mentor deliberately introduces a novice to the domain and field through "immersion in a model microcosm of the professional community" (Nakamura, 2011, p. 197). This model could provide a paradigm for further research and application in the environmental domain.

The emotional burdens of environmental activism can be large (Fraser et al., 2013; Eaton, 2012). Individual coping alone is probably insufficient. In an important contribution to the literature on hope, Christens et al. (2013) advance the notion of critical hopefulness, an attitude that is empirically distinct from those critical but alienated; uncritical but hopeful; or uncritical and unhopeful. Critical hopefulness maintains understanding of the deep systemic, historical, and social roots of a problem, which provides perspective and the ability to interpret present struggles in light of fundamental causes. But rather than this critical, indeed realistic, dimension being disempowering, it coexists with a perceived control over sociopolitical forces – that is, a viable alternative by relating the self to allies past and future. Critical hopefulness thus maintains high levels of both the cognitive (critical) and affective (hope and efficacy) dimensions of political empowerment. People in the critical and hopeful cluster showed higher sense of community, more participation in organizations, and greater mental well-being than those in the other groups. Critical hopefulness depends on strong community support, as provided, for example, by the southern African-American churches in the US civil rights movement.

Whereas positive psychology responds to the question "how can I live well?" sustainability as well as most other problems pose the question "how can we live well together?" In response, Harré (2011) suggests we come to view life less literally: as a game – not to say frivolously – but to give perspective on our choices. She builds on Carse's (1987) philosophy to suggest that life offers us a choice of two kinds of games:

> One is finite games, in which the object is to win and the other is infinite games in which the object is to keep the game in play. Finite games have boundaries, include only select players and have rules that must not change for the duration of the game. In contrast infinite games have horizons that move as the player moves, welcome everyone into the game and the rules must change over time or the game will cease. In fact, when infinite players sense another player is about to lose, they attempt to change the rules to prevent this.
>
> (Harré, http://www.infinite-game.net/)

Can we expand this infinite concept of play – itself no doubt part of the good life – to include the biosphere? Harré has run infinite game workshops with dozens of groups, asking them to generate infinite values: that which is of value for its own sake and makes the world truly alive. The most popular word is "love." Notably, in discussing this, many people say they mean love for all beings (Harré, personal communication). This suggests that the concept of infinite play is a promising way to approach a positive psychology of conservation.

References

Abramson, L. Y., Seligman, M., & Teasdale, J. D. (1978). Learned helplessness in humans: Critique and reformulation. *Journal of Abnormal Psychology*, *87*, 49–74.

Aknin, L., Norton, M. I., & Dunn, E. W. (2009). From wealth to well-being? Money matters, but less than people think. *Journal of Positive Psychology*, *4*, 523–527.

Albrecht, G. (2005). Solastalgia, a new concept in human health and identity. *Philosophy Activism Nature*, *3*, 41–44.

Algoe, S. B., & Haidt, J. (2009). Witnessing excellence in action: The "other-praising" emotions of elevation, gratitude, and admiration. *The Journal of Positive Psychology*, *4*(2), 105–127.

Amel, E. L., Manning, C. M., & Scott, B. A. (2009). Mindfulness and sustainable behavior: Pondering attention and awareness as means for increasing green behavior. *Ecopsychology*, *1*(1), 14–25.

Anker, P. (2002). The context of ecosystem theory. *Ecosystems*, *5*(7), 611–613.

Argyle, M. (1987). *The psychology of happiness*. New York: Methuen.

Aslan, C. E., Pinsky, M. L., Ryan, M. E., Souther, S., & Terrell, K. A. (2014). Cultivating creativity in conservation science: Creativity in conservation science. *Conservation Biology*, *28*(2), 345–353.

Atchley, R. A., Strayer, D. L., & Atchley, P. (2012). Creativity in the wild: Improving creativity reasoning through immersion in natural settings. *PLoS ONE*, *7*, 1–3.

Baumeister, R. F., Bratslavsky, E., Finkenauer, C., & Vohs, K. D. (2001). Bad is stronger than good. *Review of General Psychology*, *5*, 323–370.

Baumeister, R. F., Vohs, K. D., Aaker, J. L., & Garbinsky, E. N. (2013). Some key differences between a happy life and a meaningful life. *The Journal of Positive Psychology*, *8*(6), 505–516.

Berman, M. G., Jonides, J., & Kaplan, S. (2008). The cognitive benefits of interacting with nature. *Psychological Science*, *19*, 1207–1212.

Berman, M. G., Kross, E., Krpan, K. M., Askren, M. K., Burson, A., Deldin, P. J., et al. (2012). Interacting with nature improves cognition and affect for individuals with depression. *Journal of Affective Disorder*, *140*, 300–305.

Biswas-Diener, R. (2006). From the equator to the north pole: A study of character strengths. *Journal of Happiness Studies*, *7*, 293–310.

Biswas-Diener, R. (Ed.) (2011). *Positive psychology as social change*. New York: Springer.

Biswas-Diener, R. & Patterson, L. (2011). Positive psychology and poverty. In. R. Biswas-Diener (Ed.), *Positive psychology as social change* (pp. 125–140). New York: Springer.

Bonaiuto, M. & Alves, S. (2012). Residential places and neighborhoods: Toward healthy life, social integration, and reputable residence. In S. Clayton (Ed.), *Oxford handbook of environmental and conservation psychology* (pp. 221–247). New York: Oxford University Press.

Bonaiuto, M. (2013). *Positive environment.* Keynote paper presented at the meeting of the Third World Congress on Positive Psychology, Los Angeles, CA.

Bowerman, T. (2014). How much is too much? A public opinion research perspective. *Sustainability: Science, Practice, & Policy*, *10*(1), 14–28.

Bronk, C. K., Hill, P. L., Lapsley, D. K., Talib, T. L., & Finch, H. (2009). Purpose, hope, and life satisfaction in three age groups. *The Journal of Positive Psychology*, *4*(6), 500–510.

Brown, K. W., & Kasser, T. (2005). Are psychological and ecological well-being compatible? The role of values, mindfulness, and lifestyle. *Social Indicators Research*, *74*(2), 349–368.

Brown, K. W., & Ryan, R. M. (2003). The benefits of being present: Mindfulness and its role in psychological well-being. *Journal of Personality and Social Psychology, 84*(4), 822–848.

Buzzell, L. & Chalquist, C. (Eds.). (2009). *Ecotherapy: Healing with nature in mind*. San Francisco, CA: Sierra Club Books.

Carse, J. P. (1987). *Finite and infinite games: A vision of life as play and possibility*. New York: Ballantine.

Carter, D. M. (2011). Recognizing the role of positive emotions in fostering environmentally responsible behaviors. *Ecopsychology, 3*(1), 65–69.

Carver, C. & Scheier, M. (2001). Optimism, pessimism & self-regulation. In E. C. Chang (Ed.), *Optimism and pessimism: Implications for theory, research and practice* (pp. 31–51). Washington, DC: American Psychological Association.

Cervinka, R., Röderer, K., & Hefler, E. (2012). Are nature lovers happy? On various indicators of well-being and connectedness with nature. *Journal of Health Psychology, 17*(3), 379–388.

Chan, T. S. (2009). *Environmental sustainability as a generative concern*. Unpublished doctoral dissertation, Northwestern University, Evanston, IL.

Chawla, L. (1990). Ecstatic places. *Children's Environments Quarterly, 7*(4), 18–23.

Christens, B. D., Collura J.J. & Tahir, F. (2013). Critical hopefulness: A person-centered analysis of the intersection of cognitive and emotional empowerment. *American Journal of Community Psychology, 52*, 170–184.

Cobb, E. (1977). *The ecology of imagination in childhood*. New York: Columbia University Press. (Original work published 1959).

Corral-Verdugo, V. (2012). The positive psychology of sustainability. *Environment, Development and Sustainability, 14*(5), 651–666.

Corral-Verdugo, V., Mireles-Acosta, J., Tapia-Fonllem, C., & Fraijo-Sing, B. (2011). Happiness as correlate of sustainable behavior: A study of pro-ecological, frugal, equitable and altruistic actions that promote subjective wellbeing. *Human Ecology Review, 18*(2), 95–104.

Corral-Verdugo, V., Tapia-Fonllem, C., & Ortiz-Valdez, A. (2014). On the relationship between character strengths and sustainable behavior. *Environment and Behavior. First published on April 17, 2014.*

Cosco, N.G., Moore, R. C., & Smith, W.R. (2014). Childcare outdoor renovation as a built environment health promotion strategy: Evaluating the preventing obesity by design intervention. *American Journal of Health Promotion, 28* (3 Suppl): S27–S32

Cox, K. S. (2010). Elevation predicts domain-specific volunteerism 3 months later. *The Journal of Positive Psychology, 5*(5), 333–341

Crain, W. & Crain, E. F. (2014). The benefits of the green environment. In P. J. Landigan & R. E. Etzel (Eds.), *Textbook of children's environmental health* (pp. 162–170). New York: Oxford University Press.

Csikszentmihalyi, M. (1996). *Creativity: The psychology of discovery and invention*. New York: Harper Collins.

Csikszentmihalyi, M. (2011). Positive psychology and a positive world-view: New hope for the future of humankind. In S.I. Donaldson, M. Csikszentmihalyi & J. Nakamura (Eds.), *Applied positive psychology* (pp. 205–213). New York: Psychology Press.

Dallimer, M., Irvine, K. N., Skinner, A. M. J., Davies, Z. G., Rouquette, J. R., Maltby, L. L., et al. (2012). Biodiversity and the feel-good factor: Understanding associations between self-reported human well-being and species richness. *BioScience, 62*(1), 47–55.

Deci, E. L. & Ryan, R. M. (1985). *Intrinsic motivation and self-determination in human behavior*. New York: Plenum.

Deci, E. L. & Ryan, R. (2000). The "what" and "why" of goal pursuits: Human needs and the self-determination of behavior. *Psychological Inquiry, 11*, 227–268.

Deci, E. L. & Ryan, R. M. (2008). Facilitating optimal motivation and psychological well-being across life's domains. *Canadian Psychology, 49*(1), 14–23.

Delle Fave, A., Brdar, I., Wissing, M. P., & Vella-Brodrick, D. A. (2013). Sources and motives for personal meaning in adulthood. *The Journal of Positive Psychology, 8*(6), 517–529.

De Young, R. (1985–1986). Encouraging environmentally appropriate behavior: The role of intrinsic motivation. *Journal of Environmental Systems, 15*, 281–292.

De Young, R. (1996). Some psychological aspects of reduced consumption behavior: The role of intrinsic satisfaction and competence motivation. *Environment and Behavior*, *28*, 358–409.

De Young, R. & Kaplan, S. (1985–1986). Conservation behavior and the structure of satisfactions. *Journal of Environmental Systems*, *15*, 233–242.

Diener, E., & Emmons, R. A. (1984). The independence of positive and negative affect. *Journal of Personality and Social Psychology*, *47*, 1105–1117.

Diener, E. & Ryan, K. (2011). National accounts of well-being for public policy. In S.I. Donaldson, M. Csikszentmihalyi & J. Nakamura (Eds.), *Applied positive psychology* (pp. 15–32). New York: Psychology Press.

Dietz, T., Rosa, E. A., & York, R. (2007). Driving the human ecological footprint. *Frontiers in Ecology and the Environment*, *5*(1), 13–18.

Donaldson, S. I., & Ko, I. (2010). Positive organizational psychology, behavior, and scholarship: A review of the emerging literature and evidence base. *The Journal of Positive Psychology*, *5*(3), 177–191.

Duckworth, A.L., Peterson, C., Matthews, M.D., & Kelly, D.R. (2007). Grit: Perseverance and passion for long-term goals. *Personality Processes and Individual Differences*, *92*(6), 1087–1101.

Dunn, E., Gilbert, D., & Wilson, T. (2011). If money doesn't make you happy, you probably aren't spending it right. *Journal of Consumer Psychology*, *21*, 115–125.

Dyment, J. E., Bell, A. C. & Lucas, A. J. (2009). The relationship between school ground design and intensity of physical activity. *Children's Geographies*, *7*(3), 261–276.

Eaton, M. (2012). Environmental trauma and grief. Curriculum for the Bioregion Collection. Available at: http://serc.carleton.edu/bioregion/sustain_contemp_lc/essays/67207.html

Erikson, E. (1950). *Childhood and Society*. New York: Norton.

Feinberg, M., & Willer, R. (2011). Apocalypse soon?: Dire messages reduce belief in global warming by contradicting just-world beliefs. *Psychological Science*, *22*(1), 34–38.

Feygina, I., Jost, J. T., & Goldsmith, R. E. (2010). System justification, the denial of global warming, and the possibility of "system-sanctioned change." *Personality and Social Psychology Bulletin*, *36*(3), 326–338.

Fischer, J. L., Frederick, H. I., Niehuis, S., Sollie, D., Jordan, R. E., Corwin, M., et al. (2014). Cross-sectional and longitudinal predictors of well-being: Invariance across 25 years. *The Journal of Positive Psychology*, *9*(4), 350–365.

Fjørtoft, I. (2004). Landscape as playscape: The effects of natural environments on children's play and motor development. *Children, Youth and Environments*, *14*(2), 21–44.

Fraser, J., Pantesco, V., Plemons, K., Gupta, R., & Rank, S. J. (2013). Sustaining the conservationist. *Ecopsychology*, *5*(2), 70–79.

Fredrickson, B.L. (2001). The role of positive emotions in positive psychology. *American Psychologist*, *56*(3), 218–226.

Fredrickson, B. L. (2009). *Positivity*. New York: Crown Publishers.

Fredrickson, B. L. (2013). *Love 2.0*. New York: Hutton Street Press.

Fredrickson, B. L. & Kurtz, L. E. (2011). Cultivating positive emotions to enhance human flourishing. In S.I. Donaldson, M. Csikszentmihalyi & J. Nakamura (Eds.), *Applied positive psychology* (pp. 33–45). New York: Psychology Press.

Fredrickson, B. L. & Losada, M. F. (2005). Positive affect and the complex dynamics of human flourishing. *American Psychologist*, *60*, 678–686.

Fredrickson, L. M., & Anderson, D. H. (1999). A qualitative exploration of the wilderness experience as a source of spiritual inspiration. *Journal of Environmental Psychology*, *19*, 21–39.

Fritsche, I., & Hafner, K. (2012). The malicious effects of existential threat on motivation to protect the natural environment and the role of environmental identity as a moderator. *Environment and Behavior*, *44*(4), 570–590.

Fritsche, I., Jonas, E., Kayser, D. N., & Koranyi, N. (2010). Existential threat and compliance with pro-environmental norms. *Journal of Environmental Psychology*, *30*(1), 67–79.

Fuller, R., Irvine, K., Devine-Wright, P., Warren, P. & Gaston, K. (2007). Psychological benefits of greenspace increase with biodiversity. *Biology Letters* *3*(3), 390–394.

Furlong, M. J., Gilmore, R. & Huebner, E. S. (2014). *Handbook of positive psychology in schools* (2nd ed.). New York: Routledge.

Gardner, H., Csikszentmihalyi, M. & Damon, W. (2002). *Good work: When excellence and ethics meet.* New York: Basic Books.

Gifford, R., Scannell, L., Kormos, C., Smolova, L., Biel, A., Boncu, S., et al. (2009). Temporal pessimism and spatial optimism in environmental assessments: An 18-nation study. *Journal of Environmental Psychology*, *29*(1), 1–12.

Gillham, J., Shatté, A., Reivich, K. & Seligman, M. (2001). Optimism, pessimism and explanatory style. In E. C. Chang (Ed.), *Optimism and pessimism: Implications for theory, research and practice* (pp. 53–75). Washington, DC: American Psychological Association.

Greenberg, J., Solomon, S., & Pyszczynski, T. (1997). Terror management theory of self-esteem and cultural worldviews: Empirical assessments and conceptual refinements. In M. P. Zanna (Ed.), *Advances in experimental social psychology*, *29* (pp. 61–139). San Diego: Academic Press.

Gross, J. J. & Thompson, R. A. (2007). Emotion regulation: Conceptual foundations. In J. J. Gross (Ed.), *Handbook of emotion regulation* (pp. 3–24). New York: Guilford Press.

Grouzet, F. M. E, Kasser, T., Ahuvia, A., Fernandez-Dols, J. M., Kim, Y., Lau, S. et al. (2005). The structure of goal contents across 15 cultures. *Journal of Personality and Social Psychology*, *89*, 800–816.

Güsewell, A., & Ruch, W. (2012). Are there multiple channels through which we connect with beauty and excellence? *Journal of Positive Psychology*, *7*, 516–529.

Haidt, J. (2003). Elevation and the positive psychology of morality. In C. L. M. Keyes & J. Haidt (Eds.), *Flourishing: Positive psychology and the life well-lived* (pp. 275–289). Washington DC: American Psychological Association.

Hall, C. (2013). What will it mean to be green? Envisioning positive possibilities without dismissing loss. *Ethics, Policy & Environment*, *16*(2), 125–141.

Hanski I., von Hertzen L., Fyhrquist N., Koskinen K., Torppa K., et al. (2012). Environmental biodiversity, human microbiota, and allergy are interrelated. *Proceedings of the National Academy of Science*, *109*, 8334–8339.

Harré, N. (2011). *Psychology for a better world: Strategies to inspire sustainability.* Available at: https://cdn.auckland.ac.nz/assets/psych/about/our-people/documents/Psychology%20for%20a%20Better%20World.pdf

Harrison, P. R., & Mallett, R. K. (2013). Mortality salience motivates the defense of environmental values and increases collective ecoguilt. *Ecopsychology*, *5*(1), 36–43.

Hartig, T., Mang, M. & Evans, G. W. (1991). Restorative effects of natural environment experiences. *Environment and Behavior*, *23*(1), 3–26.

Hartig, T., Mitchell, R., de Vries, S., & Frumkin, H. (2014). Nature and health. *Annual Review of Public Health*, *35*(1), 207–228.

Harzer, C., & Ruch, W. (2012). When the job is a calling: The role of applying one's signature strengths at work. *The Journal of Positive Psychology*, *7*(5), 362–371.

Health Council of the Netherlands (2004). Nature and health: The influence of nature on social, psychological, and physical well-being. The Hague: Health Council of the Netherlands and RMNO. Publication number 2004/09E, RMNO publication number A02ae. Available at www.healthcouncil.nl

Henry, J. (2006). Strategies for achieving well-being. In Csikszentmihalyi, M. & Csikszentmihalyi, I. S. (Eds.) *A life worth living: Contributions to positive psychology* (pp. 120–142). New York: Oxford University Press.

Herzog, T.R., Black, A.M., Fountaine, K.A., & Knotts, D.J. (1997). Reflection and attentional recovery as distinctive benefits of restorative environments. *Journal of Environmental Psychology*, *17*, 165–170.

Herzog, T. R., Chen, H. & Primeau, J. (2002). Perception of the restorative potential of natural and other settings. *Journal of Environmental Psychology*, *22*(3), 295–306.

Herzog, T. R., & Strevey, S. J. (2008). Contact with nature, sense of humor, and psychological well-being. *Environment and Behavior*, *40*(6), 747–776.

Herzog, T. R., Hayes, L. J., Applin, R. C., & Weatherly, A. M. (2011). Incompatibility and mental fatigue. *Environment and Behavior*, *43*(6), 827–847.

Hill, P. L., Sumner, R., & Burrow, A. L. (2014). Understanding the pathways to purpose: Examining personality and well-being correlates across adulthood. *The Journal of Positive Psychology*, *9*(3), 227–234.

Hinds, J., & Sparks, P. (2009). Investigating environmental identity, well-being, and meaning. *Ecopsychology*, *1*(4), 181–186.

Horowitz, W. A. (1996). Developmental origins of environmental ethics: The life experiences of activists. *Ethics and Behavior*, *61*, 231–256.

Howell, A. J., Dopko, R. L., Passmore, H.-A., & Buro, K. (2011). Nature connectedness: Associations with well-being and mindfulness. *Personality and Individual Differences*, *51*(2), 166–171.

Howell, A. J., & Passmore, H. A. (2013). The nature of happiness: Nature affiliation and mental well-being. In Keyes, C. L. M. (Ed.) *Mental well-being: International contributions to the study of positive mental health* (pp. 231–257). Netherlands: Springer.

Howell, R. T., & Howell, C. J. (2008). The relation of economic status to subjective well-being in developing countries: A meta-analysis. *Psychological Bulletin*, *134*(4), 536–560.

Hurst, M., Dittmar, H., Bond, R., & Kasser, T. (2013). The relationship between materialistic values and environmental attitudes and behaviors: A meta-analysis. *Journal of Environmental Psychology*, *36*, 257–269.

Huta, V., & Ryan, R. M. (2010). Pursuing pleasure or virtue? The differential and overlapping well-being benefits of hedonic and eudaimonic motives. *Journal of Happiness Studies*, *11*, 735–762.

Ingulli, K., & Lindbloom, G. (2013). Connection to nature and psychological resilience. *Ecopsychology*, *5*(1), 52–55.

Johnsen, S. A. K. (2011). The use of nature for emotion regulation: Toward a conceptual framework. *Ecopsychology*, *3*(3), 175–185.

Jørgensen, I. S. & Nafstad H. E. (2004). Positive psychology: Historical, philosophical, and epistemological perspectives. In P. A. Linley & S. Joseph (Eds.), *Positive psychology in practice* (pp. 15–34). New York: John Wiley.

Joshanloo, M., & Weijers, D. (2014). Aversion to happiness across cultures: A review of where and why people are averse to happiness. *Journal of Happiness Studies*, *15*(3), 717–735.

Kahn, P. H. Jr., (2011). *Technological nature: Adaptation and the future of human life*. Cambridge, MA: MIT Press.

Kaiser, F. G., & Byrka, K. (2011). Environmentalism as a trait: Gauging people's prosocial personality in terms of environmental engagement. *International Journal of Psychology*, *46*(1), 71–79.

Kals, E. & Müller, M. M. (2012). Emotions and environment. In S. Clayton (Ed.), *Oxford handbook of environmental and conservation psychology* (pp. 128–147). New York: Oxford University Press.

Kals, E., Schumacher, D. & L. Mondata, L. (1999). Emotional affinity toward nature as a motivational basis to protect nature. *Environment and Behavior*, *31*, 178–202.

Kamitsis, I., & Francis, A. J. P. (2013). Spirituality mediates the relationship between engagement with nature and psychological wellbeing. *Journal of Environmental Psychology*, *36*, 136–143.

Kaplan, R., & Kaplan, S. (1989). *The experience of nature: A psychological perspective*. Cambridge University Press.

Kaplan, R. & Kaplan, S. (2008). Bringing out the best in people: A psychological perspective. *Conservation Biology*, *22*(4), 826–829.

Kaplan, S. (1990). Being needed, adaptive muddling and human-environment relationships. In R. I. Selby, K. H. Anthony, J. Choi & B. Orland (Eds.), *EDRA 21*. Oklahoma City: Environmental Design Research Association.

Kaplan, S. (1995). The restorative benefits of nature: Toward an integrative framework. *Journal of Environmental Psychology*, *15*, 169–182.

Kaplan, S. & Kaplan, R. (1982). *Cognition and environment: Functioning in an uncertain world*. New York: Praeger.

Kaplan, S., & Kaplan, R. (2009). Creating a larger role for environmental psychology: The Reasonable Person Model as an integrative framework. *Journal of Environmental Psychology*, *29*(3), 329–339.

Kasser, T. (2002). *The high price of materialism*. Cambridge, MA: MIT Press.

Kasser, T. (2009). Psychological need satisfaction, personal well-being, and ecological sustainability. *Ecopsychology*, *1*(4), 175–180

Kasser, T. (2011). Ecological challenges, materialistic values, and social change. In. R. Biswas-Diener (Ed.), *Positive psychology as social change* (pp. 89–108). New York: Springer.

Keltner, D., & Haidt, J. (2003). Approaching awe, a moral, spiritual, and aesthetic emotion. *Cognition and Emotion, 17*, 297–314.

Kinnafick, F.-E., & Thøgersen-Ntoumani, C. (2014). The effect of the physical environment and levels of activity on affective states. *Journal of Environmental Psychology, 38*, 241–251.

Kitzes, J., Wackernagel, M., Loh, J., Peller, A., Goldfinger, S., Cheng, D., & Tea, K., (2008). Shrink and share: Humanity's present and future ecological footprint. *Philosophical Transactions of the Royal Society B: Biological Sciences, 363*(1491), 467–475.

Kjellgren, A., & Buhrkall, H. (2010). A comparison of the restorative effect of a natural environment with that of a simulated natural environment. *Journal of Environmental Psychology, 30*(4), 464–472.

Korpela, K., Borodulin, K., Neuvonen, M., Paronen, O., & Tyrväinen, L. (2014). Analyzing the mediators between nature-based outdoor recreation and emotional well-being. *Journal of Environmental Psychology, 37*, 1–7.

Kretzmann, J. P. & McKnight, J. L. (1993). *Building communities from the inside out: A path toward finding and mobilizing a community's assets.* Chicago, IL: ACTA Publications.

Kroeber, A. (2011). China's consumption paradox: Causes and consequences. *Eurasian Geography and Economics, 52*(3), 330–346.

Langer, E. (2009). Mindfulness versus positive evaluation. In Lopez, S. J. & Snyder, C. R. (Eds.), *Oxford handbook of positive psychology* (2nd ed.) (pp. 279–293). New York: Oxford University Press.

Lee, K. (1993). *Compass and gyroscope: Integrating science and politics for the environment.* Washington DC: Island Press.

Leiserowitz, A. A. (2005). American risk perceptions: Is climate change dangerous? *Risk Analysis, 25*(6), 1433–1442.

Lerner, R. M. (2005). Positive youth development: A view of the issues. *Journal of Early Adolescence, 25*(1), 10–16.

Lerner, R. M. (2011). The positive youth development perspective. In S. J. Lopez, & C. R. Snyder (Eds.), *Oxford handbook of positive psychology* (2nd ed) (pp. 149–163). New York: Oxford University Press.

Litfin, K. (2010). The sacred and the profane in the ecological politics of sacrifice. In M. Maniates & J. M. Meyer (Eds.), *The environmental politics of sacrifice* (pp. 117–143). Cambridge, MA: MIT Press.

Maas, J., Verheij, R., Groenewegen, P., de Vries, S. & Spreeuwenberg, P., (2006). Green space, urbanity and health: How strong is the relationship? *Journal of Epidemiology and Community Health, 60*, 587–592.

Maniates, M. (2010). Struggling with sacrifice: Take back your time and Right2Vacation.org. In M. Maniates & J. M. Meyer (Eds.), *The environmental politics of sacrifice* (pp. 293–312). Cambridge, MA: MIT Press.

Maslow, A. H. (1954). *Motivation and personality.* New York: Harper and Row.

Markowitz, E. M. (2012). *Affective and moral roots of environmental stewardship: The role of obligation, gratitude and compassion.* Unpublished doctoral dissertation, University of Oregon, Eugene.

Markowitz, E. M., Goldberg, L. R., Ashton, M. C., & Lee, K. (2012). Profiling the "Pro-Environmental Individual": A personality perspective. *Journal of Personality, 80*(1), 81–111.

Markowitz, E. M., Slovic, P., Västfjäll, D., & Hodges, S. D. (2013). Compassion fade and the challenge of environmental conservation. *Judgment and Decision Making, 8*(4), 397–406.

Masten, A. S., Cutuli, J. J., Herbers, J. E., Reed, M-G. J. (2009). Resilience in development. In S. J. Lopez, & C. R. Snyder (Eds.), *Oxford handbook of positive psychology* (2nd ed.) (pp. 117–131). New York: Oxford University Press.

Matsuba, M. K. & Pratt, M. W. (2013). The making of an environmental activist: A developmental psychological perspective. In M. K. Matsuba, P. E. King & K. C Bronk (Eds.), *Exemplar methods and research: Strategies for investigation* (pp. 59–74). New Directions for Child and Adolescent Development No. 142. San Francisco: Jossey-Bass.

Matsuba, M. K., Pratt, M. W., Norris, J. E., Mohle, E., Alisat, S. & McAdams, D. P. (2012). Environmentalism as a context for expressing identity and generativity. *Journal of Personality, 24*, 1091–1115.

Mayer, F. S., & Frantz, C. M. (2004). The Connectedness to Nature Scale: A measure of individuals' feeling in community with nature. *Journal of Environmental Psychology, 24*, 504–515.

Mayer, F. S., Frantz, C. M., Bruehlman-Senecal, E., & Dolliver, K. (2009). Why is nature beneficial?: The role of connectedness to nature. *Environment and Behavior, 41*(5), 607–643.

Milfont, T. L., Wilson, J., & Diniz, P. (2012). Time perspective and environmental engagement: A meta-analysis. *International Journal of Psychology, 47*(5), 325–334.

Murdoch, I. (1967). *The sovereignty of good over other concepts*. New York: Cambridge University Press.

Nakamura, J. (2011). Contexts of positive adult development. In S.I. Donaldson, M. Csikszentmihalyi & J. Nakamura (Eds.), *Applied positive psychology* (pp. 185–202). New York: Psychology Press.

Nakamura, J., Shernoff, D. & Hooker, C. (2009). *Good mentoring*. San Francisco: Jossey-Bass.

Nakamura, J. & Csikszentmihalyi, M. (2009). Flow theory and research. In S. J. Lopez, & C. R. Snyder (Eds.), *Oxford handbook of positive psychology* (2nd ed) (pp. 195–206). New York: Oxford University Press.

Norem, J. K. (2001a). Defensive pessimism, optimism, and pessimism. In E. C. Chang (Ed.), *Optimism and pessimism: Implications for theory, research and practice* (pp. 77–100). Washington, DC: American Psychological Association.

Norem, J. K. (2001b). *The positive power of negative thinking*. Cambridge, MA: Perseus.

Nisbet, E. K., & Zelenski, J. M. (2011). Underestimating nearby nature: Affective forecasting errors obscure the happy path to sustainability. *Psychological Science, 22*(9), 1101–1106.

Nisbet, E. K., Zelenski, J. M., & Murphy, S. A. (2009). The nature relatedness scale: Linking individuals' connection with nature to environmental concern and behavior. *Environment and Behavior, 41*(5), 715–740.

Nisbet, E. K., Zelenski, J. M., & Murphy, S. A. (2011). Happiness is in our nature: Exploring nature relatedness as a contributor to subjective well-being. *Journal of Happiness Studies, 12*(2), 303–322.

Norgaard, K. (2011). *Living in denial*. Cambridge, MA: MIT Press.

O'Brien, C. (2012). Sustainable happiness and well-being: Future directions for positive psychology. *Psychology, 3*(12A), 1196–1201.

Ojala, M. (2012). How do children cope with global climate change? Coping strategies, engagement, and well-being. *Journal of Environmental Psychology, 32*(3), 225–233.

Parsons, R., Tassinary, L, Ulrich, R., Hebl, M., & Grossman-Alexander, M. (1998). The view from the road: Implications for stress recovery and immunization. *Journal of Environmental Psychology, 18*, 113–139.

Passmore, H.-A., & Howell, A. J. (2014). Nature involvement increases hedonic and eudaimonic well-being: A two-week experimental study. *Ecopsychology, 6*(3), 148–154.

Paulus, P. (2013). Interview: Paul Paulus on Group Creativity. *Creativity and Innovation Management, 22*(1), 96–99.

Pepping, C. A., O'Donovan, A., & Davis, P. J. (2013). The positive effects of mindfulness on self-esteem. *The Journal of Positive Psychology, 8*(5), 376–386.

Peterson, A. (2010). Ordinary and extraordinary sacrifices: Religion, everyday life, and environmental practice. In M. Maniates & J. M. Meyer (Eds.), *The environmental politics of sacrifice* (pp. 91–115). Cambridge, MA: MIT Press.

Peterson, C. & Park, N. (2009). Classifying and measuring strengths of character. In S. J. Lopez, & C. R. Snyder (Eds.), *Oxford handbook of positive psychology* (2nd ed) (pp. 25–33). New York: Oxford University Press.

Peterson, C., & Seligman, M.E.P. (2004). *Character strengths and virtues: A handbook and classification*. New York: Oxford University Press.

Pretty, J. (2004). How nature contributes to mental and physical health. *Spirituality and Health International, 5*(2), 68–78.

Pretty, J. N., Griffin, M., Sellens, M. & Pretty, C. J. (2003). Green exercise: Complementary roles of nature, exercise and diet in physical and emotional well-being and implications for public health policy. CES Occassional Paper 2003–1. University of Essex.

Pretty, J., Peacock, J., Hine, R., Sellens, M., South, N., & Griffin, M. (2007). Green exercise in the UK countryside: Effects on health and psychological well-being, and implications for policy and planning. *Journal of Environmental Planning and Management*, *50*(2), 211–231.

Rand, K. L. & Cheavens, J. S. (2011). Hope theory. In S. J. Lopez, & C. R. Snyder (Eds.), *Oxford handbook of positive psychology* (2nd ed.) (pp. 323–333). New York: Oxford University Press.

Russell, R., Guerry, A. D., Balvanera, P., Gould, R. K., Basurto, X., Chan, K. M. A., et al. (2013). Humans and nature: How knowing and experiencing nature affect well-being. *Annual Review of Environment and Resources*, *38*(1), 473–502

Ryan, R. M., Weinstein, N., Bernstein, J., Brown, K. W., Mistretta, L., & Gagné, M. (2010). Vitalizing effects of being outdoors and in nature. *Journal of Environmental Psychology*, *30*(2), 159–168.

Salovey, P. Mayer, J.D., Caruso, D. & Yoo, S. H. (2009). The positive psychology of emotional intelligence. In S. J. Lopez, & C. R. Snyder (Eds.), *Oxford handbook of positive psychology* (2nd ed.) (pp. 237–248). New York: Oxford University Press.

Sandri, O. J. (2013). Exploring the role and value of creativity in education for sustainability. *Environmental Education Research*, *19*(6), 765–778.

Sato, I., & Conner, T. S. (2013). The quality of time in nature: How fascination explains and enhances the relationship between nature experiences and daily affect. *Ecopsychology*, *5*(3), 197–204.

Schmitt, A., Gielnik, M. M., Zacher, H., & Klemann, D. K. (2013). The motivational benefits of specific versus general optimism. *The Journal of Positive Psychology*, *8*(5), 425–434.

Schwartz, S.H. (1992). Universals in the content and structure of values: Theoretical advances and empirical tests in 20 countries. In M.P. Zanna, (ed.) *Advances in Experimental Social Psychology*, *25* (pp. 1–65). Orlando: Academic Press.

Seligman, M. (2011). *Flourish*. New York: Free Press.

Seligman, M. E. P., & Csikszentmihalyi, M. (2000). Positive psychology: An introduction. *American Psychologist*, *55*(1), 5–14.

Sharot, T., Korn, C. W., & Dolan, R. J. (2011). How unrealistic optimism is maintained in the face of reality. *Nature Neuroscience*, *14*(11), 1475–1479.

Shiota, M. N., Keltner, D., & Mossman, A. (2007). The nature of awe: Elicitors, appraisals, and effects on self-concept. *Cognition and Emotion*, *21*, 944–963.

Simonton, D. K. (2009). Creativity. In S. J. Lopez, & C. R. Snyder (Eds.), *Oxford handbook of positive psychology* (2nd ed.) (pp. 261–269). New York: Oxford University Press.

Sirgy, M. J., Lee, D., Kosenko, R., Meadow, H. L., Rahtz, D., Cicic, M, Jin, G. X., et al. (1998). Does television viewership play a role in perception of quality of life? *Journal of Advertising*, *27*, 125–142.

Snyder, C. R. (2002). Hope theory: Rainbows in the mind. *Psychological Inquiry*, *13*(4), 249–275.

Spence, A., Poortinga, W., & Pidgeon, N. (2012). The psychological distance of climate change: Psychological distance of climate change. *Risk Analysis*, *32*(6), 957–972.

Staats, H., Kieviet, A., & Hartig, T. (2003). Where to recover from attentional fatigue: An expectancy-value analysis of environmental preference. *Journal of Environmental Psychology*, *23*, 147–157.

Stanton, A. L., Sullivan, S. J. & Austenfeld, J. L. (2009). Coping through emotional approach: Emerging evidence for the utility of processing and expressing emotions in responding to stressors. In S. J. Lopez, & C. R. Snyder (Eds.), *Oxford handbook of positive psychology* (2nd ed) (pp. 225–236). New York: Oxford University Press.

Steger, M. F. (2009). Meaning in life. In S. J. Lopez, & C. R. Snyder (Eds.), *Oxford handbook of positive psychology* (2nd ed) (pp. 679–687). New York: Oxford University Press.

Steger, M. F. (2012). Experiencing meaning in life: Optimal functioning at the nexus of well-being, psychopathology and spirituality. In P. T. P. Wong & P. S. Fry (Eds.), *The human quest for meaning* (2nd ed.) (pp. 165–184). New York: Routledge.

Steger, M. F., Hicks, B. M., Krueger, R. F., & Bouchard, T. J. (2011). Genetic and environmental influences and covariance among meaning in life, religiousness, and spirituality. *The Journal of Positive Psychology*, *6*(3), 181–191.

Steger, M. F., Kashdan, T. B., & Oishi, S. (2008a). Being good by doing good: Daily eudaimonic activity and well-being. *Journal of Research in Personality*, *42*(1), 22–42.

Steger, M. F., Kashdan, T. B., Sullivan, B. A., & Lorentz, D. (2008b). Understanding the search for meaning in life: Personality, cognitive style, and the dynamic between seeking and experiencing meaning. *Journal of Personality, 76*(2), 199–228.

Tennen, H. & Affleck, G. (2003).While accentuating the positive, don't eliminate the negative or Mr. in-between. *Psychological Inquiry, 14*,163–169.

Thomson, A. L., Nakamura, J., Siegel, J. T., & Csikszentmihalyi, M. (2014). Elevation and mentoring: An experimental assessment of causal relations. *The Journal of Positive Psychology, 9*(5), 402–413.

Thomson, A. L., & Siegel, J. T. (2013). A moral act, elevation, and prosocial behavior: Moderators of morality. *The Journal of Positive Psychology, 8*(1), 50–64.

Ulrich, R. S. (1984). View through a window may influence recovery from surgery. *Science, 224*(4647), 420–421.

Ulrich, R. S., Simons, R. F., Losito, B. D., Fiorito, E., Miles, M. & Zelson, M. (1991). Stress recovery during exposure to natural and urban environments. *Journal of Environmental Psychology, 11*, 201–230.

U. S. Census Bureau (2013). World population 1950–1970. Availabe at: http://www.census.gov /population/international/data/idb/worldpopgraph.php. Accessed 2 Oct 2014.

van den Berg, A. E., Hartig, T., & Staats, H. (2007). Preference for nature in urbanized societies: Stress, restoration, and the pursuit of sustainability. *Journal of Social Issues, 63*, 79–96.

Vianello, M., Galliani, E. M., & Haidt, J. (2010). Elevation at work: The effects of leaders' moral excellence. *The Journal of Positive Psychology, 5*(5), 390–411.

Walker, L. J. W. (2013). Exemplars' moral behavior is self-regarding. In M. K. Matsuba, P. E. King & K. C. Bronk (Eds.), *Exemplar methods and research: Strategies for investigation*. New Directions for Child and Adolescent Development No. 142 (pp. 27–40). San Francisco: Jossey-Bass.

Weick, K. E. (1984). Small wins: Redefining the scale of social problems. *American Psychologist, 39*, 40–49.

Weinstein, N., Przybylski, A. K., & Ryan, R. M. (2009). Can nature make us more caring? Effects of immersion in nature on intrinsic aspirations and generosity. *Personality and Social Psychology Bulletin, 35*(10), 1315–1329.

Wells, N. (2000). At home with nature: Effects of "greenness" on children's cognitive functioning. *Environment and Behavior, 32*, 775–795.

Wells, N.M. & Rollings, K. A. (2012). The natural environment in residential settings: Influences on human health and function. In S. Clayton (Ed.), *Oxford handbook of environmental and conservation psychology* (pp. 509–523). New York: Oxford University Press.

Zhang, J. W., Howell, R. T., & Iyer, R. (2014a). Engagement with natural beauty moderates the positive relation between connectedness with nature and psychological well-being. *Journal of Environmental Psychology, 38*, 55–63.

Zhang, J. W., Piff, P. K., Iyer, R., Koleva, S., & Keltner, D. (2014b). An occasion for unselfing: Beautiful nature leads to prosociality. *Journal of Environmental Psychology, 37*, 61–72.

Zimmerman, M. A. (1990). Toward a theory of learned hopefulness: A structural model analysis of participation and empowerment. *Journal of Research in Personality, 24*, 71–86.

Zullow, H. M. & Seligman, M. (1990). Pessimistic rumination predicts defeat of presidential candidates, 1900–1984. *Psychological Inquiry, 1*, 52–61.

Glossary

Adaptive management A learning-oriented approach to the management of social and natural systems, with an emphasis on deliberative engagement of stakeholders, explicit goals, monitoring and data collection, and iterative attempts to track and meet or modify goals and management choices.
Affordance The capacity of some setting to provide something an individual needs or that supports a behavior pattern; a match between perceived need and physical reality.
Anthropocentrism A value-based perspective that prioritizes the well-being of humans.
Applied behavioral analysis An approach to promoting sustainable behavior promoted by Geller, which includes three basic principles: It is focused on an observable behavior, it looks at external rather than internal factors to improve performance, and it utilizes principles of behavioral reinforcement.
Attention restoration theory The theory that the capacity for focused ("voluntary") attention gets depleted and may be restored by attending ("involuntarily") to fascinating stimuli for a period of time.
Attitude An evaluative reaction to an object or behavior that is based on beliefs about that object or behavior and that is associated with behavior toward the attitude object.
Autonomy supportive environment Derived from self-determination theory, an environment that helps individuals and groups act in ways consistent with their identity and values. Fostered by factors including empathic understanding, choice, transparency, and noncontrolling communicative style.
Availability heuristic The tendency for events and outcomes to appear more probable when they come to mind more easily.
Behavior setting A place with physical and social features that channel behavior into somewhat predictable patterns; a place where a typical set of behaviors usually occur.
Biocentrism A value-based perspective that prioritizes the well-being of nature.
Biophilia Positive emotion toward, interest in, or wish to affiliate with, living things.
Biophobia Negative emotion toward, fear of, or apprehension about living things.

Conservation Psychology: Understanding and promoting human care for nature, Second Edition.
Susan Clayton and Gene Myers.

www.wiley.com\go\clayton\conservation

Broaden-and-build theory Developed by Fredrickson, describing the idea that positive emotions encourage people to broaden their perspective to encompass a "big picture" look at a situation, and have a creative, expanded set of cognitive and behavioral responses, which in turn will build their set of behavioral skills and resources. In contrast, negative emotions encourage a relatively narrow mindset and set of behavioral responses.

Character strengths and virtues A scientific categorization of humanistic ideals developed by Peterson and Seligman; criteria include stability over time, ethical or intrinsically valuable, fulfilling, and conceptually and empirically isolatable.

Classroom-based environmental education A traditional approach that stresses the acquisition of knowledge and skills relevant to addressing environmental problems, along with the development of a sense of civic responsibility.

Clinical psychology A core psychological subdiscipline focusing on the study of mental health and well-being as well as abnormal behavior.

Cognitive dissonance A theory suggesting that holding two psychologically inconsistent beliefs or states generates an unpleasant feeling of arousal, and that people will work to reduce or eliminate this arousal. Thus, when people act in a way that is inconsistent with their attitudes, they may find it easier to change their attitudes than to live with the dissonance.

Cognitive psychology A core psychological subdiscipline focusing on mental representations and information processing.

Collective identity A self-concept based on one's status as a member of a social group, such as a family, community, or citizen. A strong collective identity tends to predict greater concern for the welfare of the collective in contrast to individual self-interest.

Commensal relationships Relationships in which one party benefits and the other is not significantly helped nor harmed.

Common pool resources Resources that are collectively owned or managed in some fashion, leading to the possibility of a "tragedy of the commons," or a more-or-less successful system of community management, depending on social, institutional, and resource factors.

Commons dilemma Described by Hardin, the commons dilemma is an example of a social trap that demonstrates the tendency of individuals to overexploit a commonly shared resource.

Community-Based Social Marketing An approach to changing behavior advocated by McKenzie-Mohr, which focuses on the social context as well as the immediate barriers and benefits to a particular behavior.

Consequentialism The ethical theory that the rightness of an action is determined by its consequences (i.e., costs or benefits) rather than by the principle(s) that guided it, or the qualities or intention of the actor.

Curtailment behaviors Behaviors that involve a reduction of consumption; they may be perceived as involving sacrifice.

Deep ecology A philosophical position that encourages a sense of identity that transcends the individual and encompasses the ecosystem, striving for a sense of similarity or shared community with the rest of nature.

Defensive pessimism A cognitive strategy based on expecting the worst and then preparing for it.

Defensive thinking Reasoning that is biased by the attempt to maintain a positive affective state.

Deontological ethics One of a family of approaches to ethics centered on duties or obligations and which typically refers all judgments back to one fundamental universalizable principle.

Depth psychology Psychological theory concerned with the relations between the unconscious, or patterns and dynamics of consciousness broadly construed.

Developmental psychology A core psychological subdiscipline focusing on impacts of early experience and changes as an organism matures.

Dispositional self-regulation A model of motivation that says people organize their behavior around the pursuit of goals, based on expectations for success that are a product of current conditions and previous experiences.

Dominionistic values Valuing experiences with nature based on controlling or dominating natural forces.

Ecological psychology Theory and research about how individual experience (particularly perception) is constituted by intimate and often biologically entrenched relations to constant environmental patterns.

Ecopsychology A family of approaches to understanding humanity's ecological crisis as rooted in the mismatch between humans' need to connect with nature and the circumstances of modern life; a therapeutic approach based on a link between mental and ecological well-being.

Education for sustainable development A lifelong, community-based approach to learning that aims to produce citizens who actively work toward a society that is both ecologically and socially sustainable.

Efficiency behaviors Behaviors that accomplish the same goals but more efficiently using fewer resources.

Egocentrism A value-based perspective that prioritizes one's own well-being.

Elaboration Likelihood Model Developed by Petty and Cacioppo, this model suggests that persuasive messages may work either by activating superficial associations or by providing deeper cognitive reflection.

Environmental citizenship A goal of environmental education: to produce people who actively engage with environmental problems, possessing not only the knowledge but also the motivation and commitment to work toward solutions.

Environmental generational amnesia The gradual loss of knowledge about what should compose a healthy ecosystem, as each new generation experiences a new level of environmental degradation as the "baseline."

Environmental identity A perception of oneself as connected to or interdependent with nature. Environmental identity comprises factors like the extent to which a person tends to interact with elements of the natural world, the personal importance of nature, and positive experiences and emotions associated with nature.

Environmental Identity (EID) scale A self-administered written scale developed by Clayton to measure an individual's level of environmental identity.

Environmental psychology A specialty within psychology that studies the reciprocal influences of people and their environments, characterized by both systematic theory and a concern for practical application.

Ethics The principles and values of a person or group; also, the philosophical study of what principles, virtues, and values *should* guide personal action or social policy.

Eudaimonism An approach to well-being focused on ongoing activities that the person chooses and which may lead to personal growth, authenticity, and a sense of meaning or larger purpose.

Evolutionary psychology A subfield of psychology that seeks to explain human tendencies and abilities as evolved adaptations that would have enhanced survival or reproduction during the environment in which humans evolved their current characteristics.

Explanatory style Events can be explained as due to factors that are internal to an individual or external, part of the situation; stable or unstable; and global or specific. Explanatory style refers to an individual's tendency to use particular types of explanation.
Extreme environments Environments that threaten survival in the absence of adequate preparation or protection.
Flow A mental state in which a person feels fully engaged in an activity, challenged but able to meet the demands of the task. Characterized by reduced self-awareness and a sense of freedom; may include an altered sense of time. Flow is a highly positive experience.
Folk biological system Concepts about living things that are held, often intuitively or "naively," by an individual or group, which show certain developmental and cross-cultural regularities as well as variations.
Foot-in-the-door effect The tendency for small actions in support of a cause to lead to further actions for the same cause.
Free-choice learning Learning that takes place in a relatively unstructured setting in a manner, and at a pace, determined by the learner's use of the available information.
Heuristic A short cut in mental reasoning that may lead to erroneous judgments.
Horticultural therapy A therapy involving gardening or exposure to plants with the goal of improving human well-being.
Humanistic values Values for nature that are based on creating emotional bonds, similar to those that might be formed with humans.
Identity A framework for organizing information about a person. Information can include personal attributes, social roles and relationships, or group memberships. An identity may be self-ascribed or imposed by others.
Implicit Association Test A reaction time-based measure that assesses the extent to which concepts are closely connected in a person's network of cognitive associations; has been used to measure the extent to which people feel connected to nature.
Learned helplessness The absence of behavior designed to escape aversive events or experiences, based on previous unsuccessful attempts to escape those experiences.
Mindfulness A quality of open or receptive awareness and attention to internal and/or external events; a state of consciousness focused on experience of the moment rather than on reflection or rumination. It is associated with subjective well-being.
Moral exclusion The philosophical, psychological, or practical denial of moral standing of some entity or group.
Moral foundations theory A theory of moral reasoning based on the idea of core moral constructs that represented adaptive responses to basic challenges faced by close-knit social groups. These core constructs tend to result in quick, intuitive moral judgments rather than conscious deliberations.
Morality A person's inner sense of right and wrong, and how he or she should behave.
Mortality salience Focused awareness of the possibility of one's death, brought about by some stimulus; according to Terror Management Theory, it prompts endorsement and protection of core values or a culturally accepted worldview.
Mutualistic relationships Relationships in which both parties benefit, although it may be in different ways.
Negativistic values Responses to nature that are based on fear, dread, or aversion.
New Environmental Paradigm A scale developed by Dunlap and Van Liere to measure a worldview that stresses the fragility of nature and the need for limits on human interventions into nature.
Parasitic relationships Relationships in which one party benefits at the cost of the other.

Physiological psychology A core psychological subdiscipline focusing on the physiological and neural processes that underlie behavior.
Place attachment Emotional attachment to a place, which may include the extent to which one is dependent on that place to fulfill one's goals.
Place-based education Education that focuses on teaching students about the natural history and cultural dimensions of their own personal locale, with the goal of encouraging a sense of attachment and relationship to place.
Place identity The component of identity that is associated with a particular locale.
Positive psychology A branch of psychology that focuses on human strengths and sources of positive experience rather than on psychological shortcomings and dysfunction.
Post-traumatic stress/growth Prolonged or delayed reactions to an extreme psychological stress including symptoms like depression, anxiety, suicide, substance abuse, and aggression. Common long-term growth responses to trauma include increased self-efficacy, social relationships, and perspective or sense of meaning.
Pragmatic ethics An approach to ethics centered on the ability of language and thought about social and other values to be improved by conscious use of experience and experimentation together with community dialogue.
Prescriptive norms A social or personal belief delineating obligatory principles, traits, or actions.
Proscriptive norms A social or personal belief delineating forbidden or sanctioned principles, trains, or actions.
Prospect Landscape qualities that allow a view outward for an action-relevant distance.
Prospect theory A theory of behavioral choice based on individuals' attitudes toward risk. It suggests in particular that people are more strongly motivated to avoid loss than to seek gain, and thus their attitudes toward a particular choice will depend on the reference point according to which they evaluate it.
Protection-motivation theory A theory developed by Lazarus that describes the role of threat appraisal in coping.
Reactance Resistance to obvious attempts at behavioral control, usually by doing the reverse of the behavior that is desired.
Refuge Landscape qualities that allow for hiding from others' view or from natural forces.
Reinforcement contingencies The positive or negative consequences of behavior for the actor.
Restorative environment An environment whose qualities support involuntary attention, usually by being fascinating, extensive in space, offering moderate levels of complexity and coherence, and being compatible with a person's goals.
Risk perception A subjective assessment of a possible threat.
Scope of justice A term denoting the realm of entities (i.e., which humans?, which non-humans?) that are taken into consideration in deliberations about justice or the extension of other moral principles; related to whether an entity is "morally considerable" or has "moral standing."
Self-determination theory A theory of motivation advanced by Edward Deci and Richard Ryan that focuses on the interaction between intrinsic and extrinsic sources of motivation for behavior, and specifically the impact of conditions that support the human needs for autonomy, competence, and relatedness.
Self-efficacy A person's perception that he or she is able to successfully complete an action. A feeling of self-efficacy predicts a greater likelihood of acting in support of one's values.

Self-handicapping Placing obstacles in the way of one's own success, so that failure can be blamed on those obstacles rather than on one's own shortcomings.

Social capital The extent and types of bonds and shared norms among people in a community. Several types have been identified, including bonding social capital, or the emotional connections and supportiveness that develop between similar people; bridging social capital, or the linkages among people and groups that are dissimilar but have been brought together; and linking social capital, or the ability of groups to influence or gain resources from external agencies or authorities.

Social psychology A core psychological subdiscipline focusing on social interaction and social influence.

Social trap A situation in which the pursuit of short-term gains by individuals leads to a long term or collective loss by the group to which the individuals belong.

Stages of Change A model described by Prochaska and DiClemente that identifies the characteristics associated with different stages of readiness for behavior change and the techniques likely to be successful at each stage.

Temporal discounting The tendency for delayed outcomes to have less significance or impact on decision-making.

Theory of Planned Behavior Developed by Ajzen to describe the relationship between attitudes, social norms, perceived control, and behavioral intention.

Transcendent experiences Experiences that seem to transcend mundane, day-to-day living and which may be perceived as having a spiritual component or as inducing a sense of humility. Often seem to occur in settings of natural grandeur.

Utilitarianism A variety of consequentialism that defines the "good" as the generation of pleasure or the avoidance of pain; the basis for modern economic theory and nineteenth to twentieth century resource conservationism, in the form of managing resource to produce the greatest good for the greatest number for the greatest time.

Value-Belief-Norm model Developed by Stern to describe the connection between values and behavior.

Values General, stable, strongly held judgments or preferences for end states or ways of acting that serve as goals that apply across different contexts.

Virtue ethics An approach to ethics emphasizing cultivation of inner character traits that define a good person, and the avoidance of vices; action is good if it expresses the virtue regardless of the consequences.

Wilderness-based therapy Behavioral or mental health care programs that employ features of wilderness such as distance from usual stresses and cues, challenging tasks, and increased group cohesion to foster benefits for participants.

Worldview An integrated set of beliefs about what is real, what is knowable, what is valuable, and what it means to be human, typically learned as part of cultural socialization.

Index

Conservation Psychology: Understanding and promoting human care for nature, Second Edition.
Susan Clayton and Gene Myers.

www.wiley.com\go\clayton\conservation